Quick Tax Facts—2006 Tax Act Changes in Context

Extended Provisions

The chart below highlights some of the key expired or expiring provisions that were extended by the Tax Relief and Health Care Act of 2006. See the Explanations in CCH's Tax Relief and Reconciliation Acts of 2006: Law and Explanation for complete discussions of all of the extended provisions.

Extended Provisions

Extended Provision	Was Scheduled to Expire On	Now Extended Through	Reported On
State and local general sales tax deduction	12/31/05	12/31/07	Form 1040, Sch A, line 5 add "ST"
Tuition and fees deduction	12/31/05	12/31/07	Form 1040, line 35 add "T"
Teacher's classroom expenses, above-the-line deduction	12/31/05	12/31/07	Form 1040, line 23 add "E"
Availability of Archer medical savings accounts (MSAs)	12/31/05	12/31/07	Forms 1099-MSA, 5498-MSA, 8853
Research credit	12/31/05	12/31/07	Form 6765
Work opportunity credit (consolidation including welfare-to-work credit for work beginning after 12/31/06)	12/31/05	12/31/07	Forms 5884, 8850
Welfare-to-work credit (repealed effective 12/31/06; consolidated with work opportunity credit for work beginning after 12/31/06)	12/31/05	12/31/06	Forms 8861, 8850
Expensing of environmental (Brownfields) remediation costs	12/31/05	12/31/07	Taxpayer's income tax return
15-year recovery for leaseholds and restaurant improvements	12/31/05	12/31/07 (property placed in service after 12/31/05)	Form 4562
Donations of scientific property and computer technology equipment	12/31/05	12/31/07	Form 8283
District of Columbia first-time homebuyer credit	12/31/05	12/31/07 (acquisitions after 12/31/05)	Forms 8859, 8844

Quick Tax Facts—2006 Tax Act Changes in Context

CCH

Extended Provision	Was Scheduled to Expire On	Now Extended Through	Reported On
Suspension of taxable income limit on depletion for marginal well production	12/31/05	12/31/07	Taxpayer's income tax return
Indian employment credit	12/31/05	12/31/07	Form 8845
Accelerated depreciation for business property on Indian reservations	12/31/05	12/31/07 (property placed in service after 12/31/05)	Form 4562
Qualified zone academy bond credit	12/31/05	12/31/07 (bonds issued after 12/31/05)	Taxpayer's income tax return
Election to include combat pay in earned income for EIC	12/31/06	12/31/07	Form 1040
Residential energy efficient property credit	12/31/07	12/31/08	Form 5695
Business solar and fuel cell energy credit	12/31/07	12/31/08	Form 3468
New energy efficient home credit	12/31/07	12/31/08	Form 8908
Renewable electricity production credit	12/31/07	12/31/08	Form 8835
Energy efficient commercial building deduction	12/31/07	12/31/08	Taxpayer's income tax return
GO Zone bonus depreciation	12/31/07	12/31/10	Form 4562
Clean renewable energy bond credit	12/31/07	12/31/08 (bonds issued after 12/31/06)	Taxpayer's income tax return
New markets credit	12/31/07	12/31/08	Form 8874
Capital gains treatment for self-created musical works	12/31/10	Permanent	Taxpayer's income tax return
Below market loans to qualified continuing care facilities	12/31/10	Permanent	Taxpayer's income tax return

LEGISLATION 2006

Tax Relief and Health Care Act of 2006

(P.L. 109-432)

As Signed by the President
on December 20, 2006

Tax Increase Prevention and Reconciliation Act of 2005

(P.L. 109-222)

As Signed by the President
on May 17, 2006

Law and Explanation

CCH Editorial Staff Publication

a Wolters Kluwer business

This publication is designed to provide accurate and authoritative information in regard to the subject matter covered. It is sold with the understanding that the publisher is not engaged in rendering legal, accounting, or other professional service. If legal advice or other expert assistance is required, the services of a competent professional person should be sought.

ISBN 13: 978-0-8080-1653-3

ISBN 10: 0-8080-1653-9

4025 W. Peterson Ave.
Chicago, IL 60646-6085
1 800 248 3248
www.CCHGroup.com

No claim is made to original government works; however, within this Product or Publication, the following are subject to CCH's copyright: (1) the gathering, compilation, and arrangement of such government materials; (2) the magnetic translation and digital conversion of data, if applicable; (3) the historical, statutory and other notes and references; and (4) the commentary and other materials.

Printed in the United States of America

Tax Relief and Reconciliation Acts of 2006:
Congress Approves Tax Reconciliation and Extenders Acts

Tax Reconciliation Act

Following passage by the House on May 10, 2006, the Senate on May 11, 2006, approved the Tax Increase Prevention and Reconciliation Act of 2005 (P.L. 109-222) by a vote of 54 to 44. President Bush signed the legislation into law on May 17, 2006. The new legislation extends $70 billion in net tax cuts, including extension of the dividend and capital gain tax rate cuts, some immediate relief from the alternative minimum tax (AMT), extension of the small business expensing thresholds, and allows high-income taxpayers a one-time Roth conversion opportunity. The measure also contains $20 billion in revenue raisers.

Key tax break extensions include the following:

1. Two-year extension of the reduced rates on dividends and capital gains through 2010;

2. Increase in the AMT exemption amounts for 2006 to a higher level than 2005;

3. Extension of the provision allowing nonrefundable credits to be claimed against the AMT;

4. Two-year extension of the Code Sec. 179 small business expensing election; and

5. Extension of the exception from Subpart F for active financing income for two years and creation of a Controlled Foreign Corporation look-through exception from Subpart F for cross-border payments of dividends, interest, rents and royalties funded with unrepatriated active income.

Also included are the following revenue raising provisions:

1. Waiver of the income limits on eligibility to convert from an IRA to a Roth IRA;

2. Manipulation of the timing of corporate estimated tax installment payments;

3. Application of earnings stripping rules to C corporations which are partners;

4. Expansion of information reporting requirements to interest on tax-exempt bonds;

5. Lengthening the amortization period for geological and geophysical expenditures for major integrated oil and gas companies;

6. Three provisions tightening the rules under the Foreign Investment in Real Property Tax Act (FIRPTA);

7. Restrictions on the tax-free treatment for certain corporate cash-rich spin-off transactions;

8. Imposition of loan and redemption requirements on pooled financing bonds;

9. Tightening of offers-in-compromise requirements;

10. Increase in the age for taxation of passive income of minors at their parents' rate;

11. New withholding requirements of certain payments by government entities;

12. Repeal of certain Foreign Sales Corporation/Extra-Territorial Income grandfather rules for certain binding contracts in order to comply with a recent World Trade Organization ruling;

13. Clarification that the domestic manufacturing deduction wage limitation may only include those wages allocable to domestic production gross receipts;

14. Several modifications to the foreign earned income and employer-provided housing exclusion rules for U.S. citizens living abroad; and

15. Extension of tax shelter penalties to accommodation parties.

Other provisions included in the legislation address a variety of areas:

1. Tax treatment of environmental cleanup funds;

2. Simplification of the active trade or business test;

3. Enhancement of veterans' access to affordable mortgages;

4. Availability of capital gains treatment for the sale of self-created music works and election of five-year amortization for a created or acquired music work;

5. Expansion of the tonnage tax option to lighter vessels;

6. Codification and extension of the exception for the Permanent University Fund from the tax-exempt arbitrage rules;

7. Acceleration of the increased limits for industrial development bonds; and

8. Revisions to the tax treatment of loans to continuing care facilities.

Extenders Act

In the final hours of the 109th Congress, the Tax Relief and Health Care Act of 2006 (P.L. 109-432) was approved by the House on December 8, 2006 by a vote of 367 to 45 and, on December 9, 2006, by the Senate by a 79 to 9 margin. The legislation includes over three dozen extensions of existing tax provisions, many of which had expired at the end of 2005 and would be retroactively extended. These include the state sales tax deduction, the above-the-line deduction for higher education tuition and fees, the above-the-line deduction for out-of-pocket teachers' expenses, the research and development credit, the welfare-to-work and work opportunity credits, and the15-year amortization of leasehold improvements. The 2006 tax forms issued by the IRS do not include these provisions, and the IRS will be required to create supplemental instructions explaining how these items are to be handled on the tax return. The legislation makes permanent several provisions of the Tax Increase Prevention and Reconciliation Act of 2005.

The legislation includes other provisions that make substantive changes to the tax law beyond simply extending existing provisions. These changes include:

1. several changes to the rules for health savings accounts including expanded funding options;

2. expansion of the domestic manufacturing deduction to activities in Puerto Rico;

3. changes in the alternative minimum tax calculation of the refundable credit amount;

4. new reporting requirements with respect to the issuance of stock under incentive stock option plans;

5. a mortgage interest deduction for mortgage insurance premiums;

6. a modification to the excise tax on unrelated business taxable income of charitable remainder trusts;

7. a variety of reforms to support whistleblowers;

8. an increase in frivolous return penalties; and

9. an expansion of qualified mortgage bonds for veterans.

Several of the provisions extended include significant modifications, including the alternative incremental credit and new alternative simplified credit for the research credit, combining and modifying the welfare-to-work and work opportunity credits, and inclusion of computer technology and equipment in the special rules for charitable contributions of scientific property used in research.

The estimated ten-year cost of the proposals is approximately $45 billion. President Bush signed the legislation on December 20, 2006.

About this Publication and CCH

In light of the passage of the Tax Reconciliation Act and Extenders Act this year, CCH is providing practitioners with a single integrated law and explanation resource, *Tax Relief and Reconciliation Acts of 2006: Law and Explanation*, encompassing both Acts. Along with the relevant Internal Revenue Code provisions, as amended by the Acts, and supporting committee reports and JCT Technical Explanation, CCH editors have put together a complete practical analysis of the new laws. Tax professionals looking for the full text of the Tax Reconciliation Act and the Extenders Act, and the text of portions of the House Committee Report accompanying H.R. 4297 (H.R. Rep. No. 109-304), the Conference Committee Report (H.R. Conf. Rep. No. 109-455) and the Joint Committee on Taxation's Technical Explanation of H.R. 6408 (JCX-50-06) can find it in this single publication. Other books and tax services relating to the new legislation can be found at CCH's website www.CCHGroup.com.

As always, CCH Tax and Accounting remains dedicated to responding to the needs of tax professionals in helping them quickly understand and work with these new laws as they take effect.

Mark A. Luscombe

Principal Analyst

CCH Tax and Accounting

December 2006

CCH Tax and Accounting Publishing
EDITORIAL STAFF

¶1 Features of This Publication

This publication is your complete guide to the Tax Increase Prevention and Reconciliation Act of 2005 (P.L. 109-222) (Tax Reconciliation Act of 2005), as signed by President Bush on May 17, 2006, and Titles I through IV of the Tax Relief and Health Care Act of 2006 (P.L. 109-432) (2006 Extenders Act), as signed by President Bush on December 20, 2006. The core portion of this publication contains the CCH Explanations of these Acts. The CCH Explanations outline all of the law changes and what they mean for you and your clients. The explanations feature practical guidance, examples, planning opportunities and strategies, as well as pitfalls to be avoided as a result of the law changes.

The law text, relevant House and committee reports which explain the intent of Congress with respect to the Tax Reconciliation Act of 2006, and Joint Committee on Taxation (JCT) Technical Explanation of the 2006 Extenders Act are reproduced following the explanations. Any new or amended Internal Revenue Code sections appear here, with changes highlighted in *italics*. You will also see the law text for portions of the Acts that did not amend the tax code. The JCT Technical Explanation that provide the legislative history of each provision follows the law text.

The publication also contains numerous other features designed to help you locate and understand the changes made by the Acts. These features include cross references to related materials, detailed effective dates, and numerous finding tables and indexes. A more detailed description of these features appears below.

TAXPAYERS AFFECTED

The first chapter of the publication, *Taxpayers Affected*, contains a detailed look at how the new laws affect specific categories of taxpayers. This chapter provides a quick reference for readers who want to know the immediate impact that the laws will have on their clients. Each section of this chapter highlights a different taxpayer type, noting the tax savings or costs that result from changes made by the Tax Reconciliation Act of 2005 and the 2006 Extenders Act. *Taxpayers Affected starts at ¶105.*

CCH EXPLANATIONS

CCH Explanations are designed to give you a complete, accessible understanding of the new laws. Explanations are arranged by subject for ease of use. There are three main finding devices you can use to locate explanations on a given topic. These are:

- A detailed table of contents at the beginning of the publication listing all of the CCH Explanations of the new laws; and

- A table of contents preceding each chapter.

Each CCH Explanation contains special features to aid in your complete understanding of the new laws. These include:

- A summary at the beginning of each explanation providing a brief overview of the new laws;

- A background or prior law discussion that puts the law changes into perspective;

- Editorial aids, including examples, cautions, planning notes, elections, comments, compliance tips, key rates and figures, and state tax consequences, that highlight the impact of the new laws;

- Charts and examples illustrating the ramifications of specific law changes;

- Captions at the end of each explanation identifying the Code sections added, amended or repealed, as well as the Act sections containing the changes;

- Cross references to the laws and committee report or JCT Technical Explanation paragraphs related to the explanation;

- A line highlighting the effective date of each law change, marked by an arrow symbol;

- References at the end of the discussion to related information in the Standard Federal Tax Reporter, Tax Research Consultant, Federal Tax Guide, Federal Estate and Gift Tax Reporter and the Federal Excise Tax Reporter.

The CCH Explanations begin at ¶205.

AMENDED CODE PROVISIONS

Changes to the Internal Revenue Code made by the Tax Reconciliation Act of 2005 and the 2006 Extenders Act appear under the heading "Code Sections Added, Amended or Repealed." *Any changed or added law text is set out in italics.* Deleted Code text, or the Code provision prior to amendment, appears in the Amendment Notes following each reconstructed Code provision. An effective date for each Code change is also provided.

The amendment notes contain cross references to the corresponding Committee Reports, JCT Technical Explanation and the CCH Explanations that discuss the new laws. *The text of the Code begins at ¶5001.*

Sections of the Tax Reconciliation Act and Extenders Act that do not amend the Internal Revenue Code appear in full text following "Code Sections Added, Amended or Repealed." *The text of these provisions appears in Act Section order beginning at ¶7005.*

COMMITTEE REPORTS

The committee reports explain the intent of Congress regarding the provisions of the Act. Included in this publication for the Tax Reconciliation Act are portions of the House Committee Report accompanying Tax Reconciliation Act of 2005 (H.R. Rep. No. 109-304) and the Conference Committee Report (H.R. Conf. Rep. No. 109-455). *The relevant portions of House Committee Report and the Conference Committee Report appears in Act Section order beginning at ¶10,001.*

The Joint Committee on Taxation (JCT) Technical Explanation for the H.R. 6408 (JCX-50-06) explains the intent of Congress regarding the provisions of the 2006 Extenders Act. There was no conference report issued for the 2006 Extenders Act. The Technical Explanation from the JCT is included in this section to aid the reader's understanding, but may not be cited as the official House, Senate or Conference Committee Report accompanying the 2006 Extenders Act.

¶1

At the end of each section, references are provided to the corresponding CCH explanations and the Internal Revenue Code provisions and links from these references to the corresponding material. *The pertinent sections of the JCT Technical Explanation appear in Act Section order beginning at ¶15,001.*

EFFECTIVE DATES

A table listing the major effective dates provides you with a reference bridge between Code Sections and Act Sections and indicates the retroactive or prospective nature of the laws explained. *The effective date table for the Tax Reconciliation Act of 2005 begins at ¶20,001. The effective date table for the 2006 Extenders Act begins at ¶20,005.*

SPECIAL FINDING DEVICES

Other special tables and finding devices in this book include:

- A table cross-referencing Code Sections to the CCH Explanations (*see ¶25,001*);
- A table showing all Code Sections added, amended or repealed (*see ¶25,005*);
- A table showing provisions of other acts that were amended (*see ¶25,010*);
- A table of Act Sections not amending the Internal Revenue Code (*see ¶25,015*); and
- An Act Section amending Code Section table (*see ¶25,020*).

IRS GUIDANCE

This publication also includes IRS guidance issued to help tax filers in 2007 claim the extended deductions and other tax advantages in the Tax Relief and Health Care Act of 2006 (P.L. 109-432). *IRS News Release IR-2006-195 and IRS Publication 600, State and General Sales Taxes, are reproduced beginning at ¶28,001.*

¶2 Table of Contents

¶3 Detailed Table of Contents

¶3

CHAPTER 2. TAX RELIEF—INDIVIDUALS

CHAPTER 3. TAX RELIEF—BUSINESSES IN GENERAL

¶3

CHAPTER 11. TIPRA—BONDS, TAX-EXEMPT ENTITIES AND ADMINISTRATION

State and Local Bonds

Tax-Exempt Entities

Administration and Procedure

Taxpayers Affected

1

TAX INCREASE PROTECTION AND RECONCILIATION ACT OF 2005 AND TAX RELIEF AND HEALTH CARE ACT OF 2006

TAX INCREASE PROTECTION AND RECONCILIATION ACT OF 2005 AND TAX RELIEF AND HEALTH CARE ACT OF 2006

¶105 Overview

Although the 109th Congress has been referred to by some critics as the 21st century equivalent of the "do nothing" Congress of the Truman era, that would not be a fair characterization of its record on tax matters. In 2006 alone, Congress managed to pass three pieces of legislation containing significant tax provisions. Starting with the Tax Increase Prevention and Reconciliation Act of 2005 (Tax Reconciliation Act of 2005) (P.L. 109-222), followed by the Pension Protection Act of 2006 (P.L. 109-280), and, finally, just before the gavel fell to adjourn the lame-duck session after the tumultuous mid-term elections, Congress delivered the Tax Relief and Health Care Act of 2006 (2006 Extenders Act) (P.L. 109-432).

The Tax Reconciliation Act of 2005 includes over 30 provisions potentially affecting almost every type of taxpayer, including individuals, businesses, corporations, pass-through entities, and tax-exempt and government entities. A number of provisions are also targeted at particular categories of individual taxpayers and industries. There are approximately $90 billion in tax breaks included in these provisions and $21 billion in revenue raisers. This legislation was constructed in a House-Senate conference committee with great difficulty to stay within budget protection guidelines and to squeeze in some relatively controversial provisions that might not have been able to pass the Senate in legislation that was not budget protected. Most of the provisions are effective either retroactive to the beginning of 2006 or as of May 17, 2006, the date of enactment.

The 2006 Extenders Act extends a number of popular tax breaks, including some of the provisions previously limited in the Tax Reconciliation Act of 2005. However, the Extenders Act also includes new provisions that expand the availability of health savings accounts (HSAs), provide a deduction for mortgage insurance premiums, and grant other tax relief.

INDIVIDUALS

¶107 Overall Effect on Individuals

Breaks for capital gains and AMT relief highlighted.—Among the big winners in the Tax Increase Prevention and Reconciliation Act of 2005 (P.L. 109-222) are investors with capital gain and dividend income who will reap the benefits of lower tax rates for two more years (¶905 and ¶920). Taxpayers who would have faced the spectre of the alternative minimum tax (AMT) can breathe a sigh of relief, at least for one more year (¶720 and ¶725). Limited relief is also provided for certain taxpayers by way of a refundable AMT credit (¶235). Current owners of traditional IRAs and those taxpayers who can afford to fund a nondeductible IRA will have to get out their calculators to see if they should take advantage of a new provision that allows conversions to Roth IRAs without income limitations and also provides a special two-year window for recognition of any income as a result of the conversion (¶705). Lenders to qualified care facilities will find more liberal rules on avoidance of imputed interest treatment (¶245).

Individuals also can be pleased with passage of the Tax Relief and Health Care Act of 2006 (P.L. 109-432). Included in the category of extenders for individuals is the deduction for state and local sales taxes (¶205), the deduction for higher education tuition and fees (¶210), and the deduction for certain classroom expenses of primary and secondary school educators (¶215).

In addition to extenders, a new provision allows a deduction for premiums paid for mortgage insurance (¶220). Health Savings Accounts (HSAs) were the subject of considerable coverage in the 2006 Extenders Act, with the emphasis on expanding their availability through less restrictive deduction limits and allowing transfers from other types of qualified health accounts such as flexible spending arrangements (FSAs) and health reimbursement accounts (HRAs), as well as, from IRAs (¶505, ¶510, ¶515, ¶520, and ¶525). Finally, Archer medical savings accounts (MSAs) were also extended (¶530).

Niche winners can be found in provisions of both the Tax Reconciliation Act of 2005 and the 2006 Tax Extenders Act, including song writers (¶240) and those amortizing musical compositions or copyrights attributable to them (¶815), military personnel receiving combat pay (¶225), veterans seeking mortgages in certain states (¶610, and¶620), certain members of the intelligence community (¶250), federal judicial officers (¶255), investors in the District of Columbia (¶340), and holders of bonds from certain Texas universities (¶615).

Not everyone will be happy.—On the other side of the tax coin, parents with children older than 13, but younger than 18, may have to adjust their investment plans if they had previously tried to take advantage of their child's lower income tax rates for items of unearned income (¶710). Managers of tax-exempt entities that enter into prohibited tax shelter transactions (¶1130) and taxpayers making offers in compromise to the IRS (¶1140) will find themselves the targets of new rules.

U.S. citizens working abroad face a mixed bag of issues resulting from the Tax Reconciliation Act of 2005. Although they may benefit generally from acceleration of the inflation adjustment applicable to the exclusion amount for compensation earned (¶1005), those working in relatively high-cost locales, may actually be worse off because of the new law's requirement that calculation of the housing and income allowances be tied together and as result of a new requirement that the exclusion amounts for compensation and housing be reflected in taking into account their other income (¶1010). Foreign persons investing in U.S. real estate will be hit with new restrictions to close purported loopholes exploited to avoid U.S. taxation (¶1020 and ¶1025). Recipients of certain government payments will be subject to withholding (¶1125).

¶107

¶108 Effect on Individuals With Capital Gain or Qualified Dividend Income

Lower capital gain and dividend rates extended.—Perhaps the most politically contentious provision in the Tax Increase Prevention and Reconciliation Act of 2005 (P.L. 109-222) extends the lowered rates on long-term capital gains and qualified dividends, previously scheduled to expire at the end of 2008, through 2010 (¶905 and ¶920). Much ink has been spilled on the effectiveness (or ineffectiveness) of these provisions on the American economy. Depending on whose press releases and studies you read, this is either the most significant or the most overhyped component of the legislation. For example, studies by the Center on Budget and Policy Priorities and the Urban-Brookings Tax Policy Center claim that the cost of maintaining the lower rates outweighs any positive long-term effects on the economy (*www.cbpp.org*; "Dividend and Capital Gains Cuts Unlikely to Yield Touted Economic Benefits"). These same groups also point out that the bulk of the benefits will be enjoyed by high income taxpayers, with 53 percent of the benefits going to those with incomes above $1 million and 90 percent to those with incomes above $100,000. However, figures from the Tax Foundation (*www.taxfoundation.org*; Fiscal Fact Sheet No. 1) and the Congressional Budget Office point out that, despite the rhetoric on the importance of capital gain relief versus relief from the alternative minimum tax (AMT), a large percentage of taxpayers potentially impacted by the AMT also have capital gain or dividend income.

Regardless of where the truth actually lies as to the overall macroeconomic benefits and effectiveness of lower capital gain and dividend rates, the "investor class," from Warren Buffett to coupon-clipping senior citizens, will receive some positive tax news from another two years of lowered rates. Recipients of long-term capital gains should, however, be aware of the potentially negative impact of the AMT on the actual rate of tax they pay.

Five-year holding period.—There will be no special capital gain treatment for property held more than five years in tax years beginning before 2011. However, a zero-percent rate will be available for capital gains (and for qualified dividends) of taxpayers who are otherwise in the 10 or 15-percent tax brackets for tax years 2008 through 2010 (¶910).

Small business stock.—The amount of excluded gain on the sale of so-called small business stock, that is treated as a tax preference item for AMT purposes, will remain at seven percent for tax years beginning in 2006 through 2010 (¶915).

Dividends passed through from RICs and REITs.—The extension of the lower rates on capital gains and qualified dividends also applies to capital gains or dividends passed through a regulated investment company (RIC) or real estate investment trust (REIT). For taxpayers who are otherwise in the 10 or 15-percent tax brackets, a five-percent rate is effective through December 31, 2007, and a zero-percent rate for tax years 2008 through 2010 (¶925).

¶109 Effect on Home Buyers and Owners

Mortgage insurance deduction.—In a somewhat surprising move, the Tax Relief and Health Care Act of 2006 (P.L. 109-432) creates a new deduction for premiums paid on private mortgage insurance (PMI) as well as for mortgage insurance premiums paid to the Veterans Administration, the Federal Housing Administration, and the Rural Housing Administration (¶220).

The provision effectively treats qualified mortgage insurance premiums as though they were payments of qualified residence interest. The new provision does have its limits though. For one, taxpayers with an adjusted gross income in excess of $110,000 ($55,000 for married persons filing separately) will not be eligible for the deduction. In addition, the availability of the deduction begins to phase out when AGI exceeds $100,000 ($50,000 for married persons filing separately). The deduction is limited to residential real estate contracts issued on or after January 1, 2007, and is available only through 2007.

Mortgage insurance is often required for first-time home buyers who do not have sufficient equity to avoid it. In a press release issued by Mortgage Insurance Companies of America (MICA), which is the trade association representing the mortgage insurance industry, the group lauded passage of the provision and noted that it will make homes more affordable for those who cannot afford the traditional 20-percent down payment. Potential home buyers who are considering a second or "piggy-back" loan as an alternative to mortgage insurance should make note of this provision.

Energy efficient property.—The Code Sec. 25D credit for energy efficient property purchased for use in a personal residence, originally enacted by the Energy Tax Incentives Act of 2005 (P.L. 109-58), has been extended through 2008 by the 2006 Extenders Act (¶230). In addition, the scope of the credit has been expanded to include all property that uses solar energy to generate electricity, not just photovoltaic property.

¶110 Effect on Taxpayers Who Itemize

Sales and use tax deduction extended.—After having been eliminated by the Tax Reform Act of 1986 (P.L. 99-514), the deduction for state and local sales taxes was resurrected by the American Jobs Creation Act of 2004 (P.L. 108-357), at least for 2004 and 2005. Now, the Tax Relief and Health Care Act of 2006 (P.L. 109-432) has extended the deduction for two more years through 2007 (¶205).

Long sought by representatives of states that do not have an income tax, such as Texas and Florida, the provision allows taxpayers to take an itemized deduction for state and local general sales taxes in lieu of taking a deduction for state and local income taxes. Even in states that do have an income tax, purchasers of big ticket items, such as autos and boats, should consider the possibility of claiming a deduction for state and local sales taxes instead of income taxes.

Mortgage insurance deduction.—The Extenders Act of 2006 creates a new deduction for premiums paid on private mortgage insurance (PMI) as well as for mortgage insurance premiums paid to the Veterans Administration, the Federal Housing Administration, and the Rural Housing Administration (¶220). Taxpayers with an adjusted gross income in excess of $110,000 ($55,000 for married persons filing separately) will not be eligible for the deduction. In addition, the availability of the deduction begins to phase out when AGI exceeds $100,000 ($50,000 for married persons filing separately). The deduction is limited to residential real estate contracts issued on or after January 1, 2007, and is available only through 2007.

¶111 Effect on Tax Protestors and Certain Taxpayers Dealing With the IRS

Penalty for frivolous submissions.—Tax protestors beware, the IRS has a new weapon in the war against frivolous tax returns and arguments. The Tax Relief and Health Care Act of 2006 (P.L. 109-432) increases the penalty for filing a frivolous tax return from $500 to $5,000 and will apply the penalty to all taxpayers and types of federal taxes (¶640). Requests for submissions that are intended to delay or impede tax administration with respect to collection due process hearings, installment agreements, and offers in compromise may be disregarded by the IRS. A penalty of $5,000 may be imposed for such a request, however, taxpayers will have the opportunity to avoid the penalty by withdrawing a request within 30 days after receiving notice from the IRS that the submission is considered frivolous. The provision also requires the IRS to publish a list of positions, arguments, requests, and submissions that have been determined to be frivolous.

Disclosure rules extended.—The 2006 Extenders Act also extends through 2007 a number of provisions relating to the disclosure of tax information (¶635). These include the disclosure of tax information (1) to facilitate combined employment tax reporting (Code Sec. 6103(d)(5)), (2) to assist in the investigation of terrorist activities, and (3) for purposes related to the income-contingent student loan repayment program. A separate amendment allows the IRS to provide tax information to governmental entities that have been formed and operated by municipalities that impose an income tax and collectively have a population in excess of 250,000.

¶112 Effect on Individuals With Alternative Minimum Taxable Income

AMT exemption extended.—Added to the Code originally in 1969 as a reaction to the public revelation that a handful of individuals with relatively high adjusted gross incomes for the time had been able to escape taxation through a variety of then legitimate tax breaks, the alternative minimum tax (AMT) has morphed into something quite different. It is now a tax that is hitting middle-class Americans, and without intervention on the part of Congress, is expected to catch many more in its web in the coming years. According to the Congressional Research Service, as many as 21 million taxpayers could otherwise be subject to the AMT in 2006 (RS22100). Particularly hard hit are taxpayers with high deduction amounts for home mortgages, state income and real property taxes, and those with large families or holding profits stemming from incentive stock options. The AMT also has a deleterious effect on taxpayers with income from long-term capital gains or qualified dividends in that it adversely impacts the effective rate of tax paid on those items of income. Although the law does contain an exemption amount based on taxpayer status, those amounts were not indexed for inflation.

Accordingly, it comes as a relief that the Tax Increase Prevention and Reconciliation Act of 2005 (P.L. 109-222) extends the increases in the individual exemption from the AMT through 2006 (¶720). The 2006 exemption amounts are $62,550 for married taxpayers filing jointly and surviving spouses, $42,500 for single taxpayers, and $31,275 for married taxpayers filing separately. Although hardly the overall AMT reform that many taxpayers (and legislators) had hoped for, this AMT "patch" will at least put off the pain for a significant number of taxpayers for one more year. Senate Finance Committee Chairman Charles Grassley (R. Iowa) and legislators from both sides of the aisle have promised more long-term AMT relief, but that has yet to materialize. Further relief is problematic. Estimates by the Congressional Budget Office indicate that complete repeal of the AMT would cost $611 billion over ten years, even if the other 2001 and 2003 tax cuts are allowed to expire.

Allowance of nonrefundable personal credits continued.—The Tax Reconciliation Act of 2005 provides additional relief by allowing certain nonrefundable personal tax credits, including the dependent care credit (Code Sec. 21), the credit for the elderly and disabled (Code Sec. 22), and the HOPE Scholarship Credit and Lifetime Learning Credit (Code Sec. 25A), to be claimed in full for purposes of the AMT as well as for purposes of the regular income tax. (¶725). As is the case with the AMT exemption amount, this relief is only good for one year—2006. This extension provision does not apply to the personal use portions of the nonrefundable tax credits for alternative motor vehicles (Code Sec. 30B) and alternative motor vehicle refueling property (Code Sec. 30C).

Targeted relief.—A provision of the Tax Relief and Health Care Act of 2006 (P.L. 109-432) provides relief targeted primarily at certain individuals who received incentive stock options prior to the bursting of the technology bubble and now find themselves with credits against the AMT that are effectively worthless (¶235).

¶113 Effect on Owners of IRAs

AGI limit on conversions lifted.—Although Roth IRAs have been part of the Code for a number of years, they have never gained quite the popularity that was originally expected when the provision was enacted. One of the major impediments to conversion from a traditional IRA to a Roth IRA is a limitation based on adjusted gross income (AGI) of $100,000. Effective beginning in 2010, the Tax Increase Prevention and Reconciliation Act of 2005 (P.L. 109-222) would remove the AGI limitation (¶705). Similar to what was done when Roth IRAs were first introduced, the Tax Reconciliation Act of 2005 would allow taxpayers to spread the recognition of income from Roth conversions done in 2010 over tax years 2011 and 2012. However, income recognition would be accelerated if a distribution occurred before 2012.

According to revenue estimates accompanying the legislation as well as a background statement issued by Senate Finance Committee Chairman Grassley (R. Iowa), this provision is considered a "revenue raiser," at least through 2015. However, it would appear that this change does create the possibility of effectively bypassing the Roth IRA contribution limits by contributing first to a nondeductible IRA and then converting at some later date to a Roth. It would also seem that the multi-stage strategy could be employed to take a rollover from a defined contribution plan, such as a 401(k), to a traditional IRA and then to a Roth IRA.

It will be interesting to see if this change is enough to create a significant uptick in Roth conversions as taxpayers will still have to be mindful of the cost/benefit factors to consider in determining whether to convert. These factors would include the time frame until he or she would have to begin receiving distributions from a traditional IRA versus when (if at all) withdrawals from the Roth IRA would begin and the availability of sufficient funds outside of the current IRA to pay any taxes due on conversion. Plus, the possibility of income tax rates rising after 2010, if the 2001 tax changes are allowed to lapse, would be another factor that must be considered in deciding if and when to take advantage of the new liberal rules on Roth IRA conversions.

Transfers from IRAs to HSAs allowed.—A provision of the Tax Relief and Health Care Act of 2006 (P.L. 109-432) allows a one-time transfer directly from an IRA to a health savings account (HSA) (¶525). Qualifying distributions would not be includible in income and would not be subject to the 10-percent additional tax on premature withdrawals from retirement accounts.

¶114 Effect on Qualified Health Account Participants

Expansion of HSAs.—A somewhat surprising series of provisions dealing with health savings accounts (HSAs) surfaced in the last days of negotiating the Tax Relief and Health Care Act of 2006 (P.L. 109-432). Unlike the more publicized extensions of existing tax provisions, these items constitute a major expansion of the tax rules governing HSAs. Among other things, the new law allows taxpayers a direct transfer of amounts held in a flexible spending account (FSA) or health reimbursement account (HRA) to an HSA (¶505). The maximum amount of such a transfer is limited to the lesser of the amount held in the FSA or HRA as of September 21, 2006, or the amount held at the time of the distribution. Such transfers would not be includible in income, nor would they be deductible. A qualifying transfer to an HSA must be made before January 1, 2012. If an employer allows any employee to make a rollover distribution from an FSA or HRA to an HSA, all employees covered under a high-deductible plan must be eligible.

Also modified is the treatment of FSAs that allow a grace period of up to two and one half months for participants to request reimbursement after the close of the year (¶505). The presence of such a grace period had inhibited individuals who also participate in an HSA from making contributions to the HSA until after the grace period had ended. Under the new rules, if the balance in a participant's FSA is zero, or if the participant elects to transfer the entire balance in his or her FSA to an HSA, coverage in the FSA will be disregarded in determining the tax deductibility of contributions to an HSA during the grace period.

Deductibility limits are also relaxed. Prior to passage of the new law, contributions to an HSA for 2007 would have been limited to the lesser of (1) the amount of the annual deductible under the plan or (2) $2,850 (in the case of self only coverage) and $5,650 (in the case of family coverage). As modified, the limitation pertaining to the amount of the annual deductible has been removed. Accordingly, only the monetary limits now apply. In addition, effective beginning in 2007, the new law moves up the date for determining cost-of-living adjustments based on the Consumer Price Index from the 12-month period ending August 31 to the period ending March 31 (¶510). The new law also provides a break for employees who become covered under a high-deductible health plan in a month other than January by allowing them to make contributions as if they had been eligible to make contributions during the entire year (¶515). Separately, the 2006 Extenders Act provides an exception to the comparable contribution requirements so as to allow employers to make larger contributions to HSAs on behalf of nonhighly compensated employees than for highly compensated employees (¶520).

Transfers from IRAs to HSAs allowed.—A related provision allows a one-time transfer directly from an IRA to an HSA (¶525). Qualifying distributions would not be includible in income and would not be subject to the 10-percent additional tax on premature withdrawals from retirement accounts. Persons who have not contributed the maximum possible amounts to an HSA previously should consider the possibilities offered by this provision.

Archer MSAs.—Archer medical savings accounts (MSAs) were also a subject of concern in the 2006 Extenders Act, which extended provisions governing these accounts through 2007 (¶530). New rules governing the timely filing of reports by the Archer MSA trustees as to the numerical limits on MSAs were also added.

Parity rules for mental health coverage in group health plans.—Participants in group health plans that provide mental health benefits should be aware that these plans are generally not allowed to impose annual or lifetime dollar caps on mental health benefits that are not imposed on substantially all medical and surgical benefits. The 2006 Extenders Act extends these parity requirements through 2007 (¶535).

¶115 Effect on Parents With Children Having Unearned Income

Kiddie tax age raised.—For families with teenage children age 14 or older who thought that having those children receive unearned income would avoid the so-called kiddie tax and, thus, reduce overall family taxation, the Tax Increase Prevention and Reconciliation Act of 2005 (P.L. 109-222) has negatively affected that planning strategy. Specifically, the Tax Reconciliation Act of 2005, has raised the upper limit of the reach of the kiddie tax to 18 for tax years after 2005 (¶710). This has the effect of exposing unearned income above $1,700 (for 2006 and 2007) of children under age 18 to taxation at the parent's income tax rate. The new law does include an exception from the kiddie tax for distributions from certain qualified disability trusts and also provides that the tax will not apply if the child is married and files a joint return with his or her spouse.

¶116 Effect on Persons Paying Higher Education Expenses

Tuition deduction extended.—The above-the-line deduction (Code Sec. 222) for tuition and other related expenses of higher education is extended through 2007 by the Tax Relief and Health Care Act of 2006 (P.L. 109-432) (¶210). For 2006 and 2007, the deduction is $4,000 in the case of a single taxpayer with an adjusted gross income (AGI) of $65,000 or less. The AGI limit is $130,000 for joint filers. A reduced deduction of $2,000 is available for a single taxpayer with an AGI of $80,000 or less and for joint filers with an AGI of $160,000 or less. Taking the deduction precludes use of the HOPE or lifetime learning credits for the same student in the same year (Code Sec. 25A).

¶117 Effect on Primary and Secondary School Educators

Classroom expenses deduction extended.—Teachers, counselors, principals, and classroom aides who work at least 900 hours during the school year are eligible to take an above-the-line deduction of up to $250 for out-of-pocket expenses to purchase classroom supplies. The deduction, which has proved to be very popular since its introduction in the Job Creation and Worker Assistance Act of 2002 (P.L. 107-147), has been extended through 2007 by the Tax Relief and Health Care Act of 2006 (P.L. 109-432) (¶215).

¶118 Effect on Song Writers and Acquirers of Musical Compositions

Capital gain treatment extended.—Would-be Paul McCartneys will be singing the praises of the Tax Increase Prevention and Reconciliation Act of 2005 (P.L. 109-222) because it provides that songwriters will be entitled to receive capital gains treatment for the sale or exchange of their songs rather than having the transaction taxed at ordinary income tax rates (¶240). The change is effective for sales or exchanges in tax years beginning after May 17, 2006, and by virtue of the Tax Relief and Health Care Act of 2006 (P.L. 109-432) is made permanent. At least according to their website (*www.nashvillesongwriters.com*), the Nashville Songwriter's Association International is claiming credit for suggesting this provision.

Amortization over five years.—The Tax Reconciliation of 2005 also changes the rules governing the capitalization of expenses incurred in creating or acquiring a musical composition, or a copyright to a musical composition. Specifically, taxpayers can elect to amortize such costs over a five-year period for property placed in service in tax years beginning after 2005 (¶815). Absent an election, other allowable depreciation methods, including the income forecast method are still available. This provision will generally benefit acquirers of musical compositions and those who employ the creators, rather than the creators themselves, because individual (nonemployee) creators may already avail themselves of a current deduction for their expenses.

¶119 Effect on Military Personnel

Special treatment for combat pay extended.—Military personnel will benefit from the Tax Relief and Health Care Act of 2006 (P.L. 109-432) because the provision granting special treatment of combat pay for purposes of the Code Sec. 32 earned income credit is extended through 2007 (¶225). Generally, such pay is excludable from income if earned while serving in a combat zone or while hospitalized during the two-year period following combat service if the hospitalization results from injuries or disease suffered during such service. Under the provision, otherwise excludable combat pay may be treated as earned income for purposes of computing the earned income credit.

¶120 Effect on Veterans

Service requirements and eligibility period for mortgage bonds modified.—The Tax Increase Prevention and Reconciliation Act of 2005 (P.L. 109-222) removed the requirement that veterans receiving loans financed with qualified veterans' mortgage bonds must have served before 1977. In addition, the eligibility period for applying for a loan following the veteran's release from the military was reduced to 25 years from 30 (¶620). These changes are effective for bonds issued on or after May 17, 2006 and involve bonds issued by the states of Alaska, Oregon, and Wisconsin. The present law governing qualified veterans' mortgage bonds issued by the states of California and Texas is not changed.

Under a provision of the Tax Relief and Health Care Act of 2006 (P.L. 109-432), effective for qualified mortgage bonds issued after December 20, 2006, and before January 1, 2008, the first-time home buyer requirement is waived for veterans regardless of when they last served on active duty or the date they applied for a loan after leaving active duty (¶610). However, this exception to the first-time home buyer rule may be used only once.

Volume limits changed.—The Tax Reconciliation Act of 2005 also changed the volume limits for veterans' mortgage bonds issued by the states of Alaska, Oregon, and Wisconsin. These new state volume limits are phased in over a five-year period beginning in 2006. Under a provision of the 2006 Extenders Act, the $25-million volume limit for veteran's bonds that can be issued in each of these three states would continue after 2010 (¶620).

¶121 Effect on Tax-Exempt Bond Investors

Reporting of interest.—Tax-exempt bond investors should note that the Tax Increase Prevention and Reconciliation Act of 2005 (P.L. 109-222) removes the exemption from the information reporting requirements for interest on such bonds (¶1105). This provision is effective for interest on tax-exempt bonds paid after 2005.

Capital expenditure limit for small issue bonds raised.—A provision that would have effectively doubled the $10 million limit on capital expenditures allowed with respect to certain qualified small issue bonds issued after September 30, 2009, was modified to cover such bonds issued after December 31, 2006 (¶1110).

New volume limits for veterans' mortgage bonds.—New volume limits are allowed for qualified veterans' mortgage bonds issued by the states of Alaska, Oregor, and Wisconsin. These new state volume limits are phased in over a five-year period beginning in 2006. Although the availability of such bonds was to expire after 2010, a provision of the Tax Relief and Health Care Act of 2006 (P.L. 109-432) extends them indefinitely (¶620).

Exception for Texas Permanent University Fund extended.—An agreement between the IRS and the Texas Permanent University Fund is codified and extended permanently. That agreement protects interest on bonds issued by the Fund from certain arbitrage restrictions (¶615).

Pooled financing bond rules tightened.—Rules governing the tax-exempt status of pooled financing bonds are tightened to require that the issuer have a reasonable expectation that at least 30 percent of the net proceeds from the bonds will be used within one year (¶1135). The issuer must also obtain written loan commitments for 30 percent of the proceeds prior to issuance. If the reasonable expectations are not met, the issuer must redeem a portion of the outstanding bonds within 90 days.

Qualified Zone Academy Bonds.—Qualified Zone Academy Bonds (QZABs) are also the subject of consideration in the Tax Relief and Health Care Act of 2006 (P.L. 109-432) (¶605). First, the availability of such bonds is extended through 2007. The new law also imposes certain arbitrage and spending requirements, as well as reporting requirements, on QZABs. The arbitrage requirements are generally those of Code Sec. 148 applicable to interest-bearing tax-exempt bonds. With respect to the spending requirement, the issuer must reasonably expect that at least 95 percent of the proceeds from the sale of the issue are to be spent for one or more qualified purposes within the five-year period beginning on the date of issuance of the QZAB and that a binding commitment with a third party to spend at least 10 percent of the proceeds from the sale of the issue will be incurred within the six-month period beginning on the date of issuance. If this 95-percent requirement is not met, the bonds can still continue to be treated as QZABs assuming the unspent proceeds are used within 90 days of the end of the five-year period to redeem any nonqualified bonds. There is also a provision allowing extension of the five-year period for reasonable cause.

¶123 Effect on U.S. Citizens Living Abroad

Exclusions for compensation and housing costs raised.—The foreign earned income exclusion for 2006 is adjusted for inflation to $82,400 under a provision of the Tax Increase Prevention and Reconciliation Act of 2005 (P.L. 109-222) (¶1005). Prior law had indicated that the inflation adjustment would not occur until after 2007. In conjunction with that change, the maximum exclusion amount for qualified housing costs is changed to $11,536 pursuant to a formula based on 30 percent of the compensation exclusion amount, minus 16 percent of the compensation exclusion, and taking into an account of the number of days of foreign residence or presence. The 30-percent amount may be subject to annual adjustment by the IRS based on geographic differences in housing costs relative to housing costs in the United States.

The combination of these changes results in a negative situation for many Americans living abroad, particularly those living in relatively high-cost locations, in comparison to the system that existed prior to passage of the Tax Reconciliation Act of 2005. Since passage of the law, the IRS has issued an adjustment pursuant to its authority, as noted above, based on geographic differences in housing costs relative to housing costs in the United States. That adjustment (Notice 2006-87, I.R.B. 2006-43, 766) ameliorates the problem for U.S. workers in some, but not all, high-cost locations currently being staffed.

Taxpayer's bracket to reflect excluded amounts.—Causing further pain for some U.S. workers based in foreign locations, the Tax Reconciliation Act of 2005 also requires that the tax bracket of individuals taking advantage of the foreign earned income exclusion will effectively ignore that fact with respect to other taxable income. Accordingly, under this "stacking rule," for a taxpayer with both excludable and includible income, the includible income will be taxed as if the excludable amount had been subject to tax (¶ 1010).

¶ 125 Effect on Foreign Persons Investing in U.S. Real Property

Tax avoidance curtailed.—Attempts by some foreign persons (defined to include nonresident alien individuals) to avoid U.S. taxation under the Foreign Investment in Real Property Tax Act of 1980 (FIRPTA) have been dealt a blow by the Tax Increase Prevention and Reconciliation Act of 2005 (P.L. 109-222). The first change concerns a clarification of the treatment of transactions involving the investment by a foreign person in a regulated investment company (RIC) or real estate investment trust (REIT) that in turn invests in a lower-tier RIC or REIT that then disposes of a U.S. real property interest (USRPI) and distributes the proceeds back to the upper-tier RIC or REIT on the premise that the proceeds could then be distributed to foreign shareholders of that entity as non-FIRPTA income. The new law requires that any such distribution retain its character as FIRPTA income (¶ 1020). An exception to the look-through rule applies for certain distributions involving regularly traded securities. The new rules also explicitly require withholding on distributions attributable to the sale of USRPIs made to a foreign person at 35 percent (unless regulations otherwise provide withholding at 15 percent).

Another change indicates that the amount of a distribution not treated as gain from the sale or exchange of a USRPI because of the exception for regularly traded securities, is not included in computing the shareholder's long-term capital gain, but is included as a dividend.

Wash-sale rule imposed.—The Tax Reconciliation Act of 2005 also adds a form of the wash-sale rule to impose FIRPTA tax on certain transfers by a foreign person (¶ 1025). The provision is aimed at those who would attempt to dispose of stock in a domestically controlled RIC or REIT during the 30-day period preceding a distribution on that stock (the ex-dividend date), that should have been treated as coming from the disposition of a USRPI, and then acquire an identical stock interest (or enter into a contract or option to do so) during the 61-day period beginning 30 days before the ex-dividend date and ending 30 days after the ex-dividend date. Exceptions to the wash-sale rule apply for certain distributions involving regularly traded securities and for distributions that are actually received.

¶127 Effect on Recipients of Certain Government Payments

Withholding imposed.—Beginning after 2010, recipients of certain types of government payments will discover that income taxes are being withheld (¶1125). Withholding will be applicable to payments to persons providing property or services made by the U.S. government, as well as state governments, including their political subdivisions and instrumentalities. An exemption is provided for state political subdivisions having less than $100 million in annual expenditures otherwise subject to withholding. The withholding rate will be three percent regardless of whether the payments are for property or services.

Payments covered under the provision include those made in conjunction with a government voucher or certificate program, including payments to a commodity producer as part of a support program. Although the new withholding rules will not apply to payments made in connection with needs-based public welfare or assistance programs, they will apply to payments for health care or other services that are not based on needs or income level of the recipient. Also excluded are payments of interest, payments for real property, payments to tax-exempt entities or foreign governments, intra-governmental payments, and payments under a classified or confidential contract.

¶129 Effect on Individuals Participating in Offers in Compromise

Payments required while offer being considered.—Taxpayers making an offer in compromise will be required to make partial payments to the IRS during the time their offer is pending (¶1140). Lump-sum offers in compromise (including those having five or fewer payments) would require a 20-percent down payment while periodic payment offers in compromise would require the taxpayer to maintain whatever proposed payment schedule they have requested. However, if the IRS fails to respond to an offer within two years of its submission, the offer would be deemed accepted. Offers in compromise submitted without the required partial payment will be returned to the taxpayer as unprocessable. Any user fee imposed must be submitted with the partial payment and would be applied to the taxpayer's outstanding tax liability. This provision is effective for offers submitted on or after July 17, 2006.

¶131 Effect on Lenders to Qualified Care Facilities

New test for imputed interest exception.—The dollar cap on loans to a continuing care facility that qualify for an exception to the imputed interest rules (adjusted for inflation to $163,300 for 2006) is removed, effective for calendar years after 2005. The exception is available for loans to a "qualified continuing care facility" under a "continuing care contract" if the lender or lender's spouse reaches age 62 before the end of the year (¶245).

The Tax Increase Prevention and Reconciliation Act of 2005 (P.L. 109-222) also modifies the definition of the terms "continuing care contract" and "qualified continuing care facility." Among other changes, a qualified continuing care facility must also include an independent living unit in addition to an assisted facility and/or a nursing facility. Further definitions of "assisted living facility" and "nursing facility" are also provided. A provision of the Tax Relief and Health Care Act of 2006 (P.L. 109-432) makes these changes concerning below-market loans to continuing care facilities permanent (¶245).

¶133 Effect on Managers of Tax-Exempt Entities in Tax Shelters

Entity managers face liability.—The Tax Increase Prevention and Reconciliation Act of 2005 (P.L. 109-222) adds a provision aimed generally at tax-exempt entities that enter into prohibited tax shelter transactions (¶1130). However, the provision also imposes a tax on any manager of a tax-exempt entity who approves of, or causes, the entity to enter into a prohibited tax shelter transaction. The tax is $20,000 per act of approval causing the entity to engage in the transaction. An entity manager is generally a person with authority, similar to that of an officer, director or trustee of an organization. In the case of an IRA, other retirement or tax-favored account (e.g., a health savings account or qualified tuition plan), the entity manager is the person who approves of or causes the entity to enter into the prohibited transaction. The provision is generally effective for tax years ending after May 17, 2006.

¶135 Effect on Recipients of Incentive Stock Options

AMT relief.—Certain recipients of incentive stock options who were unfortunate enough to be left holding options during the bursting of the technology bubble in 2000 and 2001 and, to make matters worse, wound up exposed to the alternative minimum tax (AMT) on what could best be described as "phantom" gain, will find at least some comfort in the Tax Relief and Health Care Act of 2006 (P.L. 109-432). Many of those affected found themselves possessing long-term AMT credits that were effectively of no value to them. The new law provides limited relief to these individuals in the form of a refundable credit that will be available for tax years through 2012 (¶235).

A separate provision requires employers to provide employees with a written statement containing information on the transfer of stock pursuant to an incentive stock option and certain other stock transfers involving employee stock purchase plans (¶630). The statement must be furnished by January 31 of the year following the year for which a return required under Code Sec. 6039(a), as amended, was made.

¶137 Effect on Whistleblowers

New cap and floor on recoveries.—The Tax Relief and Health Care Act of 2006 (P.L. 109-432) includes a number of changes to the rules concerning the treatment of whistleblowers who provide information to the government regarding violations of federal tax laws (¶650). The new law establishes both a floor on rewards (15 percent of the collected proceeds) as well as a ceiling (30 percent of collected proceeds). In the case of successful government actions that were based primarily on allegations from sources other than the whistleblower, the whistleblower may still be entitled to a reward of no more than 10 percent of the collected proceeds.

Additional changes.—An above-the-line deduction is provided for attorney's fees and costs incurred by a whistleblower in connection with a reward for providing tax violation information. Denials of a reward may be appealed to the Tax Court within 30 days of an adverse determination and may be assigned to a special trial judge. As part of the amendments, the IRS is required to issue guidance on administration of the rewards program within one year of the date of enactment.

¶139 Effect on District of Columbia Home Owners and Investors

D.C. tax incentives extended.—A number of tax incentives relating to the District of Columbia have been extended by the Tax Relief and Health Care Act of 2006 (P.L. 109-432) (¶340). Among these, the credit of up to $5,000 that is available to first-time home buyers of principal residences within D.C. is extended through 2007. The special zero-percent capital gains rate applicable to capital gains from the sale of certain qualified D.C. zone assets (e.g., stock or partnership interests in, or tangible property held by, a D.C. zone business) that are held for more than five years is also extended through 2007. Additional D.C. related provisions applicable to businesses were also extended for the same period.

¶141 Effect on Members of the Intelligence Community

Ownership and use test suspended.—The Tax Relief and Health Care Act of 2006 (P.L. 109-432) adds a new category to those taxpayers who are allowed to take advantage of rules permitting suspension of the five-year period governing qualification for exclusion of gain on the sale of a principal residence. Qualifying members of the intelligence community will be able to utilize this provision for any period during which they are serving on extended duty (¶250). The provision covers a broad spectrum of intelligence community members including, but not limited to, employees of the Central Intelligence Agency, the Office of the Director of National Intelligence, the National Security Agency, and the Defense Intelligence Agency, as well as employees of the Department of Defense tasked with the collection of specialized national intelligence, any intelligence elements of the armed services, the F.B.I., the Treasury Department, and Homeland Security. As is the case with other permitted beneficiaries of this provision, the maximum suspension period is 10 years.

¶143 Effect on Judicial Officers

Sale of property deferral extended to judges.—New rules under the Tax Relief and Health Care Act of 2006 (P.L. 109-432) allow certain judicial officers to utilize the provision deferring the recognition of gain from property that must be divested in order to comply with conflict-of-interest requirements (¶255). Under that provision, qualified individuals who receive a certificate of divestiture are allowed to postpone the recognition of gain on the sale of conflicted property by purchasing certain replacement property within 60 days, accompanied by a reduction in the basis of the replacement property corresponding to the amount of gain not recognized. The new law defines the term "judicial officer" to include the Chief Justice of the Supreme Court, as well as, the Associate Justices, the judges of the U.S. Courts of Appeal, U.S. district courts, and any court created by Act of Congress. It also applies to a judge' s spouse, dependent children, related minors, and where applicable, trusts.

¶145 Effect on Innocent Spouses

Tax Court to review requests for equitable relief.—The Tax Relief and Health Care Act of 2006 (P.L. 109-432) includes a provision amending Code Sec. 6015 to allow the U.S. Tax Court jurisdiction to review denials of requests for equitable relief from joint and several liability where the IRS has not determined a deficiency against the taxpayer (¶660).

BUSINESSES

¶151 Overall Effect on Businesses

The Tax Increase Prevention and Reconciliation Act of 2005 (P.L. 109-222) includes a variety of provisions that affect businesses generally and also provisions that have a particular effect on corporations, S Corporations, partnerships, regulated investment companies (RICs), real estate investment trusts (REITs), international business, and also specific types of industries.

One of the key tax breaks in the legislation is a two-year extension of the small business expensing election (¶805). Another tax break allows businesses that create or acquire music or music copyrights to amortize those costs over five years (¶815).

Businesses may also indirectly benefit from a provision clarifying that certain environmental settlement funds are not subject to income tax (¶855).

On the other side of the business ledger, the legislation includes several business provisions designed to raise revenue. One change to the Code Sec. 199 domestic manufacturing deduction clarifies that in determining the W-2 wage limit, only wages allocated to domestic manufacturing gross receipts be considered (¶810). A provision extending prohibited tax shelter transaction penalties to tax-exempt accommodation parties includes a notice requirement for the taxable entity to give notice to the tax-exempt entity that the transaction is a prohibited tax shelter transaction (¶1130).

The new law imposes penalties on the manager of a tax-exempt entity that causes the entity to be a party to a prohibited tax shelter transaction. It also tightens the IRS offer-in-compromise requirements by requiring a deposit on lump sum offers and requiring the commencement of payments on installment offers while the IRS is considering the offer (¶1140). Finally, the grandfathered protection for foreign sales corporation (FSC) binding contracts and extraterritorial income (ETI) binding contracts under the American Jobs Creation Act of 2004 is repealed (¶1045).

The Tax Relief and Health Care Act of 2006 (P.L. 109-432) adds a number of significant business-related provisions. The legislation retroactively extends many business tax breaks that had expired at the end of 2005, including the research credit (¶405), the welfare-to-work and work opportunity credits (¶410), and the fifteen-year amortization of leasehold improvements (¶305). Also extended are the new markets tax credit (¶415) and parity in the application of certain mental health benefits (¶535). The enhanced charitable deduction for computer technology and equipment is extended and both it and the charitable deduction for scientific property used in research are expanded to include assembled as well as constructed property (¶355). The expensing of environmental remediation costs is extended and expanded to include petroleum products (¶310). Some provisions from the Energy Tax Incentives Act of 2005 were also extended, including the energy efficient commercial building deduction (¶335), the qualified fuel cell and solar energy credit for depreciable or amortizable property (¶440), and the placed in service date for certain electricity produced from alternative resources (¶450). The legislation adds new reporting requirements in connection with the issuance of stock related to incentive stock options (¶630). Activities qualifying for the domestic manufacturing deduction are extended to those in Puerto Rico (¶345).

The extended research credit is modified in the second year of the extension to increase the rates of the alternative incremental credit and to create a new alternative simplified credit (¶405). The welfare-to-work credit and work opportunity credit are combined in the second year of their extension and modified to work together (¶410). The new law also changes the eligibility rules for ex-felons and food stamp recipients under the work opportunity credit. The extended new markets tax credit calls for regulations to insure proportional allocations of the credit limits to non-metropolitan counties (¶415).

Fiscal year taxpayers are provided an extended election period with respect to elections under expired Code provisions which have been retroactively extended by the Tax Relief and Health Care Act of 2006 (P.L. 109-432) (¶405).

¶153 Effect on Corporations

Multiple provisions hit corporations.—A number of provisions in the Tax Increase Prevention and Reconciliation Act of 2005 (P.L. 109-222) specifically apply to corporations. A new temporary exception from Subpart F taxation is created by providing look-through treatment for dividends, interest, rents, and royalties received by one controlled foreign corporation (CFC) from a related CFC to the extent attributable to non-Subpart F income of the payor (¶1040). The Tax Relief and Health Care Act of 2006 (P.L. 109-432) made some technical corrections to this provision (¶365). The legislation also relaxes the active business test for tax-free corporate spin-offs by permitting all corporations in the distributing corporate group and the spun-off subsidiary's affiliated group to determine if the active business test has been satisfied. This provision was made permanent by the 2006 Extenders Act (¶360). However, spin-off treatment is denied for certain transactions involving disqualified investment corporations (¶830). The Tax Reconciliation Act also codifies earnings stripping regulations involving a corporation with a direct or indirect interest in a partnership (¶840). The timing of certain corporate estimated tax payments and the amount of a number of estimated tax payments by large corporations are adjusted to produce the desired budgetary results (¶835). The special charitable deduction for corporate donations of computer technology and equipment has been extended and both it and the charitable deduction for scientific property used in research are expanded to include assembled property (¶355). A two-year economic development credit is provided for corporations qualifying for the possessions tax credit with respect to American Samoa (¶435) A capital gain exclusion is provided for conservation sales of certain mineral and geothermal interests (¶358).

¶155 Effect on Particular Geographic Areas

Puerto Rico and Virgin Islands.—The suspension of the limitation on the cover over of tax on distilled spirits for Puerto Rico and the Virgin Islands has been extended (¶690). Activities qualifying for the domestic manufacturing deduction are extended to those in Puerto Rico (¶345).

American Somoa.—A two-year economic development credit is provided for corporations qualifying for the possessions tax credit with respect to American Samoa (¶435).

District of Columbia.—Special tax incentives for investment in the District of Columbia are extended (¶340).

Gulf Opportunity Zone.—The placed-in-service deadline is extended for specified Gulf Opportunity Zone property (¶315).

¶157 Effect on S Corporations

Wage limitation clarified.—The W-2 wage limitation on the domestic manufacturing deduction is clarified to provide that S corporation shareholders who are allocated part of the qualified production activities income of the corporation are treated as being allocated their share of S corporation wages. The allocation will be limited to wages used to determine qualified production activities income (¶810).

¶159 Effect on Partnerships

Rules on domestic manufacturing deduction and earnings stripping modified.— The W-2 wage limitation on the domestic manufacturing deduction is clarified to provide that partners who are allocated part of the qualified production activities income of the partnership are treated as being allocated their share of partnership wages. The allocation will be limited to wages used to determine qualified production activities income (¶810). The legislation also codifies earnings stripping regulations involving a corporation with a direct or indirect interest in a partnership. The IRS is further granted regulatory authority to reallocate partnership debt or distributive shares of interest income or expense to prevent circumvention of the rules (¶840).

¶161 Effect on REITs

New FRPTA rules for REITs.—The Tax Increase Prevention and Reconciliation Act of 2005 (P.L. 109-222) makes several modifications to the treatment of Real Estate Investment Trusts (REITs) with respect to the Foreign Investment in Real Property Tax Act (FIRPTA) and distributions attributable to FIRPTA gains (¶1020). The extension of the lower rates on capital gains and qualified dividends also applies to capital gains or dividends passed through a REIT (¶925).

¶163 Effect on Building Contractors

The deduction for energy efficient commercial buildings is extended (¶335). The credit for new energy -efficient homes is also extended (¶445).

¶165 Effect on RICs

New FRPTA rules for RICs.—Several modifications are made to the treatment of regulated investment companies (RICs) with respect to the Foreign Investment in Real Property Tax Act (FIRPTA) and distributions attributable to FIRPTA gains (¶1020). The Tax Reconciliation Act of 2005 also clarifies generally the application of FIRPTA to RICs (¶1015). The extension of the lower rates on capital gains and qualified dividends also applies to capital gains or dividends passed through a RIC (¶925).

¶167 Effect on Small Businesses

Expensing limit extended.—Small business received a two-year extension of the increased limits of the small business expensing election under Code Sec. 179 (¶805). The legislation also clarifies that the amount of excluded gain on the sale of so-called small business stock, which is treated as a tax preference item for AMT purposes, will remain at seven percent for tax years beginning in 2006 through 2010 (¶915).

¶169 Effect on Farming

The rules are modified for the refund of excise taxes for kerosene used in aviation for farming purposes (¶670).

¶171 Effect on Banks, Finance Companies, and Securities Dealers

Active financing exemption and tax shelter penalties extended.—The Tax Increase Prevention and Reconciliation Act of 2005 (P.L. 109-222) includes a two-year extension of the exemption from Subpart F taxation for active financing income (¶1035). The extension of tax shelter penalties to tax-exempt accommodation parties includes a provision extending penalties to the manager of entities such as qualified pension plans, IRAs and similar tax-favored arrangements, with the entity manager being the person that approves or otherwise causes the entity to be a party to a prohibited tax shelter transaction (¶1130).

¶173 Effect on the Music Industry

Election for amortization of musical compositions.—The new law allows the election of a five-year amortization period for music compositions or music copyrights rather than the longer amortizations provided for under the income forecast method (¶815).

Capital gain treatment. —The music industry should benefit from the capital gain treatment for self-created musical works (¶240).

¶175 Effect on the Restaurant Industry

The 15-year amortization of qualified restaurant property has been extended (¶305).

¶177 Effect on Insurance Companies

Subpart F exemption extended.—A two-year extension of the exemption from Subpart F taxation for exempt insurance income is also included in the Tax Increase Prevention and Reconciliation Act of 2005 (P.L. 109-222) (¶1030).

Health insurance.—The Tax Relief and Health Care Act of 2006 (P.L. 109-432) should promote high deductible health insurance plans through an number of provisions designed to make health savings accounts more attractive and easier to fund (¶505, ¶510, ¶515, ¶520, and ¶525).

Mortgage insurance.—The new temporary mortgage interest deduction for mortgage insurance premiums should have a positive impact on the mortgage insurance industry (¶220). However, recipients of such mortgage interest shall also be required to file information returns (¶220).

¶179 Effect on the Energy Industry

The placed-in-service deadline is extended for the credit for electricity produced from certain renewable resources. Certain renewable resources already had a later placed-in service deadline and those were not further extended (¶450). The credit to holders of Clean Renewable Energy Bonds is extended and the limitation amounts are increased (¶625). A new 25-percent exclusion is created on the long-term capital gain from the conservation sale of a mineral or geothermal interest (¶358). The rules are modified for the refund of excise taxes for kerosene used in aviation (¶670).

¶181 Effect on Oil and Gas Companies

Amortization period for G&G costs extended.—The Tax Increase Prevention and Reconciliation Act of 2005 (P.L. 109-222) extends to five years the amortization period for geological and geophysical (G&G) costs incurred by certain major integrated oil companies (¶820).

The Tax Relief and Health Care Act of 2006 (P.L. 109-432) extends the taxable income limitation suspension provision for marginal oil and gas production (¶325). The expensing of environmental remediation costs is expanded to include petroleum products (¶310). A new 25-percent exclusion is created on the long-term capital gain from the conservation sale of a mineral or geothermal interest (¶358). Additional expenditures are permitted from LUST trust funds (¶675).

¶182 Effect on the Coal and Coke Industry

The Tax Relief and Health Care Act of 2006 (P.L. 109-432) extends the special excise tax rate for methanol and ethanol produced from coal (¶665). The extension of the placed-in-service date for electricity from alternative resources excludes refined coal and Indian coal, which already possessed later placed-in-service dates (¶450). New performance criteria are provided for the advanced coal credit with respect to sulfur dioxide removal in units designed to use subbituminous coal (¶455). The credit for producing fuels from a nonconventional source is changed to repeal the application of the phase-out to facilities producing coke or coke gas, but limiting those qualifying facilities to those that are not producing coke or coke gas from petroleum based products (¶460). A new 25-percent exclusion is created on the long-term capital gain from the conservation sale of a mineral or geothermal interest (¶358).

¶183 Effect on the Ethanol and Alternative Fuels Industry

The Tax Relief and Health Care Act of 2006 (P.L. 109-432) extends the special excise tax rate for methanol and ethanol produced from coal (¶665). Fifty percent first-year depreciation is allowed with respect to qualified cellulosic biomass ethanol plant property (¶323). The credit for producing fuels from a nonconventional source is changed to repeal the application of the phase-out to facilities producing coke or coke gas, but limiting those qualifying facilities to those that are not producing coke or coke gas from petroleum based products (¶460).

¶184 Effect on the Mining Industry

Partial expensing is permitted for advanced mine safety equipment (¶330). A new credit is also created for mine rescue team training (¶425).

¶185 Effect on Continuing Care Facilities

New definitions and imputed interest rules.—The definition of a qualified continuing care facility is modified and the imputed interest rules applicable to loans to such facilities are relaxed. The Tax Relief and Health Care Act of 2006 (P.L. 109-432) makes this provision permanent (¶245).

¶186 Effect on the Aviation Industry

The rules are modified for the refund of excise taxes for kerosene used in aviation (¶670).

¶187 Effect on the Shipping Industry

Tonnage tax election available.—The Tax Increase Prevention and Reconciliation Act of 2005 (P.L. 109-222) extends the opportunity for qualifying vessel operators to elect a tonnage tax, rather than the corporate income tax on shipping activities, to qualifying vessels of not less than 6,000 deadweight tons. The Tax Relief and Health Care Act of 2006 (P.L. 109-432) makes this provision permanent and makes the tonnage tax applicable to Great Lakes domestic shipping (¶370).

¶188 Effect on the Railroad Industry

The rules are modified with respect to the railroad track maintenance credit (¶430).

¶189 Effect on the Environmental Industry

CERCLA settlement funds not taxable.—The Tax Increase Prevention and Reconciliation Act of 2005 (P.L. 109-222) provides that settlement funds resolving claims under the Comprehensive Environmental Response, Compensation, and Liability Act (CERCLA) will be treated as beneficially owned by the U.S. government and will not be subject to federal taxation. The Tax Relief and Health Care Act of 2006 (P.L. 109-432) makes this provision permanent (¶375).

Brownfield Remediation.—The expensing of Brownfield remediation costs is extended and the definition of hazardous substance is expanded to include petroleum products (¶310).

Lust Trust Fund. —The Tax Relief and Health Care Act of 2006 (P.L. 109-432) expands authorized distributions from the Leaking Underground Storage Tank Trust Fund to include amounts to carry out the provisions of the Solid Waste Disposal Act (¶675).

¶190 Effect on the Drug Industry

Meningococcal and human papillomavirus vaccines are added to the list of taxable vaccines (¶685).

¶191 Effect on the Alcohol and Spirits Industry

The suspension of the limitation on the rum excise tax rate for Puerto Rico and the Virgin Islands has been extended (¶690).

¶192 Effect on International Business

International businesses faces changes.—A number of provisions in the Tax Increase Prevention and Reconciliation Act of 2005 (P.L. 109-222) alter the tax rules applicable to international business operations. A new temporary exception from Subpart F taxation is created by providing look-through treatment for dividends, interest, rents, and royalties received by one controlled foreign corporation (CFC) from a related CFC to the extent attributable to non-Subpart F income of the payor (¶1040). The Tax Relief and Health Care Act of 2006 (P.L. 109-432) made some technical corrections to this provision (¶365). The Subpart F exception for active financing income and exempt insurance income is also extended (¶1030 and ¶1035). The application of the Foreign Investment in Real Property Tax Act (FIRPTA) to regulated investment companies (RICs) is clarified and the treatment of distributions attributable to FIRPTA gains involving RICs and real estate investment trusts (REITs) is addressed (¶1015 and ¶1020). The Act also seeks to prevent tax avoidance on FIRPTA investments through wash sale transactions (¶1025).

The grandfathered protection for foreign sales corporation (FSC) binding contracts and extraterritorial income (ETI) binding contracts under the American Jobs Creation Act of 2004 is repealed (¶1045). The Act also extends the opportunity for qualifying vessel operators to elect a tonnage tax, rather than the corporate income tax on shipping activities, to qualifying vessels of not less than 6,000 deadweight tons (¶370).

International business may also be affected by the indexing of the foreign earned income exclusion and changes to the foreign housing cost exclusion applicable to U.S. taxpayers working abroad (¶1005 and ¶1010).

TAX-EXEMPT AND GOVERNMENT ENTITIES

¶193 Effect on Tax-Exempt Entities

Tax shelter rules affect tax exempts.—The Tax Increase Prevention and Reconciliation Act of 2005 (P.L. 109-222) extends the application of tax shelter penalties to tax-exempt accommodation parties and the managers that cause the tax exempt entity to become a party to a prohibited tax shelter transaction (¶1130). The Act also alters the definition of a qualified continuing care facility and relaxes the imputed interest rules applicable to loans to such facilities (¶245).

¶194 Effect on Charitable Remainder Trusts

The excise tax on the unrelated business taxable income of charitable remainder trusts is modified (¶680).

¶195 Effect on Government Entities

Settlement funds, withholding and reporting rules, and tax-exempt bonds.—Settlements funds resolving claims under the Comprehensive Environmental Response, Compensation, and Liability Act (CERCLA) will be treated as beneficially owned by the U.S. government and will not be subject to federal taxation. This provision has been made permanent by the Tax Relief and Health Care Act of 2006 (P.L. 109-432) (¶375).

Among two new efforts to close the tax gap (the amount by which tax obligations are underpaid or underreported) is a new requirement, effective beginning in 2011, that government entities withhold three percent on payments for property and services (¶1125). Also, payors of interest on tax-exempt state and local bonds are now subject to interest reporting requirements (¶1105).

The statutory cap on the issuance of qualified small issue bonds has been raised (¶1110). Also the rules with respect to requirements for tax-exemption for pooled financing bonds have been tightened (¶1135). The authority to issue qualified veterans' mortgage bonds has been expanded in Alaska, Oregon, and Wisconsin. This provision has been made permanent by the Tax Relief and Health Care Act of 2006 (P.L. 109-432) (¶620). Also, the new law includes an extension of the exception from the arbitrage requirements for Texas university fund bonds secured by the Permanent University Fund (¶615).

Regional tax agencies.—Regional tax agencies are treated as states for confidentiality and disclosure requirements (¶635).

Schools.—The provision for Qualified Zone Academy Bonds is extended and new rules with respect to arbitrage, spending and reporting are added (¶605).

¶196 Effect on Bonds

The provision for Qualified Zone Academy Bonds is extended and new rules with respect to arbitrage, spending and reporting are added (¶605). The credit to holders of Clean Renewable Energy Bonds is extended and the limitation amounts are increased (¶625). The use of qualified mortgage bonds to finance residences is extended to veterans without regard to the first-time homebuyer requirement (¶610). The Tax Increase Prevention and Reconciliation Act of 2005 (P.L. 109-222) changes the volume limits for veterans' mortgage bonds issued by the states of Alaska, Oregon, and Wisconsin (¶620). This provision is made permanent by the Tax Relief and Health Care Act of 2006 (P.L. 109-432) (¶620). The Tax Increase Prevention and Reconciliation Act of 2005 (P.L. 109-222) also modified the special arbitrage rules for certain funds associated with bond issues (¶615). This provision was also made permanent by the Tax Relief and Health Care Act of 2006 (P.L. 109-432).

¶197 Effect on Indian Tribes

Tribes could be hit with penalties.—The extension of tax shelter penalties to tax-exempt accommodation parties and the managers that cause the entity to participate in a prohibited tax shelter transaction includes the use of Indian tribal governments as accommodation parties (¶1130).

Tax break extensions.—The Indian employment tax credit (¶420) and the accelerated depreciation of qualified Indian Reservation property (¶320) have been extended.

¶198 Effect on Tax Qualified Retirement and Employee Benefit Plans

Tax shelter rules affect employee plans.—The extension of the tax shelter penalties to tax-exempt accommodation parties and the managers that cause the entity to participate in a prohibited tax shelter transaction includes the use of tax qualified retirement plans, IRAs, and employee benefit plans (¶1130).

High-deductible health plans.—A number of provisions are designed to make Health Savings Accounts (HSAs) more attractive and easier to fund (¶505, ¶510, ¶515, ¶520, and ¶525).

¶199 Effect on IRS Practice and Procedure

New rules for offers in compromise and information reporting.—The Tax Increase Prevention and Reconciliation Act of 2005 (P.L. 109-222) tightens the IRS offer-in-compromise requirements by requiring a deposit on lump sum offers and requiring the commencement of payments on installment offers while the IRS is considering the offer (¶1140). Information reporting requirements have been added to the law for payors of interest on tax-exempt state and local bonds (¶1105).

Disclosures.—The provisions in the law with respect to disclosures to facilitate combined employment tax reporting, return information with respect to terrorist activities, and return information with respect to student loan repayment have been extended (¶635). Information returns are also required in connection with the issuance of stock connected to incentive stock options (¶630).

Undercover operations.—The Code provision specifying the use of proceeds from IRS undercover operations has been extended (¶645).

Whistleblower reforms.—Several changes are made to help tax whistleblowers (¶650).

Frivolous tax returns and requests.—Penalties are increased for filing frivolous tax returns, and procedures are tightened for handling frivolous requests (¶640).

Suspension of interest rules.—The Tax Relief and Health Care Act of 2006 (P.L. 109-432) makes technical corrections regarding the authority to exercise reasonable cause and good faith exception (¶655).

Tax Relief—Individuals

DEDUCTIONS

TAX CREDITS

INCOME AND GAINS

CROSS REFERENCES

DEDUCTIONS

¶205 Election to Deduct State and Local General Sales Taxes Extended

SUMMARY OF NEW LAW

The election to deduct state and local general sales taxes in lieu of state and local income taxes is extended for two years through December 31, 2007.

BACKGROUND

For tax years beginning in 2004 and 2005, individual taxpayers could elect to deduct *either* state and local income taxes or state and local general sales taxes as an itemized deduction on their federal income tax returns (Code Sec. 164(b)(5)). The deduction is *either* (1) the total of actual general sales taxes paid as substantiated by accumulated receipts; or (2) an amount from IRS-generated tables plus, if any, the amount of general sales taxes paid in the purchase of a motor vehicle, boat, or other items as prescribed by the Secretary (see IRS Publication 600, "Optional State Sales Tax Tables").

General sales taxes. For purposes of the deduction, "general sales tax" means a tax imposed at one rate on the retail sales of a broad range of classes of items. Except in the case of a lower rate of tax applicable to food, clothing, medical supplies, and motor vehicles, no deduction is allowed for general sales tax at a rate other than the general rate of tax. If the state sales tax rate for motor vehicles exceeds the general sales tax rate, the excess is disregarded and the general sales tax rate is treated as the rate of tax. Thus, only the amount of tax that is equal to the general sales tax rate is allowed as a deduction.

If the amount of the general sales tax is separately stated, then to the extent it is paid by the consumer to the seller (other than in connection with the consumer's trade or business), the amount is treated as a tax imposed on, and paid by, the consumer. In addition, a *compensating use tax* is treated as a general sales tax provided:

(1) such a tax is complementary to a general sales tax; and

(2) a deduction for sales tax is allowed with respect to similar items sold at retail in the taxing jurisdiction.

The tax must be imposed on the use, storage, or consumption of an item.

> **Comment:** The election to deduct state and local general sales taxes in lieu of state and local income taxes applied only for calendar tax years 2004 and 2005.

NEW LAW EXPLAINED

Extension of election to deduct state and local general sales taxes in lieu of state and local income taxes.—The election to deduct state and local general sales taxes in

NEW LAW EXPLAINED

lieu of state and local income taxes is extended two years to apply to the 2006 and 2007 calendar tax years (Code Sec. 164(b)(5)(I), as amended by the Tax Relief and Health Care Act of 2006 (P.L. 109-432)).

> **Planning Note:** Taxpayers may elect to deduct sales taxes in lieu of local income taxes on Schedule A of Form 1040. The election may be revoked by filing an amended return for the tax year, if the period of limitation for filing a claim for refund or credit under Code Sec. 6511 has not expired. A taxpayer is permitted to deduct sales taxes in one tax year and local income taxes in another year (see Notice 2005-31, 2005-1 CB 830).

> **Comment:** The IRS has posted Publication 600, State and Local General Sales Taxes, to its website, www.IRS.gov. Publication 600 was updated to reflect the extension of the deduction and includes the state and local sales tax tables, a worksheet and instructions for figuring the deduction (IRS News Release, IR-2006-195, December 22, 2006) (see ¶ 28,001 et seq.).

▶ **Effective date.** This extension applies to tax years beginning after December 31, 2005 (Act Sec. 103(b) of the Tax Relief and Health Care Act of 2006 (P.L. 109-432)).

Law source: Law at ¶ 5240. Committee Report at ¶ 15,120.

— Act Sec. 103(a) of the Tax Relief and Health Care Act of 2006 (P.L. 109-432), amending Code Sec. 164(b)(5)(I);

— Act Sec. 103(b), providing the effective date.

Reporter references: For further information, consult the following CCH reporters.

— Standard Federal Tax Reporter, ¶ 9502.0385

— Tax Research Consultant, INDIV: 45,106.05

— Federal Tax Guide, ¶ 4265 and ¶ 6541

¶210 Deduction for Qualified Tuition and Related Expenses Extended

SUMMARY OF NEW LAW

The deduction for qualified tuition and related expenses is extended for two years, through December 31, 2007. The maximum amount deductible for 2006 and 2007 is the same as it was for 2004 and 2005: $4,000 or $2,000, depending on the taxpayer's adjusted gross income.

BACKGROUND

One of the education tax breaks included in the Economic Growth and Tax Relief Reconciliation Act of 2001 (P.L. 107-16) (EGTRRA) was an above-the-line deduction for qualified tuition and related expenses (Code Sec. 222). The provision was added

BACKGROUND

to provide taxpayers with a greater choice of available education tax benefits (S. Rep. No. 107-30). This deduction is allowed to qualifying individuals in tax years beginning after December 31, 2001. The deduction does not apply to tax years beginning after December 31, 2005 (Code Sec. 222(e)).

The term "qualified tuition and related expenses" is defined in Code Sec. 25A(f) (Code Sec. 222(d)). These expenses include tuition and fees required for the enrollment or attendance of the taxpayer, the taxpayer's spouse, or a dependent of the taxpayer, at an eligible institution of higher education for courses of instruction. Expenses connected to meals, lodging, insurance, transportation, and similar living expenses are not eligible for the deduction. The deduction is not available for expenses paid for elementary or secondary education. The expenses must be incurred in connection with enrollment during the tax year, or with an academic term beginning during the tax year or during the first three months of the next tax year (Code Sec. 222(d)(3)(B)).

The amount of qualified tuition and related expenses must be reduced by certain scholarships, educational assistance allowances, and other amounts paid for the benefit of the individual (Code Sec. 25A(g)(2)). In addition, the amount of qualified tuition expenses must be reduced by the amount of such expenses taken into account for purposes of determining any exclusion from gross income of: (1) income from certain U.S. Savings Bonds used to pay for higher education; and (2) income from a Coverdell education savings account (Code Sec. 222(c)(2)(B)). Moreover, qualified tuition expenses must be reduced by the earnings portion of distributions from a qualified tuition program if an exclusion under Code Sec. 529 is claimed with respect to expenses otherwise deductible under Code Sec. 222 (Code Sec. 222(c)(2)(B)). No deduction is allowed for any expense for which a deduction is otherwise allowed or with respect to an individual for whom a Hope Scholarship or Lifetime Learning Credit is elected for the tax year (Code Sec. 222(c)(2)(A)).

The amount of the deduction allowed depends on the taxpayer's adjusted gross income (AGI) and the tax year in which the deduction is claimed. Taxpayers whose AGI did not exceed $65,000 ($130,000 for joint filers) could deduct a maximum of $4,000 for tax years beginning in 2004 or 2005 (Code Sec. 222(b)(2)(B)(i)). Additionally, for tax years beginning in 2004 or 2005, taxpayers with an AGI of more than $65,000 ($130,000 for joint filers) but not in excess of $80,000 ($160,000 for joint filers) could deduct a maximum of $2,000 (Code Sec. 222(b)(2)(B)(ii)). These amounts are not adjusted for inflation and married individuals filing separately may not claim the deduction (Code Sec. 222(d)(4)). No deduction is allowed to any individual with respect to whom a personal exemption deduction may be claimed by another taxpayer for the tax year (Code Sec. 222(c)(3)).

For purposes of determining whether a taxpayer is eligible to take the deduction, AGI is determined: (1) without regard to the exclusions from income for foreign earned income and foreign housing costs (Code Sec. 911) and income of residents of Guam, American Samoa, the Northern Mariana Islands, and Puerto Rico (Code Secs. 931 and 933), and (2) for tax years beginning after 2004, without regard to the deduction for income attributable to domestic production activities (Code Sec. 199). However, taxable social security benefits (Code Sec. 86), the exclusion for certain

BACKGROUND

savings bond interest used to pay higher education expenses (Code Sec. 135), the exclusion for employer-provided adoption assistance (Code Sec. 137), the deductions for retirement savings (Code Sec. 219) and student loan interest payments (Code Sec. 221), and the disallowance of passive activity losses (Code Sec. 469) are taken into account in calculating AGI for purposes of the limitation (Code Sec. 222(b)(2)(C)).

NEW LAW EXPLAINED

Tuition deduction extended through 2007.—The deduction for qualified tuition and related expenses is extended to apply to tax years beginning in 2006 and 2007 (Code Sec. 222(b)(2)(B) and (e), as amended by the Tax Relief and Health Care Act of 2006 (P.L. 109-432)). The requirements for claiming the deduction under Code Sec. 222 are the same for 2006 and 2007 as they were in 2004 and 2005.

> **Compliance Pointer:** The taxpayer must include the name and taxpayer identification number (TIN) of the student for whom the expenses were paid on the taxpayer's return in order to claim the deduction (Code Sec. 222(d)(2)). As an above-the-line deduction, it can even be taken by taxpayers who do not itemize deductions.

> **Planning Note:** Taxpayers may not claim the deduction for qualified tuition and related expenses and a Hope Scholarship or Lifetime Learning Credit for the same student in the same year (Code Sec. 222(c)(2)(A)).

The maximum deduction for tax years beginning in 2006 and 2007 is $4,000 for taxpayers whose AGI does not exceed $65,000 ($130,000 for joint filers) and $2,000 for taxpayers whose AGI does not exceed $80,000 ($160,000 for joint filers) (Code Sec. 222(b)(2)(B), as amended by the 2006 Extenders Act). Taxpayers with AGI exceeding $80,000 ($160,000 for joint filers) cannot take the deduction (Code Sec. 222(b)(2)(B)(iii)).

> **Planning Note:** Unless the IRS provides otherwise, April 15, 2007, is the deadline for making elections under a provision that expired in 2006, and that has been extended for the 2006 tax year by the 2006 Extenders Act. Thus, the qualified tuition and related expenses deduction for 2006 must be claimed by April 15, 2007 (Act Sec. 123(b) of the 2006 Extenders Act).

> **Planning Note:** The IRS was required to finalize the 2006 version of Form 1040, U.S. Individual Income Tax Return, in early November. Because the form was finalized prior to the passage of the 2006 Extenders Act, it does not contain a line on which to claim the deduction for qualified tuition and related expenses. The IRS has issued guidance on claiming the deduction. Taxpayers electing to claim the qualified tuition deduction should claim the amount on line 35 of Form 1040, which was originally dedicated to the domestic production activities deduction under Code Sec. 199. Taxpayers should "code" the line with the letter "T" to indicate that the amount claimed relates to qualified tuition and related expenses. If a taxpayer claims both the tuition and domestic production deductions, the letter "B" should be placed on line 35, along with a breakdown

NEW LAW EXPLAINED

showing the amounts claimed for each deduction (IRS News Release, IR-2006-195, December 22, 2006) (see ¶28,001 et seq.).

Termination of deduction. The deduction does not apply to tax years beginning after December 31, 2007 (Code Sec. 222(e), as amended by the 2006 Extenders Act).

▶ **Effective date.** The provision applies to tax years beginning after December 31, 2005 (Act Sec. 101(c) of the Tax Relief and Health Care Act of 2006 (P.L. 109-432)).

Law source: Law at ¶5336. Committee Report at ¶15,100.

— Act Sec. 101(a) of the Tax Relief and Health Care Act of 2006 (P.L. 109-432), amending Code Sec. 222(e);

— Act Sec. 101(b), amending Code Sec. 222(b)(2)(B);

— Act Sec. 101(c), providing the effective date.

Reporter references: For further information, consult the following CCH reporters.

— Standard Federal Tax Reporter, ¶12,772.01

— Tax Research Consultant, INDIV: 60,064 and FILEIND: 9,086

— Federal Tax Guide, ¶6434

¶215 Above-the-Line Deduction for Certain Expenses of School Teachers Extended

SUMMARY OF NEW LAW

The deduction for eligible educator expenses has been extended for two years through December 31, 2007.

BACKGROUND

For tax years 2002 through 2005, eligible educators have been allowed an above-the-line deduction of up to $250 (annually) for unreimbursed expenses paid or incurred for books, supplies (other than nonathletic supplies for health or physical education courses), computer equipment (including related software and services), and other equipment, including supplementary materials used by the eligible educator in the classroom (Code Sec. 62(a)(2)(D)). For purposes of this deduction, an "eligible educator" is an individual who is a kindergarten through grade 12 teacher, instructor, counselor, principal, or aide working in a school for at least 900 hours during the school year; a "school" is any school that provides elementary or secondary education, as determined under state law (Code Sec. 62(d)(1)).

The deduction for eligible educator classroom expenses was enacted as part of the Job Creation and Worker Assistance Act of 2002 (P.L. 107-147). It applied to classroom expenses paid in 2002 and 2003 (Code Sec. 62(a)(2)(D)). This above-the-line deduction for eligible educator expenses was extended by the Working Families Tax Relief Act

BACKGROUND

of 2004 (P.L. 108-311) to apply also to tax years 2004 and 2005. The deduction applied only to the extent that the expenses exceeded the amount excludable from income for the year under Code Secs. 135 (education savings bonds), 529(c)(1) (qualified tuition programs), and 530(d)(2) (Coverdell education savings accounts). The above-the-line deduction for eligible educators is not allowed for tax years beginning after December 31, 2005.

NEW LAW EXPLAINED

Eligible educator expense deduction extended.—The deduction for eligible educator expenses has been extended for two years through December 31, 2007 (Code Sec. 62(a)(2)(D), as amended by the Tax Relief and Health Care Act of 2006 (P.L. 109-432)).

Planning Note: Unless the IRS provides otherwise, April 15, 2007, is the deadline for making elections under a provision that expired in 2006, and that has been extended for the 2006 tax year by the 2006 Extenders Act. Thus, the eligible educator expense deduction for 2006 must be claimed by April 15, 2007 (Act Sec. 123(b) of the 2006 Extenders Act).

Compliance Pointer: The IRA has issued guidance on claiming the deduction. The deduction for eligible educator expenses should be reported on line 23 of the 2006 Form 1040, which is currently designated for use for reporting the Archer MSA deduction. The IRS advises that taxpayers should indicate that they are taking eligible educator deduction by adding the letter "E" at line 23 of the 2006 Form 1040. The IRS further advises that if the taxpayer intends to claim both the eligible educator and Archer MSA deductions, that taxpayer should insert the letter "B" on line 23 and attach a breakdown showing the amounts claimed for each deduction (IRS News Release, IR-2006-195, December 22, 2006) (see ¶28,001 et seq.).

Comment: The IRS advises that teachers and other educators should save their receipts and keep a record of their qualifying expenses in a folder or envelope marked "Educator Expense Deduction," noting the amount, date and purpose for each purchase (IRS News Release IR-2005-82; IRS Tax Tip 2006-52).

▶ **Effective date.** The provision applies to tax years beginning after December 31, 2005 (Act Sec. 108(b) of the Tax Relief and Health Care Act of 2006 (P.L. 109-432)).

Law source: Law at ¶5085. Committee Report at ¶15,170.

— Act Sec. 108(a) of the Tax Relief and Health Care Act of 2006 (P.L. 109-432), amending Code Sec. 62(a)(2)(D);

— Act Sec. 108(b), providing the effective date.

Reporter references: For further information, consult the following CCH reporters.

— Standard Federal Tax Reporter, ¶6005.029

— Tax Research Consultant, INDIV: 36,364

— Federal Tax Guide, ¶6430

¶215

¶220 Deduction for Mortgage Insurance Premiums Added

SUMMARY OF NEW LAW

Premiums paid for mortgage insurance in 2007, pursuant to a contract entered into in 2007, are to be considered interest and deductible.

BACKGROUND

Typically, interest is not deductible for individuals if it is considered to be a form of personal interest (Code Sec. 163(h)(1)). However, this rule does not apply in the case of certain types of interest, such as interest on qualified residence indebtedness (Code Sec. 163(h)(2)(D)). Specifically, a deduction is allowed for interest on home acquisition indebtedness of up to $1 million (Code Sec. 163(h)(3)(B)) and on home equity indebtedness of up to $100,000 (Code Sec. 163(h)(3)(C)). Any person who receives $600 or more of mortgage interest from any individual in the course of a trade or business is required to make a return to the IRS and furnish a statement to the payor of the amount paid (Code Sec. 6050H).

Often, in cases of home acquisition loans, an individual who does not have funds sufficient for a full down payment may be required to purchase or obtain mortgage insurance. Mortgage insurance guarantees repayment of the acquisition loan in the case of the death or disability of the mortgagor. Mortgage insurance is available from many sources, such as various government programs. However, most often it is available to mortgagors from private insurance companies and allows individuals to purchase homes without having 20 percent of the amount of the purchase price available as a down payment.

The cost of the premiums for mortgage insurance are not deductible.

NEW LAW EXPLAINED

Mortgage insurance premiums treated as interest.—The new provision allows the premiums paid for qualified mortgage insurance in connection with acquisition indebtedness to be considered interest and, therefore, deductible (Code Sec. 163(h)(3)(E), as added by the Tax Relief and Health Care Act of 2006 (P.L. 109-432)). The provision does not apply to mortgage insurance contracts issued prior to January 1, 2007 (Code Sec. 163(h)(3)(H)(iii), as added by the 2006 Extenders Act) nor does it apply to premiums paid or accrued after December 31, 2007, or properly allocable to any period after December 31, 2007 (Code Sec. 163(h)(3)(E)(iv), as added by the 2006 Extenders Act).

Qualified mortgage insurance means mortgage insurance provided by the Veterans Administration (VA), the Federal Housing Administration (FHA), the Rural Housing Administration (RHA) and private mortgage insurance as defined under section 2 of the Homeowners Protection Act of 1998 (12 U.S.C. Sec. 4901) (Code Sec. 163(h)(4)(E), as added by the 2006 Extenders Act).

NEW LAW EXPLAINED

In the case of prepaid mortgage insurance, except contracts issued by the VA or the RHA, amounts paid that are allocable to periods beyond the year in which they are paid are charged to a capital account and treated as paid in the allocable year. Also, if the mortgage is satisfied before the end of its term, no deduction will be allowed for the unamortized balance of the capital account (Code Sec. 163(h)(4)(F), as added by the 2006 Extenders Act).

The rule is also subject to a phaseout. For every $1,000 by which the taxpayer's adjusted gross income exceeds $100,000, the amount of mortgage insurance premiums treated as interest is reduced by 10 percent. In the case of a married taxpayer filing separately, the amounts are lowered to $500 and $50,000. The effect of this phaseout is that the interest treatment is not allowed for a taxpayer with adjusted gross income of $110,000 or higher ($55,000 for a married taxpayer filing separately) (Code Sec. 163(h)(3)(E)(ii), as added by the 2006 Extenders Act).

> **Comment:** An alternative route is often taken by home buyers who do not have the 20 percent down payment available. A buyer can take out another loan in addition to the mortgage to acquire the necessary funds, and the interest payments on that amount are deductible. This has squeezed mortgage insurers out of the market, and many insurers believe that making the premiums deductible will encourage buyers to choose the insurance over a second loan.

Reporting requirements. Any person or party who receives more than $600 of mortgage insurance premiums from any individual during the course of the year is required to make a return for each individual in the form prescribed by the IRS. The person or party receiving the payments must also provide the individual with a written statement containing information as required by the IRS. The statement must be furnished to the payor by January 31. If the party receiving the payments is a government entity, the same reporting requirements apply to the officer or the entity designated to make the returns (Code Sec. 6050H(h), as added by the 2006 Extenders Act).

> **Compliance Pointer:** The return to be used for reporting mortgage interest received is Form 1098, Mortgage Interest Statement, and a copy of this form typically satisfies the notification requirement. At this time, it is not known whether the mortgage insurance premium reporting requirements can also be satisfied with a modified Form 1098 or if a new form will be issued.

▶ **Effective date.** The provision applies to amounts paid or accrued after December 31, 2006 (Act Sec. 419(d) of the Tax Relief and Health Care Act of 2006 (P.L. 109-432)).

Law source: Law at ¶5230 and ¶5765. Committee Report at ¶15,640.

— Act Sec. 419(a) of the Tax Relief and Health Care Act of 2006 (P.L. 109-432), adding Code Sec. 163(h)(3)(E);

— Act Sec. 419(b), adding Code Sec. 163(h)(4)(E) and (F);

— Act Sec. 419(c), adding Code Sec. 6050H(h);

— Act Sec. 419(d), providing the effective date.

Reporter references: For further information, consult the following CCH reporters.

— Standard Federal Tax Reporter, ¶9402.023 and ¶9402.025

NEW LAW EXPLAINED

— Tax Research Consultant, INDIV: 48,400 and REAL: 6,050

— Federal Tax Guide, ¶6571

TAX CREDITS

¶ 225   Election to Include Combat Pay as Earned Income Extended

SUMMARY OF NEW LAW

The present rule allowing individuals to elect to treat combat zone compensation as earned income for purposes of the earned income credit has been extended for one year through December 31, 2007.

BACKGROUND

Child-related tax benefits have an impact on millions of individual tax returns and can be particularly important to low-income families. The earned income credit is a refundable credit intended for low-income workers who have earned income, meet certain adjusted gross income thresholds, and do not have more than a limited amount of disqualified income (Code Sec. 32). In general, "earned income" includes taxable compensation from employment. The amount of the credit depends on the earned income of the taxpayer, whether the taxpayer has children, and whether those children meet the definitional requirements of Code Sec. 32(c) for a "qualifying child."

In an effort to assist military families, the earned income credit amount was increased for military families in 2004 and 2005 by offering those taxpayers the option to include combat zone compensation when calculating the earned income credit. Combat pay that would otherwise be excluded from gross income under Code Sec. 112 is treated as earned income for purposes of the earned income credit if the taxpayer so elects (Code Sec. 32(c)(2)(B)(vi)), as added by the Working Families Tax Relief Act of 2004 (P.L. 108-311)). The election to treat combat pay as earned income for purposes of the earned income credit was scheduled to terminate on December 31, 2005, but was extended through December 31, 2006, by the Gulf Opportunity Zone Act of 2005 (P.L. 109-135).

NEW LAW EXPLAINED

Combat pay election extended.—The provision provides a one-year extension, through December 31, 2007, for the election to treat combat zone compensation that is otherwise excluded from gross income under Code Sec. 112 as earned income for

NEW LAW EXPLAINED

purposes of the earned income credit (Code Sec. 32(c)(2)(B)(vi)(II)), as amended by the Tax Relief and Health Care Act of 2006 (P.L. 109-432)).

> **Comment:** The inclusion of combat pay for purposes of calculating the earned income credit may have either a positive or a negative impact on the taxpayer because the credit is phased in and phased out, depending upon the amount of earned income. Therefore, the taxpayer's particular circumstances should be carefully considered.

> **Planning Note:** Unless the IRS provides otherwise, April 15, 2007, is the deadline for making elections under a provision that expired in 2006, and that has been extended for the 2006 tax year by the 2006 Extenders Act. Thus, the election to include combat pay as earned income for purposes of the earned income credit must be elected by April 15, 2007 (Act Sec. 123(b) of the 2006 Extenders Act).

▶ **Effective date.** This provision is effective for tax years beginning after December 31, 2006 (Act Sec.106(b) of the Tax Relief and Health Care Act of 2006 (P.L. 109-432)).

Law source: Law at ¶5032. Committee Report at ¶15,150.

— Act Sec. 106(a) of the Tax Relief and Health Care Act of 2006 (P.L. 109-432), amending Code Sec. 32(c)(2)(B)(vi)(II);

— Act Sec. 106(b), providing the effective date.

Reporter references: For further information, consult the following CCH reporters.

— Standard Federal Tax Reporter, ¶4082.048

— Tax Research Consultant, INDIV: 57,258

— Federal Tax Guide, ¶2222

¶230 Residential Energy Efficient Property Credit Extended and Clarified

SUMMARY OF NEW LAW

The credit for residential energy efficient property is extended to property placed in service during 2008. For purposes of the credit, all property, not just photovoltaic property, that uses solar energy to generate electricity for use in a dwelling unit is qualifying property.

BACKGROUND

A nonrefundable tax credit is available to help individual taxpayers pay for residential alternative energy equipment (Code Sec. 25D). The residential alternative energy credit is 30 percent of a qualified solar photovoltaic property expenditure, qualified solar water heating property expenditure, or qualified fuel cell property expenditure made by the taxpayer during the year (Code Sec. 25D(a)). The maximum credit for

BACKGROUND

any tax year is $2,000 for each category of solar equipment, and $500 for each half kilowatt of capacity of fuel cell property installed during the year (Code Sec. 25D(b)). Eligible equipment must be placed in service during 2006 or 2007 (Code Sec. 25D(g)).

A qualified photovoltaic property expenditure is an expenditure for property that uses solar energy to generate electricity for use in a dwelling unit located in the United States and used as a residence by the taxpayer (Code Sec. 25D(d)(2)).

NEW LAW EXPLAINED

Credit extended through 2008 and expanded to include solar electric property beyond photovoltaic technology.—The Tax Relief and Health Care Act of 2006 (P.L. 109-432) extends the credit for residential energy efficient property an additional year so that it is available for qualified property placed in service in 2008 (Code Sec. 25D(g), as amended by the 2006 Extenders Act).

The 2006 Extenders Act also clarifies that, for purposes of the credit, all property, not just photovoltaic property, that uses solar energy to generate electricity for use in a taxpayer's dwelling is qualified property. More specifically, the new law substitutes the broader term "qualified solar electric property expenditure" for "qualified photovoltaic property expenditure" where it appears in Code Sec. 25D (Code Sec. 25D(a)(1), (b)(1)(A), (d)(2) and (e)(4)(A)(i), as amended by the 2006 Extenders Act).

> **Comment:** According to the U.S. Department of Energy, a viable alternative to photovoltaic technology for converting solar energy to electricity is Concentrating Solar Power (CSP). CSP plants generate electric power by using mirrors to concentrate the sun's energy and convert it into steam, which is then channeled through a conventional turbine generator. Within the United States, over 350 megawatts of CSP capacity exists and these plants have been operating reliably for more than 15 years. Smaller systems with home-sized capacity are under development (www.eere.energy.gov/solar).

▶ **Effective date.** No specific date is provided by the Act. The provision is, therefore, considered effective on December 20, 2006, the date of enactment of the Tax Relief and Health Care Act of 2006 (P.L. 109-432).

Law source: Law at ¶5010. Committee Reports at ¶15,400.

— Act Sec. 206(a) of the Tax Relief and Health Care Act of 2006 (P.L. 109-432), amending Code Sec. 25D(g);

— Act Sec. 206(b), amending Code Sec. 25D(a)(1), (b)(1)(A), (d)(2), and (e)(4)(A)(i).

Reporter references: For further information, consult the following CCH reporters.

— Standard Federal Tax Reporter, ¶3847.01

— Tax Research Consultant, INDIV: 57,850

— Federal Tax Guide, ¶2240

¶230

¶235 AMT Credit Relief for Individuals

SUMMARY OF NEW LAW

If an individual has a long-term unused minimum tax credit for a tax year beginning before January 1, 2013, the minimum tax credit allowable for that tax year will be not less than the greater of (1) the lesser of $5,000 or the unused credit, or (2) 20 percent of the unused credit.

BACKGROUND

An alternative minimum tax (AMT) is imposed on an individual taxpayer to the extent his or her tentative minimum tax liability exceeds the taxpayer's regular income tax liability (Code Sec. 55(a)). An individual's tentative minimum tax is the sum of: (1) 26 percent of the first $175,000 ($87,500 for married individuals filing separately) of the taxpayer's alternative minimum taxable income (AMTI) in excess of an exemption amount; and (2) 28 percent of any remaining AMTI in excess of the exemption amount (Code Sec. 55(b)(1)(A)).

An individual's AMTI is his or her regular taxable income increased by certain preference items and adjusted by recomputing certain items in a manner less favorable than that allowed in determining the taxpayer's regular taxable income (Code Sec. 55(b)(2)). These preference items and adjustments may provide a permanent reduction or deferral of a portion of the taxpayer's regular tax liability for the tax year. In other words, the AMT adjustments and preferences can cause a prepayment of regular tax attributable to certain tax items. To alleviate this problem, the amount of AMT attributable to these deferral-type adjustments generates a minimum tax credit designed to reduce the taxpayer's regular tax liability in a tax year by some or all of the AMT paid in previous tax years.

Minimum tax credit. The minimum tax credit for a given tax year is the excess, if any, of the "adjusted net minimum tax" for all prior years over the amount allowed as a minimum tax credit for those years (Code Sec. 53(b)). The minimum tax credit is allowable to the extent the regular tax for the tax year (reduced by certain other nonrefundable credits) exceeds the tentative minimum tax for the year (Code Sec. 53(c)). Unused minimum tax credits are carried forward (but not back) indefinitely as credits against regular tax liability. The minimum tax credit may not be used to offset any future AMT liability.

> **Comment:** The nonrefundable credits that reduce regular tax liability for this purpose include: (1) the nonrefundable personal credits such as the credit for child and dependent care, the child tax credit, the credit for the elderly or the disabled, the mortgage interest credit, the adoption credit, the foreign tax credit, and the general business credit; and (2) the tentative minimum tax for the carryover year.

In calculating the minimum tax credit, an individual's "adjusted net minimum tax" for any given tax year is his or her AMT liability for that year reduced by the amount of AMT that would be attributable to certain AMT adjustments and preference items

BACKGROUND

(Code Sec. 53(d)(1)(B)). This includes the adjustments for miscellaneous itemized deductions, certain itemized taxes, itemized medical expenses, interest, net investment income, the standard deduction, the deduction for personal exemptions, and the foreign tax credit. It also includes the tax preferences for percentage depletion, tax-exempt interest, the exclusion of gain on the sale of small business stock, and qualified electric vehicles.

Incentive stock options. One of the adjustments in computing the AMTI takes into account the favorable tax treatment of the exercise of an incentive stock option (ISO). For regular tax purposes, the exercise of an ISO is tax-free if the stock is not disposed of within one year of the exercise of the option or within two years of the grant of the option (Code Sec. 421). If the holding period requirements are not satisfied, the individual generally takes into account, at the exercise of the option, an amount of ordinary income equal to the excess of the fair market value of the stock on the date of the exercise over the amount paid for the stock. If the stock is sold at a loss before the required holding periods are met, the amount taken into account may not exceed the amount realized on the sale over the adjusted basis of the stock. If the stock is sold after the tax year in which the option was exercised but before the required holding periods are met, the required inclusion is made in the year the stock is sold (Reg. § 1.422-1).

Under the AMT, an exercise of an ISO by an individual is treated as an exercise of an option other than an ISO (Code Sec. 56(b)(3)). This means that the individual generally takes into account as ordinary income for purposes of computing the AMTI the excess of the fair market value of the stock at the date of the exercise over the amount paid for the stock. If the stock is sold in the same tax year the option is exercised, no adjustment in computing the AMTI is required. If the stock is sold later, for purposes of computing capital gain or loss for purposes of the AMTI, the adjusted basis of the stock includes the amount taken into account as AMTI.

Because the ISO adjustment is a deferral adjustment, it generates a minimum tax credit in the year the stock is sold. However, if the stock is sold for less than the amount paid for the stock, the loss may not be allowed in full in computing the AMTI by reason of the $3,000 limit on the deductibility of net capital losses. Therefore, the excess of the regular tax over the tentative minimum tax may not reflect the full amount of the loss and a portion of the minimum tax credit generated by the adjustment is unused.

NEW LAW EXPLAINED

Unused minimum tax credit refundable.—If an individual has a long-term unused minimum tax credit for any tax year beginning before January 1, 2013, the minimum tax credit allowable for that year will not be less than the "AMT refundable credit amount" regardless of the minimum tax credit otherwise allowed to the taxpayer (Code Sec. 53(e)(1), as added by the Tax Relief and Health Care Act of 2006 (P.L. 109-432)). Also, the additional amount of credit allowed by this provision is refundable (Code Sec. 53(e)(4), as added by the 2006 Extenders Act).

¶235

NEW LAW EXPLAINED

> **Comment:** This AMT credit relief is intended primarily for individuals who exercised incentive stock options at a profit and sold the stock later when the stock price had significantly declined. Individuals in this situation, would have had to pay an AMT on the profit in the year of the exercise, although they lost a large portion or all of the profit at the time of the stock sale. As a result, such individuals could have ended up with a large amount of minimum tax credit that they may never be able to use even if carried forward.

The AMT refundable credit amount is the greater of: (1) the lesser of $5,000 or the taxpayer's long-term unused minimum tax credit for the tax year; or (2) 20 percent of such credit (Code Sec. 53(e)(2)(A), as added by the 2006 Extenders Act). The long-term unused minimum tax credit for a tax year is the portion of the minimum tax credit attributable to the adjusted net minimum tax for tax years before the third tax year immediately preceding such tax year. For this purpose, the credits are treated as allowed on a first-in, first-out basis (Code Sec. 53(e)(3), as added by the 2006 Extenders Act).

> **Comment:** For the 2007 tax year, a taxpayer could potentially receive a refund for AMT paid in 2003 or an earlier tax year. However, a taxpayer could not recover 20 percent of the original amount of the accumulated AMT credit every year. Instead, only 20 percent of the remaining amount may be refunded. Because the AMT credit relief is temporary, taxpayers who have large AMT credits may still not be able to recover the entire amount of the credit.

The AMT refundable credit amount is phased out at the income levels applicable to the phaseout of the personal exemption deduction. Accordingly, if an individual's adjusted gross income (AGI) for a tax year exceeds certain threshold amounts (based on filing status), the AMT refundable credit amount is reduced by the applicable percentage, which is equal to two percentage points for each $2,500 ($1,250 for married individuals filing separately) by which AGI exceeds the threshold amount (Code Sec. 53(e)(2)(B)(i), as added by the 2006 Extenders Act). For purposes of this rule, AGI is determined without regard to the exclusion of certain foreign-earned income of U.S. citizens or residents living abroad, or the income-exclusion rules applicable to bona-fide residents of certain U.S. possessions (Code Sec. 53(e)(2)(B)(ii), as added by the 2006 Extenders Act).

> **Comment:** The phaseout of the AMT refundable credit begins when AGI exceeds: $225,750 for 2006 ($234,600 for 2007) for married individuals filing a joint return or a surviving spouse; $150,500 for 2006 ($156,400 for 2007) for unmarried individuals (not surviving spouse or head of household); $188,150 for 2006 ($195,500 for 2007) for heads of households; and $112,875 for 2006 ($117,300 for 2007) for married individuals filing separate returns.

Example 1: In 2010, Bob Williams files a tax return as a head of household. His AGI for the year exceeds the threshold for the phaseout of the personal exemptions, resulting in an applicable percentage of 50 percent. He has a regular tax liability is $45,000 and a tentative AMT liability of $40,000. He is not eligible to claim any credits other than the minimum tax credit. His minimum

---

NEW LAW EXPLAINED

tax credit for the year is $1.1 million (before application of the limit on the minimum tax credit), of which $1 million is long-term unused minimum tax credit. Generally, the minimum tax credit that Bob could claim would be limited to difference between his regular tax liability for the year over his tentative AMT liability for the year ($5,000).

However, under the new rule Bob may claim a minimum tax credit of $100,000 in 2010. This is the amount of his AMT refundable credit amount for the tax year (20 percent of his $1 million of long-term unused minimum tax credit reduced by the applicable percentage of 50 percent). The $5,000 credit allowed to Bob without regard to the new rule is nonrefundable. However, the additional $95,000 of credit allowed under the new rule is treated as a refundable credit. Thus, Bob has an overpayment of $55,000 ($45,000 regular tax, less $5,000 nonrefundable AMT credit, less $95,000 refundable AMT credit). The $55,000 overpayment is allowed as a refund or credit to the taxpayer. The remaining $1 million minimum tax credit is carried forward to future tax years (Joint Committee on Taxation, Technical Explanation of the Tax Relief and Health Care Act of 2006 (P.L. 109-432) (JCX-50-06)).

Example 2: Assume the same facts as in Example 1 above, except that Bob's AGI does not exceed the threshold amount for phaseout of the personal exemption. As a result, his AMT refundable credit amount for 2010 would be $200,000 (20 percent of his $1 million of long-term unused minimum tax credit). His overpayment would be $155,000, and the credit he would carry forward would be $900,000.

▶ **Effective date.** The provision applies to tax years beginning after December 20, 2006 (Act Sec. 402(c) of the Tax Relief and Health Care Act of 2006 (P.L. 109-432)).

Law source: Law at ¶5054 and ¶5785. Committee Report at ¶15,480.

— Act Sec. 402(a) of the Tax Relief and Health Care Act of 2006 (P.L. 109-432), adding Code Sec. 53(e);

— Act Sec. 402(b), amending 31 U.S.C. Sec. 1324(b)(2) and Code Sec. 6211(b)(4)(A);

— Act Sec. 402(c), providing the effective date.

Reporter references: For further information, consult the following CCH reporters.

— Standard Federal Tax Reporter, ¶4872.01 and ¶37,539.01

— Tax Research Consultant, FILEIND: 30,452

— Federal Tax Guide, ¶2825

INCOME AND GAINS

¶240 Capital Gains Treatment for Self-Created Musical Works Made Permanent

SUMMARY OF NEW LAW

A taxpayer may elect to treat the sale or exchange of musical compositions or copyrights in musical works created by the taxpayer's personal efforts (or having a basis determined by reference to the basis in the hands of the taxpayer whose personal efforts created the composition or copyrights) as the sale or exchange of a capital asset. The elective treatment has been made permanent.

BACKGROUND

The maximum tax rate on an individual's ordinary income is 35 percent. However, the maximum tax rate on the net capital gain income of an individual is only 15 percent for tax years beginning in 2006. Generally, the 15-percent rate is available for gain from the sale or exchange of a capital asset for which the taxpayer has satisfied a holding period requirement. Capital assets typically include all property held by a taxpayer with certain specified exclusions (Code Sec. 1221).

An exclusion from the definition of a capital asset applies to inventory property or property that is held by a taxpayer primarily for sale to customers in the ordinary course of business. Another exclusion applies to copyrights, literary, musical, or artistic compositions, letters or memoranda, or similar property held by the taxpayer whose personal efforts created the property (or held by a taxpayer whose basis in the property is determined by reference to the basis of the taxpayer whose personal efforts created the property). Therefore, if a taxpayer who owns copyrights in, for example, books, songs, or paintings that the taxpayer created (or a taxpayer to whom the copyrights have been transferred by the works' creator in a substituted basis transaction) sells the copyrights, gain from the sale is treated as ordinary income, not capital gain.

Charitable contributions. Generally, a taxpayer is allowed a deduction for the fair market value of property contributed to a charity. If a taxpayer makes a contribution of property that would have generated ordinary income (or short-term capital gain), the taxpayer's charitable contribution deduction is generally limited to the property's adjusted basis (Code Sec. 170(e)).

NEW LAW EXPLAINED

Capital gains treatment for self-created musical works.—The election to treat as a sale or exchange of a capital asset, the sale or exchange of musical compositions or copyrights in musical works created by the taxpayer's personal efforts (or having a basis determined by reference to the basis in the hands of the taxpayer whose personal

¶240

NEW LAW EXPLAINED

efforts created the composition or copyrights) has been made permanent (Code Sec. 1221(b)(3), as added by the Tax Increase Prevention and Reconciliation Act of 2005 (P.L. 109-222) and amended by the Tax Relief and Health Care Act of 2006 (P.L. 109-432)). No change has been made to the limitation on a taxpayer's charitable deduction for the contribution of such compositions or copyrights.

> **Comment:** The election was initially set to expire for sales and exchanges occurring on or after January 1, 2011, but was made permanent by the 2006 Extenders Act.

▶ **Effective date.** The provision applies to sales and exchanges in tax years beginning after May 17, 2006 (Act Sec. 204(c) of the Tax Increase Prevention and Reconciliation Act of 2005 (P.L. 109-222) and Act Sec. 412(b) of the Tax Relief and Health Care Act of 2006 (P.L. 109-432)).

Law source: Law at ¶5280 and ¶5580. Committee Reports at ¶10,060 and ¶15,570.

— Act Sec. 204(a) of the Tax Increase Prevention and Reconciliation Act of 2005 (P.L. 109-222), amending Code Sec. 1221(b);

— Act Sec. 204(b), amending Code Sec. 170(e)(1)(A);

— Act Sec. 412(a) of the Tax Relief and Health Care Act of 2006 (P.L. 109-432), amending Code Sec. 1221(b)(3);

— Act Sec. 204(c) of the Tax Reconciliation Act of 2005 and Act Sec. 412(b) of the 2006 Extenders Act, providing the effective date.

Reporter references: For further information, consult the following CCH reporters.

— Standard Federal Tax Reporter, ¶30,422.05

— Tax Research Consultant, SALES: 15,108.15

— Federal Tax Guide, ¶5610 and ¶5616

¶245 Modification of Treatment of Loans to Qualified Continuing Care Facilities

SUMMARY OF NEW LAW

The requirements for exemption from the below-market interest loan rules that apply to loans to continuing care facilities have been relaxed.

BACKGROUND

When a lender makes a below-market interest loan to a borrower, Code Sec. 7872 recasts the transaction as if the forgone interest is transferred to the borrower from the lender in the form of a gift, dividend, or other payment. That forgone interest is then treated as if paid back to the lender as interest. The result is that the borrower receives possibly taxable income upon the initial transaction, and the lender receives

BACKGROUND

interest income as the loan is paid back, with the borrower able to claim applicable interest deductions.

This imputed interest rule applies only to below-market loans. There are two definitions of below-market loans. In the case of a demand loan, a below-market loan exists when interest on the loan is payable at a rate lower than the short-term applicable federal rate (AFR). In the case of a term loan, a below-market loan exists when the amount loaned is larger than the present value of payments made under the loan, with present value calculated using the AFR and compounded semiannually.

The imputed interest rule does not apply in certain cases. One exception to the rule is a loan made by a qualified individual to a qualified continuing care facility (QCCF exception) (Code Sec. 7872(g)). In order to qualify for this exception, the loan must be:

- made by a lender who turns 65 before the end of the year (or whose spouse turns 65 before the end of the year) (Code Sec. 7872(g)(1));
- for an amount not exceeding $90,000, adjusted annually for inflation ($163,300 for 2006) (Code Sec. 7872(g)(2) and (5));
- made pursuant to a continuing care contract (Code Sec. 7872(g)(3)); and
- made to a qualified continuing care facility (Code Sec. 7872(g)(4)).

A continuing care contract is one made between the lender and the borrowing qualified continuing care facility. The contract must provide that the lending individual or the individual's spouse may use the qualified continuing care facility for his or her life or lives, and that he or she will live at first in an independent living unit without long-term nursing care, with additional facilities for meals and other personal care, and then will be provided long-term nursing care as required. Also, no additional substantial payment can be required if either individual needs increased personal care or long-term nursing care (Code Sec. 7872(g)(3)).

A qualified continuing care facility is one or more facilities that are designed to provide services under continuing care contracts. In addition, substantially all of the residents must be covered by continuing care contracts and substantially all of the facilities must be owned by the borrower of a loan pursuant to a continuing care contract. Finally, the facility must not be of a type typically considered to be a nursing home (Code Sec. 7872(g)(4)).

NEW LAW EXPLAINED

Requirements for loans to continuing care facilities to qualify for exception to imputed interest rules relaxed.—Continuing care facilities may qualify for the exception to the imputed interest rules (QCCF exception) under relaxed requirements provided in Code Sec. 7872(h), as added by the Tax Increase Prevention and Reconciliation Act of 2005 (P.L. 109-222) (TIPRA). If the facility qualifies as a continuing care facility under these relaxed requirements on the last day of the year in which the loan is owed, it will qualify for the exception.

> **Comment:** Note that the more stringent requirements under Code Sec. 7872(g) are still in place, but they do not apply when continuing care facilities satisfy the

NEW LAW EXPLAINED

requirements of new Code Sec. 7872(h) (Code Sec. 7872(g)(6), as added by the Tax Reconciliation Act of 2005).

The definition of a continuing care contract is slightly modified under new Code Sec. 7872(h). A qualified continuing care contract is a written contract between an individual and a qualifying continuing care facility under which: (1) the lender or lender's spouse may use a qualified continuing care facility for their life or lives; (2) the lender or lender's spouse will be provided with housing, as appropriate for their health, in an independent living unit (which has additional facilities outside such unit for meals and personal care) and in an assisted living facility or nursing facility; and (3) the lender or lender's spouse will be provided assisted living or nursing care as their health requires and as is available in the continuing care facility. Regulations and other guidance are to be issued which limit the definition of these contracts to those that provide the facilities, care and services of a qualified continuing care facility (Code Sec. 7872(h)(2), as added by the Tax Reconciliation Act of 2005).

The Code Sec. 7872(h) requirements to qualify for the QCCF exception are more lenient than the Code Sec. 7872(g) rules in a number of respects, including the following:

- Most significantly, there is no inflation-adjusted limitation on the amount of the loan.

- The loan must be made by a lender (or the lender's spouse) who is 62 (rather than 65) before the close of the year (Code Sec. 7872(h)(1), as added by the Tax Reconciliation Act of 2005).

- There is no requirement that the individual *first* reside in an independent unit without needing long-term nursing care.

- There is no requirement that long-term care be provided for no substantial additional fee.

- There is no requirement that the facilities be substantially owned by the borrower of the loan.

    Caution: Code Sec. 7872(h) does contain a more stringent requirement, however, over those of Code Sec. 7872(g)—a qualified continuing care facility must include an independent living unit in addition to an assisted living facility or nursing facility (Code Sec. 7872(h)(3)(A)(ii), as added by the Tax Reconciliation Act of 2005).

    Comment: Initially, TIPRA included a provision stating that the relaxed rules under Code Sec. 7872(h) would not apply to any calendar year after 2010 (Code Sec. 7872(h)(4), as added by the Tax Reconciliation Act of 2005). However, the Tax Relief and Health Care Act of 2006 (P.L. 109-432) eliminated the termination date, effective as if included in TIPRA (Act Sec. 425 of the 2006 Extenders Act). Therefore, the relaxed rules will apply indefinitely.

▶ **Effective date.** The amendments shall apply to calendar years beginning after December 31, 2005, with respect to loans made before, on, or after such date (Act Sec. 209(c) of the Tax Increase Prevention and Reconciliation Act of 2005 (P.L. 109-222) and Act Sec. 425(b) of the Tax Relief and Health Care Act of 2006 (P.L. 109-432)).

NEW LAW EXPLAINED

Law source: Law at ¶5105 and ¶5855. Committee Reports at ¶10,110 and ¶15,700.

— Act Sec. 209(a) of the Tax Increase Prevention and Reconciliation Act of 2005 (P.L. 109-222), redesignating Code Sec. 7872(h) as Code Sec. 7872(i) and adding new Code Sec. 7872(h);

— Act Sec. 209(b)(1), adding Code Sec. 7872(g)(6);

— Act Sec. 209(b)(2), amending Code Sec. 142(d)(2)(B);

— Act Sec. 425(a) of the Tax Relief and Health Care Act of 2006 (P.L. 109-432), striking Code Sec. 7872(h)(4);

— Act Sec. 209(c) of the Tax Reconciliation Act of 2005 and Act Sec. 425(b) of the 2006 Extenders Act, providing the effective date.

Reporter references: For further information, consult the following CCH reporters.

— Standard Federal Tax Reporter, ¶43,960.0405

— Tax Research Consultant, INDIV: 12,200, INDIV: 12,204.25 and INDIV: 12,208.20

— Federal Tax Guide, ¶3215 and ¶3223

— Federal Estate and Gift Tax Reporter, ¶7872(h)(4)

¶250 Exclusion of Gain From Sale of Principal Residence by Certain Employees of the Intelligence Community

SUMMARY OF NEW LAW

Certain employees of the intelligence community are eligible to elect to suspend the running of the five-year test period that ends on the date of the sale or exchange of a principal residence for purposes of satisfying the ownership test under Code Sec. 121.

BACKGROUND

An individual may exclude from income up to $250,000 of gain ($500,000 on a joint return in most situations) realized on the sale or exchange of a principal residence (Code Sec. 121(b)). Generally, gain may only be excluded if, during the five-year period that ends on the date of the sale or exchange, the individual owned and used the property as a principal residence for periods aggregating two years or more. A special exception to the two-out-of-five year rule exists for uniformed and foreign service personnel called to active duty away from home. These individuals may elect to suspend the five-year test period (Code Sec. 121(d)(9)). The election is made by not reporting the gain from the sale of the residence on the tax return filed for the year of the sale. The suspension period cannot last more than ten years and it may only be made with respect to one property.

BACKGROUND

When the election is made, it is effective during the period within which the individual, or his or her spouse, is on qualified official extended duty. The term "qualified official extended duty" is any extended duty while serving at a duty station that is at least 50 miles from the individual's principal residence or while residing in government quarters under government orders (Code Sec. 121(d)(9)(C)(i)). The term "extended duty" is any period of active duty due to a call or order to such duty for a period in excess of 90 days or for an indefinite time (Code Sec. 121(d)(9)(C)(iv)). An individual may revoke the election at any time.

NEW LAW EXPLAINED

Special election available to certain members of the intelligence community.— The benefits of the election to suspend the five-year test period in the ownership test for exclusion of gain from the sale of a principal residence are extended to certain employees of the intelligence community (Code Sec. 121(d)(9)(A)(iii), as added by the Tax Relief and Health Care Act of 2006 (P.L. 109-432)). An employee of the intelligence community is defined as an employee of:

(1) the Office of the Director of National Intelligence,

(2) the Central Intelligence Agency,

(3) the National Security Agency,

(4) the Defense Intelligence Agency,

(5) the National Geospacial-Intelligence Agency,

(6) the National Reconnaissance Office,

(7) any other office within the Department of Defense for the collection of specialized national intelligence through reconnaissance programs,

(8) any of the intelligence elements of the Army, the Navy, the Air Force, the Marine Corps, the Federal Bureau of Investigation, the Department of Treasury, the Department of Energy and the Coast Guard,

(9) the Bureau of Intelligence and Research of the Department of State, or

(10) any of the elements of the Department of Homeland Security concerned with the analyses of foreign intelligence information (Code Sec. 121(d)(9)(C)(iv), as added by the 2006 Extenders Act).

An employee of the intelligence community will not be treated as serving on qualified extended duty unless such duty is at a duty station located outside of the United States (Code Sec. 121(d)(9)(C)(vi), as added by the 2006 Extenders Act). The five-year test period may not be extended more than ten years (Code Sec. 121(d)(9)(B)).

▶ **Effective date.** The amendments made by this provision apply to sales or exchanges after December 20, 2006, and before January 1, 2011 (Sec. 417(e) of the Tax Relief and Health Care Act of 2006 (P.L. 109-432)).

¶250

NEW LAW EXPLAINED

Law source: Law at ¶5095. Committee Report at ¶15,620.

— Act Secs. 417(a) and (d) of the Tax Relief and Health Care Act of 2006 (P.L. 109-432), amending Code Sec. 121(d)(9);

— Act Sec. 417(b), redesignating Code Sec. 121(d)(9)(C)(iv) as Code Sec. 121(d)(9)(C)(v) and adding new Code Sec. 121(d)(9)(C)(iv);

— Act Sec. 417(c), adding Code Sec. 121(d)(9)(C)(vi);

— Act Sec. 417(e), providing the effective date.

Reporter references: For further information, consult the following CCH reporters.

— Standard Federal Tax Reporter, ¶7266.028

— Tax Research Consultant, REAL: 15,156.15

— Federal Tax Guide, ¶4426 and ¶4427

¶255 Sale of Property by Judicial Officers

SUMMARY OF NEW LAW

The deferral of gain on property disposed of by federal employees pursuant to conflict of interest rules is extended to federal judges.

BACKGROUND

Code Sec. 1001 requires that the excess of the full amount realized from the sale or disposal of property over the basis in the property is recognized as gain by the seller and is taxable at the time of the sale or disposal. However, this general requirement is subject to various exceptions, reductions and deferrals.

One such deferral may be elected by certain executive branch federal employees and related individuals who are required to divest property under conflict of interest requirements (Code Sec. 1043). In order to qualify for this special treatment, the sale must be pursuant to a certificate of divestiture stating that the divestiture is necessary to comply with conflict of interest requirements issued by the President or the Director of the Office of Government Ethics. The deferral only applies to the extent that the seller uses the proceeds realized from the sale to purchase "permitted property" within 60 days of the sale. Permitted property is any obligation of the United States (e.g. Treasury notes) or any diversified investment fund (e.g. mutual fund) approved by the Office of Government Ethics. If the deferral applies, the amount of realized gain that is not recognized reduces the basis of the purchased replacement property, essentially meaning that the basis of the disposed property is carried over to the new property.

The deferral rule is available to the spouse and dependent children of the federal employee and to any other minor whose ownership of the property is attributable to the federal employee to whom the conflict rules apply and to any trust if the

BACKGROUND

employee or the spouse, dependent children, or other minors have a beneficial interest in the income or principal of the trust property.

NEW LAW EXPLAINED

Deferral of gain option extended to judges.—The election to defer gain recognition under Code Sec. 1043 is extended to judicial officers of the United States. The deferral is available to any judicial officer who has received a certificate of divestiture from the Judicial Conference of the United States stating that divestiture is necessary to comply with conflict of interest requirements found in any rule, regulation or judicial canon. The provision applies to the spouses, dependent children and other related minors of judges and any applicable trusts in the same manner as it applies to executive branch employees (Code Sec. 1043(b), as amended by the Tax Relief and Health Care Act of 2006 (P.L. 109-432)).

Judicial officers include the Justices of the Supreme Court and the judges of the U.S courts of appeals (including the Court of Appeals for the Federal Circuit), the U.S. district courts (including the district courts in Guam, the Northern Mariana Islands and the Virgin Islands) and the U.S. Court of International Trade. Judicial officers also include the judges of the Article I courts—the Tax Court, the Court of Federal Claims, the Court of Appeals for Veterans Claims, and the Court of Appeals for the Armed Forces. Finally, a judicial officer would include any judge of a court created by act of Congress whose judges are entitled to hold office during good behavior (Code Sec. 1043(b)(6), as added by the Extenders Act of 2006).

▶ **Effective date.** The provision is effective for sales after December 20, 2006 (Act Sec. 418(c) of the Tax Relief and Health Care Act of 2006 (P.L. 109-432)).

Law source: Law at ¶5565. Committee Report at ¶15,630.

— Act Sec. 418(a)(1) of the Tax Relief and Health Care Act of 2006 (P.L. 109-432), amending Code Sec. 1043(b)(1);

— Act Sec. 418(a)(2), amending Code Sec. 1043(b)(2);

— Act Sec. 418(a)(3), amending Code Sec. 1043(b)(5)(B);

— Act Sec. 418(b), adding Code Sec. 1043(b)(6);

— Act Sec. 418(c), providing the effective date.

Reporter references: For further information, consult the following CCH reporters.

— Standard Federal Tax Reporter, ¶29,841.01

— Tax Research Consultant, SALES: 27,350

— Federal Tax Guide, ¶5468

¶255

Tax Relief—Businesses in General

SETTLEMENT FUNDS

¶375   Taxation of environmental settlement funds clarified and exemption made permanent

DEPRECIATION AND EXPENSING

¶305 15-Year MACRS Recovery Period for Qualified Leasehold Improvements and Qualified Restaurant Property Extended

SUMMARY OF NEW LAW

The 15-year MACRS recovery period is extended to apply to qualified leasehold improvement property and qualified restaurant property placed in service before January 1, 2008.

BACKGROUND

The American Jobs Creation Act of 2004 (P.L. 108-357) created a 15-year recovery period under the Modified Adjusted Cost Recovery System (MACRS) for qualified leasehold improvement property and qualified restaurant property placed in service after October 22, 2004, and before January 1, 2006, using the straight-line method and the half-year convention (unless the midquarter convention applies) (Code Sec. 168(e)(3)(E)(iv) and (v)). However, if the MACRS alternative depreciation system (ADS) is elected or otherwise applies, the recovery period remains at 39 years using the straight-line method (Code Sec. 168(g)(3)(B)).

Leasehold improvement. Generally, a leasehold improvement is considered a structural component of a building. If the improvement is made to residential rental property, it is depreciated over 27.5 years using the straight-line method beginning in the month it was placed in service. Prior to the enactment of the 2004 Jobs Act, if such an improvement was made to nonresidential real property, the improvement was treated as MACRS 39-year nonresidential real property and depreciated over 39-years using the straight-line method beginning in the month the improvement was placed in service.

"Qualified leasehold improvement property" is any improvement to an interior portion of nonresidential real property if the following requirements are satisfied:

(1) the improvement is made under, or pursuant to, a lease by the lessee, lessor or any sublessee of the interior portion;

(2) the lease is not between related persons;

(3) the interior portion of the building is to be occupied exclusively by the lessee or any sublessee of that interior portion; and

¶305

BACKGROUND

(4) the improvement is placed in service more than three years after the date the building was first placed in service by any person (Code Sec. 168(k)(3); Reg. § 1.168(k)-1(c)).

Restaurant property. Generally, a restaurant building is considered 39-year nonresidential real property. The depreciation treatment of an improvement made to an existing restaurant depends upon whether the improvement is a structural component (section 1250 property) or personal property (section 1245 property). An improvement which is section 1245 property may be separately depreciated as five-year MACRS property. Prior to the 2004 Jobs Act, if the improvement was section 1250 property, then it was depreciated beginning in the month and year that it was placed in service as 39-year real property.

"Qualified restaurant property" is any section 1250 property (structural component) which is an improvement to a building if the improvement is placed in service more than three years after the date the building was first placed in service and more than 50 percent of the building's square footage is devoted to preparation of, and seating for, on-premises consumption of prepared meals (Code Sec. 168(e)(7)).

NEW LAW EXPLAINED

Extension of 15-year MACRS recovery period for qualified leasehold improvement property and qualified restaurant property.—The 15-year MACRS recovery period is extended to apply to qualified leasehold improvement property and qualified restaurant property placed in service before January 1, 2008 (Code Sec. 168(e)(3)(E)(iv) and (v), as amended by the Tax Relief and Health Care Act of 2006 (P.L. 109-432).

> **Planning Note:** The 15-year recovery period is not elective. However, a taxpayer could effectively elect out by making an ADS election. An ADS election, however, would apply to all MACRS 15-year property placed in service by the taxpayer during the tax year, not just qualified leasehold improvement property and qualified restaurant property.

> **Comment:** The IRS has modified a previously issued Cost Segregation Audit Techniques Guide (ATG) to reflect the 15-year recovery period available for qualified leasehold improvement property and qualified restaurant improvements (IRS News Release, April 26, 2005).

▶ **Effective date.** This provision applies to property placed in service after December 31, 2005 (Act Sec. 113(b) of the Tax Relief and Health Care Act of 2006 (P.L. 109-432)).

Law source: Law at ¶5265. Committee Report at ¶15,220.

— Act Sec. 113(a) of the Tax Relief and Health Care Act of 2006 (P.L. 109-432), amending Code Sec. 168(e)(3)(E)(iv) and (v);

— Act Sec. 113(b), providing the effective date.

Reporter references: For further information, consult the following CCH reporters.

— Standard Federal Tax Reporter, ¶11,279.0311 and ¶11,279.0312

— Tax Research Consultant, DEPR: 3,156.25

— Federal Tax Guide, ¶9110

¶305

¶310 Election to Deduct Environmental Remediation Costs Extended; "Hazardous Substance" Definition Expanded

SUMMARY OF NEW LAW

The election to deduct environmental remediation costs is extended for two years to cover expenditures paid or incurred before January 1, 2008. In addition, the definition of hazardous substances is expanded to include any petroleum product.

BACKGROUND

A taxpayer may elect to deduct, for both regular and alternative minimum tax purposes, certain environmental cleanup costs in the tax year paid or incurred, rather than capitalize them. The election can only be made, however, if the costs are incurred in connection with the abatement or control of hazardous substances at a "qualified contaminated site," or a so-called "brownfield." In addition, the deduction allowed is treated as a depreciation deduction and is subject to the depreciation recapture rules as they apply to Code Sec. 1245 property (Code Sec. 198).

The election to deduct environmental cleanup costs generally applies to qualifying expenditures paid or incurred before January 1, 2006 (Code Sec. 198(h)). However, in the case of qualifying expenditures paid or incurred in connection with a qualified contaminated site located in the Gulf Opportunity Zone, a taxpayer may elect to deduct such costs if paid or incurred before January 1, 2008. In addition, expenditures paid or incurred on or after August 28, 2005, and through December 31, 2007, for the clean-up of petroleum products in the Gulf Opportunity Zone may also qualify for deduction (Code Sec. 1400N(g), as added by the Gulf Opportunity Zone Act of 2005 (P.L. 109-135)).

For these purposes, a "qualified contaminated site," or "brownfield," is any urban or rural property that is held for use in a trade or business, for the production of income, or as inventory, and which is certified by the appropriate State environmental agency as an area at or on which there has been a release, threat of release, or disposal of a hazardous substance. However, sites that are identified on the national priorities list under the Comprehensive Environmental Response, Compensation, and Liability Act of 1980 ("CERCLA") cannot qualify as targeted areas.

Hazardous substances are defined by reference to sections 101(14) and 102 of CER-CLA, subject to additional exclusions applicable to asbestos and similar substances within buildings, certain naturally occurring substances, and certain other substances released into drinking water supplies due to deterioration through ordinary use. Petroleum products generally are not regarded as hazardous substances for purposes of Code Sec. 198, except for purposes of determining qualified environmental remediation expenditures in the Gulf Opportunity Zone under Code Sec. 1400N(g).

Extension of election to deduct environmental remediation costs; expanded definition of hazardous substance.—The election to deduct environmental remediation costs is extended for two years to cover qualifying expenditures paid or incurred before January 1, 2008 (Code Sec. 198(h), as amended by the Tax Relief and Health Care Act of 2006 (P.L. 109-432)). The general tax law principle regarding expensing versus capitalization of expenditures continues to apply to environmental remediation efforts not specifically covered under Code Sec. 198. Thus, depending upon the specific situation, these costs may need to be capitalized.

> **Planning Note:** Unless (or until) the IRS provides otherwise, April 15, 2007, is the deadline for making elections under a provision that expired in 2005, and that has been extended for the 2006 tax year by the 2006 Extenders Act. Thus, the election to deduct environmental remediation costs for 2006 must be elected by April 15, 2007 unless the IRS provides otherwise (Act Sec. 123(b) of the 2006 Extenders Act).

Hazardous substance. In addition to the definition contained in the Comprehensive Environmental Response, Compensation, and Liability Act of 1980 (CERCLA), the term "hazardous substance" is expanded to include any petroleum product, as defined in Code Sec. 4612(a)(3), which includes crude oil, crude oil condensates, and natural gasoline. In general, the term includes toxic pollutants and hazardous chemical wastes.

> **Planning Note:** The legislative history of the Code Sec. 198 election makes clear that asbestos and similar substances within buildings, certain natural substances (e.g., radon) and other substances released into drinking water due to deterioration through ordinary use are not considered to be hazardous substances.

▶ **Effective date.** The amendments made by this provision will apply to expenditures paid or incurred after December 31, 2005 (Act Sec. 109(c) of the Tax Relief and Health Care Act of 2006 (P.L. 109-432)).

Law source: Law at ¶5320. Committee Report at ¶15,180.

— Act Sec. 109(a) of the 2006 Extenders Act, amending Code Sec. 198(h);

— Act Sec. 109(b), amending Code Sec. 198(d)(1);

— Act Sec. 109(c), providing the effective date.

Reporter references: For further information, consult the following CCH reporters.

— Standard Federal Tax Reporter, ¶12,465.01

— Tax Research Consultant, BUSEXP: 18,756

— Federal Tax Guide, ¶7402

¶315 Extended Placed-in-Service Deadline for Certain Gulf Opportunity Zone Property

SUMMARY OF NEW LAW

The placed-in-service deadline for claiming 50-percent bonus depreciation on non-residential real and residential rental property located in specified counties and parishes in the Gulf Opportunity Zone is extended from December 31, 2008 to December 31, 2010. Personal property used in such realty also qualifies for the extended deadline.

BACKGROUND

A 50-percent bonus depreciation deduction is available for qualified Gulf Opportunity Zone property acquired on or after August 28, 2005, and placed in service on or before December 31, 2007, in the case of personal property, and on or before December 31, 2008 in the case of nonresidential real property and residential rental property (Code Sec. 1400N(d), as added by the Gulf Opportunity Zone Act of 2005 (P.L. 109-135); Notice 2006-77, I.R.B. 2006-33). No written binding contract for the acquisition may be in effect before August 28, 2005.

To qualify for the 50-percent bonus allowance substantially all (80 percent of more) of the use of the property must be in the Gulf Opportunity Zone (also referred to as the GO Zone or core disaster area) in the active conduct of a trade or business. In general, the GO Zone is the area of the Gulf Coast that was declared a disaster area by President Bush as a result of Hurricane Katrina and for which individual or public assistance is authorized (Code Sec. 1400M(1), as added by P.L. 109-135). See IRS Publication 4492 (January 2006) for a list of counties and parishes located in Alabama, Louisiana, and Mississippi that are within the GO Zone.

Only newly constructed real property qualifies for the GO Zone bonus deduction because the first or original use of the property in the GO Zone must begin with the taxpayer (Code Sec. 1400N(d)(2)(A)(iii)). However, if used real property is rehabilitated (e.g., first story water damage to an existing building is repaired), the cost of rehabilitation will usually qualify for the additional depreciation allowance.

Taxpayers other than estates, trusts, and certain noncorporate lessors may elect to claim a Code Sec. 179 expense deduction on the cost of qualifying section 179 property acquired by purchase. The maximum allowable Code Sec. 179 expense allowance ($108,000 in 2006 and $112,000 in 2007) is increased by the lesser of $100,000 or the cost of qualified section 179 Gulf Opportunity Zone property placed in service in the tax year. The investment limit ($430,000 in 2006 and $450,000 in 2007) is increased by the lesser of $600,000 or the amount of qualified section 179 Gulf Opportunity Zone property placed in service during the tax year (Code Sec. 1400N(e), as added by P.L. 109-135). The increases in the dollar and investment limits apply to qualified section 179 Gulf Opportunity Zone property acquired on or after August 28, 2005, and placed in service before January 1, 2008 (Code Sec. 1400N(d)(2)(A), (e)(2)).

NEW LAW EXPLAINED

Two-year extension of GO Zone bonus depreciation placed-in-service deadline for nonresidential real and residential rental property located in specified counties and parishes.—The December 31, 2008 deadline for placing nonresidential real property and new residential rental property in service in order to qualify for the 50 percent GO Zone bonus depreciation allowance is extended to December 31, 2010, if the property is located in a county or parish in which one or more hurricanes that occurred during 2005 damaged more than 60 percent of occupied housing units (Code Sec. 1400N(d)(6), as added by the Tax Relief and Health Care Act of 2006 (P.L. 109-432)). However, bonus depreciation may only be claimed on the portion of the building that is completed before January 1, 2010. Thus, any adjusted basis attributable to manufacture, construction, or production of the real property from January 1, 2010 through December 31, 2010 does not qualify for the 50-percent GO Zone depreciation allowance (Code Sec. 1400N(d)(6)(D), as added by the 2006 Extenders Act).

The new law also provides that personal property used in the building, such as furniture and computers that are amortizable over three years, will qualify for the 50 percent allowance if placed in service not later than 90 days after the building is placed in service (Code Sec. 1400N(d)(6)(B)(ii)(II), as added by the 2006 Extenders Act).

Types of qualifying property. The extended placed-in-service date applies to "specified Gulf Opportunity Zone extension property," which is defined as:

(1) nonresidential real property or residential rental property placed in service by the taxpayer on or before December 31, 2010, or

(2) in the case of a taxpayer who placed a building described above in service on or before December 31, 2010,

- MACRS property with a recovery period of 20 years or less
- computer software that is not amortizable under Code Sec. 197
- water utility property described in Code Sec. 168(e)(5)
- qualified leasehold improvement property

if substantially all (80 percent or more) of the use of the property is in the building and the property is placed in service within 90 days after the building is placed in service (Code Sec. 1400N(d)(6)(B), as added by the 2006 Extenders Act). (The building itself, however, must be placed in service no later than December 31, 2010).

Qualified leasehold improvement property is any section 1250 property which is an improvement to an interior portion of a building that is nonresidential real property and which is made under or pursuant to a lease by the lessee, sublessee, or lessor. The improvement must be placed in service more than three years after the date the building was first placed in service by any person. In addition, the interior of the building must be occupied exclusively by the lessee or sublessee. The lease may not be between related persons (Code Sec. 168(k)(3), as added by P.L. 107-147; Reg. § 1.168(k)-1(c)(1)). Qualified leasehold improvement property placed in service after

NEW LAW EXPLAINED

October 22, 2004 and on or before December 31, 2007 may be depreciated under MACRS over 15 years using the straight-line method. The placed-in-service deadline for qualified leasehold improvement property has been extended two years from December 31, 2005 to December 31, 2007. See ¶ 305.

Only pre-January 1, 2010 basis of real property eligible for bonus depreciation. Although the placed-in-service deadline for nonresidential real property and residential rental property located in a specified portion of the GO Zone is extended to December 31, 2010, only the adjusted basis of the property attributable to manufacture, construction, or production before January 1, 2010 qualifies for the 50-percent bonus depreciation allowance (Code Sec. 1400N(d)(6)(D), as added by the 2006 Extenders Act).

> **Comment:** This limitation to pre-January 1, 2010 progress expenditures only applies to real property. Thus, the cost of a building's personal property elements qualify for the bonus deduction even if the personal property is acquired and placed in service after December 31, 2009, so long as the building is placed in service by December 31, 2010 and the personal property is placed in service within 90 days after the building's placed-in-service date.

> **Comment:** When a taxpayer purchases or constructs a new building, a cost segregation study is often performed. Certain elements of the building are identified and depreciated over a shorter recovery period as personal property. Under the new provision, it appears that the extended placed-in-service date also applies to these personal property components as well as to unattached personal property used in the building, such as furniture and personal computers. However, such personal property must be placed in service by the taxpayer no later than 90 days after the date that the building is placed in service and the building must be placed in service on or before December 31, 2010.

Specified portions of GO Zone defined. The extended placed-in-service deadline applies to property substantially all of the use of which is in one or more "specified portions of the GO Zone." The term "specified portions of the GO Zone" means any county or parish located in the GO Zone in which hurricanes occurring during 2005 (e.g., Hurricanes Katrina, Rita, and Wilma) damaged (in the aggregate) more than 60 percent of occupied housing units (Code Sec. 1400N(d)(6)(C), as added by the 2006 Extenders Act).

> **Comment:** The IRS will identify the counties and parishes that qualify under the provision using data compiled by the Office of the Federal Coordinator for Gulf Cost Rebuilding at the Department of Homeland Security and available at www.dhs.gov/xlibrary/assets/GulfCoast_HousingDamageEstimates 021206.pdf (Joint Committee on Taxation, Technical Explanation of the Tax Relief and Health Care Act of 2006 (P.L. 109-432) (JCX-50-06)).

> **Caution:** Buildings and personal property placed in service inside of the GO Zone but outside of a "specified portion" of the GO Zone (as defined above) do not qualify for the extended placed-in-service deadline. As noted in the *Background* section above, the unextended deadlines are December 31, 2007 for personal property and December 31, 2008 for nonresidential real property and residential rental property. Accordingly, if a building is located outside of the

NEW LAW EXPLAINED

specified portions of the GO Zone, elements of such a building identified in a cost segregation study as personal property appear to be subject to the December 31, 2007 placed-in-service deadline rather than the December 31, 2008 placed-in-service deadline for real property.

Example 1: A new commercial building is placed in service by a taxpayer on June 1, 2008. A cost segregation study indicates that 20 percent of the building's adjusted basis is attributable to personal property elements that are MACRS five-year property. If the building is not located in a "specified portion" of the GO Zone, only 80 percent of the building's adjusted basis will qualify for the 50-percent bonus depreciation deduction, assuming that the personal property components are considered placed in service at the same time as the building is placed in service. The personal property elements do not qualify because they were not placed in service by the December 31, 2007 deadline for personal property located outside of a specified portion of the GO Zone.

Example 2: Assume the same facts as in Example 1, except that the building is located in a "specified portion" of the GO Zone and is placed in service on June 1, 2010. In this situation, the entire adjusted basis of the building attributable to personal property components identified in a cost segregation study qualify for the 50-percent bonus allowance (including any personal property elements placed in service within 90 days after the building is placed in service). However, with respect to the portion of the adjusted basis not attributable to personal property, only progress expenditures through December 31, 2009 are taken into account in computing the bonus allowance.

Example 3: Assume the same facts as in Example 1, except that the building is placed in service by the taxpayer on December 31, 2009 in a specified portion of the GO Zone. In this case, the entire adjusted basis of the building as of December 31, 2009, including all personal property components identified in a cost segregation study, qualify for the 50-percent bonus depreciation allowance. Any additional personal property components installed and placed in service in the building within 90 days after December 31, 2009 will also qualify. Any components added after December 31, 2009 that are real property do not qualify because they are considered post-December 31, 2009 progress expenditures.

Extended placed-in-service date does not apply to additional section 179 allowance. The extension of the placed-in-service date deadline does not apply for purposes of the increased Code Sec. 179 expensing limit for section 179 property that is also Gulf Opportunity Zone property (Code Sec. 1400N(e)(2), as amended by the 2006 Extenders Act). Thus, Gulf Opportunity Zone property that is section 179 property cannot qualify for the increased section 179 allowance unless it is placed in service by December 31,

NEW LAW EXPLAINED

2007, even if the property is used in a building located in a specified portion of the Gulf Opportunity Zone.

▶ **Effective date.** The provision is effective for tax years ending on or after August 28, 2005 (Act Sec. 120(c) of the Tax Relief and Health Care Act of 2006 (P.L. 109-432) and Act Sec. 101(c) of the Gulf Opportunity Zone Act of 2005 (P.L. 109-135).

Law source: Law at ¶5626. Committee Report at ¶15,290.

— Act Sec. 120(a) of the Tax Relief and Health Care Act of 2006 (P.L. 109-432), adding Code Sec. 1400N(d)(6);

— Act Sec. 120(b) amending Code Sec. 1400N(e)(2);

— Act Sec. 120(c), providing the effective date.

Reporter references: For further information, consult the following CCH reporters.

— Standard Federal Tax Reporter, ¶32,487.024

— Tax Research Consultant, DEPR: 3,650

— Federal Tax Guide, ¶9132

¶320   Accelerated MACRS Recovery Periods for Qualified Indian Reservation Property

SUMMARY OF NEW LAW

The Modified Accelerated Cost Recovery System (MACRS) recovery periods that apply to qualified Indian reservation property have been extended for two years through December 31, 2007.

BACKGROUND

A business incentive designed to encourage the purchase of depreciable property for use on Indian reservations shortens the modified accelerated cost recovery system (MACRS) recovery periods for "qualified Indian reservation property" (Code Sec. 168(j)). In addition, the MACRS depreciation deduction allowed for regular tax purposes using these shortened recovery periods also applies for alternative minimum tax (AMT) purposes (Code Sec. 168(j)(3)). Consequently, there is no AMT depreciation adjustment. This incentive was last extended through December 31, 2005 by the Working Families Tax Relief Act of 2004 (P.L. 108-311).

The following chart shows the shortened recovery periods.

BACKGROUND

Property Class	Recovery Period
3-year property	2 years
5-year property	3 years
7-year property	4 years
10-year property	6 years
15-year property	9 years
20-year property	12 years
39-year nonresidential real property	22 years

Comment: The recovery period for MACRS 27.5-year residential rental property used on an Indian reservation is not shortened.

The incentive applies to "qualified Indian reservation property." Qualified Indian reservation property is MACRS 3-, 5-, 7-, 10-, 15-, 20-year property and 39-year nonresidential real property that meets all of these requirements:

- the property must be used predominantly in the active conduct of a trade or business within an Indian reservation,

- the property may not be used or located outside an Indian reservation on a regular basis,

- the property may not be acquired (directly or indirectly) from a related person (as defined by Code Sec. 465(b)(3)(C)), and

- the property may not be used for certain gaming purposes.

NEW LAW EXPLAINED

Expiration date of special MACRS Indian reservation property depreciation periods extended through December 31, 2007.—The shortened modified accelerated cost recovery system (MACRS) recovery periods that apply to qualified Indian reservation property have been extended for two years through December 31, 2007. Thus, the shortened recovery periods will continue to apply to qualified Indian reservation property placed in service before January 1, 2008 (Code Sec. 168(j)(8), as amended by the Tax Relief and Health Care Act of 2006 (P.L. 109-432)).

▶ **Effective date.** The provision applies to property placed in service after December 31, 2005 (Act Sec. 112(b) of the Tax Relief and Health Care Act of 2006 (P.L. 109-432)).

Law source: Law at ¶5265. Committee Report at ¶15,210.

— Act Sec. 112(a) of the Tax Relief and Health Care Act of 2006 (P.L. 109-432), amending Code Sec. 168(j)(8);

— Act Sec. 112(b) of the 2006 Extenders Act, providing the effective date.

Reporter references: For further information, consult the following CCH reporters.

— Standard Federal Tax Reporter, ¶11,279.0311

— Tax Research Consultant, DEPR: 3,156.55

— Federal Tax Guide, ¶9110

¶323 50-Percent Deduction for Certain Biomass Ethanol Plant Property

SUMMARY OF NEW LAW

A 50-percent additional depreciation allowance may be claimed on the adjusted basis of qualified cellulosic biomass ethanol plant property acquired and placed in service after December 20, 2006 and before January 1, 2013.

BACKGROUND

Cellulosic ethanol has an energy content three times higher than corn ethanol and reduces greenhouse gas emissions by 85 percent over reformulated gasoline. Starch ethanol, such as ethanol produced from corn, only reduces greenhouse gas emission emissions by 18 percent to 29 percent. President Bush called for expanded use of cellulosic ethanol in his State of the Union address delivered January 31, 2006.

NEW LAW EXPLAINED

50-percent depreciation allowance for cellulosic biomass ethanol plant property.—A 50-percent additional depreciation allowance may be claimed on the adjusted basis of qualified cellulosic biomass ethanol plant property (QCBEPP) acquired and placed in service after December 20, 2006 and before January 1, 2013. The original use of the property must begin with the taxpayer (Code Sec. 168(l), as added by the Tax Relief and Health Care Act of 2006 (P.L. 109-432)). Regular MACRS depreciation deductions are computed on the adjusted basis of the property after reduction by the 50 percent allowance (Code Sec. 168(l) (1) (B), as added by the 2006 Extenders Act).

No AMT adjustment required. The deduction is claimed in full for purposes of determining alternative minimum tax liability. In addition, all MACRS depreciation deductions claimed on the QCBEPP are allowed in full in computing AMT (i.e., no depreciation adjustment is required) (Code Sec. 168(l) (6), as added by the 2006 Extenders Act).

> **Comment:** These are the same rules that apply to property on which the 30- or 50-percent bonus depreciation deduction under Code Sec. 168(k) is claimed. The bonus deduction and regular MACRS deductions on bonus depreciation property are allowed in full under the AMT (Code Sec. 168(k)(2)(G)).

Qualified cellulosic biomass ethanol plant property (QCBEPP) defined. To qualify as QCBEPP:

(1) the property must be depreciable and used in the United States solely to produce cellulosic biomass ethanol;

(2) the taxpayer must acquire the property by purchase (with the meaning of Code Sec. 179(d)) after December 20, 2006, the date of enactment of the 2006 Extenders Act;

¶323

NEW LAW EXPLAINED

(3) no written binding contract for the purchase of the property may be in effect on or before December 20, 2006;

(4) the original use of the property must commence with the taxpayer after December 20, 2006 (see below for special rules relating to sale-leasebacks and syndicated leasing transactions);

(5) the property must be placed in service by the taxpayer before January 1, 2013 (Code Sec. 168(l)(2), as added by the 2006 Extenders Act).

Cellulosic biomass ethanol means ethanol produced by enzymatic hydrolysis of any lignocellulosic or hemicellulosic matter that is available on a renewable or recurring basis (Code Sec. 168(l)(3), as added by the 2006 Extenders Act).

> **Comment:** Lignocellulosic or hemicellulosic matter that is available on a renewable or recurring basis includes (but is not limited to) bagasse (from sugar cane), corn stalks, and switchgrass (Joint Committee on Taxation, Technical Explanation of the Tax Relief and Health Care Act of 2006 (P.L. 109-432) (JCX-50-06)).

> **Comment:** Since original use of the property must commence with the taxpayer, only new property may qualify as QCBEPP.

> **Comment:** An acquisition of property is considered made by purchase within the meaning of Code Sec. 179(d) unless the property (1) is acquired from a person whose relationship to the taxpayer bars recognition of a loss in any transaction between them under Code Sec. 267 or Code Sec. 707(b); (2) is acquired in a transfer between members of a controlled group of corporations (substituting 50 percent for the 80 percent that would otherwise apply with respect to stock ownership requirements); (3) has a substituted basis (in whole or in part); or (4) has a stepped-up basis determined under Code Sec. 1014(a) relating to inherited property (Code Sec. 179(d)(2); Reg. § 1.179-4(c)).

Property manufactured, constructed, or produced by or for a taxpayer. Property manufactured, constructed, or produced by the taxpayer for the taxpayer's own use may qualify as QCBEPP if the taxpayer begins the manufacture, construction, or production of the property after December 20, 2006, and the property is placed in service before January 1, 2013. Property manufactured, constructed, or produced for the taxpayer by another person under a contract that is entered into prior to the manufacture, construction, or production of the property is considered manufactured, constructed, or produced by the taxpayer (Code Sec. 168(l)(5), as added by the 2006 Extenders Act).

Sale-leasebacks. A limited exception to the original use requirement applies to sale-leasebacks. The rule applies to property originally placed in service after December 20, 2006, by a person who sells it to the taxpayer and then leases it from the taxpayer within three months after the date that the property was originally placed in service. In this situation, the property is treated as originally placed in service by the taxpayer (rather than the seller) and the placed-in-service date is deemed to occur no earlier than the date that the property is used under the leaseback (Code Sec. 168(l)(5), as added by the 2006 Extenders Act).

Syndication transactions. The ultimate purchaser in a syndicated leasing transaction may be able to qualify for the 50-percent deduction. If property is originally placed in

NEW LAW EXPLAINED

service by a lessor after December 20, 2006, and is sold by the lessor or any later purchaser within three months after the date the property was originally placed in service by the lessor, and the user of the property does not change during this three-month period, then the purchaser of the property in the last sale is considered to be the original user of the property and the property is treated as originally placed in service not earlier than the date of the last sale by the purchaser of the property in the last sale (Code Sec. 168(l)(5), as added by the 2006 Extenders Act).

Limitation on certain users and related parties. Property is not QCBEPP if the user of the property (as of the date on which the property is originally placed in service) or a person related (within the meaning of Code Sec. 267(b) or Code Sec. 707(b)) to such user or to the taxpayer had a written binding contract in effect for the acquisition of the property at any time on or before December 20, 2006, or in the case of property manufactured, constructed, or produced for such user's or person's own use, the manufacture, construction, or production of the property began at any time on or before December 20, 2006 (Code Sec. 168(l)(5), as added by the 2006 Extenders Act).

> **Comment:** The rules relating to manufactured, constructed, or produced property, sale leasebacks, syndication transactions, and limitations on certain users and related parties are borrowed directly from Code Sec. 168(k)(2)(E) except that the date of enactment of the 2006 Extenders Act is substituted for September 10, 2001 (the effective date of the Code Sec. 168(k) bonus depreciation provision) and the January 1, 2013 termination date of the QCBEPP provision is substituted for the January 1, 2005 (the termination date of the bonus depreciation provision). Thus, taxpayers should be able to rely on the related regulations issued under Code Sec. 168(k) for additional guidance.

Tax-exempt bond-financed property excluded. Property financed with tax-exempt bonds cannot qualify as QCBEPP and, therefore, does not qualify for the additional deduction (Code Sec. 168(l)(4)(B), as added by the 2006 Extenders Act).

Mandatory ADS property excluded. Property required to be depreciated under the MACRS alternative depreciation system (ADS) does not qualify as QCBEPP. The deduction is not denied if a taxpayer merely elects to depreciate the QCBEPP using ADS (Code Sec. 168(l)(4)(A), as added by the 2006 Extenders Act).

Election out. A taxpayer may elect not to claim the deduction with respect to any class of property for any tax year. The election out applies to all property in the class for which the election out is made and which is placed in service during the tax year.

> **Comment:** QCBEPP placed in service during a tax year may consist of various MACRS property classes, e.g., 5-year property, 7-year property, 10-year property, etc. The election out is made at the property class level. A taxpayer may make an election out for some or all of the property classes (Code Sec. 168(l)(4)(C), as added by the 2006 Extenders Act).

Recapture when property loses QCBEPP status. Recapture of the deduction is required in a tax year in which QCBEPP ceases to be QCBEPP. The recapture amount is computed in a similar manner to the recapture of the Code Section 179 deduction when section 179 property ceases to be used more than 50 percent in the active conduct of a taxpayer's trade or business during any year of the section 179 prop-

NEW LAW EXPLAINED

erty's MACRS recovery period (Code Sec. 168(l)(7), as added by the 2006 Extenders Act).

> **Comment:** QCBEPP could lose its status as QCBEPP if it becomes subject to ADS or is no longer used solely to produce cellulosic biomass ethanol.

> **Comment:** The 50-percent GO Zone bonus depreciation allowance (Code Sec. 1400N(d) is also required to be recaptured by applying rules similar to those applicable to section 179 property. Under guidance issued by the IRS in Notice 2006-77, I.R.B. 2006-40, the benefit derived from claiming the GO Zone additional first year depreciation deduction for the property is equal to the excess of the total depreciation claimed (including the GO Zone additional first year depreciation deduction) for the property for the tax years before the recapture year over the total depreciation that would have been allowable for the tax years before the recapture year had the GO Zone additional first year depreciation deduction not been claimed. The amount recaptured is treated as ordinary income for the recapture year. For the recapture year and subsequent tax years, the taxpayer's depreciation deductions are determined as if no GO Zone additional first year depreciation deduction was claimed with respect to the property.

Coordination with Code Sec. 179C election to expense refineries. The 50-percent deduction for QCBEPP does not apply to any QCBEPP with respect to which the taxpayer claims the 50-percent deduction allowed by Code Sec. 179C for qualified refinery property.

> **Comment:** The potential for a duplicative deduction exists because qualified refinery property can include a facility that processes biomass via gas into a liquid fuel.

▶ **Effective date.** The provision applies to property placed in service after December 20, 2006 in tax years ending after December 20, 2006 (Act Sec. 209(b) of the Tax Relief and Health Care Act of 2006 (P.L. 109-432)).

Law source: Law at ¶5265. Committee Reports at ¶15,430.

— Act Sec. 209(a) of the Tax Relief and Health Care Act of 2006 (P.L. 109-432), adding Code Sec. 168(l);

— Act Sec. 209(b), providing the effective date.

Reporter references: For further information, consult the following CCH reporters.

— Standard Federal Tax Reporter, ¶11,279.01 and ¶12,137E.01

— Federal Tax Guide, ¶9110

¶325 Suspension of Taxable Income Limit on Percentage Depletion for Oil and Gas Produced from Marginal Properties

SUMMARY OF NEW LAW

The suspension of the percentage depletion limitation for oil and gas produced from marginal properties is extended for two years through December 31, 2007.

BACKGROUND

Code Sec. 613A imposes substantial limitations on the allowance for percentage depletion of oil and gas wells. Code Sec. 613A(c) allows percentage depletion only with respect to up to 1,000 barrels of average daily production of domestic crude oil or the equivalent amount of natural gas (6 million cubic feet) to independent producers and royalty owners. For producers of both oil and natural gas, this limitation applies on a combined basis. This deduction is limited to 65-percent of the taxpayer's taxable income for the year (Code Sec. 613A(d)). Amounts disallowed under this provision are treated as a deduction in the succeeding tax year subject, again, to the 65-percent limitation.

The percentage depletion allowance for producers and royalty owners of oil and natural gas produced from marginal wells cannot exceed 100-percent of the tax-payer's net income from the property (computed without allowances for depletion) (Code Sec. 613(a)). This 100-percent net income limitation requires percentage depletion to be calculated on a property-by-property basis. The 100-percent of net income limitation on percentage depletion applies independently of the 65-percent taxable income limitation. The 100-percent of net income limitation was suspended for tax years after December 31, 1997, and before January 1, 2006.

NEW LAW EXPLAINED

Extension of suspension of taxable income limit with respect to marginal production.—The temporary suspension of the taxable income limit on the percentage depletion allowance for oil and gas produced from marginal wells has been extended to include tax years 2006 and 2007. Thus, the limitation on the amount of a percentage depletion deduction to 100 percent of the net income from an oil or gas producing property does not apply to domestic oil and gas produced from marginal properties during tax years beginning after December 31, 1997, and before January 1, 2008 (Code Sec. 613A(c)(6)(H), as amended by the Tax Relief and Health Care Act of 2006 (P.L. 109-432)).

> **Comment:** Marginal production means domestic crude oil or natural gas that is produced from a property that is a stripper well property for the calendar year in which the tax year begins or a property in which substantially all of the production during such calendar year is heavy oil (Code Sec. 613A(c)(6)(D)).

NEW LAW EXPLAINED

▶ **Effective date.** The provision applies to tax years beginning after December 31, 2005 (Act Sec. 118(b) of the Tax Relief and Health Care Act of 2006 (P.L. 109-432)).

Law source: Law at ¶5410. Committee Report at ¶15,270.

— Act Sec. 118(a) of the Tax Relief and Health Care Act of 2006 (P.L. 109-432), amending Code Sec. 613A(c)(6)(H);

— Act Sec. 118(b), providing the effective date.

Reporter references: For further information, consult the following CCH reporters.

— Standard Federal Tax Reporter, ¶23,988.038

— Tax Research Consultant, FARM: 15,300

— Federal Tax Guide, ¶9645

¶330 Expensing Election for Mine Safety Equipment

SUMMARY OF NEW LAW

A taxpayer may make an election to expense 50 percent of the cost of advanced mine safety equipment paid or incurred after December 20, 2006.

BACKGROUND

Largely in response to the explosion at the Sago Mine in West Virginia that claimed the lives of 12 miners in early 2006, Congress enacted the Mine Improvement and New Emergency Response (MINER) Act, (P.L. 109-236) on June 15, 2006. The Act requires coal mine operators to improve accident preparedness by providing: (1) emergency air supplies; (2) self-rescuer caches, maintenance, and replacement; (3) escapeways and flame-resistant directional lifelines; (4) emergency training; and (5) wireless communication between underground and the surface and electronic tracking of trapped persons.

Code Sec. 179 allows a current deduction for most types of depreciable assets placed in service during a tax year. However, the deduction is limited to $100,000 of qualifying section 179 property per year. Furthermore, many mining companies are ineligible to expense any amount due the investment limitation which reduces the $100,000 deduction limit by $1 for each dollar of qualifying section 179 property in excess of $400,000 that is placed in service during the tax year. The deduction is also denied if the company does not have taxable income in the tax year the section 179 property is placed in service. A section 179 deduction denied for this reason may be carried forward to a nonloss year.

Depreciable assets used in mining that are not expensed are generally treated as 7-year property under MACRS (Asset Class 10.0 of Rev. Proc. 87-56, 1987-2 CB 674).

50-percent expensing election for advanced mine safety equipment.—A taxpayer may elect to deduct 50 percent of the cost of qualified advanced mine safety equipment in the tax year that the equipment is placed in service (Code Sec. 179E, as added by the Tax Relief and Health Care Act of 2006 (P.L. 109-432)). The amount expensed is not capitalized. The election only applies to new property placed in service after December 20, 2006 and on or before January 1, 2009. (Code Sec. 179E(c) and (g), as added by the 2006 Extenders Act; Act Sec. 404(c) of the 2006 Extenders Act).

The election is made on the taxpayer's tax return and must specify the equipment to which the election applies. The IRS may prescribe regulations governing other aspects of the election (Code Sec. 179E(b)(1), as added by the 2006 Extenders Act).

The election may only be revoked with IRS consent (Code Sec. 179E(b)(2), as added by the 2006 Extenders Act).

Qualified advanced mine safety equipment. Qualified advanced mine safety equipment is defined as advanced mine safety equipment property for use in any underground mine located in the United States the original use of which commences with the taxpayer and which is placed in service after December 20, 2006 (Code Sec. 179E(c), as added by the 2006 Extenders Act).

> **Comment:** The original use must commence with the taxpayer. This means the property must be new. Used property does not qualify even if its first use at a mine is by the taxpayer.

Advanced mine safety equipment property. Advanced mine safety equipment property includes any of the following:

(1) An emergency communication technology or device which allows a miner to maintain constant communication with an individual who is not in the mine;

(2) An electronic identification and location device which allows an individual who is not in the mine to track at all times the movements and location of miners working in or at the mine;

(3) An emergency oxygen-generating, self-rescue device which provides oxygen for at least 90 minutes;

(4) Pre-positioned supplies of oxygen which in combination with self-rescue devices can be used to provide each miner on a shift the ability to survive for at least 48 hours if trapped in the mine;

(5) A comprehensive atmospheric monitoring system which monitors the levels of carbon monoxide, methane, and oxygen that are present in all areas of the mine and which can detect smoke in the case of a fire in a mine (Code Sec. 179E(d), as added by the 2006 Extenders Act).

> **Comment:** The new law also provides a tax credit for mine rescue team training costs. See ¶425.

Coordination with Code Sec. 179. The cost of any mine safety equipment which is expensed under Code Sec. 179 may not be taken into account in computing the 50-percent deduction for advance mine safety equipment (Code Sec. 179E(e), as

¶330

NEW LAW EXPLAINED

added by the 2006 Extenders Act). In other words, the section 179 expense deduction first reduces the cost of the advanced mine safety equipment before the calculation of the 50-percent deduction.

> **Example:** CoalCo pays $300,000 for qualifying equipment. If CoalCo elects to expense $100,000 under Code Sec. 179 only $200,000 may be taken into account in computing the deduction for mine safety equipment ($300,000 – $100,000). The mine safety equipment expensing deduction is $100,000 ($200,000 × 50%). The remaining $100,000 is depreciated under MACRS.

Basis reduction. The basis of qualified advanced mine safety equipment must be reduced by the amount deducted under this provision (Joint Committee on Taxation, Technical Explanation of the Tax Relief and Health Care Act of 2006 (P.L. 109-432) (JCX-50-06)).

Capitalization not required. Amounts expensed under this provision need not be capitalized even if the expenditures would otherwise constitute a permanent improvement that increases the value of the property (Code Sec. 263(a)(1)(L), as added by 2006 Extenders Act).

Corporate earnings and profits computation. For purposes of computing the earnings and profits of a corporation, any amount deducted under this provision is allowed as a deduction ratably over five tax years beginning with the tax year in which the deduction is claimed (Code Sec. 312(k)(3)(B), as amended by the 2006 Extenders Act).

Recapture upon sale or disposition. The deduction is subject to recapture as ordinary income under the Code Sec. 1245 depreciation recapture rules (Code Sec. 1245(a)(2)(C) and (3)(C), as amended by the 2006 Extenders Act).

Reporting requirement. The deduction for qualified advance mine safety equipment may not be claimed for a tax year unless the taxpayer files a report with the IRS containing any information with respect to the operation of the taxpayer's mine that the IRS may require (Code Sec. 179E(f), as amended by the 2006 Extenders Act).

Termination date. The deduction does not apply to property placed in service after December 31, 2008 (Code Sec. 179E(g), as added by the 2006 Extenders Act).

> **Caution Note:** If a taxpayer purchased and paid for advanced mine safety equipment on or before December 20, 2006 it will not qualify for the deduction even if it is placed in service after December 20, 2006 and on or before December 31, 2008. The costs for the equipment must be paid or incurred after December 20, 2006.

▶ **Effective date.** The provision applies to costs paid or incurred after December 20, 2006 (Act Sec. 404(c) of the Tax Relief and Health Care Act of 2006 (P.L. 109-432)).

Law source: Law at ¶5315, ¶5341, ¶5347, and ¶5590. Committee Report at ¶15,490.

— Act Sec. 404(a) of the Tax Relief and Health Care Act of 2006 (P.L. 109-432), adding Code Sec. 179E;

NEW LAW EXPLAINED

— Act Sec. 404(b), adding Code Sec. 263(a)(1)(L); amending Code Sec. 312(k)(3)(B), and amending Code Sec. 1245(a)(2)(C) and (3)(C);

— Act Sec. 404(c), providing the effective date.

Reporter references: For further information, consult the following CCH reporters.

— Standard Federal Tax Reporter, ¶12,126.01

— Federal Tax Guide, ¶25,299

OTHER DEDUCTIONS

¶335 Deduction for Energy Efficient Commercial Building Property Extended

SUMMARY OF NEW LAW

The deduction for costs associated with energy efficient commercial building property is extended for one year and expires with respect to property placed in service after December 31, 2008.

BACKGROUND

A taxpayer may deduct the cost of certain energy efficiency improvements installed on or in a depreciable building located in the U.S., effective for improvements placed in service after December 31, 2005 and before January 1, 2008 (Code Sec. 179D). The deduction applies to "energy efficient commercial building property," which is defined as depreciable property that is installed as part of a building's (1) interior lighting systems, (2) heating, cooling, ventilation, and hot water systems, or (3) envelope, and is part of a certified plan to reduce the total annual energy and power costs of these systems by at least 50 percent in comparison to a reference building that meets specified minimum standards. The deduction is limited to the product of $1.80 and the total square footage of the building, reduced by the aggregate amount deducted in any prior tax year.

A taxpayer may also claim a partial deduction for the costs of property that meet energy savings targets set by the IRS in Notice 2006-52, I.R.B. 2006-26, 1175. The deduction is determined by substituting $.60 for $1.80.

Generally, the deduction is claimed by the building's owner. However, in the case of a public building, the person primarily responsible for designing the property may claim the deduction. The deduction reduces the depreciable basis of the building and is treated as a depreciation deduction for Code Sec. 1245 recapture purposes (Code Sec. 1245(a)(3)(C)).

The Department of Energy will create and maintain a list of the software that must be used to calculate power consumption and energy costs for purposes of certifying the

BACKGROUND

required energy savings necessary to claim the deduction. This list will be available to the public at http://www.eere.energy.gov/buildings/info/tax_credit_2006.html (Notice 2006-52). The certification need not be attached to the taxpayer's return but must be retained as part of the taxpayer's books and records.

NEW LAW EXPLAINED

Deduction extended through 2008.—The new law extends the deduction for energy-efficient commercial building property so that it is available for qualified property placed into service in 2008 (Code Sec. 179D(h), as amended by the Tax Relief and Health Care Act of 2006 (P.L. 109-432).

▶ **Effective date.** No specific effective date is provided by the Act. The provision is, therefore, considered effective on December 20, 2006, the date of enactment.

Law source: Law at ¶5310. Committee Reports at ¶15,380.

— Act Sec. 204 of the Tax Relief and Health Care Act of 2006 (P.L. 109-432), amending Code Sec. 179D(h).

Reporter references: For further information, consult the following CCH reporters.

— Standard Federal Tax Reporter, ¶12,138D.01

— Tax Research Consultant, BUSEXP: 18,950

— Federal Tax Guide, ¶8365

¶340 Tax Incentives for Investment in the District of Columbia

SUMMARY OF NEW LAW

The District of Columbia enterprise zone provisions and the D.C. homebuyer credit are extended for two years.

BACKGROUND

Parts of the District of Columbia are treated as an empowerment zone, called the District of Columbia Enterprise Zone (the "DC Zone") (Code Sec. 1400). The designation of the area as the DC Zone is scheduled to end on December 31, 2005 (Code Sec. 1400(f)).

As with other empowerment zones, special tax incentives are provided for the DC Zone in order to attract businesses to the area. The DC Zone receives special tax-exempt financing incentives that apply to bonds issued from January 1, 1998, through December 31, 2005 (Code Sec. 1400A). Generally, the limit on the amount of bonds that can be allocated to a particular DC Zone business is $15 million and the bonds

BACKGROUND

may be issued only while the DC Zone designation is in effect. This is higher than the $3 million that can be allocated to a particular enterprise zone business in an empowerment zone or enterprise community (Code Sec. 1400A and Code Sec. 1394(c)).

Another tax break for DC Zone businesses is an exclusion from income for qualified capital gain from the sale or exchange of a DC Zone asset held for more than five years (Code Sec. 1400B). The DC Zone assets, including DC Zone business stock, DC Zone partnership interests and DC Zone business property, must be acquired before January 1, 2006, and the gain cannot be attributable to periods before January 1, 1998, or after December 31, 2010 (Code Sec. 1400B(e)(2)).

First-time homebuyers of a principal residence in the District of Columbia are allowed a credit of up to $5,000 of the purchase price of the residence. The maximum amount of the credit is $2,500 for each married taxpayer filing a separate return (Code Sec. 1400C(a) and (e)(1)(A)). The credit phases out for individual taxpayers with adjusted gross income between $70,000 and $90,000 ($110,000 and $130,000 for joint filers) (Code Sec. 1400C(b)). A first-time homebuyer means any individual who did not have a present ownership interest in a principal residence in the District of Columbia in the one-year period ending on the date of the purchase of the residence to which the credit applies (Code Sec. 1400C(c)).

To qualify for the credit, the residence must have been purchased after August 4, 1997, and before January 1, 2006 (Code Sec. 1400C(i)). If the DC residence is newly constructed by the taxpayer, the date that the taxpayer first occupies the residence is treated as the purchase date (Code Sec. 1400C(e)(2)(B)).

NEW LAW EXPLAINED

D.C. enterprise zone and homebuyer credit provisions extended.—The Tax Relief and Health Care Act of 2006 (P.L. 109-432) extends the designation of the applicable DC area as the DC Enterprise Zone for two years through December 31, 2007 (Code Sec. 1400(f), as amended by the Tax Relief and Health Care Act of 2006 (P.L. 109-432)). The DC Zone tax-exempt bond financing incentives have also been extended to apply to bonds issued from January 1, 1998 through December 31, 2007 (Code Sec. 1400A(b), as amended by the 2006 Extenders Act).

With respect to the zero percent capital gains rate provisions of Code Sec. 1400B, the 2006 Extenders Act: (1) extends the DC Zone business stock acquisition date from January 1, 2006, to January 1, 2008 (Code Sec. 1400B(b), as amended by the 2006 Extenders Act); (2) extends the ending date of the period to which "qualified capital gains" may be attributable from December 31, 2010 to December 31, 2012 (Code Sec. 1400B(e)(2), as amended by the 2006 Extenders Act); and (3) extends the ending date of the period during which qualified capital gains from the sales and exchanges of interests in partnerships and S corporations that are DC businesses may be determined from December 31, 2010, to December 31, 2012 (Code Sec. 1400B(g)(2), as amended by the 2006 Extenders Act).

¶340

NEW LAW EXPLAINED

The termination of the first-time homebuyer credit for DC is extended from January 1, 2006, to January 1, 2008 (Code Sec. 1400C(i), as amended by the 2006 Extenders Act).

> **Compliance Tip:** Taxpayers eligible for the District of Columbia first-time homebuyer credit must file Form 8859, District of Columbia First-Time Homebuyer Credit, with their Form 1040 to claim the credit.

▶ **Effective date.** The amendments made by this section are generally effective after December 31, 2005, except that the conforming amendments of Act Sec. 110(c)(2) are effective on December 20, 2006 (Act Secs. 110(a)(2), 110(b)(2), 110(c)(3) and 110(d)(2) of the Tax Relief and Health Care Act of 2006 (P.L. 109-432)).

Law source: Law at ¶5611, 5614, 5617, 5620, and 5623. Committee Report at ¶15,190.

— Act Sec. 110(a)(1) of the Tax Relief and Health Care Act of 2006 (P.L. 109-432), amending Code Sec. 1400(f);

— Act Sec. 110(b)(1), amending Code Sec. 1400A(b);

— Act Sec. 110(c)(1), amending Code Sec. 1400B(b);

— Act Sec. 110(c)(2)(A), amending Code Sec. 1400B(e)(2);

— Act Sec. 110(c)(2)(B), amending Code Sec. 1400B(g)(2);

— Act Sec. 110(c)(2)(C), amending Code Sec. 1400F(d);

— Act Sec. 110(d)(1), amending Code Sec. 1400C(i);

— Act Secs. 110(a)(2), (b)(2), (c)(3) and (d)(2) providing the effective dates.

Reporter references: For further information, consult the following CCH reporters.

— Standard Federal Tax Reporter, ¶32,423.01, ¶32,425.01 and ¶32,429.01

— Tax Research Consultant, BUSEXP: 57,056.30

— Federal Tax Guide, ¶2226 and ¶8590

¶345 Code Sec. 199 Deduction Allowable with Respect to Production Activities in Puerto Rico

SUMMARY OF NEW LAW

For purposes of the domestic production activities deduction under Code Sec. 199, a taxpayer may take into account its Puerto Rico business activity to calculate its domestic production gross receipts (DPGR) and qualified production activities income (QPAI). To be eligible, however, all of the taxpayer's gross receipts from Puerto Rican sources must be subject to U.S. income taxation. In addition, the taxpayer can take into account wages paid to U.S. citizens who are bona fide residents of Puerto Rico for purposes of the 50-percent W-2 wage limitation. These provisions are only effective for the first two tax years beginning after 2005 and before 2008.

BACKGROUND

Generally, a taxpayer may claim a deduction equal to a percentage of the lesser of its taxable income (or adjusted gross income (AGI) for individual taxpayers and estates and trusts) or its qualified production activities income (QPAI) (Code Sec. 199). For tax years beginning in 2005 and 2006, the maximum deduction is three percent of the lesser of such income. For tax years beginning in 2007 through 2009, the percentage increases to six percent and for tax years after 2009, the percentage increases to nine percent.

The amount of the deduction is also limited to 50 percent of the W-2 wages paid by the taxpayer to its employees for the calendar year ending during the tax year (Code Sec. 199(b)). For this purpose, "wages" includes any amount paid by the taxpayer to its employees for employment which are deemed to be wages subject to income tax withholding under Code Sec. 3401. For example, remuneration paid for services performed by a U.S. citizen in Puerto Rico (unless the employer is the United States or one of its agencies) will not be considered "wages" if it is reasonable to believe that the employee-citizen will be a bona fide resident of Puerto Rico during the calendar year (Code Sec. 3401(a)(8)(C)). However, wages will include the total amount of elective deferrals made by the employee to a qualified retirement plan (401(k), 403(b), SIMPLE, SEP), compensation deferred to a Code Sec. 457 plan, as well as Roth IRA contributions considered to be elective deferrals under Code Sec. 402A, for the calendar year (see Rev. Proc. 2006-22).

> **Comment:** For tax years beginning before May 18, 2006, the W-2 wage limitation is based upon all "wages" paid by the taxpayer to all employees, regardless of whether it is related to its domestic production activities. However, for tax years beginning after May 17, 2006, the limitation only includes the W-2 wages properly allocable to the taxpayer's domestic production gross receipts (DPGR). In other words, only those wages which the taxpayer deducts in calculating its QPAI will be considered to determine the W-2 wage limit.

Qualified production activities income. A taxpayer's QPAI is its DPGR attributable to the actual conduct of a trade or business during the tax year, less the cost of goods sold allocable to DPGR, other deductions or expenses directly allocable to DPGR, and a ratable share of any other deductions or expenses which are not directly allocable to DPGR or any other class of income (Code Sec. 199(c)). DPGR are the gross receipts of the taxpayer that are derived from:

(1) the lease, license, sale, exchange of other disposition of any:

- qualifying production property (i.e., tangible personal property) manufactured, produced, grown or extracted by the taxpayer in whole or in significant part within the United States;

- qualified film produced by the taxpayer within the United States; or

- electricity, natural gas, or potable water produced by the taxpayer in the United States;

(2) the construction of real property that is performed by the taxpayer in the United States in the ordinary course of an taxpayer's construction trade or business; and

¶345

BACKGROUND

(3) architectural or engineering services that are performed by the taxpayer in the ordinary course of its architectural or engineering trade or business in the United States with respect to the construction of real property that is located in the United States.

For this purpose, the "United States" is defined as including all 50 states and the District of Columbia, as well as the territorial waters of the United States, and the seabed and subsoil of those submarine areas that are adjacent to the territorial waters of the United States and over which the U.S. has exclusive rights, in accordance with international law, with respect to the exploration and exploitation of natural resources (Reg. § 1.199-3(h), effective for tax years beginning after May 31, 2006; Notice 2005-14, § § 3.04(6), 4.04(6), and Proposed Reg. § 1.199-3(g), effective for tax years beginning before June 1, 2006). The "United States" does not include possessions and territories of the United States or the airspace or space over the United States and these areas.

> **Comment:** The inclusion of territorial waters, the seabed and the subsoil of submarine areas makes this definition of the "United States" similar to the one used for purposes of mineral exploitation, and somewhat broader than the one used for most other tax purposes. See Code Sec. 638 and Reg. § 301.7701(b)-1(c)(2)(ii), respectively.

NEW LAW EXPLAINED

Puerto Rico deemed part of United States.—The new law provides that Puerto Rico will be considered part of the "United States" for purposes of determining the domestic production gross receipts (DPGR) of a taxpayer if all of the taxpayer's gross receipts from sources in Puerto Rico are taxable (Code Sec. 199(d)(8)(A), as added by the Tax Relief and Health Care Act of 2006 (P.L. 109-432)). Consequently, if a taxpayer has gross receipts from qualified production activites within the Commonwealth of Puerto Rico, then such receipts will be considered DPGR. However, this rule will only apply if *all* of the taxpayer's gross receipts from Puerto Rican sources are currently taxable for U.S. federal income tax purposes. For example, a controlled foreign corporation (CFC) would not be eligible for the Code Sec. 199 deduction under this provision (Joint Committee on Taxation, Technical Explanation of the Tax Relief and Health Care Act of 2006 (P.L. 109-432) (JCX-50-06)).

> **Example 1:** Dunder Mifflin is a U.S. corporation that manufactures all of its paper products at its facilities in Georgia and Puerto Rico. It then sells the products to customers through sales offices in the eastern United States. All of the gross receipts derived by Dunder Mifflin, and not just the gross receipts from products manufactured in Georgia, will be considered DPGR because Puerto Rico is considered part of the United States for purposes of the Code Sec. 199 deduction.

¶345

NEW LAW EXPLAINED

The treatment of Puerto Rico as part of the United States for purposes of the Code Sec. 199 deduction will only apply with respect to the first two tax years of the taxpayer beginning after 2005 and before 2008. This means that for calendar-year taxpayers, the rule will apply only for 2006 and 2007. For fiscal-year taxpayers, this means that the rule will apply for any tax year beginning in 2006 and 2007.

> **Comment:** The 2006 Extenders Act did not extend the geographic reach of the domestic production activities deduction to the U.S. Virgin Islands or other U.S. territories and possessions. Thus, gross receipts derived from qualifying production activities in these locations will *not* be considered DPGR because the activities are not deemed to have occurred in the "United States."

W-2 wage limit. If a taxpayer has gross receipts from Puerto Rican sources that are considered DPGR, then remuneration paid by the taxpayer to a U.S. citizen who is a bona fide resident of Puerto Rico for services performed in Puerto Rico may be considered "wages" for purposes of calculating the 50-percent W-2 wage limitation (Code Sec. 199(d)(8)(B), as added by the 2006 Extenders Act).

> **Example 2:** Assume the same facts as in Example 1 above, except that Dunder Mifflin employes 20 people at its facilities in Puerto Rico. All 20 of the employees are U.S. citizens that the company reasonably believes are bona fide residents of Puerto Rico. Thus, the remuneration paid by Dunder Mifflin to the employees may be considered "wages" for purposes of calculating the 50-percent wage limitation on its domestic production activities deduction. This is true, even though the remuneration is not considered "wages" subject to withholding and therefore are not reported on the employees' W-2 forms.

▶ **Effective date.** The amendments made by this provision shall apply to tax years beginning after December 31, 2005 (Act Sec. 401(b) of the Tax Relief and Health Care Act of 2006 (P.L. 109-432)).

Law source: Law at ¶5330. Committee Reports at ¶15,470.

— Act Sec. 401(a) of the Tax Relief and Health Care Act of 2006 (P.L. 109-432), redesignating Code Sec. 199(d)(8) as (d)(9) and adding a new Code Sec. 199(d)(8);

— Act Sec. 401(b), providing the effective date.

Reporter references: For further information, consult the following CCH reporters.

— Standard Federal Tax Reporter, ¶12,476.01

— Tax Research Consultant, BUSEXP: 6,000

— Federal Tax Guide, ¶8320 and ¶8325

¶345

¶355 Deduction for Charitable Contributions of Computers or Scientific Research Property

SUMMARY OF NEW LAW

The enhanced corporate deduction for charitable contributions of computers is extended two years and is set to expire for contributions made during any tax year beginning after December 31, 2007. In addition, the enhanced corporate deduction for charitable contributions of computers, as well as the enhanced corporate deduction for charitable contributions of scientific property used for research, are expanded to include property assembled by the taxpayer, in addition to property constructed by the taxpayer.

BACKGROUND

Corporations are entitled to a charitable contributions deduction limited to 10 percent of the corporation's taxable income, computed without adjustments for: (1) the deduction for charitable contributions, (2) the deductions for certain dividends received and for dividends paid on certain preferred stock of public utilities, (3) any net operating loss carryback, and (4) any capital loss carryback (Code Sec. 170(b)(2)). Generally, for contributions of property, the deduction is limited to the corporation's basis in the property up to 10 percent of the corporation's taxable income (Code Sec. 170(e)).

Certain corporate contributions, however, qualify for preferred treatment. An enhanced charitable deduction is available to C corporations for: (1) qualified contributions of scientific property used for research ("qualified research contributions"); and (2) qualified contributions of computer technology and/or equipment ("qualified computer contributions"). The enhanced charitable deduction is equal to the corporate donor's basis in the donated property plus one-half of the ordinary income that would have been realized if the property had been sold. However, the deduction cannot exceed twice the corporation's basis in the property (Code Sec. 170(e)(4)(A) and (6)(A)).

Qualified research contributions. Qualified contributions of scientific property used for research means donations of tangible personal property that is inventory or stock in trade of the donor and that is constructed by the donor and contributed within two years of the substantial completion of its construction (Code Sec. 170(e)(4)(B)). For property to qualify as self-constructed, the cost of parts, other than parts manufactured by the donor or a related company, may not exceed 50 percent of the donor's basis in the property (Code Sec. 170(e)(4)(C)). The property itself must be scientific equipment at least 80 percent of the use of which by the donee is for research, experimentation or research training in the United States in physical or biological sciences.

Further, the donee must be a college or university or an exempt scientific research organization. The donee must be the original user of the property, and the property must not have been transferred by the donee in exchange for money, other property

BACKGROUND

or services. Finally, the donor must receive written assurance from the donee that it will use the property in accordance with the conditions for the enhanced deduction.

Qualified computer contributions. Qualified donations of computer technology and equipment include contributions of computer software, computer or peripheral equipment, and fiber optic cable related to computer use that are to be used within the United States for educational purposes (Code Sec. 170(e)(6)(F)). An eligible donee includes:

(1) an educational organization that normally maintains a regular faculty and curriculum and has regularly enrolled students in attendance at the place where its educational activities are regularly conducted;

(2) a tax-exempt entity that is organized primarily for purposes of supporting elementary and secondary education;

(3) a private foundation that, within 30 days after receipt of the contribution, contributes the property to an eligible donee described in (1) and (2) above, and notifies the donor of the contribution (Code Secs. 170(e)(6)(B) and (C)); or

(4) a public library, as defined in the Library Services and Technology Act (20 U.S.C. §9122(2)(A)) (Code Sec. 170(e)(6)(B)(i)(III)).

The enhanced charitable deduction for contributions of computer technology and/or equipment to schools or public libraries expired for contributions made during any tax year beginning after December 31, 2005 (Code Sec. 170(e)(6)(G)).

NEW LAW EXPLAINED

Enhanced deductions for charitable contributions of computers and scientific research property.—The new law retroactively extends for two years the enhanced charitable deduction for computer technology and/or equipment. The deduction is now set to expire for contributions made during any tax year beginning after December 31, 2007 (Code Sec. 170(e)(6)(G), as amended by the Tax Relief and Health Care Act of 2006 (P.L. 109-432)).

In addition, under the 2006 Extenders Act, property assembled by the donor corporation, as well as property constructed by the donor corporation, is eligible for both the enhanced deduction for contributions of computer technology and/or equipment and the enhanced deduction for contributions of scientific property for research (Code Sec. 170(e)(4)(B) and 170(e)(6)(B), as amended by the 2006 Extenders Act).

> **Caution:** According to the Joint Committee on Taxation, Technical Explanation of the Tax Relief and Health Care Act of 2006 (P.L. 109-432) (JCX-50-06), there is no intention that old or used components assembled by the donor corporation into computer technology or scientific property qualify for the enhanced deduction.

▶ **Effective date.** These provisions are effective for contributions made in tax years beginning after December 31, 2005 (Act Sec. 116(a)(2) and (b)(3) of the Tax Relief and Health Care Act of 2006 (P.L. 109-432)).

¶355

NEW LAW EXPLAINED

Law source: Law at ¶5280. Committee Report at ¶15,250.

— Act Sec. 116(a) of the Tax Relief and Health Care Act of 2006 (P.L. 109-432), amending Code Sec. 170(e)(6)(G);

— Act Sec. 116(b)(1), amending Code Sec. 170(e)(4)(B)(ii) and 170(e)(4)(B)(iii);

— Act Sec. 116(b)(2), amending Code Sec. 170(e)(6)(B)(ii) and 170(e)(6)(D);

— Act Sec. 116(a)(2) and (b)(3), providing the effective date.

Reporter references: For further information, consult the following CCH reporters.

— Standard Federal Tax Reporter, ¶11,680.037

— Tax Research Consultant, CCORP: 9,358

— Federal Tax Guide, ¶6591

CORPORATIONS

¶358 Capital Gains Exclusion for Conservation Sales of Certain Mineral and Geothermal Interests

SUMMARY OF NEW LAW

Twenty-five percent of otherwise recognizable long-term capital gain from a "conservation sale" of a qualifying mineral or geothermal interest located on specified Federal land in the Rocky Mountain Front area may be excluded from the seller's gross income.

BACKGROUND

Mining on Federal lands in the West is very controversial, pitting those eager to protect the environment and tourism against those supporting development of natural resources to increase America's energy independence. A temporary moratorium on oil, gas, and mineral exploration in the Lewis and Clark National Forest lands located in the Rocky Mountain Front area in Montana has been in force since 1997. Montana's U.S. Senators have sought to broaden and make the ban permanent.

NEW LAW EXPLAINED

Twenty-five percent capital gains exclusion for sales of certain mineral and geothermal interests located on Federal land for conservation purposes.—The new law provides that 25 percent of otherwise recognizable long-term capital gain from a "conservation sale" of a qualifying mineral or geothermal interest may be excluded from gross income, effective for sales occurring on or after December 20, 2006 (Act Sec. 403(c), Division C of the Tax Relief and Health Care Act of 2006 (P.L. 109-432)). Non-tax

NEW LAW EXPLAINED

provisions of the law include a permanent ban on oil, gas, and mineral exploration along Montana's Rocky Mountain Front (Act Sec. 403(b)(1), Division C of the 2006 Extenders Act). The exclusion provides an incentive for existing leaseholders to sell their leases to governments or nonprofit organizations that would retire them.

> **Comment:** The tax break potentially applies to approximately 60 current leases on the front, according to Sen. Max Baucus, D-Mont.

Conservation sale defined. A conservation sale is a sale of a qualifying mineral or geothermal interest to an "eligible entity" that provides the seller with a "qualifying letter of intent" guaranteeing perpetual use of the property for conservation purposes (Act Sec. 403(c)(3), Division C of the Extenders Act). As explained below, a sale of a qualifying mineral or geothermal interest is a sale of a taxpayer's entire interest in a mineral or geothermal deposit located on "eligible Federal land" located in the Rocky Mountain Front area. An eligible entity is a specified tax-exempt entity, including a Federal, State, or local government or an agency or department thereof, or a nonprofit organization. A sale pursuant to an order of condemnation or eminent domain is not a conservation sale. In such cases a deferral of gain may be available under the involuntary conversion rules (Code Sec. 1033).

Eligible Federal land. The qualifying mineral or geothermal interest must be an interest in a deposit located on "eligible Federal land." Eligible Federal land means:

(1) Bureau of Land Management land and any Federally-owned minerals located south of the Blackfeet Indian Reservation and East of the Lewis and Clark National Forest to the Eastern edge of R. 8 W., beginning in T. 29 N. down to and including T. 19 N. and all of T. 18 N., R. 7 W;

(2) Forest Service land and any Federally-owned minerals located in the Rocky Mountain Division of the Lewis and Clark National Forest, including the approximately 356,111 acres of land made unavailable for leasing by the August 28, 1997, Record of Decision for the Lewis and Clark National Forest Oil and Gas Leasing Environmental Impact Statement and that is located from T. 31 N. to T. 16 N. and R. 13 W. to R. 7 W.; and

(3) Forest Service land and any Federally-owned minerals located within the Badger Two Medicine area of the Flathead National Forest, including the land located in T. 29 N. from the Western edge of R. 16 W. to the Eastern edge of R. 13 W. and the land located in T. 28 N., Rs. 13 and 14 W. (Act Sec. 403(a), Division C of the 2006 Extenders Act).

> **Comment:** Eligible Federal land is depicted on a map entitled "Rocky Mountain Front Mineral Withdrawal Area," dated December 31, 2006 (Act Sec. 403(a), Division C of the 2006 Extenders Act). The map is on file and available for inspection in the Office of the Chief of the Forest Service (Joint Committee on Taxation, Technical Explanation of the Tax Relief and Health Care Act of 2006 (P.L. 109-432) (JCX-50-06)).

Sale of entire interest required. The 25-percent long-term capital gain exclusion does not apply unless the taxpayer sells its entire interest in the mineral or geothermal deposit located on the eligible Federal land (Act Sec. 403(c)(4), Division C of the 2006 Extenders Act).

NEW LAW EXPLAINED

A taxpayer has not sold its entire interest if the interest was divided before the sale in order to avoid this requirement (or the rule contained in Code Sec. 170(f)(3)(A) which denies a charitable contribution deduction for certain contributions of partial interests in property) (Act Sec. 403(c)(4)(B)(i), Division C of the 2006 Extenders Act).

> **Comment:** The partial interest rules contained in Reg. § 1.170A-7(a)(2)(i), relating to charitable contributions of partial interests, are to be applied similarly for purposes of this provision (Joint Committee on Taxation, Technical Explanation of the Tax Relief and Health Care Act of 2006 (P.L. 109-432) (JCX-50-06)).

A taxpayer may retain an interest in deposits other than the mineral or geothermal deposit located on the eligible Federal land. Such interests may be retained even if the deposits they include are contiguous to and were acquired in the same conveyance as the mineral or geothermal deposit located on the eligible Federal land (Act Sec. 403(c)(4)(B)(ii), Division C of the 2006 Extenders Act).

Types of qualifying tax-exempt purchasers. The sale of the taxpayer's interest in the mineral or geothermal deposit must be to an "eligible entity." An eligible entity means:

(1) A Federal, State, or local government (i.e., entities described in Code Sec. 170(c)(1)); or

(2) An agency or department of a Federal, State, or local government operated primarily for one of the three conservation purposes listed in Code Sec. 170(h)(4)(A)(i), (ii), or (iii), namely,

- the preservation of land areas for outdoor recreation by, or the education of, the general public,

- the protection of a relatively natural habitat of fish, wildlife, or plants, or similar ecosystem, or

- the preservation of open space (including farmland and forest land) where such preservation is for the scenic enjoyment of the general public, or pursuant to a clearly delineated Federal, State, or local governmental conservation policy, and will yield a significant public benefit.

(3) A tax-exempt entity described in Code Sec. 170(b)(1)(A)(vi) or Code Sec. 170(h)(3)(B) organized and operated at all times primarily for one or more of the conservation purposes listed in item (2), above.

> **Comment:** In general, Code Sec. 170(b)(1)(A)(vi) describes a corporation, trust, or community chest, fund, or foundation which is tax-exempt under Code Sec. 501(a) and normally receives a substantial part of its support (exclusive of income received in the exercise or performance of the function constituting the basis for its exemption) from a governmental unit or from direct or indirect contributions from the general public. Code Sec. 170(h)(3)(B) describes a tax-exempt Code Sec. 501(c)(3) organization permitted to accept a qualified conservation contribution.

Tax-exempt purchaser must provide qualifying letter of intent. The eligible entity must provide the taxpayer with a written letter of intent at the time of the sale that includes

NEW LAW EXPLAINED

the following statement (Act Secs. 403(c)(3)(B), (5)(B), Division C of the 2006 Extenders Act):

"The transferee's intent is that this acquisition will serve 1 or more of the conservation purposes specified in clause (i), (ii), or (iii) of section 170(h)(4)(A) of the Internal Revenue Code of 1986, that the transferee's use of the deposits so acquired will be consistent with section 170(h)(5) of such Code, and that the use of the deposits will continue to be consistent with such section, even if ownership or possession of such deposits is subsequently transferred to another person."

> **Comment:** Use consistent with Code Sec. 170(h)(5) requires protection of the conservation purpose in perpetuity and a ban on surface mining (Joint Committee on Taxation, Technical Explanation of the Tax Relief and Health Care Act of 2006 (P.L. 109-432) (JCX-50-06)).

> **Comment:** The provision does not contain a formal election out. However, the Joint Committee's explanation indicates that a taxpayer may, in effect, elect out by intentionally failing to satisfy one or more of the provision's requirements. For example, the taxpayer may fail to obtain the required letter of intent from the qualified tax-exempt purchaser (Joint Committee on Taxation, Technical Explanation of the Tax Relief and Health Care Act of 2006 (P.L. 109-432) (JCX-50-06)).

Reporting requirements. The IRS may impose reporting requirements necessary to further the purpose that any conservation use be in perpetuity (Act Sec. 403(c)(7), Division C of the 2006 Extenders Act).

Excise tax penalty on subsequent transfer by tax-exempt purchaser. An excise tax penalty is imposed on the tax-exempt purchaser (i.e. the "eligible entity" that purchased the qualifying mineral or geothermal interest) if ownership or possession is transferred by sale, exchange, or lease to another person unless:

(1) the subsequent transferee is also an eligible entity that provides a qualifying letter of intent; or

(2) the subsequent transferee is not an eligible entity but provides a qualifying letter of intent and the IRS is satisfied that the transfer remains consistent with the perpetual protection of the conservation purpose and ban on surface mining (Act Sec. 403(c)(6), Division C of the 2006 Extenders Act).

If a transfer to a subsequent transferee that is an eligible entity is not subject to the excise tax penalty, the penalty can be imposed on the eligible entity that is a subsequent transferee if the eligible entity later transfers the mineral or geothermal interest in a disqualifying transfer not described in (1) or (2), above (Act Sec. 403(c)(6)(A)(ii)), Division C of the 2006 Extenders Act).

> **Comment:** Act Sec. 403(c)(6)(A) provides that the tax is only imposed on transfers by eligible entities. Thus, it does not appear that the tax may be on a subsequent transferee described in (2) above (i.e., a ineligible entity) that makes a disqualifying transfer. Presumably, this result is unintended.

The excise tax is only imposed on the first disqualifying transfer. Once imposed, it does not apply to any later transfers (Act Sec. 403(c)(6)(D)(iii), Division C of the 2006 Extenders Act).

NEW LAW EXPLAINED

The excise tax is equal to the sum of (1) 20 percent of the fair market value of the transferred interest at the time of the disqualifying transfer and (2) the product of the highest rate of income tax imposed on C corporations times any gain or income realized by the transferor (Act Sec. 403(c)(6)(B), Division C of the 2006 Extenders Act).

The penalty is treated as an excise tax to which the deficiency procedures of subtitle F of the Internal Revenue Code apply (i.e., Code Secs. 6001 and following) (Act Sec. 403(c)(6)(E), Division C of the 2006 Extenders Act).

▶ **Effective date.** The provision applies to sales occurring on or after December 20, 2006 (Act Sec. 403(d), Division C of the Tax Relief and Health Care Act of 2006 (P.L. 109-432)).

Law source: Law at ¶7090. Committee Report at ¶15,720.

— Act Sec. 403(a), (b), and (c), Division C of the Tax Relief and Health Care Act of 2006 (P.L. 109-432);

— Act Sec. 403(d), Division C, providing the effective date.

Reporter references: For further information, consult the following CCH reporters.

— Standard Federal Tax Reporter, ¶5504.025

— Tax Research Consultant, INDIV: 33,300

— Federal Tax Guide, ¶4850

¶360 Modified Active Business Test for Tax-Free Distributions of Controlled Corporation Stock

SUMMARY OF NEW LAW

For purposes of the active business requirement under Code Sec. 355, all members of the separate affiliated group of the distributing or controlled corporation are treated as one corporation and the "substantially all" active business stock test does not apply to distributions occurring after May 17, 2006.

BACKGROUND

A distribution of property by a corporation to its shareholders is generally a taxable event for both the distributing corporation and the shareholders (Code Secs. 301 and 311). However, a distribution of stock or securities of a controlled corporation may qualify for tax-free treatment if it meets the Code Sec. 355 requirements (Code Sec. 355(a) and (c)).

One of the requirements is the active business test (Code Sec. 355(b)). The test generally requires that both the distributing corporation and the controlled corporation be engaged in the active conduct of a trade or business immediately after the distribution (Code Sec. 355(b)(1)).

BACKGROUND

For this purpose, a corporation is treated as engaged in the active conduct of a trade or business if (1) it is directly engaged in the active conduct of a trade or business, or (2) substantially all of its assets consist of stock and securities of a controlled corporation that is directly engaged in the active conduct of a trade or business (Code Sec. 355(b)(2)(A)). The IRS has taken the position that the "substantially all" requirement is satisfied if such stock or securities constitute at least 90 percent of the fair market value of the corporation's gross assets (Rev. Proc. 96-30, 1996-1 CB 696).

In addition, the trade or business must have been conducted actively for at least five years prior to the distribution and must not have been acquired in a taxable transaction during that five-year period (Code Sec. 355(b)(2)(B) and (C)). An exception applies for certain assets acquired in a taxable transaction as part of an expansion of an existing qualifying business (Reg. § 1.355-3(b)(ii)).

Finally, control of a corporation conducting such trade or business must not have been acquired in a taxable transaction during the five-year period ending on the date of the distribution (Code Sec. 355(b)(2)(D)).

NEW LAW EXPLAINED

Modified active business test.—For distributions occurring after May 17, 2006, a corporation is treated as meeting the active business requirement only if it is engaged in the active conduct of a trade or business (Code Sec. 355(b)(3)(A), as added by the Tax Increase Prevention and Reconciliation Act of 2005 (P.L. 109-222) and amended by the Tax Relief and Health Care Act of 2006 (P.L. 109-432)). In order to determine if this condition is satisfied, all members of the corporation's separate affiliated group are treated as one corporation. For this purpose, the separate affiliated group of the corporation consists of that corporation as the common parent and all corporations affiliated with it through Code Sec. 1504(a)(1)(B) stock ownership, without regard to whether such corporations are includible corporations under Code Sec. 1504(b) (Code Sec. 355(b)(3)(B), as added by the Tax Reconciliation Act of 2005).

> **Comment:** Thus, a corporation that is not part of a separate affiliated group may no longer use the "substantially all" test to satisfy the active business requirement. Instead, it must be directly engaged in the active conduct of a trade or business.

> **Comment:** The House Committee clarifies that the modifications to the active business test are intended to simplify the planning for corporate groups that use holding company structures to engage in Code Sec. 355 distributions. Prior to these changes, a corporate group planning to undertake a spin-off under Code Sec. 355 very often had first to arrange elaborate corporate restructurings to place active businesses in certain entities to satisfy the active business test. If the transaction involved a chain of corporations with a holding company on the top, then the business activity requirements with respect to its subsidiaries were harsher than if the top-tier corporation was directly engaged in some business activity (House Committee Report (H.R. Rep. No. 109-304)).

¶360

NEW LAW EXPLAINED

Transition rule. The modified active business requirement does not apply to a distribution in a transaction which is (a) made pursuant to an agreement that was binding on May 17, 2006, and at all times thereafter, (b) described in a ruling request submitted to the IRS on or before May 17, 2006, or (c) described on or before May 17, 2006 in a public announcement or a filing with the Securities and Exchange Commission. The distributing corporation may irrevocably elect out of the application of this transition rule (Code Sec. 355(b)(3)(C), as added by the Tax Reconciliation Act of 2005).

> **Comment:** The IRS has issued guidance for making an election under Code Sec. 355(b)(3)(C) with respect to transactions described in the transition rule. A distributing corporation that wants tax-free treatment of such a transaction under Code Sec. 355 is not required to make an affirmative election if the transaction either conforms to the active business test of Code Sec. 355(b) before its modification, or to the modified test under the new Code Sec. 355(b)(3). However, a corporation must make the election under Code Sec. 355(b)(3)(C) if the purpose of the election is to disqualify the distribution under Code Sec. 355(a). The election is made by including a statement on or with the distributing corporation's return filed by the due date (including extensions) for filing its original return for the tax year in which the distribution occurs. If the transaction is described in the transition rule and the corporation does not desire tax-free treatment and requires Code Sec. 355(b)(2)(A) to apply to ensure taxable treatment, then it is not required to file the election, but must report the distribution as taxable. (Notice 2006-81, I.R.B. 2006-40, 595).

Certain pre-enactment distributions. A special rule applies for purposes of determining the continued qualification under Code Sec. 355(b)(2)(A) of a distribution made on or before May 17, 2006 as a result of an acquisition, disposition, or other restructuring that occurs after such date. Such distribution is treated as made on the date of the post-enactment acquisition, disposition, or restructuring for purposes of applying the modified active business requirement (Code Sec. 355(b)(3)(D), as added by the Tax Reconciliation Act of 2005 and amended by the 2006 Extenders Act).

▶ **Effective date.** The provision is effective on May 17, 2006, the date of enactment of the Tax Increase Prevention and Reconciliation Act of 2005 (P.L. 109-222) (Act Sec. 410(b) of the Tax Relief and Health Care Act of 2006 (P.L. 109-432)).

Law source: Law at ¶5355. Committee Reports at ¶10,040 and ¶15,550.

— Act Sec. 202 of the Tax Increase Prevention and Reconciliation Act of 2005 (P.L. 109-222), adding Code Sec. 355(b)(3);

— Act Sec. 410(a) of the Tax Relief and Health Care Act of 2006 (P.L. 109-432), amending Code Sec. 355(b)(3)(A) and (D);

— Act Sec. 410(b), providing the effective date.

Reporter references: For further information, consult the following CCH reporters.

— Standard Federal Tax Reporter, ¶16,466.038

— Tax Research Consultant, REORG: 30,106

— Federal Tax Guide, ¶12,343

¶365 Look-Through Treatment for Related Controlled Foreign Corporation Payments

SUMMARY OF NEW LAW

A look-through rule applies to dividends, interest, rents and royalties received by a controlled foreign corporation (CFC) from a related CFC. Under the rule, amounts are excluded from foreign personal holding company income if paid from nonsubpart F income or income that is not effectively connected income. The rule generally applies to tax years beginning after December 31, 2005, and before January 1, 2009.

BACKGROUND

U.S. shareholders that own stock in a foreign corporation would typically expect to be taxed on the earnings of the foreign corporation only when the earnings are repatriated or distributed to the U.S. shareholders. Under the subpart F rules, however, a taxpayer may be currently taxed on certain types of income earned by the foreign corporation, even though the income is not repatriated or distributed (Code Secs. 951-965).

The subpart F rules apply to U.S. shareholders that own at least 10 percent of the voting stock of a controlled foreign corporation (CFC) (Code Sec. 951). A CFC is a foreign corporation with at least 50 percent of its stock owned (by vote or value) by 10-percent U.S. shareholders (Code Sec. 957).

One of the main categories of subpart F income is foreign base company income. Foreign base company income is made up of several categories of income, one of which is foreign personal holding company income (FPHCI). FPHCI generally includes dividends, interest, rents, royalties and annuities.

Dividends and interest may be excluded from FPHCI if received from a related corporation that is created or organized under the law of the same country where the CFC was created or organized. An exception however, requires that a substantial part of the related corporation's assets must be engaged in a trade or business in the CFC's country. Rents and royalties received from a related corporation may also be excluded from FPHCI if the property is used in the same country where the CFC is created or organized (Code Sec. 954(c)(3)).

> **Comment:** The general rule that allows a U.S. company to defer its earnings in its foreign subsidiary is intended to provide a competitive advantage for U.S.-based companies operating abroad. The subpart F rules, however, target and prevent deferral for certain types of easily movable income that could be earned through a foreign corporation solely for the tax benefits.

NEW LAW EXPLAINED

Look-through treatment for cross-border payments between CFCs.—A new look-through rule applies to dividend, interest, rents and royalty payments received by a

NEW LAW EXPLAINED

controlled foreign corporation (CFC) from a related CFC (Code Sec. 954(c)(6), as added by the Tax Increase Prevention and Reconciliation Act of 2005 (P.L. 109-222) and amended by the Tax Relief and Health Care Act of 2006 (P.L. 109-432)). Provided the payments are attributable and allocable to neither subpart F income nor income that is effectively connected to a U.S. trade or business (ECI), the amounts are excluded from foreign personal holding company income (FPHCI). Thus, an exception from FPHCI for related person payments does not necessarily depend upon meeting the same-country requirement. Cross-border payments can be made between subsidiaries, of amounts that otherwise would be FPHCI, as long as the amounts are generated from an active business.

> **Comment:** The 2006 Extenders Act added the requirement that the payment must not be attributable or properly allocable to income of a related party that is treated as ECI. When added by the Tax Reconciliation Act of 2005, the look-through rule prohibited only payments from subpart F income. Thus, U.S.-source effectively connected income, which is specifically excluded from subpart F income, could qualify for the exception. Excluding payments from ECI insures that active foreign earnings are the earnings that are redeployed under the exception (Joint Committee on Taxation, Technical Explanation of the Tax Relief and Health Care Act of 2006 (P.L. 109-432) (JCX-50-06)).

For the look-through rule to apply, the payments must be received or accrued from a related CFC (Code Sec. 954(c)(6)(A), as added by the Tax Reconciliation Act of 2005 and amended by the 2006 Extenders Act). A related CFC is a CFC that controls the CFC, is controlled by the CFC, or a CFC that is controlled by the same person or persons that control the other CFC. Control means ownership of more than 50 percent of the CFC's stock (by vote or value) (Code Sec. 954(d)(3); House Committee Report, H.R. Rep. No. 109-304) for the Tax Reconciliation Act of 2005.

To determine whether payments are neither attributable and allocable to subpart F income nor ECI, rules similar to the CFC look-through rules used for calculating the foreign tax credit limitation apply (Code Sec. 954(c)(6)(A), as added by the Tax Reconciliation Act of 2005 and amended by the 2006 Extenders Act). Under the CFC look-through rules, rents and royalties are generally treated as income in a separate foreign tax credit limitation basket to the extent the income is allocated to the CFC's income in the same basket. The income is allocated in the same manner that deductions would be allocated under Reg. §1.861-8 through Temporary Reg. §1.861-14T (Code Sec. 904(d)(3)(C); Reg. §1.904-5(c)(3)). While a similar rule applies to interest income, interest income paid or accrued by a CFC to a U.S. shareholder (related person interest) must first be allocated to the CFC's passive FPHCI (Code Secs. 904(d)(3)(C) and 954(b)(5); Reg. §1.904-5(c)(2)). Dividends are treated as paid pro rata out of all of the CFC's earnings and profits in the separate foreign tax credit limitation baskets (Code Sec. 904(d)(3)(D); Reg. §1.904-5(c)(4)).

> **Example:** Near, a U.S. corporation owns 100 percent of the stock of Far, a Country X corporation. Far Corporation owns 100 percent of the stock of Farther, a Country Y corporation. Near manufactures, in the United States, the

NEW LAW EXPLAINED

parts needed to assemble greenhouses. Far Corporation purchases these parts and then uses them to manufacture greenhouses in Country X. Farther Corporation solicits orders for the greenhouses from customers in Country Y. Farther's income consists solely of the commissions it earns from its solicitations. Farther Corporation pays a dividend to Far Corporation from Farther's only income, the commission income. The commission income is nonsubpart F income because Farther is selling the property on behalf of Far, a related CFC, for use in Country Y, where Farther is incorporated. Thus, the dividend will not be characterized as FPHCI under the look-through rule and no immediate tax must be paid by Near on the dividend (see, Regs. § 1.954-3(a)(1)(i) and 1.954-3(a)(3)). In effect, Near is allowed to take active foreign earnings from one business and reinvest the earnings in another business without penalty.

Interest includes factoring income. The look-through rule also applies to interest, including factoring income that is treated as the equivalent of interest under Code Sec. 954(c)(1)(E) (Code Sec. 954(c)(6)(A), as added by the Tax Reconciliation Act of 2005). Factoring income is generally income, other than stated interest, from the acquisition and collection or disposition of a factored receivable (Reg. § 1.954-2(h)(4)). A factored receivable is an account receivable or other evidence of indebtedness that arises from the disposition of property or the performance of services, acquired by someone other than the seller or the person performing services (Reg. § 1.954-2(h)(4)(iii)).

Example: Far Corporation, a controlled foreign corporation, acquires an account receivable from the sale of property by an unrelated corporation for $95, less than the $100 face amount of the receivable on the acquisition date. The account bears stated interest after 30 days. On day 40, Far receives $100, plus stated interest from the obligor. The amount received by Far, other than the stated interest, is factoring income and is the equivalent of interest (Reg. § 1.954-2(h)(iv), *Example 1*).

Regulations to prevent abuse. The IRS is authorized to issue regulations to carry out the rules and prevent abuse of the look-through exception (Code Sec. 954(c)(6)(A), as added by the Tax Reconciliation Act of 2005 and amended by the 2006 Extenders Act). According to the Joint Committee on Taxation, the regulations, might, for example, prevent the look-through rule from applying to interest that is deemed to arise under related-party factoring arrangements under Code Sec. 864(d), or other transactions that would result in a deduction without a corresponding inclusion of subpart F income (Joint Committee on Taxation, Technical Explanation of the Tax Relief and Health Care Act of 2006 (P.L. 109-432) (JCX-50-06)).

Period for applying the look-through rule. The provision applies to tax years of foreign corporations beginning after December 31, 2005, and before January 1, 2009, and to tax years of U.S. shareholders with or within which such tax years of foreign corporations end (Code Sec. 954(c)(6)(B), as added by the Tax Reconciliation Act of 2005).

¶365

NEW LAW EXPLAINED

Comment: The House Committee Report (H.R. Rep. No. 109-304) for the Tax Reconciliation Act of 2005 states that the look-through rule is needed to make U.S. companies and U.S. workers more competitive by allowing these companies to reinvest active foreign earnings without incurring immediate additional tax, a tax that is not imposed on companies in many other foreign countries. The Committee believes that this will result in more sales abroad and goods produced in the United States.

Senator John Kyl, R-Arizona, of the Senate Finance Committee expanded on this point when he introduced an identical (except for the effective date) look-through rule in S. 750, on April 11, 2005. Senator Kyl noted that the traditional model for operating a global business has changed since the first subpart F rules were introduced in 1962. Today, in order to operate efficiently, a U.S.-based manufacturer may have to establish specialized manufacturing sites, distribution hubs and service centers. Additionally, financial institutions have established foreign subsidiaries with headquarters in a financial center and branches in multiple countries in the same geographic region ("hub and spoke" operation). According to Senator Kyl, the current rules have put the U.S. companies at a significant disadvantage when they deploy active foreign earnings cross-border to respond to market or investment opportunities because of the current U.S. tax on cross-border payments.

Practical Analysis: Lowell D. Yoder and Martin J. Collins, of McDermott Will & Emery, comment that Congress has further culled the subpart F rules so that active income is not subject to U.S. tax until such income is repatriated to the United States—a welcome change for U.S.-based multinationals in the ever-increasing competitive global economy. Not so long ago, in the fall of 2004, Congress simplified or eliminated several anti-deferral provisions by passing the American Jobs Creation Act of 2004 ("Jobs Act"). In the Jobs Act, *inter alia*, foreign base company shipping was repealed, gain on certain partnership interest was granted look-through treatment and the foreign personal holding company and the foreign investment company rules were repealed. Now, as part of the Tax Increase Prevention and Reconciliation Act of 2005 (P.L. 109-222) ("Tax Reconciliation Act of 2005"), Congress has taken a major step towards permitting deferral for most active earnings by passing the CFC look-through rule. The obvious exceptions to deferral for active income that remain are (1) income from sales of product or goods that fail the foreign base company sales rules in Code Sec. 954(d), and (2) income from services that fail the foreign base company services rules in Code Sec. 954(e). As territorial tax system discussions gain more footing around Washington and around the country, one is left to wonder whether Congress is testing the waters.

What is the CFC look-through rule? The Tax Reconciliation Act of 2005 provides that dividends, interest, rents and royalties received or accrued from related CFCs attributable to non–subpart F income of the payor should not be subpart F income to the recipient CFC under look-through rules similar to the rules of Code Sec. 904(d)(3)(C) and (D). What does this mean? A few immediate observations are noteworthy (some may be readily apparent).

NEW LAW EXPLAINED

- Active earnings derived by related CFCs will be able to be distributed *vis-à-vis* interest payments on borrowings or dividends on shares whether or not the CFCs are located in the same country. Thus, the need to test the location of assets to ensure the same country exception is satisfied is no longer necessary. For many multinationals, the new rule should make their offshore treasury functions more straightforward.

- The tables have reversed with respect to royalties paid by related CFCs versus royalties paid from unrelated parties. Previously, royalties paid by related CFCs generated subpart F income unless the same-country exception or high-tax exception was met. The new rule changes this result; however, royalty payments from unrelated parties must continue to traverse the somewhat restrictive standards of ensuring that the CFC-licensor is actively engaged in licensing the specific type of IP.

- For companies with *Brown Group* ramifications in their structure, a review of such structures may be warranted to determine if less complex arrangements are available, *i.e.,* structures that do not involve partnerships. The same can be said for "superholdco" type structures where entities below a foreign holding company are checked.

- The new rule is effective for tax years beginning after December 31, 2005, and before January 1, 2009. Yes, the new rule is temporary (if you are optimistic, you may add, "for the time being"). Thus, U.S. multinationals will place a wager if they decide to restructure to benefit from the new rule. Although there are no guarantees, the fact that CFC look-through passed alongside the extension of the active financing exception to subpart F income is encouraging.

In short, the CFC look-through rule will provide greater flexibility to U.S.-based multinationals in reducing current U.S. taxation on active CFC earnings. Arguably, this change is consistent with the beginnings of subpart F where there was more concern with a shifting of income from the United States as opposed to a shifting of active earnings from one foreign jurisdiction to another foreign jurisdiction.

Technical Corrections. Following the enactment of the CFC look-through rule on May 17, 2006, technical corrections that would amend Code Sec. 954(c)(6) were introduced in Congress a few different times. At the end of the 109th Congress, technical corrections amending Code Sec. 954(c)(6) were passed as part of the Tax Relief and Health Care Act of 2006 (P.L. 109-432). Only two of the three introduced provisions were included in the 2006 Extenders Act:

(i) A fix to Code Sec. 954(c)(6) to preclude taxpayers from taking advantage of the exclusion of effectively connected income ("ECI") from subpart F income (Code Sec. 952(b)) at one CFC and then excluding from a second CFC's subpart F income (under Code Sec. 954(c)(6)) a payment (e.g., interest) from the first CFC attributable to its U.S.-source ECI income. Such a scheme would have the effect of reducing U.S. tax on the payor-CFC's ECI and, at the same time, excluding the payment from the second CFC's subpart F income under the CFC look-through rule. Obviously, this result is inconsistent with the purpose of Code Sec. 954(c)(6) which is to permit CFCs to redeploy their active earnings as dictated by their business needs.

NEW LAW EXPLAINED

> (ii) Additional wording to clarify the anti-abuse part of Code Sec. 954(c)(6)(A) (last sentence).
>
> A third provision that would have precluded taxpayers from gaining an unintended advantage through the interaction of the accumulated deficit rule of Code Sec. 952(c)(1)(B) (or the chain-deficit rule in Code Sec. 952(c)(1)(C)) and Code Sec. 954(c)(6) was not included in the final passage of technical corrections. Treasury and the IRS, however, should have the ability to write the necessary rule to preclude an unintended advantage resulting from the interaction of Code Sec. 952(c)(1)(B) (or Code Sec. 952(c)(1)(C)) and Code Sec. 954(c)(6) by virtue of the anti-abuse rule in Code Sec. 954(c)(6)(A) (arguably the same authority was sufficient to preclude the ECI scheme described above without technical corrections). Hence, taxpayers should think twice before attempting to juxtapose two pro-taxpayer statutory provisions to achieve an unintended result (Cf. *Gen. Elec. Co.*, 83-2 USTC ¶9532, 3 ClsCt 289 (1983) (taxpayer barred from juxtaposing two nonrecognition provisions to achieve an unintended result).

▶ **Effective date.** The provision applies to tax years of foreign corporations beginning after December 31, 2005, and to tax years of U.S. shareholders with or within which such tax years of foreign corporations end (Act Sec. 103(b)(2) of the Tax Increase Prevention and Reconciliation Act of 2005 (P.L. 109-222) and Act Sec. 426(a)(2) of the Tax Relief and Health Care Act of 2006 (P.L. 109-432)).

Law source: Law at ¶5555. Committee Reports at ¶10,027 and ¶15,710.

— Act Sec. 103(b)(1) of the Tax Increase Prevention and Reconciliation Act of 2005 (P.L. 109-222), adding Code Sec. 954(c)(6);

— Act Sec. 426(a)(1) of the Tax Relief and Health Care Act of 2006 (P.L. 109-432), amending Code Sec. 954(c)(6)(A);

— Act Sec. 103(b)(2) of the Tax Reconciliation Act of 2005 and Act Sec. 426(a)(2) of the 2006 Extenders Act, providing the effective dates.

Reporter references: For further information, consult the following CCH reporters.

— Standard Federal Tax Reporter, ¶28,543.0252

— Tax Research Consultant, INTLOUT: 9,106.10

— Federal Tax Guide, ¶17,440 and ¶17,445

¶370 Tonnage Tax Rules Modified

SUMMARY OF NEW LAW

The minimum vessel tonnage limit that must be met to meet the definition of a "qualifying vessel," for purposes of the alternative tax on qualifying shipping activities (referred to as the "tonnage tax"), is decreased from 10,000 deadweight tons to 6,000 deadweight tons. In addition, a corporation that elects to apply the tonnage tax regime may further elect to treat "qualified zone domestic trade" as use in U.S.

SUMMARY OF NEW LAW

foreign trade for the sole purpose of not disqualifying a qualifying vessel from the tonnage tax regime.

BACKGROUND

For tax years beginning after October 22, 2004, a corporation that operates one or more "qualifying vessels" can elect the application of a "tonnage tax" instead of the corporate tax on income from qualifying shipping activities (Code Sec. 1352). Qualifying shipping activity income is not included in an electing corporation's gross income. The qualifying shipping activities of an electing corporation are treated as a separate trade or business activity distinct from all other activities conducted by the corporation.

An electing corporation is subject to tax on income from qualifying shipping activities at the maximum corporate income tax rate on its notional shipping income. The corporation's notional shipping income is derived from the net tonnage of the corporation's qualifying vessels (Code Sec. 1353). The electing corporation's tax, therefore, is the tonnage tax (which is equal to the maximum corporate rate multiplied by the notional shipping income for the tax year) plus the corporate tax on nonqualifying activity income.

For purposes of the tonnage tax, a "qualifying vessel" is a self-propelled (or combination self-propelled and non-self-propelled) U.S. flag vessel of not less than 10,000 "deadweight" tons used exclusively in the U.S. foreign trade during the period that the election to apply the tonnage tax is in effect (Code Sec. 1355(a)(4)).

> **Comment:** According to the Joint Committee on Taxation, Technical Explanation of the Tax Relief and Health Care Act of 2006 (P.L. 109-432) (JCX-50-06), "deadweight measures the lifting capacity of a ship expressed in long tons (2,240 lbs.), including cargo, crew, and consumables such as fuel, lube oil, drinking water, and stores. It is the difference between the number of tons of water a vessel displaces without such items on board and the number of tons it displaces when fully loaded."

An electing corporation will be treated as continuing to use a qualifying vessel in U.S. foreign trade during any period of temporary use in U.S. domestic trade (not exceeding 30 days during the tax year) if the corporation gives timely notice of such temporary use to the IRS (Code Sec. 1355(f)). The notice will be deemed timely if it is given by the due date (including extensions) for the corporation's tax return for the tax year in which the temporary cessation began. The temporary use period (for qualifying vessels used in U.S. domestic trade) continues until the earlier of the date on which: (1) an electing corporation abandons its intention to resume operations of the vessel in U.S. foreign trade; or (2) the corporation resumes operation of the vessel in U.S. foreign trade.

NEW LAW EXPLAINED

Tonnage tax expanded.—For purposes of the tonnage tax, the definition of a "qualifying vessel" is expanded to include U.S. flag vessels of not less than 6,000 deadweight tons used exclusively in the U.S. foreign trade (Code Sec. 1355(a)(4), as amended by the Tax Increase Prevention and Reconciliation Act of 2005 (P.L. 109-222) and the Tax Relief and Health Care Act of 2006 (P.L. 109-432)). The change is retroactively effective for tax years beginning after December 31, 2005.

> **Comment:** The threshold change from 10,000 deadweight tons to 6,000 deadweight tons was a temporary change under the Tax Increase Prevention and Reconciliation Act of 2005 (P.L. 109-222). The Tax Relief and Health Care Act of 2006 (P.L. 109-432) made the change permanent.

Qualified zone domestic trade. The 2006 Extenders Act allows a corporation that elects to apply the tonnage tax regime ("electing corporation") to further elect to treat "qualified zone domestic trade" (referred to in the title of new Code Sec. 1355(g) as "Great Lakes Domestic Shipping") as U.S. foreign trade so as not to disqualify an otherwise qualifying vessel from the tonnage tax regime (Code Sec. 1355(g)(1)(A), as added by the 2006 Extenders Act). "Qualified zone domestic trade" refers to the transportation of goods or passengers between locations in the "qualified zone" (as defined, below), so long as the transportation is in the U.S. domestic trade (Code Sec. 1355(g)(4)(A), as added by the 2006 Extenders Act).

> **Comment:** As noted in the Joint Committee on Taxation, Technical Explanation of the Tax Relief and Health Care Act of 2006 (P.L. 109-432) (JCX-50-06), qualified zone domestic trade does not include the transportation of goods or passengers between a U.S. port in the qualifying zone and a U.S. port outside of the zone (or *vice versa*). Such transportation is considered U.S. domestic trade.

The term, "qualified zone," is defined as the Great Lakes Waterway and the St. Lawrence Seaway (Code Sec. 1355(g)(4)(B), as added by the 2006 Extenders Act).

> **Comment:** According to the Joint Committee Explanation, this region "consists of the deep-draft waterways of Lake Superior, Lake Michigan, Lake Huron (including Lake St. Clair), Lake Erie, and Lake Ontario, connecting deep-draft channels, including the Detroit River, the St. Clair River, the St. Marys River, and the Welland Canal, and the waterway between the port of Sept-Iles, Quebec and Lake Ontario, including all locks, canals, and connecting and contiguous waters that are part of these deep-draft waterways."

Although the election to treat qualified zone domestic trade as U.S. foreign trade does not disqualify an otherwise qualifying vessel from the tonnage tax regime, the election does not cause qualified zone domestic trade activities to be treated as qualifying shipping activities. As a result, such activities do not qualify for the tonnage tax regime. Instead, the IRS is directed to establish rules for the proper allocation of income, expenses, losses, and deductions between the qualified shipping activities of a qualifying vessel and its other activities (Code Sec. 1355(g)(3), as added by the 2006 Extenders Act).

The rules under Code Sec. 1355(f), pertaining to temporary use in U.S. domestic trade, do not apply to a qualifying vessel with respect to its use in a qualified zone where an electing corporation makes a qualified zone domestic trade election (Code

NEW LAW EXPLAINED

Sec. 1355(g)(1)(B), as added by the 2006 Extenders Act). Thus, there is no requirement that the electing corporation provide notice of the election to the IRS. Further, the qualifying vessel does not lose its status as a qualifying vessel if the use of the vessel in the qualified zone exceeds 30 days during the tax year.

In the event that an electing corporation that has made a qualified zone domestic trade election with respect to a qualifying vessel uses such vessel in the U.S. domestic trade (other than qualified zone domestic trade) for a temporary period of no more than 30 days, it is treated as using such vessel in qualified zone domestic trade. However, it must provide notice of such use to the IRS no later than the due date (including extensions) of the corporation's tax return for the tax year in which the temporary period begins. The notice must state that the electing corporation temporarily operates, or has operated, in the U.S. domestic trade (other than qualified zone domestic trade) a qualifying vessel that had been used in the U.S. foreign trade or qualified zone domestic trade, and that it intends to resume operating such vessel in the U.S. foreign trade or qualified zone domestic trade (Code Sec. 1355(g)(2), as added by the 2006 Extenders Act).

The period of allowable temporary use of a qualifying vessel in the U.S. domestic trade continues until the earlier of (a) the date on which the electing corporation relinquishes its intention to resume operation of the vessel in the U.S. foreign trade or qualified zone domestic trade, or (b) the electing corporation resumes operation of the vessel in the U.S. foreign trade or qualified zone domestic trade. If a qualifying vessel is operated in the U.S. domestic trade (other than qualified zone domestic trade) for more than 30 days during the tax year, then usage in the U.S. domestic trade (other than qualified zone domestic trade) during such year may not be disregarded and the vessel is no longer qualified (Code Sec. 1355(g)(2), as added by the 2006 Extenders Act).

> **Example:** A vessel is used for 120 days during the tax year in qualified zone domestic trade and 180 days during the tax year in the U.S. foreign trade. It is used for 35 days in the tax year in the U.S. domestic trade that is not qualified zone domestic trade. It is not treated as a qualifying vessel.

The IRS is authorized to issue regulations relating to the tonnage tax, as necessary or appropriate (Code Sec. 1355(h), as redesignated by the 2006 Extenders Act). The Joint Committee Explanation notes that the IRS may specify the time, manner and other conditions for making, maintaining, and terminating the qualified zone domestic trade election.

▶ **Effective date.** This provision regarding the reduction in minimum vessel tonnage is effective for tax years beginning after December 31, 2005 (Act Sec. 413(b) of the Tax Relief and Health Care Act of 2006 (P.L. 109-432); Act Sec. 205(b) of the Tax Increase Prevention and Reconciliation Act of 2005 (P.L. 109-222)). The provision regarding the election to treat qualified zone domestic trade as U.S. foreign trade is effective for tax years beginning after December 20, 2006 (Act Sec. 415(b) of the 2006 Extenders Act).

¶370

NEW LAW EXPLAINED

Law source: Law at ¶5605. Committee Reports at ¶10,070, ¶15,580 and ¶15,600.

— Act Sec. 205(a) of the Tax Increase Prevention and Reconciliation Act of 2005 (P.L. 109-222), amending Code Sec. 1355(a)(4);

— Act Sec. 413(a) of the Tax Relief and Health Care Act of 2006 (P.L. 109-432), amending Code Sec. 1355(a)(4);

— Act Sec. 415(a) of the 2006 Extenders Act, redesignating Code Sec. 1355(g) as Code Sec. 1355(h) and adding new Code Sec. 1355(g);

— Act Sec. 205(b) of the 2005 Tax Reconciliation Act of 2005 and Act Secs. 413(b) and 415(b) of the 2006 Extenders Act, providing the effective dates.

Reporter references: For further information, consult the following CCH reporters.

— Standard Federal Tax Reporter, ¶31,928.021

— Tax Research Consultant, INTL: 3,610

— Federal Tax Guide, ¶17,140

SETTLEMENT FUNDS

¶375 Taxation of Environmental Settlement Funds Clarified and Exemption Made Permanent

SUMMARY OF NEW LAW

Certain escrow accounts, settlement funds or similar funds established to resolve claims brought under the Comprehensive Environmental Response, Compensation, and Liability Act of 1980 (CERCLA) (P.L. 96-510) are treated as beneficially owned by the United States and, thus, exempt from federal income tax. The exemption, which was originally set to expire for funds established after 2010, has been made permanent.

BACKGROUND

Businesses began establishing designated settlement funds to resolve claims arising from alleged tortious acts. Thus, Congress added Code Sec. 468B to define when economic performance occurred and to determine the appropriate year for deducting payments into these funds. A designated settlement fund is defined as a fund:

• established pursuant to a court order;

• into which only qualified payments may be transferred;

• that extinguishes completely the taxpayer's tort liability arising out of personal injury, death or property damage;

• administered by persons, a majority of whom are independent of the taxpayer;

BACKGROUND

- that under the terms of the fund, the taxpayer or any related person may not hold any beneficial interest in the income or corpus of the fund; and

- the taxpayer elects to be treated as a designated settlement fund under Code Sec. 468B (Code Sec. 468B(d)(2)).

In general, for certain payments or transfers made to a fund, economic performance occurs when payments are made to the fund, rather than to the injured party (Code Sec. 468B(a)).

Generally, these designated settlement funds are subject to federal income taxation as a separate entity at the maximum estate and trust rate on its gross income, less any administrative costs and incidental expenses. These costs must be incurred in connection with operating the fund and deductible for the purposes of determining the taxable income of a corporation (Code Sec. 468B(b)(1) and (2)). The Technical and Miscellaneous Revenue Act of 1988 (P.L. 100-647) further clarified the taxation of these funds by providing that nothing in the law shall prevent these designated settlement funds from current income taxation (Code Sec. 468B(g)).

One use of this type of settlement fund or escrow account is to finance the cleanup of hazardous waste sites under the direction of the Environmental Protection Agency (EPA). These "environmental" funds or accounts are established in consent decrees between the EPA and the settling parties under the jurisdiction of the federal courts. The EPA then uses the fund or account to resolve claims brought under the Comprehensive Environmental Response, Compensation and Liability Act of 1980 (CERCLA) (P.L. 96-510).

NEW LAW EXPLAINED

Clarification of taxation of certain environmental settlement funds.—Certain environmental settlement funds are treated as beneficially owned by the United States and, therefore, are exempt from taxation (Code Sec. 468B(g)(2), as added by the Tax Increase Prevention and Reconciliation Act of 2005 (P.L. 109-222)). The funds considered beneficially owned by the United States and exempt from taxation under Code Sec. 468B are escrow accounts, settlement funds or similar funds:

- that are established under a consent decree entered by a U.S. District Court judge;

- that are created to receive settlement payments as directed by a government entity for the sole purpose of resolving and satisfying one or more liability claims brought under the Comprehensive Environmental Response, Compensation and Liability Act of 1980 (CERCLA) (P.L. 96-510);

- that designate the authority and control over the expenditures of the fund, including the expenditure of contributions and the net earnings on the contributions, to a governmental entity; and

- that disburse all remaining funds at termination to a governmental entity for use in accordance with applicable law (Code Sec. 468B(g)(2), as added by the Tax Reconciliation Act of 2005).

¶375

NEW LAW EXPLAINED

"Governmental entities" include the United States, any State or political subdivision, the District of Columbia, any possession of the United States, and any agency or instrumentality of the these entities (Code Sec. 468B(g)(2), as added by the Tax Reconciliation Act of 2005).

> **Comment:** The tax treatment of designated settlement funds or escrow accounts was apparently causing a delay in settling claims brought under CERCLA and limiting the ultimate amount of funds available to the Environment Protection Agency (EPA) to clean up hazardous waste sites. To encourage settling claims brought under CERCLA and to increase the amount of funds available, the exemption was enacted.

Tax exemption made permanent. As originally enacted, the tax exemption for environmental settlement funds and escrow accounts was scheduled to expire for funds or accounts established after December 31, 2010. The exemption has now been made permanent and will apply to qualifying environmental settlement funds and escrow accounts established after May 17, 2006 (Act Sec. 409(a) of the Tax Relief and Health Care Act of 2006 (P.L. 109-432), striking Code Sec. 468B(g)(3)).

▶ **Effective date.** The amendments clarifying the tax treatment of certain environmental settlement funds shall apply to accounts and funds established after May 27, 2006 (Act Sec. 201(b) of the Tax Increase Prevention and Reconciliation Act of 2005 (P.L. 109-222) and Act Sec. 409(b) of the Tax Relief and Health Care Act of 2006 (P.L. 109-432)).

Law source: Law at ¶5405. Committee Reports at ¶10,030 and ¶15,540.

— Act Sec. 201(a) of the Tax Increase Prevention and Reconciliation Act of 2005 (P.L. 109-222), amending Code Sec. 468B(g);

— Act Sec. 409(a) of the Tax Relief and Health Care Act of 2006 (P.L. 109-432), striking Code Sec. 468B(g)(3);

— Act Sec. 201(b) of the Tax Reconciliation Act of 2005 and Act Sec. 409(b) of the 2006 Extenders Act, providing the effective date.

Reporter references: For further information, consult the following CCH reporters.

— Standard Federal Tax Reporter, ¶21,951.046

— Tax Research Consultant, ACCTNG: 12,214.20

— Federal Tax Guide, ¶15,535 and ¶15,540

Tax Relief—Business Tax Credits

BUSINESS INCENTIVES

ENERGY CREDITS

CROSS REFERENCE

BUSINESS INCENTIVES

¶405 Research Credit Extended and Modified

SUMMARY OF NEW LAW

The research credit is extended for two years, through December 31, 2007. In addition, for tax years ending after December 31, 2006, the rates used to compute the

SUMMARY OF NEW LAW

research credit under the alternative incremental credit are increased and taxpayers can elect to compute the credit under a third method, the alternative simplified credit.

BACKGROUND

In order to encourage businesses to increase their spending on research and development of new technologies, products, and services, a research credit is available under Code Sec. 41. The credit applies to incremental increases in qualified research paid or incurred by a business, to increases in basic research payments made by a business to universities and certain other qualified organizations, and to payments made or incurred by a business to an energy research consortium. The credit applies to amounts paid or incurred (1) before July 1, 1995, and (2) after June 30, 1996 and before December 31, 2005 (Code Sec. 41(h)(1)). Expenditures made after June 30, 1995, and before July 1, 1996, are not eligible for the credit.

Under the general rule, the amount of the credit is equal to the sum of:

(1) 20 percent of the excess of a company's qualified research expenses for the tax year over its base amount;

(2) 20 percent of the excess of its qualified research payments made during the tax year over the average annual payments made during a base period; and

(3) 20 percent of all payments made during the tax year to an energy research consortium (Code Sec. 41(a)).

The base amount is computed by multiplying the taxpayer's fixed-base percentage by the taxpayer's average gross receipts for the four preceding tax years (Code Sec. 41(c)(1)). A taxpayer's fixed-base percentage is the ratio that its total qualified research expenditures for 1984 through 1988 bears to its total gross receipts for that period (subject to a maximum ratio of .16). Start-up companies are assigned a fixed-base percentage of three percent (Code Sec. 41(c)(3)).

Qualified research expenses include expenses incurred with respect to in-house research, contract research, and basic research conducted by certain entities. There are basically four categories of expenses to which the credit applies, the first three of which refer to in-house research activities: (1) wages for employees involved in the research activity, (2) costs of supplies used in research, (3) payments to others for the use of computer time in qualified research (except if the taxpayer, or a person with whom the taxpayer must aggregate expenditures in computing the credit, receives or accrues any amount from another person for computer use), and (4) 65 percent of costs of contracting with another party to conduct research on the taxpayer's behalf (75 percent of costs paid to a qualified research consortium and 100 percent of costs paid for energy research to eligible small businesses, universities, and federal laboratories) (Code Sec. 41(b)(1) through (3)).

An alternative incremental research credit may be elected which allows a business to calculate the research credit at reduced rates based upon the amount of research expenses over a lower base (fixed-base percentages). Once the election is made, it

¶405

BACKGROUND

applies to all succeeding tax years unless revoked with the consent of the IRS. Under this method, the credit is equal to the sum of:

(1) 2.65 percent of that portion of the qualified research expenses that exceed one percent, but not more than 1.5 percent, of the average annual gross receipts for the four preceding tax years;

(2) 3.2 percent of that portion of the qualified research expenses that exceed 1.5 percent, but not more than two percent of the average annual gross receipts for the four preceding tax years; and

(3) 3.75 percent of that portion of the qualified research expenses that exceed two percent of the average annual gross receipts for the four preceding tax years (Code Sec. 41(c)(4)).

Comment: When it was first enacted in 1981, the research credit was to terminate after four and one-half years. However, it has been subject to several extensions over the years and was even allowed to expire at one point without the extension being made retroactive to the prior termination date. The latest extension was in 2004, for a period of eighteen months. Manufacturing associations continue to lobby to make the credit permanent so that they can rely on the tax incentive to make long-term plans for research projects.

NEW LAW EXPLAINED

Extension of the research credit.—The research credit is extended for two years for qualified research expenses paid or incurred after December 31, 2005, and before January 1, 2008 (Code Sec. 41(h)(1)(B), as amended by the Tax Relief and Health Care Act of 2006 (P.L. 109-432).

The clinical drug testing credit (orphan drug credit) under which qualified clinical testing expenses are defined in part by reference to qualified research expenses is also amended to reflect the extension of the research credit for two years (Code Sec. 45C(b)(1)(D), as amended by the 2006 Extenders Act).

Planning Note: Unless the IRS provides otherwise, April 15, 2007, is the deadline for making elections under a provision that expired in 2006, and that has been extended for the 2006 tax year by the 2006 Extenders Act (Act Sec. 123(a) of the 2006 Extenders Act). Thus, any elections with respect to the research credit for 2006 must be made by April 15, 2007.

Increase in alternative incremental credit rates.—The rates used to calculate the three tiers of the alternative incremental credit are increased, for tax years ending after December 31, 2006, to:

(1) three percent of the portion of the qualified research expenses that exceed one percent, but not more than 1.5 percent of the average annual gross receipts for the four preceding tax years;

(2) four percent of the portion of the qualified research expenses that exceed 1.5 percent, but not more than two percent of the average annual gross receipts for the four preceding tax years; and

NEW LAW EXPLAINED

(3) five percent of the portion of the qualified research expenses that exceed two percent of the average annual gross receipts for the four preceding tax years (Code Sec. 41(c)(4)(A), as amended by the 2006 Extenders Act).

Transitional rule for fiscal year taxpayers. The amount of the alternative incremental credit for 2006-2007 fiscal year taxpayers is computed by adding (1) the credit calculated as if it were extended but the rates not increased, and multiplied by a fraction that is the number of days in the tax year before January 1, 2007, over the total number of days in the tax year and (2) the credit calculated using the increased rates and multiplied by a fraction that is the number of days in the tax year after December 31, 2006, over the total number of days in the tax year (Act Sec. 104(b)(3) of the 2006 Extenders Act).

Alternative simplified credit for qualified research expenses.—The 2006 Extenders Act allows taxpayers, at their election, to compute the research credit under a third method—the alternative simplified credit. Under the alternative simplified credit, a taxpayer can claim an amount equal to 12 percent of the amount by which the qualified research expenses exceeds 50 percent of the average qualified research expenses for the three preceding tax years (Code Sec. 41(c)(5)(A), as added by the 2006 Extenders Act). If the taxpayer has no qualified research expenses for any of the preceding three tax years, then the credit is equal to six percent of the qualified research expenses for the current tax year (Code Sec. 41(c)(5)(B), as added by the 2006 Extenders Act). As with the alternative incremental credit, an election to calculate the research credit using the alternative simplified credit is effective for all succeeding tax years unless revoked with the consent of the IRS (Code Sec. 41(c)(5)(C), as added by the 2006 Extenders Act).

Transitional rule for fiscal year taxpayers. The amount of the alternative simplified credit for 2006-2007 fiscal year taxpayers is computed by adding (1) the credit calculated under the general rule or the alternative incremental credit, if elected, as if it were extended but the rates not increased, and multiplied by a fraction that is the number of days in the tax year before January 1, 2007, over the total number of days in the tax year and (2) the credit calculated using the increased rates and multiplied by a fraction that is the number of days in the tax year after December 31, 2006, over the total number of days in the tax year (Act Sec. 104(c)(4) of the 2006 Extenders Act).

> **Practice Pointer:** Since the alternative simplified credit is applicable to tax years ending after December 31, 2006, 2006-2007 fiscal year taxpayers may elect to compute the research credit under both the alternative incremental credit and the alternative simplified credit for the specified transitional tax year (Act Sec. 104(c)(4)(B)(ii) of the 2006 Extenders Act). For example, a fiscal year taxpayer electing the alternative simplified method would compute the research credit under the alternative incremental credit for the portion of the tax year prior to January 1, 2007, and the alternative simplified credit for the portion of the tax year after December 31, 2006. The alternative incremental credit election will then be treated as revoked for all tax years after the 2006-2007 fiscal tax year.

Coordination of alternative simplified credit and alternative incremental credit. If a taxpayer has already elected the alternative incremental credit, the alternative simplified credit election cannot be made unless the alternative incremental credit is revoked with the

NEW LAW EXPLAINED

consent of the IRS (Code Sec. 41(c)(5)(C), as added by the 2006 Extenders Act). Likewise, a taxpayer cannot elect the alternative incremental credit if the alternative simplified credit is elected unless the alternative simplified credit is revoked with the consent of the IRS (Code Sec. 41(c)(4)(B), as amended by the 2006 Tax Relief Act). However, under a special transition rule, if the alternative incremental credit is elected for the tax year that includes January 1, 2007, the alternative incremental credit is treated as if it was revoked with the consent of the IRS upon election of the alternative simplified credit (Act Sec. 104(c)(2) of the 2006 Extenders Act).

> **Example:** Estecorp, Inc., a calendar-year corporation formed in 2001, had $2 million of qualified research expenses and $20 million in annual gross receipts during 2007. In 2004, 2005, and 2006, Estecorp had qualified research expenses of $500,000, $1 million, and $1.5 million, respectively. Estecorp elected to compute its research credit under the alternative incremental credit in 2003 and has never revoked the election. If Estecorp elects to compute its research credit under the alternative simplified credit for 2007, the alternative incremental credit is treated as revoked with the consent of the IRS. Under the alternative simplified credit, Estecorp can claim a research credit of $60,000 (50 percent of three-year average research expenses ($500,000) x 12 percent).

Compliance Pointer: The research credit is computed on Form 6765, Credit for Increasing Research Activities, and, as a component of the general business credit, is subject to the carryforward and carryback rules of Code Sec. 39.

▶ **Effective date.** The extension provision applies to amounts paid or incurred after December 31, 2005 (Act Sec. 104(a)(3) of the Tax Relief and Health Care Act of 2006 (P.L. 109-432)). The increase in the alternative incremental credit rates and the addition of the alternative simplified credit apply to tax years ending after December 31, 2006 (Act Secs. 104(b)(2) and 104(c)(3) of the 2006 Extenders Act). For transition rules, see the explanations above.

Law source: Law at ¶5036 and ¶5042. Committee Report at ¶15,130.

— Act Sec. 104(a)(1) of the Tax Relief and Health Care Act of 2006 (P.L. 109-432), amending Code Sec. 41(h)(1)(B);

— Act Sec. 104(a)(2), amending Code Sec. 45C(b)(1)(D);

— Act Sec. 104(b)(1), amending Code Sec. 41(c)(4)(A);

— Act Sec. 104(c)(1), redesignating former Code Sec. 41(c)(5) and (6) as Code Sec. 41(c)(6) and (7), respectively, and adding new Code Sec. 41(c)(5);

— Act Secs. 104(a)(3), 104(b)(2) and (3), and 104(c)(2)-(4), providing the effective dates.

Reporter references: For further information, consult the following CCH reporters.

— Standard Federal Tax Reporter, ¶4362.01

— Tax Research Consultant, BUSEXP: 54,164.10 and BUSEXP: 54,172

— Federal Tax Guide, ¶2450

¶405

¶410 Work Opportunity and Welfare-to-Work Credits Extended, Consolidated

SUMMARY OF NEW LAW

The work opportunity tax credit and the welfare-to-work credit are extended one year, through December 31, 2006. The work opportunity tax credit and the welfare-to-work credit are combined, amended and extended for 2006 and 2007.

BACKGROUND

The work opportunity tax credit provides employers with an incentive to hire individuals from eight targeted groups that have a particularly high unemployment rate or other special employment needs (Code Sec. 51). The credit was designed to help such employers offset the costs of hiring, training, and supervising workers who have little, if any, work experience and few prospects for employment.

Employers hiring members of the following groups are eligible for the credit:

(1) families eligible to receive benefits under the Temporary Assistance for Needy Families (TANF) program (Code Sec. 51(d)(2));

(2) high-risk youth (Code Sec. 51(d)(5));

(3) qualified ex-felons (Code Sec. 51(d)(4));

(4) vocational rehabilitation referrals (Code Sec. 51(d)(6));

(5) qualified summer youth employees (Code Sec. 51(d)(7));

(6) qualified veterans (Code Sec. 51(d)(3));

(7) qualified food stamp recipients (Code Sec. 51(d)(8)); and

(8) persons receiving certain Supplemental Security Income benefits (Code Sec. 51(d)(9)).

An employer must obtain certification from a state employment security agency that an individual is a member of a targeted group (Code Sec. 51(d)(12)).

The credit is equal to 40 percent of up to $6,000 of the targeted employee's qualified first-year wages ($3,000 for qualified summer youth employees), provided the employee completes a minimum of 400 hours of service (Code Sec. 51(a), (b), (c) and (d)). Thus, the maximum credit per targeted employee is $2,400 ($1,200 for qualified summer youth employees). The credit is reduced to 25 percent for employees who complete less than 400 hours of service, and no credit is allowed for employees who complete less than 120 hours of service (Code Sec. 51(i)(3)). An employer's business expense deduction for wages is reduced by the amount of the work opportunity tax credit (Code Sec. 280C(a)).

The work opportunity credit was enacted by the Small Business Jobs Protection Act of 1996 (P.L. 104-188), replacing the targeted jobs tax credit. As enacted, it applied to wages paid or incurred to a qualified individual who begins work for the employer after September 30, 1996, and before October 1, 1997. The credit, however, has been

BACKGROUND

extended over the years. Most recently, the Working Families Tax Relief Act of 2004 (P.L. 108-311) extended the credit to wages paid or incurred to a qualified individual who began work for an employer before January 1, 2006.

A welfare-to-work credit of $8,500 per individual is allowed to employers for qualified first- and second-year wages paid to qualified long-term family assistance recipients (Code Sec. 51A). The purpose of the credit is to provide employers with an incentive to hire long-term welfare recipients, to promote the transition from welfare to work by increasing access to employment, and to encourage employers to provide these individuals with training, health coverage, dependent care and better job attachment.

The credit is generally equal to 35 percent of the first $10,000 of eligible wages paid in the first year of employment, plus 50 percent of the first $10,000 of eligible wages paid in the second year of employment (Code Sec. 51A(a) and (b)). Special rules apply to agricultural and railroad labor (Code Sec. 51A(b)(5)(C)). If a welfare-to-work tax credit is allowed to an employer for an individual for any tax year, that individual is not deemed to be a member of a targeted group for that tax year for purposes of the Code Sec. 51 work opportunity tax credit (Code Sec. 51A(e)).

Enacted by the Taxpayer Relief Act of 1997 (P.L. 105-34), the credit originally applied to wages paid to employees who started work for the employer after December 31, 1997 and before May 1, 1999. The credit was extended several times and was last extended by the Working Families Tax Relief Act of 2004 (P.L. 108-311) to cover wages paid to employees who start work no later than December 31, 2005.

Excess business credits, such as the work opportunity credit and the welfare-to-work credit, may be carried back to the tax year preceding the unused credit year, and carried forward to each of the 20 tax years following the unused credit year (Code Sec. 39(a)(1)).

NEW LAW EXPLAINED

Extension and consolidation of the work opportunity credit and the welfare-to-work credit.—The work opportunity tax credit and the welfare-to-work credit are retroactively extended for one year through December 31, 2006 (Code Sec. 51(c)(4)(B), as amended by the Tax Relief and Health Care Act of 2006 (P.L. 109-432)).

> **Compliance Pointer:** Employers claiming the credit are to use Form 5884, Work Opportunity Credit. Form 8850, Pre-Screening Notice and Certification Request for the Work Opportunity and Welfare-to-Work Credits, is to be used in the pre-screening and certification process. Form 8850 must be sent, along with the appropriate U.S. Department of Labor form, to the state's designated certification agency no later than 28 days after the individual begins work.

> **Planning Note:** Unless the IRS provides otherwise, April 15, 2007, is the deadline for making elections under a provision that expired in 2006, and that has been extended for the 2006 tax year by the 2006 Extenders Act. Thus, the work opportunity tax credit and the welfare-to-work credit for 2006 must be elected by April 15, 2007 (Act Sec. 123(b) of the 2006 Extenders Act).

¶410

NEW LAW EXPLAINED

Amendment, consolidation and extension of credits.—For individuals who begin work for the employer after December 31, 2006 and on or before December 31, 2007, the work opportunity tax credit and the welfare-to-work credit are combined, amended and extended. The Code Sec. 51A incentives for employing long-term family assistance recipients are consolidated with the work opportunity credit by adding long-term family assistance recipients as the ninth targeted group under Code Sec. 51. The separate welfare-to-work credit of Code Sec. 51A is thus repealed (Code Sec. 51(d)(1)(I), as added by the 2006 Extenders Act).

For second-year wages of long-term family assistance recipients, 50 percent of the qualified second-year wages may be included in the calculation of the work opportunity credit. In lieu of applying the $6,000 per year limitation of Code Sec. 51(b)(3), a maximum of $10,000 may be taken into account for qualified first-year wages and qualified second-year wages for long-term family assistance recipients (Code Sec. 51(e), as added by the 2006 Extenders Act).

> **Planning Note:** The combined credit follows the work opportunity tax credit definition of wages under Code Sec. 51(c). The definition does not include (1) amounts paid by the employer for educational assistance that would have been excludable under a Code Sec. 127 program, prior to expiration, (2) health plan coverage for the employee, but not more than the applicable premium defined under Code Sec. 4980B(f)(4), and (3) dependent care assistance excludable under Code Sec. 129.

> **Comment:** The definition of "qualified second-year wages" remains the same as it was under the separate welfare-to-work credit (Code Sec. 51(e)(2), as added by the 2006 Extenders Act). The special rules for agricultural and railway employees are also the same as they were under the welfare-to-work credit (Code Sec. 51(e)(3), as added by the 2006 Extenders Act).

The following changes to Code Sec. 51 apply to the combined work opportunity tax credit and welfare-to-work credit. The separate provision for the welfare-to-work credit (Code Sec. 51A) is repealed (Code Sec. 51(d)(1)(I), as added by the 2006 Extenders Act).

Family income disregarded for eligibility. A "qualified ex-felon" is no longer required to be an individual certified as a member of an economically disadvantaged family. The requirement for eligibility as a qualified ex-felon based on a six-month family income of 70 percent or less of the Bureau of Labor Statistics lower living standard is removed. (Code Sec. 51(d)(4), as amended by the 2006 Extenders Act).

Increase in age limit for food stamp recipients. The maximum age for food stamp eligibility is increased from 25 to 40. The category of "qualified food stamp recipient" is expanded to any individual who is certified as having attained the age of 18 but not the age of 40 on the hiring date (Code Sec. 51(d)(8)(A), as amended by the 2006 Extenders Act).

Extension of filing deadline. The deadline for an employer to file the pre-screening notice with the designated local agency as part of a written request for the individual to be treated as a member of a targeted group is extended. Under the amended provision, the employer must submit the notice, signed by the employer and the

¶410

NEW LAW EXPLAINED

individual, no later than the 28th day after the individual begins work for the employer (Code Sec. 51(d)(12)(A)(ii)(II), as amended by the 2006 Extenders Act).

▶ **Effective date.** The extension of the credits is effective for wages paid or incurred to a qualified individual who begins work for the employer after December 31, 2005 (Act Sec. 105(f)(1) of the Tax Relief and Health Care Act of 2006 (P.L. 109-432)). The consolidation of the credits and other modifications are effective for wages paid or incurred to a qualified individual who begins work for the employer after December 31, 2006 (Act Sec. 105(f)(2), as added by the 2006 Extenders Act).

Law source: Law at ¶5052 and ¶5053. Committee Report at ¶15,140.

— Act Sec. 105(a), amending Code Sec. 51(c)(4)(B) and Code Sec. 51A(f);
— Act Sec. 105(b), amending Code Sec. 51(d)(4);
— Act Sec. 105(c), amending Code Sec. 51(d)(8)(A)(i);
— Act Sec. 105(d), amending Code Sec. 51(d)(12)(A)(ii)(II);
— Act Sec. 105(e), adding Code Sec. 51(d)(I), redesignating Code Sec. 51(d)(10)-(12) as Code Sec. 51(d)(11)-(13), respectively, adding new Code Sec. 51(d)(10), adding Code Sec. 51(e), and striking Code Sec. 51A;
— Act Sec. 105(f), providing the effective date.

Reporter references: For further information, consult the following CCH reporters.

— Standard Federal Tax Reporter, ¶4803.01 and ¶4825.01
— Tax Research Consultant, BUSEXP: 54,250 and BUSEXP: 54,850
— Federal Tax Guide, ¶2800 and ¶2822

¶415 New Markets Tax Credit Extended and Modified

SUMMARY OF NEW LAW

The new markets tax credit is extended through 2008, permitting up to $3.5 billion in qualified equity investments for that calendar year.

BACKGROUND

The Internal Revenue Code does not offer many incentives for taxpayers to either invest in, or make loans to, small businesses located in low-income communities. One such incentive is provided by Code Sec. 45D, which was added by the Community Renewal Tax Relief Act of 2000 (P.L. 106-554). Code Sec. 45D provides a new markets tax credit for qualified equity investments made to acquire stock in a corporation, or a capital interest in a partnership, that is a qualified community development entity (CDE). The amount of the credit allowable to the investor is (1) a five-percent credit for the first three years from the date that the equity interest was purchased from the CDE, and (2) a six-percent credit for each of the following four years (Code Sec. 45D(a)(2)). The credit is determined by applying the applicable percentage (five or

BACKGROUND

six) to the amount paid to the CDE for the investment at its original issue (Code Sec. 45D(a)(1)). The credit is subject to recapture in certain circumstances (Code Sec. 45D(g)).

There is a national limitation with respect to the new markets tax credit. The maximum annual amount of qualified equity investments is capped at $2 billion for calendar years 2004 and 2005. In 2006 and 2007, the cap is $3.5 billion (Code Sec. 45D(f)(1)). The Secretary of the Treasury is authorized to allocate the amounts among qualified CDEs, giving preference (in part) to any entity with a record of successfully providing capital or technical assistance to disadvantaged businesses or communities (Code Sec. 45D(f)(2)).

A qualified CDE includes any domestic corporation or partnership: (1) whose primary mission is serving or providing investment capital for low-income communities or persons; (2) that maintains accountability to the residents of low-income communities by their representation on any governing board of or any advisory board to the CDE; and (3) that is certified by the Secretary of the Treasury as being a qualified CDE (Code Sec. 45D(c)). A qualified equity investment means stock (other than nonqualified preferred stock) in a corporation or a capital interest in a partnership that is acquired directly from a CDE for cash. Substantially all of the investment proceeds must be used by the CDE to make qualified low-income community investments, as defined in Code Sec. 45D(d) (Code Sec. 45D(b)(1)).

One category of qualified low-income community investments is any capital or equity investment in (or loan to) any qualified active low-income community business (Code Sec. 45D(d)(1)(A)). For purposes of Code Sec. 45D, the term "low-income community" means any population census tract with either (1) a poverty rate of at least 20 percent or (2) median family income that does not exceed 80 percent of metropolitan area median family income (or in the case of a non-metropolitan census tract, does not exceed 80 percent of statewide median family income) (Code Sec. 45D(e)(1)). A modification is made for census tracts within high migration rural counties (Code Sec. 45D(e)(5)).

The Secretary of the Treasury is directed to prescribe regulations that address several specified areas relating to the credit (Code Sec. 45D(i)).

NEW LAW EXPLAINED

Extension of new markets tax credit.—The Code Sec. 45D new markets tax credit is extended through 2008, permitting up to $3.5 billion in qualified equity investments for that calendar year (Code Sec. 45D(f)(1)(D), as amended by the Tax Relief and Health Care Act of 2006 (P.L. 109-432)). As a result, the $3.5 billion amount will be in effect for calendar years 2006, 2007, and 2008.

Direction to issue regulations. The provision also requires the Secretary of the Treasury to issue regulations that ensure that non-metropolitan counties receive a proportional allocation of qualified equity investments (Code Sec. 45D(i)(6), as added by the 2006 Extenders Act).

¶415

NEW LAW EXPLAINED

▶ **Effective date.** The provision takes effect on December 20, 2006 (Act Sec. 102(c) of the Tax Relief and Health Care Act of 2006 (P.L. 109-432)).

Law source: Law at ¶5044. Committee Report at ¶15,110.

— Act Sec. 102(a) of the Tax Relief and Health Care Act of 2006 (P.L. 109-432), amending Code Sec. 45D(f)(1)(D);

— Act Sec. 102(b), adding Code Sec. 45D(i)(6);

— Act Sec. 102(c), providing the effective date.

Reporter references: For further information, consult the following CCH reporters.

— Standard Federal Tax Reporter, ¶4490.01

— Tax Research Consultant, BUSEXP: 54,900

— Federal Tax Guide, ¶2490

¶420 Indian Employment Tax Credit Extended

SUMMARY OF NEW LAW

The Indian employment tax credit is extended for two years through December 31, 2007.

BACKGROUND

The Omnibus Budget Reconciliation Act of 1993 (P.L. 103-66) provided tax incentives to stimulate economic development and encourage investment in Indian reservations. A nonrefundable income tax credit is allowed for the first $20,000 of qualified wages and health insurance costs paid or incurred for qualified employees who work on an Indian reservation (Code Sec. 45A).

The credit is equal to 20 percent of the employer's costs for a qualified employee's wages and health insurance that exceed the amount the employer paid or incurred for such costs during 1993. Employees are qualified employees if they or their spouses are enrolled members of an Indian tribe, who work within an Indian reservation, and whose principal place of abode while employed is on or near the reservation where they are working. Employees whose total wages exceed $30,000 per year (as adjusted for inflation) during the tax year are not qualified employees.

Originally scheduled to expire in 2003, the credit was extended through December 31, 2004 by the Job Creation and Worker Assistance Act of 2002 (P.L. 107-147) and extended through December 31, 2005 by the Working Families Tax Relief Act of 2004 (P.L. 108-311).

NEW LAW EXPLAINED

Extension of Indian employment tax credit.—The Indian employment tax credit is extended for two years through December 31, 2007 (Code Sec. 45A(f), as amended by the Tax Relief and Health Care Act of 2006 (P.L. 109-432)).

> **Compliance Pointer:** Employers should use Form 8845, Indian Employment Tax Credit, to compute the credit. Form 8845 is to be attached to the employer's tax return.

> **Planning Note:** Unless the IRS provides otherwise, April 15, 2007 is the deadline for making elections under a provision that expired in 2006, and that has been extended for the 2006 tax year by the 2006 Extenders Act. Thus, the Indian employment tax credit for 2006 must be elected by April 15, 2007 (Act Sec. 123(b) of the 2006 Extenders Act).

▶ **Effective date.** The amendments made by this section apply to tax years beginning after December 31, 2005 (Act Sec. 111(b) of the Tax Relief and Health Care Act of 2006 (P.L. 109-432)).

Law source: Law at ¶5040. Committee Report at ¶15,200.

— Act Sec. 111(a) of the Tax Relief and Health Care Act of 2006 (P.L. 109-432), amending Code Sec. 45A(f);

— Act Sec. 111(b) of the 2006 Tax Extenders Act, providing the effective date.

Reporter references: For further information, consult the following CCH reporters.

— Standard Federal Tax Reporter, ¶4440.01

— Tax Research Consultant, BUSEXP: 54,700

— Federal Tax Guide, ¶2775

¶425 Mine Rescue Team Training Tax Credit Added

SUMMARY OF NEW LAW

The mine rescue training team credit can be claimed by eligible mine employers as a general business credit, in an amount equal to the lesser of 20 percent of training program costs or $10,000.

BACKGROUND

Most mining operations establish a centralized team that responds to mine accidents within the general area where the company operates. Currently, there are no tax incentives available, other than the deduction for ordinary and necessary costs of doing business, to mining companies to encourage the training of miners in mine safety and rescue. The spate of recent mine accidents, with the resulting tragic loss of life, has spurred Congress into taking action to encourage not only additional mine safety training but also the establishment of local mine rescue teams.

NEW LAW EXPLAINED

Mine rescue team training tax credit.—Eligible employers are entitled to a new credit for mine rescue team training expenses in tax years beginning after December 31, 2005, but before January 1, 2009. The credit amount is equal to the lesser of—

(1) 20 percent of the training program costs paid or incurred during the tax year for each qualified mine rescue team employee, including wages paid while attending the training program; or

(2) $10,000 (Code Sec. 45N(a), as added by the Tax Relief and Health Care Act of 2006 (P.L. 109-432)).

An eligible employer is any taxpayer that employs individuals as miners in underground mines located in the United States (Code Sec. 45N(c), as added by the 2006 Extenders Act). A qualified mine rescue team employee is a full-time miner employee who is eligible for more than six months of the tax year to serve as a mine rescue team member because he or she has either:

(1) completed at minimum an initial 20 hour instruction course as approved by the Mine Safety and Health Administration's Office of Education Policy and Development; or

(2) received at least 40 hours of refresher training (Code Sec. 45N(b), as added by the 2006 Extenders Act).

Wages are defined as all compensation including noncash benefits under Code Sec. 3306(b), but without regard to any dollar limitation stated in that section (Code Sec. 45N(d), as added by the 2006 Extenders Act).

The mine rescue team training credit is a part of and subject to the limitations and carryover rules of the general business credit (Code Sec. 38(b), as amended by the 2006 Extenders Act).

> **Comment:** Code Sec. 196 was not amended to allow the claiming of any unused carryforward mine rescue training team credit in the year following the final carryforward year.

To prevent any double benefits that may arise from claiming this credit, Code Sec. 280C is amended to disallow a deduction for the amount of any mine rescue team training credit determined for the tax year (Code Sec. 280C(e), as added by the 2006 Extenders Act). Finally, the credit is set to terminate for tax years beginning after December 31, 2008 (Code Sec. 45N(e), as added by the 2006 Extenders Act).

▶ **Effective date.** The provision applies to tax years beginning after December 31, 2005 (Act Sec. 405(e) of the Tax Relief and Health Care Act of 2006 (P.L. 109-432)).

Law source: Law at ¶5034, ¶5049 and ¶5344. Committee Report at ¶15,500.

— Act Sec. 405(a) of the Tax Relief and Health Care Act of 2006 (P.L. 109-432), adding Code Sec. 45N;

— Act Sec. 405(b), amending Code Sec. 38(b);

— Act Sec. 405(c), adding Code Sec. 280C(e);

— Act Sec. 405(e), providing the effective date.

NEW LAW EXPLAINED

Reporter references: For further information, consult the following CCH reporters.

— Standard Federal Tax Reporter, ¶4251.01

¶430 Railroad Track Maintenance Credit Modified

SUMMARY OF NEW LAW

The definition of qualified railroad track expenditures is modified to include gross expenditures for maintaining railroad track owned or leased as of January 1, 2005 by a Class II or Class III railroad, determined without regard to any consideration for such expenditures given by the Class II or Class III railroad that made the track assignment.

BACKGROUND

The American Jobs Creation Act of 2004 (P.L. 108-357) added the railroad track maintenance credit as part of the general business credit to assist small and mid-sized railroads in upgrading their tracks and related infrastructure, and maintaining those railroads as a viable alternative to shipping freight via over-the-road trucking. The railroad track maintenance credit is equal to 50 percent of any qualified railroad track maintenance expenditures paid or incurred by an eligible taxpayer during the tax year (Code Sec. 45G(a)). Taxpayers eligible to claim the credit include any Class II or Class III railroad, and any person who transports property using the rail facilities of a Class II or Class III railroad or who furnishes railroad-related property or services to a Class II or Class III railroad, but only with respect to miles of railroad track assigned to such person by the railroad (Code Sec. 45G(c)). Railroads are classified as Class I, Class II or Class III by the Surface Transportation Board of the Department of Transportation (Code Sec. 45G(g)(1)).

The credit is available for qualified railroad track maintenance expenditures paid or incurred during tax years beginning after December 31, 2004, and before January 1, 2008 (Code Sec. 45G(f)). For this purpose, qualified railroad track maintenance expenditures include expenditures (whether or not otherwise chargeable to capital account) for maintaining railroad track (including roadbed, bridges, and related track structures) owned or leased as of January 1, 2005, by a Class II or Class III railroad (Code Sec. 45G(d)). Qualified expenditures can be ordinary or capital, but the taxpayer's basis in the track is reduced by the allowable credit (Code Sec. 45G(e)(3)).

The railroad track maintenance credit is limited to the product of (1) $3,500, and (2) the sum of the number of miles of railroad track owned or leased by an eligible taxpayer as of the close of its tax year and assigned to the eligible taxpayer by a Class II or Class III railroad that owns or leases the track at the close of the tax year. Each mile of railroad track may be taken into account only once, either by the owner or by the owner's assignee, in computing the limitation. The credit is also limited with respect to the total number of miles of track owned or leased by the Class II or Class

BACKGROUND

III railroad and assigned to the Class II or Class III railroad for purposes of the credit (Code Sec. 45G(b)).

> **Compliance Pointer:** The credit is claimed on Form 8900, Qualified Railroad Track Maintenace Credit.

NEW LAW EXPLAINED

Modified definition of qualified railroad track expenditures.—The definition of qualified railroad track expenditures is modified to include gross expenditures (whether or not otherwise chargeable to capital account) for maintaining railroad track (including roadbed, bridges, and related track structures) owned or leased as of January 1, 2005 by a Class II or Class III railroad, determined without regard to any consideration for such expenditures given by the Class II or Class III railroad that made the assignment of the track (Code Sec. 45G(d), as amended by the Tax Relief and Health Care Act of 2006 (P.L. 109-432)).

> **Comment:** The Joint Committee on Taxation clarifies, that, under the modified definition, qualified railroad track maintenance expenditures are not reduced by the discount amount in the case of discounted freight shipping rates, the increment in a markup of the price for track materials, or by debt forgiveness or cash payments made by the Class II or Class III railroad to the assignee as consideration for the expenditures. Consideration received directly or indirectly from persons other that the Class II or Class III railroad, however, does reduce the amount of qualified railroad track maintenance expenditures. The Committee further states that no inference is intended under the provision as to whether or not such consideration is or is not includable in the assignee's income for federal tax purposes (Joint Committee on Taxation, Technical Explanation of the Tax Relief and Health Care Act of 2006 (P.L. 109-432) (JCX-50-06)).

▶ **Effective date.** The provision applies to tax years beginning after December 31, 2004 (Act Sec. 423(b) of the Tax Relief and Health Care Act of 2006 (P.L. 109-432); Act Sec. 245(e) of the American Jobs Creation Act of 2004 (P.L. 108-357)).

Law source: Law at ¶5046. Committee Report at ¶15,680.

— Act Sec. 423(a) of the Tax Relief and Health Care Act of 2006 (P.L. 109-432), amending Code Sec. 45G(d);

— Act Sec. 423(b), providing the effective date.

Reporter references: For further information, consult the following CCH reporters.

— Standard Federal Tax Reporter, ¶4496.01

— Tax Research Consultant, BUSEXP: 55,050

¶430

¶435 American Samoa Economic Development Credit Added

SUMMARY OF NEW LAW

A temporary, two-year credit is provided for qualifying possessions corporations operating in American Samoa.

BACKGROUND

Certain domestic corporations with a substantial portion of business operations in U.S. possessions are eligible for a possession tax credit under Code Sec. 936. This credit offsets the U.S. tax imposed on taxable non-U.S.-source income from: (1) the active conduct of a trade or business within a U.S. possession; (2) the sale or exchange of substantially all of the assets used by the taxpayer in such a trade or business; or (3) qualified possessions investment. For purposes of the credit, the possessions include, among other places, American Samoa. U.S. corporations with activities in Puerto Rico are eligible for the Code Sec. 30A economic activity credit, which is calculated under the rules set forth in Code Sec. 936. The Code Sec. 936 credit expires for tax years beginning after December 31, 2005 (Code Sec. 936(j)).

In order to qualify for the possession tax credit, a U.S. corporation must satisfy two gross income tests (Code Sec. 936(a)(2)). First, 80 percent or more of its gross income for the three-year period immediately preceding the close of the tax year must be from sources within a U.S. possession. Second, 75 percent or more of the corporation's gross income during the same period must be from the active conduct of a trade or business within a U.S. possession. The general rules for determining the source of the income apply. The possession tax credit is available only to a corporation that qualifies as an existing credit claimant. A determination as to whether that corporation is an existing credit claimant is made separately for each possession.

Existing credit claimant. An existing credit claimant is a corporation that was actively conducting a trade or business within a possession on October 13, 1995, and elected the benefits of the possession tax credit in an election in effect for its tax year that included October 13, 1995 (Code Sec. 936(j)(9)). Although a corporation can also qualify as an existing credit claimant if it acquires all of an existing credit claimant's trade or business, status as an existing claimant is lost if a substantial new line of business is added (Code Sec. 936(j)(9)(B)).

Economic activity-based limitation. The possession tax credit is computed separately for each possession with respect to which the corporation is an existing credit claimant. For tax years beginning after December 13, 1993, the credit is subject to either an economic activity-based limitation or an income-based limit (Code Sec. 936(a)(4)). Under the economic activity-based limit, the amount of the credit for the tax year may not exceed an amount equal to the sum of:

BACKGROUND

(1) 60 percent of the possession corporation's "qualified possession wages" and "allocable employee fringe benefit expenses";

(2) 15 percent of the depreciation deductions allowable for the tax year under Code Sec. 167 with respect to short-life qualified tangible property (three-year or five-year property to which Code Sec. 168 applies);

(3) 40 percent of the depreciation deductions allowable for the tax year under Code Sec. 167 with respect to medium-life qualified tangible property (seven-year or 10-year property to which Code Sec. 168 applies);

(4) 65 percent of the depreciation deductions allowable for the tax year under Code Sec. 167 with respect to long-life qualified tangible property (property that is not described in (2) or (3) above and to which Code Sec. 168 applies); and

(5) in certain cases, a portion of the taxpayer's possession income taxes.

Income based limitation/reduced credit election. As an alternative to the economic activity limitation, a possession corporation may elect to apply a limit equal to the applicable percentage of the credit that would otherwise be allowable with respect to possession business income; currently, that applicable percentage is 40 percent (Code Sec. 936(a)(4)(B)(ii)).

Repeal and transition rules. The Code Sec. 936 possession tax credit is not available to new claimants for any tax year beginning after 1995. The credit is phased out for existing credit claimants over a period including tax years beginning before 2006. The amount of the credit available during the phase-out period is generally reduced by special limitation rules. The special limitation rules do not apply, however, to existing credit claimants for income from activities in Guam, American Samoa, and the Northern Mariana Islands. As previously noted, the Code Sec. 936 credit is repealed for all possessions, including American Samoa, for all tax years beginning after 2005 (Code Sec. 936(j)).

NEW LAW EXPLAINED

Credit with respect to American Samoa allowed for two tax years.—A U.S. corporation that is an existing credit claimant with respect to American Samoa, and that elected the application of Code Sec. 936 for its last tax year beginning before January 1, 2006, is allowed a credit for two tax years (Act Sec. 119(a) of the Tax Relief and Health Care Act of 2006 (P.L. 109-432)). The credit is based on the economic-based limitation rules described above (Code Sec. 30A(d)).

Note: The temporary credit with respect to American Samoa is not part of the Code but is computed based on the rules in Code Secs. 30A and 936.

Comment: A House Committee Report (H.R. Rep. No. 109-304) explained that because the tuna canning industry is the largest employer in American Samoa as well as the primary beneficiary of the possession tax credit, the expiration of the possession tax credit would negatively impact the economy in American Samoa. Accordingly, the committee concluded that the credit should be extended to provide time for the development of a comprehensive long-term policy with respect to American Samoa. Similarly, according to a Joint Committee on Taxation report, the two-year credit allowed by the 2006 Extenders Act "is intended to provide additional time for the development of a comprehensive, long-term

NEW LAW EXPLAINED

economic policy toward American Samoa" (Joint Committee on Taxation, Technical Explanation of the Tax Relief and Health Care Act of 2006 (P.L. 109-432) (JCX-50-06)).

Comment: Deputy Assistant Secretary of the Interior for Insular Affairs David B. Cohen, in a March 1, 2006 statement before the Senate Committee on Energy and Natural Resources, reiterated the Administration's support for a temporary extension of the possession tax credit to allow the American Samoa government to develop a diversified private sector economy. He noted that the American Samoa tuna canneries have relied on the possession tax credit to counter the great competitive disadvantage in labor costs as compared to countries such as Thailand and the Philippines. He explained that it is likely that once trade advantages are expanded to other countries and regions, the canneries will leave, and American Samoa would be left with no viable industry and no major employer.

Determination of credit amount. The amount of the credit under the provision is equal to the sum of the amounts used in computing the corporation's economic activity-based limitation (described above) with respect to American Samoa, except that no credit is allowed for the amount of any American Samoa income taxes (Act Sec. 119(b)(1) of the 2006 Extenders Act). Accordingly, the amount of the credit for any qualifying corporation equals the sum of:

(1) 60 percent of the corporation's qualified American Samoa wages and allocable employee fringe benefit expenses; and

(2) 15 percent of the corporation's depreciation allowances with respect to short-life qualified American Samoa tangible property, plus 40 percent of the corporation's depreciation allowances with respect to medium-life qualified American Samoa tangible property, plus 65 percent of the corporation's depreciation allowances with respect to long-life qualified American Samoa tangible property.

Foreign tax credit allowed. The rule in Code Sec. 936(c) that denies a credit or deduction for any possessions or foreign tax paid with respect to taxable income taken into account in computing the Code Sec. 936 credit does not apply with respect to the credit allowed by the provision (Act Sec. 119(b)(3) of the 2006 Extenders Act).

Definition of terms. Any term used in the provision that is also used in Code Secs. 30A or 936 has the same meaning given to such term by Code Secs. 30A or 936 (Act Sec. 119(c) of the 2006 Extenders Act).

▶ **Effective date.** The provision applies to the first two tax years of a qualifying corporation that begin after December 31, 2005, and before January 1, 2008 (Act Sec. 119(d) of the Tax Relief and Health Care Act of 2006 (P.L. 109-432)).

Law source: Law at ¶7050. Committee Report at ¶15,280.

— Act Sec. 119(a)-(c) of the Tax Relief and Health Care Act of 2006 (P.L. 109-432);

— Act Sec. 119(d), providing the effective date.

Reporter references: For further information, consult the following CCH reporters.

— Standard Federal Tax Reporter, ¶4059.01, ¶28,394.01 and ¶28,394.031

— Tax Research Consultant, INTL: 27,070.15

¶430

ENERGY CREDITS

¶440 Enhanced Business Energy Credit Rates Extended

SUMMARY OF NEW LAW

The business energy credit rates in effect for 2006 and 2007 are extended to include property placed in service in 2008.

BACKGROUND

The energy credit under Code Sec. 48 is one component of the investment tax credit. The nonrefundable credit is 10 percent of the taxpayer's basis in qualified energy property. For property placed in service in 2006 and 2007, the credit percentage is increased to 30 percent for (1) qualified fuel cell property, (2) equipment that uses solar energy to generate electricity to heat or cool a structure (including provide hot water) or provide solar process heat, and (3) equipment that illuminates the inside of a structure using fiber-optic distributed sunlight. For stationary microturbine property and other energy property, the credit remains at 10 percent (Code Sec. 48(a)).The increased 30 percent rate for fuel cell property and property that generates solar electricity or process heat is not available for property placed in service after 2007. Furthermore, fuel cell property, microturbine property, and property that illuminates the inside of a structure using fiber-optic distributed sunlight no longer qualify as energy property at all for property placed in service after 2007 under the old law (Code Sec. 48(c)).

NEW LAW EXPLAINED

Energy credit extended for property placed in service in 2008.—The new law extends the business energy credit at current credit rates through December 31, 2008 (Code Sec. 48, as amended by the Tax Relief and Health Care Act of 2006 (P.L. 109-432)). As a result, fuel cell property, microturbine property, and property that illuminates the inside of a structure using fiber-optic distributed sunlight continue to qualify as energy property as long as they are placed in service before January 1, 2009. Moreover, the increased 30 percent rate applies with respect to property placed in service during 2008 if the property is (1) qualified fuel cell property, (2) equipment that uses solar energy to generate electricity to heat or cool a structure (including provide hot water) or provide solar process heat, or (3) equipment used to illuminate the inside of a structure using fiber-optic distributed sunlight.

▶ **Effective date.** No specific date is provided by the Act. The provision is, therefore, considered effective on December 20, 2006, the date of enactment.

Law source: Law at ¶5050. Committee Report at ¶15,410.

— Act Sec. 207 of the Tax Relief and Health Care Act of 2006 (P.L. 109-432), amending Code Sec. 48.

NEW LAW EXPLAINED

Reporter references: For further information, consult the following CCH reporters.

— Standard Federal Tax Reporter, ¶4671.021

— Tax Research Consultant, BUSEXP: 51,100

— Federal Tax Guide, ¶2725

¶445 Credit for New Energy-Efficient Homes Extended

SUMMARY OF NEW LAW

The homebuilder's credit for new energy efficient homes is extended through 2008.

BACKGROUND

As part of the general business credit, eligible contractors may claim a credit of up to $2,000 for each qualified new energy efficient home that they construct or manufacture (Code Sec. 38(b)(23); Code Sec. 45L). A qualified energy efficient home must be located in the United States, its construction must be substantially completed after August 8, 2005, it must be acquired for use as a residence during the tax year, and it must be certified to meet prescribed energy-saving requirements (Code Sec. 45L(b)(2)). The credit is reduced to $1,000 for manufactured homes that meet a less stringent set of energy-savings requirements (Code Sec. 45L(c)). The credit is effective for qualified new energy efficient homes acquired after December 31, 2005, in tax years ending after that date (Energy Tax Incentives Act of 2005 (P.L. 109-58), Act § 1332(a)). The credit does not apply to any home acquired after December 31, 2007 (Code Sec. 45L(g)).

NEW LAW EXPLAINED

Homebuilder's credit extended through 2008.—The homebuilder's credit for new energy efficiency homes is extended for one year. Accordingly, the credit expires for energy efficient homes acquired after December 31, 2008 (Code Sec. 45L(g), as amended by the Tax Relief and Health Care Act of 2006 (P.L. 109-432)).

▶ **Effective date.** No specific effective date is provided by the Act. The provision is, therefore, considered effective on December 20, 2006, the date of enactment.

Law source: Law at ¶5048. Committee Reports at ¶15,390.

— Act Sec. 205 of the Tax Relief and Health Care Act of 2006 (P.L. 109-432), amending Code Sec. 45L(g).

NEW LAW EXPLAINED

Reporter references: For further information, consult the following CCH reporters.
— Standard Federal Tax Reporter, ¶4500L.01 and ¶4500L.021
— Tax Research Consultant, BUSEXP: 55,352
— Federal Tax Guide, ¶2604

¶450 Qualifying Energy Resources Credit Extended

SUMMARY OF NEW LAW

The placed-in-service dates for qualified wind, closed-loop biomass, open-loop biomass, geothermal or solar energy, small irrigation power, landfill gas, and gas combustion facilities are extended to include facilities placed in operation before January 1, 2009.

BACKGROUND

A nonrefundable tax credit is available for the domestic production of electricity from certain "qualified energy resources" (QERs) (Code Sec. 45(a)). Electricity from the following QERs qualify for the credit: (1) wind, (2) closed-loop biomass, (3) open-loop biomass, (4) geothermal energy, (5) solar energy, (6) small irrigation power, (7) municipal solid waste, and (8) qualified hydroelectric production. In addition, the credit is available for the sale of refined coal produced at a refined coal production facility and the sale of Indian coal (coal produced on an Indian reservation). In order to be eligible for the credit, the electricity must be produced at qualified facilities, which are defined as:

(1) wind energy facilities placed in service after 1993 and before January 1, 2008;

(2) closed-loop biomass facilities placed in service after 1992 and before January 1, 2008, or facilities placed in service and modified before January 1, 2008, to use closed-loop biomass to co-fire with coal, with other biomass, or with both;

(3) open-loop biomass facilities using agricultural livestock waste nutrients placed in service after October 22, 2004 and before January 1, 2008, and other open-loop biomass facilities using certain wood waste or waste from forest-related or agricultural resources placed in service before January 1, 2008;

(4) geothermal facilities placed in service after October 22, 2004 and before January 1, 2008;

(5) small irrigation power facilities placed in service after October 22, 2004 and before January 1, 2008;

(6) landfill gas facilities placed in service after October 22, 2004 and before January 1, 2008;

(7) trash combustion facilities (including the addition of new units at an existing facility on or before October 22, 2004, that result in increased electricity produc-

BACKGROUND

tion at the entire facility) placed in service after October 22, 2004 and before January 1, 2008;

(8) refined coal production facilities placed in service after October 22, 2004 and before January 1, 2009;

(9) qualified hydropower facilities, including (a) hydroelectric dams placed in service on or before August 8, 2005, to which efficiency improvements or additions to capacity are added after August 8, 2005 and before January 1, 2008, or (b) nonhydroelectric dams placed in service before August 8, 2005, to which turbines or other generating devices are added after August 8, 2005 and before January 1, 2008; and

(10) Indian coal production facilities placed in service before January 1, 2009.

NEW LAW EXPLAINED

"Placed in service" dates for qualified facilities extended.—The placed-in-service-date for wind energy, closed-loop biomass, open-loop biomass, geothermal small irrigation power, landfill gas, trash combustion and qualified hydropower facilities is extended to include facilities placed in service before January 1, 2009 (Code Sec. 45(d), as amended by the Tax Relief and Health Care Act of 2006 (P.L. 109-432)).

Caution: The placed in service dates for refined coal production facilities (after October 22, 2004 and before January 1, 2009) and Indian coal production facilities (before January 1, 2009) remain the same and are now consistent with the other qualified facilities.

▶ **Effective date.** No specific effective date is provided by the Act. The provision is, therefore, considered effective on December 20, 2006, the date of enactment.

Law source: Law at ¶5038. Committee Report at ¶15,350.

— Act Sec. 201 of the Tax Relief and Health Care Act of 2006 (P.L. 109-432), amending Code Sec. 45(d).

Reporter references: For further information, consult the following CCH reporters.

— Standard Federal Tax Reporter, ¶4415.01 and ¶4415.03

— Tax Research Consultant, BUSEXP: 54,554

— Federal Tax Guide, ¶2575

¶450

¶455 Qualifying Advanced Coal Project Credit Performance Standards Modified for Sulfur Dioxide Removal

SUMMARY OF NEW LAW

The credit for advanced coal projects is amended to add a performance standard for sulfur dioxide removal in electric generation units designed to use subbituminous coal.

BACKGROUND

The Energy Tax Incentives Act of 2005 (P.L. 109-58) added the qualifying advanced coal project credit (Code Sec. 48A) to the investment credit provisions of Code Sec. 46 (Code Sec. 46(3)). The credit is available only to taxpayers who have applied for and received certification that their project satisfies the relevant requirements. The IRS, in consultation with the Department of Energy, certifies project applicants and the IRS allocates the credits. Certifications are issued using a competitive bidding process.

The amount of the qualifying advanced coal project credit for a tax year is (1) 20 percent of the qualified investment for the tax years for integrated gasification combined cycle (IGCC) projects, and (2) 15 percent of the qualified investment for the tax year for projects using other technologies (Code Sec. 48A(a)).

In order for an electric generation unit to be treated as advanced coal-based generation technology it must be designed to meet a number of performance requirements (Code Sec. 48A(f)(1)). One of those requirements is that the electric generation unit must be designed to achieve a 99-percent reduction in sulfur dioxide.

NEW LAW EXPLAINED

Performance requirement relating to sulfur dioxide removal is changed.—An electric generation unit designed to use subbituminous coal will meet the advanced coal-based technology standard for sulfur removal if it either (1) is designed to remove 99 percent of the sulfur dioxide or (2) achieves an emission limit of 0.04 pounds of sulfur dioxide per million BTU on a 30-day average (Code Sec. 48A(f)(1), as amended by the Tax Relief and Health Care Act of 2006 (P.L. 109-432)).

> **Comment:** On November 30, 2006, the IRS announced that it had allocated nearly $1 billion in investment tax credits to nine planned clean coal projects. This amount included projects under both the qualifying advanced coal project credit (Code Sec. 48A) and the qualifying gasification project credit (Code Sec. 48B). Among the tax credits issued, two went to IGCC bituminous coal projects, one to an IGCC lignite project and two to non-IGCC advanced coal electricity generation projects. The Department of Energy did not certify any IGCC subbituminous coal projects. Bituminous coal is found primarily in the eastern states;

NEW LAW EXPLAINED

the western states' and Alaska's coal resources are predominantly subbituminous.

Basin Electric Power Cooperative (Basin), one of the largest electric generation and transmission cooperatives in the United States, distributes electricity to 1.8 million consumers in nine central and western states. Basin submitted an IGCC subbituminous coal project for certification, but it was rejected. Ron Harper, Basin CEO and general manager, stated that, "We're disappointed that the Department of Energy chose not to certify any subbituminous clean coal technology projects." Harper added that if there was another opportunity to apply for the investment tax credit in the future for an IGCC power plant, Basin would consider submitting a second application. Prior to notification that its IGCC project had not been certified, Basin passed a resolution stating that the "one size fits all" emission reduction requirements "significantly disadvantages the western power producers." The resolution urged the congressional delegation in its distribution area to include the substance of Basin's resolutions in legislation changing air emission requirements, including a recommendation that emission standards "take into account regional differences and maintain fuel diversity." Senator Norm Coleman, R-Minn., a member of the congressional delegation in Basin's distribution area, introduced the change to the sulfur dioxide removal performance requirement. The IRS stated that of the approximately $650 million in additional tax credits available for allocation to clean coal projects in 2007, $267 million will be available for IGCC subbituminous coal projects.

▶ **Effective date.** This provision applies with respect to applications for certifications under Code Sec. 48A(d)(2) submitted after October 2, 2006 (Act Sec. 203(b) of the Tax Relief and Health Care Act of 2006 (P.L. 109-432)).

Law source: Law at ¶5051. Committee Reports at ¶15,370.

— Act Sec. 203(a) of the Tax Relief and Health Care Act of 2006 (P.L. 109-432), amending Code Sec. 48A(f)(1);

— Act Sec. 203(b), providing the effective date.

Reporter references: For further information, consult the following CCH reporters.

— Standard Federal Tax Reporter, ¶4675.01

— Tax Research Consultant, BUSEXP: 51,702.15

¶460 Credit Modified for Producing Fuel from a Nonconventional Source—Coke or Coke Gas Facilities

SUMMARY OF NEW LAW

The phase-out limitation for coke or coke gas otherwise eligible for the tax credit for producing fuel from a nonconventional source is repealed. Qualifying facilities do not include facilities that produce petroleum-based coke or coke gas.

BACKGROUND

The Energy Tax Incentives Act of 2005 (P.L. 109-58) extended the tax credit for producing fuel from a nonconventional source to facilities producing coke or coke gas. The credit can be claimed for coke or coke gas (1) produced in facilities that were placed in service before January 1, 1993, or after June 30, 1998, and before January 1, 2010, and (2) sold during the period beginning on the later of January 1, 2006, or the date the facility is placed in service, and ending on the date that is four years after the date such period began (Code Sec. 45K(g)(1)).

Special rules. Special rules are provided for determining the amount of the credit allowed solely as a result of the coke and coke gas provision contained in Code Sec. 45K(g)(1). The amount of qualified fuels sold during the tax year for which a credit can be claimed cannot exceed an average barrel-of-oil equivalent of 4000 barrels per day with respect to any facility. Days prior to the date the facility is placed in service are not taken into account in determining the average (Code Sec. 45K(g)(2)(A)).

The tax credit is generally equal to $3.00 (adjusted for inflation) multiplied by the number of barrel-of-oil equivalents of qualified fuels produced and sold during the tax year. Generally, the credit for fuel produced in 2005 is $6.79 per barrel-of-oil equivalent. For fuels sold after 2005, in determining the amount of the credit related to facilities producing coke or coke gas, the $3.00 credit amount is adjusted for inflation using 2004 as the base year instead of 1979 (Code Sec. 45K(g)(2)(B)). The credit allowed as a result of Code Sec. 45K(g) does not apply to any facility producing qualified fuels that received a credit under Code Sec. 45K for the tax year or any preceding tax year as a result of the provisions of Code Sec. 45K(f). (Code Sec. 45K(g)(2)(c)).

Phase-out of credit. The nonconventional source fuel credit is reduced (but not below zero) over a $6 (inflation-adjusted) phase-out period as the reference price of oil exceeds $23.50 per barrel (also adjusted for inflation) (Code Sec. 45K(b)). The reference price is the IRS's estimate of the annual average wellhead price per barrel for all domestic crude oil. The credit did not phase-out for 2005 because the reference price for that year of $50.26 did not exceed the inflation threshold adjustment amount of $51.35.

Beginning with tax years ending after December 31, 2005, the nonconventional source fuel credit is part of the Code Sec. 38 general business credit. Thus, subject to some

BACKGROUND

limitations, any unused credits can be carried forward 20 years or back one year (Code Sec. 39).

NEW LAW EXPLAINED

Treatment of coke and coke gas facilities.—The nonconventional source fuel credit phase-out provisions under Code Sec. 45K(b)(1) do not apply to coke or coke gas otherwise eligible for the credit for producing fuel from a nonconventional source (Code Sec. 45K(g)(2)(D), as added by the Tax Relief and Health Care Act of 2006 (P.L. 109-432)).

The new law also clarifies that a coke and coke gas facility, for purposes of the nonconventional source fuel credit, does not include facilities that produce petroleum-based coke or coke gas (Code Sec. 45K(g)(1), as amended by 2006 Extenders Act).

> **Caution Note:** The Energy Tax Incentives Act of 2005 (P.L. 109-58), which extended the nonconventional source fuel credit to coke and coke gas facilities, did not provide a definition of "facility." The new changes to Code Sec. 45K(g) made by the Tax Relief and Health Care Act of 2006 (P.L. 109-432), still do not resolve the issue of what constitutes a "facility." However, the Joint Committee on Taxation, Description and Technical Explanation of the Energy Tax Incentives Act of 2005 (JCX-60-05) stated that the "conferees understand that a single facility for the production of coke or coke gas is generally composed of multiple coke ovens or similar structures."

▶ **Effective date.** This provision applies to fuel produced and sold after December 31, 2005, in tax years ending after that date (Act Sec. 211(c) of the Tax Relief and Health Care Act of 2006 (P.L. 109-432); Act Sec. 1321(b) of the Energy Tax Incentives Act of 2005 (P.L. 109-58)).

Law source: Law at ¶5047. Committee Reports at ¶15,450.

— Act Sec. 211(a) of the Tax Relief and Health Care Act of 2006 (P.L. 109-432), adding Code Sec. 45K(g)(2)(D);

— Act Sec. 211(b), amending Code Sec. 45K(g)(1);

— Act Sec. 211(c), providing the effective date.

Reporter references: For further information, consult the following CCH reporters.

— Standard Federal Tax Reporter, ¶4500H.055

— Tax Research Consultant, BUSEXP: 54,302.05 and BUSEXP: 54,510

¶460

Tax Relief—Health and Medical Benefits

5

HEALTH PLANS

HEALTH PLANS

¶505 Qualified HSA Distributions Allowed from FSAs and HRAs

SUMMARY OF NEW LAW

An HSA can receive a one-time distribution from a health FSA or HRA. Eligibility and comparable contribution rules for HSAs are modified.

BACKGROUND

Employers can offer two devices to help employees pay medical expenses. Health flexible spending arrangements (also known as flexible spending accounts or FSAs) allow employees to use their own pre-tax wages to pay medical expenses, while health reimbursements accounts (HRAs) allow employees to use employer contributions for medical expenses. These arrangements can affect an employee's participation in a health savings account (HSA).

FSAs. An FSA is normally funded by diverting some of the employee's pre-tax compensation into the account. These funds can be used to pay or reimburse medical

BACKGROUND

expenses incurred by the employee and the employee's spouse and dependents. Foregone compensation that is used to pay qualified medical expenses is not included in the employee's gross income or wages. Health FSAs that are offered as salary reduction agreements are subject to the general requirements for cafeteria plans and, thus, cannot provide deferred compensation (Code Sec. 125(d)(2)). These FSAs are subject to a "use it or lose it" rule that prevents employees from carrying funds over from one year to the next by requiring them to forfeit any amounts that are not spent for the year. Generally, the medical expenses must be paid or incurred by the end of the plan year, but employers may provide a two-and-one-half-month grace period (Notice 2005-42, 2005-1 CB 1204). If the FSA allows reimbursements during a grace period, the employee generally cannot make contributions to an HSA until the first month following the end of the grace period, even if the employee's health FSA has no unused benefits as of the end of the prior plan year (Notice 2005-86, I.R.B. 2005-49, 1075).

HRAs. HRAs are also employer-maintained arrangements that can be used for medical expenses. As with FSAs, funds in an HRA are excluded from an employee's gross income and wages as long as they are used to pay or reimburse medical expenses incurred by the employee and the employee's spouse and dependents. HRAs differ from FSAs in three significant ways. First, HRAs are funded by the employer, rather than by the employee. Second, HRAs are not subject to the use-it-or-lose-it rule, so amounts remaining in an HRA at the end of the year may be carried forward to following years. Third, HRA funds can be used to pay medical insurance premiums, while FSAs cannot (Notice 2002-45, 2002-2 CB 93).

HSAs. HSAs share some features of health FSAs and HRAs, but they also have three distinctive features. First, FSAs and HRAs are tied to employment, but HSAs are not. HSAs can be provided and/or funded by employers, but they can also be established and funded by individuals. Second, because HSAs are not tied to employment, they are fully portable; an HSA remains the account holder's property regardless of where or whether the account holder is employed. Third, HSA funds can be invested by the account holder. The investment income is tax-free if it is used to pay qualified medical expenses, or if it is distributed after the account holder dies, becomes disabled, or turns 65 (Code Sec. 223).

HSA eligibility. To be eligible for an HSA, an individual generally must have a high deductible health plan (HDHP), with no other coverage other than permitted insurance or permitted coverage. Permitted insurance is generally limited to insurance related to workers' compensation liabilities, tort liabilities and liabilities arising from the ownership of property (such as automobile insurance); insurance for a specified disease or illness; or insurance that provides a fixed payment for each period of hospitalization. Permitted coverage is coverage for accidents, disability, dental care, vision care, or long-term care (Code Sec. 223(c)). For purposes of these rules, FSAs and HRAs constitute other coverage, unless the FSA or HRA is for a limited purpose, is suspended, is a post-deductible account, or is a retirement HRA (Rev. Rul. 2004-45, 2004 CB 971). Thus, most employees who are eligible for health FSAs or HRAs are not eligible for HSAs.

¶505

BACKGROUND

Comparable contributions. Employer contributions to employee HSAs that are not made through a cafeteria plan generally must satisfy the comparable contribution rule. This rule requires the employer to contribute the same amount or the same percentage of the HDHP deductible limit to all comparable employees who have the same kind of coverage from the employer's HDHP. If all employees who are eligible individuals do not contribute the same amount to their HSAs and, consequently, do not receive comparable contributions to their HSAs, the comparability rules are not satisfied, even if the employer makes the same contribution amount available to each employee. Employers are subject to a 35-percent excise tax on HSA contributions that do not satisfy the comparable contribution rule (Code Sec. 4980G; Notice 2004-25, 2004-1 CB 727).

NEW LAW EXPLAINED

FSAs and HRAs can roll over funds to HSAs; some FSA coverage disregarded for purposes of HSA eligibility.—An employer can make a one-time transfer of funds from an employee's health flexible savings arrangement (FSA) or health reimbursement account (HRA) to the employee's health savings account (HSA). The comparable contribution rules are modified for the rollover contributions. For purposes of the permitted insurance rules for HSA eligibility, FSAs with no account balance are disregarded.

Qualified HSA distribution. A qualified HSA distribution must be made directly by the employer into the employee's HSA before January 1, 2012 (Code Sec. 106(e)(2)(B), as added by the Tax Relief and Health Care Act of 2006 (P.L. 109-432)). The FSA or HRA that allows the qualified HSA distribution continues to qualify as an FSA or an HSA (Code Sec. 106(e)(1), as added by the 2006 Extenders Act). Each FSA or HRA may allow only one distribution to the employee's HSA (Code Sec. 106(e), as added by the 2006 Extenders Act). The amount of the distribution cannot exceed the lesser of the balance in the FSA or HRA as of:

- September 21, 2006, or
- the date of the distribution (Code Sec. 106(e)(2), as added by the 2006 Extenders Act).

The balance in the FSA or HRA is determined on a cash basis; that is, expenses that have been incurred but not paid or reimbursed as of the date of the determination are not taken into account (Joint Committee on Taxation, Technical Explanation of the Tax Relief and Health Care Act of 2006 (P.L. 109-432) (JCX-50-06)).

Qualified HSA distributions are treated as employer contributions and as rollover contributions. Thus, they are excludable from gross income and wages for employment tax purposes, they are not taken into account in applying the maximum deduction limitation for other HSA contributions (see ¶ 510), they are not deductible, and they do not have to be in cash (Code Sec. 106(e)(4)(C) and (5)(A), as added by the 2006 Extenders Act; Joint Committee on Taxation, Technical Explanation of the Tax Relief and Health Care Act of 2006 (P.L. 109-432) (JCX-50-06)).

NEW LAW EXPLAINED

> **Example 1:** On September 21, 2006, the balance in Mei's health FSA is $2,000. On January 1, 2008, the balance in her FSA is $3,000. On June 30, 2008, the balance in her FSA is $1,500. On January 1, 2008, Mei's FSA can make a qualified HSA distribution of up to $2,000 (the lesser of her balance on September 21, 2006, and her balance on the distribution date). If instead the FSA makes the qualified HSA distribution on June 30, 2008, it cannot exceed $1,500. In either case, the amount of the distribution is not includible in Mei's income, is not deductible by her, and does not count against the annual maximum tax deductible contribution that can be made to her HSA (Joint Committee on Taxation, Technical Explanation of the Tax Relief and Health Care Act of 2006 (P.L. 109-432) (JCX-50-06)).

Comparable contributions. Generally, the comparable contribution rules do not apply to qualified HSA distributions. However, if an employer allows any employee to make a qualified HSA distribution, it must allow all employees who are covered under an HDHP plan of the employer to make qualified HSA distributions. A 35-percent excise tax applies if this requirement is not met (Code Sec. 105(e)(5)(B), as added by the 2006 Extenders Act).

HSA eligibility. The HSA account holder must remain eligible for an HSA during the testing period following the qualified HSA distribution; that is, the account holder must be covered only by a high deductible health plan (HDHP), permitted insurance, and/or permitted coverage (Code Sec. 106(e)(4)(B), as added by the 2006 Extenders Act). The testing period begins with the month in which the qualified HSA distribution is contributed to the HSA, and ends on the last day of the 12th month following that month (Code Sec. 106(e)(4)(A), as added by the 2006 Extenders Act). An HSA account holder who fails to qualify as an eligible individual during the testing period must include the qualified HSA distribution in income for the tax year of the first day during the test period when the account holder is not an eligible individual (Code Sec. 106(e)(3)(A)(i), as added by the 2006 Extenders Act; Joint Committee on Taxation, Technical Explanation of the Tax Relief and Health Care Act of 2006 (P.L. 109-432) (JCX-50-06)). The account holder must also pay an additional tax equal to 10 percent of the distribution (Code Sec. 106(e)(3)(A)(ii), as added by the 2006 Extenders Act). These rules do not apply if the account holder ceases to be an eligible individual by reason of death or disability (Code Sec. 106(e)(3)(B), as added by the 2006 Extenders Act). Similar rules apply to part-year eligibility (see ¶ 515) and qualified HSA funding distributions from IRAs (see ¶ 525).

> **Example 2:** On September 21, 2006, the balance in Mei's health FSA is $2,000. On January 1, 2008, the balance in her FSA is $3,000. On January 1, 2008, her FSA makes a qualified HSA distribution of $2,000 (the lesser of her balance on September 21, 2006, and her balance on the distribution date). On June 1, 2008, Mei enrolls in a comprehensive health insurance plan and, thus, ceases to be an eligible individual. The $2,000 distribution to her HSA is included in her gross

NEW LAW EXPLAINED

income, and she is liable for an additional $200 in tax (Joint Committee on Taxation, Technical Explanation of the Tax Relief and Health Care Act of 2006 (P.L. 109-432) (JCX-50-06)).

Caution Note: According to the Joint Committee on Taxation, qualified HSA distributions are intended to assist individuals to transfer to HDHPs from other types of health plans, such as traditional or comprehensive insurance. Thus, an HSA account holder who takes advantage of a qualified HSA distribution is effectively locked into a HDHP for the following year.

FSA coverage disregarded for HSA eligibility purposes. For purposes of determining whether an individual is eligible for an HSA, FSA coverage is disregarded for tax years beginning after December 31, 2006, during any period immediately following the end of the FSA plan year if:

- the balance in the individual's FSA at the end of the plan year is zero; or
- the individual is making a qualified HSA distribution in an amount equal to the remaining balance (Code Sec. 223(c)(1)(iii), as added by the 2006 Extenders Act).

However, the present law rule that individuals are not eligible if they have coverage under a general purpose health FSA or HRA continues to apply. Thus, for example, if the health FSA or HRA from which the contribution is made is a general purpose health FSA or HRA and the individual remains eligible under the arrangement after the distribution to the HSA, the individual is not an eligible individual (Joint Committee on Taxation, Technical Explanation of the Tax Relief and Health Care Act of 2006 (P.L. 109-432) (JCX-50-06)).

Example 3: As of December 31, 2006, Joe's health FSA balance is zero. Because the balance is zero, coverage under the FSA during the period from January 1, 2007, until March 15, 2007 (the grace period) is disregarded in determining if tax deductible contributions can be made to his HSA for that period. Similarly, if the entire balance in Joe's health FSA as of December 31, 2006, is distributed and contributed to his HSA, coverage during the health FSA grace period is disregarded (Joint Committee on Taxation, Technical Explanation of the Tax Relief and Health Care Act of 2006 (P.L. 109-432) (JCX-50-06)).

It is intended that the Secretary of the Treasury will provide guidance with respect to the timing of health FSA distributions contributed to an HSA in order to facilitate the rollovers and the establishment of HSAs. For example, it is intended that the Secretary will provide rules under which coverage is disregarded if, before the end of a year, an individual elects HDHP coverage and elects to contribute any remaining FSA balance to an HSA, even if the trustee-to-trustee transfer cannot be completed until the following plan year. Similar rules apply for the general provision allowing amounts from a health FSA or HRA to be contributed to an HSA in order to facilitate such contributions at the beginning of an employee's first year of HSA eligibility. The provision does not modify the permitted health FSA grace period allowed under existing IRS guidance (Joint

NEW LAW EXPLAINED

Committee on Taxation, Technical Explanation of the Tax Relief and Health Care Act of 2006 (P.L. 109-432) (JCX-50-06)).

▶ **Effective date.** The amendments providing for qualified HSA distributions and modifying the comparable contribution rules apply to distributions on or after December 20, 2006 (Act Sec. 302(c)(1) of the Tax Relief and Health Care Act of 2006 (P.L. 109-432)). The amendments providing for disregarded FSA coverage are effective on December 20, 2006 (Act Sec. 302(c)(2) of the Tax Relief and Health Care Act of 2006 (P.L. 109-432)).

Law source: Law at ¶5090 and ¶5339. Committee Reports at ¶15,460.

— Act Sec. 302(a) of the Tax Relief and Health Care Act of 2006 (P.L. 109-432), adding Code Sec. 106(e);

— Act Sec. 302(b), adding Code Sec. 223(c)(1)(B)(iii);

— Act Sec. 302(c), providing the effective date.

Reporter references: For further information, consult the following CCH reporters.

— Standard Federal Tax Reporter, ¶6803.025

— Tax Research Consultant, INDIV: 42,454

— Federal Tax Guide, ¶4131, ¶4152 and ¶4510

¶510 Limitation on Health Savings Account Contributions

SUMMARY OF NEW LAW

Contributions to HSAs are no longer limited to the annual deductible under the high deductible health plan. The Consumer Price Index for HSA-related cost-of-living adjustments is determined for the 12 month period ending on March 31.

BACKGROUND

Code Sec. 223 permits individuals with a high deductible health plan to establish a health savings account (HSA). In general, HSAs are trusts created or organized in the United States exclusively for the purpose of paying for the qualified medical expenses of the account holder and his or her spouse and dependents. Such accounts provide tax-favored treatment for current medical expenses and for savings for future medical expenses.

A high deductible health plan (HDHP) is one that has an annual deductible of at least $1,000 for self-coverage and $2,000 for family coverage, and an out-of-pocket expense limit that is no more than $5,000 for self-coverage and $10,000 for family coverage (Code Sec. 223(c)(2)). These amounts are adjusted annually for inflation (Code Sec. 223(g)). For 2006, the annual deductible amounts are $1,050 for self-coverage and $2,100 for family coverage. The out-of-pocket expense limits for 2006 are $5,250 for self-coverage and $10,500 for family coverage (Rev. Proc. 2005-70, I.R.B. 2005-47, 979).

BACKGROUND

For 2007, the annual deductible amounts are $1,100 for self-coverage and $2,200 for family coverage. The out-of-pocket expense limits for 2007 are $5,500 for self-coverage and $11,000 for family coverage (Rev. Proc. 2006-53, I.R.B. 2006-48, 996).

Within limits, cash contributions made to an HSA by an eligible individual are deductible from that individual's income (Code Sec. 223(a)). To the extent that contributions from an individual's employer do not exceed the annual limit on HSA contributions, they are excluded from the individual's income and exempt from employment taxes. An employee cannot deduct employer contributions that are also excluded from the employee's income. Contributions from an employer that exceed the annual limit on contributions are included in the employee's income as compensation subject to income and employment taxes (Code Sec. 223(d)(4)(C)).

The maximum annual deductible contribution that can be made to an individual's HSA is the lesser of (1) the annual deductible under the individual's high deductible plan or (2) $2,250 for an individual with self-only coverage and $4,500 for an individual with family coverage (Code Sec. 223(b)). The amounts in (2) are adjusted annually for inflation in $50 increments (Code Sec. 223(g)). For 2006, the contribution limits are $2,700 per person and $5,450 per family (Rev. Proc. 2005-70, I.R.B. 2005-47, 979). For 2007, the contribution limits are $2,850 per person and $5,650 per family (Rev. Proc. 2006-53, I.R.B. 2006-48, 996).

The annual contribution limit is the sum of the limits determined separately for each month, based on the individual's status and health plan coverage as of the first day of the month (Code Sec. 223(b)(2)). The annual contribution limits are increased for individuals who have attained age 55 by the end of the tax year (Code Sec. 223(b)(3)).

Contributions from all sources are aggregated for purposes of the annual limit. The maximum annual contribution limit for an HSA is reduced by the aggregate amount that is contributed by the individual's employer and excluded from individual's income and the aggregate amount of any contributions to the individual's Archer medical savings account (MSA) under Code Sec. 220 (Code Sec. 223(b)(4)).

Annual cost-of-living adjustments are made to the high deductible health plan requirements and to the deductible contribution limitations. Any increase is rounded to the nearest multiple of $50. The adjustments are determined under Code Sec. 1(f)(3) for the calendar year in which the affected tax year begins. The Consumer Price Index for any calendar year is the average of the CPI as of the close of the 12 month period ending on August 31 of that calendar year (Code Secs. 223(g) and 1(f)(4)).

NEW LAW EXPLAINED

Annual plan deductible limit on health savings account contribution limitation repealed.—The Tax Relief and Health Care Act of 2006 (P.L. 109-432) modifies the limit on the annual deductible contributions that can be made to an HSA so that the maximum deductible contribution is not limited to the annual deductible under the high deductible health plan (HDHP) (Code Sec. 223(b), as amended by the 2006 Extenders Act). Thus, the maximum aggregate annual contribution that can be made to an HSA is

NEW LAW EXPLAINED

$2,250 for an individual with self-only coverage and $4,500 for an individual with family coverage. These amounts are adjusted annually for inflation.

> **Comment:** Because of the difference between the annual contribution limit and the definition of an HDHP, this provision can greatly increase the ability of an HSA to shelter income. For instance, a taxpayer with family coverage under an HDHP in 2007 can have a deductible as low as $2,200, but can make deductible HSA contributions of $5,650. This means that even if the taxpayer pays the full deductible during the year, an additional $3,450 escapes taxation in 2007 and remains in the HSA to grow tax-free. Eventual distributions of that extra $3,450, along with the income it earns, will also be tax-free as along as they are made for qualified medical expenses or after the taxpayer dies, becomes disabled, or reaches the age of 65.

Cost-of-living adjustments.—In the case of HSA-related inflation adjustments made for any tax year beginning after 2007, the Consumer Price Index for a calendar year is the average of the CPI as of the close of the 12 month period ending on March 31 of the calendar year (rather than August 31). The affected adjustments apply to dollar amounts for the high-deductible health plan requirements and the deductible contribution limits. The Secretary of Treasury must publish the adjusted amounts for a year no later than June 1 of the preceding calendar year (Code Sec. 223(g)(1), as amended by the 2006 Extenders Act).

▶ **Effective date.** The repeal of the annual deductible limitation on HSA contributions applies to tax years beginning after December 31, 2006 (Act Sec. 303(c) of the Tax Relief and Health Care Act of 2006 (P.L. 109-432)). With respect to the change in the computation of cost-of-living adjustments applicable to HSAs, no specific effective date is provided by the Act. The provision is, therefore, considered effective on December 20, 2006, the date of enactment.

Law source: Law at ¶5339. Committee Reports at ¶15,460.

— Act Sec. 303(a) of the Tax Relief and Health Care Act of 2006 (P.L. 109-432), amending Code Sec. 223(b)(2);

— Act Sec. 303(b), amending Code Sec. 223(d)(1)(A)(ii)(I);

— Act Sec. 304, amending Code Sec. 223(g)(1);

— Act Sec. 303(c), providing the effective date.

Reporter references: For further information, consult the following CCH reporters.

— Standard Federal Tax Reporter, ¶12,785.033

— Tax Research Consultant, INDIV: 42452.05 and COMPEN: 45,064.15

— Federal Tax Guide, ¶4152

¶510

¶515 Part-Year HDHP Coverage Does Not Reduce Annual Limitation on HSA Contributions

SUMMARY OF NEW LAW

The annual limit on HSA contributions is not reduced for taxpayers who are eligible individuals for less than the entire year.

BACKGROUND

An individual with a high deductible health plan (and certain other permitted coverage) is eligible to contribute to a health savings account (HSA) in order to receive tax-favored treatment for current medical expenses and for savings for future medical expenses. Eligible individuals must not be covered by any other health plan that is not a high-deductible health plan (HDHP) or by any health plan that provides coverage for any benefit that is covered under the high-deductible health plan. Exceptions include plans covering only accidents, disability, dental care, vision care, or long-term care, and certain liability insurance (Code Sec. 223(c)(1)). In addition, individuals who may be claimed as a dependent on another taxpayer's return and individuals who are entitled to Medicare benefits are not eligible individuals (Code Secs. 223(c)(6) and (c)(7)). Eligibility for an HSA is determined on a monthly basis.

The maximum annual deductible contribution that can be made to an individual's HSA is the lesser of (1) the annual deductible under the individual's high deductible plan or (2) $2,250 for an individual with self-only coverage and $4,500 for an individual with family coverage (Code Sec. 223(b)(2)). These amounts are adjusted annually for inflation in $50 increments (Code Sec. 223(g)). The annual contribution limits are increased for individuals who have attained age 55 by the end of the tax year (Code Sec. 223(b)(3)).

The annual contribution limit is the sum of the limits determined separately for each month, based on an individual's status and health plan coverage on the first day of the month (Code Sec. 223(b)(2)). Therefore, the limit is reduced if the individual is not covered by a high deductible health plan for the entire year.

NEW LAW EXPLAINED

Full annual HSA contribution limit applies to taxpayers who are eligible individuals during last month of the year.—For purposes of the annual limit on deductible contributions to a health savings account (HSA), a taxpayer who is an eligible individual during the last month of a tax year is treated as an eligible individual during every month of that tax year (Code Sec. 223(b)(8)(A)(i), as added by the Tax Relief and Health Care Act of 2006 (P.L. 109-432)). For the months in which the taxpayer is treated as an eligible individual, the taxpayer is also treated as having been enrolled in the same high deductible health plan (HDHP) in which the taxpayer is enrolled during the last month of the tax year (Code Sec. 223(b)(8)(A)(ii), as added by the 2006 Extenders Act).

NEW LAW EXPLAINED

Thus, the limitation on deductible contributions is not reduced if the taxpayer becomes an eligible individual after January of the tax year.

A recapture provision applies if the taxpayer obtains health insurance other than an HDHP and permitted coverage during the testing period and, thus, ceases to be an eligible individual. The taxpayer must include in gross income the amount of otherwise deductible contributions attributable to the months preceding the month in which the taxpayer was an eligible individual. An additional 10 percent tax applies to the amount of includible income (Code Sec. 223(b)(8)(B)(i), as added by the 2006 Extenders Act). An exception applies if the taxpayer ceases to be an eligible individual because of death or disability (Code Sec. 223(b)(8)(B)(ii), as added by the 2006 Extenders Act).

The testing period is the period beginning with the last month of the tax year for which the individual was an eligible individual and ending on the last day of the 12th month following that month (Code Sec. 223(b)(8)(B)(iii), as added by the 2006 Extenders Act). See ¶505 and ¶525 for similar rules for HSA contributions from health flexible spending accounts and individual retirement accounts.

> **Example:** Susan Smith enrolls in the HD high deductible health plan in December of 2007 and qualifies as an eligible individual in that month. Smith was not an eligible individual in any other month of 2007. She may make Health Savings Account contributions as if she had been enrolled in the HD plan for all of that year. If Smith stops coverage under the HD plan in June of 2008 and thus ceases to be an eligible individual, an amount equal to the HSA deduction attributable to treating her as an eligible individual from January 2007 through November 2007 is included in her income in 2008. A 10 percent additional tax also applies to the amount includible in income in 2008 (Joint Committee on Taxation, Technical Explanation of the Tax Relief and Health Care Act of 2006 (P.L. 109-432) (JCX-50-06)).

▶ **Effective date.** The provision applies to tax years beginning after December 31, 2006 (Act Sec. 305(b) of the Tax Relief and Health Care Act of 2006 (P.L. 109-432)).

Law source: Law at ¶5339. Committee Reports at ¶15,460.

— Act Sec. 305(a) of the Tax Relief and Health Care Act of 2006 (P.L. 109-432), adding Code Sec. 223(b)(8);

— Act Sec. 305(b), providing the effective date.

Reporter references: For further information, consult the following CCH reporters.

— Standard Federal Tax Reporter, ¶12,785.025 and ¶12,785.033

— Tax Research Consultant, INDIV: 42,452.05 and COMPEN: 45,064.15

— Federal Tax Guide, ¶4152

¶515

¶520 Comparable Contribution Rules for Employer Contributions to HSAs Modified

SUMMARY OF NEW LAW

Employers may make larger HSA contributions for nonhighly compensated employees than for highly compensated employees.

BACKGROUND

Employers are permitted to make contributions to the health savings accounts (HSAs) of their employees (Code Sec. 223). An employer is penalized if it fails to make comparable HSA contributions on behalf of all employees with comparable coverage during the same period (Code Sec. 4980G(a)). The comparability rules and requirements of Code Sec. 4980E, relating to Archer Medical Savings Accounts (MSAs), apply to HSAs (Code Sec. 4980G(b)). Generally, contributions are considered comparable if they are either of the same amount or the same percentage of the annual deductible limit under the high deductible health plan covering the employees. The comparability rule is applied separately to part-time employees (those customarily employed fewer than 30 hours a week) and to other employees. The comparability rule does not apply to amounts transferred from an employee's HSA, health flexible spending account (FSA), or Archer MSA or to contributions made through a cafeteria plan (Code Sec. 4980E(d)).

If employer contributions do not satisfy the comparability rule during a period, then the employer is subject to an excise tax equal to 35 percent of the aggregate amount contributed by the employer to HSAs of employees for that period (Code Sec. 4980E(b)). In the case of a failure to comply with the comparability rule due to reasonable cause and not willful neglect, the IRS may waive part or all of the tax imposed to the extent that the payment of the tax would be excessive relative to the failure involved (Code Sec. 4980E(c)). For purposes of the comparability rule, employers under common control are aggregated (Code Sec. 4980E(e)).

NEW LAW EXPLAINED

Exception to comparable contribution requirements for employer contributions to HSAs.—An exception to the comparable contribution requirements for health savings accounts (HSAs) allows employers to make larger HSA contributions for nonhighly compensated employees than for highly compensated employees (Code Sec. 4980G(d), as added by the Tax Relief and Health Care Act of 2006 (P.L. 109-432)). Highly compensated employees include any employee who was (1) a five-percent owner at any time during the year or the preceding year; or (2) for the preceding year, (a) had compensation from the employer in excess of $100,000 (for 2007, indexed for inflation) and (b) if elected by the employer, was in the group consisting of the top 20 percent of employees when ranked based on compensation (Code Sec. 414(q). Nonhighly compen-

NEW LAW EXPLAINED

sated employees are those employees not included in the definition of highly compensated employees.

The exception applies only to the treatment of nonhighly compensated employees versus highly compensated employees. Employers must continue to make available comparable contributions on behalf of all nonhighly compensated employees with comparable coverage during the same period. For example, an employer is permitted to make a $1,000 contribution to the HSA of each nonhighly compensated employee for a year without making contributions to the HSA of each highly compensated employee (Joint Committee on Taxation, Technical Explanation of the Tax Relief and Health Care Act of 2006 (P.L. 109-432) (JCX-50-06)).

▶ **Effective date.** The provision applies to tax years beginning after December 31, 2006 (Act Sec 306(b) of the Tax Relief and Health Care Act of 2006 (P.L. 109-432)).

Law source: Law at ¶5690. Committee Reports at ¶15,460.

— Act Sec. 306(a) of the Tax Relief and Health Care Act of 2006 (P.L. 109-432), adding Code Sec. 4980G(d);

— Act Sec. 306(b), providing the effective date.

Reporter references: For further information, consult the following CCH reporters.

— Standard Federal Tax Reporter, ¶34,619M.01

— Tax Research Consultant, INDIV: 42,456.05 and COMPEN: 45,064.15

— Federal Tax Guide, ¶4152

¶525 Qualified HSA Funding Distributions Allowed from IRAs

SUMMARY OF NEW LAW

A one-time transfer of funds can be made to an HSA from most IRAs.

BACKGROUND

HSAs. Health savings accounts (HSAs) are tax-advantaged savings and investment vehicles that allow taxpayers to use tax-free money to pay medical expenses. To be eligible for an HSA, an individual generally must have a high deductible health plan (HDHP), with no other coverage other than permitted insurance or permitted coverage. An individual's HDHP coverage is either self-only coverage or family coverage, which is anything other than self-only coverage (Code Sec. 223(c)).

HSA contributions up to an inflation-adjusted annual limit are deductible from the account holder's income. The amount of the limit is lower for individuals with self-only coverage, and higher for individuals with family coverage (Code Sec. 223(b)). For purposes of the limit, all contributions from all sources to all of the account

BACKGROUND

holder's HSAs are aggregated (Code Sec. 223(a)). Contributions generally must be made in cash, but noncash contributions can be rolled over from other HSAs and from Archer Medical Savings Accounts (Code Sec. 223(f)(5)). Excess contributions are not deductible, and they are subject to a six-percent excise tax (Code Secs. 223(f)(3) and 4973(a)(5)).

HSA distributions are fully excluded from gross income as long as they are used to pay qualified medical expenses, or they are made after the account holder dies, becomes disabled, or turns 65 (Code Sec. 223(f)).

IRAs. Individual retirement arrangements (also known as individual retirement accounts or IRAs) are tax-advantaged savings and investment vehicles that allow individuals to save for retirement (Code Sec. 408). In a traditional IRA, contributions are generally deductible and distributions are taxable to the extent they are attributable to accumulated earnings (Code Secs 219 and 408(d)). In a Roth IRA, contributions are taxable, but qualified distributions are generally tax-free (Code Sec. 409A(c) and (d)). A simplified employee pension (SEP) is an arrangement in which an employer makes contributions to traditional IRAs on behalf of its employees (Code Sec. 409(k)). A savings incentive match plan for employees (SIMPLE plan) is a simplified retirement plan for certain small employers. A SIMPLE can be an IRA for each employee (a SIMPLE IRA), or it can be part of a 401(k) arrangement (Code Sec. 408(p)). SEP and SIMPLE IRAs are subject to a number of special rules.

NEW LAW EXPLAINED

A qualified HSA funding distribution can roll over funds from most IRAs to an HSA.—A health savings account (HSA) can receive a one-time rollover distribution from the account holder's individual retirement arrangement (IRA). This qualified HSA funding distribution:

(1) must be contributed to the individual's HSA,

(2) must be contributed in a direct trustee-to-trustee transfer, and

(3) cannot be made from a SEP or a SIMPLE IRA (Code Sec. 408(d)(9)(B), as added by the Tax Relief and Health Care Act of 2006 (P.L. 109-432)).

Generally, an individual may elect only one lifetime qualified HSA funding distribution. However, if the distribution is made during a month when the individual has self-only coverage, and the individual later switches to family coverage during the same tax year, the individual can make an additional qualified HSA funding distribution (Code Sec. 408(d)(9)(C)(ii), as added by the 2006 Extenders Act).

The amount that can be distributed from the IRA and contributed to an HSA is limited to the otherwise maximum deductible contribution amount to the HSA, which depends on whether the individual has self-only coverage or family coverage (see ¶ 510). This annual limit also applies to any additional qualified additional HSA funding distributions that is allowed in the year the individual switches from self-only coverage to family coverage (Code Sec. 408(d)(9)(C), as added by the 2006 Extenders Act). The amount that can otherwise be contributed to the HSA for the year of the qualified HSA funding

NEW LAW EXPLAINED

distribution is reduced by the amount contributed from the IRA. The HSA account holder cannot deduct the amount of the qualified HSA funding distribution as a contribution to the HSA (Code Sec. 223(b)(4)(C), as added by the 2006 Extenders Act).

> **Comment:** This new rollover rule enables an individual who had made less than the permitted amount of HSA contributions to "top off" the HSA tax free.

Amounts distributed from an IRA that would otherwise be includible in gross income are excludible to the extent the distribution is a qualified HSA funding distribution. The distributions also are not subject to the 10-percent additional tax on early distributions (Code Sec. 408(d)(9)(A), as added by 2006 Extenders Act). In determining the extent to which amounts distributed from the IRA would otherwise be includible in income, the aggregate amount distributed from the IRA is treated as includible in income to the extent of the aggregate amount that would have been includible if all amounts were distributed from all IRAs of the same type. In other words, in the case of a traditional IRA, there is no pro-rata distribution of basis. As under present law, this rule is applied separately to Roth IRAs and other IRAs (Code Sec. 408(d)(9)(E), as added by 2006 Extenders Act).

> **Planning Note:** An individual with a choice between rolling over amounts from a traditional IRA or from a Roth IRA would be well advised to roll over from the traditional IRA. Roth IRA contributions are taxed, but traditional IRA contributions are not. Since qualified HSA distributions are also tax-free, amounts rolled over from a traditional IRA escape tax as fully as do direct contributions to an HSA.

An individual who elects a qualified HSA funding distribution must remain eligible for an HSA during the testing period. The testing period begins with the month of the contribution and ends on the last day of the 12th month following the month of the contribution. If the individual does not remain an eligible individual during the testing period, the amount of the IRA distribution and HSA contribution is includible in the individual's gross income for the tax year of the first day during the testing period that the individual is not an eligible individual. A 10-percent additional tax also applies to the amount includible. These rules do not apply if the individual ceases to be eligible for an HSA because of death or disability (Code Sec. 408(d)(9)(D), as added by the 2006 Extenders Act). See ¶505 and ¶520 for similar rules applicable to HSA contributions from FSAs and HRAs, and to the contribution limitation for part-year coverage.

▶ **Effective date.** The amendments are effective for tax years beginning after December 31, 2006 (Act Sec. 307(c) of the Tax Relief and Health Care Act of 2006 (P.L. 109-432)).

Law source: Law at ¶5339 and ¶5370. Committee Reports at ¶15,460.

— Act Sec. 307(a) of the Tax Relief and Health Care Act of 2006 (P.L. 109-432), adding Code Sec. 408(d)(9);

— Act Sec. 307(b), adding Code Sec. 223(b)(4)(C);

— Act Sec. 307(c), providing the effective date.

Reporter references: For further information, consult the following CCH reporters.

— Standard Federal Tax Reporter, ¶18,922.0326 and ¶18,922.033

¶525

NEW LAW EXPLAINED

— Tax Research Consultant, COMPEN: 45,064.40 and COMPEN: 45,212

— Federal Tax Guide, ¶4152 and ¶11,445

¶530 Archer Medical Savings Accounts

SUMMARY OF NEW LAW

Individuals may establish a new Archer medical savings account (MSA) through the 2007 calendar year unless the IRS indicates the numerical threshold is met earlier. Trustees of Archer MSAs have until March 20, 2007 to report the number of accounts established in calendar year 2005 and 2006, respectively.

BACKGROUND

Employees of small employers and self-employed individuals have the option to establish Archer medical savings accounts (MSAs) to pay for medical expenses, a concept similar to establishing an individual retirement account (IRA) for retirement purposes (Code Sec. 220). Participation in an Archer MSA is conditioned upon the individual being covered by an employer-sponsored high-deductible health plan (HDHP). However, an individual will not be eligible to participate if he or she is covered under any other health plan in addition to the HDHP.

For this purpose, an HDHP is a health insurance plan (not merely a reimbursement arrangement) with deductibles and out-of-pocket limitations that are indexed for inflation. For tax years beginning in 2007, the annual deductible for an HDHP for individual coverage must be at least $1,900 and not more than $2,850. For family coverage, the annual deductible of the HDHP must be at least $3,750 and not more than $5,650. The maximum out-of-pocket expenses for 2007 under the HDHP, including the deductible, must not be more than $3,750 for individuals and not more than $6,900 for family coverage.

Contributions and distributions. Contributions to an Archer MSA can be made either by the participant or the individual's employer. Contributions by a participant are deductible from gross income, and contributions made by the employer are excluded from the individual's gross income (unless if made through a cafeteria plan (Code Sec. 125)). Although employer contributions must be reported on the employee's W-2 for the tax year, they are not subject to income tax withholding or other employment taxes. All contributions to an Archer MSA account are subject to an annual limitation, which is a percentage of the deductible of the HDHP (65 percent for individual coverage and 75 percent for family coverage).

Amounts earned in an Archer MSA are not subject to current taxation. Distributions from the account, however, are included in gross income unless they are made for qualified medical expenses of the participant, his or her spouse, or dependents. Distributions may also be excluded from gross income if they are rolled over to

BACKGROUND

another Archer MSA or a health savings account (HSA), or are made incident to the participant's divorce. If an Archer MSA distribution is included in gross income, then an additional 15 percent tax will apply unless the distribution is made after the participant turns age 65, or the participant's death or disability.

Numerical limitations. Generally, new Archer MSAs may not be established after 2005. However, the prohibition against new accounts may be cut off earlier if the number of taxpayers who benefit from Archer MSAs exceeds 750,000 for a particular tax year. To determine if this threshold is met, each person who is a trustee of an Archer MSA must report to the IRS by August 1 of each calendar year the number of accounts established before July 1 of that year. The IRS must then announce by October 1 whether the threshold is met. After the cutoff date (i.e., December 31, 2005, or the date announced by the IRS if earlier), contributions may only be made to existing Archer MSAs. Special rules prevent year-end adoptions of Archer MSAs for purposes of avoiding the cutoff date.

NEW LAW EXPLAINED

Archer MSAs available in 2006 and 2007.—The availability of Archer MSAs has been extended by allowing taxpayers to establish new accounts through 2007 (unless the 750,000 threshold is met in an earlier tax year) (Code Sec. 220(i)(2) and (i)(3)(B), as amended by the Tax Relief and Health Care Act of 2006 (P.L. 109-432)). Trustees of Archer MSAs who were required to report to the IRS by August 1 of 2005 or 2006 on the number of accounts established in those respective calendar years will be considered to meet this requirement if they file the report by March 20, 2007 (Act Sec. 117(c)(1) of the 2006 Extenders Act). In addition, the IRS' determination and publication of whether the 750,000 threshold level was met for either the 2005 or 2006 calendar year will be treated as timely made if it is made by April 19, 2007 (Act Sec. 117(c)(2) of the 2006 Extenders Act). If the IRS determines that threshold level will be met for either the 2005 or 2006 calendar year, then the cut-off date for establishing a new Archer MSA for 2005 or 2006 will be April 19, 2007.

> **Planning Note:** There is little incentive for an individual to participate in a new Archer MSA given the more advantageous tax treatment of heath savings accounts (HSAs). HSAs are generally identical to Archer MSAs, except that an individual's participation does not have to be tied to his or her employment. In addition, the definition of a HDHP under an HSA is less restrictive. For example, the annual deductible under an HDHP for 2007 must be at least $1,100 for individual coverage and $2,200 for family coverage, there is no maximum deductible limit, and the maximum out-of-pocket expenses, including the deductible, must be more than $5,500 for individual coverage and $11,000 for family coverage. Like Archer MSAs, these figures are indexed annually for inflation.

> **Planning Note:** Unlike Archer MSAs, HSAs are permanent and not subject to any limitation on the number of new accounts that may be established during a calendar year or the year when they can be established. However, taxpayers in a number of States may be unable to take advantage of either Archer MSAs or

NEW LAW EXPLAINED

HSAs. This is because either State insurance law prohibits the selling of HDHPs or State tax law undermines the federal tax advantages of such accounts.

▶ **Effective date.** No specific effective date is provided by the Act. The provisions is, therefore, considered effective on December 20, 2006, the date of enactment.

Law source: Law at ¶5333. Committee Report at ¶15,260.

— Act Sec. 117(a) and (b) of the Tax Relief and Health Care Act of 2006 (P.L. 109-432), amending Code Sec. 220(i) and (j);

— Act Sec. 117(c).

Reporter references: For further information, consult the following CCH reporters.

— Standard Federal Tax Reporter, ¶12,675.01 and ¶12,675.05

— Tax Research Consultant, INDIV: 42,454 and RETIRE: 66,452

— Federal Tax Guide, ¶4153

¶535 Parity in Application of Certain Limits to Mental Health Benefits

SUMMARY OF NEW LAW

The mental health parity requirements under the Code, ERISA and the Public Health Service Act are extended through December 31, 2007.

BACKGROUND

Under the Code Sec. 9812 mental health parity requirements, group health plans that provide both medical and surgical benefits and mental health benefits cannot impose aggregate lifetime or annual dollar limits on mental health benefits if such limits are not imposed on substantially all medical and surgical benefits (Code Sec. 9812(a)).

The mental health parity requirements do not affect the terms and conditions relating to the amount, duration, or scope of mental health benefits under the plan, except as specifically provided with respect to parity in the imposition of aggregate lifetime limits and annual limits. Nor do they require group health plans to provide mental health benefits (Code Sec. 9812(b)). Small employers, as defined in Code Sec. 4980D(d), are exempt from the mental health parity requirements. The parity provisions also do not apply if their application would result in an increase of at least one percent in the cost under the plan (Code Sec. 9812(c)).

Employers whose group health plans fail to comply with the mental health parity rules are subject to the Code Sec. 4980D excise tax. The excise tax is equal to $100 per day per individual during the period of noncompliance (Code Sec. 4980D(b)(1)). The maximum tax that can be imposed during a tax year cannot exceed the lesser of 10 percent of the employer's group health plan expenses for the prior year or $500,000

BACKGROUND

(Code Sec. 4980D(c)(3)). No excise tax is imposed if the IRS determines that the person otherwise liable for the tax did not know and could not have reasonably known that such noncompliance existed (Code Sec. 4980D(c)(1)).

The Employee Retirement Income Security Act of 1974 (ERISA) and the Public Health Service Act (PHSA) impose similar mental health parity requirements (Act Sec. 712 of ERISA; Act Sec. 2705 of PHSA). The Code, ERISA and PHSA mental health parity requirements are all scheduled to expire with respect to benefits for services furnished after December 31, 2006 (Code Sec. 9812(f); Act Sec. 712(f) of ERISA; Act Sec. 2705(f) of PHSA).

NEW LAW EXPLAINED

Mental health parity requirements extended.—The mental health parity requirements under the Code are extended through December 31, 2007 (Code Sec. 9812(f)(3), as amended by the Tax Relief and Health Care Act of 2006 (P.L. 109-432)). The corresponding ERISA and PHSA mental health parity provisions are also extended through December 31, 2007 (Act Sec. 712(f) of ERISA and Act Sec. 2705(f) of PHSA, as amended by the 2006 Extenders Act).

▶ **Effective date.** No specific effective date is provided by the Act. The provision is, therefore, considered effective on December 20, 2006, the date of enactment.

Law source: Law at ¶5920 and ¶7040. Committee Report at ¶15,240.

— Act Sec. 115(a) of the Tax Relief and Health Care Act of 2006 (P.L. 109-432), amending Code Sec. 9812(f)(3);

— Act Sec. 115(b), amending Act Sec. 712(f) of the Employee Retirement Income Security Act of 1974;

— Act Sec. 115(c), amending Act Sec. 2705(f) of the Public Health Service Act.

Reporter references: For further information, consult the following CCH reporters.

— Standard Federal Tax Reporter, ¶44,088.01

— Tax Research Consultant, INDIV: 42,514

— Federal Tax Guide, ¶21,475

Tax Relief—Bonds, Administration, and Excise Taxes

6

¶685   Addition of meningococcal and human papillomavirus vaccines to list of taxable vaccines

¶690   Cover over of tax on rum

CROSS REFERENCE

Tax Incentive for sale of existing mineral and geothermal rights (*see ¶358*)

BONDS

¶605 Qualified Zone Academy Bond Program Extended

SUMMARY OF NEW LAW

The qualified zone academy bond program is extended for two years through 2007. Spending, arbitration and reporting requirements are added.

BACKGROUND

Traditionally, states and local school districts issue bonds to fund school renovation and expansion projects. Under Code Sec. 103(a), the interest earned on these bonds is exempt from federal taxes. The tax-exempt nature of these bonds makes them attractive to many investors, and, therefore, the issuing authorities can sell them with a lower interest rate than the rate applicable to standard corporate bonds.

The Taxpayer Relief Act of 1997 (P.L. 105-34) created a new financial tool known as a qualified zone academy bond (QZAB) that can be used by state education agencies to encourage the formation of partnerships between public schools and local businesses. QZAB issuers do not pay tax-exempt interest to the bond holders. Instead, bond holders receive a federal income tax credit and must report income in the amount of the credit (Code Sec. 1397E(a) and (g)). The school district or other issuer is then only responsible for repaying the amount borrowed. Bonds of this sort are known generally as tax credit bonds. Since 1997, tax credit bonds have also been authorized to provide temporary financial assistance to Louisiana, Mississippi and Alabama after 2005's major hurricanes (Gulf tax credit bonds under Code Sec. 1400N(l)) and to subsidize clean electricity generation by public and nonprofit electric companies (clean renewable energy bonds, or CREBs, under Code Sec. 54).

Although tax credit bonds are not tax-exempt bonds, some of the requirements that apply to tax-exempt bonds have been imposed on tax credit bonds. In particular, both Gulf tax credit bonds and CREBs are subject to arbitrage and reporting requirements. QZABs are not subject to those requirements.

QZABs are bonds issued by a state or local government where at least 95 percent of the funds raised are to be used for a "qualified purpose" at certain public schools

BACKGROUND

(qualified zone academies), which provide education or training below the college level. Qualified purposes include:

- rehabilitating or repairing the facility;
- providing equipment for use at the academy;
- developing course materials for use at the academy; or
- training teachers and others at the academy.

Qualified zone academies must be located in empowerment zones or enterprise communities, or there must be a reasonable expectation that at least 35 percent of the students will be eligible for free or reduced-cost lunches under the National School Lunch Act. In addition, the local educational agency that establishes the academy must get commitments from private businesses to contribute equipment, technical assistance or training, employees' services, or other property or services with a value equal to at least 10 percent of the present value of the bond proceeds (Code Sec. 1397E(d)).

Banks, insurance companies, and certain corporate lenders may hold QZABs (Code Sec. 1397E(d)(6)). The credit is allowed to eligible taxpayers holding a QZAB on the credit allowance date (the anniversary of the issuance of the bond) for each year in which the bond is held (Code Sec. 1397E(f)(1)). The credit may be claimed against regular income tax and alternative minimum tax (AMT) liability. However, the amount of the credit is includible in a bond holder's income as if it were an interest payment on the bond (Code Sec. 1397E(g); Reg. § 1.1397E-1(a)).

The amount of the credit is equal to the daily credit rate determined by the Treasury Department on the first day there is a binding contract for the sale or exchange of the bond, multiplied by the face amount of the bond (Code Sec. 1397E(b); Reg. § 1.1397E-1(b)). The credit rate for QZABs is published daily by the Bureau of Public Debt on its Internet site for State and Local Government Bonds (https://www.publicdebt.treas.gov/SZ/SPESQZABRate). (For example, the QZAB rate on December 14, 2006 for a 16-year bond was 5.58%.).

Up to $400 million in QZABs may be issued nationally in each calendar year beginning in 1998 and ending in 2005 (Code Sec. 1397E(e)(1)). The annual $400 million amount is allocated to the states based on their population below the poverty level (Code Sec. 1397E(e)(2)). Each state's educational agency is responsible for apportionment of the allocation within its boundaries. A state is permitted a two-year carryforward of unused annual QZAB allocations.

This provision, originally due to expire in 2001, was extended to calendar years 2002 and 2003 by the Job Creation and Worker Assistance Act of 2002 (P.L. 107-147), and later extended to 2004 and 2005 by the Working Families Tax Relief Act of 2004 (P.L. 108-311).

NEW LAW EXPLAINED

Extension and amendment of qualified zone academy bond program.—The qualified zone academy bond (QZAB) program is extended for two years. Thus, up to $400

NEW LAW EXPLAINED

million in QZABs may be issued nationally for calendar years 2006 and 2007. Additionally, new spending, arbitrage and reporting requirements are instituted for QZABs.

> **Comment:** The arbitrage and reporting requirements are identical to those that currently apply to CREBs and Gulf tax credit bonds (Code Secs. 54 and 1400N(l)). The spending requirements are nearly identical to the CREBs spending requirements. The IRS may issue guidance on these new requirements, as it did in the case of CREBs and Gulf tax credit bonds (see Notice 2005-98, 2005-2 CB 1211 and Notice 2006-41, I.R.B. 2006-18, 857).

Spending requirements. In order for a bond to be a QZAB, the issuer must reasonably have the following expectations regarding the spending of the bond proceeds as of the date of issuance:

- at least 95 percent of the proceeds from the issue will be spent for one or more qualified QZAB purposes within the 5-year period beginning on the date the QZAB is issued;

- a binding commitment with a third party to spend at least 10 percent of the proceeds from the issue will be entered into within six months of the date the QZAB is issued; and

- the QZAB purposes will be completed with due diligence, and the proceeds from the sale of the issue will be spent with due diligence (Code Sec. 1397E(f)(1), as added by the Tax Relief and Health Care Act of 2006 (P.L. 109-432)).

Prior to expiration of the 5-year period for spending the QZAB proceeds for qualified purposes, the issuer may request an extension of this time period. The IRS may grant the extension if the failure to satisfy the 5-year requirement is due to reasonable cause, and the issuer will continue to exercise due diligence in pursuing QZAB purposes (Code Sec. 1397E(f)(2), as added by the 2006 Extenders Act).

To the extent that the issuer fails to meet the 95 percent spending requirement by the end of the 5-year period (or at the end of the extension period, if an extension was granted), the bonds will still qualify as QZABs if all unspent proceeds are used within 90 days from the end of the 5-year period (or the extension period) to redeem any "nonqualified" bonds. The amount of the nonqualified bonds required to be redeemed is to be determined as it is for the redemption of exempt facility bonds under Code Sec. 142) (Code Sec. 1397E(f)(3), as added by the 2006 Extenders Act; Joint Committee on Taxation, Technical Explanation of the Tax Relief and Health Care Act of 2006 (P.L. 109-432) (JCX-50-06)).

Arbitrage rules. A bond is not a QZAB unless the issuer meets the arbitrage requirements of Code Sec. 148 with respect to the issue (Code Sec. 1397E(g), as added by the 2006 Extenders Act). Generally, these requirements are satisfied if the proceeds of the issue are not reasonably expected to be used to acquire higher yielding investments or replace funds that are used to acquire higher yielding investments. A bond will not be treated as an arbitrage bond if a special rebate is paid to the United States. According to the Joint Committee on Taxation, the Code Sec. 148 rules and regulations apply for purposes of determining the yield restriction and the arbitrage rebate for QZABs. For arbitrage purposes, the yield on an issue is computed by taking into account all payments of interest on the bond, regardless of whether the bonds are

NEW LAW EXPLAINED

issued at par, premium or discount. The credit, while included in income to the bond holder, is not treated as interest (Joint Committee on Taxation, Technical Explanation of the Tax Relief and Health Care Act of 2006 (P.L. 109-432) (JCX-50-06).

Reporting required. Issuers of QZABs are required to submit reports to the IRS that are similar to those required of tax-exempt bond issuers under Code Sec. 149(e) (Code Sec. 1397E(h)). That provision requires issuers to file a statement identifying the issuer and listing details of the issue not later than the 15th day of the second month after the end of the calendar quarter in which the bond is issued.

> **Compliance Pointer:** Tax-exempt entities must use Form 8038, Information Return for Tax-Exempt Private Activity Bond Issue, for information reporting. The IRS will likely issue guidance on the reporting requirement.

▶ **Effective date.** The provision extending the authority to issue QZABs applies to obligations issued after December 31, 2005 (Act Sec. 107(c)(1) of the Tax Relief and Health Care Act of 2006 (P.L. 109-432)). The spending, arbitrage and reporting requirements apply to obligations issued after December 20, 2006, the date of enactment, pursuant to allocations of the national zone academy bond limitation for calendar years after 2005 (Act Sec. 107(c)(2) of the 2006 Extenders Act).

Law source: Law at ¶5055, ¶5608 and ¶5626. Committee Report at ¶15,160.

— Act Sec. 107(a) of the Tax Relief and Health Care Act of 2006 (P.L. 109-432), amending Code Sec. 1397E(e)(1);

— Act Sec. 107(b)(1)(A), adding Code Sec. 1397E(d)(1)(E);

— Act Sec. 107(b)(1)(B), redesignating Code Sec. 1397E(f), (g), (h), and (i), as (i), (j), (k), and (l), respectively, and adding new Code Sec. 1397E(f), (g) and (h);

— Act Sec. 107(b)(2), amending Code Secs. 54(l)(3)(B) and 1400N(l)(7)(B)(ii);

— Act Sec. 107(c), providing the effective date.

Reporter references: For further information, consult the following CCH reporters.

— Standard Federal Tax Reporter, ¶32,407.01 and ¶32,407.04

— Tax Research Consultant, BUSEXP: 57,150

— Federal Tax Guide, ¶8501

¶610 Veterans Need Not Be First-Time Homebuyers to Receive Subsidized Mortgages Funded by Qualified Mortgage Bonds

SUMMARY OF NEW LAW

The first-time homebuyer requirement is eliminated for veterans obtaining mortgage loans financed by certain qualified mortgage bonds.

BACKGROUND

State and local government entities are authorized to issue tax-exempt bonds and use the proceeds to fund home mortgage loans to qualified borrowers. Mortgage lending programs funded by qualified mortgage bonds help support home ownership for middle and lower income individuals. Programs supported by qualified veterans' mortgage bonds are aimed exclusively at veterans. Bonds are qualified mortgage bonds paying tax-exempt interest if certain requirements relating to the bonds and the funded loans are met (Code Sec. 143). Requirements with regard to the funded loans include income limitations for borrowers, as well as limitations on the location and purchase price of the home. In addition, loans funded by qualified mortgage bonds generally cannot be made to any borrower who had an ownership interest in a principal residence in the three years preceding the execution of the mortgage (the "first-time homebuyer" requirement) (Code Sec. 143(d)).

NEW LAW EXPLAINED

First-time homebuyer restriction temporarily eliminated for veterans.—Veterans who served in the active military and did not receive a dishonorable discharge may, one time only, receive a loan financed by qualified mortgage bonds even if they don't satisfy the first-time homebuyer requirement. This suspension of the first-time homebuyer requirement applies for bonds issued after December 20, 2006 and before January 1, 2008 (Code Sec. 143(d)(2)(D), as added by the Tax Relief and Health Care Act of 2006 (P.L. 109-432)).

> **Comment:** The suspension of the first-time homebuyer rule applies to ultimate borrowers who are military veterans, but it is not restricted to loans financed by bonds issued under qualified veterans' mortgage bond programs. Any state and local mortgage lending program funded by qualified mortgage bonds may change its rules or procedures to allow loans to veterans who were ineligible under the prior law because they failed to satisfy the first-time homebuyer requirement. For 2006 changes to the rules governing qualified veterans' mortgage bond programs in particular, see ¶620.

▶ **Effective date.** The provision applies to bonds issued after December 20, 2006, the date of enactment (Act Sec. 416(b) of the Tax Relief and Health Care Act of 2006 (P.L. 109-432)).

Law source: Law at ¶5130. Committee Reports at ¶15,610.

— Act Sec. 416(a) of the Tax Relief and Health Care Act of 2006 (P.L. 109-432), adding Code Sec. 143(d)(2)(D);

— Act Sec. 416(b), providing the effective date.

Reporter references: For further information, consult the following CCH reporters.

— Standard Federal Tax Reporter, ¶7786.04

— Tax Research Consultant, SALES: 51,350

— Federal Tax Guide, ¶4787 and ¶4790

¶610

¶615 Exception from Arbitrage Restrictions for Certain Texas University Bonds Made Permanent

SUMMARY OF NEW LAW

The exception from the arbitrage requirements for bonds secured by the Texas Permanent University Fund is extended to all such bonds issued after May 17, 2006.

BACKGROUND

The arbitrage restrictions on municipal bonds generally provide that interest on such a bond is not exempt from federal income tax if the bond proceeds are invested in materially higher earning investments or if the debt service on the bonds is secured by or paid (directly or indirectly) from such investments.

An exception to the arbitrage restrictions, enacted in 1984, provides that the pledging of investment earnings from the Texas Permanent University Fund as security for certain bonds issued by the University of Texas and Texas A&M Systems will not result in those bonds losing their exempt status (Act Sec. 648 of the Deficit Reduction Act of 1984 (P.L. 98-369)). The exception only applies to an amount of tax-exempt bonds that does not exceed 20 percent of the value of the Fund. The Texas state constitution provision governing the Fund was amended in 1999 to allow the payment of bond interest from the Fund's corpus if the investment earnings were insufficient. As a result of this change, the Fund no longer satisfies the requirements of the federal statutory exception. The IRS has agreed to continue to apply the 1984 exception for the Fund's benefit, pending introduction of corrective legislation (Conference Committee Report (H.R. Conf. Rep. No. 109-455)).

The House Ways and Means Committee stated that "the Committee does not believe that the Fund should lose the benefits of the 1984 exception from the tax-exempt bond arbitrage restrictions by adopting a more modern approach to the management of Fund distributions" (House Committee Report (H.R. Rep. No. 109-304)).

NEW LAW EXPLAINED

Exception from arbitrage restrictions for bonds secured by Texas Permanent University Fund made permanent.—The special exception to the arbitrage restrictions for bonds secured by the Texas Permanent University Fund has been made permanent (Act Sec. 414(a) of the Tax Relief and Health Care Act of 2006 (P.L. 109-432); Act Sec. 206 of the Tax Increase Prevention and Reconciliation Act of 2005 (P.L. 109-222)).

> **Comment:** The Tax Increase Prevention and Reconciliation Act of 2005 (P.L. 109-222) amended the language of the Deficit Reduction Act of 1984 (P.L. 98-369) to reflect the change to the Texas constitution and extended the special exception to the arbitrage restrictions so that it applied to bonds issued after May 17, 2006

NEW LAW EXPLAINED

and before August 31, 2009. The 2006 Extenders Act eliminates the 2009 termination provision.

▶ **Effective date.** The provision is effective on May 17, 2006, the date of enactment of the Tax Increase Prevention and Reconciliation Act of 2005 (P.L. 109-222) (Act Sec. 206 of the Tax Increase Prevention and Reconciliation Act of 2006 and Act Sec. 414(b) of the Tax Relief and Health Care Act of 2006 (P.L. 109-432)).

Law source: Law at ¶7075. Committee Reports at ¶15,590.

— Act Sec. 206 of the Tax Increase Prevention and Reconciliation Act of 2005 (P.L. 109-222);

— Act Sec. 414(a) of the Tax Relief and Health Care Act of 2006 (P.L. 109-432), amending Act Sec. 206 of the Tax Increase Prevention and Reconciliation Act of 2005 (P.L. 109-222);

— Act Sec. 414(b), providing the effective date.

Reporter references: For further information, consult the following CCH reporters.

— Standard Federal Tax Reporter, ¶7889.021

— Tax Research Consultant, SALES: 51,500

— Federal Tax Guide, ¶4075

¶620 Authorization for Qualified Veterans' Mortgage Bonds Expanded in Some States

SUMMARY OF NEW LAW

Alaska, Oregon and Wisconsin may expand eligibility for participation in their qualified veterans' mortgage programs. Also, the existing annual limit on the amount of tax-exempt bonds which can be issued to fund the programs in those states is reset beginning with calendar year 2006.

BACKGROUND

Qualified veterans' mortgage bonds are private activity bonds the proceeds of which are used to fund state programs that make mortgage loans to certain veterans (Code Sec. 143(b)). In the early 1980s, Congress became concerned that state qualified veterans' mortgage programs were expanding too quickly, and costing the federal government too much in revenue losses (Joint Committee on Taxation, General Explanation of the Revenue Provisions of the Deficit Reduction Act of 1984, JCS-41-84 (December 31, 1984)). The Deficit Reduction Act of 1984 (P.L. 98-369) restricted the availability of veterans' mortgage bonds to states which already had issued them, imposed volume limitations, and restricted the cohort of veterans eligible for the assistance. As a result, only five states—California, Texas, Wisconsin, Oregon, and Alaska—retain the authority to operate programs issuing qualified veterans' mortgage bonds.

BACKGROUND

The amount of the bonds that participating states can issue each year to fund qualified veterans' bond programs is limited on a state-by-state basis under a limit separate from that imposed on other private activity bonds. The state veterans limit for each state was generally based on the average amount of the bonds it issued annually between 1979 and 1985. Eligible veterans were a small and shrinking group; only those who served on active duty at some time before 1977 and who applied for the financing before the date 30 years after the date the veteran last left active service could borrow under the state programs. Mortgage loans under the programs could be made only to first-time homebuyers for the purchase of their principal residences and could not be used to refinance existing mortgages.

Some of the states authorized to issue veterans mortgage bonds lobbied for amendments to the law to allow loans to more recent veterans and increase the total amounts available for lending under the programs.

NEW LAW EXPLAINED

Expansion of qualified veterans' mortgage bond authorization for Alaska, Oregon and Wisconsin.—The definition of qualified veteran is expanded for purposes of qualified veterans' mortgage programs, but only for Alaska, Oregon, and Wisconsin. In those three states, subsidized mortgage loans may now be offered to all veterans of active duty, as long as the financing is applied for before the date 25 years after the veteran last left active service (Code Sec. 143(l)(4), as amended by the Tax Increase Prevention and Reconciliation Act of 2005 (P.L. 109-222)). This change is effective with respect to bonds issued on or after May 17, 2006 (Act Sec. 203(a)(2) of the Tax Reconciliation Act of 2005).

> **Comment:** As a result of the reduction of the window from 30 years after service to 25 years after service, only individuals who left active duty after May 17, 1981, are able to benefit from the new provision.

> **Planning Note:** Interested veterans in the affected states (particularly those nearing the end of their 25 year eligibility period) should contact their respective state administrative agencies: the Alaska Housing Finance Corporation (http://www.ahfc.state.ak.us/loans/veterans.cfm), the Oregon Department of Veterans' Affairs (http://www.oregon.gov/ODVA/loans.shtml), or the Wisconsin Department of Veterans Affairs (http://dva.state.wi.us/Ben_mortgageloans.asp).

The annual limits on the amount of qualified veterans' mortgage bonds that Alaska, Oregon and Wisconsin may issue (the state veterans limits) are also reset (Code Sec. 143(l)(3)(B), as amended by the Tax Reconciliation Act of 2005 and the Tax Relief and Health Care Act of 2006 (P.L. 109-432)). The limits will increase beginning with calendar year 2006 until they reach $25,000,000 in calendar year 2010 and thereafter. The specific dollar amounts for each year are shown in the table below:

¶620

NEW LAW EXPLAINED

State Veterans Limits for Alaska, Oregon and Wisconsin
(Code Sec. 143(l)(3)(B), as amended by the
Tax Reconciliation Act of 2005 and the 2006 Extenders Act)

2006	$ 5,000,000
2007	10,000,000
2008	15,000,000
2009	20,000,000
2010 and thereafter	25,000,000

If a state does not use its full issuing authority in one year, the unused amount is lost. It does not carry over to future years (Conference Committee Report (H.R. Conf. Rep. No. 109-455)).

Qualified veterans' mortgage loan programs offered by California and Texas continue to be subject to the existing law (Code Sec. 143(l)(3)(B), as amended by the Tax Reconciliation Act of 2005 and the 2006 Extenders Act and Code Sec. 143(l)(4)(B), as amended by the Tax Reconciliation Act of 2005).

> **Comment:** Under the Tax Reconciliation Act of 2005 the bond limits for Alaska, Oregon and Wisconsin were to be reduced to zero for 2011 and thereafter. However, the 2006 Extenders Act eliminates the termination.

> **Comment:** A separate provision of the 2006 Extenders Act temporarily eliminates the first-time homebuyer requirement for veterans whether they are borrowing from a generally available qualified mortgage loan program or from a qualified veterans mortgage loan program. See ¶610.

▶ **Effective date.** The provision applies to allocations of State volume limit after April 5, 2006 (Act Sec. 411(b) of the Tax Relief and Health Care Act of 2006 (P.L. 109-432); Act Sec. 203(b)(2) of the Tax Increase Prevention and Reconciliation Act of 2005 (P.L. 109-222)).

Law source: Law at ¶5130. Committee Reports at ¶10,050 and ¶15,560.

— Act Sec. 203(a)(1) of the Tax Increase Prevention and Reconciliation Act of 2005 (P.L. 109-222), amending Code Sec. 143(l)(4);

— Act Sec. 203(b)(1), amending Code Sec. 143(l)(3)(B);

— Act Sec. 203(a)(2) and (b)(2), providing the effective dates;

— Act Sec. 411(a) of the Tax Relief and Health Care Act of 2006 (P.L. 109-432), amending Code Sec. 143(l)(3)(B);

— Act Sec. 411(b), providing the effective date.

Reporter references: For further information, consult the following CCH reporters.

— Standard Federal Tax Reporter, ¶7786.04

— Tax Research Consultant, SALES: 51,372.15

— Federal Tax Guide, ¶4790

¶620

¶625 Tax Credit Bonds to Subsidize Non-Profits' Production of Renewable Energy Electricity

SUMMARY OF NEW LAW

The clean renewable energy bonds (CREBs) program is extended one year. An additional $400 million of CREBs may be issued through December 31, 2008. The maximum amount of CREBs that may be allocated to qualified projects of governmental bodies is increased by $250 million.

BACKGROUND

The Energy Tax Incentives Act of 2005 (P.L. 109-58) authorized the issuance of up to $800 million of tax credit bonds, known as clean renewable energy bonds (CREBs), during 2006 and 2007 to finance capital expenditures by tax-exempt electricity producers to increase their capacity to produce electricity from clean renewable sources (Code Sec. 54). The bonds may be issued by governmental bodies, cooperative electricity companies, or cooperative lenders owned by cooperative electricity companies. These bonds provide a federal subsidy to allow nonprofit electricity providers, including cooperatives and government-owned utilities, to compete more evenly with for-profit companies that can take advantage of the existing tax credit under Code Sec. 45. The $800 million national limit was required to be allocated among qualified projects at the discretion of the IRS, except that not more than $500 million was allowed to be allocated to government projects (Code Sec. 54(f)).

Unlike tax-exempt bonds, CREBs are not interest-bearing obligations. Instead, a taxpayer holding a CREB on one or more allowance dates during a tax year is allowed a credit equivalent to the interest that the bond would otherwise pay (Code Sec. 54(a)). The credit accrues quarterly and is generally equal to 25 percent of the annual credit for the bond, though a pro rata reduction applies for the quarters in which the bond is issued, redeemed or matures. The annual credit is equal to the face amount of the bond multiplied by a credit rate determined by the IRS. The credit rate is the rate that the IRS estimates will allow the issuance of bonds with a specified maturity without discount and without interest cost to the issuer (Code Sec. 54(b)). Credit rates are issued daily and reported at https://www.publicdebt.treas.gov/SZ/ SPESRates?type=CREBS. The amount of the credit allowed to the taxpayer must be included in gross income and treated as interest income (Code Sec. 54(g)).

The credit is available with respect to bonds issued after December 31, 2005, and before January 1, 2008.

> **Comment:** The IRS announced that 610 projects for state and local governmental borrowers and for electrical cooperative borrowers would receive volume cap allocations of the initial authority to issue CREBs. Overall, the IRS received applications from 40 different states totaling approximately $2.6 billion in CREBs requests. Out of the 700-plus applications received by the April 26, 2006 deadline, 610 government and electrical cooperative projects—which ranged in scale from $23,000 to $80 million—were chosen to receive the tax credit bond financ-

ing. The $800 million maximum amount of CREBs authorized for the time period between January 1, 2006 and December 31, 2007, have been allocated.

Planning Note: In IRS Notice 2005-98, the IRS provided guidance on the CREBs volume cap application process and indicated that CREBs volume cap allocations would be made based on a "smallest-to-largest" project amount methodology, beginning with the project requesting the smallest dollar amount and proceeding to projects for successively larger dollar amounts until the entire national volume cap is consumed. In IRS Notice 2006-7, the IRS described four provisions that it anticipated would be included in temporary and proposed regulations that will provide guidance to holders and issuers of CREBs, including guidance on what constitutes a qualified project and the rules under which a state or political subdivision may issue CREBs.

Potentially qualified types of projects include wind facilities, closed loop biomass facilities, open loop biomass facilities, geothermal or solar facilities, small irrigation power facilities, landfill gas facilities, trash combustion facilities, refined coal production facilities and certain hydropower facilities.

NEW LAW EXPLAINED

Extension of CREBs program and increase in amount that can be issued.—An additional $400 million of CREBs may be issued, raising the national limitation on the amount of bonds to $1.2 billion (Code Sec. 54(f)(1), as amended by the Tax Relief and Health Care Act of 2006 (P.L. 109-432)). The amount of CREBs that the IRS can allocate to finance qualified projects by qualified governmental bodies is increased by $250 million, raising that limitation to $750 million (Code Sec. 54(f)(2), as amended by the 2006 Extenders Act). The authority to issue CREBs is extended through December 31, 2008 (Code Sec. 54(m), as amended by the 2006 Extenders Act).

▶ **Effective date.** The provisions increasing the total amount of CREBs that may be issued by $400 million and extending the authority to issue such bonds through December 31, 2008, apply to bonds issued after December 31, 2006 (Act Sec. 202(b)(1) of the Tax Relief and Health Care Act of 2006 (P.L. 109-432)). The provision to increase the amount of CREBs that may be allocated to qualified projects of governmental bodies by $250 million is effective for allocations or reallocations after December 31, 2006 (Act Sec. 202(b)(2) of the 2006 Extenders Act).

Law source: Law at ¶5055. Committee Report at ¶15,360.

— Act Sec. 202(a)(1) of the Tax Relief and Health Care Act of 2006 (P.L. 109-432), amending Code Sec. 54(f)(1);

— Act Sec. 202(a)(2), amending Code Sec. 54(f)(2);

— Act Sec. 202(a)(3), amending Code Sec. 54(m);

— Act Sec. 202(b), providing the effective date.

Reporter references: For further information, consult the following CCH reporters.

— Standard Federal Tax Reporter, ¶4880.03

— Tax Research Consultant, BUSEXP: 54,558

— Federal Tax Guide, ¶2612

¶625

RETURNS

¶630 Corporations Must File Information Returns Regarding Certain Stock Options

SUMMARY OF NEW LAW

Corporate employers must file an information return with the IRS with regard to the transfer of stock to an employee if the transfer is made in connection with the exercise of an option obtained by the employee through an employee stock purchase plan or through an incentive stock option program.

BACKGROUND

Corporate employers must provide payee information to an employee to whom the corporation transfers stock under certain conditions if the transfer is made in connection with the exercise of an option obtained by the employee through an employee stock purchase plan (ESPP) or through an incentive stock option (ISO) program.

Under an ESPP, employers may grant employees a right to purchase stock at a discount. Employees are not taxed on the option's receipt or exercise. If an employee satisfies holding period requirements, disposition of the stock results in capital gain or loss rather than ordinary income. To qualify for this treatment, the option price must be at least 85 percent of the fair market value of the stock when the option is granted or exercised. In the event the option price is between 85 percent and 100 percent of the value of the stock at the time the option was granted, a portion of the price received upon disposition is treated as ordinary income by the employee (Code Sec. 423(c)).

An ISO is an employee stock option granted to a key employee that gives the employee the right to purchase stock of the employer without realizing income either when the option is granted or when the employee exercises it. Assuming ISO requirements are met, the employee is first taxed upon disposition of the option stock, and any resulting gain is taxed as a capital gain rather than ordinary income. Even if all the ISO requirements are met, however, a transfer of stock through exercise of an ISO may subject to the employee to current taxation under the alternative minimum tax.

Corporate employers must provide payee information to any employee to whom the corporation transfers stock during a calendar year if the transfer was made (1) in connection with the exercise of an incentive stock option, or (2) under an employee stock purchase plan where the option price is between 85 and 100 percent of the value of the stock. The information must be provided by January 31 of the following calendar year (Code Sec. 6039(a)). Failure to correctly provide such statements may subject the corporation to a penalty (Code Secs. 6722 and 6723(d)(2)(B)).

¶630

Corporate employers must file information returns with the IRS.—The new law requires corporate employers to file information returns with the IRS regarding transfers of stock to employees within any calendar year if the transfer is (1) made in connection with the exercise of an incentive stock option, or (2) made under an employee stock purchase plan where the option price is between 85 and 100 percent of the value of the stock (Code Sec. 6039(a), as amended by the Tax Relief and Health Care Act of 2006 (P.L. 109-432)). Failure to correctly file this information return may subject the corporation to penalties that normally apply to failures to correctly file information returns (Code Sec. 6724(d)(1)(B), as amended by the 2006 Extenders Act).

Comment: The IRS is given the task of filling in the details through regulations.

As under the old law, the corporation must continue to provide payee information to its employees regarding these stock transfers. The new law provides that the corporation must furnish each person it names in its information return with a written payee statement by January 31 of the following calendar year setting forth the information that the IRS may require (Code Sec. 6039(b), as added by the 2006 Extenders Act). As under the old law, failure to correctly provide this information may subject the corporation to a penalty (Code Sec. 7624(d)(2)(B), as amended by the 2006 Extenders Act).

▶ **Effective date.** The provision applies to calendar years beginning after December 20, 2006 (Act Sec. 403(d) of the Tax Relief and Health Care Act of 2006 (P.L. 109-432)).

Law source: Law at ¶5740 and ¶5820. Committee Reports at ¶15,480.

— Act Sec. 403(a) of the Tax Relief and Health Care Act of 2006 (P.L. 109-432), amending Code Sec. 6039(a);

— Act Sec. 403(b), redesignating Code Sec. 6039(b) and (c) as Code Sec. 6039(c) and (d), and adding new Code Sec. 6039(b);

— Act Sec. 403(c), amending Code Sec. 6724(d)(1)(B) and (2)(B);

— Act Sec. 403(d), providing the effective date.

Reporter references: For further information, consult the following CCH reporters.

— Standard Federal Tax Reporter, ¶35,606.01

— Tax Research Consultant, PENALTY: 3,204.05

— Federal Tax Guide, ¶22,084

¶630

¶635 IRS Disclosure of Information Authority Extended and Expanded

SUMMARY OF NEW LAW

The IRS's authority to disclose certain tax return information is extended for one year through December 31, 2007, and the definition of "State" is broadened to include regional income tax agencies.

BACKGROUND

In general, a taxpayer's return and return information is considered confidential and cannot be disclosed by the IRS, federal employees, or other persons who have access to the information (Code Sec. 6103). However, there are a number of exceptions to this nondisclosure rule that allow a taxpayer's return and return information to be disclosed for specific purposes set forth in the statute, including (1) disclosures to facilitate combined federal and state employment tax reporting, (2) disclosures related to establishing an appropriate income-contingent repayment amount for certain student loans, and (3) disclosures related to a terrorist incident, threat, or activity. The IRS's ability to disclose such tax return information is authorized through December 31, 2006.

Disclosures related to employment tax reporting. Under one exception to the requirement of confidentiality of tax returns and return information, the IRS can disclose taxpayer identity information and signatures in order to carry out a combined federal and state employment tax reporting program approved by the Secretary of the Treasury (Code Sec. 6103(d)(5)(A)). The disclosure may be made to any agency, body or commission of any state for the purpose of carrying out the tax-reporting program.

Disclosures related to student loans. A second exception to the general rule of confidentiality permits disclosure of returns and return information to establish an appropriate repayment amount for certain student loans under an income-contingent loan repayment program (Code Sec. 6103(l)(13)). This disclosure permits the Secretary of the Treasury, upon written request from the Secretary of Education, to disclose to officers and employees of the Department of Education return information with respect to a taxpayer whose student loan repayment amounts are based on the taxpayer's income. The information that may be disclosed is limited to taxpayer identity information, filing status and adjusted gross income.

Disclosures related to terrorist activities. Under a third exception to the general rule of nondisclosure, returns and return information may be disclosed for the purpose of investigating terrorist incidents, threats, or activities or analyzing intelligence concerning such activities (Code Sec. 6103(i)(3) and (i)(7)). A "terrorist incident, threat, or activity" can involve either an act of domestic terrorism or international terrorism as defined in Code Sec. 6103(b)(11) and 18 U.S.C. §§ 2331(1) and 2331(5). Disclosure may be made to the extent necessary to apprise the head of the federal law enforcement agency responsible for investigating such terrorist incident, threat or activity. The head of this agency may disclose the return information to officers and employ-

BACKGROUND

ees of the agency to the extent necessary to investigate and respond (Code Sec. 6103(i)(3)(C)(i)). Disclosure may also be made to the Department of Justice for use in preparing an application for an *ex parte* court order for disclosure, if there is reasonable cause to believe that the return and return information are relevant to a matter relating to such terrorist incident, threat or activity and the return or return information is sought for use in a federal investigation, analysis or proceeding involving terrorism (Code Sec. 6103(i)(3)(C)(ii)).

To the extent the federal law enforcement agency can show that it is involved in a response and investigation of a terrorist incident, threat or activity and can articulate the specific reason why disclosure may be relevant to a terrorist incident, threat or activity, the IRS, upon written request, may disclose return information to officers and employees of the federal law enforcement agency. The head of the federal law enforcement agency may disclose return information to officers and employees of any state or local law enforcement agency, but only if such agency is part of a team with the federal law enforcement agency (Code Sec. 6103(i)(7)(A)(ii)).

NEW LAW EXPLAINED

Disclosure authority extended and expanded.—The IRS's authority to disclose certain tax return information is extended for one year through December 31, 2007 (Code Sec. 6103, as amended by the Tax Relief and Health Care Act of 2006 (P.L. 109-432)). Specifically, the IRS's authority to disclose information related to employment tax reporting is extended through December 31, 2007 (Code Sec. 6103(d)(5)(B), as amended by the 2006 Extenders Act); the IRS's authority to disclose information related to terrorist activities is similarly extended (Code Sec. 6103(i)(3)(C)(iv) and 6103(i)(7)(E), as amended by the 2006 Extenders Act); and the IRS's disclosure authority relating to information on student loans is also extended through the end of 2007 (Code Sec. 6103(l)(13)(D), as amended by the 2006 Extenders Act).

Regional income tax agencies treated as states. The definition and applicability of the term "State" has been expanded as it applies to the confidentiality and disclosure by the IRS of income tax return information (Code Sec. 6103(b)(5), as amended by the 2006 Extenders Act). Specifically, the term "State" is expanded to include any governmental entity formed and operated by a "qualified group of municipalities" with which the Secretary has entered into an agreement regarding disclosure. A "qualified group of municipalities" consists of two or more municipalities which:

(1) each impose a tax on income or wages;

(2) each administers the laws relating to the imposition of such taxes under the authority of a state statute; and

(3) collectively have a population in excess of 250,000 (under the most recent decennial U.S. census data available).

Comment: The addition of this provision permits smaller municipalities to band together to establish a regional income tax agency and have available the same information-sharing with the IRS that municipalities in excess of 250,000 already

NEW LAW EXPLAINED

could avail themselves of via Code Sec. 6103(b)(5)(B), prior to amendment by the 2006 Extenders Act.

Any inspection of, or disclosure to, a regional income tax agency of income tax information by the IRS may only be for the purpose—and to the extent necessary—for the administration of the tax laws of the member municipalities. The regional income tax agency must not redisclose tax information to its member municipalities in any form that can be associated or identified, directly or indirectly, with any particular taxpayer (Code Sec. 6103(d)(6), as added by the 2006 Extenders Act). The agency may, however, disclose data to its member municipalities if it is in a form which precludes any such identification.

Certification requirement. Regional income tax agencies that have entered into such information-sharing agreements with the IRS are required to conduct on-site reviews of all of their contractors and agents with access to returns or return information to assess the contractor's efforts to safeguard the federal tax information (Code Sec. 6103(a)(5)(B)(iii), as amended by the 2006 Extenders Act). Such reviews must take place every three years, or at the mid-point of any contract or agreement whose duration is less than three years. This review should cover the safeguards deemed appropriate by the Secretary, including secure storage, restricted access, computer security and any other pertinent concerns, whether or not specifically contained in the regional agency's agreement with the IRS. Nothing in such agreements prevents the IRS from requiring additional safeguards or conducting further safeguard reviews as needed prior to making any disclosures (Joint Committee on Taxation, Technical Explanation of the Tax Relief and Health Care Act of 2006 (P.L. 109-432) (JCX-50-06)).

The regional income tax agency is required to submit a report of its review findings to the IRS. In addition, each such agency is required to submit an annual certification that such contractors and agents are maintaining compliance with the requirements necessary to safeguard the confidentiality of federal tax information. Such certification must include:

(1) name and address of each contractor and agent;

(2) a description of the contract or agreement; and

(3) the duration of the contract or agreement (Code Sec. 6103(a)(5)(B)(iii), as amended by the 2006 Extenders Act).

▶ **Effective date.** The amendments covering disclosure authority apply to disclosures and requests made after December 31, 2006 (Act Secs. 122(a)(2), 122(b)(2), 122(c)(2), and 421(c) of the Tax Relief and Health Care Act of 2006 (P.L. 109-432)).

Law source: Law at ¶5770. Committee Reports at ¶15,310, ¶15,320, ¶15,330 and ¶15,660.

— Act Sec. 122(a)(1) of the Tax Relief and Health Care Act of 2006 (P.L. 109-432), amending Code Sec. 6103(d)(5)(B);

— Act Sec. 122(b)(1), amending Code Sec. 6103(i)(3)(C)(iv) and 6103(i)(7)(E);

— Act Sec. 122(c)(1), amending Code Sec. 6103(l)(13)(D);

— Act Sec. 421(a), amending Code Sec. 6103(b)(5);

NEW LAW EXPLAINED

— Act Sec. 421(b), adding Code Sec. 6103(d)(6);

— Act Secs. 122(a)(2), 122(b)(2), 122(c)(2), and 421(c), providing the effective date.

Reporter references: For further information, consult the following CCH reporters.

— Standard Federal Tax Reporter, ¶36,894.026

— Tax Research Consultant, IRS: 9150

— Federal Tax Guide, ¶22,221

— Federal Estate and Gift Tax Reporter, ¶6103(b)(5)

¶640 Frivolous Tax Submissions

SUMMARY OF NEW LAW

The civil penalty for frivolous tax returns is increased from $500 to $5,000, and applies to all taxpayers and all types of federal taxes. In addition, the $5,000 civil penalty applies to any request for a collection due process hearing, an installment agreement, or an offer-in-compromise that raises frivolous arguments. The Secretary will prescribe, and periodically revise, a list of positions identified as frivolous.

BACKGROUND

A significant deterrent to the use of tax protest tactics is the immediately-assessable penalty under Code Sec. 6702 against taxpayers who file tax protest documents. A $500 penalty can be imposed upon any individual (1) who files a purported federal income tax return that either does not contain information from which the substantial correctness of reported tax liability can be determined, or contains information that indicates the tax liability shown is substantially incorrect; and (2) whose conduct is due to a frivolous position or a desire (as shown on the purported return) to delay or impede administration of the income tax law (Code Sec. 6702(a)). The penalty is in addition to any other penalty provided by law (Code Sec. 6702(b)).

The penalty is not based on tax liability; an underpayment or understatement of tax is not necessary for the penalty to be imposed. Liability arises immediately with the filing of the frivolous return, and there is no requirement of advance notice, such as that included in the deficiency procedures. Taxpayers must pay the entire penalty before seeking judicial review of its imposition. Suits contesting this penalty may be brought only in the federal District Courts and the Claims Court.

The penalty is intended to attack a variety of tax protest activities, including:

(1) irregular Forms 1040 not in processible form;

(2) references to spurious constitutional arguments instead of required completion of a tax form;

(3) forms on which there is insufficient information to calculate tax liability;

BACKGROUND

(4) presentation of information that is clearly inconsistent, such as the listing of only a few dependents by a person who claims 99 exemptions;

(5) "gold standard" or "war tax" deductions; and

(6) deliberate use of incorrect tax tables.

A "frivolous issue" is one without basis in fact or law, or that espouses a position held by the courts to be frivolous or groundless (Rev. Proc. 2006-2, I.R.B. 2006-1, 89).

The IRS has been investigating promoters of frivolous arguments and referring cases to the Department of Justice for criminal prosecution. In addition to tax, interest and the $500 penalty, taxpayers who file frivolous income tax returns may be subject to civil penalties of 20 or 75 percent of any underpaid tax. Those who pursue frivolous tax cases in court may face an additional penalty of up to $25,000 (IRS News Release IR-2005-27, March 14, 2005).

Requests for collection due process hearings; applications for offers-in-compromise or install-ment agreements. A person who is given a notice before levy or of the filing of a notice of lien for unpaid federal taxes may request a collection due process hearing (Code Secs. 6320 and 6330). An issue may not be raised at a hearing if (1) the issue was raised and considered at a previous hearing upon filing of notice of lien or in any other previous proceeding; and (2) the person seeking to raise the issue participated meaningfully in the hearing or proceeding (Code Sec. 6330(c)(4)). Neither the provisions for hearing requests on notices of lien or levy, nor the provisions for applications for offers-in-compromise or installment tax payment agreements, contain express rules for dealing with frivolous requests or submissions (Code Secs. 6159, 6320, 6330 and 7122).

NEW LAW EXPLAINED

Penalty for frivolous tax returns increased; penalty for frivolous tax submissions imposed.—The civil penalty for frivolous tax returns is increased from $500 to $5,000, and now applies to *all* federal taxes, not just to income tax. The penalty also applies to a "person" who filed the return, not just to an "individual" (Code Sec. 6702(a), as amended by the Tax Relief and Health Care Act of 2006 (P.L. 109-432)). The definition of the term "person" includes an individual, a trust, estate, partnership, association, company or corporation (Code Sec. 7701(a)(1)). In addition, a penalty of $5,000 is imposed on any person who submits a specified frivolous submission (Code Sec. 6702(b)(1), as added by the 2006 Extenders Act). The Secretary of the Treasury will prescribe and periodically revise a list of frivolous positions, but the list will not include any position for which the taxpayer has a reasonable basis under Code Sec. 6662(d)(2)(B)(ii)(II) (Code Sec. 6702(c), as added by the 2006 Extenders Act).

These penalties are in addition to any other penalty provided by law (Code Sec. 6702(e), as added by the 2006 Extenders Act). The Secretary can reduce the penalties in order to promote compliance with and administration of the federal tax laws (Code Sec. 6702(d), as added by the 2006 Extenders Act). If a person withdraws a submission within 30 days after receiving notice from the Secretary that it is a specified frivolous submission, the

NEW LAW EXPLAINED

penalty will not be imposed (Code Sec. 6702(b)(3), as added by the 2006 Extenders Act).

Specified frivolous submissions. A "specified frivolous submission" is a specified submission that either (1) is based on a position that the Secretary has identified as frivolous in his prescribed frivolous positions list; or (2) reflects a desire to delay or impede the administration of federal tax laws (Code Sec. 6702(b)(2)(A), as added by the 2006 Extenders Act). A "specified submission" is:

(1) a request for a hearing after—

- the IRS files a notice of lien under Code Sec. 6320; or
- the taxpayer receives a pre-levy Collection Due Process Hearing Notice under Code Sec. 6330; and

(2) an application relating to—

- agreements for payment of tax liability in installments under Code Sec. 6159;
- compromises under Code Sec. 7122; or
- taxpayer assistance orders under Code Sec. 7811 (Code Sec. 6702(b)(2)(B), as added by the 2006 Extenders Act).

Written requests for collection due process hearings; frivolous hearing requests or issues. Hearing requests before levy or after the IRS files a notice of lien must be in writing and must state the grounds for the requested hearing (Code Secs. 6330(b)(1) and 6320(b)(1), as amended by the 2006 Extenders Act). A request for a hearing, or any portion of it, that meets either requirement for a specified frivolous submission will be treated as if it were never submitted, and will not be subjected to any further administrative or judicial review (Code Sec. 6330(g), as added by the 2006 Extenders Act; Code Sec. 6320(c), as amended by the 2006 Extenders Act). Further, an issue cannot be raised at a pre-levy hearing if it meets either requirement for a specified frivolous submission (Code Sec. 6330(c)(4), as amended by the 2006 Extenders Act).

> **Comment:** The Code Sec. 6330(c)(4) provision precluding frivolous issues from being raised at pre-levy hearings also applies to issues raised at hearings after the IRS files a notice of lien (Code Sec. 6320(c)).

Frivolous applications for offers-in-compromise and installment agreements. Any portion of an application for an offer-in-compromise under Code Sec. 7122 or for an installment agreement under Code Sec. 6159 will be treated as if it were never submitted and will not be subjected to any further administrative or judicial review, if that portion of the application meets either requirement for a specified frivolous submission (Code Sec. 7122(f), as added by the 2006 Extenders Act).

> **Comment:** The IRS has issued a news release announcing updated guidance which describes and rebuts frivolous arguments that taxpayers should avoid when filing their tax returns (IRS News Release IR-2006-45, March 16, 2006). The IRS has also recently updated a document entitled "The Truth About Frivolous Tax Arguments" (November 30, 2006; available at www.irs.com), that addresses

NEW LAW EXPLAINED

false arguments about the legality of not paying taxes or filing returns. Some of the more common frivolous "legal" arguments include:

(1) the filing of a tax return and payment of the tax is voluntary;

(2) wages, tips and other compensation received for personal services are not income;

(3) the taxpayer is not a "citizen" of the United States, thus not subject to the federal income tax laws;

(4) taxpayers can refuse to pay income tax based on constitutional amendment claims;

(5) the IRS is not an agency of the United States; and

(6) the Tax Court lacks authority to decide legal issues.

▶ **Effective date.** The provision applies to submissions made and issues raised after the date on which the Secretary of the Treasury first prescribes a list under Code Sec. 6702(c), as amended by Act Sec. 407(a) of the Tax Relief and Health Care Act of 2006 (P.L. 109-432) (Act Sec. 407(f) of the Tax Relief and Health Care Act of 2006 (P.L. 109-432)).

Law source: Law at ¶5790, ¶5795, ¶5810 and ¶5830. Committee Report at ¶15,520.

— Act Sec. 407(a) of the Tax Relief and Health Care Act of 2006 (P.L. 109-432), amending Code Sec. 6702;

— Act Sec. 407(b), adding Code Sec. 6330(g), and amending Code Sec. 6330(b)(1) and (c)(4);

— Act Sec. 407(c), amending Code Sec. 6320(b)(1) and (c);

— Act Sec. 407(d), adding Code Sec. 7122(f);

— Act Sec. 407(f), providing the effective date.

Reporter references: For further information, consult the following CCH reporters.

— Standard Federal Tax Reporter, ¶40,043.01

— Tax Research Consultant, PENALTY: 100 and PENALTY: 3,204.05

— Federal Tax Guide, ¶22,591

— Federal Estate and Gift Tax Reporter, ¶7122(g)

PENALTIES AND IRS AUTHORITY

¶645 Extension of Authority for Undercover Operations

SUMMARY OF NEW LAW

The IRS's authority to use amounts obtained in an undercover operation to pay for additional expenses of the operation is extended for one year through December 31, 2007.

BACKGROUND

In general, the use of government funds is restricted by requiring receipts to be deposited in the general fund of the U.S. Treasury and by requiring expenses to be paid out of appropriated funds. However, IRS undercover operations are exempt from these restrictions. The exemption allows the IRS to use proceeds from an undercover operation to pay additional expenses of the operation that are necessary for the detection and prosecution of offenses and criminal violations of the internal revenue laws (Code Sec. 7608(c)).

The exemption was originally enacted as part of the Anti-Drug Abuse Act of 1988 (P.L. 100-690). Although the provision was allowed to lapse for a four-and-a-half-year period during the 1990s, it was reinstated in 1996 and has been regularly extended since then. The most recent extension granted the IRS authority to use the proceeds from undercover operations through December 31, 2006 (Gulf Opportunity Zone Act of 2005 (P.L. 109-135)).

NEW LAW EXPLAINED

IRS permitted to churn income earned in undercover operations before 2007.— The IRS's authority under current law to use proceeds obtained from an undercover operation to pay additional expenses incurred in conducting the operation has been extended for one year through December 31, 2007 (Code Sec. 7608(c)(6), as amended by the Tax Relief and Health Care Act of 2006 (P.L. 109-432)). Without such authority, the IRS might be hindered in conducting undercover operations by having to deposit all income from such operations into the general fund of the U.S. Treasury and to pay all expenses out of appropriated funds.

▶ **Effective date.** No specific effective date is provided by the Act. The provision is, therefore, considered effective on December 20, 2006, the date of enactment.

Law source: Law at ¶5840. Committee Reports at ¶15,300.

— Act Sec. 121 of the Tax Relief and Health Care Act of 2006 (P.L. 109-432), amending Code Sec. 7608(c)(6).

Reporter references: For further information, consult the following CCH reporters.

— Standard Federal Tax Reporter, ¶42,885.01

— Tax Research Consultant, IRS: 63,170

¶650 Whistleblower Reforms

SUMMARY OF NEW LAW

The reward program has been reformed and enhanced, and a Whistleblower Office will be established and administered within the IRS.

¶650

BACKGROUND

Individuals who provide information to the government relating to violations of internal revenue laws may be entitled to receive a reward from the IRS for their efforts. Although certain guidelines have been established, both the grant and the amount of the reward are at the discretion of the IRS. The IRS has administratively set the maximum reward limit at 15 percent of the amounts recovered, up to a maximum of $10 million. However these percentage and dollar limits can be increased as a result of a special arrangement with the IRS. The 15 percent limit is reduced to 10 percent for non-specific information that (1) results in an investigation and (2) assists in the determination of tax liabilities. If the information provided results in an investigation, but otherwise did not directly assist in the determination of tax liabilities, the percentage limit is reduced to one percent.

The minimum reward is $100, and no reward will be paid if the recovery is so small that the reward would be less than $100 when calculated at the maximum percentage limit described above. Amounts may be paid based on taxes, fines and penalties actually collected based on the information provided, but may not be based on any interest amounts collected. Rewards may be granted for information on either criminal or civil violations.

NEW LAW EXPLAINED

Whistleblower reforms.—The reward program has been reformed and enhanced, and a Whistleblower Office will be established and administered within the IRS (Code Sec. 7623, as amended by the Tax Relief and Health Care Act of 2006 (P.L. 109-432)).

Reward amounts have been increased in several ways. First, if the IRS proceeds with *any* administrative or judicial action based on information provided by an individual, the individual *shall* receive a reward based on the amounts collected. Therefore, the IRS's discretion whether or not to make a reward in such cases is greatly reduced. Second, the reward will be at least 15 percent, and no more than 30 percent, of the collected amount (Code Sec. 7623(b)(1), as added by the 2006 Extenders Act). In addition, the prohibition against including interest amounts collected when calculating the size of rewards has been removed and, therefore, will be included in any such calculations (Code Sec. 7623(a), as amended by the 2006 Extenders Act). The amount of the reward will be determined by the Whistleblower Office based upon a determination of the extent to which the information substantially contributed to the administrative or judicial action and recovery.

In situations where the Whistleblower Office determines that the IRS's actions were based on an individual's allegations (rather than specific information), and those allegations arose from:

(1) a judicial or administrative hearing;

(2) a governmental report, hearing, audit or investigation; or

(3) the news media,

NEW LAW EXPLAINED

then a lesser reward is appropriate and a maximum reward amount would be 10 percent of the recovered funds (Code Sec. 7623(b)(2), as added by the 2006 Extenders Act). Again, the Whistleblower Office will consider the significance of the individual's contribution to the information resulting in the recovery. The Whistleblower Office may reduce a reward if it determines that the claim was brought by an individual who planned and initiated the actions that led to an underpayment of tax or violation of the Internal Revenue Code. If the individual is actually convicted of criminal conduct arising from his or her role, then the Whistleblower Office shall deny an award (Code Sec. 7623(b)(3), as added by the 2006 Extenders Act).

The size of any reward provided under this program may be appealed within 30 days of its determination. The appeal should be made to the Tax Court, which is granted jurisdiction with respect to these matters (Code Sec. 7623(b)(4), as added by the 2006 Extenders Act). Tax Court review of an award determination may be assigned to a special trial judge (Code Sec. 7443A(b)(6), as added by the 2006 Extenders Act).

These new parameters for the rewards program apply when an individual's information or allegations implicate any type of taxpayer entity (such as a corporation), but if the information implicates an individual taxpayer, these whistleblower awards only apply if the individual taxpayer against whom they are made:

(1) has a gross income in excess of $200,000 for any tax year involved in the administrative or judicial action; and

(2) the tax, penalties, interest, additions to tax, plus any additional amounts in dispute exceed $2,000,000 (Code Sec. 7623(b)(5), as added by the 2006 Extenders Act).

In addition, no award will be given unless the information submitted to the IRS is submitted under penalty of perjury (Code Sec. 7623(b)(6)(C), as added by the 2006 Extenders Act). No contract with the IRS is necessary to receive such an award (Code Sec. 7623(b)(6)(A), as added by the 2006 Extenders Act).

Deduction permitted. An above-the-line deduction is permitted for costs and attorney's fees paid in connection with any whistleblower award for providing information regarding violations of the tax laws. However, no such deduction shall exceed the amount includible in the taxpayer's gross income as a result of such award (Code Sec. 62(a)(21), as added by the 2006 Extenders Act).

Whistleblower Office. The IRS is required to establish a Whistleblower Office through which it will administer a whistleblower program. Within one year of enactment, the IRS is also required to issue guidance regarding the operation of the Office and how it will administer the reward program. The Whistleblower Office will analyze information provided to it by individuals, and determine whether to:

(1) investigate the matter itself, or

(2) assign the matter to an appropriate IRS office (Act Sec. 406(b) of the 2006 Extenders Act).

The Treasury Inspector General for Tax Administration (TIGTA) issued a report in June, 2006, entitled *The Informant's Rewards Program Needs More Centralized Manage-*

NEW LAW EXPLAINED

ment Oversight (2006-30-092) that contains recommendations for centralizing management of the rewards program and reducing the processing time for claims. It is expected that these recommendations will be considered by the IRS while drafting the details of its administrative plans for operating the Whistleblower Office (Joint Committee on Taxation, Technical Explanation of the Tax Relief and Health Care Act of 2006 (P.L. 109-432) (JCX-50-06)).

In addition, the Secretary of the Treasury is required to conduct annual studies and make annual reports to Congress on the effectiveness of the whistleblower reward program. The Secretary is to include in those reports any legislative or administrative recommendations that the Secretary believes might improve the administration of the program (Act Sec. 406(c) of the 2006 Extenders Act).

▶ **Effective date.** This provision is applicable to information provided on or after December 20, 2006 (Act Sec. 406(d) of the Tax Relief and Health Care Act of 2006 (P.L. 109-432)).

Law source: Law at ¶5085, ¶5835 and ¶5845. Committee Reports at ¶15,510.

— Act Sec. 406(a)(1) of the Tax Relief and Health Care Act of 2006 (P.L. 109-432), amending Code Sec. 7623;

— Act Sec. 406(a)(2), amending Code Sec. 7443A(b)-(c);

— Act Sec. 406(a)(3), adding Code Sec. 62(a)(21);

— Act Sec. 406(d), providing the effective date.

Reporter references: For further information, consult the following CCH reporters.

— Standard Federal Tax Reporter, ¶42,957.01

— Tax Research Consultant, IRS: 63,060.05

¶655 Modification of Suspension of Interest Rules

SUMMARY OF NEW LAW

A technical correction to a non-Code provision clarifies that the Secretary of the Treasury may delegate authority to his delegate to permit interest suspension where taxpayers have acted reasonably and in good faith with respect to certain listed and reportable transactions.

BACKGROUND

In general, interest and penalties continue to accrue during periods for which taxes were due but remain unpaid, regardless of whether the taxpayer was aware that the taxes were due. The accumulation of interest and penalties can quickly transform a tax debt into a debt that poses a financial hardship for the average taxpayer. In an effort to address this problem, and following congressional hearings on IRS collection

BACKGROUND

activities, the IRS Restructuring and Reform Act of 1998 (P.L. 105-206) added a special rule for abating interest and penalties that accrue unknown to the taxpayer.

Under this special rule, the accrual of interest and penalties will be suspended after 18 months unless the IRS provides a notice to the taxpayer specifically stating the taxpayer's liability and the basis for that liability within 18 months following the later of: (1) the original due date of the return (without regard to extensions) or (2) the date on which a timely filed return is filed. Returns filed prior to the due date are considered, for this purpose, to have been filed on the due date. Interest and penalties resume 21 days after the IRS sends this required notice to the taxpayer. The 18-month suspension period was scheduled to be reduced to 12 months beginning with tax years beginning on or after January 1, 2004; however, the American Jobs Creation Act of 2004 (P.L. 108-357) made the 18-month suspension period permanent (Code Sec. 6404(g), as amended by the 2004 Jobs Act).

This special rule is available only to individuals who file a timely tax return and is applied separately to each item or adjustment. The special rule does not apply where the taxpayer has self-assessed the tax; further, it does not apply to the failure-to-pay penalty, in the case of fraud, or regarding criminal penalties. The suspension of interest rules do not apply with respect to listed transactions and undisclosed reportable transactions for interest accruing on or before October 3, 2004. This exception for listed transactions and undisclosed reportable transactions originally applied only to interest accruing after October 3, 2004. Taxpayers remain eligible for the rules suspending the accrual of interest if, as of December 14, 2005, the year in which the underpayment occurred is barred by the statute of limitations or a closing agreement has been entered into with respect to the transaction (Act Sec. 903(d)(2) of the 2004 Jobs Act, as amended by Act Sec. 303(a)(2) of the Gulf Opportunity Zone Act of 2005 (P.L. 109-135)). Further, under a special rule, a taxpayer is eligible for the suspension of interest, on a transaction-by-transaction basis, if participating in the IRS settlement initiative described in IRS Announcement 2005-80, I.R.B. 2005-46, 967, and if he entered into a settlement agreement or initiative by January 23, 2006. Also, if a taxpayer files a return for a tax year and then files an amended return or other signed, written document showing that the taxpayer owes additional tax for the tax year, the 18-month period runs from the latest date on which such documents were provided (Code Sec. 6404(g)(1), as amended by the 2005 Gulf Zone Act).

In addition, under the 2004 Jobs Act, as amended by the 2005 Gulf Zone Act, the Secretary of the Treasury may permit the suspension of interest where taxpayers have acted reasonably and in good faith. For provisions that are included in the Code, Code Sec. 7701(a)(11) clarifies that the term "Secretary of the Treasury" means the Secretary in his non-delegable capacity, and the term "Secretary" means the Secretary or his delegate. However, Act Sec. 903 of the 2004 Jobs Act (as modified) is a non-Code provision. Therefore, only the Secretary of the Treasury could determine whether taxpayers had acted reasonably and in good faith. Consequently, a clarification that the Secretary may delegate authority under Act Sec. 903 of the 2004 Jobs Act (as modified) was needed.

¶655

NEW LAW EXPLAINED

Authority to exercise good faith exception.—The provision provides a technical correction to Act Sec. 903 of the American Jobs Creation Act of 2004 (P.L. 108-357), as modified by Act Sec. 303 of the Gulf Opportunity Zone Act of 2005 (P.L. 109-135), clarifying that the Secretary of the Treasury may delegate authority under Act Sec. 903 of the 2004 Jobs Act, as modified, to permit interest suspension where taxpayers have acted reasonably and in good faith with respect to certain listed and reportable transactions. The provision adds the words "or the Secretary's delegate" after reference to the Secretary of the Treasury to make this clear (Act Sec. 426(b)(1) of the Tax Relief and Health Care Act of 2006 (P.L. 109-432)).

▶ **Effective date.** This provision applies to documents provided on or after December 21, 2005 (Act Sec. 903(d)(2)(B)(iii) of the American Jobs Creation Act of 2004, as amended by Act Sec. 303 of the Gulf Opportunity Zone Act of 2005 and Act Sec. 426(b)(2) of the Tax Relief and Health Care Act of 2006 (P.L. 109-432)).

Law source: Law at ¶7085. Committee Reports at ¶15,710.

— Act Sec. 426(b)(1) of the Tax Relief and Health Care Act of 2006 (P.L. 109-432), amending Act Sec. 903(d)(2)(B)(iii) of the American Jobs Creation Act of 2004 (P.L. 108-357), as amended by Act Sec. 303(a) of the Gulf Opportunity Zone Act of 2005 (P.L. 109-135);

— Act Sec.426(b)(2), providing the effective date.

Reporter references: For further information, consult the following CCH reporters.

— Standard Federal Tax Reporter, ¶38,580.037

— Tax Research Consultant, PENALTY: 3350

— Federal Tax Guide, ¶22,596

TAX COURT

¶660 U.S. Tax Court Jurisdiction Expanded to Review Denials of Equitable Innocent Spouse Relief

SUMMARY OF NEW LAW

The U.S. Tax Court has statutory jurisdiction to review the IRS's denial of equitable innocent spouse relief in situations where the IRS has not asserted a deficiency against the taxpayer.

BACKGROUND

Code Sec. 6015 allows married taxpayers to seek relief from the joint and several liability imposed by Code Sec. 6013(d)(3) on joint filers. This relief is commonly referred to as "innocent spouse relief". Code Sec. 6015(f), in particular, allows the IRS

BACKGROUND

to provide "equitable relief" when it would be inequitable to hold one spouse liable for any unpaid tax or deficiency resulting from a joint return.

Code Sec. 6015(e) provides the U.S. Tax Court with jurisdiction to review denials of innocent spouse relief. The Tax Court and two federal appellate courts have held that Code Sec. 6015(e) does not give the U.S. Tax Court jurisdiction to review denials of Code Sec. 6015(f) "equitable relief" when the IRS has not asserted a deficiency against the petitioning taxpayer (*D.B. Billings,* 127 T.C. 7, Dec. 56,572; *G.A.Ewing,* CA-9, 2006-1 USTC ¶50,191, 439 F.3d 1009; *T.E. Bartman,* CA-8, 2006-1 USTC ¶50,298, 446 F.3d 785). Based primarily on these decisions, the IRS stated that it will move to dismiss for lack of jurisdiction any case under Code Sec. 6015(f) where a deficiency has not been asserted against the taxpayer (Chief Counsel Notice CC-2006-020, September 8, 2006, 2006ARD 175-1).

NEW LAW EXPLAINED

Jurisdiction to review denials of equitable innocent spouse relief expanded.— The U.S. Tax Court has jurisdiction to review denials of innocent spouse relief under the equitable relief provisions of Code Sec. 6015(f) where the IRS has not determined a deficiency against the taxpayer (Code Sec. 6015(e)(1), as amended by the Tax Relief and Health Care Act of 2006 (P.L. 109-432)).

Taxpayers who request equitable relief are treated in the same manner as taxpayers against whom a deficiency has been assessed. Thus, the rules regarding filing requirements and past litigation apply to these taxpayers (Code Sec. 6015(e)(1)(A)(i)(II) and (g)(2), as amended by the 2006 Extenders Act). In addition, the various rules regarding notice and collection also apply to cases arising under Code Sec. 6015(f) (Code Sec. 6015(e)(1)(B), (e)(4), (e)(5), and (h)(2), as amended by the 2006 Extenders Act).

▶ **Effective date.** This provision applies with respect to liability for taxes arising or remaining unpaid on or after December 20, 2006 (Act Sec. 408(c), Division C of the Tax Relief and Health Act of 2006 (P.L. 109-432)).

Law source: Law at ¶5720. Committee Report at ¶15,530.

— Act Sec. 408(a), Division C of the Tax Relief and Health Care Act of 2006 (P.L. 109-432), amending Code Sec. 6015(e)(1);

— Act Sec. 408(b)(1)-(3), Division C of the 2006 Extenders Act, amending Code Sec. 6015(e)(1)(A) and (B);

— Act Sec. 408(b)(4)-(5), Division C of the 2006 Extenders Act, amending Code Sec. 6015(e)(4) and (5);

— Act Sec. 408(b)(6), Division C of the 2006 Extenders Act, amending Code Sec. 6015(g)(2);

— Act Sec. 408(b)(7), Division C of the 2006 Extenders Act, amending Code Sec. 6015(h)(2);

— Act Sec. 408(c), Division C of the 2006 Extenders Act, providing the effective date.

Reporter references: For further information, consult the following CCH reporters.

— Standard Federal Tax Reporter, ¶35,192.028

— Tax Research Consultant, IRS: 18,052.20

— Federal Tax Guide, ¶22,054

¶660

EXCISE TAXES

¶665 Tax Benefits for Ethanol Produced from Coal Extended

SUMMARY OF NEW LAW

The favorable tax benefits accorded to qualified methanol or ethanol fuel produced from coal have been extended through December 31, 2008.

BACKGROUND

Ethanol is often blended into gasoline to reduce emissions, increase octane, and extend gasoline stocks. Recent high oil and gasoline prices have led to increased interest in alternatives to petroleum fuels for transportation. The promotion of these fuel alternatives, including ethanol fuel, has been an ongoing goal of U.S. energy policy. This has led to the establishment of significant federal initiatives beneficial to the ethanol industry, including tax incentives, import tariffs, and mandates for ethanol use. In fact, the Energy Policy Act of 2005 (P.L. 109-58, § 1501) established a renewable fuel standard that sets a target to increase renewable fuel production to 7.5 billion gallons per year by 2012. This target is expected to be met primarily with ethanol.

Today, most ethanol is made from corn or other biomass. However, ethanol can be produced from coal, and according to www.alternativefuelsworld/node/2.com, the American coal industry is actively promoting the manufacture of gasified coal.

As part of U.S. energy policy, qualified methanol or ethanol is taxed at reduced rates relative to other fuels—12.35 cents per gallon for qualified methanol and 13.25 cents per gallon for qualified ethanol. "Qualified methanol or ethanol" is any liquid that is at least 85 percent methanol, ethanol, or other alcohol produced from coal or peat. These favorable tax rates are scheduled to expire after September 30, 2007.

The ethanol tax subsidies originally were enacted in 1978 to promote development of alternative fuels at a time when oil prices were projected to exceed $50 per barrel. The subsidies were assumed to be temporary measures that would allow these fuels to become economical without permanent federal subsidies. Since 1978, however, the tax benefits for qualified ethanol and methanol have been extended a number of times.

NEW LAW EXPLAINED

Tax benefits extended for qualified methanol and ethanol fuel produced from coal.—The lower tax rates for qualified methanol and qualified ethanol have been extended until January 1, 2009 (Code Sec. 4041 (b) (2) (D), as amended by the Tax Relief

NEW LAW EXPLAINED

and Health Care Act of 2006 (P.L. 109-432)). Thus, through December 31, 2008, ethanol derived from coal or peat is taxed at a rate of 13.25 cents per gallon (Code Sec. 4041(b)(2)(A)(ii) and (C)(ii), as amended by the 2006 Extenders Act) and methanol derived from coal or peat is taxed at a rate of 12.35 cents per gallon (Code Sec. 4041(b)(2)(A)).

The 2006 Extenders Act also clarified the heading of Code Sec. 4041(b)(2)(B) by providing that "qualified methanol and ethanol," as those terms are defined in the tax code, are produced from coal.

▶ **Effective date.** No specific effective date is provided by the Act. The provision is, therefore, considered effective on December 20, 2006, the date of enactment.

Law source: Law at ¶5660. Committee Report at ¶15,420.

— Act Sec. 208(a) of the Tax Relief and Health Care Act of 2006 (P.L. 109-432), amending Code Sec. 4041(b)(2)(D);

— Act Sec. 208(b), amending Code Sec. 4041(b)(2)(C)(ii);

— Act Sec. 208(c), amending Code Sec. 4041(b)(2)(B).

Reporter references: For further information, consult the following CCH reporters.

— Tax Research Consultant, BUSEXP: 54,106 and EXCISE: 3,104.05

— Federal Tax Guide, ¶21,030

— Federal Excise Tax Reporter, ¶5700.065

¶670 Refunds for Kerosene Used in Aviation

SUMMARY OF NEW LAW

Ultimate purchasers of aviation fuel used for an *exempt* aviation fuel purpose, such as in crop dusting, air ambulances, and aircraft engaged in foreign trade, may now make a claim for refund of the 24.3 cents per gallon excise tax, or may waive the right to their ultimate vendors. Previously, that right belonged only to the ultimate vendor of such fuel. The partial refund of 2.5 cents per gallon for fuel put to a *taxable* use in noncommercial aviation must still be taken by the ultimate vendor of the fuel.

BACKGROUND

In most instances, kerosene is the fuel used to power an aircraft. There is a 24.4 cents per gallon federal excise tax on kerosene upon its removal from a refinery or terminal, entry into the United States, or sale. A reduced rate of tax applies, however, in the case of kerosene used in aviation. Generally, the rate is 21.8 cents per gallon for kerosene used in noncommercial aviation and 4.3 cents per gallon for kerosene used in commercial aviation. Both commercial and noncommercial aviation fuel are also subject to an additional tax of 0.1 cents that funds the Leaking Underground Storage Tank (LUST) trust fund.

BACKGROUND

Commercial aviation is defined as any use of an aircraft in the business of transporting persons or property for compensation or hire by air. It does not include seaplanes that take off or land on water, aircraft used for skydiving, small aircraft on nonestablished lines, or transportation for affiliated group members (Code Sec. 4083(b)). All aviation other than commercial aviation is considered noncommercial aviation.

The reduced rates for kerosene used in aviation (21.9 cents and 4.4 cents) apply only if the kerosene is removed directly from a terminal into the fuel tank of an aircraft. Certain refueler trucks, tankers and wagons are treated as a terminal if the requirements of Code Sec. 4081(a)(3) are met. If fuel is not removed directly into the fuel tank of an aircraft, it is subject to the higher 24.4 cents per gallon rate generally applicable to kerosene. If the kerosene is then used in commercial aviation, however, the *purchaser* of the fuel (i.e., the aircraft operator in most cases) may obtain a refund of 20 cents per gallon (the difference between the 24.4 cent rate and the 4.4 cent rate), or may waive that right to the ultimate vendor.

On the other hand, a purchaser has no right to file a refund concerning taxes paid on kerosene used as a fuel in *noncommercial* aviation; that right belongs to the ultimate vendor exclusively. Therefore, if kerosene taxed at 24.4 cents per gallon is then used in taxable noncommercial aviation, the *ultimate vendor* of the fuel may obtain a refund of 2.5 cents per gallon (the difference between the 24.4 cent rate and the 21.9 cent rate).

Similarly, if the fuel is taxed at 24.4 cents per gallon then is put to an exempt use, the *ultimate vendor* of the fuel may obtain a full 24.3 cent refund (except in the case of exports, the 0.1 cent per gallon LUST trust fund tax is nonrefundable). In order to claim the refund, the ultimate vendor must be registered with the IRS and must have omitted the tax from the price of the fuel, repaid the tax to the purchaser, or provided the IRS with the purchaser's written consent to the vendor receiving the refund (Code Sec. 6427(l)(5)(B)).

The following uses of kerosene are exempt from tax and therefore subject to a full 24.3 cents per gallon refund to the ultimate vendor:

- on a farm for farming purposes;
- in foreign trade;
- in military vessels and aircraft;
- exclusive use of a state or local government;
- exclusive use by a nonprofit educational organization;
- for export or shipment to a possession of the United States (24.4 cent refund);
- in a World War II aircraft museum;
- for certain helicopter and fixed-wing ambulance uses; and
- off-highway business use.

Even though the rule giving the ultimate vendor exclusive rights to a refund is generally limited to kerosene put to a noncommercial or exempt *aviation* use, there is a separate rule for kerosene sold to a state or local government (Code Sec. 6427(l)(6)(A)). Under that rule, the ultimate registered vendor is the proper claimant

BACKGROUND

for a refund concerning any kerosene used by a state or local government, even if that kerosene is not used in aviation. A special rule applies in the case of credit card sales by state or local governments; under this rule, if certain conditions are met, the credit card issuer may make the refund claim.

NEW LAW EXPLAINED

Modification of refund rules for noncommercial aviation fuel.—The Tax Relief and Health Care Act of 2006 (P.L. 109-432), with certain exceptions, makes the ultimate purchaser the proper claimant for all refunds of the excise taxes imposed by Code Secs. 4041 and 4081 on any kerosene used in aviation. An ultimate purchaser may, however, waive and assign its right to a registered ultimate vendor. To claim a refund, in addition to being registered with the IRS, the ultimate vendor must have omitted the tax from the price of the fuel, repaid the tax to the purchaser, or provided the IRS with the purchaser's written consent to the vendor receiving the refund (Code Sec. 6427(l)(4)(C)(i), as amended by the 2006 Extenders Act).

As a result of this ultimate purchaser rule applying generally to aviation kerosene, purchasers of kerosene used for an *exempt* aviation purpose now have the right to claim the refund. Therefore, ultimate purchasers who put kerosene to exempt uses, such as in crop dusting, in air ambulances, and in aircraft engaged in foreign trade, may now claim a refund of the 24.3 cents per gallon excise tax, or may waive the right to their registered ultimate vendors. The rules applicable to state and local governments, however, remain unchanged. Thus, if kerosene is purchased by a state or local government without the use of a credit card, the ultimate vendor is still the proper refund claimant if it is registered with the IRS (Code Sec. 6427(l)(4)(C)(i), as amended by the 2006 Extenders Act, making reference to Code Sec. 6427(l)(5), as redesignated by the 2006 Extenders Act).

An exception to this general rule applies, however, to kerosene used for a taxable purpose in noncommercial aviation. Such kerosene, if not removed directly from a terminal into the fuel tank of an aircraft, is subject in the first instance to the 24.4 cents per gallon rate that applies to all kerosene. Then, 2.5 cents per gallon (the difference between the general 24.4 cents per gallon rate on kerosene and the 21.9 cents per gallon reduced rate for kerosene used in noncommercial aviation) is refundable. But the refund remains payable only to the ultimate vendor of the aviation kerosene (Code Sec. 6427(l)(4)(C)(ii), as amended by the 2006 Extenders Act).

In sum then, concerning the right to claim a refund of taxes paid on kerosene used in aviation, an *ultimate purchaser* rule continues to apply to kerosene used in commercial aviation and now applies as well to kerosene used in tax-exempt aviation, whereas the *ultimate vendor* rule continues to apply to kerosene put to taxable uses in noncommercial aviation.

Pending claims. These new rules apply to kerosene sold after September 30, 2005. They apply, therefore, to sales of kerosene for tax-exempt aviation for which the ultimate vendor may have already made a refund claim under the prior rules. But under the new

¶670

NEW LAW EXPLAINED

rules, the right to receive a refund for those sales has been retroactively transferred to the ultimate purchaser. Consequently, the 2006 Extenders Act adds a special rule for kerosene sold for use in aviation after September 30, 2005, and before December 20, 2006. Specifically, for kerosene sold during this period, the ultimate purchaser is treated as having waived and assigned the right to a refund under Code Sec. 6427(l)(1) to the ultimate vendor if the ultimate vendor (1) has not included the tax in the price of the fuel and has not collected the tax from the ultimate purchaser; (2) has repaid the tax to the ultimate purchaser; or (3) has filed the written consent of the ultimate purchaser to allow the ultimate vendor to claim the refund (Act Sec. 420(c)(2) of the 2006 Extenders Act).

Special rule for aviation kerosene used on a farm. The 2006 Extenders Act generally gives the ultimate purchaser of kerosene put to a tax-exempt use the right to claim a refund for kerosene sold after September 30, 2005. But the ultimate purchaser of kerosene used in aviation on a farm for farming purposes is granted the refund right all the way back to January 1, 2005 (i.e., kerosene purchased after December 31, 2004, and before October 1, 2005) (Act Sec. 420(d)(1) of the 2006 Extenders Act).

This special rule for farm-use aviation kerosene has several limitations. First, any refund claim made by an ultimate purchaser of aviation kerosene used on a farm is reduced by any payments made to the ultimate vendor (Act Sec. 420(d)(1) of the 2006 Extenders Act). Second, refund claims by the ultimate purchaser under this provision must be filed within three months of December 20, 2006, the date of enactment (Act Sec. 420(d)(3) of the 2006 Extenders Act). Third, no refund under this rule can exceed the tax imposed on the kerosene under Code Sec. 4041 or Code Sec. 4081 (Act Sec. 420(d)(4) of the 2006 Extenders Act). Also, refund claims under the rule may not duplicate claims filed under Code Sec. 6427(l) (Joint Committee on Taxation, Technical Explanation of the Tax Relief and Health Care Act of 2006 (P.L. 109-432) (JCX-50-06)). If duplicate refund claims are filed, the taxpayer may be subject to penalties under the tax code (Act Sec. 420(d)(5) of the 2006 Extenders Act).

▶ **Effective date.** The new rules generally apply to kerosene sold after September 30, 2005 (Act Sec. 420(c) of the Tax Relief and Health Care Act of 2006 (P.L. 109-432)). The special rule for kerosene used in aviation on a farm for a farming purpose is effective on December 20, 2006.

Law source: Law at ¶5665, ¶5800, ¶5860 and ¶5865. Committee Report at ¶15,650.

— Act Sec. 420(a) of the Tax Relief and Health Care Act of 2006 (P.L. 109-432), amending Code Sec. 6427(l)(4);

— Act Sec. 420(b), striking Code Sec. 6427(l)(5), and redesignating Code Sec. 6427(l)(6) as (l)(5); amending Code Secs. 4082(d)(2)(B), 6427(i)(4)(A), 6427(l)(1), 9502(d) and 9503(c)(7).

— Act Sec. 420(c), providing the effective date.

— Act Sec. 420(d), providing a special rule for kerosene used in aviation on a farm for farming purposes.

Reporter references: For further information, consult the following CCH reporters.

— Tax Research Consultant, EXCISE: 24,310

¶670

NEW LAW EXPLAINED

— Federal Tax Guide, ¶21,060

— Federal Excise Tax Reporter, ¶9215.047 and ¶49,685.13

¶675 LUST Trust Fund Expenditures

SUMMARY OF NEW LAW

Expenditures may now be made from the Leaking Underground Storage Tank (LUST) trust fund in order to carry out a number of monitoring, prevention, detection and compliance initiatives relating to underground storage tanks—initiatives effected by recent amendments to the Solid Waste Disposal Act (SWDA).

BACKGROUND

The Leaking Underground Storage Tank (LUST) trust fund was created by the Superfund Revenue Act of 1986 (P.L. 99-499) to pay cleanup and related costs with respect to petroleum storage tanks that have no solvent owner, as well as for those tanks whose owner or operator refuses or is unable to comply with an urgent corrective order. In addition, the fund provides grants to states carrying out these purposes. The LUST trust fund is financed by a 0.1 cent per gallon tax on the manufacture, sale or use of gasoline, diesel, kerosene or alternative fuels/special motor fuels (other than liquefied petroleum gas or other liquefied natural gas), including their use on inland waterways (Code Secs. 4041(d), 4042 and 4081(a)). The Energy Policy Act of 2005 (P.L. 109-58) extended the LUST trust fund tax through September 30, 2011.

Under Code Sec. 9508(c), amounts in the LUST trust fund can be used only to carry out section 9003(h) of the Solid Waste Disposal Act (SWDA) as in effect on October, 17, 1986, the date of enactment of the Superfund Amendments and Reauthorization Act of 1986 (P.L. 99-499). Generally, if any expenditure is made from the LUST trust fund that is not permitted by Code Sec. 9508, no further amounts may be appropriated to the fund (Code Sec. 9508(e)). This spending restriction applies despite any provision to the contrary that is not contained in either the Internal Revenue Code or a revenue act, even if that provision is enacted subsequently or seeks to waive this restriction (Joint Committee on Taxation, Technical Explanation of the Tax Relief and Health Care Act of 2006 (P.L. 109-432) (JCX-50-06)).

Besides extending the LUST tax, the Energy Policy Act of 2005, through amendments to provisions outside of the tax code—amendments to the Solid Waste Disposal Act—broadened the uses of the LUST trust fund. Specifically, it authorized trust fund money to be used to carry out a number of monitoring, prevention, detection and compliance initiatives relating to leaking underground storage tanks.

Further, as discussed above, under Code Sec. 9508(c), amounts in the LUST trust fund can be used to carry out section 9003(h) of SWDA, but only as in effect on October 17,

BACKGROUND

1986. The Energy Policy Act of 2005, however, amended section 9003(h) as well, adding, for example, a provision allowing the EPA and states to use LUST trust fund money to correct releases of fuels containing oxygenated fuel additives, such as MTBE and ethanol, that threaten human health or the environment.

Public Law 109-168, which was enacted on January 10, 2006, made some technical corrections to the Solid Waste Disposal Act, as amended by the Energy Policy Act of 2005. Those corrections concerned the regulation of underground tanks and government-owned tanks. That law also extended the authorization for LUST trust fund appropriations through 2011.

Although the Energy Policy Act of 2005 and Public Law 109-168 amended the Solid Waste Disposal Act, neither law amended Code Sec. 9508 to permit the new expenditures from the LUST trust fund (JCX-50-06).

NEW LAW EXPLAINED

New LUST trust fund expenditures have been authorized.—Expenditures from the Leaking Underground Storage Tank (LUST) trust fund are now permitted to carry out various sections of the Solid Waste Disposal Act (SWDA) as in effect on January 10, 2006 (Code Sec. 9508(c), as amended by the Tax Relief and Health Care Act of 2006 (P.L. 109-432)). Thus, LUST trust fund money can now be used to carry out certain amendments to SWDA made by the Energy Policy Act of 2005 (P.L. 109-58) and Public Law 109-168. Specifically, LUST trust fund expenditures are now authorized in connection with the following:

- various requirements imposed on states to protect groundwater, including tank monitoring, proof of financial responsibility by tank manufacturers and installers to pay for corrective actions, and certification or licensure of tank installers (section 9003(i) of SWDA)
- compliance of government-owned tanks with release detection, prevention, and correction regulations (section 9003(j) of SWDA)
- the directive to the EPA to allot at least 80 percent of the trust funds made available to the states for the LUST cleanup program (section 9004(f) of SWDA)
- the requirement that the EPA or the states conduct compliance inspections of underground storage tanks every three years (section 9005(c) of SWDA)
- the addition of operator training requirements (section 9010 of SWDA)
- tank release prevention and compliance (section 9011 of SWDA)
- the prohibition from delivering fuel to ineligible tanks (section 9012 of SWDA)
- the strategy for addressing tanks on tribal lands (section 9013 of SWDA)

In addition, while expenditures from the trust fund were permitted to carry out section 9003(h) of SWDA as in effect on October 17, 1986, now expenditures are permitted to carry out section 9003(h) of SWDA as amended by the Energy Policy Act of 2005. Thus, the EPA and states may now use LUST trust fund money to correct releases of fuels containing oxygenated fuel additives, such as MTBE and ethanol, that threaten human

NEW LAW EXPLAINED

health or the environment (Joint Committee on Taxation, Technical Explanation of the Tax Relief and Health Care Act of 2006 (P.L. 109-432) (JCX-50-06)).

▶ **Effective date.** The provision is effective on December 20, 2006 (Act Sec. 210(c) of the Tax Relief and Health Care Act of 2006 (P.L. 109-432)).

Law source: Law at ¶5870 and ¶7060. Committee Report at ¶15,440.

— Act Sec. 210(a) of the Tax Relief and Health Care Act of 2006 (P.L. 109-432), amending Code Sec. 9508(c);

— Act Sec. 210(b), amending section 9014(2) of the Solid Waste Disposal Act;

— Act Sec. 210(c), providing the effective date.

Reporter references: For further information, consult the following CCH reporters.

— Tax Research Consultant, EXCISE: 3104.05

— Federal Excise Tax Reporter, ¶5700.0129

¶680 Charitable Remainder Trusts Tax Modification

SUMMARY OF NEW LAW

A 100 percent excise tax is imposed on the unrelated business taxable income of charitable remainder trusts.

BACKGROUND

A charitable remainder trust, i.e. a charitable remainder annuity trust (CRAT) or a charitable remainder unitrust (CRUT), is exempt from Federal income taxation, unless it has unrelated business taxable income. If a charitable remainder trust has any unrelated business taxable income, the trust is taxable on all of its income as a complex trust and is allowed the same deductions as a complex trust, including a deduction for distributions to the income beneficiaries.

A CRAT is required to pay, at least annually, a fixed dollar amount of at least five percent (but not more than 50 percent) of the initial value of the trust to a noncharity for the life of an individual or for a period of 20 years or less, with the remainder passing to charity (Code Sec. 664(d)(1)).

> **Example:** John Brennan created a charitable trust with property valued at $100,000. The trust provides a life income only for Mrs. Brennan, with the trust remainder payable to a charity at her death. The trust pays Mrs. Brennan an annual income of $5,000 for her lifetime (5% of the initially valued $100,000 property placed in trust). The trust is a CRAT.

BACKGROUND

A CRUT generally is required to pay, at least annually, a fixed percentage of at least five percent (but not more than 50 percent) of the fair market value of the trust's assets determined at least annually to a noncharity for the life of an individual or for a period of 20 years or less, with the remainder passing to charity (Code Sec. 664(d)(2)).

Example: John Brennan funds a charitable trust with securities valued at $100,000. Annual trust payments are to be made to Brennan, himself, for 15 years, with trust remainder going to a charity at the end of that period. The trust provides for the amount of the annual payments to be based on 5% of the net fair market value of the trust's assets at the end of each year. At the end of the first year, the trust fund is still valued at $100,000, at which time the trust distributes $5,000 to Brennan. At the end of the second year, the trust property is valued at $120,000, and the trust distributes $6,000 to Brennan. The value of the trust property drops down to $110,000 at the end of the third year, at which time the trust distributes $5,500 to Brennan. The trust is a CRUT.

A trust does not qualify as a CRAT or CRUT unless the value of the remainder interest in the trust is at least 10 percent of the value of the assets contributed to the trust.

Pursuant to Code Sec. 664(b), deductions from a CRAT or a CRUT are treated in the following order as:

(1) ordinary income to the extent of the trust's current and previously undistributed ordinary income for the trust's year in which the distribution occurred;

(2) capital gains to the extent of the trust's current capital gain and previously undistributed capital gain for the trust's year in which the distribution occurred;

(3) other income (such as tax-exempt income) to the extent of the trust's current and previously undistributed other income for the trust's year in which the distribution occurred; and

(4) corpus.

Generally, distributions to the extent they are characterized as income are includable in the income of the beneficiary for the year that the annuity or unitrust amount is required to be distributed, even though the annuity or unitrust amount is not distributed until after the close of the trust's tax year (Reg. § 1.664-1(d)(4)).

NEW LAW EXPLAINED

Excise tax imposed on unrelated business taxable income of charitable remainder trusts.—Charitable remainder trusts (i.e., charitable remainder annuity or unitrusts) are subject to a 100-percent excise tax on their unrelated business taxable income. Trusts subject to this tax will retain their tax-exempt status (Code Sec. 664(c)(2)(A), as added by the Tax Relief and Health Care Act of 2006 (P.L. 109-432)). This rule replaces the prior rule that took away the income tax exemption of a charitable remainder trust for any year in which the trust has any unrelated business taxable

NEW LAW EXPLAINED

income (Code Sec. 664(c), prior to amendment by the 2006 Extenders Act). The tax is treated as if it is imposed under the excise tax rules that apply to private foundations and other tax-exempt organizations, other than the rules for abatement of first and second-tier taxes (i.e., Code Secs. 4940-4958) (Code Sec. 664(c)(2)(B), as added by the 2006 Extenders Act).

The unrelated business taxable income is considered income of the trust for purposes of determining the character of the distribution made to the beneficiary. Consistent with present law, the tax is treated as paid from corpus (Joint Committee on Taxation, Technical Explanation of the Tax Relief and Health Care Act of 2006 (P.L. 109-432) (JCX-50-06)).

The claim preclusion rule under Code Sec. 6212(c), which generally prevents the IRS from filing an additional deficiency notice once a taxpayer files a Tax Court petition challenging the deficiency, applies to this tax (Code Sec. 664(c)(2)(C), as added by the 2006 Extenders Act).

▶ **Effective date.** This provision applies to tax years beginning after December 31, 2006 (Act Sec. 424(b) of the Tax Relief and Health Care Act of 2006 (P.L. 109-432)).

Law source: Law at ¶5420. Committee Reports at ¶15,690.

— Act Sec. 424(a) of the Tax Relief and Health Care Act of 2006 (P.L. 109-432), amending Code Sec. 664(c);

— Act Sec. 424(b), providing the effective date.

Reporter references: For further information, consult the following CCH reporters.

— Standard Federal Tax Reporter, ¶24,468.01

— Tax Research Consultant, ESTGIFT: 45,200

— Federal Tax Guide, ¶19,250

— Federal Estate and Gift Tax Reporter, ¶664(c)

¶685 Addition of Meningococcal and Human Papillomavirus Vaccines to List of Taxable Vaccines

SUMMARY OF NEW LAW

Any meningococcal vaccine and any vaccine against the human papillomavirus is added to the list of taxable vaccines.

BACKGROUND

To provide funding for the Vaccine Trust Fund under the National Vaccine Injury Compensation Program, a 75 cents-per-dose manufacturer's excise tax is imposed on

BACKGROUND

the sale of the following vaccines routinely recommended for administration to children: diphtheria, pertussis, tetanus, measles, mumps, rubella, polio, haemophilus influenza type B (HIB), hepatitis A, hepatitis B, chicken pox, rotavirus gastroenteritis, streptococcus pneumoniae and trivalent vaccines against influenza. Vaccines containing more than one taxable vaccine component are taxed at a rate of 75 cents multiplied by the number of components.

The National Vaccine Injury Compensation Program is a no-fault federal insurance system created to compensate individuals who are injured or die due to the administration of these vaccines. Individuals who suffer injuries following the administration of taxable vaccines after September 30, 1988, must pursue their claims under the compensation program before bringing civil tort actions under State law.

NEW LAW EXPLAINED

Addition of vaccines to taxable list.—Any meningococcal vaccine and any vaccine against the human papillomavirus is added to the list of taxable vaccines (Code Sec. 4132(a)(1)(O), as added by the Tax Relief and Health Care Act of 2006 (P.L. 109-432)).

▶ **Effective date.** These amendments to the list of taxable vaccines are effective for sales, uses, and deliveries as follows:

(1) *Sales, etc.* The amendments apply to sales and uses on or after the first day of the first month which begins more than four weeks after December 20, 2006, the date of enactment (Act Sec. 408(c)(1) of the Tax Relief and Health Care Act of 2006 (P.L. 109-432)).

(2) *Deliveries.* For purposes of paragraph (1) and Code Sec. 4131, in the case of sales on or before the effective date in (1) for which delivery is made after that date, the delivery date is considered the sale date (Act Sec. 408(c)(2) of the 2006 Extenders Act).

Law source: Law at ¶5670. Committee Reports at ¶15,530.

— Act Sec. 408(a) and Act Sec. 408(b) of the Tax Relief and Health Care Act of 2006 (P.L. 109-432), adding Code Sec. 4132(a)(1)(O);

— Act Sec. 408(c), providing the effective date.

Reporter references: For further information, consult the following CCH reporters.

— Tax Research Consultant, EXCISE: 6160.05

— Federal Tax Guide, ¶21,710

— Federal Excise Tax Reporter, ¶12,375.01 and ¶12,575.01

¶690 Cover Over of Tax on Rum

SUMMARY OF NEW LAW

The $13.25 per proof gallon cover over amount for rum brought into the United States is extended through December 31, 2007.

BACKGROUND

A $13.50 per proof gallon excise tax is imposed on all distilled spirits produced in, or imported into, the United States (Code Sec. 5001(a)(1)). This excise tax does not apply to distilled spirits that are exported from the United States or to distilled spirits that are consumed in U.S. possessions, such as Puerto Rico and the Virgin Islands.

Puerto Rico and the Virgin Islands receive a payment ("cover over") limited to the amount of $10.50 per proof gallon of the excise tax imposed on rum brought into the United States (Code Sec. 7652(f)). The payment is made with respect to all rum entering the United States on which tax is paid, not just rum originating in the two possessions. The cover over payment limit was temporarily set at $13.25 per proof gallon for the period July 1, 1999, through December 31, 2005.

Tax amounts from rum produced in Puerto Rico are covered over to Puerto Rico, and tax amounts from rum produced in the Virgin Islands are covered over to the Virgin Islands. Tax amounts from rum produced in neither Puerto Rico nor the Virgin Islands are divided and covered over to the two possessions under a formula. All amounts covered over are subject to the dollar limitation.

NEW LAW EXPLAINED

Increased cover over limit extended.—The $13.25 per proof gallon cover over amount to Puerto Rico and Virgin Islands for rum brought into the United States is extended for two more years, through December 31, 2007 (Code Sec. 7652(f)(1), as amended by the Tax Relief and Health Care Act of 2006 (P.L. 109-432)). Beginning on January 1, 2008, the cover over amount reverts to $10.50 per proof gallon.

▶ **Effective date.** The provision applies to articles brought into the United States after December 31, 2005 (Act Sec. 114(b) of the Tax Relief and Health Care Act of 2006 (P.L. 109-432)).

Law source: Law at ¶5850. Committee Report at ¶15,230.

— Act Sec. 114(a) of the Tax Relief and Health Care Act of 2006 (P.L. 109-432), amending Code Sec. 7652(f)(1);

— Act Sec. 114(b), providing the effective date.

Reporter references: For further information, consult the following CCH reporters.

— Standard Federal Tax Reporter, ¶42,968F.01

— Federal Tax Guide, ¶21,740

— Federal Excise Tax Reporter, ¶58,275.01

¶690

TIPRA—Individuals

7

CROSS REFERENCES

Capital gains rates for individuals (*see ¶905*)

Dividends rates for individuals (*see ¶920*)

Foreign income and housing exclusions (*see ¶1005*)

Tax rate on nonexcluded foreign income (*see ¶1010*)

¶705 Elimination of Income Limits on Roth IRA Conversions

SUMMARY OF NEW LAW

The $100,000 AGI limit on the conversion of a traditional IRA to a Roth IRA is eliminated effective for tax years beginning after December 31, 2009. For conversions in 2010, taxpayers can recognize conversion income ratably in 2011 and 2012. For conversions after 2010, all of the conversion income has to be recognized in the year of conversion.

BACKGROUND

There are two kinds of individual retirement accounts (IRAs): the traditional IRA and the Roth IRA. Both are subject to the same contribution limit of $4,000 ($8,000 for married couples filing jointly) in 2006 and the same catch-up contribution limit of

BACKGROUND

$1,000 for taxpayers age 50 or older ($2,000 for joint filers if each spouse qualifies) (Code Secs. 219(b)(5) and 408A(c)(2)). Both allow income on funds held in the account to grow tax free (Code Secs. 408(e)(1) and 408A(a)). There are major differences, however.

First, contributions to a traditional IRA are deductible if certain conditions are met, while contributions to a Roth IRA are never deductible. A contribution to a traditional IRA may not be fully deductible if the taxpayer or the taxpayer's spouse is an active participant in an employer-sponsored retirement plan (Code Sec. 219(g)). Taxpayers who cannot make deductible (or fully deductible) contributions to a traditional IRA may make nondeductible contributions up to the maximum annual contribution limit. A taxpayer may also elect to treat deductible contributions as nondeductible contributions. Distributions or portions of distributions treated as a return of nondeductible contributions are not taxed (Code Sec. 408(o)).

Second, distributions from traditional IRAs (unless they are returns of nondeductible contributions) are taxable (Code Sec. 408(d)(1)), while qualified distributions from a Roth IRA are not. A Roth IRA distribution is not qualified unless it is made more than five years after the first tax year for which the taxpayer or the taxpayer's spouse made a contribution to a Roth IRA for the taxpayer (Code Sec. 408A(d)(2)(B)). Distributions that are not qualified are taxable.

Third, eligibility to make nondeductible contributions to a traditional IRA is not limited by income, while eligibility to make contributions to a Roth IRA is subject to modified adjusted gross income limits. The maximum Roth IRA contribution is phased out between $150,000 to $160,000 in the case of married taxpayers filing jointly; between $0 and $10,000 for married taxpayers filing separate returns; and between $95,000 to $105,000 for all other taxpayers (Code Sec. 408A(c)(3)(A)).

Fourth, the required minimum distribution (RMD) rules apply to traditional IRAs, but not to Roth IRAs during the lifetime of the owner (Code Sec. 408A(d)(5)). The RMD rules are designed to ensure that a retirement account is distributed and taxed during the individual's retirement years, rather than saved in the tax deferred account for the next generation. The RMD rules for traditional IRAs require distributions to begin no later than April 1 of the calendar year after the year in which the taxpayer reaches age $70\frac{1}{2}$. Distributions must be made by December 31 of each year after the year the taxpayer reaches that age (Code Secs. 408(a)(6), (b)(3) and 401(a)(9); Reg § 1.408-1).

Fifth, taxpayers cannot contribute to a traditional IRA after reaching age $70\frac{1}{2}$, but they can continue contributing to a Roth IRA as long as they have earned income (Code Secs. 219(d)(1) and 408A(d)(4)).

Conversion of traditional IRA to Roth IRA. A taxpayer can convert a traditional IRA to a Roth IRA but only if the taxpayer's adjusted gross income does not exceed $100,000 (Code Sec. 408A(c)(3)(B)). A required minimum distribution from an IRA is not taken into account for purposes of determining the $100,000 limit (Code Sec. 408A(c)(3)(C)(i)). A married taxpayer filing a separate return is prohibited from making a conversion (Code Sec. 408A(c)(3)(B)). The amount converted is treated as distributed from the traditional IRA and, thus, is included in the taxpayer's income,

BACKGROUND

but the 10-percent additional tax for early withdrawals does not apply (Code Sec. 408A(d)(3)(A)(ii)).

Ordering rules for distributions from converted Roth IRAs. Ordering rules apply to determine which amounts are withdrawn for tax purposes where a Roth IRA contains both conversion and contributed amounts, or conversion amounts from different years. Under these rules, regular Roth IRA contributions are deemed to be withdrawn first, then conversion contributions on a first-in, first-out basis, then earnings. Distributions of conversion contributions are treated as made first from the portion that was required to be included in income as a result of the conversion (Code Sec. 408A(d)(4)(B)).

NEW LAW EXPLAINED

Income limit on conversions eliminated.—For tax years beginning after December 31, 2009, the Tax Increase Prevention and Reconciliation Act of 2005 (P.L. 109-222) eliminates the $100,000 adjusted gross income limitation on a conversion of a traditional IRA to a Roth IRA (Code Sec. 408A(c), as amended by the Tax Reconciliation Act of 2005). This provision does not sunset.

Ratable inclusion in gross income over two-tax-year spread. For conversions in 2010, the taxpayer recognizes the conversion amount ratably in adjusted gross income (AGI) in 2011 and 2012 unless the taxpayer elects to recognize it all in 2010 (Code Sec. 408A(d)(3)(A)(iii), as amended by the Tax Reconciliation Act of 2005).

> **Comment:** The two-tax-year spread for recognizing conversion income is modeled on (and in the Code now takes the place of) a provision providing a four-tax-year spread for conversions in 1998.

> **Example 1:** Jack has a traditional IRA with a value of $100 consisting of deductible contributions and earnings. He does not have a Roth IRA. He converts the traditional IRA to a Roth IRA in 2010, and as a result of the conversion, has $100 in gross income. Unless Jack elects otherwise, $50 of the income is included in income in 2011, and $50 is included in income in 2012.

> **Planning Note:** If the tax rate reductions made by the Economic Growth and Tax Relief Reconciliation Act of 2001 (P.L. 107-16) are allowed to sunset as scheduled after 2010, recognizing all of the conversion income in 2010 might be the best tax strategy for many taxpayers.

No special provision is made for years after 2010, so taxpayers making conversions in 2011 and thereafter will have to recognize the entire amount of conversion income in the tax year of conversion.

Acceleration of income for distributions before 2012. For taxpayers who opt to include a 2010 conversion in income ratably in 2011 and 2012, distribution of conversion amounts before 2012 results in acceleration of income. The amount included in

NEW LAW EXPLAINED

income in the year of the distribution is increased by the amount distributed. The amount included in income in 2011 and in 2012 is the lesser of:

- half of the amount includible in income as a result of the conversion, or
- the remaining portion of the amount includible in income that was not already included in income (Code Sec. 408A(d)(3)(E)(i), as amended by the Tax Reconciliation Act of 2005).

Example 2: Jack from Example 1 takes a post-conversion distribution of $20 in 2010. The distribution is not a qualified distribution and, under the ordering rules, all of it is attributable to amounts includible in gross income as a result of the conversion. Under the accelerated inclusion rule, $20 is included in income in 2010. The amount included in income in 2011 is $50, which is the lesser of (1) $50 (half of the income resulting from the conversion), or (2) $80 (the remaining untaxed income from the conversion). The amount included in 2012 is $30, which is the lesser of (1) $50 (half of the income resulting from the conversion) or (2) $30 (the remaining untaxed income from the conversion). The result is that instead of including $50 in income in 2011, and $50 in 2012, Jack has $20 in income in 2010, $50 in 2011, and $30 in 2012.

Comment: The above example is based on an example in the Conference Committee Report (H.R. Conf. Rep. No. 109-455). The example in the report used a figure of $70 instead of $80 for the remaining income from the conversion in 2011. That appears to be a mistake because as of 2011, only $20 of the $100 has been taxed.

Although the elimination of the $100,000 income limit for Roth conversions is billed as a revenue enhancer, it opens the door to some serious tax savings for higher income taxpayers, not only by enabling them to take advantage of Roth conversions, but also by allowing them to use a traditional IRA as a conduit to Roth IRAs for contributions and rollovers that would otherwise be prohibited.

Planning Note: The income limits on both kinds of IRAs have prevented higher income taxpayers from making deductible contributions to traditional IRAs or any contributions to Roth IRAs. They could always make nondeductible contributions to a traditional IRA, but such contributions have a limited pay-off (no current deduction, tax on account income is deferred rather than eliminated, required minimum distributions). A taxpayer could avoid these problems by making nondeductible contributions to a traditional IRA and then converting it to a Roth IRA, but this option was not available for upper income taxpayers who would have the most to benefit from such a conversion. With the elimination of the income limit for tax years after December 31, 2009, higher income taxpayers can begin now to make nondeductible contributions to a traditional IRA and then convert them to a Roth IRA in 2010. In all likelihood, there will be little to tax on the converted amount. They could continue making nondeductible IRA contributions in the future and roll them over into a Roth IRA periodically. Thus,

¶705

NEW LAW EXPLAINED

the elimination of the income limit for converting to a Roth IRA also effectively eliminates the income limit for contributing to a Roth IRA.

Example 3: Ralph and Wilma are a married couple with $300,000 in income. They are not eligible to contribute to a Roth IRA because their adjusted gross income exceeds the $160,000 Roth IRA eligibility limit. Beginning in 2006, the couple makes the maximum allowed nondeductible IRA contribution ($8,000 in 2006 and 2007, and $10,000 in 2008, 2009, and 2010). In 2010, their account is worth $60,000, with $46,000 of that amount representing nondeductible contributions that are not taxed upon conversion. The couple rolls over the $60,000 in their traditional IRA into a Roth IRA. They must include $14,000 in income (the amount representing their deductible contributions), which they can recognize either in 2010, or ratably in 2011 and 2012. Assuming they have sufficient earned income each year thereafter (until reaching age 70½) , the couple can continue to make the maximum nondeductible contributions to a traditional IRA and quickly roll over these funds into their Roth IRA, thereby avoiding significant taxable growth in the assets that would have to be recognized upon distribution from a traditional IRA. There is no sunset on this strategy.

Planning Note: Contributions to a Code Sec. 401(k) plan (or CODA plan) cannot be rolled over directly into a Roth IRA. However, they can be rolled over into a traditional IRA and then, under the strategy discussed above, into a Roth IRA.

Married taxpayers filing separate returns. Married taxpayers who file separate returns are no longer prohibited from converting amounts in a traditional IRA into a Roth IRA. Thus, they can make a conversion under the same rules that apply to other taxpayers (Code Sec. 408A(c)(3)(B)(ii), repealed by the Tax Reconciliation Act of 2005).

Conforming amendments. The rule that excludes required minimum distributions from income for purposes of the $100,000 adjusted gross income limit for making Roth conversions is removed along with the $100,000 limit (Code Sec. 408A(c)(3)(C)(i), as amended by the Tax Reconciliation Act of 2005).

Planning Note: In deciding whether to convert a traditional IRA to a Roth IRA, a key factor is whether the taxpayer anticipates being in a higher or lower tax bracket after retirement. The traditional IRA tax deferral works well for individuals who fall into a lower tax bracket during retirement. It is often the case, however, that high-income taxpayers end up in the same or a higher bracket.

The effect of required distribution rules on the taxpayer is another consideration in conversion. These rules apply only to traditional IRAs. Most retirees do not feel a pinch from required distributions because they are living off of the account—indeed their problem is in not distributing the account too soon. In contrast, higher income taxpayers who do not need to draw down the account experience the required minimum distribution rules as a nuisance since they force a portion of the assets out of the tax-favored account. Because these rules do not apply to a Roth IRA, it is an ideal tax-free vehicle for preserving assets for the next generation. Note too that the heirs of an inherited IRA are taxed just as

NEW LAW EXPLAINED

the taxpayer was. Thus, if a traditional IRA outlasts the taxpayer, the beneficiaries still have to pay tax on account distributions. In contrast, since Roth IRA distributions are not taxable to the taxpayer, they also are not taxable to the taxpayer's heirs.

Another Roth IRA advantage for high income taxpayers is that there is no prohibition against contributing after age 70½ (as long as they have sufficient earned income) as there is with traditional IRAs. Of course, the traditional prohibition is hardly a hardship for most retirees, who rarely have extra money at that age, but it does make a Roth IRA even more attractive for higher-income individuals who do.

Caution Note: In spite of all the advantages of a Roth IRA, a conversion is advisable only if the taxpayer can readily pay the tax. If the tax is paid out of a distribution from the converted IRA, that amount is also taxed; and if the distribution counts as an early withdrawal, it is also subject to an additional 10-percent penalty. Taking a large taxable distribution may also have a negative effect on income-sensitive tax benefits. Finally, state law creditor protection is common for traditional IRAs, but less so for Roth IRAs.

▶ **Effective date.** The provision applies to tax years beginning after December 31, 2009 (Act Sec. 512(c) of the Tax Increase Prevention and Reconciliation Act of 2005 (P.L. 109-222)).

Law source: Law at ¶5380. Committee Report at ¶10,260.

— Act Sec. 512(a)(1) of the Tax Increase Prevention and Reconciliation Act of 2005 (P.L. 109-222), repealing Code Sec. 408A(c)(3)(B), and redesignating Code Sec. 408A(c)(3)(C) and (D) as Code Sec. 408A(c)(3)(B) and (C) respectively;

— Act Sec. 512(a)(2), amending redesignated Code Sec. 408A(c)(3)(B)(i);

— Act Sec. 512(b)(1), amending Code Sec. 408A(d)(3)(A)(iii);

— Act Sec. 512(b)(2), amending Code Sec. 408A(d)(3)(E); and

— Act Sec. 512(c), providing the effective date.

Reporter references: For further information, consult the following CCH reporters.

— Standard Federal Tax Reporter, ¶18,930.032 and ¶18,930.033

— Tax Research Consultant, RETIRE: 66,706 and RETIRE: 66,760.10

— Federal Tax Guide, ¶11,460

¶710 Increased Age Limit for Kiddie Tax

SUMMARY OF NEW LAW

The age of minor children whose investment income is subject to tax at the parent's higher rate is increased from under age 14 to under age 18. Distributions from qualified disability trusts are treated as earned income of the child; therefore, the distributions are exempt from the kiddie tax.

BACKGROUND

The amount of investment income of a child under the age of 14 that exceeds the annual inflation adjusted amount ($1,700 in 2006) is generally taxed at the parents' highest marginal rate. This is referred to as the kiddie tax. Investment income includes all taxable income other than earned income; therefore, it is also referred to as unearned income. Investment income includes taxable interest, ordinary dividends, capital gains, rents and royalties. It also includes taxable social security benefits, pension and annuity income and income (other than earned income) received as the beneficiary of a trust. Earned income refers to wages, tips, salaries, professional fees or other amounts received as pay for work actually done (Code Secs. 1(g)(4) and 911(d)(2)(A)).

The kiddie tax is designed to lessen the effectiveness of intra-family transfers of income-producing property, which shift income produced from such property from the parent's high marginal tax rate to the child's generally lower tax bracket, thereby reducing the family's overall income tax liability. The kiddie tax applies if a child is under age 14 before the close of the tax year and either parent is alive at the close of such year, regardless of whether the child may be claimed as a dependent on the parent's return (Code Sec. 1(g)(2)).

Net investment income is the total of all investment income (other than tax-exempt income) reduced by the sum of the adjustments to income related to investment income plus the larger of:

(1) $850 (in 2006) plus the itemized deductions connected with producing the investment income, or

(2) $1,700 (in 2006) (Code Sec. 1(g)(4); Rev. Proc. 2005-70, I.R.B. 2005-47, 979; IRS Publication 929, Tax Rules for Children and Dependents (2005)).

In 2006, a child's net investment income in excess of $1,700 will be taxed at the parents' rate if the parent's rate is higher than the child's rate. However, the amount of the net investment income for any tax year cannot exceed the child's taxable income for such year (Code Sec. 1(g)(4)(B)).

The imposition of the kiddie tax requires a calculation of the parent's allocable parental tax (Code Sec. 1(g)(3)). Allocable parental tax is the hypothetical increase in tax to the parent that results from adding the child's net investment income to the parent's taxable income (Code Sec. 1(g)(3)(A)). If the parent has more than one child subject to the kiddie tax, the net investment income of all children is combined, and a single kiddie tax is calculated. Each child is then calculated a proportionate share of a hypothetical increase, based upon the child's net investment income relative to the aggregate net investment income of all the parent's children subject to the tax (Code Sec. 1(g)(3)(B)).

NEW LAW EXPLAINED

Age increased to under 18 for application of kiddie tax; qualified disability trust distributions not subject to kiddie tax.—The age of a child whose unearned income is taxed at the parent's higher tax rate is increased from under age 14 to under age 18

NEW LAW EXPLAINED

(Code Sec. 1(g)(2)(A), as amended by the Tax Increase Prevention and Reconciliation Act of 2005 (P.L. 109-222)). The amendment is effective for tax years beginning after December 31, 2005.

> **Comment:** The application of the kiddie tax has been expanded to include investment income of children age 14 to under age 18. Prior to the amendment, investment income of a child age 14 and up was includible in the child's gross income and taxed at the child's tax rate. As amended, the kiddie tax will cease to apply when the child is 18 years old as of the close of the tax year.

> **Planning Note:** Since the age increase is effective for tax year 2006, this amendment has immediate impact. Parents who had planned to sell a child's college stock portfolio in 2006 when the child reaches 14 now have to wait for more years if they intend to take advantage of the child's lower tax rate. If the parents plan to postpone a sale until 2008 when the child's capital gains rate could be zero, then they have to make sure that the child reaches 18 by then, otherwise, the gain will still be taxed at the parent's presumably higher rate.

> **Compliance Pointer:** Unless the parent elects to include the child's income on the parent's return, the child must file a separate return to report his or her income. The child must attach Form 8615, Tax for Children Under Age 14 Who Have Investment Income of More Than $1,600 (which has to be revised to reflect the amendments and the annual inflation adjustments) to his or her return. Form 8814, Parent's Election to Report Child's Interest and Dividends, has to be filed if the parent elects to report the child's unearned income on the parent's return. If the election is made, the child is treated as having no income; hence, the child does not have to file a return (IRS Publication 929, Tax Rules for Children and Dependents (2005)).

> **Comment:** The parent's deductions and credits that are based on the adjusted gross income, as well as income-based phaseouts, limitations and floors are affected when the child's income is included on the parent's return. In addition, certain deductions that the child would have been entitled to take on his or her own return are lost. If the child received tax-exempt interest from a private activity bond, that item is considered a tax preference of the parent for alternative minimum tax purposes (Conference Committee Report (H.R. Conf. Rep. No. 109-455)).

Exception. The kiddie tax rules do not apply to a child who files a joint return for the tax year, effective for tax years beginning after December 31, 2005 (Code Sec. 1(g)(2)(C), as added by the Tax Reconciliation Act of 2005).

> **Comment:** The unearned income of a child who is age 17 and married in 2006 is not subject to the kiddie tax if the child files a joint return for tax year 2006. The child's eligibility to file a joint return is not enough to avoid application of the kiddie tax. The child must actually file a joint return for the tax year. There are now three circumstances in which the kiddie tax rules do not apply:

> (1) the child is 18 years old as of the close of the tax year;

> (2) neither parent is alive at the close of the tax year; or

NEW LAW EXPLAINED

(3) the child is married and files a joint return for the tax year (Code Sec. 1(g)(2), as amended by the Tax Reconciliation Act of 2005).

Distributions from qualified disability trusts. Any distribution under Code Secs. 652 and 662 to a child who is a beneficiary of a qualified disability trust as defined in Code Sec. 642(b)(2)(C)(ii) is treated as the child's earned income for the tax year the distribution was received (Code Sec. 1(g)(4)(C), as added by the Tax Reconciliation Act of 2005). Earned income treatment excludes the distribution from application of the kiddie tax rules. Any amount required to be included in the child's gross income from the qualified disability trust distributions is taxed at the child's tax rate.

▶ **Effective date.** The amendments apply to tax years beginning after December 31, 2005 (Act Sec. 510(d) of the Tax Increase Prevention and Reconciliation Act of 2005 (P.L. 109-222)).

Law source: Law at ¶5005. Committee Report at ¶10,240.

— Act Sec. 510(a) of the Tax Increase Prevention and Reconciliation Act of 2005 (P.L. 109-222), amending Code Sec. 1(g)(2)(A);

— Act Sec. 510(b), adding Code Sec. 1(g)(4)(C);

— Act Sec. 510(c), amending Code Sec. 1(g)(2)(A) and (B) and adding Code Sec. 1(g)(2)(C);

— Act Sec. 510(d), providing the effective date.

Reporter references: For further information, consult the following CCH reporters.

— Standard Federal Tax Reporter, ¶3280.01, ¶3280.022 and ¶3280.025

— Tax Research Consultant, FILEIND: 100, FILEIND: 15,052.20, INDIV: 100, INDIV: 18,154 and INDIV: 18,156,

— Federal Tax Guide, ¶1070

¶715 Capital Gains Treatment for Self-Created Musical Works

SUMMARY OF NEW LAW

A taxpayer may elect to treat the sale or exchange of musical compositions or copyrights in musical works created by the taxpayer's personal efforts (or having a basis determined by reference to the basis in the hands of the taxpayer whose personal efforts created the composition or copyrights) as the sale or exchange of a capital asset. The election was added by the Tax Increase Prevention and Reconciliation Act of 2005 (P.L. 109-222) and made permanent by the Tax Relief and Health Care Act of 2006 (P.L. 109-432) (see ¶240).

¶720 Alternative Minimum Tax Exemption Amount

SUMMARY OF NEW LAW

The alternative minimum tax exemption amount for individuals is increased for tax years beginning in 2006.

BACKGROUND

In addition to all other tax liabilities, an individual is subject to an alternative minimum tax (AMT) to the extent that his or her tentative minimum tax exceeds the amount of regular income tax owed (Code Sec. 55). An individual's tentative minimum tax is generally equal to the sum of: (1) 26 percent of the first $175,000 ($87,500 for a married taxpayer filing a separate return) of the taxpayer's alternative minimum taxable income (AMTI); and (2) 28 percent of the taxpayer's remaining AMTI (Code Sec. 55(b)(1)(A)).

AMTI is the individual's regular taxable income recomputed with certain adjustments and increased by certain tax preferences (Code Sec. 56). A specified amount of AMTI is exempt from tax based on the taxpayer's filing status. For example, the exemption amount for tax years prior to 2001 was: (1) $45,000 for married individuals filing a joint return and surviving spouses; (2) $33,750 for unmarried individuals; and (3) $22,500 for married individuals filing separate returns (Code Sec. 55(d)(1), prior to amendment by the Economic Growth and Tax Relief Reconciliation Act of 2001 (P.L. 107-16)).

The exemption amounts, however, are not indexed for inflation. Consequently, the number of individuals affected by the AMT has increased each tax year. To alleviate this problem, the exemption amount was increased for tax years beginning in 2001 through 2005. The exemption amount that applied for tax years beginning in 2001 and 2002 was: (1) $49,000 for married individuals filing a joint return and surviving spouses; (2) $35,750 for unmarried individuals; and (3) $24,500 for married individuals filing separate returns (Code Sec. 55(d)(1), as amended by the Economic Growth and Tax Relief Reconciliation Act of 2001 (P.L. 107-16)).

The exemption amount for tax years beginning in 2003 through 2005 was: (1) $58,000 for married individuals filing a joint return and surviving spouses; (2) $40,250 for unmarried individuals; and (3) $29,000 for married individuals filing separate returns (Code Sec. 55(d)(1), as amended by the Jobs and Growth Tax Relief Reconciliation Act of 2003 (P.L. 108-27) and the Working Families Tax Relief Act of 2004 (P.L. 108-311)). For tax years beginning after 2005, the AMT exemption amount for individuals is scheduled to revert to the exemption amounts that applied prior to 2001.

> **Comment:** The exemption amount for corporations, and estates or trusts, have remained unchanged during this period. The exemption amount is $40,000 for a corporation and $22,500 for an estate or trust.

Regardless of the tax year, the AMT exemption amount is phased out for taxpayers with high AMTI. The exemption amount is reduced by an amount equal to 25 percent of the amount by which the taxpayer's AMTI for the tax year exceeds: (1) $150,000 in

BACKGROUND

the case of married individuals filing a joint return, surviving spouses and corporations; (2) $112,500 in the case of unmarried individuals; and (3) $75,000 in the case of married individuals filing separate returns, or an estate or trust (Code Sec. 55(d)(3)). These threshold amounts are not indexed for inflation.

NEW LAW EXPLAINED

Extension of AMT exemption amounts.—The alternative minimum tax (AMT) exemption amount for individuals is increased for tax years beginning in 2006, to:

- $62,550 for married individuals filing a joint return and surviving spouses;
- $42,500 for unmarried individuals; and
- $31,275 for married individuals filing separate returns (Code Sec. 55(d)(1)(A) and (B), as amended by the Tax Increase Prevention and Reconciliation Act of 2005 (P.L. 109-222)).

The $40,000 exemption amount for corporations and the $22,500 exemption amount for estates or trusts remains unchanged for tax years beginning in 2006.

> **Comment:** Absent another legislative extension, the AMT exemption amounts for individuals are scheduled to revert for tax years beginning after 2006 to the amounts that applied prior to the 2001 tax year. Thus, the exemption amounts would be: (1) $45,000 for married individuals filing a joint return and surviving spouses; (2) $33,750 for unmarried individuals; and (3) $22,500 for married individuals filing separate returns.

> **Caution Note:** Although the AMT exemption amounts for individuals is increased for 2006, the threshold levels for the calculation of the phase-out remain unchanged. Thus, the exemption amount for tax years beginning in 2006 is still reduced by 25 percent for each $1 of alternative minimum taxable income (AMTI) in excess of: (1) $150,000 in the case of married individuals filing a joint return, surviving spouses and corporations; (2) $112,500 in the case of unmarried individuals; and (3) $75,000 in the case of married individuals filing separate returns or an estate or a trust.

▶ **Effective date.** The amendments made by this section shall apply to tax years beginning after December 31, 2005 (Act Sec. 301(b) of the Tax Increase Prevention and Reconciliation Act of 2005 (P.L. 109-222)).

Law source: Law at ¶5080. Committee Report at ¶10,120.

— Act Sec. 301(a) of the Tax Increase Prevention and Reconciliation Act of 2005 (P.L. 109-222), amending Code Sec. 55(d)(1)(A) and (B);

— Act Sec. 301(b), providing the effective date.

Reporter references: For further information, consult the following CCH reporters.

— Standard Federal Tax Reporter, ¶5101.035 and ¶5101.036

— Tax Research Consultant, FILEIND: 100 and FILEIND: 30,400

— Federal Tax Guide, ¶1320 and ¶1430

¶725 Nonrefundable Personal Credits Offset Against Regular Tax and Alternative Minimum Tax Liability Extended

SUMMARY OF NEW LAW

The provision allowing nonrefundable personal tax credits to the full extent of the individual's regular tax and alternative minimum tax liability is extended to tax years beginning in 2006.

BACKGROUND

The nonrefundable personal tax credits available to individual taxpayers include the dependent care credit, the credit for the elderly and disabled, the adoption credit, the child tax credit, the credit for interest on certain home mortgages, the education credits, the savers' credit, the credit for certain nonbusiness energy property, the credit for residential energy efficient property, the personal use portion of the alternative motor vehicle credit, the personal use portion of the alternative motor vehicle refueling property credit, and the District of Columbia first-time homebuyer credit.

> **Comment:** The credit for certain nonbusiness energy property, the credit for residential energy efficient property, the alternative motor vehicle credit, and the alternative motor vehicle refueling property credit were added by the Energy Tax Incentives Act of 2005 (P.L. 109-58) and generally apply to properties placed in service after December 31, 2005 (Code Secs. 25C, 25D, 30B and 30C). The alternative motor vehicle credit and the refueling property credit may be claimed for business as well as nonbusiness use.

The total amount of personal credits a taxpayer may claim is limited based on the taxpayer's tax liability. The nonrefundable personal credits, with certain exceptions, are subject to the limitation set forth in Code Sec. 26. However, the personal use portions of the credits for alternative motor vehicles and alternative motor vehicle refueling property are subject to the limitations found at Code Secs. 30B(g)(2) and 30C(d)(2), respectively. The adoption credit, the child tax credit and the savers' credit are also subject to separate limitations provided in Code Secs. 23(b)(4), 24(b)(3) and 25B(g), respectively.

For tax years beginning in 2000 through 2005, the nonrefundable personal credits are allowed to the extent of the full amount of the taxpayer's regular tax and alternative minimum tax liability. The regular tax liability, however, must first be reduced by the amount of any applicable foreign tax credit (Code Sec. 26(a)(2)(A)).

For tax years beginning after 2005, the aggregate amount of nonrefundable personal credits, except for the adoption credit, the child tax credit and the savers' credit, is limited to the excess of the taxpayer's regular tax liability over the tentative minimum tax liability, determined without regard to the alternative minimum tax foreign tax credit (Code Sec. 26(a)(1)). The personal use portions of the alternative motor vehicle

BACKGROUND

and alternative motor vehicle refueling property credits are limited to the excess of the taxpayer's regular tax liability, reduced by all other nonrefundable credits plus the foreign tax credit and the credit for qualified electric vehicles, over the tentative minimum tax liability (Code Secs. 30B(g)(2) and 30C(d)(2)). Thus, all nonrefundable personal credits, except for the child tax credit, the adoption credit and the savers' credit, will be able to only offset regular tax liability to the extent it exceeds the tentative minimum tax.

The adoption credit, the child tax credit and the savers' credit are allowed to the full extent of the taxpayer's regular tax and alternative minimum tax liability for any tax year to which Code Sec. 26(a)(2) does not apply (Code Secs. 23(b)(4), 24(b)(3) and 25B(g)).

> **Comment:** Only these three credits, therefore, may be claimed against both the regular tax and minimum tax liability for tax years after 2005. However, the savers' credit is scheduled to terminate for tax years beginning after 2006.

NEW LAW EXPLAINED

Nonrefundable personal credits allowed against regular tax and alternative minimum tax liability for tax years beginning in 2006.—For tax years beginning in 2006, the nonrefundable personal tax credits are allowed to the full extent of the taxpayer's regular tax and alternative minimum tax liability. For this purpose, the regular tax liability is first reduced by the amount of any applicable foreign tax credit (Code Sec. 26(a)(2), as amended by the Tax Increase Prevention and Reconciliation Act of 2005 (P.L. 109-222)).

> **Comment:** This extension provision does not apply to the personal use portions of the nonrefundable tax credits for alternative motor vehicles and alternative motor vehicle refueling property. The personal use portion of these credits, therefore, is limited to the excess of the taxpayer's regular tax liability, reduced by all other nonrefundable credits plus the foreign tax credit and the credit for qualified electric vehicles, over the tentative minimum tax (Code Secs. 30B(g)(2) and 30C(d)(2)).

▶ **Effective date.** The provision applies to tax years beginning after December 31, 2005 (Act Sec. 302(b) of the Tax Increase Prevention and Reconciliation Act of 2005 (P.L. 109-222)).

Law source: Law at ¶5030. Committee Report at ¶10,130.

— Act Sec. 302(a) of the Tax Increase Prevention and Reconciliation Act of 2005 (P.L. 109-222), amending Code Sec. 26(a)(2);

— Act Sec. 302(b), providing the effective date.

Reporter references: For further information, consult the following CCH reporters.

— Standard Federal Tax Reporter, ¶3851.01

— Tax Research Consultant, INDIV: 57,200, INDIV: 57,350, INDIV: 57,450, INDIV: 57,550 and INDIV: 57,852

— Federal Tax Guide, ¶1320 and ¶2050

¶730 Treatment of Loans to Qualified Continuing Care Facilities Modified

SUMMARY OF NEW LAW

The requirements for exemption from the below-market interest loan rules for loans to continuing care facilities are relaxed. The provision was added by the Tax Increase Prevention and Reconciliation Act of 2005 (P.L. 109-222) and made permanent by the Tax Relief and Health Care Act of 2006 (P.L. 109-432) (see ¶245).

TIPRA—Businesses

8

DEDUCTIONS

CORPORATIONS

SETTLEMENT FUNDS

DEDUCTIONS

¶805 Extension of Increased Expensing for Small Business

SUMMARY OF NEW LAW

The $100,000 expensing limit for qualified depreciable property is extended two years, through 2009.

BACKGROUND

Code Sec. 179 permits taxpayers that purchase tangible depreciable property to deduct the cost of the property in the year that it is placed in service. This deduction is in lieu of depreciating the property and recovering the cost over a number of years through the modified accelerated cost recovery system (MACRS). The Jobs and Growth Tax Relief Reconciliation Act of 2003 (JGTRRA) (P.L. 108-27) increased the maximum dollar amount that could be deducted under Code Sec. 179 from $25,000 to $100,000 for tax years beginning in 2003, 2004, and 2005 (Code Sec. 179(b)(1)).

> **Caution Note:** The Code Sec. 179 deduction is not available to estates, trusts, and certain noncorporate lessors (Code Sec. 179(d)(4) and (5)).

> **Comment:** The $100,000 limit was adjusted for inflation in 2004 and 2005 (Code Sec. 179(b)(5)). The inflation-adjusted limit for 2004 was $102,000 (Rev. Proc. 2003-85, 2003-2 CB 1184) and the limit for 2005 was $105,000 (Rev. Proc. 2004-71, 2004-2 CB 970).

The American Jobs Creation Act of 2004 (AJCA) (P.L. 108-357) extended for an additional two years the changes made to the Code Sec. 179 expense allowance by JGTRRA. As a result, the $100,000 amount (as adjusted for inflation) applies for tax years beginning in 2006 and 2007. The inflation-adjusted limit for 2006 is $108,000 (Rev. Proc. 2005-70, I.R.B. 2005-47, 979) and for 2007 is $112,000 (Rev. Proc. 2006-53, I.R.B. 2006-48, 996).

For tax years beginning after 2002, the $100,000 limit is reduced dollar-for-dollar (but not below zero) by the amount by which the cost of qualifying property placed in service during the tax year exceeds $400,000 (Code Sec. 179(b)(2)). The $400,000 limit, which is adjusted for inflation, applies to tax years beginning before 2008.

> **Comment:** The inflation-adjusted investment limitation for 2005 was $420,000 (Rev. Proc. 2004-71, 2004-2 CB 970), the limit for 2006 is $430,000 (Rev. Proc. 2005-70, I.R.B. 2005-47, 979) and the limit for 2007 is $450,000 (Rev. Proc. 2006-53, I.R.B. 2006-48, 996).

Example: In 2006, Lotton Company, a manufacturing firm, purchases a machine for use in its business. The cost of the machine, which meets the definition of Code Sec. 179 property, is $460,000. Because the cost of this qualified property exceeds the $430,000 investment limitation in effect for 2006, the $108,000 deduction limitation must be reduced by $30,000 ($460,000 − $430,000). Therefore, Lotton Company may expense $78,000 under Code Sec. 179.

The amount of the Code Sec. 179 deduction cannot exceed the aggregate amount of taxable income that is derived from the active conduct of any trade or business during the tax year (Code Sec. 179(b)(3)(A)). An amount disallowed because of this taxable income limitation can be carried forward (Code Sec. 179(b)(3)(B)).

In general, only new or used tangible Code Sec. 1245 property purchased for use in the active conduct of a trade or business and which is depreciable under MACRS qualifies for expensing under Code Sec. 179 (Code Sec. 179(d)(1)). Certain "off-the-shelf" computer software that is otherwise amortizable over three years under Code Sec.

BACKGROUND

167(f)(1) also qualifies for expensing under this rule (Code Sec. 179(d)(1)(A)(ii)). The expense deduction for the cost of a sports utility vehicle (SUV) is limited to $25,000. This $25,000 limitation applies to an SUV that is not subject to the luxury car depreciation caps because its gross vehicle weight rating exceeds 6,000 pounds (Code Sec. 179(b)(6)).

An election under Code Sec. 179 is generally made on the taxpayer's original return for the tax year to which the election relates (Code Sec. 179(c)(1)). As a result of the changes made by JGTRRA, an election may be revoked or modified by the taxpayer on an amended return without the permission of the IRS. Once the revocation is made, it is irrevocable (Code Sec. 179(c)(2)).

Additional Code Sec. 179 incentives are provided in certain circumstances. For example, the maximum allowable Code Sec. 179 expense allowance can be increased by the lesser of $100,000 or the cost of qualified section 179 Gulf Opportunity Zone property placed in service in the tax year. The investment limit is increased by the lesser of $600,000 or the amount of qualified section 179 Gulf Opportunity Zone property placed in service during the tax year (Code Sec.1400N(e)). In addition, the otherwise applicable expensing limitation amount is increased by an additional $35,000 in the case of qualifying section 179 property placed in service in the New York Liberty Zone (Code Sec. 1400L(f)), an empowerment zone (Code Sec. 1397A), or a renewal community (Code Sec. 1400J).

NEW LAW EXPLAINED

Two-year extension for increased Code Sec. 179 expensing limits.—The Tax Increase Prevention and Reconciliation Act of 2005 (P.L. 109-222) extends for an additional two years (2008 and 2009) the changes made to the Code Sec. 179 expense allowance by the Jobs and Growth Tax Relief Reconciliation Act of 2003 (JGTRRA) (P.L. 108-27), which were previously extended through 2007 by the American Jobs Creation Act of 2004 (AJCA) (P.L. 108-357). As a result, for tax years beginning in 2003, 2004, 2005, 2006, 2007, 2008, and 2009, the Code Sec. 179 dollar limitation is $100,000 and the investment limitation is $400,000 (each as adjusted for inflation) (Code Sec. 179(b)(1) and (2), as amended by the Tax Increase Prevention and Reconciliation Act of 2005 (P.L. 109-222)). These limits will return to the pre-2003 $25,000 and $200,000 amounts, respectively, for tax years beginning in 2010 and thereafter, absent further action by Congress.

> **Comment:** The $100,000 and $400,000 amounts will continue to be adjusted for inflation for tax years beginning in 2008 and 2009 (Code Sec. 179(b)(5), as amended by the Tax Reconciliation Act of 2005).

Off-the-shelf computer software will continue to be considered Code Sec. 179 property for tax years beginning in 2008 and 2009 (Code Sec. 179(d)(1)(A)(ii), as amended by the Tax Reconciliation Act of 2005).

Consistent with the two-year extension of the increased expensing amount, a taxpayer may file an amended return to revoke or change a Code Sec. 179 election made

NEW LAW EXPLAINED

with respect to property placed in service in a tax year that begins in 2003, 2004, 2005, 2006, 2007, 2008, or 2009 (Code Sec. 179(c)(2), as amended by the Tax Reconciliation Act of 2005).

▶ **Effective date.** No specific effective date is provided by the Act. The provision is, therefore, considered effective on May 17, 2006, the date of enactment.

Law source: Law at ¶5305. Committee Report at ¶10,010.

— Act Sec. 101 of the Tax Increase Prevention and Reconciliation Act of 2005 (P.L. 109-222), amending Code Sec. 179(b), (c), and (d).

Reporter references: For further information, consult the following CCH reporters.

— Standard Federal Tax Reporter, ¶12,126.01 and ¶12,126.03

— Tax Research Consultant, DEPR: 100, DEPR: 12,000, DEPR: 12,100 and DEPR: 12,104

— Federal Tax Guide, ¶9130

¶810 Modification of W-2 Wages Limitation on Manufacturing Deduction

SUMMARY OF NEW LAW

All W-2 wages used to determine the wage limitation on the domestic production deduction must be allocable to the taxpayer's domestic production gross receipts. W-2 wages allocated by a pass-through entity are no longer limited to a percentage of the entity's allocated qualified production activities income.

BACKGROUND

The manufacturing deduction allows qualified taxpayers to deduct an amount equal to a phased-in percentage of the lesser of (1) taxable income (or, if the taxpayer is an individual, adjusted gross income), or (2) qualified production activities income (Code Sec. 199). The phased-in percentage is three percent in 2005 and 2006; six percent in 2007 through 2009; and nine percent after 2009. The amount of the deduction is also limited to 50 percent of the taxpayer's qualified W-2 wages (Code Sec. 199(b)).

QPAI and DPGR. Qualified production activities income (QPAI) is based on the taxpayer's domestic production gross receipts (DPGR). DPGR are gross receipts derived from the taxpayer's qualifying production activities. Qualifying production activities are specified dispositions of certain types of property manufactured, produced, grown or extracted in the U.S., and specified construction, architectural and engineering services performed in the U.S. To calculate QPAI, DPGR is reduced by the cost of goods sold and other deductions, expenses and losses that are properly allocable to those receipts, under rules provided by the Secretary of the Treasury (Code Sec. 199(c)).

¶810

BACKGROUND

W-2 wages. W-2 wages are wages paid by the taxpayer with respect to the taxpayer's employment of employees during the calendar year ending during the tax year for which the manufacturing deduction is claimed. The taxpayer's employees are limited to those defined in Code Sec. 3121(d)(1) and (2) (that is, common-law employees and corporate officers). W-2 wages are the sum of wages described in Code Sec. 3401(a) (wages paid as remuneration for services of an employee for an employer), plus the total amount of elective deferrals described in Code Sec. 402(g)(3); compensation deferred under Code Sec. 457; and, for tax years beginning after 2005, the amount of designated Roth contributions as defined in Code Sec. 402A. W-2 wages do not include any amount that is not properly included on a Form W-2, Wage and Tax Statement, filed with the Social Security Administration on or before the 60th day after its due date (including extensions) (Code Sec. 199(b)(2); Notice 2005-14, I.R.B. 2005-7, 498; Proposed Reg. § 1.199-2).

Pass-through entities. For pass-through entities, such as partnerships and S corporations, the manufacturing deduction is calculated and claimed at the level of the partners or shareholders. They are allocated their proper shares of the entity's items that are attributable to QPAI; cost of goods sold and other expenses and deductions that are allocated to those items; and gross receipts that are included in those items. The portion of the entity's W-2 wages that can be taken into account by the partner or shareholder is the lesser of:

- that person's allocable share of the entity's wages (allocated in the same manner as the entity's wage expense); or

- twice the phased-in percentage (three, six or nine percent) of that person's share of the entity's QPAI (Code Sec. 199(d)(1)(A); Notice 2005-14, I.R.B. 2005-7, 498; Proposed Reg. § 1.199-5).

NEW LAW EXPLAINED

W-2 wages allocable to DPGR.—For purposes of the W-2 wage limitation on the amount of the manufacturing deduction, W-2 wages are limited to the amount that is properly allocable to the taxpayer's domestic production gross receipts (DPGR), as determined for purposes of the taxpayer's qualified production activities income (QPAI) (Code Sec. 199(b)(2)(B), as added by the Tax Increase Prevention and Reconciliation Act of 2005 (P.L. 109-222)). Thus, the wage limitation is 50 percent of the wages that the taxpayer deducts in calculating its QPAI.

> **Comment:** Prior to this change, the wage limit on the domestic manufacturing deduction was 50 percent of *all* of the taxpayer's W-2 wages. This change reduces the wage limit for taxpayers whose operations include activities that do not qualify for the manufacturing deduction.

> **Comment:** For tax years beginning after May 17, 2006, three methods are provided for calculating wages under Reg. § 1.199-2(e)(1) ("(e)(1) wages"). Under Temporary Reg. § 1.199-2T(e)(2), W-2 wages include only (e)(1) wages allocable to DPGR (Rev. Proc. 2006-47, I.R.B. 2006-45, 869, and T.D. 9293, I.R.B. 2006-48, 957). Rev. Proc. 2006-22, I.R.B. 2006-22, 1033, provides methods for calculating

NEW LAW EXPLAINED

W-2 wages, for tax years beginning on or after January 1, 2005, and on or before May 17, 2006.

Comment: According to the Conference Committee Report, the Treasury Secretary's current authority to provide rules for allocating cost of goods sold and other expenses, losses and deductions in determining QPAI is extended to the proper allocation of wages (Conference Committee Report (H.R. Conf. Rep. No. 109-455)). The IRS has provided methods for allocating cost of goods sold and other items to DPGR, but it has not provided any particular rules for allocating wages.

QPAI limit on wages from pass-through entity eliminated. For pass-through entities, the QPAI limitation on the amount of wages that can be taken into account by a partner or shareholder is eliminated. Thus, a person who is allocated QPAI from a pass-through entity is treated as having W-2 wages in an amount equal to that person's allocable share of the entity's W-2 wages, as determined under regulations prescribed by the Treasury Secretary (Code Sec. 199(d)(1)(A)(iii), as amended by the Tax Reconciliation Act of 2005).

▶ **Effective date.** The provision is effective with respect to tax years beginning after May 17, 2006 (Act Sec. 514(c) of the Tax Increase Prevention and Reconciliation Act of 2005 (P.L. 109-222)).

Law source: Law at ¶5330. Committee Report at ¶10,280.

— Act Sec. 514(a) of the Tax Increase Prevention and Reconciliation Act of 2005 (P.L. 109-222), amending Code Sec. 199(b)(2);

— Act Sec. 514(b), amending Code Sec. 199(a) and (d)(1)(A)(iii);

— Act Sec. 514(c), providing the effective date.

Reporter references: For further information, consult the following CCH reporters.

— Standard Federal Tax Reporter, ¶12,476.013

— Tax Research Consultant, BUSEXP: 6,050, BUSEXP: 6,054, BUSEXP: 6,206 and BUSEXP: 6,214

— Federal Tax Guide, ¶8315

¶815 Amortization of Costs of Creating or Acquiring Musical Compositions and Copyrights

SUMMARY OF NEW LAW

A taxpayer may elect to ratably amortize expenses paid or incurred in creating or acquiring a musical composition or a copyright to a musical composition over five-years, effective for expenses with respect to property placed in service in tax years beginning after December 31, 2005, and before January 1, 2011.

BACKGROUND

In general, the uniform capitalization rules (UNICAP) apply to the production of all tangible personal property and to the purchase and holding of property for resale. Tangible personal property includes a film, sound recording, video tape, book, or similar property. The UNICAP rules do not apply to any personal property acquired during any tax year for resale if the average annual gross receipts of the taxpayer for the 3-tax year period ending with the tax year preceding such tax year do not exceed $10,000,000 (Code Sec. 263A(b)(2)).

Code Sec. 263A(h) provides an exception from the uniform capitalization rules for the qualified creative expenses of free-lance writers, photographers, and artists if those expenses are otherwise currently deductible.

The exception only applies to individuals and certain closely held personal service corporations. A writer is defined as any individual whose personal efforts in a trade or business (other than as an employee) create or may reasonably be expected to create a literary manuscript, musical composition (including any accompanying words), or dance score. Expenses paid or incurred by a personal service corporation (as defined in Code Sec. 269A(b)) that directly relate to the activities of a qualified employee-owner qualify for the exception to the extent that the expenses would qualify if paid or incurred directly by the employee-owner. A qualified employee-owner for these purposes is defined as any writer, photographer, or artist who is an employee-owner of the personal service corporation and who (alone or in conjunction with members of the employee-owner's family) owns substantially all of the corporation's stock.

A limited safe-harbor allows certain taxpayers to elect to recover their capitalized creative property costs over three years (Notice 88-62, 1988-1 CB 548). Under this rule, 50 percent of qualified costs are deducted in the tax year paid or incurred and the remaining costs are recovered equally in each of the two successive tax year.

For purposes of the safe harbor, qualified creative costs are those incurred by a self-employed individual in the production of creative properties such as films, sound recordings, musical and dance compositions including accompanying words, and other similar properties. The properties must be created predominantly by the individual efforts of the taxpayer. A corporation or partnership qualifies under this safe-harbor rule if it is substantially owned by an individual and family members.

> **Comment:** Notice 88-62, 1988-1 CB 548, was issued prior to the enactment of Code Sec. 263A(h) by the Technical and Miscellaneous Revenue Act of 1988 (P.L. 100-647). Certain taxpayers who are not exempt from the UNICAP rules by virtue of Code Sec. 263A(h) (e.g., partners) may continue to qualify for three-year amortization under Notice 88-62.

The capitalized costs of producing creative property that is not exempt from the UNICAP rules by reason of Code Sec. 263A(h) or the safe-harbor election provided by Notice 88-62 may not be recovered until the project is placed in service (i.e., the year in which it can begin generating income). Cost recovery is then usually based on the income forecast method.

The income forecast method may be used to depreciate films and video tapes, sound recordings, copyrights, books, and patents unless the property is an amortizable

BACKGROUND

section 197 intangible. Amortizable section 197 intangibles are not eligible for the income forecast method and must be amortized over 15 years (Code Sec. 167(g)(6)). Interests in musical compositions and copyrights are not considered amortizable section 197 intangibles unless acquired as part of the acquisition of a trade or business (Code Sec. 197(e)(4)).

Under the income forecast method, the cost of an asset is multiplied by a fraction, the numerator of which is the net income from the asset for the tax year, and the denominator of which is the total net income to be derived from the asset before the close of the 10th tax year following the tax year in which the asset is placed in service (Code Sec. 167(g)(1)(A)). The unrecovered adjusted basis of the property as of the beginning of the 10th tax year is claimed as a depreciation deduction in the 10th tax year after the year in which the property is placed in service (Code Sec. 167(g)(1)(C)).

NEW LAW EXPLAINED

Election to amortize expenses incurred in creating or acquiring musical compositions or music copyrights.—The new law allows a taxpayer to elect five-year amortization of capitalized expenses paid or incurred in creating or acquiring a musical composition (including the accompanying words) or a copyright to a musical composition if the expenses could otherwise be recovered using the income forecast method (Code Sec. 167(g)(8), as added by the Tax Increase Prevention and Reconciliation Act of 2005 (P.L. 109-222)).

> **Comment:** Expenses that may be claimed as a current deduction under present law remain currently deductible.

If any expense is capitalized and amortized under this provision it may not be depreciated or amortized using any other method (e.g., the income forecast method) (Code Sec. 167(g)(8)(B), as added by the Tax Reconciliation Act of 2005). In other words no duplicate deductions are allowed for the same expense.

The election applies to all musical compositions and copyrights placed in service during the tax year for which the election is made. The time and procedures for making the election will be prescribed by the IRS (Code Sec. 167(g)(8)(D), as added by the Tax Reconciliation Act of 2005).

Amortization period. The expenses are amortized ratably over the five-year period beginning with the month in which the musical composition or copyright is placed in service (Code Sec. 167(g)(8)(A), as added by the Tax Reconciliation Act of 2005).

> **Comment:** This provision will benefit taxpayers who acquire copyrights that are not amortizable under Code Sec. 197. It will also benefit taxpayers who acquire rather than create musical compositions and employers of employees who create musical compositions. In the case of the creation of a musical composition, individuals (who do not create the composition in their status as an employee) are generally allowed to claim a current deduction for their expenses as a result of the exemption from the UNICAP rules provided by Code Sec. 263A(h) or to amortize their expenses over three years under the Notice 88-62 safe harbor. See *Background* section above.

¶815

NEW LAW EXPLAINED

Planning Note: The new election to amortize over five years is not available to individuals who are exempted from UNICAP under Code Sec. 263A(h). A taxpayer who is not exempt from UNICAP by reason of Code Sec. 263(a)(h) but remains eligible for the three-year amortization election under the Notice 88-62 safe harbor election may also qualify to elect five-year amortization under the new provision. The new five-year amortization provision, however, is less beneficial because the amortization period is two years longer and also begins when the property is placed in service. The three-year amortization period, on the other hand, begins in the tax year that the expenses are paid or incurred.

Comment: In the absence of this new provision (and assuming that the exemption under Code Sec. 263A(h) and the three-year amortization election of Notice 88-62 do not apply), capitalized expenses of creating or acquiring a musical composition or acquiring a copyright would generally be recovered using the income forecast method (Code Sec. 167(g)) over an 11-year period beginning in the year that income is first generated from the property. Under the income forecast method deductions are largest in the tax years in which the most income is produced from the property. In some cases the deductions allowed in the initial years under the income forecast method could be significantly larger than the ratable deduction allowed in the same period under the new law.

Exceptions. The new five-year amortization election does not apply to a musical composition or copyright if:

(1) the related expenses are qualified creative expense as defined in Code Sec. 263A(h) (i.e., the property is exempted from UNICAP as explained in the *Background* section, above);

(2) a simplified UNICAP method for property acquired for resale applies (i.e., the simplified resale method for inventory authorized by Code Sec. 263A(i)(2) and described in Reg. § 1.263A-3(d)(1) has been elected); or

(3) the composition or copyright is an amortizable Code Sec. 197 intangible (Code Sec. 167(g)(8)(C)(ii), as added by the Tax Reconciliation Act of 2005).

Comment: With regard to item (2), the new law refers to "simplified procedures established under section *263A(j)(2).*" Code Sec. 263A(j) does not exist. It appears the reference was intended to be to Code Sec. 263A(i)(2).

Comment: A musical composition or a copyright to a musical composition is amortizable under Code Sec. 197 only if acquired as part of the acquisition of a trade or business or a substantial portion thereof (Code Sec. 197(e)(4)). Self-created intangibles are generally excluded from the scope of Code Sec. 197 (Code Sec. 197(c)(2)).

Termination date. The election may not be made for any tax year beginning after December 31, 2010 (Code Sec. 167(g)(8)(D), as added by the Tax Reconciliation Act of 2005).

▶ **Effective date.** The provision applies to expenses paid or incurred with respect to property placed in service in tax years beginning after December 31, 2005 (Act Sec. 207(b) of the Tax Increase Prevention and Reconciliation Act of 2005 (P.L. 109-222)).

¶815

NEW LAW EXPLAINED

Law source: Law at ¶5255. Committee Report at ¶10,090.

— Act Sec. 207(a) of the Tax Increase Prevention and Reconciliation Act of 2005 (P.L. 109-222), adding Code Sec. 167(g)(8);

— Act Sec. 207(b), providing the effective date.

Reporter references: For further information, consult the following CCH reporters.

— Standard Federal Tax Reporter, ¶11,009.044

— Tax Research Consultant, DEPR: 15,162, DEPR: 15,556 and DEPR: 21,552

— Federal Tax Guide, ¶9020

¶820 Geological and Geophysical Expenditures Amortization Period Extended to Five-Years for Major Integrated Oil Companies

SUMMARY OF NEW LAW

Certain major integrated oil companies are required to amortize geological and geophysical expenditures over a five-year period instead of a 24-month period.

BACKGROUND

Geological and geophysical expenditures are costs incurred for the purpose of obtaining and accumulating data that will serve as the basis for the acquisition and retention of mineral properties by taxpayers exploring for minerals, including gas and oil. Courts have found these expenses are capital in nature, and are allocable to the property acquired or retained. IRS guidance on how to allocate such expenses incurred in a project area to particular areas of interest, if any, is found in Rev. Rul. 77-188, 1977-1 CB 76, as amplified by Rev. Rul. 83-105, 1983-2 CB 51. Historically, if no area of interest was found, the costs were taken as a loss in the year the project area was abandoned.

The Energy Tax Incentives Act of 2005 (P.L. 109-58) simplified the treatment of geological and geophysical expenses. Such expenses paid or incurred in connection with oil and gas exploration or development in the United States must be amortized ratably over a 24-month period beginning on the mid-point of the tax-year that the expenses were paid or incurred (Code Sec. 167(h)(1) and (h)(2)). This is the exclusive method for claiming these expenses (Code Sec. 167(h)(3)). Thus, in the case of property abandoned or retired during the 24-month amortization period, any remaining basis may not be recovered in the year of abandonment (Code Sec. 167(h)(4)).

NEW LAW EXPLAINED

Amortization period of geological and geophysical expenditures extended to five years for major integrated oil companies.—Certain major integrated oil companies will be required to amortize ratably over a five-year period, instead of a 24-month period, geological and geophysical expenses paid or incurred (Code Sec. 167(h)(5), as added by the Tax Increase Prevention and Reconciliation Act of 2005 (P.L. 109-222)). A major integrated oil company, subject to the five-year amortization provision, is defined as a producer of crude oil that:

(1) has an average worldwide production of crude oil of at least 500,000 barrels for the tax year (Code Sec. 167(h)(5)(B)(i), as added by the Tax Reconciliation Act of 2005);

(2) has gross receipts in excess of $1 billion for its last tax year ending during calendar year 2005 (Code Sec. 167(h)(5)(B)(ii), as added by the Tax Reconciliation Act of 2005); and

(3) has an ownership interest in a crude oil refiner of 15 percent or more as defined with reference to the rules under Code Sec. 613A (Code Sec. 167(h)(5)(B)(iii), as added by the Tax Reconciliation Act of 2005).

Comment: Code Sec. 167(h)(5)(B)(iii), in defining an ownership interest for purposes of the major integrated oil company definition, modifies the rule, under Code Sec. 613A(d)(3), that provides that a taxpayer is "related" to a refiner if a five-percent or more ownership interest in either the taxpayer or the refiner is held by the other person or a third party has such an ownership interest in both parties. For purposes of Code Sec. 167(h)(5)(B)(iii), a taxpayer is "related" to a refiner if a 15-percent or more ownership interest in either the taxpayer or the refiner is held by the other person or a third party has such an ownership interest in both parties.

Code Sec. 167(h)(5)(B)(iii) then provides that a taxpayer is a major integrated oil company if Code Sec. 613A(c) does not apply by reason of Code Sec. 613A(d)(4), determined using the modified version of Code Sec. 613A(d)(3) (Code Sec. 167(h)(5)(B)(iii)(I), as added by the Tax Reconciliation Act of 2005). In addition, the retailer exclusion under Code Sec. 613A(d)(2) is not to be regarded in determining whether Code Sec. 613A(c) does not apply (Code Sec. 167(h)(5)(B)(iii)(II), as added by the Tax Reconciliation Act of 2005).

Caution Note: Basically, Code Sec. 167(h)(5)(B)(iii) is a variation of the definition of an "integrated oil company" as defined in Code Sec. 291(b)(4). In an earlier version of this bill, the text defined a "major integrated oil company" in accordance with that definition. The definition of "major integrated oil company" provided in new Code Sec. 167(h)(5)(b)(i), (b)(ii) and (b)(iii) is significantly different from the Code Sec. 291(b)(4) definition of an "integrated oil company". The new law specifically defines major integrated oil companies. It is not applicable to all integrated oil companies, as defined in Code Sec. 291(b)(4).

In determining whether a taxpayer has an average worldwide production of crude oil of at least 500,000 barrels for the tax year and gross receipts in excess of $1 billion for its last tax year ending during calendar year 2005 (see (1) and (2), above), taxpayers

NEW LAW EXPLAINED

treated as a single employer under Code Sec. 52(a) or (b) are treated as one person (Code Sec. 167(h)(5)(B), as added by the Tax Reconciliation Act of 2005).

In the case of a short tax year, the Code Sec. 448(c)(3)(B) rule requiring gross receipts for a tax year of less than 12 months to be annualized by multiplying the gross receipts for the short period by 12 and dividing the result by the number of months in the short period, will apply (Code Sec. 167(h)(5)(B), as added by the Tax Reconciliation Act of 2005).

▶ **Effective date.** This provision applies to amounts paid or incurred after May 17, 2006 (Act Sec. 503(b) of the Tax Increase Prevention and Reconciliation Act of 2005 (P.L. 109-222)).

Law source: Law at ¶5255. Committee Report at ¶10,170.

— Act Sec. 503(a) of the Tax Increase Prevention and Reconciliation Act of 2005 (P.L. 109-222), adding Code Sec. 167(h)(5);

— Act Sec. 503(b), providing the effective date.

Reporter references: For further information, consult the following CCH reporters.

— Standard Federal Tax Reporter, ¶11,009.047

— Tax Research Consultant, FARM: 100 and FARM: 21,134

— Federal Tax Guide, ¶9661

CORPORATIONS

¶825   Active Business Test for Tax-Free Distributions of Controlled Corporation Stock Modified

SUMMARY OF NEW LAW

For purposes of the active business requirement under Code Sec. 355, all members of the separate affiliated group of the distributing or controlled corporation are treated as one corporation and the "substantially all" active business stock test does not apply. The active business test was modified by the Tax Increase Prevention and Reconciliation Act of 2005 (P.L. 109-222). The modifications were made permanent by the Tax Relief and Health Care Act of 2006 (P.L. 109-432) (see ¶360).

¶830   Tax-Free Stock Distribution Rules Inapplicable to Disqualified Investment Corporations

SUMMARY OF NEW LAW

Code Sec. 355 does not apply to a distribution in which either the distributing or controlled corporation is a disqualified investment corporation and any person, who did not hold a 50-percent or greater interest in such a corporation before the distribution, holds such interest after the distribution.

BACKGROUND

A distribution of property by a corporation to its shareholders is generally taxable to both the distributing corporation and the shareholders (Code Secs. 301 and 311). However, a distribution of stock or securities of a controlled corporation may qualify for a tax-free treatment if it meets the Code Sec. 355 requirements (Code Sec. 355(a) and (c)).

Generally, the distribution must be made to the shareholders with respect to their stock and to security holders in exchange for their securities. The distributed stock or securities must be of a corporation controlled by the distributing corporation. "Control" means possessing at least 80 percent of the total vote and at least 80 percent of the total number of shares. In addition, the distributing corporation must distribute all of the controlled corporation stock or securities, or enough stock to constitute an 80-percent control. In the last case, however, it must establish to the IRS that the retention of any stock or securities is not part of a tax-avoidance plan. Further, both the distributing corporation and the controlled corporation must meet the stringent active business test of Code Sec. 355(b). The final requirement for non-recognition treatment is that the transaction is not used as a "device" to distribute earnings and profits to shareholders without the payment of tax on dividends (Code Sec. 355(a)).

> **Comment:** A transaction is not considered to be a "device" if the distribution would have been treated by the shareholder as a redemption constituting a sale or exchange of stock, rather than as a dividend, provided Code Sec. 355 had not applied.

NEW LAW EXPLAINED

Code Sec. 355 inapplicable to disqualified investment corporations.—The Code Sec. 355 rules do not apply to distributions in which (a) either the distributing corporation or the controlled corporation is a disqualified investment corporation immediately after the transaction in which the distribution occurs, and (b) any person, who did not hold a 50-percent or greater interest in such a disqualified investment corporation immediately before the transaction, holds such an interest immediately after the transaction (Code Sec. 355(g)(1), as added by the Tax Increase Prevention and Reconciliation Act of 2005 (P.L. 109-222)).

NEW LAW EXPLAINED

Disqualified investment corporation. In the case of distributions occurring after the end of the one-year period beginning on May 17, 2006, a disqualified investment corporation is any distributing or controlled corporation having investment assets with a fair market value that is two-thirds or more of the fair market value of all its assets. For distributions occurring during such one-year period, the fair market value of the investment assets is increased to three-quarters or more of the fair market value of all of the corporation's assets (Code Sec. 355(g)(2)(A), as added by the Tax Reconciliation Act of 2005).

Investment assets. Investment assets include cash, corporate stock or securities, partnership interests, debt instruments, options, forward contracts, futures contracts, notional principal contracts, derivatives, foreign currency, or any similar asset (Code Sec. 355(g)(2)(B)(i), as added by the Tax Reconciliation Act of 2005).

An exception applies for assets used in certain financial trades or businesses if substantially all of the income of the business is derived from persons who are not related to the person conducting the business. To qualify for the exception, the assets must be held for use in the active and regular conduct of (1) a lending or finance business within the meaning of Code Sec. 954(h)(4), (2) a banking business conducted through a bank, a domestic building and loan association, or any similar institution that may be specified by the IRS, or (3) an insurance business, the conduct of which is licensed, authorized, or regulated by an applicable insurance regulatory body (Code Sec. 355(g)(2)(B)(ii), as added by the Tax Reconciliation Act of 2005).

Another exception applies to any security (as defined in Code Sec. 475(c)) held by a dealer in securities that is subject to the mark-to-market accounting method under Code Sec. 475(a) (Code Sec. 355(g)(2)(B)(iii), as added by the Tax Reconciliation Act of 2005).

In addition, stock or securities in a 20-percent controlled entity (with respect to the distributing or controlled corporation) are not considered investment assets. This exception also applies to debt instruments , options, derivatives, or forward, futures, or notional principal contracts issued by such a controlled entity. A look-through rule applies to treat the distributing or controlled corporation as owning its ratable share of assets of any 20-percent controlled entity. For the purpose of this exception, a 20-percent controlled entity means a corporation in which the distributing or controlled corporation owns (directly or indirectly) stock meeting the Code Sec. 1504(a)(2) requirements, except that "20 percent" is substituted for "80 percent" and any Code Sec. 1504(a)(4) preferred stock is not taken into account (Code Sec. 355(g)(2)(B)(iv), as added by the Tax Reconciliation Act of 2005).

Further, a partnership interest or a debt instrument or other evidence of indebtedness issued by a partnership is also not treated as an investment asset in certain cases. This exception applies if one or more of the partnership's trades or businesses are taken into account (or would be taken into account if the 5-year business history requirement of Code Sec. 355(b)(2)(B) is disregarded) by the distributing or controlled corporation in order to determine if the distribution satisfies the active business requirement of Code Sec. 355(b). For this purpose, the distributing or controlled corporation is treated as

NEW LAW EXPLAINED

owning its ratable share of the assets of the partnership (Code Sec. 355(g)(2)(B)(v), as added by the Tax Reconciliation Act of 2005).

50-percent or greater interest. To determine if any person holds a 50-percent or greater interest in a disqualified investment corporation immediately after the distribution, the "vote or value" test of Code Sec. 355(d)(4) is used. For this purpose, the attribution rules of Code Sec. 318 apply (Code Sec. 355(g)(3), as added by the Tax Reconciliation Act of 2005).

> **Comment:** This means that where a person holds 50 percent of the voting power (but not the value) of the distributing corporation prior to the transaction, and 50 percent of the value of either the distributing or controlled corporation immediately after the transaction, the disqualified investment corporation rules apply (Conference Committee Report (H.R. Conf. Rep. No. 109-455)).

Transaction. For purposes of the disqualified investment corporation rules, the term "transaction" also means a series of transactions (Code Sec. 355(g)(4), as added by the Tax Reconciliation Act of 2005).

Regulations. The IRS is granted regulatory power to carry out the purpose, and to prevent the avoidance, of the disqualified investment corporation rules. The regulations may address the use of related persons, intermediaries, pass-thru entities, options, or other arrangements. The regulations may also treat assets unrelated to the trade or business of the corporation as investment assets if investment assets were used to acquire those assets prior to the distribution. The IRS is also authorized to issue regulations that may exclude from the application of the disqualified investment corporation rules a distribution that is not a redemption treated as a sale or exchange under Code Sec. 302. Finally, the regulations may modify the attribution rules for purposes of this provision (Code Sec. 355(g)(5), as added by the Tax Reconciliation Act of 2005).

> **Comment:** The Conference Committee clarifies that the authority of the IRS to issue regulations is not limited to the situations specifically mentioned in the text of the provision. The IRS may address any other situation if it is necessary to carry out, or prevent the avoidance of, the purposes of the disqualified investment corporation rules (Conference Committee Report (H.R. Conf. Rep. No. 109-455)).

▶ **Effective date.** This provision applies to distributions after May 17, 2006 (Act Sec. 507(b)(1) of the Tax Increase Prevention and Reconciliation Act of 2005 (P.L. 109-222)).

Transition rule. This provision does not apply to any distribution pursuant to a transaction that is (a) made pursuant to an agreement which was binding on May 17, 2006, the date of enactment, and at all times thereafter, (b) described in a ruling request submitted to the IRS on or before such date, or (c) described on or before such date in a public announcement or in a filing with the Securities and Exchange Commission (Act Sec. 507(b)(2) of the Tax Reconciliation Act of 2005).

Law source: Law at ¶5355. Committee Report at ¶10,210.

— Act Sec. 507(a) of the Tax Increase Prevention and Reconciliation Act of 2005 (P.L. 109-222), adding Code Sec. 355(g);

— Act Sec. 507(b), providing the effective date.

NEW LAW EXPLAINED

Reporter references: For further information, consult the following CCH reporters.

— Standard Federal Tax Reporter, ¶ 16,466.01

— Tax Research Consultant, REORG: 30,100 and REORG: 30,113

— Federal Tax Guide, ¶ 12,340

¶835 Corporate Estimated Tax Payments

SUMMARY OF NEW LAW

For certain large corporations, the estimated tax payment required in July, August or September of 2006, 2012 and 2013 is increased by a stated percentage above the amount otherwise due. In addition, a percentage of estimated tax payments of all corporations due in September 2010 and 2011 is deferred until October 1 of those years.

BACKGROUND

Generally, corporations are required to make quarterly estimated tax payments. For calendar-year corporations, estimated payments are due on April 15, June 15, September 15 and December 15. Payments by fiscal-year corporations are due on the 15th day of the fourth, sixth, ninth and twelfth months of the corporation's tax year. In either case, if any due date falls on a Saturday, Sunday or legal holiday, the payment is due on the first following business day. A penalty may apply if a corporation's quarterly payment is underpaid (Code Sec. 6655).

NEW LAW EXPLAINED

Payment of corporate estimated taxes.—For corporations with assets of $1,000,000,000 or more (determined as of the end of the preceding tax year), the new law requires a larger estimated tax payment in the July-August-September quarter of the years 2006, 2012 and 2013 (Act Sec. 401(1) of the Tax Increase Prevention and Reconciliation Act of 2005 (P.L. 109-222)). Affected corporations must pay:

- 105 percent of the amount otherwise due in July, August or September of 2006;

- 106.25 percent of the amount otherwise due in July, August or September of 2012; and

- 100.75 percent of the amount otherwise due in July, August or September of 2013.

The amount of the next required installment after each of these payments is then reduced to reflect the prior increased amount. Thus, an affected corporation must pay:

NEW LAW EXPLAINED

- 95 percent of the amount otherwise due in October, November or December of 2006;
- 93.75 percent of the amount otherwise due in October, November or December of 2012; and
- 99.25 percent of the amount otherwise due in October, November or December of 2013.

Deferred payments. For all corporations, the new law also provides that 20.5 percent of the estimated tax payment otherwise due in September, 2010 is not due until October 1, 2010 (Act Sec. 401(2) of the Tax Reconciliation Act of 2005). Additionally, 27.5 percent of the required installment otherwise due in September, 2011 is not due until October 1, 2011 (Act Sec. 401(3) of the Tax Reconciliation Act of 2005).

> **Comment:** The legislative history of the Act provides no insight on the purpose of the acceleration and deferral of estimate tax payments in the above years. However, because the federal government's fiscal year begins on October 1st, it appears that Congress is moving revenues from one fiscal year to another in order to meet budgetary requirements.

▶ **Effective date.** No specific effective date is provided by the Act. The provision is, therefore, considered effective on May 17, 2006, the date of enactment.

Law source: Law at ¶7020. Committee Report at ¶10,140.

— Act Sec. 401 of the Tax Increase Prevention and Reconciliation Act of 2005 (P.L. 109-222).

Reporter references: For further information, consult the following CCH reporters.

— Standard Federal Tax Reporter, ¶39,575.021

— Tax Research Consultant, CCORP: 45,654 and FILEBUS: 6,054.05

— Federal Tax Guide, ¶12,055 and ¶22,511

¶840 Application of Earnings Stripping Rules to Corporate Partners

SUMMARY OF NEW LAW

A corporate partner's distributive share of the partnership's interest income or expense is treated as the partner's interest income or expense, and its share of the partnership's liabilities is treated as the partner's liabilities for purposes of applying the earnings stripping rules to that partner.

BACKGROUND

Various earnings stripping rules apply to limit the ability of U.S. corporations to reduce the U.S. tax on their U.S.-source income. Code Sec. 163(j) specifically addresses earnings stripping involving interest payments. It generally limits a corporation's interest expense deduction for disqualified interest paid or accrued during the tax year. Disallowed interest may be carried forward indefinitely and is treated as

BACKGROUND

disqualified interest paid or accrued in any succeeding tax year (Code Sec. 163(j)(1)). Disqualified interest is generally interest paid or accrued to certain related persons exempt from U.S. tax, or unrelated persons in certain cases where related persons guarantee the debt (Code Sec. 163(j)(3)).

The limitation applies in years in which the corporation has an excess interest (i.e., the excess of the corporation's net interest expense over 50 percent of it adjusted taxable income) and its debt-to-equity ratio exceeds 1.5. For this purpose, the corporation's adjusted taxable income is generally taxable income computed without regard to deductions for net interest expense, net operating losses, depreciation, amortization and depletion. Excess limitation, which is the excess (if any) of the 50-percent limit over a corporation's net interest expense for a given year, can be generally carried forward three years (Code Sec. 163(j)(2)).

The IRS is granted regulatory authority, pursuant to which it may issue regulations to prevent the avoidance of the purpose of these rules, to provide for appropriate adjustments in the case of affiliated corporations, and to coordinate these rules with the branch profits tax provisions of Code Sec. 884 (Code Sec. 163(j)(8)).

Although Code Sec. 163(j) does not specifically apply to partnerships, proposed regulations, issued in 1991, generally provide that a partner's proportionate share of the partnership's liabilities is treated as liabilities incurred directly by the partner for purposes of applying the earnings stripping limitation to interest payments by a corporate partner (Proposed Reg. § 1.163(j)-3(b)(3)). In addition, interest paid or accrued to a partnership is treated as paid or accrued to the partners in proportion to their distributive shares of the partnership's interest income. Similarly, interest expense paid or accrued by a partnership is treated as paid or accrued by the partners in proportion to their distributive shares of the partnership's interest expense (Proposed Reg. §§ 1.163(j)-2(e)(4) and (5)).

NEW LAW EXPLAINED

Application of the earnings stripping rules to corporate partners.—Except to the extent provided by regulations, if a corporation owns a direct or indirect interest in a partnership, the corporation's distributive share of the partnership's interest income or expense is treated as interest income or expense of the corporation for purposes of applying the earnings stripping rules to that corporation. In addition, the corporation's share of the partnership's liabilities is treated as liabilities of the corporation for this purpose (Code Sec. 163(j)(8), as added by the Tax Increase Prevention and Reconciliation Act of 2005 (P.L. 109-222)).

> **Comment:** This amendment addresses the concern that corporations may use partnerships to avoid the application of the earnings stripping rules. The Tax Reconciliation Act of 2005 basically codifies the approach of the 1991 proposed regulations, discussed in the Background above.

The IRS is granted regulatory authority to reallocate shares of partnership debt, or distributive shares of the partnership's interest income or expense, as may be appro-

NEW LAW EXPLAINED

priate to carry out the purpose of the earnings stripping rules applicable to corporate partners (Code Sec. 163(j)(9)(D), as added by the Tax Reconciliation Act of 2005).

> **Comment:** Without such regulatory power, the earnings stripping rules applicable to corporate partners can be circumvented through allocations of partnership interest income or expense, or partnership liabilities, to or away from partners (Conference Committee Report (H.R. Conf. Rep. No. 109-455)).

▶ **Effective date.** The provision applies to tax years beginning on or after May 17, 2006 (Act Sec. 501(c) of the Tax Increase Prevention and Reconciliation Act of 2005 (P.L. 109-222)).

Law source: Law at ¶5230. Committee Report at ¶10,150.

— Act Sec. 501(a) of the Tax Increase Prevention and Reconciliation Act of 2005 (P.L. 109-222), redesignating Code Sec. 163(j)(8) as Code Sec. 163(j)(9) and adding new Code Sec. 163(j)(8);

— Act Sec. 501(b), amending Code Sec. 163(j)(9)(B) and (C) and adding Code Sec. 163(j)(9)(D);

— Act Sec. 501(c), providing the effective date.

Reporter references: For further information, consult the following CCH reporters.

— Standard Federal Tax Reporter, ¶9406N.01

— Tax Research Consultant, BUSEXP: 21,210

— Federal Tax Guide, ¶6555

¶845 Decrease in Minimum Vessel Tonnage Limit

SUMMARY OF NEW LAW

The minimum vessel tonnage limit that must be met to meet the definition of a "qualifying vessel," for purposes of the alternative tax on qualifying shipping activities (referred to as the "tonnage tax"), is decreased from 10,000 deadweight tons to 6,000 deadweight tons. The provision was added by the Tax Increase Prevention and Reconciliation Act of 2005 (P.L. 109-222) and made permanent by the Tax Relief and Health Care Act of 2006 (P.L. 109-432) (see ¶370).

SETTLEMENT FUNDS

¶855 Taxation of Designated Settlement Funds Clarified

SUMMARY OF NEW LAW

The provision exempts from income taxation certain escrow accounts, settlement funds or similar funds established to resolve claims brought under the Comprehensive Environmental Response, Compensation, and Liability Act of 1980 (CERCLA) (P.L. 96-510) by designating these funds as being beneficially owned by the United States. The exemption was added by the Tax Increase Prevention and Reconciliation Act of 2005 (P.L. 109-222) and made permanent by the Tax Relief and Health Care Act of 2006 (P.L. 109-432) (see ¶375).

TIPRA—Capital Gains and Dividends

CROSS REFERENCE

Capital gains treatment for self-created music (*see ¶240*)

¶905 Reduced Capital Gains Rate for Individuals, Estates & Trusts Extended Through 2010

SUMMARY OF NEW LAW

The maximum capital gains tax rate for noncorporate taxpayers will remain at 15 percent for tax years beginning on or before December 31, 2010. The capital gain rate for taxpayers in the 10- or 15-percent rate brackets will remain at five percent through December 31, 2007, and will be zero for tax years 2008 through 2010.

BACKGROUND

Gain from sales of personal investments is generally taxed at a maximum capital gains tax rate of 15 percent (five percent for individuals in the 10- or 15-percent tax bracket) (Code Sec. 1(h)(1), as amended by the Jobs and Growth Tax Relief Reconciliation Act of 2003 (JGTRRA) (P.L. 108-27)). The five-percent capital gain rate (for 10- and 15-percent bracket taxpayers) drops to zero percent for tax years beginning after December 31, 2007 (Code Sec. 1(h)(1)(B)).

The reduced capital gains rates of 15 percent or five percent apply to individuals, estates and trusts. The same rates apply for purposes of both the regular tax and the

BACKGROUND

alternative minimum tax (AMT). Corporate taxpayers do not currently have a special tax rate for capital gains.

Capital gains eligible for the 15-percent and five-percent rates include most long-term gains from sales of capital assets. A capital asset must be held for more than 12 months in order for the sales proceeds to be classified as long-term capital gain. The 15-percent and five-percent capital gain rates do not apply to sales of collectibles (artwork, sports memorabilia, antiques, etc.), which are subject to a maximum rate of 28 percent. Unrecaptured Section 1250 gain is subject to a maximum rate of 25 percent. Unrecaptured Section 1250 gain is generally the portion of gain attributable to depreciation claimed on the property that is not recaptured as ordinary income. Sales of small business stock are also taxed at 28 percent, as they were before the enactment of JGTRRA.

The reduced capital gains rates are subject to a "sunset" provision and will expire for tax years beginning after December 31, 2008 (Act Sec. 303 of JGTRRA). At that time, the rates in effect prior to the enactment of JGTRRA will be reinstated. Prior to JGTRRA, the maximum long-term capital gains tax rate for individuals was 20 percent (Code Sec. 1(h)(1)(C), prior to amendment by JGTRRA). A lower rate of 10 percent applied for individuals in a 10- or 15-percent tax bracket (Code Sec. 1(h)(1)(B)). However, if the capital asset was owned for at least five years, a maximum capital gains rate of 18 percent (eight percent for individuals in the 10- or 15-percent tax bracket) could be applied (Code Sec. 1(h)(2)). The maximum capital gains rates applicable prior to JGTRRA (e.g., 20 or 10 percent, or 18 percent or eight percent for five-year property) was also used when computing an individual's alternative minimum tax liability (Code Sec. 55(b)(3)).

NEW LAW EXPLAINED

15-percent and five-percent rates for capital gains extended through 2010.—The maximum rate applicable to long-term capital gain for taxpayers other than corporations will remain at 15 percent (five percent for individuals with taxable income in the 10- or 15-percent tax brackets) for tax years beginning in 2006, 2007, 2008, 2009, and 2010. The reduced rates will expire for tax years beginning after December 31, 2010 (Act Sec. 102 of the Tax Increase Prevention and Reconciliation Act of 2005 (P.L. 109-222)). For taxpayers in the 10- or 15-percent tax brackets, the maximum capital gain rate will be five percent for 2006 and 2007, and will be reduced to zero percent for 2008, 2009 and 2010. The zero percent rate will expire for tax years beginning after December 31, 2010 (Act Sec. 102 of the Tax Reconciliation Act of 2005). The reduced rates apply to individuals, estates, and trusts for sales of capital assets that are held for more than 12 months. The reduced rates apply for both the regular income tax and the alternative minimum tax (AMT).

> **Comment:** The reduced rates were scheduled to expire in tax years beginning after December 31, 2008. The old rates will now go back into effect in tax years beginning after December 31, 2010.

NEW LAW EXPLAINED

Comment: The zero percent capital gain rate was intended to apply for only one year (2008) when the reduced rates were originally enacted. Because Code Sec. 1(h)(1)(B) was not amended by the new law to revise the 2008 date, the zero percent rate now applies for three tax years (i.e., tax years beginning in 2008, 2009 and 2010).

New Sunset Date. The provisions and amendments of Title III of JGTRRA relating to the reduced rates on long-term capital gain will not apply to tax years beginning after December 31, 2010. After the sunset date, the Code will be applied and administered as if the amendments had not been enacted (Act Sec. 102 of the Tax Reconciliation Act of 2005; Act Sec. 303 of the Jobs and Growth Tax Relief Reconciliation Act of 2003 (P.L. 108-27)).

▶ **Effective date.** No specific effective date is provided by the Act. The provision is, therefore, considered effective on May 17, 2006, the date of enactment.

Law source: Law at ¶7010. Committee Report at ¶10,020.

— Act Sec. 102 of the Tax Increase Prevention and Reconciliation Act of 2005 (P.L. 109-222), amending Act Sec. 303 of the Jobs and Growth Tax Relief Reconciliation Act of 2003 (P.L. 108-27).

Reporter references: For further information, consult the following CCH reporters.

— Standard Federal Tax Reporter, ¶3285.021, ¶5101.042 and ¶32,792.04

— Tax Research Consultant, FILEIND: 15,054.15, SALES: 100, SALES: 15,000, SALES: 15,200 and SALES: 15,204.05

— Federal Tax Guide, ¶5581

¶910 Five-Year Property

SUMMARY OF NEW LAW

Gains from five-year property will continue to be taxed in a manner similar to other long-term capital gains, without special treatment, effective for tax years beginning before December 31, 2010. The maximum rate applicable to long-term capital gain, including gain from sales of five-year property, will remain at 15 percent (five percent for individuals with taxable income in the 10- or 15-percent tax brackets) for tax years beginning before December 31, 2010.

BACKGROUND

From 2001 until mid 2003, individuals were eligible for a special lower capital gains tax rate on sales of property that was held for more than five years (i.e., "qualified five-year gain"). The maximum applicable rate on qualified five-year gain was 18 percent (eight percent for those in the 10- or 15-percent brackets) (Code Sec. 1(h)(2),

BACKGROUND

prior to amendment by the Jobs and Growth Tax Relief Reconciliation Act of 2003 (JGTRRA) (P.L. 108-27)).

JGTRRA eliminated the special capital gain treatment for capital assets held for more than five years (Code Sec. 1(h)(2), repealed by JGTRRA). Since JGTRRA generally lowered the maximum capital gains tax rates to 15 percent (five percent for taxpayers in the 15- or 10-percent brackets), it was not necessary to have special rules for five-year property.

The JGTRRA section which repealed the five-year property rules, and which enacted the generally applicable reduced capital gains rates, is subject to a "sunset" provision. The sunset provision causes the law to expire for tax years beginning after December 31, 2008 (Act Sec. 303 of JGTRRA). At that time, the rates in effect prior to the enactment of JGTRRA will be reinstated, and the special rules for five-year property will also be reinstated. Prior to JGTRRA, the maximum long-term capital gains tax rate for individuals was 20 percent (Code Sec. 1(h)(1)(C), prior to amendment by JGTRRA). A lower rate of 10 percent applied for individuals in a 10- or 15-percent tax bracket (Code Sec. 1(h)(1)(B), prior to amendment by JGTRRA). Under the five-year property rules, if the capital asset was owned for at least five years, a maximum capital gains rate of 18 percent (eight percent for individuals in the 10- or 15-percent tax bracket) could be applied (Code Sec. 1(h)(2), prior to repeal by JGTRRA).

NEW LAW EXPLAINED

Sunset date for repeal of five-year property rules extended to 2010.—There will be no special capital gain treatment for five-year property in tax years beginning before December 31, 2010 (Act Sec. 303 of the Jobs and Growth Tax Relief Reconciliation Act of 2003 (JGTRRA) (P.L. 108-27), as amended by Act Sec. 102 of the Tax Increase Prevention and Reconciliation Act of 2005 (P.L. 109-222)). The maximum rate applicable to long-term capital gain, including gain from sales of five-year property, will remain at 15 percent (five percent for individuals with taxable income in the 10- or 15-percent tax brackets) for tax years beginning before December 31, 2010. A zero percent rate will replace the five percent rate for tax years beginning after December 31, 2007, and before December 31, 2010 (Code Sec. 1(h)(1)(B)). The reduced rates apply to individuals, estates, and trusts for sales of capital assets that are held for more than 12 months. The reduced rates apply for both the regular income tax and the alternative minimum tax (AMT). See ¶ 905.

> **Comment:** The zero percent capital gain rate was intended to apply for only one year (2008) when the reduced rates were originally enacted. Because Code Sec. 1(h)(1)(B) was not amended to revise the 2008 date, the zero percent rate now applies for three tax years (2008, 2009 and 2010).

New Sunset Date. The provisions and amendments of Title III of JGTRRA, including those relating to the repeal of the special capital gain rates for property held for more than five years, will not apply to tax years beginning after December 31, 2010. After the sunset date, the Code will be applied and administered as if the amendments had

NEW LAW EXPLAINED

not been enacted (Act Sec. 102 of the Tax Reconciliation Act of 2005; Act Sec. 303 of the Jobs and Growth Tax Relief Reconciliation Act of 2003 (P.L. 108-27))

▶ **Effective date.** No specific effective date is provided by the Act. The provision is, therefore, considered effective on May 17, 2006, the date of enactment.

Law source: Law at ¶7010. Committee Report at ¶10,020.

— Act Sec. 102 of the Tax Increase Prevention and Reconciliation Act of 2005 (P.L. 109-222), amending Act Sec. 303 of the Jobs and Growth Tax Relief Reconciliation Act of 2003 (P.L. 108-27).

Reporter references: For further information, consult the following CCH reporters.

— Standard Federal Tax Reporter, ¶3285.03

— Tax Research Consultant, FILEIND: 15,054.15, SALES: 15,000, SALES: 15,200 and SALES: 15,204.05

— Federal Tax Guide, ¶5581

¶915 AMT Special Treatment for Sales of Small Business Stock Extended Through 2010

SUMMARY OF NEW LAW

The amount of excluded gain from sales of small business stock that is treated as a tax preference item under the alternative minimum tax will remain at seven percent for tax years beginning on or before December 31, 2010 (2006, 2007, 2008, 2009, and 2010).

BACKGROUND

Noncorporate investors may exclude up to 50 percent of the gain realized on the sale or exchange of small business stock, if certain conditions are satisfied (Code Sec. 1202(a)(1)). Small business stock must be issued by a C corporation, and at least 80 percent of the corporation's assets must be invested in assets used in the active conduct of a business. The corporation's aggregate assets at the time the stock is issued must not exceed $50 million (Code Secs. 1202(c), (d) and (e)). In order for a sale of small business stock to qualify for special treatment, the stock must have been issued after August 10, 1993, and the investor must have held it for more than five years (Code Sec. 1202(b)).

If the small business stock qualifies for this 50-percent exclusion, any recognized gain from the sale or exchange of the stock is subject to a maximum capital gains rate of 28 percent (Code Sec. 1(h)(4)(A)(ii)). For purposes of alternative minimum tax calculations, seven percent of the 50-percent gain exclusion (or, looked at another way, 3.5 percent of the total gain on the small business stock sale) is treated as a tax preference item (Code Sec. 57(a)(7)).

NEW LAW EXPLAINED

AMT rule for small business stock sales extended through 2010.—The amount of excluded gain from a sale of small business stock that is treated as a tax preference item in computing alternative minimum taxable income (AMTI) will remain at seven percent for tax years beginning on or before December 31, 2010 (Act Sec. 102 of the Tax Increase Prevention and Reconciliation Act of 2005 (P.L. 109-222); Act Sec. 303 of the Jobs and Growth Tax Relief Reconciliation Act of 2003 (JGTRRA) (P.L. 108-27)). Thus, 3.5 percent of the total gain on a small business stock sale is treated as a tax preference item for calendar years 2006 through 2010 (seven percent of the 50 percent of gain that is excluded from income under Code Sec. 1202) (Code Sec. 57(a)(7)).

> **Comment:** After 2010, the rules governing alternative minimum tax (AMT) treatment of sales of small business stock will revert to their status prior to the enactment of JGTRRA. Under the law prior to the enactment of JGTRRA, 42 percent of the gain exclusion for small business stock sales (21 percent of the investor's total realized gain) was treated as a tax preference item when computing AMTI. If the stock qualified under the five-year holding period for capital assets, 28 percent of the excluded gain was classified as a tax preference item (Code Sec. 57(a)(7)).

New Sunset Date. The provisions and amendments of Title III of JGTRRA will not apply to tax years beginning after December 31, 2010. After the sunset date, the Code will be applied and administered as if the amendments had not been enacted (Act Sec. 102 of the Tax Reconciliation Act of 2005; Act Sec. 303 of the Jobs and Growth Tax Relief Reconciliation Act of 2003 (P.L. 108-27)).

▶ **Effective date.** No specific effective date is provided by the Act. The provision is, therefore, considered effective on May 17, 2006, the date of enactment.

Law source: Law at ¶7010. Committee Report at ¶10,020.

— Act Sec. 102 of the Tax Increase Prevention and Reconciliation Act of 2005 (P.L. 109-222), amending Act Sec. 303 of the Jobs and Growth Tax Relief Reconciliation Act of 2003 (P.L. 108-27).

Reporter references: For further information, consult the following CCH reporters.

— Standard Federal Tax Reporter, ¶5307.045

— Tax Research Consultant, SALES: 15,000, SALES: 15,300 and FILEIND: 30,256

— Federal Tax Guide, ¶1400 and ¶5586

¶920 Reduced Dividends Tax Rate Extended Through 2010

SUMMARY OF NEW LAW

The maximum tax rate on qualified dividends will remain at 15 percent for tax years beginning on or before December 31, 2010. The rate for dividends for taxpayers in the

SUMMARY OF NEW LAW

10- or 15-percent rate brackets will remain at five percent through December 31, 2007, and will be zero for tax years 2008 through 2010.

BACKGROUND

The top federal tax rate for qualified dividends received by an individual, estate or trust is 15 percent (five percent for those whose incomes fall in the 10- or 15-percent rate brackets) (Code Sec. 1(h)(11), as added by the Jobs and Growth Tax Relief Reconciliation Act of 2003 (JGTRRA) (P.L. 108-27)). A zero-percent rate applies to taxpayers in the 10- or 15-percent brackets for 2008 only.

The reduced dividend rate applies only to qualified dividends, which generally means taxable stock dividends. Dividends from investments in tax-deferred retirement vehicles such as regular IRAs, 401(k)s and deferred annuities are taxed at ordinary income rates, not at the dividend rate.

Qualified dividends include dividends paid by a domestic corporation or a qualified foreign corporation. The underlying stock must have been held for at least 61 days during the 121-day period beginning 60 days before the ex-dividend date. There are restrictions on use of the special rate if the underling stock was part of a short sale, and several other restrictions. Corporate stock dividends passed through to investors by a mutual fund or other regulated investment company, partnership, real estate investment trust, or held by a common trust fund are eligible for the reduced rate, assuming the distribution would otherwise be classified as qualified dividend income.

The reduced rates for dividends are subject to a "sunset" provision under which the special rates will expire for tax years beginning after December 31, 2008 (Act Sec. 303 of JGTRRA). At that time, the rates in effect prior to the enactment of JGTRRA will be reinstated. Prior to JGTRRA, there was no special maximum tax rate on dividends, and dividends were included in the taxpayer's ordinary income and taxed at the otherwise applicable tax rates (which are now 10, 15, 25, 28, 33, or 35 percent, depending on the taxpayer's taxable income level).

NEW LAW EXPLAINED

15 percent maximum rate on dividends extended through 2010.—The maximum rate applicable to dividends will remain at 15 percent (five percent for individuals with taxable income in the 10- or 15-percent tax brackets) for tax years beginning before December 31, 2010 (Act Sec. 102 of the Tax Increase Prevention and Reconciliation Act of 2005 (P.L. 109-222)). The five-percent rate for taxpayers in the 10- or 15-percent brackets will be reduced to zero for tax years beginning after December 31, 2007, and before December 31, 2010 (i.e., 2008, 2009, and 2010) (Code Sec. 1(h)(1)(B)). The rate on dividends is the same as the rate on capital gains (see ¶ 905). The reduced rates apply for both the regular income tax and the alternative minimum tax (AMT).

> **Comment:** The zero-percent dividend rate was intended to apply for only one year (2008) when the reduced rates were originally enacted. Because Code Sec.

NEW LAW EXPLAINED

1(h)(1)(B) was not amended to revise the 2008 date, the zero-percent rate now applies for three tax years (2008, 2009 and 2010 for a taxpayer using a calendar tax year).

New Sunset Date. The provisions and amendments of Title III of JGTRRA relating to the reduced dividend rate will not apply to tax years beginning after December 31, 2010. After the sunset date, the Code will be applied and administered as if the amendments had not been enacted (Act Sec. 102 of the Tax Reconciliation Act of 2005; Act Sec. 303 of the Jobs and Growth Tax Relief Reconciliation Act of 2003 (P.L. 108-27))

▶ **Effective date.** No specific effective date is provided by the Act. The provision is, therefore, considered effective on May 17, 2006, the date of enactment.

Law source: Law at ¶7010. Committee Report at ¶10,020.

— Act Sec. 102 of the Tax Increase Prevention and Reconciliation Act of 2005 (P.L. 109-222), amending Act Sec. 303 of the Jobs and Growth Tax Relief Reconciliation Act of 2003 (P.L. 108-27).

Reporter references: For further information, consult the following CCH reporters.

— Standard Federal Tax Reporter, ¶3285.05

— Tax Research Consultant, FILEIND: 15,054.15, CCORP: 6,062 and SALES: 15,202.55

— Federal Tax Guide, ¶3205

¶925   Dividends and Capital Gains Paid Through Mutual Funds and REITS

SUMMARY OF NEW LAW

The maximum tax rate applicable to dividends or capital gains passed through a RIC (mutual fund) or REIT will remain at 15 percent through 2010. For taxpayers in the 10- or 15-percent bracket, the rate will remain at five percent through December 31, 2007, and will be zero for tax years 2008 through 2010. The special rules enacted to coordinate RIC and REIT distributions with the reduced rates on capital gains and dividends are also extended through 2010.

BACKGROUND

A regulated investment company (RIC) (mutual fund) is a corporation or common trust fund that invests in stocks and securities and satisfies a number of complex tests relating to income, assets, and other matters. RICs are taxed as corporations but can deduct their dividends. The shareholders of a RIC are taxed on distributions from RICs under the general rules applying to dividends. However, if the distributing RIC designates a distribution as a capital gain dividend, the shareholder treats it as capital gain.

BACKGROUND

Special reduced tax rates apply to capital gains and qualified dividends (see ¶905 and ¶920). Capital gains and dividends are generally taxed at a maximum capital gains tax rate of 15 percent (five percent for individuals in the 10- or 15-percent tax bracket) (Code Sec. 1(h)(1), as amended by the Jobs and Growth Tax Relief Reconciliation Act of 2003 (JGTRRA) (P.L. 108-27)). A zero percent rate will replace the five-percent rate for tax years beginning after December 31, 2007 (Code Sec. 1(h)(1)(B)).

For a RIC distribution, the amount that will be treated as dividends for purposes of the 95-percent test is limited to "qualified dividend income" as described in Code Sec. 1(h)(11)(B) (Code Sec. 854(b)(5) , as added by JGTRRA). The aggregate amount that may be designated by a RIC as a dividend for purposes of the dividends received deduction may not exceed the aggregate amount of dividends received by the RIC during the tax year (Code Sec. 854(b)(1)(B)). The same restriction applies with respect to the amount that may be designated by the RIC as a dividend for purposes of claiming the lower rates on dividends (Code Sec. 854(b)(1)(B)).

A real estate investment trust (REIT) is similar to a RIC that invests in real estate. A REIT is taxed on its income as a separate taxpayer, but it can deduct its dividends paid. However, if the distributing REIT designates a distribution as a capital gain dividend, the shareholders treat it as capital gain.

The amount of dividends paid by a REIT that will qualify for the reduced rate may not exceed the amount of aggregate qualifying dividends received by the REIT if the amount of aggregate qualifying dividends received by the REIT is less than 95 percent of its gross income (Code Sec. 857(c)(2)(A)). A REIT is treated as receiving qualified dividend income (i.e., amounts which may be treated as dividends for purposes of the 95-percent gross income test) in an amount equal to the sum of:

(1) the excess of REIT taxable income computed under Code Sec. 857(b)(2) for the preceding tax year over the tax payable by the REIT under Code Sec. 857(b)(1) for that preceding tax year, and

(2) the excess of the income subject to tax by reason of the application of the Code Sec. 337(d) regulations for the preceding tax year over the tax payable by the REIT on that income for the preceding tax year (Code Sec. 857(c)(2)(B)).

In determining the amount of aggregate dividends received by a RIC, for purposes of applying the 95-percent gross income test, distributions received by a RIC from a qualifying REIT may be considered dividends (Code Sec. 854 (b)(1)(B)(i)).

The reduced capital gains and dividends rates, as well as the coordinating rules for RICs and REITS, are subject to a "sunset" provision. The sunset provision causes the special rules and reduced rates to expire for tax years beginning after December 31, 2008 (Act Sec. 303 of JGTRRA). At that time, the rules in effect prior to the enactment of the 2003 Jobs Act will be reinstated. Prior to JGTRRA, the maximum long-term capital gains tax rate for individuals was 20 percent (Code Sec. 1(h)(1)(C), prior to amendment by JGTRRA). A lower rate of 10 percent applied for individuals in a 10- or 15-percent tax bracket (Code Sec. 1(h)(1)(B)).

Dividend and capital gain rules for RICs and REITS extended through 2010.—
The special rules for coordinating RIC and REIT distributions with the reduced rates for capital gains and dividends have been extended through tax years beginning on or before December 31, 2010 (Act Sec. 102 of the Tax Increase Prevention and Reconciliation Act of 2005 (P.L. 109-222); Act Sec. 303 of the Jobs and Growth Tax Relief Reconciliation Act of 2003 (JGTRRA) (P.L. 108-27)).

New Sunset Date. The provisions and amendments of Title III of JGTRRA, which enacted the coordinating dividend and capital gain rules for RICs and REITs, will not apply to tax years beginning after December 31, 2010. After this date, the Code will be administered as if the law changes had not been enacted (Act Sec. 102 of the Tax Reconciliation Act of 2005; Act Sec. 303 of the Jobs and Growth Tax Relief Reconciliation Act of 2003 (P.L. 108-27)).

▶ **Effective date.** No specific effective date is provided by the Act. The provision is, therefore, considered effective on May 17, 2006, the date of enactment.

Law source: Law at ¶7010. Committee Report at ¶10,020.

— Act Sec. 102 of the Tax Increase Prevention and Reconciliation Act of 2005 (P.L. 109-222), amending Act Sec. 303 of the Jobs and Growth Tax Relief Reconciliation Act of 2003 (P.L. 108-27).

Reporter references: For further information, consult the following CCH reporters.

— Standard Federal Tax Reporter, ¶3285.057

— Tax Research Consultant, CCORP: 6,062, RIC: 3,254, RIC: 6,150 and SALES: 15,202.55

— Federal Tax Guide, ¶16,600 and ¶16,670

TIPRA—International Taxation 10

FOREIGN EARNED INCOME

FOREIGN EARNED INCOME

¶1005 Modification of Foreign Income and Housing Exclusions

SUMMARY OF NEW LAW

The foreign earned income exclusion limitation is indexed for inflation beginning in 2006. In addition, the base housing amount used in calculating the foreign housing

SUMMARY OF NEW LAW

cost exclusion is tied to the foreign earned income exclusion limitation, and a 30-percent limitation applies in determining the amount of reasonable foreign housing expenses.

BACKGROUND

U.S. citizens and resident aliens are generally taxed on their worldwide income, regardless of where the income is earned or received. A U.S. citizen who earns income in a foreign country may also be taxed on that income by the foreign host country, thus leading to possible double taxation. A number of provisions in the Code provide mitigation to this potential inequity, including the foreign earned income exclusion and the foreign housing cost exclusion.

Foreign earned income exclusion/deduction. For tax years beginning in 2002 through 2007, qualified individuals who live and work abroad may elect to exclude from gross income up to $80,000 of foreign earned income, as well as certain employer-provided housing costs (Code Sec. 911(b)(2)(D); Reg. § 1.911-1(a)). Individuals with self-employment income are also entitled to deduct certain non-employer-provided housing costs (Code Sec. 911(c)(3)). The sum of the exclusions and deduction may not exceed a taxpayer's foreign earned income for the year (Code Sec. 911(d)(7)). Moreover, a taxpayer's foreign tax credit is reduced by the amount of the credit that is attributable to excluded income. Beginning in tax years after 2007, the exclusion amount is scheduled to be adjusted annually for inflation (Code Sec. 911(b)(2)(D)(ii)).

To qualify for the foreign earned income exclusion, a taxpayer must have a tax home in a foreign country and meet either the bona fide residence or physical presence test. Under these tests:

(1) *Bona Fide Residence Test.*—the individual must be a bona fide resident of a foreign country for an uninterrupted period which includes an entire tax year (e.g., January 1 through December 31, for calendar year taxpayers) (Code Sec. 911(d)(1)(A)), or

(2) *Physical Presence Test.*—the individual must be physically present in the foreign country during at least 330 full days during 12 consecutive months (Code Sec. 911(d)(1)(B)).

The amount of foreign earned income excluded is the lesser of the foreign earned income in excess of the housing exclusion (see below) or the annual dollar limit multiplied by a fraction. The numerator of the fraction is the number of qualifying days in the tax year in which the individual meets the 330-day test. The denominator is 365 (366 for leap years). If the individual has been a bona-fide resident for the entire tax year, the fraction is equal to one, which would result in the exclusion of all foreign earned income up to $80,000 for tax years prior to 2008 (Reg. § 1.911-3(d)(2)).

Foreign Earned Income. For this purpose, foreign earned income is income earned by the taxpayer as an employee or from a trade or business engaged in by the taxpayer in a foreign country (Code Sec. 911(d)(2). The place of receipt of the earned income is

¶1005

BACKGROUND

not relevant. The term "earned income" means wages or professional fees, and other amounts received as compensation for personal services rendered.

Foreign earned income does not include: (1) the value of meals or lodging excluded from gross income; (2) pension or annuity payments, including social security benefits; (3) payments from the U.S. or any agency or instrumentality of the of the U.S.; (4) amounts included in gross income due to employer's contributions to a nonexempt employee trust or to a nonqualified annuity contract; (5) amounts included in gross income because moving expenses may not be deducted against excludable foreign income; and (6) amounts received after the close of the first tax year after the tax year in which the services were performed (Code Sec. 911(b)(1)(B); Reg. § 1.911-3(c)).

Foreign Housing Exclusion/Deduction. Individuals who meet the bona fide residency test or the physical presence test may deduct or exclude a "housing cost amount" (Code Sec. 911(a)(2)). The "housing cost amount" is defined as the excess of the taxpayer's "housing expenses" over a base housing amount (Code Sec. 911(c)(1)). The housing cost amount is calculated by:

(1) Determining the annual salary of a U.S. government worker who is on step 1 of a grade GS-14.

(2) Taking 16 percent of the amount determined above, figured on a daily basis.

(3) Multiplying the amount in step 2 by the number of days in the tax year that either the bona fide residence test or the physical presence test is met.

(4) Deducting the amount in step 3, "the base amount," from the "housing expenses" of the individual.

The foreign housing exclusion is claimed by individuals with "employer-provided amounts" such as salary, while the "foreign housing deduction" is claimed by self-employed individuals (Code Sec. 911(c)(2) and (c)(3)).

Foreign housing expenses. The term "housing expenses" means the reasonable expenses (not lavish or extravagant under the circumstances) paid or incurred in the tax year for housing in a foreign country for the individual and his or her spouse and dependents (if they reside with the individual) (Code Sec. 911(c)(2)(A)). Included are expenses attributable to housing such as rent, the fair rental value of employer-provided property, utilities, insurance, nondeductible occupancy taxes, nonrefundable fees paid for securing a lease, rental of furniture, household repairs, and residential parking. Interest and taxes (including the share of interest and taxes of a member of a housing cooperative) are not included, however. Also not included are expenses for such things as house improvements, purchased furniture, mortgage payments, and reimbursed expenses which are excludable from income.

In certain instances, housing expenses eligible for the housing cost amount exclusion or deduction can include the cost of maintaining a second foreign household (Code Sec. 911(c)(2)(B)). To qualify, the household must be maintained for the individual's spouse or dependents, and the individual must show that there are "adverse living conditions" at the individual's tax home (meaning that it is dangerous or unhealthful to live there). An individual is never allowed to deduct the cost of more than one second foreign household at the same time.

¶1005

BACKGROUND

The housing exclusion applies when amounts are considered paid with "employer-provided" amounts. Employer-provided amounts are any amounts paid or incurred on behalf of the individual by the employer. The amounts must be paid in connection with foreign earned income that is taxable (before taking into account the foreign earned income exclusion). However, the housing costs do not need to be paid directly by the employer to qualify. For example, any salary paid by the employer to the employee is considered an employer-provided amount.

The housing exclusion is the lesser of: (1) the portion of the housing amount that is paid for with employer-provided amounts; or (2) the taxpayer's foreign earned income (Reg. § 1.911-4(d)). The housing exclusion is determined before computing the foreign earned income exclusion. Moreover, taxpayers who elect to use the housing exclusion must use the full amount of the exclusion. Once an individual claims the exclusion, the foreign tax credit (or deduction) cannot be claimed for taxes paid on the income excluded.

Foreign housing cost deduction. Only individuals who have self-employment income may take the foreign housing deduction (Code Sec. 911(c)(3)(A)). The deduction is taken "above-the-line," meaning that it is deducted from gross income and is not subject to the limits that apply to deductions from adjusted gross income. The housing deduction cannot exceed foreign earned income, less the foreign earned income exclusion and the housing exclusion. In addition, a housing cost amount deduction in excess of this limit can be carried forward one year, to the next tax year only (Code Sec. 911(c)(3)(C)(i)). The amount carried forward can be deducted only to the extent that it is needed to come up with the maximum deduction allowed because of the limitation. In other words, the current year's housing cost amount deduction is taken before the carryforward is allowed.

NEW LAW EXPLAINED

Exclusions for citizens living abroad modified.—The provision reforms the rules applicable to U.S. citizens living and working abroad by accelerating the indexing of the foreign earned income exclusion limitation. Inflation adjustments now apply in tax years beginning in calendar years after 2005, rather than after 2007, as under present law (Code Sec. 911(b)(2)(D)(ii), as amended by the Tax Increase Prevention and Reconciliation Act of 2005 (P.L. 109-222)). Thus, using current U.S. Bureau of Labor Statistics Consumer Price Index data, the 2006 limitation is $82,400 (Conference Committee Report (H.R. Conf. Rep. No. 109-455)).

The provision also ties the employer-provided housing exclusion to the foreign earned income maximum exclusion amount (Code Sec. 911(c)(1)(B)(i), as amended by the Tax Reconciliation Act of 2005). Accordingly, the base housing amount is 16 percent of the foreign earned income exclusion limitation computed on a daily basis—instead of the present law 16 percent of the grade GS-14, step 1 amount—multiplied by the number of days of foreign residence or presence in that year.

Foreign housing expenses. The provision also applies an objective standard in determining the amount of reasonable foreign housing expenses that may be excluded (Code

NEW LAW EXPLAINED

Sec. 911(c)(2)(A), as added by the Tax Reconciliation Act of 2005). Reasonable foreign housing expenses in excess of the base housing amount remain excluded from gross income, but the amount of the exclusion is limited to 30 percent of the taxpayer's foreign earned income exclusion limitation, computed on a daily basis, multiplied by the number of days of foreign residence or presence in that year.

For example, the maximum foreign housing cost exclusion in 2006, assuming the taxpayer lives year-round in a foreign residence, is $11,536 [($82,400 × 30 percent) – ($82,400 × 16 percent)]. Further, the provision grants the Secretary with authority to issue regulations or other guidance providing for the adjustment of this 30-percent housing cost limitation based on geographic differences in housing costs relative to housing costs in the United States (Code Sec. 911(c)(2)(B), as added by the Tax Reconciliation Act of 2005).

> **Comment:** The Conference Report also noted the Conferees' intention to allow the Secretary to use publicly available data, such as the Quarterly Report Indexes published by the U.S. Department of State, or other deemed reliable information, in making adjustments to this new limitation. Accordingly, the Secretary may adjust the 30-percent limitation annually, either upward or downward (Conference Committee Report (H.R. Conf. Rep. No. 109-455)). Adjustments to the limitations on housing expenses for specific locations have been issued, for tax years beginning on or after January 1, 2006. The adjustments are in a table derived from the Living Quarters Allowance Table prepared by the Office of Allowance of the U.S. State Department of State, as of August 20, 2006 (Notice 2006-87, I.R.B. 2006-43, 766).

See ¶1010 for a discussion of the rates of tax applicable to nonexcluded income for citizens living abroad.

▶ **Effective date.** The provision is effective for tax years beginning after December 31, 2005 (Act Sec. 515(d) of the Tax Increase Prevention and Reconciliation Act of 2005 (P.L. 109-222)).

Law source: Law at ¶5505. Committee Report at ¶10,290.

— Act Sec. 515(a) of the Tax Increase Prevention and Reconciliation Act of 2005 (P.L. 109-222), amending Code Sec. 911(b)(2)(D)(ii);

— Act Sec. 515(b), amending Code Sec. 911(c)(1), redesignating Code Sec. 911(c)(2) and (3) as Code Sec. 911(c)(3) and (4), and adding new Code Sec. 911(c)(2);

— Act Sec. 515(d), providing the effective date.

Reporter references: For further information, consult the following CCH reporters.

— Standard Federal Tax Reporter, ¶28,049.025 and ¶28,049.031

— Tax Research Consultant, EXPAT: 12,000, EXPAT: 12,102, EXPAT: 12,152, INDIV: 6,060, INDIV: 63,306 and INTLOUT: 6,454

— Federal Tax Guide, ¶17,280

¶1010 Tax Rates Applicable to Nonexcluded Foreign Income

SUMMARY OF NEW LAW

A "stacking rule" applies to the foreign earned income and foreign housing cost exclusions to determine tax rates applicable to nonexcluded income.

BACKGROUND

U.S. citizens and resident aliens are generally taxed on their worldwide income, regardless of where the income is earned or received. A U.S. citizen who earns income in a foreign country may also be taxed on that income by the foreign host country, thus leading to possible double taxation. A number of provisions in the Code provide some mitigation to this potential inequity, including the foreign earned income exclusion and the foreign housing cost exclusion.

Foreign earned income exclusion/deduction. For tax years beginning in 2002 through 2007, qualified individuals who live and work abroad may elect to exclude from gross income up to $80,000 of foreign earned income (adjusted annually for inflation, see ¶1005), as well as certain employer-provided housing costs (Code Sec. 911(b)(2)(D); Reg. §1.911-1(a)). Individuals with self-employment income are also entitled to deduct certain non-employer-provided housing costs (Code Sec. 911(c)(3)). The sum of the exclusions and deduction may not exceed a taxpayer's foreign earned income for the year (Code Sec. 911(d)(7)). Moreover, a taxpayer's foreign tax credit is reduced by the amount of the credit that is attributable to excluded income.

The amount excludable is the lesser of the foreign earned income in excess of the housing exclusion or the annual dollar limit multiplied by a fraction. The numerator of the fraction is the number of qualifying days in the tax year in which the individual is physically present in the foreign country (not to be less than 330 days). The denominator is 365 (366 for leap years). If the individual has been a bona-fide resident for the entire tax year, the fraction is equal to one, which would result in the exclusion of all foreign earned income up to the dollar limit (Reg. §1.911-3(d)(2)).

Foreign housing exclusion/deduction. Individuals who meet a bona fide residency test or the physical presence test may deduct or exclude a "housing cost amount" (Code Sec. 911(a)(2)). The foreign housing exclusion is claimed by individuals with "employer-provided amounts" such as salary, while the "foreign housing deduction" is claimed by self-employed individuals (Code Secs. 911(c)(2) and (c)(3)).

The housing exclusion applies when amounts are considered paid with "employer-provided" amounts. Employer-provided amounts are any amounts paid or incurred on behalf of the individual by the employer. The amounts must be paid in connection with foreign earned income that is taxable (before taking into account the foreign earned income exclusion). However, the housing costs do not need to be paid directly by the employer to qualify. For example, any salary paid by the employer to the employee is considered an employer-provided amount.

BACKGROUND

The housing exclusion is the lesser of: (1) the portion of the housing amount that is paid for with employer-provided amounts; or (2) the taxpayer's foreign earned income (Reg. § 1.911-4(d)). The housing exclusion is determined before computing the foreign earned income exclusion. Moreover, taxpayers who elect to use the housing exclusion must use the full amount of the exclusion. Once an individual claims the exclusion, the foreign tax credit (or deduction) cannot be claimed for taxes paid on the income excluded.

Foreign housing cost deduction. Only individuals who have self-employment income may take the foreign housing deduction (Code Sec. 911(c)(3)(A)). The deduction is taken "above-the-line," meaning that it is deducted from gross income and is not subject to the limits that apply to deductions from adjusted gross income. The housing deduction cannot exceed foreign earned income, less the foreign earned income exclusion and the housing exclusion. In addition, a housing cost amount deduction in excess of this limit can be carried forward one year, to the next tax year only (Code Sec. 911(c)(3)(C)(i)). The amount carried forward can be deducted only to the extent that it is needed to come up with the maximum deduction allowed because of the limitation. In other words, the current year's housing cost amount deduction is taken before the carryforward is allowed.

U.S. tax liability. As a general rule, U.S. citizens and resident aliens living abroad are allowed the same deductions as citizens and residents living in the United States, including: charitable contributions, medical expenses, mortgage interest, and real estate taxes on a personal residence. The general rule does not apply, however, where expenses are definitely related to income that is excludable under the foreign earned income exclusion (Code Sec. 911(d)(6)). Thus, a taxpayer may not deduct unreimbursed employee business expenses against wage income that was excluded as foreign earned income. However, personal exemptions, qualified retirement contributions, and the deduction for alimony paid are not subject to this disallowance because they do not relate to any particular type of income. In addition, a taxpayer remains subject to tax on nonexcluded income, after deductions, starting in the lowest tax rate bracket.

NEW LAW EXPLAINED

Rates of tax applicable to nonexcluded income for citizens living abroad determined.—The provision applies a "stacking rule" to ensure that U.S. citizens living abroad are subject to the same U.S. tax rates as individuals living and working in the United States. Thus income that has been excluded from gross income as either foreign earned income or as a foreign housing allowance is included for purposes of determining the regular tax rate under Code Sec. 1 and the tentative minimum tax rate under Code Sec. 55 applicable to the nonexcluded income (Code Sec. 911(f), as added by the Tax Increase Prevention and Reconciliation Act of 2005 (P.L. 109-222)). Accordingly, the regular tax is equal to the *excess*, if any, of the tax which would be imposed if the taxpayer's taxable income were *increased* by the excluded amount, over the tax which would be imposed if the taxpayer's taxable income were *equal* to the amount excluded (Code Sec. 911(f)(1), as added by the Tax Reconciliation Act of 2005). The tentative

NEW LAW EXPLAINED

minimum tax is equal to the *excess*, if any, of the amount which would be the tentative minimum tax if the taxpayer's taxable excess were *increased* by the amount excluded, over the amount which would be the tentative minimum tax if the taxpayer's taxable excess were *equal* to the excluded amount (Code Sec. 911(f)(2), as added by the Tax Reconciliation Act of 2005).

Example: An individual with $80,000 of foreign earned income that is excluded under Code Sec. 911, who also has $20,000 in other taxable, nonexcluded income (after deductions), would be subject to tax on that $20,000 at the rate or rates applicable to taxable income in the range of $80,000 to $100,000 (Conference Committee Report (H.R. Conf. Rep. No. 109-455)).

For purposes of determining the applicable tax rates under the new provision, the excluded amount is reduced by the aggregate amount of any deductions or exclusions disallowed under Code Sec. 911(d)(6), which denies a double benefit for those amounts which are properly allocable or chargeable to the excluded income (Code Sec. 911(f), as added by the Tax Reconciliation Act of 2005).

See ¶1005 for a discussion on further modifications made to the foreign earned income and foreign housing exclusions for citizens living abroad.

▶ **Effective date.** The provision is effective for tax years beginning after December 31, 2005 (Act Sec. 515(d) of the Tax Increase Prevention and Reconciliation Act of 2005 (P.L. 109-222)).

Law source: Law at ¶5505. Committee Report at ¶10,290.

— Act Sec. 515(c) of the Tax Increase Prevention and Reconciliation Act of 2005 (P.L. 109-222), redesignating Code Sec. 911(f) as (g) and adding new Code Sec. 911(f);

— Act Sec. 515(d), providing the effective date.

Reporter references: For further information, consult the following CCH reporters.

— Standard Federal Tax Reporter, ¶28,049.01

— Tax Research Consultant, EXPAT: 100, EXPAT: 12,000, EXPAT: 12,100, EXPAT: 12,150 and EXPAT: 12,204

— Federal Tax Guide, ¶17,280 and ¶17,285

¶1010

U.S. REAL PROPERTY INTERESTS

¶1015 FIRPTA Definition of Regulated Investment Company Modified

SUMMARY OF NEW LAW

The Foreign Investment in Real Property Tax Act (FIRPTA) rules apply to regulated investment companies (RICs) only if the RICs are United States real property holding companies, or would be if the regularly traded stock and domestically controlled entity exceptions did not apply.

BACKGROUND

The Foreign Investment in Real Property Tax Act (FIRPTA), as part of the Omnibus Budget Reconciliation Act of 1980 (P.L. 96-499) and codified in Code Sec. 897, provides that any gain realized by a foreign person (i.e., a nonresident alien individual or a foreign corporation) from the disposition of a U.S. real property interest is taken into account as if the taxpayer received income effectively connected with the conduct of a U.S. trade or business. Thus, the nonresident alien or foreign corporation is taxed on the net gain in the same manner as a U.S. citizen or domestic corporation and must report the gain on a U.S. tax return.

A U.S. real property interest includes real property located in the United States or the Virgin Islands (Code Sec. 897(c)(1)(A)(i) and Reg. §1.897-1(b)). A U.S. real property interest also includes any interest in a domestic corporation, unless the taxpayer establishes that the corporation was not a U.S. real property holding corporation (USRPHC) during the five-year period ending on the date of disposition of the interest (Code Sec. 897(c)(1)(A)(ii)). A corporation is a USRPHC if the fair market value (FMV) of all of its U.S. real property interests equals or exceeds 50 percent of the sum of the FMV of its real property interests within and outside the United States and any other assets used or held for use in a trade or business (Code Sec. 897(c)(2)).

Special rules apply to interests in qualified investment entities, i.e., real estate investment trusts (REITs) and regulated investment companies (RICs) or mutual funds) (Code Sec. 897(h)(4)(A)). Generally, any distribution by a qualified investment entity to a nonresident alien individual or a foreign corporation, attributable to gain from a sale or exchange of a U.S. real property interest by the qualified investment entity, will be treated as gain recognized by the nonresident alien individual or foreign corporation from the sale or exchange of a U.S. real property interest (Code Sec. 897(h)(1)).

A U.S. real property interest does not include any interest in a domestically controlled qualified investment entity (Code Sec. 897(h)(2)). The term "domestically controlled qualified investment entity" means any qualified investment entity (RIC or REIT) in which at all times during the testing period less than 50 percent in value of the stock

BACKGROUND

was held directly or indirectly by foreign persons (Code Sec. 897(h)(4)(B)). The testing period is the shortest of:

(1) the period beginning on June 19, 1980 and ending on the date of the disposition or distribution;

(2) the five-year period ending on the date of the disposition or distribution; or

(3) the period during which the qualified investment entity was in existence (Code Sec. 897(h)(4)(D)).

In addition, stock in a publicly traded domestic corporation is not treated as a U.S. real property interest if such interest is regularly traded on an established securities market and is held by a person owning five percent or less of that class of stock (Code Sec. 897(c)(3)).

NEW LAW EXPLAINED

Modification of qualified investment entity definition.—The definition of a qualified investment entity has been modified for purposes of applying the Foreign Investment in Real Property Tax Act (FIRPTA) rules. A qualified investment entity includes (1) any real estate investment trust (REIT), and (2) any regulated investment company (RIC) that is a U.S. real property holding corporation (USRPHC) or would be a USRPHC if the exceptions for regularly traded stock (Code Sec. 897(c)(3)) and domestically controlled entities (Code Sec. 897(h)(2)) did not apply to the RIC's interest in any REIT or other RIC (Code Sec. 897(h)(4)(A)(i), as amended by the Tax Increase Prevention and Reconciliation Act of 2005 (P.L. 109-222)).

Thus, distributions by a RIC to foreign shareholders after December 31, 2004, attributable to the sale of any U.S. real property interest will not be treated as FIRPTA income unless the RIC itself is a USRPHC (or would be as noted above). For a discussion of the tax treatment of REIT and RIC distributions attributable to FIRPTA gains, see ¶ 1020.

A domestic corporation is a USRPHC if the fair market value (FMV) of its U.S. real property interests equals or exceeds 50 percent of the sum of the FMVs of its U.S. real property interests, its interests in real property located outside the United States, plus any of its other assets used or held for use in a trade or business (Code Sec. 897(c)(2)).

> **Comment:** Effectively, for a RIC to satisfy the qualified investment entity definition after 2004, the FMV of the RIC's U.S. real property interests must equal or exceed 50 percent of the FMVs of its U.S. and foreign real property interests and any other of its assets which are used or held for use in a trade or business.

For purposes of determining whether a RIC is a USRPHC, the following rules (which except certain interests from U.S. real property interest treatment) *do not* apply to any REIT or RIC:

(1) Stock regularly traded on an established securities market is not treated as a U.S. real property interest unless a person owns more than five percent of the stock during the shorter of:

NEW LAW EXPLAINED

    (a) the period after June 18, 1980, during which the person held the stock; or

    (b) the five-year period ending on the date of disposition (Code Sec. 897(c)(3) and (c)(1)(A)(ii)).

(2) If at all times during the testing period foreign persons hold directly or indirectly less than 50 percent in value of a qualified investment entity's stock, then the qualified investment entity is domestically controlled and is not a U.S. real property interest (Code Sec. 897(h)(2) and (h)(4)(B)). The testing period is the shortest of the period:

    (a) beginning on June 19, 1980 and ending on the date of the disposition or distribution;

    (b) the five-year period ending on the date of the disposition or distribution; or

    (c) the period during which the qualified investment entity was in existence (Code Sec. 897(h)(4)(D)).

Comment: According to the Conference Committee Report, in order to determine if a RIC is a USRPHC, a RIC must include as U.S. real property interests its holdings of RIC or REIT stock if the RIC or REIT is a USRPHC. The fact that the RIC or REIT stock is regularly traded on an established securities market or that the RIC owns less than five percent of the stock does not affect the application of this special rule. In addition, the RIC must include its interests in any domestically controlled RIC or REIT that is a USRPHC (Conference Committee Report (H.R. Conf. Rep. No. 109-455)).

Comment: The amendment does not alter the fact that the definition of a qualified investment entity will not include a RIC after December 31, 2007. However, see ¶1020 for a discussion of a limited purpose extension.

▶ **Effective date.** This amendment shall take effect after December 31, 2004 (Act Sec. 504(b) of the Tax Increase Prevention and Reconciliation Act of 2005 (P.L. 109-222)).

Law source: Law at ¶5480. Committee Report at ¶10,180.

— Act Sec. 504(a) of the Tax Increase Prevention and Reconciliation Act of 2005 (P.L. 109-222), amending Code Sec. 897(h)(4)(A)(i)(II);

— Act Sec. 504(b), providing the effective date.

Reporter references: For further information, consult the following CCH reporters.

— Standard Federal Tax Reporter, ¶27,711.033

— Tax Research Consultant, INTL: 3,500 and RIC: 3,258

— Federal Tax Guide, ¶17,115

¶1020 FIRPTA Rules for Look-Through Distributions Expanded

SUMMARY OF NEW LAW

The FIRPTA look-through distribution rule is expanded to include distributions made *to* a qualified investment entity. The REIT exception to the look-through rule for distributions of stock regularly traded on an established U.S. securities market has been extended to RICs that are U.S. real property holding corporations (USRPHCs). For purposes of the FIRPTA distribution and wash sale rules and general withholding rules, a RIC USRPHC that receives a distribution from a REIT attributable to gain from the sale of a U.S. real property interest is treated as a qualified investment entity, whether the distribution is before or after December 31, 2007. A RIC USRPHC is required to withhold 35 percent from any distribution to a nonresident alien individual or a foreign corporation that is treated as gain realized from the sale or exchange of a U.S. real property interest. Dividend treatment is accorded to RIC USRPHC distributions that comply with an exception for regularly traded stock.

BACKGROUND

Pursuant to the Foreign Investment in Real Property Tax Act (FIRPTA), nonresident aliens and foreign corporations are taxed on the net gain from a disposition of a U.S. real property interest, including a disposition of an interest in a U.S. real property holding corporation. Such distributions are treated as income effectively connected with the conduct of a U.S. trade or business and the foreign distributees are required to file U.S. tax returns to report that income (Code Sec. 897(a)(1)).

A look-through rule applies to distributions by qualified investment entities, i.e., real estate investment trusts (REITs) and regulated investment companies (RICs), (Code Sec. 897(h)(4)(A)). Generally, any distribution by a qualified investment entity to a nonresident alien individual or a foreign corporation that is attributable to gain from a sale or exchange of a U.S. real property interest by the qualified investment entity will be treated as gain recognized by the nonresident alien individual or foreign corporation from the sale or exchange of a U.S. real property interest (Code Sec. 897(h)(1)). Such REIT distributions are subject to withholding at 35 percent (Reg. § 1.1445-8). Regulations have not been issued regarding withholding on similar RIC distributions.

If less than 50 percent in value of the stock of a RIC or REIT is held directly or indirectly by foreign persons at all times during the shorter of:

- the period beginning on June 19, 1980 and ending on the date of the disposition or distribution,

- the 5-year period ending on the date of the disposition or distribution, or

- the period during which the qualified investment entity was in existence (Code Sec. 897(h)(4)(D)),

BACKGROUND

then an interest in the RIC or REIT is not treated as a U.S. real property interest because the RIC or REIT is domestically controlled (Code Sec. 897(h)(4)(B) and (h)(2)). Furthermore, the look-through rule does not apply to REIT distributions if:

- the distribution is received with respect to any class of stock that is regularly traded on an established securities market in the United States, and

- the foreign distributee did not own more than five percent of the class of stock at any time during the one-year period ending on the date of distribution (Code Sec. 897(h)(1)).

If the regularly traded stock exception applies, the distribution is treated by the REIT and the foreign shareholder as a distribution of an ordinary dividend subject to 30 percent, or a lower treaty rate, withholding.

The general rule for distributions by qualified investment entities to non-U.S. investors does not apply to REIT distributions if the stock of the REIT is regularly traded on an established securities market in the U.S. and the foreign distributee did not own more than five percent of the class of stock at any time during the one year period ending on the date of the distribution (Code Sec. 897(h)(1)). Effectively, a capital gain distribution is treated as an ordinary dividend and the foreign investor is not required to file a U.S. tax return. This exception to the general rule regarding distributions by qualified investment entities to non-U.S. investors does not apply to RICs.

> **Comment:** The term qualified investment entity does not include a RIC after December 31, 2007 (Code Sec. 897(h)(4)(A)(ii)).

NEW LAW EXPLAINED

Tax treatment of FIRPTA gain distributions modified—The Tax Increase Prevention and Reconciliation Act of 2005 (P.L. 109-222) made several changes related to the Foreign Investment in Real Property Act (FIRPTA). These changes include expansion of the FIRPTA distribution rules, extension of the regularly traded securities exception to publicly traded regulated investment company (RIC) U.S. Real Property Holding Corporations (USRPHCs), modification of the RIC termination date, required withholding on RIC USRPHC distributions, and treatment of certain RIC capital gain distributions as dividends.

FIRPTA distributions rule expanded. The FIRPTA look-through distribution rule is expanded to include distributions made *to* a qualified investment entity. Any distribution by a qualified investment entity (RIC USRPHC, or a real estate investment trust (REIT)) to a nonresident alien individual, a foreign corporation, or other qualified investment entity that is attributable to gain from a sale or exchange of a U.S. real property interest by the qualified investment entity will be treated as gain recognized by the nonresident alien individual, foreign corporation, or other qualified investment entity from the sale or exchange of a U.S. real property interest (Code Secs. 897(h)(1) and 897(h)(4)(A)(i)(II) as amended by the Tax Reconciliation Act of 2005.

NEW LAW EXPLAINED

Comment: For a RIC to satisfy the qualified investment entity definition for dispositions in tax years beginning after December 31, 2004, the fair market value (FMV) of the RIC's U.S. real property interests must equal or exceed 50 percent of the FMVs of its U.S. and foreign real property interests and any other of its assets which are used or held for use in a trade or business. Simply put, the RIC must be a USRPHC. See ¶1015 for a discussion of the modification of the RIC definition for FIRPTA purposes.

Comment: Extending application of the look-through distribution rule to include distributions made *to* a RIC USRPHC, or *to* a REIT, directly affects investments in tiered qualified investment entities that allowed foreign investors to argue that the FIRPTA rules did not apply. The argument was based on the lower tier RIC or REIT disposing of the U.S. real property interest, distributing the proceeds to the upper tier domestic RIC or REIT that then distributed alleged non-FIRPTA income to its foreign shareholders. The distributions now retain their character as FIRPTA income when distributed by a RIC USRPHC or a REIT to other qualified investment entities (RIC USRPHCs or REITs).

Regularly-traded securities exception. Under certain circumstances, the capital gain distributions of a publicly traded RIC USRPHC are not treated as gain recognized from the sale or exchange of a U.S. real property interest. The look-through rule does not apply to distributions from a REIT, or from a RIC USRPHC, if:

(1) the shareholder distributee is a nonresident alien individual or a foreign corporation;

(2) the distribution is received with respect to any class of stock that is regularly traded on an established securities market in the United States; and

(3) the shareholder distributee did not own more than five percent of the class of stock at any time during the one-year period ending on the date of distribution (Code Sec. 897(h)(1), as amended by the Tax Reconciliation Act of 2005).

Comment: The exception to the look-through rule that applied to REIT stock regularly traded on an established U.S. securities market has been extended to RIC USRPHCs. Since these distributions will not be treated as effectively connected income, the foreign investors will not be required to file U.S. tax returns. These distributions, however, are recharacterized as dividends and are subject to ordinary dividend withholding rules (Code Sec. 852(b)(3)(E), as added by the Tax Reconciliation Act of 2005; Conference Committee Report (H.R. Conf. Rep. No. 109-455)).

Comment: The regularly traded stock exception under Code Sec. 897(h)(1), as amended by the Tax Reconciliation Act of 2005, has a one year holding period rather than the five year period that applies to the regularly traded stock exception under Code Sec. 897(c)(3).

Comment: If a RIC does not qualify as a USRPHC, the RIC's distributions from sales of U.S. real property interests to foreign distributees that do not meet the regularly traded stock exception can be designated by the RIC as non-taxable long- or short-term capital gain (Conference Committee Report (H.R. Conf. Rep. No. 109-455)).

¶1020

NEW LAW EXPLAINED

Withholding on RIC USRPHC distributions. A REIT or RIC USRPHC is required to withhold 35 percent from any distribution to a nonresident alien individual or a foreign corporation that is treated as gain realized from the sale or exchange of a U.S. real property interest (Code Sec. 1445(e)(6), as added by the Tax Reconciliation Act of 2005). The withholding percent may be reduced to 15 percent by regulations (20 percent in tax years beginning after 2010).

> **Comment:** An existing regulation provides for 35 percent withholding on REIT distributions, but is silent on the issue of withholding on RIC distributions (Reg. § 1.1445-8(c)(2)). The withholding obligation of qualified investment entities (REITS and RIC USRPHCs) on distributions to nonresident alien individuals and foreign corporations that result in gain attributable to a U.S. real property interest has now been codified.

Dividend treatment for certain RIC capital gain distributions. The amount of a distribution from a RIC USRPHC that is not treated as gain from the sale or exchange of a U.S. real property interest under Code Sec. 897(h)(1) because of the regularly traded stock exception is not included in computing the shareholder's long-term capital gain, but is included in the shareholder's gross income as a dividend from a RIC (Code Sec. 852(b)(3)(E), as added by the Tax Reconciliation Act of 2005). Similarly, the distribution amount is not treated as a short-term capital gain, but as a dividend (Code Sec. 871(k)(2)(E), as added by the Tax Reconciliation Act of 2005).

> **Comment:** A capital gain distribution from a publicly traded RIC USRPHC is not treated as gain from the sale or exchange of a U.S. real property interest if the foreign distributee owns five percent or less of the stock at any time during the one-year period ending on distribution and the stock is regularly traded on an established U.S. securities market. The distribution is includable in the foreign shareholder's gross income as a dividend from a RIC.

Modification of RIC termination date. For purposes of applying the FIRPTA look-through rule of Code Sec. 897(h)(1), the wash sale rule of Code Sec. 897(h)(5), and the withholding rules of Code Sec. 1445, a RIC USRPHC is treated as a qualified investment entity with respect to any distribution that it makes to a nonresident alien individual or a foreign corporation that is attributable to a distribution it received from a REIT, whether before or after December 31, 2007 (Code Sec. 897(h)(4)(A)(ii), as amended by the Tax Reconciliation Act of 2005). See ¶1025 for a discussion of the FIRPTA wash sale rules.

▶ **Effective date.** The amendments apply to tax years of qualified investment entities beginning after December 31, 2005, except that no withholding is required under Code Secs. 1441, 1442 or 1445 with respect to any distribution before May 17, 2006 if such amount was not otherwise required to be withheld under any such section as in effect before such amendments (Act Sec. 505(d) of the Tax Increase Prevention and Reconciliation Act of 2005 (P.L. 109-222)).

Law source: Law at ¶5430, ¶5455, ¶5480 and ¶5630. Committee Report at ¶10,190.

— Act Sec. 505(a) of the Tax Increase Prevention and Reconciliation Act of 2005 (P.L. 109-222), amending Code Sec. 897(h)(1) and 897(h)(4)(A)(ii);

NEW LAW EXPLAINED

— Act Sec. 505(b), redesignating Code Sec. 1445(e)(6) as Code Sec. 1445(e)(7) and adding new Code Sec. 1445(e)(6);

— Act Sec. 505(c)(1), adding Code Sec. 852(b)(3)(E);

— Act Sec. 505(c)(2), adding Code Sec. 871(k)(2)(E);

— Act Sec. 505(d), providing the effective date.

Reporter references: For further information, consult the following CCH reporters.

— Standard Federal Tax Reporter, ¶27,711.033, ¶32,792.01 and ¶32,792.04

— Tax Research Consultant, INTLIN: 6,112, INTLIN: 6,112.20, RIC: 3,250 and RIC: 3,258

— Federal Tax Guide, ¶17,115 and ¶18,635

¶1025 FIRPTA Rules Apply to Wash Sale Transactions

SUMMARY OF NEW LAW

A nonresident alien, foreign corporation, or qualified investment entity that disposes of an interest in a domestically controlled qualified investment entity within 30 days prior to a distribution of FIRPTA income by that entity and acquires a substantially identical interest in the entity within a 61 day period, must pay FIRPTA tax on an amount equal to the amount of the distribution that was not taxed because of the disposition.

BACKGROUND

The Foreign Investment in Real Property Tax Act (FIRPTA) added Code Secs. 897 and 1445 governing the imposition and collection of tax on dispositions of U.S. real property interests held by nonresident alien individuals or foreign corporations. FIRPTA provides that any gain realized by a foreign person from the disposition of a U.S. real property interest is taken into account as if the taxpayer received income effectively connected with the conduct of a U.S. trade or business (Code Sec. 897(a)). Thus, a nonresident alien or foreign corporation is taxed on the net gain in the same manner as a U.S. citizen or domestic corporation and must report the gain on a U.S. tax return.

The term U.S. real property interest does not include any interest in a domestically controlled qualified investment entity (Code Sec. 897(h)(2)). A qualified investment entity is any real estate investment trust (REIT) and any regulated investment company (RIC) (Code Sec. 897(h)(4)(A)). The term "domestically controlled qualified investment entity" means any REIT or RIC in which at all times during the testing period less than 50 percent in value of the stock was held directly or indirectly by foreign persons (Code Sec. 897(h)(4)(B)). The testing period is the shortest of:

BACKGROUND

(1) the period beginning on June 19, 1980 and ending on the date of the disposition or distribution;

(2) the 5-year period ending on the date of the disposition or distribution; or

(3) the period during which the qualified investment entity was in existence (Code Sec. 897(h)(4)(D)).

A wash sale occurs if stock or securities are sold at a loss and the seller acquires substantially identical stock or securities 30 days before or after the sale. Loss deductions are disallowed where they result from wash sales of stock or securities (Code Sec. 1091(a)). The law is silent on the applicability of the FIRPTA rules to wash sale transactions.

NEW LAW EXPLAINED

Wash sale transaction produces U.S. real property gain.—If an interest in a domestically controlled qualified investment entity is disposed of by a nonresident alien, foreign corporation, or qualified investment entity in an applicable wash sales transaction prior to a distribution by that domestically controlled qualified investment entity, the nonresident alien, foreign corporation, or qualified investment entity is treated as having gain from the sale or exchange of a U.S. real property interest (Code Sec. 897(h)(5)(A)), as added by the Tax Increase Prevention and Reconciliation Act of 2005 (P.L. 109-222)). The amount of the gain is equal to the portion of the wash sale disposition that would have been treated as gain from the sale or exchange of a U.S. real property interest (resulting from the distribution by the domestically controlled qualified investment entity), but for the wash sale disposition.

> **Comment:** Generally the FIRPTA rules do not apply to the sale of stock in domestically controlled qualified investment entities because an interest in a domestically controlled qualified investment entity is not a U.S. real property interest (Code Sec. 897(h)(2)). However, when a wash sale transaction is involved, the disposition of an interest in a domestically controlled qualified investment entity by a nonresident alien, foreign corporation, or qualified investment entity is treated as gain from the sale or exchange of a U.S. real property interest.

Applicable wash sales transaction. An applicable wash sales transaction is any transaction (or series of transactions) in which a nonresident alien, foreign corporation, or qualified investment entity disposes of an interest in a domestically controlled qualified investment entity during the 30-day period preceding the ex-dividend date of a distribution by the domestically controlled qualified investment entity that would have been treated as gain from the sale or exchange of a U.S. real property interest. The nonresident alien, foreign corporation, or qualified investment entity must then acquire, or enter into a contract or option to acquire, a substantially identical interest in such entity during the 61-day period beginning with the 1st day of the 30-day period preceding the ex-dividend date of the distribution (Code Sec. 897(h)(5)(B)(i), as added by the Tax Reconciliation Act of 2005). A nonresident alien, foreign corporation, or qualified investment entity is treated as having acquired any interest acquired by a related party as defined in Code Sec. 267(b) or Code Sec.

NEW LAW EXPLAINED

707(b)(1), including any interest that the related party has entered into any contract or option to acquire.

Comment: The wash sale transaction covers a period of 61 days; the 30 days before and the 30 days after the ex-dividend date, plus the ex-dividend date itself.

Comment: The following elements are required for a wash sale transaction to produce U.S. real property gain:

- disposition of an interest in a qualified investment entity by a nonresident alien, a foreign corporation, or a qualified investment entity;

  — A *qualified investment entity* is a regulated investment company (RIC) that is a U.S. real property holding corporation (USRPHC), or a real estate investment trust (REIT) (Code Sec. 897(h)(4)(A), as amended by the Tax Reconciliation Act of 2005). See ¶1015 for a discussion of the modification of the RIC definition for FIRPTA purposes.

  — A corporation is a *U.S. real property holding corporation* (USRPHC) if the fair market value (FMV) of its U.S. real property interests equals or exceeds 50 percent of the sum of the FMVs of its real property interests within and outside the United States and any other assets used or held for use in a trade or business (Code Sec. 897(c)(2)).

- the qualified investment entity (RIC USRPHC or REIT) must be domestically controlled;

  — The term *domestically controlled qualified investment entity* means that less than 50 percent in value of the stock of the RIC USRPHC, or REIT, was held directly or indirectly by foreign persons at all times during the shortest of: (a) the period between June 19, 1980 and the disposition date; (b) the 5-year period ending on the disposition date; or (c) the period during which the qualified investment entity was in existence (Code Sec. 897(h)(4)(B); Code Sec. 897(h)(4)(D)).

- the disposition must take place during the 30-day period preceding the ex-dividend date of a distribution by the REIT or RIC USRPHC that would have been treated as gain from the sale or exchange of a U.S. real property interest by the nonresident alien, foreign corporation, or qualified investment entity; and

- the reacquisition, or entry into a contract or option for reacquisition, of a substantially identical interest in the REIT or RIC USRPHC by the nonresident alien, foreign corporation, qualified investment entity, or a related party, must take place during the 61-day period beginning with the first day of the 30-day period preceding the ex-dividend date of the distribution.

Substitute dividend payments. A substitute dividend payment is the payment received by a foreign person for the transfer of shares of stock in a securities lending or sale-repurchase transaction (Reg. § 1.861-3(a)(6)). The payment represents the amount of dividend distributions the transferor would have received on the stock. Substitute dividend payments are treated as FIRPTA gain by treating the foreign shareholder

¶1025

NEW LAW EXPLAINED

(nonresident alien, foreign corporation, or qualified investment entity) of the domestically controlled RIC USRPHC or REIT as if it had received a FIRPTA distribution that is treated as U.S. effectively connected income when a wash sale transaction is involved (Code Sec. 897(h)(5)((B)(ii), as added by the Tax Reconciliation Act of 2005). To prevent avoidance of tax on investments of foreign persons in U.S. real property through wash sale transactions, the Treasury is authorized to issue regulations specifying similar arrangements subject to FIRPTA gain treatment.

Exceptions. There are two situations that are not treated as applicable wash sales transactions. First, if the nonresident alien, foreign corporation, or qualified investment entity actually receives a distribution from a RIC USRPHC, or a REIT, that is gain from the sale or exchange of a U.S. real property interest with respect to the interest disposed of or acquired, the transaction is not an applicable wash sales transaction (Code Sec. 897(h)(5)(B)(iii), as added by the Tax Reconciliation Act of 2005). Second, a transaction is not treated as an applicable wash sales transaction if it involves the disposition of any class of stock in a qualified investment entity that is regularly traded on an established U.S. securities market, as long as the nonresident alien, foreign corporation or qualified investment entity did not own more than five percent of the class of stock at any time during the one-year period ending on the ex-dividend date of the distribution (Code Sec. 897(h)(5)(B)(iv), as added by the Tax Reconciliation Act of 2005).

> **Comment:** Persons who sell stock that is regularly traded on an established U.S. securities market and do not own more than five percent of such stock during the one year period ending on the distribution date do not have FIRPTA income even if there is a wash sale transaction because they would not have been subject to FIRPTA tax if they had received the dividend instead of disposing of the stock (Conference Committee Report (H.R. Conf. Rep. No. 109-455)).

Related party. For purposes of an applicable wash sales transaction, a person is related to any person if one of the following relationships exists, as specified in Code Secs. 267(b) and 707(b)(1).

(1) Members of the same immediate family, including only brothers and sisters (whether whole or half-blood), wife or husband, ancestors (parents, grandparents, etc.), and lineal descendants (children, grandchildren, etc.).

(2) An individual and a corporation if more than 50 percent in value of the outstanding stock is owned, directly or indirectly, by or for that individual.

(3) Two corporations that are members of the same controlled group

(4) A trust fiduciary and a corporation if more than 50 percent in value of the outstanding stock is owned, directly or indirectly, by or for the trust, or by or for the grantor of the trust

(5) A grantor and fiduciary, and the fiduciary and beneficiary, of any trust.

(6) Fiduciaries of two different trusts, and the fiduciary and beneficiary of two different trusts, if both trusts have the same grantor.

(7) Tax-exempt educational and charitable organizations and a person or a member of that person's family who, directly or indirectly, controls such an organization.

NEW LAW EXPLAINED

(8) A corporation and a partnership if the same persons own more than 50 percent in value of the outstanding stock of the corporation, and more than 50 percent of the capital or profit interest in the partnership.

(9) Two S corporations if the same persons own more than 50 percent of the value in the outstanding stock of each corporation.

(10) An S corporation and a C corporation if the same persons own more than 50 percent in value of the outstanding stock of each corporation.

(11) An executor of an estate and a beneficiary of that estate except in the case of a sale or exchange in satisfaction of a pecuniary bequest.

(12) A partnership and a person owning, directly or indirectly, more than 50 percent of the capital interest, or the profits interest, in such partnership.

(13) Two partnerships in which the same persons own, directly or indirectly, more than 50 percent of the capital interests or profits interests.

Withholding. Although the disposition of a U.S. real property interest by a foreign person or entity is generally subject to withholding, a disposition by a nonresident alien, foreign corporation, or qualified investment entity that is treated as a disposition of U.S. real property solely by reason of the wash sale rule is not subject to withholding (Code Sec. 1445(b)(8), as added by the Tax Reconciliation Act of 2005).

▶ **Effective date.** The amendments apply to tax years beginning after December 31, 2005, except that the amendments do not apply to any distribution, or substitute dividend payment, occurring before the date that is 30 days after May 17, 2006 (Act Sec. 506(c) of the Tax Increase Prevention and Reconciliation Act of 2006 (P.L. 109-222)).

Law source: Law at ¶5480 and ¶5630. Committee Report at ¶10,190.

— Act Sec. 506(a) of the Tax Increase Prevention and Reconciliation Act of 2005 (P.L. 109-222), adding Code Sec. 897(h)(5);

— Act Sec. 506(b), adding Code Sec. 1445(b)(8);

— Act Sec. 506(c), providing the effective date.

Reporter references: For further information, consult the following CCH reporters.

— Standard Federal Tax Reporter, ¶27,711.01 and ¶32,792.01

— Tax Research Consultant, INTL: 3,500 and INTLIN: 6,056

— Federal Tax Guide, ¶17,115 and ¶18,635

¶1025

CONTROLLED FOREIGN CORPORATIONS

¶1030 Subpart F Exceptions for Insurance Income Extended

SUMMARY OF NEW LAW

The temporary exceptions from subpart F income for certain insurance and insurance investment income are extended through 2008.

BACKGROUND

Under the subpart F rules, certain income earned by a controlled foreign corporation (CFC) may be currently taxed to U.S. shareholders, even though the earnings are not distributed to the shareholders (Code Sec. 951-965). For this purpose, a CFC is a foreign corporation with at least 50 percent of its stock owned (by vote or value) by 10-percent U.S. shareholders (Code Sec. 957). A U.S. shareholder is a shareholder that owns at least 10 percent of the voting stock of a foreign corporation (Code Sec. 951(b)).

A CFC's subpart F income that is currently taxed to its U.S. shareholders is made up of the following three categories of income:

(1) insurance income (Code Sec. 953);

(2) foreign base company income (Code Sec. 954); and

(3) income related to international boycotts and other violations of public policy (Code Sec. 952(a)(3)-(5)).

A CFC's subpart F insurance income is the corporation's income that is attributable to issuing or reinsuring an insurance or annuity contract. The income must be the type of income that would be taxed (with some modifications) under the rules of sub-chapter L, if the income were earned by a U.S. insurance company (Code Sec. 953(a)).

Foreign base company income is made up of several categories of income, one of which is foreign personal holding company income (FPHCI). FPHCI is generally passive type income, such as dividend, interest, rent and royalty income (Code Sec. 954(c)).

Temporary exception for insurance income. Under a temporary exception, the "exempt insurance income" of a qualifying insurance company or a qualifying insurance company branch is not considered subpart F income. In general, exempt insurance income is income from insuring or reinsuring risks in the home country and other risks outside of the United States, if certain requirements are met. The income must be treated as earned by the company or its branch in the home country under the home country's tax laws (Code Sec. 953(e)).

The definition of a "qualifying insurance company" is intended to make sure that the exception applies to income from active insurance operations. Thus, a qualifying

BACKGROUND

insurance company is a CFC that meets the following requirements (Code Sec. 953(e)(3) and (6)):

(1) it is regulated in its home country (i.e., country where the CFC is created or organized) as an insurance or reinsurance company and is allowed by the applicable insurance regulatory body to sell insurance, reinsurance or annuity contracts to unrelated persons;

(2) more than 50 percent of the aggregate net written premiums on the contracts of the CFC and each qualifying insurance company branch are from covering home country risks with respect to unrelated persons; and

(3) the CFC is engaged in the insurance business and would be taxed under subchapter L, if it were a U.S. company.

A "qualifying insurance company branch" is, in general, a separate and clearly identified qualified business unit of the CFC (under Code Sec. 989) that is a qualifying insurance company. The branch must maintain its own books and records, and must be allowed to sell insurance by the applicable insurance regulatory body in its home country (i.e., the country where the unit has its principal office) (Code Sec. 953(e)(4)).

"Exempt insurance income" is income attributable to an exempt contract (Code Sec. 953(a) and 953(e)(1)(A)). An exempt contract is an insurance or annuity contract issued or reinsured by a qualifying insurance company or a qualifying insurance company branch in connection with risks located outside of the United States (Code Sec. 953(e)(2)(A)). However, the qualifying insurance company or branch must separately meet a minimum home country requirement—more than 30 percent of net premiums on exempt contracts must cover home country risks with respect to unrelated persons (Code Sec. 953(e)(1)(C) and (2)(B)). Additionally, exempt income will not include income from covering home country risks if, as a result of an arrangement, another company receives a substantially equal amount of consideration for covering non-home country risks (Code Sec. 953(e)(1)(B)).

If risks from both the home country and non-home country are covered under the contract, the income is not exempt unless the qualifying insurance company or branch conduct substantial activities in its home country with respect to the insurance business. Additionally, substantially all of the activities necessary to give rise to the contract must be performed in the home country (Code Sec. 953(e)(2)(C)).

Temporary exception for insurance investment income. Under a temporary exception, subpart F FPHIC does not include certain investment income of a qualifying insurance company or a qualifying insurance company branch (Code Sec. 954(i)).

The exception applies to "qualified insurance income" received by a qualifying insurance company or a qualifying insurance company branch from an unrelated person. A qualifying insurance company and a qualifying insurance company branch are defined in the same way for both the subpart F insurance income exception, see above, and this exception (Code Sec. 954(i)(6)).

Qualifying insurance company income is income from the investment of assets allocable to exempt contracts in an amount equal to:

BACKGROUND

(1) one-third of the premiums earned during the tax year on the property, casualty or health insurance contracts; and

(2) 10 percent of the loss reserves for life insurance or annuity contracts (Code Sec. 954(i)(2)(B)).

Qualified insurance income is also income from the investment of:

(1) loss reserves that are allocable to exempt contracts; and/or

(2) 80 percent of unearned premiums from exempt contracts (Code Sec. 954(i)(2)(A)).

An exempt contract is defined the same way for both the subpart F insurance company exception, see above, and this exception. Thus, the amounts invested are allocable to the insuring or reinsuring of risks in the home country and other risks outside of the United States, if certain requirements are met (Code Sec. 954(i)(6)).

Application of temporary exceptions. The temporary exceptions from subpart F for insurance income apply to tax years of a foreign corporation beginning after December 31, 1998, and before January 1, 2007, and to tax years of U.S. shareholders with and within which such tax years of foreign corporations end (Code Sec. 953(e)(10)).

NEW LAW EXPLAINED

Temporary exceptions from subpart F income for insurance income extended two years.—The temporary exception from subpart F insurance income for "exempt insurance income" of a qualifying insurance company or a qualifying insurance company branch is extended for two years, through 2008 (Code Sec. 953(e)(10), as amended by the Tax Increase Prevention and Reconciliation Act of 2005 (P.L. 109-222)). In general, exempt insurance income is income from issuing or reinsuring risks in the home country and other risks outside of the United States, if certain requirements are met (Code Sec. 953(e)(1)).

The temporary exception from foreign personal holding company income for "qualified insurance income" of a qualifying insurance company or a qualifying insurance company branch is also extended for two years, through 2008 (Code Sec. 953(e)(10), as amended by the Tax Reconciliation Act of 2005). The exception generally applies to certain income from the investment of amounts attributable to the insuring or reinsuring of risks in the home country and other risks outside of the United States, if certain requirements are met (Code Sec. 954(i)).

The temporary exceptions apply to tax years of a foreign corporation beginning after December 31, 1998, and before January 1, 2009, and to tax years of U.S. shareholders with or within which any such tax years of the foreign corporation ends (Code Sec. 953(e)(10), as amended by the Tax Reconciliation Act of 2005).

For tax years beyond the extension, Code Sec. 953(a), which defines subpart F insurance income, is applied as if the tax year of the foreign corporation began in 1998 (Code Sec. 953(e)(10), as amended by the Tax Reconciliation Act of 2005). Consequently, only income attributable to insuring or reinsuring home country risks is

NEW LAW EXPLAINED

excluded from subpart F insurance income. However, that income from issuing home country risks could be subpart F income if, as a result of an arrangement, another corporation receives a substantially equal amount for insuring non-home country risks (Code Sec. 953(a), prior to amendment by the Tax and Trade Relief Extension Act of 1998 (P.L. 105-277)).

> **Comment:** Prior to the Tax Reform Act of 1986 (P.L. 99-514), exceptions from subpart F were provided for income earned in the active conduct of a banking, financing or similar business, or from certain investments made by insurance companies. The exceptions were eliminated by P.L. 99-514 and the income was subject to tax on a current basis under the general subpart F rules. Beginning in 1997, Congress has enacted five temporary exceptions from the subpart F rules, for periods between one and five years: Taxpayer Relief Act of 1997 (P.L. 105-34), one year; Tax and Trade Relief Extension Act of 1998 (P.L. 105-277) one year; Tax Relief Extension Act of 1999 (P.L. 106-170), two years, Job Creation and Worker Assistance Act of 2002 (P.L. 107-147), five years; and the Tax Increase Prevention and Reconciliation Act of 2005 (P.L. 109-222), two years).

See ¶1035 for a discussion of the temporary exceptions from subpart F income for income earned in the active conduct of a banking, financing or similar business.

▶ **Effective date.** No specific effective date is provided by the Act. The provision is, therefore, considered effective on May 17, 2006, the date of enactment.

Law source: Law at ¶5530. Committee Report at ¶10,022.

— Act Sec. 103(a)(1) of the Tax Increase Prevention and Reconciliation Act of 2005 (P.L. 109-222), amending Code Sec. 953(e)(10).

Reporter references: For further information, consult the following CCH reporters.

— Standard Federal Tax Reporter, ¶28,518.066

— Tax Research Consultant, INTLOUT: 100, INTLOUT: 9,102, INTLOUT: 9,102.35 and INTLOUT: 9,106.30

— Federal Tax Guide, ¶17,445

¶1035 Subpart F Exceptions for Active Financing Income Extended

SUMMARY OF NEW LAW

The exceptions from subpart F income for so-called active financing income have been extended through 2008.

BACKGROUND

Under the subpart F rules, certain income earned by a controlled foreign corporation (CFC) may be currently taxed to U.S. shareholders, even though the earnings are not

BACKGROUND

distributed to the shareholders (Code Secs. 951-965). For this purpose, a CFC is a foreign corporation with at least 50 percent of its stock owned (by vote or value) by 10-percent U.S. shareholders (Code Sec. 957). A U.S. shareholder is a shareholder that owns at least 10 percent of the voting stock of a foreign corporation (Code Sec. 951(b)).

A CFC's subpart F income that is currently taxed to its U.S. shareholders is made up of the following three categories of income:

(1) insurance income (Code Sec. 953);

(2) foreign base company income (Code Sec. 954); and

(3) income related to international boycotts and other violations of public policy (Code Sec. 952(a)(3)-(5)).

Foreign base company income is made up of several categories of income, one of which is foreign personal holding company income (FPHCI). FPHCI is generally passive type income, such as dividend, interest, rent and royalty income (Code Sec. 954(c)).

FPHCI also includes the excess of gains over losses on the sale of non-inventory property (Code Sec. 954(c)(1)(B)). A regular dealer exception applies to gains from this type of property, if the gain is derived from a transaction entered into in the ordinary course of a dealer's trade or business, including a bona fide hedging transaction. However, dealers must treat interest, dividends, and equivalent amounts as FPHCI (Code Sec. 954(c)(2)(C)).

Another category of foreign base company income is foreign base company services income. Foreign base company services income is income from the performance of services outside of the CFC's home country, for, or on behalf of, a related person (Code Sec. 954(e)).

Temporary exceptions from subpart F income for active financing income. Income derived in the active conduct of a banking, finance or similar business, or in an insurance business (see ¶1030) (so-called active financing income) is temporarily excepted from subpart F income. The temporary exceptions apply to tax years of a foreign corporation beginning after December 31, 1998, and before January 1, 2007, and to tax years of U.S. shareholders with or within which any such tax year of the foreign corporation ends (Code Sec. 954(h)(9)).

Under the exceptions, FPHCI does not include the active financing income of a CFC or its qualified business unit (QBU) (as defined under Code Sec. 989(a)). For the exception to apply, the CFC must be predominately engaged in the active conduct of a banking, financing or similar business and must conduct substantial activity with respect to that business. Further, the income must be earned by the CFC or its qualified business unit (QBU) in the active conduct of the business (Code Sec. 954(h)(2) and (3)). Only income earned in transactions with customers located outside of the United States where substantially all of the activities of the transaction are conducted in the corporation's or QBU's home country (i.e., where the CFC is created or organized or where the QBU has its principal office) is excepted. For cross-border transactions, the corporation or QBU must conduct substantial activities with respect

BACKGROUND

to the business in the home country. The income must also be treated as earned by the corporation or QBU in its home country (Code Sec. 954(h)(3) and (5)(B)).

FPHCI also does not temporarily include income with respect to a securities dealer's interest, dividends and equivalent amounts from transactions, including hedging transactions, entered into in the ordinary course of the dealer's trade or business as a securities dealer. The income must be attributable to the dealer's activities in the country where the dealer is created or organized (or where the QBU of the dealer has its principal office and conducts substantial business activity) (Code Sec. 954(c)(2)(C)(ii)).

Finally, income that falls within the following temporary exceptions is not considered foreign base company services income (Code Sec. 954(e)(2)):

(1)   the temporary exception from subpart F insurance income under Code Sec. 953(e), see ¶ 1030,

(2)   the temporary exception from FPHCI for insurance investment income under Code Sec. 954(i), see ¶ 1030,

(3)   the temporary exception from FPHCI for securities dealers under Code Sec. 954(c)(2)(C)(ii), see above, and

(4)   the temporary exception from FPHCI for income derived in the active conduct of a banking, financing or similar business, see above.

NEW LAW EXPLAINED

Exceptions from subpart F for active financing income extended two years.— Temporary exceptions from subpart F income for so-called active financing income, are extended for two years, through 2008. The extension applies to the temporary exceptions from foreign personal holding company income for:

(1)   income derived in the active conduct of a banking, financing or similar business under Code Sec. 954(h), and

(2)   income derived in the ordinary course of a security dealer's trade or business under Code Sec. 954(c)(2)(C)(ii).

The extension also applies to the temporary exception from foreign base company services income for income that falls within the other temporary exceptions for active financing income (Code Sec. 954(e)(2)).

See ¶ 1030 for a discussion of the extension of the temporary exceptions from subpart F insurance income under Code Sec. 953(e) and from foreign personal holding company income for insurance investment income under Code Sec. 954(i).

The temporary exceptions apply to tax years of foreign corporations beginning after December 31, 1998, and before January 1, 2009, and to tax years of U.S. shareholders with or within which any such tax year of the foreign corporation ends (Code Sec. 954(h)(9), as amended by the Tax Increase Prevention and Reconciliation Act of 2005 (P.L. 109-222)).

¶1035

NEW LAW EXPLAINED

Comment: According to the Senate Summary of the Tax Reconciliation Act of 2005, the active financing exception generally applies to U.S. based financial services and insurance industries and to domestic manufacturers who finance sales of large equipment to foreign customers.

Comment: Prior to the Tax Reform Act of 1986 (P.L. 99-514), exceptions from subpart F were provided for income earned in the active conduct of a banking, financing or similar business, or from certain investments made by insurance companies. The exceptions were eliminated by P.L. 99-514 and the income was subject to tax on a current basis under the general subpart F rules. Beginning in 1997, Congress has enacted five temporary exceptions from the subpart F rules, for periods between one and five years: Taxpayer Relief Act of 1997 (P.L. 105-34), one year; Tax and Trade Relief Extension Act of 1998 (P.L. 105-277) one year; Tax Relief Extension Act of 1999 (P.L. 106-170), two years, Job Creation and Worker Assistance Act of 2002 (P.L. 107-147), five years; and Tax Increase Prevention and Reconciliation Act of 2005 (P.L. 109-222), two years).

▶ **Effective date.** No specific effective date is provided by the Act. The provision is, therefore, considered effective on May 17, 2006, the date of enactment.

Law source: Law at ¶5555. Committee Report at ¶10,022.

— Act Sec. 103(a)(2) of the Tax Increase Prevention and Reconciliation Act of 2005 (P.L. 109-222), amending Code Sec. 954(h)(9).

Reporter references: For further information, consult the following CCH reporters.

— Standard Federal Tax Reporter, ¶28,543.0662

— Tax Research Consultant, INTLOUT: 9,106, INTLOUT: 9,106.30 and INTLOUT: 9,110

— Federal Tax Guide, ¶17,445

¶1040 Look-Through Treatment for Related Controlled Foreign Corporation Payments

SUMMARY OF NEW LAW

A look-through rule applies to dividends, interest, rents and royalties received by a controlled foreign corporation (CFC) from a related CFC. Under the rule, amounts are excluded from foreign personal holding company income if paid from nonsubpart F income. The rule generally applies to tax years beginning after December 31, 2005, and before January 1, 2009. The look-through rule was added by the Tax Increase Prevention Act of 2005 (P.L. 109-222) and modified by the Tax Relief and Health Care Act of 2006 (P.L. 109-432) (see ¶365).

FSC/ETI

¶1045 Repeal of FSC/ETI Binding Contract Relief Measures

SUMMARY OF NEW LAW

The provision repeals both the foreign sales corporation (FSC) binding contract relief and the extraterritorial income (ETI) binding contract relief measures. The general transition rule allowing the retention of a specified percentage of ETI benefits through 2006 remains in effect.

BACKGROUND

In 1998, the European Union requested that a World Trade Organization (WTO) Dispute Settlement Panel determine whether the foreign sales corporation (FSC) export incentive scheme that the United States had applied since 1984 was consistent with U.S. obligations under the WTO rules, including the WTO Agreement on Subsidies and Countervailing Measures and the Agreement on Agriculture. Through the FSC regime, which was itself enacted by the United States in response to objections from its trading partners that the favorable tax deferral treatment of Domestic International Sales Corporations (DISCs) constituted an export subsidy that violated U.S. commitments under the General Agreement on Tariffs and Trade (GATT), the predecessor organization to the WTO, the United States provided tax benefits to certain qualifying foreign sales corporations under Code Secs. 921 through 927. Foreign sales corporations were subsidiaries of U.S. parent corporations that engaged in export sales on behalf of the U.S. corporation.

On October 8, 1999, a WTO Panel ruled that the FSC provisions did not comply with the United States' WTO obligations. The United States appealed the ruling but was unsuccessful. In February 2000, the WTO Appellate Body affirmed the Panel's ruling and gave the United States a period of time to implement the rulings by repealing the FSC provisions or face WTO-approved retaliatory measures. The WTO's ruling in 2000 was significant in that it formally recognized that export-related tax benefits bestowed by a national tax regime could create the same kind of obstacle and economic distortion to the free flow of goods and capital in the international marketplace as trade tariffs once caused. Accordingly, later in 2000, the United States repealed the FSC rules and enacted a new regime under the FSC Repeal and Extraterritorial Income (ETI) Exclusion Act of 2000 (P.L. 106-519). Under this regime, an exclusion from gross income applied with regard to "extraterritorial income," which was a taxpayer's gross income attributable to foreign trading gross receipts, if certain criteria were met.

In 2002, once again in response to a complaint filed by the European Union, the WTO held that the ETI regime also constituted an impermissible export subsidy. Again, the United States was given a period of time in which to implement the WTO ruling. Absent U.S. compliance, it authorized the European Union to initiate retaliatory

BACKGROUND

measures against the United States by applying retaliatory duties to select U.S. exports; the European Union began applying those duties on March 1, 2004. Those retaliatory duties were discontinued in January 2005 after Congress passed the American Jobs Creation Act of 2004 (P.L. 108-357) which repealed the ETI exclusion.

While the repeal contained in the Jobs Act was generally effective for transactions after December 31, 2004, it provided a general transition rule under which taxpayers could retain 100 percent of their ETI benefits for transactions prior to 2005, 80 percent for transactions during 2005, and 60 percent of their otherwise-applicable ETI benefits for transactions during 2006. In addition, the legislation that repealed both the FSC and ETI regimes contained clauses permitting U.S. corporations that had signed contracts in effect by a certain date to retain the tax benefits existing at the time those contracts became binding. This, in effect, "grandfathered" those tax benefits in, despite the repeal of the underlying legislation. These clauses are what is referred to as binding contract relief measures.

In February 2006, a WTO ruling held that the ETI general transition rule and the FSC and ETI binding contract relief measures were prohibited export subsidies. The European Union could reinstitute its retaliatory duties against U.S. exports if Congress did not repeal these provisions. While neither the Senate nor the House versions of the tax reconciliation legislation contained a provision addressing this matter, Conference Committee conferees took up the matter and drafted a provision that would repeal both FSC and ETI binding contract relief measures and, thus, avoid the reinstatement of retaliatory duties against U.S. exports that was scheduled to begin on May 16, 2006.

NEW LAW EXPLAINED

Transition rules for binding contracts repealed.—The provision repeals the foreign sales corporation (FSC) binding contract relief measure under which certain existing contracts were permitted under a grandfathering clause (Act Sec. 513(a) of the Tax Increase Prevention and Reconciliation Act of 2005 (P.L. 109-222), amending Section 5(c)(1) of the FSC Repeal and Extraterritorial Income Exclusion Act of 2000 (P.L. 106-519)). Accordingly, transactions occurring in the ordinary course of a trade or business after December 31, 2001, that were engaged in pursuant to a binding contract between an FSC or related person and an unrelated party which was itself in effect on September 30, 2000, and thereafter are no longer transactions permitted under the FSC transition rule (the "FSC" binding contract relief).

Similarly, the provision repeals the extraterritorial income (ETI) binding contract relief measure (Act Sec. 513(b) of the Tax Reconciliation Act of 2005, striking Section 101(f) of the American Jobs Creation Act of 2004 (P.L. 108-357)). Therefore, transactions occurring in the ordinary course of a trade or business that were engaged in pursuant to a binding contract between a taxpayer and an unrelated party which was itself in effect on September 17, 2003, and thereafter are no longer transactions permitted under the transition rule (the "ETI" binding contract relief). Despite the fact that these specific-

NEW LAW EXPLAINED

application transition rules no longer apply, the general transition rule allowing the retention of a specified percentage of ETI benefits through 2006 remains in effect.

> **Comment:** A European Union spokesperson announced on May 11, 2006, that, given the repeal of the WTO-incompatible tax breaks for U.S. companies, it would withdraw the reintroduction of sanctions foreseen for May 16 (European Union Press Release No. 34/06, May 11, 2006).

▶ **Effective date.** The provision is effective for tax years beginning after May 17, 2006 (Act Sec. 513(c) of the Tax Increase Prevention and Reconciliation Act of 2005 (P.L. 109-222)).

Law source: Law at ¶7025. Committee Report at ¶10,270.

— Act Sec. 513(a) of the Tax Increase Prevention and Reconciliation Act of 2005 (P.L. 109-222), amending Section 5(c)(1) of the FSC Repeal and Extraterritorial Income Exclusion Act of 2000 (P.L. 106-519);

— Act Sec. 513(b), striking Section 101(f) of the American Jobs Creation Act of 2004 (P.L. 108-357);

— Act Sec. 513(c), providing the effective date.

Reporter references: For further information, consult the following CCH reporters.

— Standard Federal Tax Reporter, ¶28,406.01

— Tax Research Consultant, INTLOUT: 12,054, INTLOUT: 12,056 and INTLOUT: 15,000

— Federal Tax Guide, ¶17,310

¶1045

TIPRA—Bonds, Tax-Exempt Entities and Administration

11

STATE AND LOCAL BONDS

TAX-EXEMPT ENTITIES

ADMINISTRATION AND PROCEDURE

STATE AND LOCAL BONDS

¶1105 Reporting Requirements for Payors of Interest on Tax-Exempt State and Local Bonds

SUMMARY OF NEW LAW

Payors of interest on tax-exempt state and local bonds must report interest payments to the IRS and payees.

BACKGROUND

Code Sec. 6049(a) requires a payor of interest aggregating 10 dollars or more in a calendar year to report such payments to the IRS. Additionally, any nominee of 10 dollars or more in interest who subsequently pays out that interest must also report such payments. This requirement ensures that the interest is reported at some point in the chain of payment.

The interest payments are reported on Form 1096, Annual Summary and Transmittal of U.S. Information Returns, and Form 1099-INT, Interest Income. Regulations require Form 1099-INT to include information regarding the aggregate amount of the payments and the name, address and taxpayer identification number of the payee (Reg. §1.6049-4(b)). In addition, Code Sec. 6049(c) requires the payor to mail to the payee a return indicating the aggregate amount of interest paid for the tax year and contact information for the payor. Generally, a copy of the Form 1099-INT is sufficient for this purpose.

There are several exceptions to the interest reporting rules. One exception applies to interest that is exempt from tax, such as the interest on state or local bonds under Code Sec. 103. A payor of interest on a tax-exempt bond is not required to report the interest (Code Sec. 6049(b)(2)(B)).

NEW LAW EXPLAINED

Payors of interest on state and local bonds must report payments.—The exception from the interest reporting requirement for payors of interest on tax-exempt state and local bonds is eliminated. Payors of interest on these tax-exempt bonds aggregating 10 dollars or more per calendar year must now report such payments to the IRS (Code Sec. 6049(b)(2), as amended by the Tax Increase Prevention and Reconciliation Act of 2005 (P.L. 109-222)).

> **Comment:** Tax-exempt interest is a component of several calculations required to be made by taxpayers. For example, interest from a qualified private activity bond is a preference item for purposes of calculating the alternative minimum tax (Joint Committee on Taxation, Description of the Chairman's Modification to the Provisions of the "Tax Relief Act of 2005" (JCX-77-05)). Allowing payors of tax-exempt interest an exception from the interest reporting rules may allow taxpayers who are payees of such interest to either purposely or accidentally fail to report the interest. Eliminating the exception is likely a way for the IRS to curtail such underreporting.

> **Compliance Pointer:** The IRS has provided guidance on the new information reporting requirements for interest paid on tax-exempt municipal bonds (see Notice 2006-93, I.R.B. 2006-44, 798).

▶ **Effective date.** The amendments apply to interest earned after December 31, 2005 (Act Sec. 502(c) of the Tax Increase Prevention and Reconciliation Act of 2005 (P.L. 109-222)).

¶1105

NEW LAW EXPLAINED

Law source: Law at ¶5755. Committee Report at ¶10,160.

— Act Sec. 502(a) of the Tax Increase Prevention and Reconciliation Act of 2005 (P.L. 109-222), striking Code Sec. 6049(b)(2)(B) and redesignating Code Sec. 6049(b)(2)(C) and (D) as Code Sec. 6049(b)(2)(B) and (C), respectively;

— Act Sec. 502(b), amending Code Sec. 6049(b)(2)(C), as redesignated;

— Act Sec. 502(c), providing the effective date.

Reporter references: For further information, consult the following CCH reporters.

— Standard Federal Tax Reporter, ¶36,037.021

— Tax Research Consultant, FILEBUS: 9,158 and FILEBUS: 9,258.05

— Federal Tax Guide, ¶22,125

¶1110 Accelerated Expansion of Qualified Small-Issue Bond Limit

SUMMARY OF NEW LAW

For bonds issued after December 31, 2006, the first $10,000,000 of capital expenditures will not count against the elective face amount limit for qualified small issue bonds, effectively raising the elective cap from $10,000,000 to $20,000,000.

BACKGROUND

Interest on certain private activity bonds is excludable from gross income if at least 95 percent of the bond proceeds is to be used to finance private business manufacturing facilities or the acquisition of certain agricultural land or equipment. An issue of these "qualified small-issue bonds" generally cannot have an aggregate authorized face amount in excess of $1,000,000. At the election of the issuer, the maximum aggregate face amount of an issue may be increased to $10,000,000. However, if the election is made, certain capital expenditures of the business made during the six-year period beginning three years before the date of issue and ending three years after the date of issue are treated as part of the face amount of the issue (Code Sec. 144(a)).

For bonds issued after September 30, 2009, the first $10,000,000 of capital expenditures will not count against the face amount limit if the election to use the increased limit is made, effectively raising the cap from $10,000,000 to $20,000,000 (Code Sec. 144(a)(4)(G)).

> **Caution Note:** This expansion of the elective limit already applies for certain bond issues used to finance facilities with respect to which an urban development action grant has been made under Act Sec. 119 of the Housing and Community Development Act of 1974 (Code Sec. 144(a)(4)(F)).

Effective date for expanded limit accelerated.—The first $10,000,000 of capital expenditures will not count against the face amount limit for qualified small issue bonds if the election to use the increased limit is made for any bonds issued after December 31, 2006 (Code Sec. 144(a)(4)(G), as amended by the Tax Increase Prevention and Reconciliation Act of 2005 (P.L. 109-222)). Thus, for bonds issued after December 31, 2006, the elective cap increases from an aggregate of $10,000,000 to $20,000,000.

▶ **Effective date.** No specific date is provided by the Act. The provision is, therefore, considered effective on May 17, 2006, the date of enactment.

Law source: Law at ¶5155. Committee Report at ¶10,100.

— Act Sec. 208(a) of the Tax Increase Prevention and Reconciliation Act of 2005 (P.L. 109-222), amending Code Sec. 144(a)(4)(G);

— Act Sec. 208(b), amending Code Sec. 144(a)(4)(F).

Reporter references: For further information, consult the following CCH reporters.

— Standard Federal Tax Reporter, ¶7814.04

— Tax Research Consultant, SALES: 51,304.05 and SALES: 51,304.15

— Federal Tax Guide, ¶4793

¶1115 Authorization for Qualified Veterans' Mortgage Bonds Expanded in Some States

SUMMARY OF NEW LAW

Alaska, Oregon and Wisconsin may expand eligibility for participation in their qualified veterans' mortgage programs. Also, the existing annual limit on the amount of tax-exempt bonds which can be issued to fund the programs in those states is reset, beginning with calendar year 2006. The provision was added by the Tax Increase Prevention and Reconciliation Act of 2005 (P.L. 109-222) and modified by the Tax Relief and Health Care Act of 2006 (P.L. 109-432) (see ¶620).

¶1120 Special Exception from Arbitrage Restrictions for Certain Texas University Bonds Extended

SUMMARY OF NEW LAW

The exception from the arbitrage requirements for Texas University bonds secured by the Permanent University Fund was initially extended through August 30, 2009 by the Tax Increase Prevention and Reconciliation Act of 2005 (P.L. 109-222), but then

SUMMARY OF NEW LAW

made permanent by the Tax Relief and Health Care Act of 2006 (P.L. 109-432) (see ¶615).

TAX-EXEMPT ENTITIES

¶1125 Withholding on Certain Payments Made by Government Entities

SUMMARY OF NEW LAW

Beginning in 2011, federal, state and local government entities will be required to withhold three percent on certain payments made for property or services. The payments and amounts withheld must be reported to the IRS.

BACKGROUND

Employers are required to withhold income tax on wages paid to employees, including wages and salaries of employees and elected officials of federal, state and local government units. Withholding rates vary depending on the amount of wages paid, the length of the payroll period and the number of withholding allowances that employee claims.

Certain non-wage payments are also subject to mandatory or voluntary withholding, such as certain gambling proceeds, FICA and Railroad Retirement taxes, interest and dividends if the payee has not provided a valid taxpayer identification number, unemployment compensation benefits and Social Security payments. Many payments, including payments made by government entities, are not subject to withholding. For example, no tax is generally withheld from payments made to workers who are not classified as employees (independent contractors).

Reporting requirements. Numerous reporting requirements are imposed on payors that enable the IRS to verify the correctness of taxpayers' returns. For example, every person engaged in a trade or business generally is required to file information returns for each calendar year for payments of $600 or more made in the course of the payor's trade or business. Information reporting requirements exist for employers required to deduct and withhold tax from employees' income. Furthermore, any service recipient engaged in a trade or business and paying for services is required to make a return when the aggregate of payments is $600 or more. Government entities are also required to make an information return, reporting certain payments to corporations as well as to individuals. The head of every federal executive agency that enters into certain contracts is required to file an information return containing information about the contractor and the contract.

NEW LAW EXPLAINED

Withholding on certain payments made by government entities.—Beginning in 2011, the federal government, every state and local government and their political subdivisions and instrumentalities (including multi-state agencies) are required to withhold tax at the rate of three percent on certain payments to persons providing any property or services. Any payment made in connection with a government voucher or certificate program that acts as a payment for services or property is subject to the withholding requirement (Code Sec. 3402(t)(1), as added by the Tax Increase Prevention and Reconciliation Act of 2005 (P.L. 109-222)). The withholding requirement applies even if the government entity making the payment is not the recipient of the property or services.

> **Example:** Payments made by the federal government to a commodity producer under a government commodity support program are subject to the withholding requirement (Conference Committee Report (H.R. Conf. Rep. No. 109-455)).

Payments not subject to withholding. The withholding requirement does not apply to any payment:

(1) except as provided in (2) below, which is subject to withholding under any other provision of Chapter 1 regarding income taxes and surtaxes or under Chapter 3 regarding withholding of tax on nonresident aliens and foreign corporations,

(2) which is subject to withholding under Code Sec. 3406 and from which amounts are being withheld under such section,

(3) of interest,

(4) for real property,

(5) to any governmental entity subject to the requirements of Code Sec. 3402(t)(1), any tax-exempt entity or any foreign government,

(6) made pursuant to a classified or confidential contract described in Code Sec. 6050M(e)(3),

(7) made by a political subdivision of a state (or any instrumentality thereof) which makes less than $100 million of such payments annually,

(8) which is made with respect to a public assistance or public welfare program, eligibility for which is determined by a needs or income test, and

(9) to any government employee not otherwise excludable with respect to their services as an employee (Code Sec. 3402(t)(2), as added by the Tax Reconciliation Act of 2005).

> **Example:** Payments under government programs providing food vouchers or medical assistance to low-income individuals are not subject to withholding under the provision. However, payments under government programs to pro-

NEW LAW EXPLAINED

> vide health care or other services that are not based on the needs or income of the recipients are subject to withholding, including programs where eligibility is based on the age of the recipient.

Information reporting requirements. For purposes of the liability for the tax under Code Sec. 3403 and the return and payment requirements under Code Sec. 3404, payments to any person for property or services which are subject to withholding are treated as if such payments were wages paid by an employer to an employee. This same treatment applies for purposes of so much of subtitle F (Procedure and Administration), except Code Sec. 7205, as relates to the collection of income tax at source on wages under Chapter 24 (Code Sec. 3402(t)(3), as added by the Tax Reconciliation Act of 2005).

> **Comment:** It is expected that prior to 2011, the IRS will issue guidance with respect to the forms and procedures for reporting the amounts withheld from qualifying payments.

▶ **Effective date.** The provision applies to payments made after December 31, 2010 (Act Sec. 511(b) of the Tax Increase Prevention and Reconciliation Act of 2005 (P.L. 109-222)).

Law source: Law at ¶5655. Committee Report at ¶10,250.

— Act Sec. 511(a) of the Tax Increase Prevention and Reconciliation Act of 2005 (P.L. 109-222), adding Code Sec. 3402(t);

— Act Sec. 511(b), providing the effective date.

Reporter references: For further information, consult the following CCH reporters.

— Standard Federal Tax Reporter, ¶33,590A.01

— Tax Research Consultant, FILEBUS: 18,410

¶1130 Tax Involvement of Exempt Organizations in Tax Shelter Transactions

SUMMARY OF NEW LAW

A tax-exempt entity that is a party to a prohibited tax shelter transaction or becomes a party to a subsequently listed transaction at any time during the tax year must pay an excise tax. An entity that knows, or has reason to know, a transaction was a prohibited tax shelter transaction at the time it became a party to the transaction must also pay an excise tax.

BACKGROUND

An individual, trust, estate, partnership, association, company or corporation that participates in a reportable transaction (including a listed transaction) and who is required to file a tax return must make a disclosure by attaching Form 8886,

BACKGROUND

Reportable Transaction Disclosure Statement, to their tax return. Reportable transactions include:

(1) listed transactions that have been determined by the IRS to be tax avoidance transactions;

(2) confidential transactions which are offered to a taxpayer under conditions of confidentiality for which the taxpayer has paid a minimum fee to an advisor;

(3) loss transactions;

(4) transactions with a significant book-tax difference; and

(5) transactions involving a brief asset holding period.

Transactions with significant book-tax differences have been recently removed as a category from list of reportable transactions (Notice 2006-6). A penalty ranging from $10,000 to $200,000 is imposed for failing to disclose a reportable transaction (Code Sec. 6707A).

A material advisor with respect to any reportable transaction must timely file an information return. The information return must include:

(1) information identifying and describing the transaction;

(2) information describing any potential tax benefits expected to result from the transaction; and

(3) such other information prescribed by the IRS.

The amount of the penalty for failure to file the information return is $50,000. If the penalty is with respect to a listed transaction, the amount of the penalty is increased to the greater of (1) $200,000, or (2) 50 percent of the gross income derived by such person with respect to the aid, assistance, or advise that is provided on the transaction before the date the information return that includes the transaction is filed.

NEW LAW EXPLAINED

Excise tax imposed on certain exempt organizations involved in tax shelters.—A tax-exempt entity that is a party to a prohibited transaction at any time during the tax year in which it becomes a party or is a party to a subsequently listed transaction must pay an excise tax (Code Sec. 4965(a)(1), as added by the Tax Increase Prevention and Reconciliation Act of 2005 (P.L. 109-222)). The amount of tax is the highest unrelated business taxable income tax rate times the greater of:

(1) the entity's net income (after taking into account any income tax imposed with respect to the transaction) for the tax year attributable to the prohibited tax shelter transaction, or

(2) 75 percent of the proceeds received by the entity which are attributable to the prohibited tax shelter transaction.

If an entity is a party to a subsequently listed transaction at any time during the tax year, the entity must pay an excise tax at the highest unrelated business taxable income rate times the greater of:

NEW LAW EXPLAINED

(1) any income that is properly allocable to the period beginning on the later of: (a) the date the transaction is identified by the IRS as a listed transaction, or (b) the first day of the tax year; or

(2) 75 percent of the proceeds received by the entity which are attributable to such transaction and are properly allocable to the period beginning on the later of: (a) the date the transaction is identified as a listed transaction, or (b) the first day of the tax year (Code Sec. 4965(b)(1)(A), as added by the Tax Reconciliation Act of 2005).

A tax-exempt entity that is a party to a prohibited tax shelter transaction at any time during the tax year *and knows or has reason to know* the transaction is a prohibited tax shelter transaction must pay a larger excise tax. The amount of the tax is the greater of:

(1) 100 percent of the entity's net income (after taking into account any income tax imposed with respect to the transaction) for such tax year attributable to the prohibited tax shelter transaction, or

(2) 75 percent of the proceeds received by the entity which are attributable to the prohibited tax shelter transaction (Code Sec. 4965(b)(1)(B), as added by the Tax Reconciliation Act of 2005).

> **Comment:** According to the Conference Committee Report (H.R. Conf Rep. No. 109-455), in order for an entity or entity manager to have reason to know that a transaction is a prohibited tax shelter transaction, the entity or manager must have knowledge of sufficient facts that would lead a reasonable person to conclude that the transaction is a prohibited tax shelter transaction. Generally, the presence of certain factors may indicate that the entity or manager has a responsibility to inquire further about whether a transaction is a prohibited tax shelter transaction. These factors include: whether a transaction is extraordinary for the entity; promises an exceptional return considering the amount invested; or the transaction is of significant size, either in an absolute sense or relative to the receipts of the entity. The IRS has issued a notice in Q&A format, which discusses the new rules (Notice 2006-65, I.R.B. 2006-31, 102).

Prohibited tax shelter transaction. A prohibited tax shelter transaction is one that the IRS determines is a listed transaction under Code Sec. 6707A(c)(2) or a prohibited reportable transaction. A prohibited reportable transaction is any confidential transaction or any transaction with contractual protection that is a Code Sec. 6707A(c)(1) reportable transaction (Code Sec. 4965(e)(1), as added by the Tax Reconciliation Act of 2005).

A *subsequently listed transaction* is a transaction that is not a tax shelter prohibited transaction at the time a tax-exempt entity participates in the transaction, but the transaction subsequently is determined by the IRS to be a prohibited tax shelter transaction (Code Sec. 4965(e)(2), as added by the Tax Reconciliation Act of 2005).

Tax-exempt entities. The rules generally apply to all tax-exempt organizations and entities under Code Sec. 501(c) or (d), including charitable and other organizations described in Code Sec. 170(c) (other than the United States), Indian tribal governments, qualified pension plans, qualified annuity plans and contracts, individual

NEW LAW EXPLAINED

retirement arrangements, and similar tax-favored savings arrangements (such as Coverdell education savings accounts, health savings accounts, and qualified tuition plans) (Code Sec. 4965(c), as added by the Tax Reconciliation Act of 2005).

Entity manager. An entity manager who approves an entity as, or otherwise causes such entity to be, a party to a prohibited tax shelter transaction at any time during the tax years and knows or has reason to know that the transaction is a prohibited tax shelter transaction must pay a tax in the amount of $20,000 for each approval (Code Sec. 4965(b)(2), as added by the Tax Reconciliation Act of 2005). An entity manager is an exempt organization manager, a private foundation manager or a person with authority or responsibility similar to that exercised by an officer, director or trustee of an organization (Code Sec. 4965(a)(2), as added by the Tax Reconciliation Act of 2005).

IRS regulations. The IRS may provide guidance regarding the determination of the allocation of net income of a tax-exempt entity attributable to a transaction to various periods, including before and after the listing of the transaction or the date which is 90 days after May 17, 2006 (Code Sec. 4965(f), as added by the Tax Reconciliation Act of 2005).

Coordination with other taxes and penalties. The excise tax imposed on entering into prohibited tax shelter transaction is in addition to any other tax, addition to tax or penalty (Code Sec. 4965(g), as added by the Tax Reconciliation Act of 2005).

Disclosure requirements. A tax-exempt entity must file a disclosure to the IRS of the entity's participation in any prohibited tax shelter transaction and the identity of any other party participating in such transaction which is known by the entity (Code Sec. 6033(a), as amended by the Tax Reconciliation Act of 2005). Likewise, any taxable party to a prohibited tax shelter transaction must provide a statement disclosing to any tax-exempt entity which is a party to the transaction that the transaction is a prohibited tax shelter transaction (Code Sec. 6011, as amended by the Tax Reconciliation Act of 2005).

Penalty for nondisclosure. A tax-exempt entity or the entity manager in the case of certain tax-exempt entities in the case of qualified pension plans, qualified annuity plans and contracts, individual retirement arrangements, and similar tax-favored savings arrangements (such as Coverdell education savings accounts, health savings accounts, and qualified tuition plans) who fails to file a disclosure under Code Sec. 6033(a)(2) must pay $100 for each day the failure continues. The maximum penalty with respect to one disclosure must not exceed $50,000. The IRS may make a written demand on any tax-exempt entity subject to the penalty. The demand must specify a reasonable future date by which the disclosure must be filed. Any person who fails to comply with such demand must pay $100 for each day after the expiration of the time specified in the demand during which the failure continues. The maximum penalty for failures with respect to any one disclosure must not exceed $10,000 (Code Sec. 6652(c), as amended by the Tax Reconciliation Act of 2005).

▶ **Effective date.** The provision applies to tax years ending after May 17, 2006, with respect to transactions before, on, or after such date, except that no tax under Code Sec. 4965(a) shall apply with respect to income or proceeds that are properly allocable to any period ending on or before August 15, 2006, the date which is 90 days after such date of

NEW LAW EXPLAINED

enactment, May 17, 2006 (Act Sec. 516(d)(1) of the Tax Increase Prevention and Reconciliation Act of 2005 (P.L. 109-222)). The provisions relating to disclosure requirements under Code Sec. 4965(b) and (c) apply to disclosures the due date for which are after May 17, 2006 (Act Sec. 516(d)(2) of the Tax Reconciliation Act of 2005).

Law source: Law at ¶5680, ¶5705, ¶5730 and ¶5805. Committee Report at ¶10,300.

— Act Sec. 516(a) of the Tax Increase Prevention and Reconciliation Act of 2005 (P.L. 109-222), adding Code Sec. 4965;

— Act Sec. 516(b)(1), redesignating Code Sec. 6033(a)(2) as (3) and adding new Code Sec. 6033(a)(2);

— Act Sec. 516(b)(2), redesignating Code Sec. 6011(g) as (h) and adding new Code Sec. 6011(g);

— Act Sec. 516(c), redesignating Code Sec. 6652(c)(3) and (4) as (4) and (5), respectively, and adding new Code Sec. 6652(c)(3);

— Act Sec. 516(d), providing the effective date.

Reporter references: For further information, consult the following CCH reporters.

— Standard Federal Tax Reporter, ¶35,141.001, ¶34,315.01, ¶35,425.01 and ¶39,490.0218

— Tax Research Consultant, EXEMPT: 6,252, EXEMPT: 12,252.15 and PENALTY: 3,208.15

— Federal Tax Guide, ¶16,001 and ¶22,237

¶1135 Rules on Pooled Financing Bonds Tightened

SUMMARY OF NEW LAW

Pooled financing bonds will be tax-exempt only if the issuer reasonably expects to use 30% of the net proceeds within one year, written loan commitments for 30% of the proceeds are in place before issuance, and the bonds will be redeemed within 90 days to the extent that the required reasonable expectations for use after one year and three years are not in fact met. The written commitment requirement does not apply to any issuer that is a state (or an integral part of a state) issuing bonds to finance loans to subordinate governments within the state or a state-created entity providing financing for certain water-infrastructure projects. Also, pooled financing bonds will count in determining the issuer's eligibility for the small issuer exception to the arbitrage rebate requirement.

BACKGROUND

State and local governments frequently issue bonds and use the proceeds to finance their activities. According to the Bond Market Association, there are approximately 86,000 municipal bond issuers, ranging in size from the state of California to school districts serving only a few hundred students. Interest on municipal bonds is generally excluded from the bondholders' gross income (Code Sec. 103(a)). As a result, the

BACKGROUND

issuers of these bonds can pay a lower rate of interest than issuers of taxable bonds. The income tax foregone by the federal government is an indirect subsidy to the state and local government issuers.

Smaller government entities that may be lacking in resources, expertise, and market leverage are able to obtain the benefits of tax-exempt financing by participating in pooled financing arrangements. Under a pooled financing arrangement, a single entity issues a bond, the proceeds of which are then used to make or finance loans to other governmental entities ("conduit borrowers"). There is no requirement that the issuer know who the conduit borrowers will be before issuing the bonds. If more than $5 million of the proceeds of an issue are to be reloaned (other than to finance private activities or veterans' mortgages), a reasonable expectation requirement applies. In such cases the bonds will be tax-exempt only if the issuer reasonably expects that at least 95 percent of the net proceeds of the issue will be loaned out within three years after the date of issuance (Code Sec. 149(f)(2)).

The exclusion for municipal bond interest does not apply to arbitrage bonds (Code Sec. 103(b)(2)). An arbitrage bond is any bond that is part of an issue if any part of the proceeds of the issue is reasonably expected to be used or intentionally is used to acquire higher-yielding investments (Code Sec. 148). In certain situations arbitrage profits will not result in the bond losing its exemption, as long as the arbitrage profits are paid over to the federal government (an "arbitrage rebate").

There is a small issuer exception to the arbitrage rebate requirement. No rebate is required with respect to an issue if (Code Sec. 148(f)(4)(D)):

(1) the issuer is a governmental unit with general taxing powers;

(2) the issue does not include any private activity bonds;

(3) 95 percent or more of the net proceeds of the issue are to be used for local governmental activities of the issuer or a subordinate governmental unit; and

(4) the issuer is reasonably expected not to issue more than $5 million in tax-exempt bonds, other than private activity bonds, during the year.

In determining whether an issuing governmental unit has exceeded the $5 million annual limit, any pooled financing bonds issued to make loans to other governmental units with general taxing powers that are not subordinate to the issuer are disregarded.

> **Comment:** A number of instances have been reported in which pooled financing bonds were issued but few or no loans were made from the proceeds. Issuance of unnecessary bonds overburdens the municipal bond market, raising the cost of financing for all issuers. The Joint Committee on Taxation has suggested that changes in the rules are appropriate to reduce the burden on the bond market and improve the efficiency of the tax expenditure (Options to Improve Tax Compliance and Reform Tax Expenditures, Joint Committee on Taxation (JCS-02-05)).

NEW LAW EXPLAINED

Pooled financing rules tightened.—The rules for tax-exempt pooled financing arrangements are tightened in several ways. First, an additional reasonable expectation requirement now applies. While prior law required only that the issuer reasonably expect that 95 percent of the issue's net proceeds would be used within three years, now the issuer must also reasonably expect that at least 30 percent of the net proceeds will be used within one year after the date of issuance (Code Sec. 149(f)(2)(A), as amended by the Tax Increase Prevention and Reconciliation Act of 2005 (P.L. 109-222)).

Second, the issuer must obtain, before the date of issuance, written loan commitments identifying the ultimate potential borrowers of at least 30 percent of the net proceeds of the issue (Code Sec. 149(f)(4)(A), as added by the Tax Reconciliation Act of 2005). A loan commitment exists only if the issuer is committed to loan funds to the borrower identified in the commitment and the borrower has applied for and agreed to execute a loan in a specified amount to finance a specifically identified project and, as part of the application, has paid a nonrefundable commitment fee in an amount commensurate with fees customarily paid for similar loan commitments (Joint Committee on Taxation Description of the Chairman's Modification of the Tax Relief Act of 2005 (JCX-77-05)). This loan commitment requirement does not apply if the issuer of the pooled financing bonds is (Code Sec. 149(f)(4)(B), as added by the Tax Reconciliation Act of 2005):

(1) a state (or an integral part of a state) that will use the proceeds to make or finance loans to subordinate governmental entities of the state; or

(2) a state-created entity providing financing for water-infrastructure projects through the federally-sponsored State Revolving Fund program.

> **Comment:** The Environmental Protection Agency operates both a Clean Water State Revolving Fund and a Drinking Water State Revolving Fund. It is not clear whether the exception applies to entities providing financing through one or both.

Third, to the extent that the required reasonable expectations for use (30 percent within one year and 95 percent within three years) are not in fact met, the issuer must use proceeds of the issue to redeem a portion of the outstanding bonds within 90 days.

> **Example:** If, as of the date one year after the date of issuance of pooled bonds, only 25 percent of the net proceeds (received as of that date) have been used to make or finance qualifying loans, the issuer must use 5 percent of those net proceeds to redeem outstanding bonds of the issue. If after three years have passed, 80 percent of the net proceeds of the same issue have been used to make or finance loans (and five percent were used to redeem bonds after the one-year mark), another 10 percent of the proceeds must be used to redeem outstanding bonds (Code Sec. 149(f)(5), as added by the Tax Reconciliation Act of 2005).

Finally, pooled financing bonds are not disregarded in determining whether an issuer has issued $5 million or more in bonds for purposes of the small issuer exception to the

NEW LAW EXPLAINED

arbitrage rebate requirement (Act Sec. 508(c) of the Tax Reconciliation Act of 2005, striking Code Sec. 148(f)(4)(D)(ii)(II)).

> **Comment:** The provision which passed the Senate on this issue required that issuers must obtain binding loan commitments for and reasonably expect to use 50 percent of the issue proceeds within the first year. Representatives of the issuer community, while recognizing that some abuses of the pooled financing rules have occurred, suggested that this provision would push too far in the opposite direction. Requiring small borrowers with varying and unpredictable needs to sign binding loan commitments may discourage them from participating in pooled financing arrangements and result in increases in their borrowing costs. If requiring redemptions of unused proceeds results, as intended, in issuers reducing the size of their bond issues, more issues will be required to finance the same amount of activity, resulting in increased costs (Bond Market Association, Letter to Sens. Grassley and Baucus, Comments on JCS-02-05, March 1, 2005). In conference these concerns were addressed by reducing the required percentage from 50 to 30 percent.

▶ **Effective date.** The provision is effective with respect to bonds issued after May 17, 2006 (Act Sec. 508(e) of the Tax Increase Prevention and Reconciliation Act of 2005 (P.L. 109-222)).

Law source: Law at ¶5055, ¶5180, and ¶5205. Committee Report at ¶10,220.

— Act Sec. 508(a) of the Tax Increase Prevention and Reconciliation Act of 2005 (P.L. 109-222), amending Code Sec. 149(f)(2)(A);

— Act Sec. 508(b), redesignating Code Sec. 149(f)(4) and (5) as Code Sec. 149(f)(6) and (7), respectively, and adding new Code Sec. 149(f)(4) and (5);

— Act Sec. 508(c), striking Code Sec. 148(f)(4)(D)(ii)(II);

— Act Sec. 508(d), amending Code Secs. 149(f)(1), 149(f)(7)(B), and 54(l)(2);

— Act Sec. 508(e), providing the effective date.

Reporter references: For further information, consult the following CCH reporters.

— Standard Federal Tax Reporter, ¶7905.035

— Tax Research Consultant, SALES: 51,070 and SALES: 51,556.15

— Federal Tax Guide, ¶4075

ADMINISTRATION AND PROCEDURE

¶1140 Offers in Compromise

SUMMARY OF NEW LAW

Taxpayers who submit offers in compromise are required to make nonrefundable partial payments to the IRS for their offers to be considered. An offer will be deemed accepted if it has not been rejected within 24 months after it is submitted to the IRS.

¶1140

BACKGROUND

The IRS is authorized to compromise unpaid tax liabilities, including interest and penalties, for less than the amount owed (Code Sec. 7122). An offer in compromise must be based upon one or more of the following grounds:

- Doubt as to liability - The taxpayer disputes the existence or amount of the correct tax liability;

- Doubt as to collectibility - The taxpayer is unable to pay the liability in full based upon the value of his or her assets and income; and

- Effective tax administration - Collection of the full amount of unpaid tax liability would cause the taxpayer economic hardship or based upon other compelling public policy or equity considerations (Reg. § 301.7122-1(b)).

An offer in compromise must be submitted on a Form 656, Offer in Compromise. Taxpayers submitting offers in compromise based upon doubt as to collectibility or effective tax administration must also submit collection information statements with their offers (Form 433A for individual taxpayers; Form 433B for business taxpayers) (Reg. § 301.7122-1(d)(1)).

The IRS imposes a user fee of $150 for each offer in compromise submitted. The fee is not required, however, for offers in compromise based solely upon doubt as to liability or filed by low income taxpayers (Reg. § 300.3(b)). The user fee is applied against the amount of an offer, unless the taxpayer requests that it be refunded, if the offer is (1) accepted to promote effective tax administration, or (2) accepted based upon doubt as to collectibility and collection of more than the amount offered would create economic hardship within the meaning of Reg. § 301.6343-1. The fee is otherwise nonrefundable once an offer is accepted for processing by the IRS (Reg. § 300.3(b)). Taxpayers may, but are not required to, submit a deposit with the filing of an offer in compromise or while an offer is pending. Any deposit will be refunded if the offer is rejected, unless the taxpayer has authorized the IRS to apply the deposit to the liability for which the offer was submitted (Reg. § 301.7122-1(h)).

The decision to accept or reject an offer in compromise is left to the discretion of the Secretary of the Treasury. The determination is based upon all of the facts and circumstances of the offer (Reg. § 301.7122-1(c)). Each offer in compromise that is properly submitted to the IRS undergoes a thorough review process, during which the IRS usually requests additional information and supporting documents from the taxpayer. Because of the taxpayer-specific nature of each offer examination, the review process is typically lengthy, often taking at least 12 months to complete.

Offers in compromise can be paid in one of three ways:

- a lump-sum payment of the compromised amount paid within 90 days of the acceptance of the offer;

- short-term deferred payments for up to 24 months; or

- deferred payments over the remaining statutory period for collecting the tax.

¶1140

NEW LAW EXPLAINED

Partial payments required with submission of offers in compromise.—Taxpayers are required to make nonrefundable partial payments with the submission of any offer in compromise on or after July 16, 2006. Taxpayers who submit a lump-sum offer in compromise must include a payment of 20 percent of the amount offered. Taxpayers who submit a periodic payment offer in compromise must include payment of the first proposed installment with the offer and continue making payments under the terms proposed while the offer is being evaluated (Code Sec. 7122(c), as added by the Tax Increase Prevention and Reconciliation Act of 2005 (P.L. 109-222); see also Notice 2006-68, I.R.B. 2006-31, 105).

> **Comment:** A Joint Committee on Taxation Report noted that some taxpayers abuse the offer in compromise process by concealing information and making frivolous offers and that the IRS's lengthy review process for offers may lead to a substantial delay in the government's collection of the compromised liability. According to the Committee Report, it is expected that this provision will increase and accelerate payments to the government without discouraging most taxpayers from making offers or further burdening the IRS (JCT Report, Options to Improve Tax Compliance and Reform Tax Expenditures (JCS-02-05)). However, the required prepayment may discourage or prevent many taxpayers from filing offers. For example, taxpayers who intend to borrow against their assets to obtain the necessary funds for an offer are likely to have difficulty securing loans. If a taxpayer intends to borrow against the equity in a home to fund a lump-sum offer, and the home is already encumbered by a tax lien, the taxpayer will likely find it difficult to find a willing lender without any guarantee that the offer will be accepted and the tax lien released. Given the IRS's lengthy review process, taxpayers may also be reluctant to submit deferred payment offers. For example, a taxpayer who submits an offer for 12 installment payments may make all 12 payments during the time it takes the IRS to evaluate the offer, and then have the offer rejected.

Offers in compromise that are submitted to the IRS without the required partial payments will be returned to the taxpayer as unprocessable (Code Sec. 7122(d)(3)(C), as amended by the Tax Reconciliation Act of 2005). Additionally, taxpayers who fail to make payments under the terms of a periodic payment offer will be deemed to have withdrawn their offers (Code Sec. 7122(c)(1)(B), as added by the Tax Reconciliation Act of 2005). However, the new law authorizes the IRS to issue regulations waiving the payment requirement for offers based solely on doubt as to liability or filed by low income taxpayers (Code Sec. 7122(c)(2)(C), as added by the Tax Reconciliation Act of 2005). The IRS has issued guidance on the waiver requirements. The guidance applies until regulations are issued (see Notice 2006-68, I.R.B. 2006-31, 105).

> **Planning Note:** Generally, a lump-sum offer in compromise refers to an offer in which one lump-sum payment is made within 90 days of the offer's acceptance. For the purposes of the partial payment requirement, however, lump-sum offers include any offer that will be paid in five or fewer installments (Code Sec. 7122(c)(1)(A)(ii), as added by the Tax Reconciliation Act of 2005). If the payment is less than 20 percent of the required amount, the IRS may accept the offer for

NEW LAW EXPLAINED

processing and then solicit payment for the remaining 20 percent of the payment (see Notice 2006-68, I.R.B. 2006-31, 105).

Application of partial payments and user fee. The required partial payments are applied to the taxpayer's unpaid liability and are not refundable. However, taxpayers may specify the liability to which they want their payments applied (Code Sec. 7122(c)(2)(A), as added by the Tax Reconciliation Act of 2005). Additionally, under the new law, the user fee is applied to the taxpayer's outstanding tax liability (Code Sec. 7122(c)(2)(B), as added by the Tax Reconciliation Act of 2005).

> **Planning Note:** If an offer in compromise is ultimately accepted by the IRS, the application of the required partial payments and user fee will be irrelevant. However, taxpayers submitting offers should consider whether it is advantageous to direct the application of their payments toward certain tax liabilities in the event their offers are rejected. For example, a taxpayer who submits an offer in compromise for several different years may decide to apply his or her partial payments to the most recently assessed liabilities rather than older liabilities with less time remaining on the statute of limitations for collection.

Offers automatically deemed accepted. Under the new law, any offer in compromise that is not rejected within 24 months of the date it is submitted is deemed to be accepted. However, any period during which the tax liability to be compromised is in dispute in any judicial proceeding is not taken into account in determining the expiration of the 24 month period (Code Sec. 7122(f), as added by the Tax Reconciliation Act of 2005).

> **Comment:** It is not unusual for the IRS to take more than 12 months to evaluate an offer in compromise. By enacting this provision, it appears that Congress is encouraging the IRS to speed up the offer review process and reduce the backlog of pending offers. However, some commentators have expressed concern that imposing strict time limits on the IRS may lead the IRS to reject some offers that have not been fully evaluated but would otherwise be deemed accepted after a certain number of months had passed. An earlier bill (the Safe, Accountable, Flexible, Efficient Transportation Equity Act of 2005) contained a version of this provision that would have reduced the timeframe for "deemed acceptance" from 24 months to 12 months after five years. It is likely, however, that such a restricted timeframe would make it even more difficult for the IRS to fully evaluate more complex offers.

▶ **Effective date.** This provision applies to offers in compromise submitted on and after July 16, 2006, the date which is 60 days after the date of enactment, May 17, 2006 (Act Sec. 509(d) of the Tax Increase Prevention and Reconciliation Act of 2005 (P.L. 109-222)).

Law source: Law at ¶5780 and ¶5830. Committee Report at ¶10,230.

— Act Sec. 509(a) of the Tax Increase Prevention and Reconciliation Act of 2005 (P.L. 109-222), redesignating Code Sec. 7122(c) and (d) as Code Sec. 7122(d) and (e), respectively, and adding new Code Sec. 7122(c);

— Act Sec. 509(b), amending Code Sec. 7122(d)(3) and adding new Code Sec. 7122(f);

— Act Sec. 509(c), amending Code Sec. 6159(f);

— Act Sec. 509(d), providing the effective date.

NEW LAW EXPLAINED

Reporter references: For further information, consult the following CCH reporters.

— Standard Federal Tax Reporter, ¶41,130.01, ¶41,130.023 and ¶41,130.024

— Tax Research Consultant, FILEIND: **21,154.40, IRS:** 42,100, IRS: 42,106 and IRS: 42,116

— Federal Tax Guide, ¶22,641

— Federal Estate and Gift Tax Reporter, ¶22,120.03

Code Sections Added, Amended Or Repealed

[¶ 5001]

INTRODUCTION.

The Internal Revenue Code provisions amended by the Tax Increase Prevention and Reconciliation Act of 2005 (P.L. 109-222) and the Tax Relief and Health Care Act of 2006 (P.L. 109-432) are shown in the following paragraphs. Deleted Code material or the text of the Code Section prior to amendment appears in the amendment notes following each amended Code provision. *Any changed or added material is set out in italics.*

[¶ 5005] CODE SEC. 1. TAX IMPOSED.

* * *

(g) CERTAIN UNEARNED INCOME OF MINOR CHILDREN TAXED AS IF PARENT'S INCOME.—

* * *

(2) CHILD TO WHOM SUBSECTION APPLIES.—This subsection shall apply to any child for any taxable year if—

(A) such child has not attained *age 18* before the close of the taxable year,

(B) either parent of such child is alive at the close of the taxable year, *and*

(C) *such child does not file a joint return for the taxable year.*

* * *

(4) NET UNEARNED INCOME.—For purposes of this subsection—

* * *

(C) *TREATMENT OF DISTRIBUTIONS FROM QUALIFIED DISABILITY TRUSTS.—For purposes of this subsection, in the case of any child who is a beneficiary of a qualified disability trust (as defined in section 642(b)(2)(C)(ii)), any amount included in the income of such child under sections 652 and 662 during a taxable year shall be considered earned income of such child for such taxable year.*

* * *

[CCH Explanation at ¶710. Committee Reports at ¶10,240.]

Amendments

● 2006, Tax Increase Prevention and Reconciliation Act of 2005 (P.L. 109-222)

P.L. 109-222, § 510(a):

Amended Code Sec. 1(g)(2)(A) by striking "age 14" and inserting "age 18". **Effective** for tax years beginning after 12-31-2005.

P.L. 109-222, § 510(b):

Amended Code Sec. 1(g)(4) by adding at the end a new subparagraph (C). **Effective** for tax years beginning after 12-31-2005.

P.L. 109-222, § 510(c):

Amended Code Sec. 1(g)(2) by striking "and" at the end of subparagraph (A), by striking the period at the end of subparagraph (B) and inserting ", and", and by inserting after subparagraph (B) a new subparagraph (C). **Effective** for tax years beginning after 12-31-2005.

[¶ 5010] CODE SEC. 25D. RESIDENTIAL ENERGY EFFICIENT PROPERTY.

(a) ALLOWANCE OF CREDIT.—In the case of an individual, there shall be allowed as a credit against the tax imposed by this chapter for the taxable year an amount equal to the sum of—

(1) 30 percent of the *qualified solar electric property expenditures* made by the taxpayer during such year,

(2) 30 percent of the qualified solar water heating property expenditures made by the taxpayer during such year, and

(3) 30 percent of the qualified fuel cell property expenditures made by the taxpayer during such year.

[CCH Explanation at ¶230. Committee Reports at ¶15,400.]
Amendments
• **2006, Tax Relief and Health Care Act of 2006 (P.L. 109-432)**

P.L. 109-432, Division A, §206(b)(1):

Amended Code Sec. 25D(a)(1) by striking "qualified photovoltaic property expenditures" and inserting "qualified solar electric property expenditures". **Effective** 12-20-2006.

(b) LIMITATIONS.—

(1) MAXIMUM CREDIT.—The credit allowed under subsection (a) (determined without regard to subsection (c)) for any taxable year shall not exceed—

(A) $2,000 with respect to any *qualified solar electric property expenditures,*

* * *

[CCH Explanation at ¶230. Committee Reports at ¶15,400.]
Amendments
• **2006, Tax Relief and Health Care Act of 2006 (P.L. 109-432)**

P.L. 109-432, Division A, §206(b)(1):

Amended Code Sec. 25D(b)(1)(A) by striking "qualified photovoltaic property expenditures" and inserting "qualified solar electric property expenditures". **Effective** 12-20-2006.

(d) DEFINITIONS.—For purposes of this section—

* * *

(2) *QUALIFIED SOLAR ELECTRIC PROPERTY EXPENDITURE.*—The term *"qualified solar electric property expenditure"* means an expenditure for property which uses solar energy to generate electricity for use in a dwelling unit located in the United States and used as a residence by the taxpayer.

* * *

[CCH Explanation at ¶230. Committee Reports at ¶15,400.]
Amendments
• **2006, Tax Relief and Health Care Act of 2006 (P.L. 109-432)**

P.L. 109-432, Division A, §206(b)(2)(A)-(B):

Amended Code Sec. 25D(d)(2) by striking "qualified photovoltaic property expenditure" and inserting "qualified solar electric property expenditure", and in the heading by striking "[Q]UALIFIED PHOTOVOLTAIC PROPERTY EXPENDITURE" and inserting "QUALIFIED SOLAR ELECTRIC PROPERTY EXPENDITURE". **Effective** 12-20-2006.

(e) SPECIAL RULES.—For purposes of this section—

* * *

(4) DOLLAR AMOUNTS IN CASE OF JOINT OCCUPANCY.—In the case of any dwelling unit which is jointly occupied and used during any calendar year as a residence by two or more individuals the following rules shall apply:

(A) MAXIMUM EXPENDITURES.—The maximum amount of expenditures which may be taken into account under subsection (a) by all such individuals with respect to such dwelling unit during such calendar year shall be—

(i) $6,667 in the case of any *qualified solar electric property expenditures,*

* * *

[CCH Explanation at ¶230. Committee Reports at ¶15,400.]

Amendments

• 2006, Tax Relief and Health Care Act of 2006 (P.L. 109-432)

P.L. 109-432, Division A, §206(b)(1):

Amended Code Sec. 25D(e)(4)(A)(i) by striking "qualified photovoltaic property expenditures" and inserting "quali-

fied solar electric property expenditures". **Effective** 12-20-2006.

(g) TERMINATION.—The credit allowed under this section shall not apply to property placed in service after *December 31, 2008.*

[CCH Explanation at ¶230. Committee Reports at ¶15,400.]

Amendments

• 2006, Tax Relief and Health Care Act of 2006 (P.L. 109-432)

P.L. 109-432, Division A, §206(a):

Amended Code Sec. 25D(g) by striking "December 31, 2007" and inserting "December 31, 2008". **Effective** 12-20-2006.

[¶5030] CODE SEC. 26. LIMITATION BASED ON TAX LIABILITY; DEFINITION OF TAX LIABILITY.

(a) LIMITATION BASED ON AMOUNT OF TAX.—

* * *

(2) SPECIAL RULE FOR TAXABLE YEARS 2000 THROUGH *2006.*—For purposes of any taxable year beginning during 2000, 2001, 2002, 2003, 2004, *2005, or 2006,* the aggregate amount of credits allowed by this subpart for the taxable year shall not exceed the sum of—

(A) the taxpayer's regular tax liability for the taxable year reduced by the foreign tax credit allowable under section 27(a), and

(B) the tax imposed by section 55(a) for the taxable year.

* * *

[CCH Explanation at ¶725. Committee Reports at ¶10,130.]

Amendments

• 2006, Tax Increase Prevention and Reconciliation Act of 2005 (P.L. 109-222)

P.L. 109-222, §302(a)(1)-(2):

Amended Code Sec. 26(a)(2) by striking "2005" in the heading thereof and inserting "2006", and by striking "or

2005" and inserting "2005, or 2006". **Effective** for tax years beginning after 12-31-2005.

[¶5032] CODE SEC. 32. EARNED INCOME.

* * *

(c) DEFINITIONS AND SPECIAL RULES.—For purposes of this section—

* * *

(2) EARNED INCOME.—

* * *

(B) For purposes of subparagraph (A)—

* * *

(vi) in the case of any taxable year ending—

(I) after the date of the enactment of this clause, and

(II) before January 1, *2008,*

a taxpayer may elect to treat amounts excluded from gross income by reason of section 112 as earned income.

* * *

[CCH Explanation at ¶ 225. Committee Reports at ¶ 15,150.]

Amendments

• **2006, Tax Relief and Health Care Act of 2006 (P.L. 109-432)**

P.L. 109-432, Division A, § 106(a):

Amended Code Sec. 32(c)(2)(B)(vi)(II) by striking "2007" and inserting "2008". **Effective** for tax years beginning after 12-31-2006.

[¶ 5034] CODE SEC. 38. GENERAL BUSINESS CREDIT.

* * *

(b) CURRENT YEAR BUSINESS CREDIT.—For purposes of this subpart, the amount of the current year business credit is the sum of the following credits determined for the taxable year:

* * *

(29) the Hurricane Rita employee retention credit determined under section 1400R(b),

(30) the Hurricane Wilma employee retention credit determined under section 1400R(c) , *plus*

(31) *the mine rescue team training credit determined under section 45N(a).*

* * *

[CCH Explanation at ¶ 425. Committee Reports at ¶ 15,500.]

Amendments

• **2006, Tax Relief and Health Care Act of 2006 (P.L. 109-432)**

P.L. 109-432, Division A, § 405(b):

Amended Code Sec. 38(b) by striking "and" at the end of paragraph (29), by striking the period at the end of para-graph (30) and inserting ", plus", and by adding at the end a new paragraph (31). **Effective** for tax years beginning after 12-31-2005.

[¶ 5036] CODE SEC. 41. CREDIT FOR INCREASING RESEARCH ACTIVITIES.

* * *

(c) BASE AMOUNT.—

* * *

(4) ELECTION OF ALTERNATIVE INCREMENTAL CREDIT.—

(A) IN GENERAL.—At the election of the taxpayer, the credit determined under subsection (a)(1) shall be equal to the sum of—

(i) *3 percent* of so much of the qualified research expenses for the taxable year as exceeds 1 percent of the average described in subsection (c)(1)(B) but does not exceed 1.5 percent of such average,

(ii) *4 percent* of so much of such expenses as exceeds 1.5 percent of such average but does not exceed 2 percent of such average, and

(iii) *5 percent* of so much of such expenses as exceeds 2 percent of such average.

(B) ELECTION.—An election under this paragraph shall apply to the taxable year for which made and all succeeding taxable years unless revoked with the consent of the Secretary.

(5) *Election of alternative simplified credit.—*

(A) *In general.—At the election of the taxpayer, the credit determined under subsection (a)(1) shall be equal to 12 percent of so much of the qualified research expenses for the taxable year as exceeds 50 percent of the average qualified research expenses for the 3 taxable years preceding the taxable year for which the credit is being determined.*

(B) *Special rule in case of no qualified research expenses in any of 3 preceding taxable years.—*

(i) *Taxpayers to which subparagraph applies.—The credit under this paragraph shall be determined under this subparagraph if the taxpayer has no qualified research expenses in any one of the 3 taxable years preceding the taxable year for which the credit is being determined.*

(ii) *Credit rate.—The credit determined under this subparagraph shall be equal to 6 percent of the qualified research expenses for the taxable year.*

(C) *Election.—An election under this paragraph shall apply to the taxable year for which made and all succeeding taxable years unless revoked with the consent of the Secretary. An election under this paragraph may not be made for any taxable year to which an election under paragraph (4) applies.*

(6) *Consistent treatment of expenses required.—*

(A) *In general.—*Notwithstanding whether the period for filing a claim for credit or refund has expired for any taxable year taken into account in determining the fixed-base percentage, the qualified research expenses taken into account in computing such percentage shall be determined on a basis consistent with the determination of qualified research expenses for the credit year.

(B) *Prevention of distortions.—*The Secretary may prescribe regulations to prevent distortions in calculating a taxpayer's qualified research expenses or gross receipts caused by a change in accounting methods used by such taxpayer between the current year and a year taken into account in computing such taxpayer's fixed-base percentage.

(7) *Gross receipts.—*For purposes of this subsection, gross receipts for any taxable year shall be reduced by returns and allowances made during the taxable year. In the case of a foreign corporation, there shall be taken into account only gross receipts which are effectively connected with the conduct of a trade or business within the United States, the Commonwealth of Puerto Rico, or any possession of the United States.

* * *

[CCH Explanation at ¶405. Committee Reports at ¶15,130.]

Amendments

• **2006, Tax Relief and Health Care Act of 2006 (P.L. 109-432)**

P.L. 109-432, Division A, §104(b)(1)(A)-(C):

Amended Code Sec. 41(c)(4)(A) by striking "2.65 percent" and inserting "3 percent", by striking "3.2 percent" and inserting "4 percent", and by striking "3.75 percent" and inserting "5 percent". **Effective** generally for tax years ending after 12-31-2006. For a transition rule, see Act Sec. 104(b)(3), below.

P.L. 109-432, Division A, §104(b)(3), provides:

(3) Transition rule.—

(A) In general.—In the case of a specified transitional taxable year for which an election under section 41(c)(4) of the Internal Revenue Code of 1986 applies, the credit determined under section 41(a)(1) of such Code shall be equal to the sum of—

(i) the applicable 2006 percentage multiplied by the amount determined under section 41(c)(4)(A) of such Code

(as in effect for taxable years ending on December 31, 2006), plus

(ii) the applicable 2007 percentage multiplied by the amount determined under section 41(c)(4)(A) of such Code (as in effect for taxable years ending on January 1, 2007).

(B) Definitions.—For purposes of subparagraph (A)—

(i) Specified transitional taxable year.—The term "specified transitional taxable year" means any taxable year which ends after December 31, 2006, and which includes such date.

(ii) Applicable 2006 percentage.—The term "applicable 2006 percentage" means the number of days in the specified transitional taxable year before January 1, 2007, divided by the number of days in such taxable year.

(iii) Applicable 2007 percentage.—The term "applicable 2007 percentage" means the number of days in the specified transitional taxable year after December 31, 2006, divided by the number of days in such taxable year.

P.L. 109-432, Division A, § 104(c)(1):

Amended Code Sec. 41(c) by redesignating paragraphs (5) and (6) as paragraphs (6) and (7), respectively, and by inserting after paragraph (4) a new paragraph (5). **Effective** generally for tax years ending after 12-31-2006. For transition rules, see Act Sec. 104(c)(2) and (4), below.

P.L. 109-432, Division A, § 104(c)(2) and (4), provide:

(2) TRANSITION RULE FOR DEEMED REVOCATION OF ELECTION OF ALTERNATIVE INCREMENTAL CREDIT.—In the case of an election under section 41(c)(4) of the Internal Revenue Code of 1986 which applies to the taxable year which includes January 1, 2007, such election shall be treated as revoked with the consent of the Secretary of the Treasury if the taxpayer makes an election under section 41(c)(5) of such Code (as added by this subsection) for such year.

* * *

(4) TRANSITION RULE FOR NONCALENDAR TAXABLE YEARS.—

(A) IN GENERAL.—In the case of a specified transitional taxable year for which an election under section 41(c)(5) of the Internal Revenue Code of 1986 (as added by this subsection) applies, the credit determined under section 41(a)(1) of such Code shall be equal to the sum of—

(i) the applicable 2006 percentage multiplied by the amount determined under section 41(a)(1) of such Code (as in effect for taxable years ending on December 31, 2006), plus

(ii) the applicable 2007 percentage multiplied by the amount determined under section 41(c)(5) of such Code (as in effect for taxable years ending on January 1, 2007).

(B) DEFINITIONS AND SPECIAL RULES.—For purposes of subparagraph (A)—

(i) DEFINITIONS.—Terms used in this paragraph which are also used in subsection (b)(3) shall have the respective meanings given such terms in such subsection.

(ii) DUAL ELECTIONS PERMITTED.—Elections under paragraphs (4) and (5) of section 41(c) of such Code may both apply for the specified transitional taxable year.

(iii) DEFERRAL OF DEEMED ELECTION REVOCATION.—Any election under section 41(c)(4) of the Internal Revenue Code of 1986 treated as revoked under paragraph (2) shall be treated as revoked for the taxable year after the specified transitional taxable year.

(h) TERMINATION.—

(1) IN GENERAL.—This section shall not apply to any amount paid or incurred—

(A) after June 30, 1995, and before July 1, 1996, or

(B) after December 31, *2007*.

* * *

[CCH Explanation at ¶ 405. Committee Reports at ¶ 15,130.]

Amendments

• **2006, Tax Relief and Health Care Act of 2006 (P.L. 109-432)**

P.L. 109-432, Division A, § 104(a)(1):

Amended Code Sec. 41(h)(1)(B) by striking "2005" and inserting "2007". **Effective** for amounts paid or incurred after 12-31-2005.

[¶ 5038] CODE SEC. 45. ELECTRICITY PRODUCED FROM CERTAIN RENEWABLE RESOURCES, etc. [sic]

* * *

(d) QUALIFIED FACILITIES.—For purposes of this section:

(1) WIND FACILITY.—In the case of a facility using wind to produce electricity, the term "qualified facility" means any facility owned by the taxpayer which is originally placed in service after December 31, 1993, and before *January 1, 2009*.

(2) CLOSED-LOOP BIOMASS FACILITY.—

(A) IN GENERAL.—In the case of a facility using closed-loop biomass to produce electricity, the term "qualified facility" means any facility—

(i) owned by the taxpayer which is originally placed in service after December 31, 1992, and before *January 1, 2009*, or

(ii) owned by the taxpayer which before *January 1, 2009*, is originally placed in service and modified to use closed-loop biomass to co-fire with coal, with other biomass, or with both, but only if the modification is approved under the Biomass Power for Rural Development Programs or is part of a pilot project of the Commodity Credit Corporation as described in 65 Fed. Reg. 63052.

* * *

(3) OPEN-LOOP BIOMASS FACILITIES.—

(A) IN GENERAL.—In the case of a facility using open-loop biomass to produce electricity, the term "qualified facility" means any facility owned by the taxpayer which—

(i) in the case of a facility using agricultural livestock waste nutrients—

(I) is originally placed in service after the date of the enactment of this subclause and before *January 1, 2009*, and

(II) the nameplate capacity rating of which is not less than 150 kilowatts, and

(ii) in the case of any other facility, is originally placed in service before *January 1, 2009*.

(B) CREDIT ELIGIBILITY.—In the case of any facility described in subparagraph (A), if the owner of such facility is not the producer of the electricity, the person eligible for the credit allowable under subsection (a) shall be the lessee or the operator of such facility.

(4) GEOTHERMAL OR SOLAR ENERGY FACILITY.—In the case of a facility using geothermal or solar energy to produce electricity, the term "qualified facility" means any facility owned by the taxpayer which is originally placed in service after the date of the enactment of this paragraph and before *January 1, 2009* (January 1, 2006, in the case of a facility using solar energy). Such term shall not include any property described in section 48(a)(3) the basis of which is taken into account by the taxpayer for purposes of determining the energy credit under section 48.

(5) SMALL IRRIGATION POWER FACILITY.—In the case of a facility using small irrigation power to produce electricity, the term "qualified facility" means any facility owned by the taxpayer which is originally placed in service after the date of the enactment of this paragraph and before *January 1, 2009*.

(6) LANDFILL GAS FACILITIES.—In the case of a facility producing electricity from gas derived from the biodegradation of municipal solid waste, the term "qualified facility" means any facility owned by the taxpayer which is originally placed in service after the date of the enactment of this paragraph and before *January 1, 2009*.

(7) TRASH COMBUSTION FACILITIES.—In the case of a facility which burns municipal solid waste to produce electricity, the term "qualified facility" means any facility owned by the taxpayer which is originally placed in service after the date of the enactment of this paragraph and before *January 1, 2009*. Such term shall include a new unit placed in service in connection with a facility placed in service on or before the date of the enactment of this paragraph, but only to the extent of the increased amount of electricity produced at the facility by reason of such new unit.

* * *

(9) QUALIFIED HYDROPOWER FACILITY.—In the case of a facility producing qualified hydroelectric production described in subsection (c)(8), the term "qualified facility" means—

(A) in the case of any facility producing incremental hydropower production, such facility but only to the extent of its incremental hydropower production attributable to efficiency improvements or additions to capacity described in subsection (c)(8)(B) placed in service after the date of the enactment of this paragraph and before *January 1, 2009*, and

(B) any other facility placed in service after the date of the enactment of this paragraph and before *January 1, 2009*.

* * *

[CCH Explanation at ¶450. Committee Reports at ¶15,350.]

Amendments

• **2006, Tax Relief and Health Care Act of 2006 (P.L. 109-432)**

P.L. 109-432, Division A, §201:

Amended Code Sec. 45(d) by striking "January 1, 2008" each place it appears and inserting "January 1, 2009". **Effective** 12-20-2006.

[¶ 5040] CODE SEC. 45A. INDIAN EMPLOYMENT CREDIT.

* * *

(f) TERMINATION.—This section shall not apply to taxable years beginning after December 31, 2007.

[CCH Explanation at ¶ 420. Committee Reports at ¶ 15,200.]

Amendments

• 2006, Tax Relief and Health Care Act of 2006
(P.L. 109-432)

P.L. 109-432, Division A, §111(a):

Amended Code Sec. 45A(f) by striking "2005" and inserting "2007". **Effective** for tax years beginning after 12-31-2005.

[¶ 5042] CODE SEC. 45C. CLINICAL TESTING EXPENSES FOR CERTAIN DRUGS FOR RARE DISEASES OR CONDITIONS.

* * *

(b) QUALIFIED CLINICAL TESTING EXPENSES.—For purposes of this section—

(1) QUALIFIED CLINICAL TESTING EXPENSES.—

* * *

(D) SPECIAL RULE.—For purposes of this paragraph, section 41 shall be deemed to remain in effect for periods after June 30, 1995, and before July 1, 1996, and periods after December 31, 2007.

* * *

[CCH Explanation at ¶ 405. Committee Reports at ¶ 15,130.]

Amendments

• 2006, Tax Relief and Health Care Act of 2006
(P.L. 109-432)

P.L. 109-432, Division A, §104(a)(2):

Amended Code Sec. 45C(b)(1)(D) by striking "2005" and inserting "2007". **Effective** for amounts paid or incurred after 12-31-2005.

[¶ 5044] CODE SEC. 45D. NEW MARKETS TAX CREDIT.

* * *

(f) NATIONAL LIMITATION ON AMOUNT OF INVESTMENTS DESIGNATED.—

(1) IN GENERAL.—There is a new markets tax credit limitation for each calendar year. Such limitation is—

(A) $1,000,000,000 for 2001,

(B) $1,500,000,000 for 2002 and 2003,

(C) $2,000,000,000 for 2004 and 2005, and

(D) $3,500,000,000 for 2006, 2007, and 2008.

* * *

[CCH Explanation at ¶ 415. Committee Reports at ¶ 15,110.]

Amendments

• 2006, Tax Relief and Health Care Act of 2006
(P.L. 109-432)

P.L. 109-432, Division A, § 102(a):

Amended Code Sec. 45D(f)(1)(D) by striking "and 2007"
and inserting ", 2007, and 2008". Effective 12-20-2006.

(i) REGULATIONS.—The Secretary shall prescribe such regulations as may be appropriate to carry out this section, including regulations—

* * *

(4) which impose appropriate reporting requirements,

(5) which apply the provisions of this section to newly formed entities, *and*

(6) *which ensure that non-metropolitan counties receive a proportional allocation of qualified equity investments.*

[CCH Explanation at ¶ 415. Committee Reports at ¶ 15,110.]

Amendments

• 2006, Tax Relief and Health Care Act of 2006
(P.L. 109-432)

P.L. 109-432, Division A, § 102(b):

Amended Code Sec. 45D(i) by striking "and" at the end of paragraph (4), by striking the period at the end of para-

graph (5) and inserting ", and", and by adding at the end a new paragraph (6). Effective 12-20-2006.

[¶ 5046] CODE SEC. 45G. RAILROAD TRACK MAINTENANCE CREDIT.

* * *

(d) QUALIFIED RAILROAD TRACK MAINTENANCE EXPENDITURES.—For purposes of this section, the term "qualified railroad track maintenance expenditures" means *gross* expenditures (whether or not otherwise chargeable to capital account) for maintaining railroad track (including roadbed, bridges, and related track structures) owned or leased as of January 1, 2005, by a Class II or Class III railroad *(determined without regard to any consideration for such expenditures given by the Class II or Class III railroad which made the assignment of such track).*

* * *

[CCH Explanation at ¶ 430. Committee Reports at ¶ 15,680.]

Amendments

• 2006, Tax Relief and Health Care Act of 2006
(P.L. 109-432)

P.L. 109-432, Division A, § 423(a)(1)-(2):

Amended Code Sec. 45G(d) by inserting "gross" after "means", and by inserting "(determined without regard to

any consideration for such expenditures given by the Class II or Class III railroad which made the assignment of such track)" after "Class II or Class III railroad". Effective as if included in the amendment made by section 245(a) of the American Jobs Creation Act of 2004 (P.L. 108-357) [effective for tax years beginning after 12-31-2004.—CCH].

[¶ 5047] CODE SEC. 45K. CREDIT FOR PRODUCING FUEL FROM A NONCONVENTIONAL SOURCE.

* * *

(g) EXTENSION FOR FACILITIES PRODUCING COKE OR COKE GAS.—Notwithstanding subsection (e)—

(1) IN GENERAL.—In the case of a facility for producing coke or coke gas *(other than from petroleum based products)* which was placed in service before January 1, 1993, or after June 30, 1998, and before January 1, 2010, this section shall apply with respect to coke and coke gas produced in such facility and sold during the period—

(A) beginning on the later of January 1, 2006, or the date that such facility is placed in service, and

(B) ending on the date which is 4 years after the date such period began.

(2) SPECIAL RULES.—In determining the amount of credit allowable under this section solely by reason of this subsection—

* * *

(D) NONAPPLICATION OF PHASEOUT.—*Subsection (b)(1) shall not apply.*

[CCH Explanation at ¶ 460. Committee Reports at ¶ 15,450.]

Amendments

• **2006, Tax Relief and Health Care Act of 2006 (P.L. 109-432)**

P.L. 109-432, Division A, § 211(a):

Amended Code Sec. 45K(g)(2) by adding at the end a new subparagraph (D). **Effective** as if included in section 1321 of the Energy Policy Act of 2005 (P.L. 109-58) [**effective** for fuel produced and sold after 12-31-2005, in tax years ending after such date.—CCH].

P.L. 109-432, Division A, § 211(b):

Amended Code Sec. 45K(g)(1) by inserting "(other than from petroleum based products)" after "coke or coke gas". **Effective** as if included in section 1321 of the Energy Policy Act of 2005 (P.L. 109-58) [**effective** for fuel produced and sold after 12-31-2005, in tax years ending after such date.—CCH].

[¶ 5048] CODE SEC. 45L. NEW ENERGY EFFICIENT HOME CREDIT.

* * *

(g) TERMINATION.—This section shall not apply to any qualified new energy efficient home acquired after *December 31, 2008.*

[CCH Explanation at ¶ 445. Committee Reports at ¶ 15,390.]

Amendments

• **2006, Tax Relief and Health Care Act of 2006 (P.L. 109-432)**

P.L. 109-432, Division A, § 205:

Amended Code Sec. 45L(g) by striking "December 31, 2007" and inserting "December 31, 2008". **Effective** 12-20-2006.

[¶ 5049] *CODE SEC. 45N. MINE RESCUE TEAM TRAINING CREDIT.*

(a) AMOUNT OF CREDIT.—*For purposes of section 38, the mine rescue team training credit determined under this section with respect to each qualified mine rescue team employee of an eligible employer for any taxable year is an amount equal to the lesser of—*

(1) *20 percent of the amount paid or incurred by the taxpayer during the taxable year with respect to the training program costs of such qualified mine rescue team employee (including wages of such employee while attending such program), or*

(2) *$10,000.*

(b) QUALIFIED MINE RESCUE TEAM EMPLOYEE.—*For purposes of this section, the term "qualified mine rescue team employee" means with respect to any taxable year any full-time employee of the taxpayer who is—*

(1) *a miner eligible for more than 6 months of such taxable year to serve as a mine rescue team member as a result of completing, at a minimum, an initial 20-hour course of instruction as prescribed by the Mine Safety and Health Administration's Office of Educational Policy and Development, or*

(2) *a miner eligible for more than 6 months of such taxable year to serve as a mine rescue team member by virtue of receiving at least 40 hours of refresher training in such instruction.*

(c) ELIGIBLE EMPLOYER.—*For purposes of this section, the term "eligible employer" means any taxpayer which employs individuals as miners in underground mines in the United States.*

(d) WAGES.—*For purposes of this section, the term "wages" has the meaning given to such term by subsection (b) of section 3306 (determined without regard to any dollar limitation contained in such section).*

(e) TERMINATION.—*This section shall not apply to taxable years beginning after December 31, 2008.*

[CCH Explanation at ¶425. Committee Reports at ¶15,500.]

Amendments

• 2006, Tax Relief and Health Care Act of 2006
(P.L. 109-432)

P.L. 109-432, Division A, §405(a):

Amended subpart D of part IV of subchapter A of chapter 1 by adding at the end a new Code Sec. 45N. **Effective** for tax years beginning after 12-31-2005.

[¶5050] CODE SEC. 48. ENERGY CREDIT.

(a) ENERGY CREDIT.—

* * *

(2) ENERGY PERCENTAGE.—

(A) IN GENERAL.—The energy percentage is—

(i) 30 percent in the case of—

* * *

(II) energy property described in paragraph (3)(A)(i) but only with respect to periods ending before *January 1, 2009,* and

* * *

(3) ENERGY PROPERTY.—For purposes of this subpart, the term "energy property" means any property—

(A) which is—

* * *

(ii) equipment which uses solar energy to illuminate the inside of a structure using fiber-optic distributed sunlight but only with respect to periods ending before *January 1, 2009,*

* * *

[CCH Explanation at ¶440. Committee Reports at ¶15,410.]

Amendments

• 2006, Tax Relief and Health Care Act of 2006
(P.L. 109-432)

P.L. 109-432, Division A, §207(1):

Amended Code Sec. 48[(a)] by striking "January 1, 2008" both places it appears and inserting "January 1, 2009". **Effective** 12-20-2006.

(c) QUALIFIED FUEL CELL PROPERTY; QUALIFIED MICROTURBINE PROPERTY.—For purposes of this subsection—

(1) QUALIFIED FUEL CELL PROPERTY.—

* * *

(E) TERMINATION.—The term "qualified fuel cell property" shall not include any property for any period after *December 31, 2008.*

(2) QUALIFIED MICROTURBINE PROPERTY.—

* * *

(E) TERMINATION.—The term "qualified microturbine property" shall not include any property for any period after *December 31, 2008.*

[CCH Explanation at ¶440. Committee Reports at ¶15,410.]

Amendments

• 2006, Tax Relief and Health Care Act of 2006
(P.L. 109-432)

P.L. 109-432, Division A, §207(2):

Amended Code Sec. 48[(c)] by striking "December 31, 2007" both places it appears and inserting "December 31, 2008". Effective 12-20-2006.

[¶5051] CODE SEC. 48A. QUALIFYING ADVANCED COAL PROJECT CREDIT.

* * *

(f) ADVANCED COAL-BASED GENERATION TECHNOLOGY.—

(1) IN GENERAL.—For the purpose of this section, an electric generation unit uses advanced coal-based generation technology if—

(A) the unit—

(i) uses integrated gasification combined cycle technology, or

(ii) except as provided in paragraph (3), has a design net heat rate of 8530 Btu/kWh (40 percent efficiency), and

(B) the unit is designed to meet the performance requirements in the following table:

Performance characteristic:	Design level for project:
SO_2 (percent removal)	99 percent
NO_x (emissions)	0.07 lbs/MMBTU
PM* (emissions)	0.015 lbs/MMBTU
Hg (percent removal)	90 percent

For purposes of the performance requirement specified for the removal of SO_2 in the table contained in subparagraph (B), the SO_2 removal design level in the case of a unit designed for the use of feedstock substantially all of which is subbituminous coal shall be 99 percent SO_2 removal or the achievement of an emission level of 0.04 pounds or less of SO_2 per million Btu, determined on a 30-day average.

* * *

[CCH Explanation at ¶455. Committee Reports at ¶15,370.]

Amendments

• 2006, Tax Relief and Health Care Act of 2006
(P.L. 109-432)

P.L. 109-432, Division A, §203(a):

Amended Code Sec. 48A(f)(1) by adding at the end a new flush sentence. Effective with respect to applications for certification under Code Sec. 48A(d)(2) submitted after 10-2-2006.

[¶5052] CODE SEC. 51. AMOUNT OF CREDIT.

* * *

(c) WAGES DEFINED.—For purposes of this subpart—

* * *

(4) TERMINATION.—The term "wages" shall not include any amount paid or incurred to an individual who begins work for the employer—

(A) after December 31, 1994, and before October 1, 1996, or

(B) after December 31, 2007.

[CCH Explanation at ¶410. Committee Reports at ¶15,140.]
Amendments
• **2006, Tax Relief and Health Care Act of 2006 (P.L. 109-432)**

P.L. 109-432, Division A, §105(a):

Amended Code Sec. 51(c)(4)(B) by striking "2005" and inserting "2007". **Effective** for individuals who begin work for the employer after 12-31-2005.

(d) MEMBERS OF TARGETED GROUPS.—For purposes of this subpart—

(1) IN GENERAL.—An individual is a member of a targeted group if such individual is—

* * *

(G) a qualified food stamp recipient,

(H) a qualified SSI recipient, *or*

(I) a long-term family assistance recipient.

* * *

(4) QUALIFIED EX-FELON.—The term "qualified ex-felon" means any individual who is certified by the designated local agency—

(A) as having been convicted of a felony under any statute of the United States or any State, *and*

(B) as having a hiring date which is not more than 1 year after the last date on which such individual was so convicted or was released from prison.

* * *

(8) QUALIFIED FOOD STAMP RECIPIENT.—

(A) IN GENERAL.—The term "qualified food stamp recipient" means any individual who is certified by the designated local agency—

(i) as having attained age 18 but not age 40 on the hiring date, and

(ii) as being a member of a family—

(I) receiving assistance under a food stamp program under the Food Stamp Act of 1977 for the 6-month period ending on the hiring date, or

(II) receiving such assistance for at least 3 months of the 5-month period ending on the hiring date, in the case of a member of a family who ceases to be eligible for such assistance under section 6(o) of the Food Stamp Act of 1977.

* * *

(10) LONG-TERM FAMILY ASSISTANCE RECIPIENT.—The term "long-term family assistance recipient" means any individual who is certified by the designated local agency—

(A) as being a member of a family receiving assistance under a IV-A program (as defined in paragraph (2)(B)) for at least the 18-month period ending on the hiring date,

(B)(i) as being a member of a family receiving such assistance for 18 months beginning after August 5, 1997, and

(ii) as having a hiring date which is not more than 2 years after the end of the earliest such 18-month period, or

(C)(i) as being a member of a family which ceased to be eligible for such assistance by reason of any limitation imposed by Federal or State law on the maximum period such assistance is payable to a family, and

(ii) as having a hiring date which is not more than 2 years after the date of such cessation.

(11) HIRING DATE.—The term "hiring date" means the day the individual is hired by the employer.

(12) DESIGNATED LOCAL AGENCY.—The term "designated local agency" means a State employment security agency established in accordance with the Act of June 6, 1933, as amended (29 U.S.C. 49-49n).

(13) SPECIAL RULES FOR CERTIFICATIONS.—

(A) IN GENERAL.—An individual shall not be treated as a member of a targeted group unless—

(i) on or before the day on which such individual begins work for the employer, the employer has received a certification from a designated local agency that such individual is a member of a targeted group, or

(ii)(I) on or before the day the individual is offered employment with the employer, a pre-screening notice is completed by the employer with respect to such individual, and

(II) not later than the *28th day* after the individual begins work for the employer, the employer submits such notice, signed by the employer and the individual under penalties of perjury, to the designated local agency as part of a written request for such a certification from such agency.

For purposes of this paragraph, the term "pre-screening notice" means a document (in such form as the Secretary shall prescribe) which contains information provided by the individual on the basis of which the employer believes that the individual is a member of a targeted group.

* * *

[CCH Explanation at ¶ 410. Committee Reports at ¶ 15,140.]

Amendments

• **2006, Tax Relief and Health Care Act of 2006 (P.L. 109-432)**

P.L. 109-432, Division A, § 105(b):

Amended Code Sec. 51(d)(4) by adding "and" at the end of subparagraph (A), by striking ", and" at the end of subparagraph (B) and inserting a period, and by striking all that follows subparagraph (B). **Effective** for individuals who begin work for the employer after 12-31-2006. Prior to being stricken, all that follows Code Sec. 51(d)(4)(B) read as follows:

(C) as being a member of a family which had an income during the 6 months immediately preceding the earlier of the month in which such income determination occurs or the month in which the hiring date occurs, which, on an annual basis, would be 70 percent or less of the Bureau of Labor Statistics lower living standard.

Any determination under subparagraph (C) shall be valid for the 45-day period beginning on the date such determination is made.

P.L. 109-432, Division A, § 105(c):

Amended Code Sec. 51(d)(8)(A)(i) by striking "25" and inserting "40". **Effective** for individuals who begin work for the employer after 12-31-2006.

P.L. 109-432, Division A, § 105(d):

Amended Code Sec. 51(d)(12)(A)(ii)(II) by striking "21st day" and inserting "28th day". **Effective** for individuals who begin work for the employer after 12-31-2006.

P.L. 109-432, Division A, § 105(e)(1):

Amended Code Sec. 51(d)(1) by striking "or" at the end of subparagraph (G), by striking the period at the end of subparagraph (H) and inserting ", or", and by adding at the end a new subparagraph (I). **Effective** for individuals who begin work for the employer after 12-31-2006.

P.L. 109-432, Division A, § 105(e)(2):

Amended Code Sec. 51(d) by redesignating paragraphs (10) through (12) as paragraphs (11) through (13), respectively, and by inserting after paragraph (9) a new paragraph (10). **Effective** for individuals who begin work for the employer after 12-31-2006.

(e) CREDIT FOR SECOND-YEAR WAGES FOR EMPLOYMENT OF LONG-TERM FAMILY ASSISTANCE RECIPIENTS.—

(1) IN GENERAL.—With respect to the employment of a long-term family assistance recipient—

(A) the amount of the work opportunity credit determined under this section for the taxable year shall include 50 percent of the qualified second-year wages for such year, and

(B) in lieu of applying subsection (b)(3), the amount of the qualified first-year wages, and the amount of qualified second-year wages, which may be taken into account with respect to such a recipient shall not exceed $10,000 per year.

(2) QUALIFIED SECOND-YEAR WAGES.—For purposes of this subsection, the term "qualified second-year wages" means qualified wages—

(A) which are paid to a long-term family assistance recipient, and

(B) which are attributable to service rendered during the 1-year period beginning on the day after the last day of the 1-year period with respect to such recipient determined under subsection (b)(2).

(3) SPECIAL RULES FOR AGRICULTURAL AND RAILWAY LABOR.—If such recipient is an employee to whom subparagraph (A) or (B) of subsection (h)(1) applies, rules similar to the rules of such subparagraphs shall apply except that—

(A) such subparagraph (A) shall be applied by substituting "$10,000" for "$6,000", and

(B) such subparagraph (B) shall be applied by substituting "$833.33" for "$500".

* * *

[CCH Explanation at ¶410. Committee Reports at ¶15,140.]

Amendments

• **2006, Tax Relief and Health Care Act of 2006 (P.L. 109-432)**

P.L. 109-432, Division A, §105(e)(3):

Amended Code Sec. 51 by inserting after subsection (d) a new subsection (e). **Effective** for individuals who begin work for the employer after 12-31-2006.

⟫→ *Caution: Code Sec. 51A, below, was repealed by P.L. 109-432, applicable to individuals who begin work for the employer after December 31, 2006.*

[¶5053] CODE SEC. 51A. TEMPORARY INCENTIVES FOR EMPLOYING LONG-TERM FAMILY ASSISTANCE RECIPIENTS.

(a) DETERMINATION OF AMOUNT.—For purposes of section 38, the amount of the welfare-to-work credit determined under this section for the taxable year shall be equal to—

(1) 35 percent of the qualified first-year wages for such year, and

(2) 50 percent of the qualified second-year wages for such year.

(b) QUALIFIED WAGES DEFINED.—For purposes of this section—

(1) IN GENERAL.—The term "qualified wages" means the wages paid or incurred by the employer during the taxable year to individuals who are long-term family assistance recipients.

(2) QUALIFIED FIRST-YEAR WAGES.—The term "qualified first-year wages" means, with respect to any individual, qualified wages attributable to service rendered during the 1-year period beginning with the day the individual begins work for the employer.

(3) QUALIFIED SECOND-YEAR WAGES.—The term "qualified second-year wages" means, with respect to any individual, qualified wages attributable to service rendered during the 1-year period beginning on the day after the last day of the 1-year period with respect to such individual determined under paragraph (2).

(4) ONLY FIRST $10,000 OF WAGES PER YEAR TAKEN INTO ACCOUNT.—The amount of the qualified first-year wages, and the amount of qualified second-year wages, which may be taken into account with respect to any individual shall not exceed $10,000 per year.

(5) WAGES.—

(A) IN GENERAL.—The term "wages" has the meaning given such term by section 51(c), without regard to paragraph (4) thereof.

(B) CERTAIN AMOUNTS TREATED AS WAGES.—The term "wages" includes amounts paid or incurred by the employer which are excludable from such recipient's gross income under—

(i) section 105 (relating to amounts received under accident and health plans),

(ii) section 106 (relating to contributions by employer to accident and health plans),

(iii) section 127 (relating to educational assistance programs), but only to the extent paid or incurred to a person not related to the employer, or

(iv) section 129 (relating to dependent care assistance programs).

The amount treated as wages by clause (i) or (ii) for any period shall be based on the reasonable cost of coverage for the period, but shall not exceed the applicable premium for the period under section 4980B(f)(4).

(C) SPECIAL RULES FOR AGRICULTURAL AND RAILWAY LABOR.—If such recipient is an employee to whom subparagraph (A) or (B) of section 51(h)(1) applies, rules similar to the rules of such subparagraphs shall apply except that—

(i) such subparagraph (A) shall be applied by substituting "$10,000" for "$6,000", and

(ii) such subparagraph (B) shall be applied by substituting "$833.33" for "$500".

(c) LONG-TERM FAMILY ASSISTANCE RECIPIENTS.—For purposes of this section—

(1) IN GENERAL.—The term "long-term family assistance recipient" means any individual who is certified by the designated local agency (as defined in section 51(d)(11))—

(A) as being a member of a family receiving assistance under a IV-A program (as defined in section 51(d)(2)(B)) for at least the 18-month period ending on the hiring date,

(B)(i) as being a member of a family receiving such assistance for 18 months beginning after the date of the enactment of this section, and

(ii) as having a hiring date which is not more than 2 years after the end of the earliest such 18-month period, or

(C)(i) as being a member of a family which ceased to be eligible after the date of the enactment of this section for such assistance by reason of any limitation imposed by Federal or State law on the maximum period such assistance is payable to a family, and

(ii) as having a hiring date which is not more than 2 years after the date of such cessation.

(2) HIRING DATE.—The term "hiring date" has the meaning given such term by section 51(d).

(d) CERTAIN RULES TO APPLY.—

(1) IN GENERAL.—Rules similar to the rules of section 52, and subsections (d)(11), (f), (g), (i) (as in effect on the day before the date of the enactment of the Taxpayer Relief Act of 1997), (j), and (k) of section 51, shall apply for purposes of this section.

(2) CREDIT TO BE PART OF GENERAL BUSINESS CREDIT, ETC.—References to section 51 in section 38(b), 280C(a), and 1396(c)(3) shall be treated as including references to this section.

(e) COORDINATION WITH WORK OPPORTUNITY CREDIT.—If a credit is allowed under this section to an employer with respect to an individual for any taxable year, then for purposes of applying section 51 to such employer, such individual shall not be treated as a member of a targeted group for such taxable year.

(f) TERMINATION.—This section shall not apply to individuals who begin work for the employer after December 31, 2007.

[CCH Explanation at ¶410. Committee Reports at ¶15,140.]

Amendments

• **2006, Tax Relief and Health Care Act of 2006 (P.L. 109-432)**

P.L. 109-432, Division A, §105(a):

Amended Code Sec. 51A(f) by striking "2005" and inserting "2007". Effective for individuals who begin work for the employer after 12-31-2005.

P.L. 109-432, Division A, §105(e)(4)(A):

Repealed Code Sec. 51A. Effective for individuals who begin work for the employer after 12-31-2006.

[¶ 5054] CODE SEC. 53. CREDIT FOR PRIOR YEAR MINIMUM TAX LIABILITY.

* * *

(e) SPECIAL RULE FOR INDIVIDUALS WITH LONG-TERM UNUSED CREDITS.—

(1) IN GENERAL.—If an individual has a long-term unused minimum tax credit for any taxable year beginning before January 1, 2013, the amount determined under subsection (c) for such taxable year shall not be less than the AMT refundable credit amount for such taxable year.

(2) AMT REFUNDABLE CREDIT AMOUNT.—For purposes of paragraph (1)—

(A) IN GENERAL.—The term "AMT refundable credit amount" means, with respect to any taxable year, the amount equal to the greater of—

(i) the lesser of—

(I) $5,000, or

(II) the amount of long-term unused minimum tax credit for such taxable year, or

(ii) 20 percent of the amount of such credit.

(B) PHASEOUT OF AMT REFUNDABLE CREDIT AMOUNT.—

(i) IN GENERAL.—In the case of an individual whose adjusted gross income for any taxable year exceeds the threshold amount (within the meaning of section 151(d)(3)(C)), the AMT refundable credit amount determined under subparagraph (A) for such taxable year shall be reduced by the applicable percentage (within the meaning of section 151(d)(3)(B)).

(ii) ADJUSTED GROSS INCOME.—For purposes of clause (i), adjusted gross income shall be determined without regard to sections 911, 931, and 933.

(3) LONG-TERM UNUSED MINIMUM TAX CREDIT.—

(A) IN GENERAL.—For purposes of this subsection, the term "long-term unused minimum tax credit" means, with respect to any taxable year, the portion of the minimum tax credit determined under subsection (b) attributable to the adjusted net minimum tax for taxable years before the 3rd taxable year immediately preceding such taxable year.

(B) FIRST-IN, FIRST-OUT ORDERING RULE.—For purposes of subparagraph (A), credits shall be treated as allowed under subsection (a) on a first-in, first-out basis.

(4) CREDIT REFUNDABLE.—For purposes of this title (other than this section), the credit allowed by reason of this subsection shall be treated as if it were allowed under subpart C.

[CCH Explanation at ¶ 235. Committee Reports at ¶ 15,480.]

Amendments

• **2006, Tax Relief and Health Care Act of 2006 (P.L. 109-432)**

P.L. 109-432, Division A, § 402(a):

Amended Code Sec. 53 by adding at the end a new subsection (e). **Effective** for tax years beginning after 12-20-2006.

[¶ 5055] CODE SEC. 54. CREDIT TO HOLDERS OF CLEAN RENEWABLE ENERGY BONDS.

* * *

(f) LIMITATION ON AMOUNT OF BONDS DESIGNATED.—

(1) NATIONAL LIMITATION.—There is a national clean renewable energy bond limitation of $1,200,000,000.

(2) ALLOCATION BY SECRETARY.—The Secretary shall allocate the amount described in paragraph (1) among qualified projects in such manner as the Secretary determines appropriate, except that the Secretary may not allocate more than $750,000,000 of the national clean renewable

energy bond limitation to finance qualified projects of qualified borrowers which are governmental bodies.

* * *

[CCH Explanation at ¶ 625. Committee Reports at ¶ 15,360.]

Amendments

• **2006, Tax Relief and Health Care Act of 2006 (P.L. 109-432)**

P.L. 109-432, Division A, § 202(a)(1):

Amended Code Sec. 54(f)(1) by striking "$800,000,000" and inserting "$1,200,000,000". **Effective** for bonds issued after 12-31-2006.

P.L. 109-432, Division A, § 202(a)(2):

Amended Code Sec. 54(f)(2) by striking "$500,000,000" and inserting "$750,000,000". **Effective** for allocations or reallocations after 12-31-2006.

(l) OTHER DEFINITIONS AND SPECIAL RULES.—For purposes of this section—

* * *

(2) POOLED FINANCING BOND.—The term "pooled financing bond" shall have the meaning given such term by *section 149(f)(6)(A)*.

(3) PARTNERSHIP; S CORPORATION; AND OTHER PASS-THRU ENTITIES.—

* * *

(B) NO BASIS ADJUSTMENT.—In the case of a bond held by a partnership or an S corporation, rules similar to the rules under *section 1397E(l)* shall apply.

* * *

[CCH Explanation at ¶ 605 and ¶ 1135. Committee Reports at ¶ 10,220 and ¶ 15,160.]

Amendments

• **2006, Tax Relief and Health Care Act of 2006 (P.L. 109-432)**

P.L. 109-432, Division A, § 107(b)(2):

Amended Code Sec. 54(l)(3)(B) by striking "section 1397E(i)" and inserting "section 1397E(l)". **Effective** for obligations issued after 12-20-2006 pursuant to allocations of the national zone academy bond limitation for calendar years after 2005.

• **2006, Tax Increase Prevention and Reconciliation Act of 2005 (P.L. 109-222)**

P.L. 109-222, § 508(d)(3):

Amended Code Sec. 54(l)(2) by striking "section 149(f)(4)(A)" and inserting "section 149(f)(6)(A)". **Effective** for bonds issued after 5-17-2006.

(m) TERMINATION.—This section shall not apply with respect to any bond issued after *December 31, 2008*.

[CCH Explanation at ¶ 625. Committee Reports at ¶ 15,360.]

Amendments

• **2006, Tax Relief and Health Care Act of 2006 (P.L. 109-432)**

P.L. 109-432, Division A, § 202(a)(3):

Amended Code Sec. 54(m) by striking "December 31, 2007" and inserting "December 31, 2008". **Effective** for bonds issued after 12-31-2006.

[¶ 5080] CODE SEC. 55. ALTERNATIVE MINIMUM TAX IMPOSED.

* * *

(d) EXEMPTION AMOUNT.—For purposes of this section—

(1) EXEMPTION AMOUNT FOR TAXPAYERS OTHER THAN CORPORATIONS.—In the case of a taxpayer other than a corporation, the term "exemption amount" means—

(A) $45,000 (*$62,550 in the case of taxable years beginning in 2006*) in the case of—

(i) a joint return, or

(ii) a surviving spouse,

(B) $33,750 ($42,500 *in the case of taxable years beginning in 2006*) in the case of an individual who—

(i) is not a married individual, and

(ii) is not a surviving spouse,

(C) 50 percent of the dollar amount applicable under paragraph (1)(A) in the case of a married individual who files a separate return, and

(D) $22,500 in the case of an estate or trust.

For purposes of this paragraph, the term "surviving spouse" has the meaning given to such term by section 2(a), and marital status shall be determined under section 7703.

* * *

[CCH Explanation at ¶720. Committee Reports at ¶10,120.]

Amendments

• **2006, Tax Increase Prevention and Reconciliation Act of 2005 (P.L. 109-222)**

P.L. 109-222, §301(a)(1)-(2):

Amended Code Sec. 55(d)(1) by striking "$58,000" and all that follows through "2005" in subparagraph (A) and inserting "$62,550 in the case of taxable years beginning in 2006", and by striking "$40,250" and all that follows through "2005" in subparagraph (B) and inserting "$42,500 in the case of taxable years beginning in 2006". **Effective** for tax years beginning after 12-31-2005. Prior to amendment, Code Sec. 55(d)(1)(A)-(B) read as follows:

(A) $45,000 ($58,000 in the case of taxable years beginning in 2003, 2004, and 2005) in the case of—

(i) a joint return, or

(ii) a surviving spouse,

(B) $33,750 ($40,250 in the case of taxable years beginning in 2003, 2004, and 2005) in the case of an individual who—

(i) is not a married individual, and

(ii) is not a surviving spouse,

[¶5085] CODE SEC. 62. ADJUSTED GROSS INCOME DEFINED.

(a) GENERAL RULE.—For purposes of this subtitle, the term "adjusted gross income" means, in the case of an individual, gross income minus the following deductions:

* * *

(2) CERTAIN TRADE AND BUSINESS DEDUCTIONS OF EMPLOYEES.—

* * *

(D) CERTAIN EXPENSES OF ELEMENTARY AND SECONDARY SCHOOL TEACHERS.—In the case of taxable years beginning during 2002, 2003, 2004, *2005, 2006, or 2007*, the deductions allowed by section 162 which consist of expenses, not in excess of $250, paid or incurred by an eligible educator in connection with books, supplies (other than nonathletic supplies for courses of instruction in health or physical education), computer equipment (including related software and services) and other equipment, and supplementary materials used by the eligible educator in the classroom.

* * *

(21) *ATTORNEYS FEES RELATING TO AWARDS TO WHISTLEBLOWERS.—Any deduction allowable under this chapter for attorney fees and court costs paid by, or on behalf of, the taxpayer in connection with any award under section 7623(b) (relating to awards to whistleblowers). The preceding sentence shall not apply to any deduction in excess of the amount includible in the taxpayer's gross income for the taxable year on account of such award.*

Nothing in this section shall permit the same item to be deducted more than once.

[CCH Explanation at ¶215 and ¶650. Committee Reports at ¶15,170 and ¶15,510.]

Amendments

• **2006, Tax Relief and Health Care Act of 2006 (P.L. 109-432)**

P.L. 109-432, Division A, §108(a):

Amended Code Sec. 62(a)(2)(D) by striking "or 2005" and inserting "2005, 2006, or 2007". **Effective** for tax years beginning after 12-31-2005.

P.L. 109-432, Division A, §406(a)(3):

Amended Code Sec. 62(a) by inserting after paragraph (20) a new paragraph (21). **Effective** for information provided on or after 12-20-2006.

[¶5090] CODE SEC. 106. CONTRIBUTIONS BY EMPLOYER TO ACCIDENT AND HEALTH PLANS.

* * *

(e) FSA AND HRA TERMINATIONS TO FUND HSAS.—

(1) IN GENERAL.—A plan shall not fail to be treated as a health flexible spending arrangement or health reimbursement arrangement under this section or section 105 merely because such plan provides for a qualified HSA distribution.

(2) QUALIFIED HSA DISTRIBUTION.—The term "qualified HSA distribution" means a distribution from a health flexible spending arrangement or health reimbursement arrangement to the extent that such distribution—

(A) does not exceed the lesser of the balance in such arrangement on September 21, 2006, or as of the date of such distribution, and

(B) is contributed by the employer directly to the health savings account of the employee before January 1, 2012.

Such term shall not include more than 1 distribution with respect to any arrangement.

(3) ADDITIONAL TAX FOR FAILURE TO MAINTAIN HIGH DEDUCTIBLE HEALTH PLAN COVERAGE.—

(A) IN GENERAL.—If, at any time during the testing period, the employee is not an eligible individual, then the amount of the qualified HSA distribution—

(i) shall be includible in the gross income of the employee for the taxable year in which occurs the first month in the testing period for which such employee is not an eligible individual, and

(ii) the tax imposed by this chapter for such taxable year on the employee shall be increased by 10 percent of the amount which is so includible.

(B) EXCEPTION FOR DISABILITY OR DEATH.—Clauses (i) and (ii) of subparagraph (A) shall not apply if the employee ceases to be an eligible individual by reason of the death of the employee or the employee becoming disabled (within the meaning of section 72(m)(7)).

(4) DEFINITIONS AND SPECIAL RULES.—For purposes of this subsection—

(A) TESTING PERIOD.—The term "testing period" means the period beginning with the month in which the qualified HSA distribution is contributed to the health savings account and ending on the last day of the 12th month following such month.

(B) ELIGIBLE INDIVIDUAL.—The term "eligible individual" has the meaning given such term by section 223(c)(1).

(C) TREATMENT AS ROLLOVER CONTRIBUTION.—A qualified HSA distribution shall be treated as a rollover contribution described in section 223(f)(5).

(5) TAX TREATMENT RELATING TO DISTRIBUTIONS.—For purposes of this title—

(A) IN GENERAL.—A qualified HSA distribution shall be treated as a payment described in subsection (d).

(B) COMPARABILITY EXCISE TAX.—

(i) IN GENERAL.—Except as provided in clause (ii), section 4980G shall not apply to qualified HSA distributions.

(ii) FAILURE TO OFFER TO ALL EMPLOYEES.—In the case of a qualified HSA distribution to any employee, the failure to offer such distribution to any eligible individual covered under a high deductible health plan of the employer shall (notwithstanding section 4980G(d)) be treated for purposes of section 4980G as a failure to meet the requirements of section 4980G(b).

[CCH Explanation at ¶505. Committee Reports at ¶15,460.]
Amendments
• **2006, Tax Relief and Health Care Act of 2006**
(P.L. 109-432)

P.L. 109-432, Division A, §302(a):

Amended Code Sec. 106 by adding at the end a new subsection (e). **Effective** for distributions on or after 12-20-2006.

[¶5095] CODE SEC. 121. EXCLUSION OF GAIN FROM SALE OF PRINCIPAL RESIDENCE.

* * *

(d) SPECIAL RULES.—

* * *

(9) *UNIFORMED SERVICES, FOREIGN SERVICE, AND INTELLIGENCE COMMUNITY.*—

(A) IN GENERAL.—At the election of an individual with respect to a property, the running of the 5-year period described in subsections (a) and (c)(1)(B) and paragraph (7) of this subsection with respect to such property shall be suspended during any period that such individual or such individual's spouse is serving on qualified official extended *duty*—

(i) *as a member of the uniformed services,*

(ii) *as a member of the Foreign Service of the United States, or*

(iii) *as an employee of the intelligence community.*

* * *

(C) QUALIFIED OFFICIAL EXTENDED DUTY.—For purposes of this paragraph—

* * *

(iv) EMPLOYEE OF INTELLIGENCE COMMUNITY.—*The term "employee of the intelligence community" means an employee (as defined by section 2105 of title 5, United States Code) of—*

(I) *the Office of the Director of National Intelligence,*

(II) *the Central Intelligence Agency,*

(III) *the National Security Agency,*

(IV) *the Defense Intelligence Agency,*

(V) *the National Geospatial-Intelligence Agency,*

(VI) *the National Reconnaissance Office,*

(VII) *any other office within the Department of Defense for the collection of specialized national intelligence through reconnaissance programs,*

(VIII) *any of the intelligence elements of the Army, the Navy, the Air Force, the Marine Corps, the Federal Bureau of Investigation, the Department of Treasury, the Department of Energy, and the Coast Guard,*

(IX) *the Bureau of Intelligence and Research of the Department of State, or*

(X) *any of the elements of the Department of Homeland Security concerned with the analyses of foreign intelligence information.*

(v) EXTENDED DUTY.—*The term "extended duty" means any period of active duty pursuant to a call or order to such duty for a period in excess of 90 days or for an indefinite period.*

(vi) SPECIAL RULE RELATING TO INTELLIGENCE COMMUNITY.—*An employee of the intelligence community shall not be treated as serving on qualified extended duty unless such duty is at a duty station located outside the United States.*

* * *

[CCH Explanation at ¶250. Committee Reports at ¶15,620.]

Amendments

• **2006, Tax Relief and Health Care Act of 2006 (P.L. 109-432)**

P.L. 109-432, Division A, §417(a):

Amended Code Sec. 121(d)(9)(A) by striking "duty" and all that follows and inserting "duty—" and new clauses (i)-(iii). **Effective** for sales or exchanges after 12-20-2006 and before 1-1-2011. Prior to amendment, Code Sec. 121(d)(9)(A) read as follows:

(A) IN GENERAL.—At the election of an individual with respect to a property, the running of the 5-year period described in subsections (a) and (c)(1)(B) and paragraph (7) of this subsection with respect to such property shall be suspended during any period that such individual or such individual's spouse is serving on qualified official extended duty as a member of the uniformed services or of the Foreign Service of the United States.

P.L. 109-432, Division A, §417(b):

Amended Code Sec. 121(d)(9)(C) by redesignating clause (iv) as clause (v) and by inserting after clause (iii) a new clause (iv). **Effective** for sales or exchanges after 12-20-2006 and before 1-1-2011.

P.L. 109-432, Division A, §417(c):

Amended Code Sec. 121(d)(9)(C), as amended by Act Sec. 417(b), by adding at the end a new clause (vi). **Effective** for sales or exchanges after 12-20-2006 and before 1-1-2011.

P.L. 109-432, Division A, §417(d):

Amended the heading for Code Sec. 121(d)(9). **Effective** for sales or exchanges after 12-20-2006 and before 1-1-2011. Prior to amendment, the heading for Code Sec. 121(d)(9) read as follows:

MEMBERS OF UNIFORMED SERVICES AND FOREIGN SERVICE

[¶5105] CODE SEC. 142. EXEMPT FACILITY BOND.

* * *

(d) QUALIFIED RESIDENTIAL RENTAL PROJECT.—For purposes of this section—

* * *

(2) DEFINITIONS AND SPECIAL RULES.—For purposes of this subsection—

* * *

(B) INCOME OF INDIVIDUALS; AREA MEDIAN GROSS INCOME.—The income of individuals and area median gross income shall be determined by the Secretary in a manner consistent with determinations of lower income families and area median gross income under section 8 of the United States Housing Act of 1937 (or, if such program is terminated, under such program as in effect immediately before such termination). Determinations under the preceding sentence shall include adjustments for family size. *Subsections (g) and (h) of section 7872 shall not apply in determining the income of individuals under this subparagraph.*

* * *

[CCH Explanation at ¶245. Committee Reports at ¶10,110.]

Amendments

• **2006, Tax Increase Prevention and Reconciliation Act of 2005 (P.L. 109-222)**

P.L. 109-222, §209(b)(2):

Amended Code Sec. 142(d)(2)(B) by striking "Section 7872(g)" and inserting "Subsections (g) and (h) of section

7872". **Effective** for calendar years beginning after 12-31-2005, with respect to loans made before, on, or after such date.

[¶5130] CODE SEC. 143. MORTGAGE REVENUE BONDS: QUALIFIED MORTGAGE BOND AND QUALIFIED VETERANS' MORTGAGE BOND.

* * *

(d) 3-YEAR REQUIREMENT.—

* * *

(2) EXCEPTIONS.—For purposes of paragraph (1), the proceeds of an issue which are used to provide—

(A) financing with respect to targeted area residences,

(B) qualified home improvement loans and qualified rehabilitation loans,

(C) financing with respect to land described in subsection (i)(1)(C) and the construction of any residence thereon, *and*

(D) *in the case of bonds issued after the date of the enactment of this subparagraph and before January 1, 2008, financing of any residence for a veteran (as defined in section 101 of title 38, United States Code), if such veteran has not previously qualified for and received such financing by reason of this subparagraph,*

shall be treated as used as described in paragraph (1).

* * *

[CCH Explanation at ¶ 610. Committee Reports at ¶ 15,610.]

Amendments

• **2006, Tax Relief and Health Care Act of 2006 (P.L. 109-432)**

P.L. 109-432, Division A, §416(a):

Amended Code Sec. 143(d)(2) by striking "and" at the end of subparagraph (B), by adding "and" at the end of subpara-

graph (C), and by inserting after subparagraph (C) a new subparagraph (D). **Effective** for bonds issued after 12-20-2006.

(l) ADDITIONAL REQUIREMENTS FOR QUALIFIED VETERANS' MORTGAGE BONDS.—An issue meets the requirements of this subsection only if it meets the requirements of paragraphs (1), (2), and (3).

* * *

(3) VOLUME LIMITATION.—

* * *

(B) *STATE VETERANS LIMIT.*—

(i) IN GENERAL.—*In the case of any State to which clause (ii) does not apply, the State veterans limit for any calendar year is the amount equal to*—

(I) the aggregate amount of qualified veterans bonds issued by such State during the period beginning on January 1, 1979, and ending on June 22, 1984 (not including the amount of any qualified veterans bond issued by such State during the calendar year (or portion thereof) in such period for which the amount of such bonds so issued was the lowest), divided by

(II) the number (not to exceed 5) of calendar years after 1979 and before 1985 during which the State issued qualified veterans bonds (determined by only taking into account bonds issued on or before June 22, 1984).

(ii) ALASKA, OREGON, AND WISCONSIN.—*In the case of the following States, the State veterans limit for any calendar year is the amount equal to*—

(I) *$25,000,000 for the State of Alaska,*

(II) *$25,000,000 for the State of Oregon, and*

(III) *$25,000,000 for the State of Wisconsin.*

(iii) PHASEIN.—*In the case of calendar years beginning before 2010, clause (ii) shall be applied by substituting for each of the dollar amounts therein an amount equal to the applicable percentage of such dollar amount. For purposes of the preceding sentence, the applicable percentage shall be determined in accordance with the following table:*

For Calendar Year:	Applicable percentage is:
2006	20 percent
2007	40 percent
2008	60 percent
2009	80 percent.

(iv) [Stricken.]

* * *

(4) QUALIFIED VETERAN.—*For purposes of this subsection, the term "qualified veteran" means*—

(A) *in the case of the States of Alaska, Oregon, and Wisconsin, any veteran*—

(i) *who served on active duty, and*

(ii) *who applied for the financing before the date 25 years after the last date on which such veteran left active service, and*

(B) *in the case of any other State, any veteran—*

(i) *who served on active duty at some time before January 1, 1977, and*

(ii) *who applied for the financing before the later of—*

(I) *the date 30 years after the last date on which such veteran left active service, or*

(II) *January 31, 1985.*

* * *

[CCH Explanation at ¶ 620. Committee Reports at ¶ 10,050 and ¶ 15,560.]

Amendments

• 2006, Tax Relief and Health Care Act of 2006 (P.L. 109-432)

P.L. 109-432, Division A, § 411(a):

Amended Code Sec. 143(l)(3)(B) by striking clause (iv). **Effective** as if included in section 203 of the Tax Increase Prevention and Reconciliation Act of 2005 (P.L. 109-222) [effective for allocations of State volume limit after 4-5-2006.—CCH]. Prior to being stricken, Code Sec. 143(l)(3)(B)(iv) read as follows:

(iv) TERMINATION.—The State veterans limit for the States specified in clause (ii) for any calendar year after 2010 is zero.

• 2006, Tax Increase Prevention and Reconciliation Act of 2005 (P.L. 109-222)

P.L. 109-222, § 203(a)(1):

Amended Code Sec. 143(l)(4). **Effective** for bonds issued on or after 5-17-2006. Prior to amendment, Code Sec. 143(l)(4) read as follows:

(4) QUALIFIED VETERAN.—For purposes of this subsection, the term "qualified veteran" means any veteran—

(A) who served on active duty at some time before January 1, 1977, and

(B) who applied for the financing before the later of—

(i) the date 30 years after the last date on which such veteran left active service, or

(ii) January 31, 1985.

P.L. 109-222, § 203(b)(1)(A)-(C):

Amended Code Sec. 143(l)(3)(B) by redesignating clauses (i) and (ii) as subclauses (I) and (II), respectively, and moving such clauses 2 ems to the right, by amending the matter preceding subclause (I), as [re]designated by Act Sec. 203(b)(1)(A), and by adding at the end new clauses (ii)-(iv). **Effective** for allocations of State volume limit after 4-5-2006. Prior to amendment, the matter preceding subclause (I) of Code Sec. 143(l)(3)(B) read as follows:

(B) STATE VETERANS LIMIT.—A State veterans limit for any calendar year is the amount equal to—

[¶ 5155] CODE SEC. 144. QUALIFIED SMALL ISSUE BOND; QUALIFIED STUDENT LOAN BOND; QUALIFIED REDEVELOPMENT BOND.

(a) QUALIFIED SMALL ISSUE BOND.—

* * *

(4) $10,000,000 LIMIT IN CERTAIN CASES.—

* * *

(F) AGGREGATE AMOUNT OF CAPITAL EXPENDITURES WHERE THERE IS URBAN DEVELOPMENT ACTION GRANT.—In the case of any issue 95 percent or more of the net proceeds of which are to be used to provide facilities with respect to which an urban development action grant has been made under section 119 of the Housing and Community Development Act of 1974, capital expenditures of not to exceed $10,000,000 shall not be taken into account for purposes of applying subparagraph (A)(ii). This subparagraph shall not apply to bonds issued after *December 31, 2006.*

(G) ADDITIONAL CAPITAL EXPENDITURES NOT TAKEN INTO ACCOUNT.—With respect to bonds issued after *December 31, 2006,* in addition to any capital expenditure described in subparagraph (C), capital expenditures of not to exceed $10,000,000 shall not be taken into account for purposes of applying subparagraph (A)(ii).

* * *

[CCH Explanation at ¶1110. Committee Reports at ¶10,100.]

Amendments

• **2006, Tax Increase Prevention and Reconciliation Act of 2005 (P.L. 109-222)**

P.L. 109-222, §208(a):

Amended Code Sec. 144(a)(4)(G) by striking "September 30, 2009" and inserting "December 31, 2006". **Effective** 5-17-2006.

P.L. 109-222, §208(b):

Amended Code Sec. 144(a)(4)(F) by striking "September 30, 2009" and inserting "December 31, 2006". **Effective** 5-17-2006.

[¶5180] CODE SEC. 148. ARBITRAGE.

* * *

(f) Required Rebate to the United States.—

* * *

(4) Special Rules for Applying Paragraph (2).—

* * *

(D) Exception for Governmental Units Issuing $5,000,000 or Less of Bonds.—

* * *

(ii) Aggregation of Issuers.—For purposes of subclause (IV) of clause (i)—

(I) an issuer and all entities which issue bonds on behalf of such issuer shall be treated as 1 issuer,

(II) all bonds issued by a subordinate entity shall, for purposes of applying such subclause to each other entity to which such entity is subordinate, be treated as issued by such other entity, and

(III) an entity formed (or, to the extent provided by the Secretary, availed of) to avoid the purposes of such subclause (IV) and all other entities benefiting thereby shall be treated as 1 issuer.

* * *

[CCH Explanation at ¶1135. Committee Reports at ¶10,220.]

Amendments

• **2006, Tax Increase Prevention and Reconciliation Act of 2005 (P.L. 109-222)**

P.L. 109-222, §508(c):

Amended Code Sec. 148(f)(4)(D)(ii) by striking subclause (II) and by redesignating subclauses (III) and (IV) as subclauses (II) and (III), respectively. **Effective** for bonds issued after 5-17-2006. Prior to being stricken, Code Sec. 148(f)(4)(D)(ii)(II) read as follows:

(II) all bonds issued by a governmental unit to make loans to other governmental units with general taxing powers not subordinate to such unit shall, for purposes of applying such subclause to such unit, be treated as not issued by such unit.

[¶5205] CODE SEC. 149. BONDS MUST BE REGISTERED TO BE TAX EXEMPT; OTHER REQUIREMENTS.

* * *

(f) Treatment of Certain Pooled Financing Bonds.—

(1) In General.—Section 103(a) shall not apply to any pooled financing bond unless, with respect to the issue of which such bond is a part, the requirements of *paragraphs (2), (3), (4), and (5)* are met.

(2) Reasonable Expectation Requirement.—

(A) In General.—The requirements of this paragraph are met with respect to an issue if the issuer reasonably expects that—

(i) as of the close of the 1-year period beginning on the date of issuance of the issue, at least 30 percent of the net proceeds of the issue (as of the close of such period) will have been used directly or indirectly to make or finance loans to ultimate borrowers, and

(ii) as of the close of the 3-year period beginning on such date of issuance, at least 95 percent of the net proceeds of the issue (as of the close of such period) will have been so used.

* * *

(4) WRITTEN LOAN COMMITMENT REQUIREMENT.—

(A) IN GENERAL.—The requirement of this paragraph is met with respect to an issue if the issuer receives prior to issuance written loan commitments identifying the ultimate potential borrowers of at least 30 percent of the net proceeds of such issue.

(B) EXCEPTION.—Subparagraph (A) shall not apply with respect to any issuer which—

(i) is a State (or an integral part of a State) issuing pooled financing bonds to make or finance loans to subordinate governmental units of such State, or

(ii) is a State-created entity providing financing for water-infrastructure projects through the federally-sponsored State revolving fund program.

(5) REDEMPTION REQUIREMENT.—The requirement of this paragraph is met if to the extent that less than the percentage of the proceeds of an issue required to be used under clause (i) or (ii) of paragraph (2)(A) is used by the close of the period identified in such clause, the issuer uses an amount of proceeds equal to the excess of—

(A) the amount required to be used under such clause, over

(B) the amount actually used by the close of such period,

to redeem outstanding bonds within 90 days after the end of such period.

(6) POOLED FINANCING BOND.—For purposes of this subsection—

(A) IN GENERAL.—The term "pooled financing bond" means any bond issued as part of an issue more than $5,000,000 of the proceeds of which are reasonably expected (at the time of the issuance of the bonds) to be used (or are intentionally used) directly or indirectly to make or finance loans to 2 or more ultimate borrowers.

(B) EXCEPTIONS.—Such term shall not include any bond if—

(i) section 146 applies to the issue of which such bond is a part (other than by reason of section 141(b)(5)) or would apply but for section 146(i), or

(ii) section 143(l)(3) applies to such issue.

(7) DEFINITION OF LOAN; TREATMENT OF MIXED USE ISSUES.—

(A) LOAN.—For purposes of this subsection, the term "loan" does not include—

(i) any loan which is a nonpurpose investment (within the meaning of section 148(f)(6)(A), determined without regard to section 148(b)(3)), and

(ii) any use of proceeds by an agency of the issuer unless such agency is a political subdivision or instrumentality of the issuer.

(B) PORTION OF ISSUE TO BE USED FOR LOANS TREATED AS SEPARATE ISSUE.—If only a portion of the proceeds of an issue is reasonably expected (at the time of issuance of the bond) to be used (or is intentionally used) as described in *paragraph (6)(A)*, such portion and the other portion of such issue shall be treated as separate issues for purposes of determining whether such portion meets the requirements of this subsection.

* * *

[CCH Explanation at ¶ 1135. Committee Reports at ¶ 10,220.]

Amendments

• **2006, Tax Increase Prevention and Reconciliation Act of 2005 (P.L. 109-222)**

P.L. 109-222, § 508(a):

Amended Code Sec. 149(f)(2)(A). **Effective** for bonds issued after 5-17-2006. Prior to amendment, Code Sec. 149(f)(2)(A) read as follows:

(A) IN GENERAL.—The requirements of this paragraph are met with respect to an issue if the issuer reasonably expects that as of the close of the 3-year period beginning on the date of issuance of the issue, at least 95 percent of the net proceeds of the issue (as of the close of such period) will have been used directly or indirectly to make or finance loans to ultimate borrowers.

P.L. 109-222, § 508(b):

Amended Code Sec. 149(f) by redesignating paragraphs (4) and (5) as paragraphs (6) and (7), respectively, and by inserting after paragraph (3) new paragraphs (4) and (5). **Effective** for bonds issued after 5-17-2006.

P.L. 109-222, § 508(d)(1):

Amended Code Sec. 149(f)(1) by striking "paragraphs (2) and (3)" and inserting "paragraphs (2), (3), (4), and (5)". **Effective** for bonds issued after 5-17-2006.

P.L. 109-222, § 508(d)(2):

Amended Code Sec. 149(f)(7)(B), as redesignated by Act Sec. 508(b), by striking "paragraph (4)(A)" and inserting "paragraph (6)(A)". **Effective** for bonds issued after 5-17-2006.

[¶ 5230] CODE SEC. 163. INTEREST.

* * *

(h) DISALLOWANCE OF DEDUCTION FOR PERSONAL INTEREST.—

* * *

(3) QUALIFIED RESIDENCE INTEREST.—For purposes of this subsection—

* * *

(E) MORTGAGE INSURANCE PREMIUMS TREATED AS INTEREST.—

(i) IN GENERAL.—Premiums paid or accrued for qualified mortgage insurance by a taxpayer during the taxable year in connection with acquisition indebtedness with respect to a qualified residence of the taxpayer shall be treated for purposes of this section as interest which is qualified residence interest.

(ii) PHASEOUT.—The amount otherwise treated as interest under clause (i) shall be reduced (but not below zero) by 10 percent of such amount for each $1,000 ($500 in the case of a married individual filing a separate return) (or fraction thereof) that the taxpayer's adjusted gross income for the taxable year exceeds $100,000 ($50,000 in the case of a married individual filing a separate return).

(iii) LIMITATION.—Clause (i) shall not apply with respect to any mortgage insurance contracts issued before January 1, 2007.

(iv) TERMINATION.—Clause (i) shall not apply to amounts—

(I) paid or accrued after December 31, 2007, or

(II) properly allocable to any period after such date.

(4) OTHER DEFINITIONS AND SPECIAL RULES.—For purposes of this subsection—

* * *

(E) QUALIFIED MORTGAGE INSURANCE.—The term "qualified mortgage insurance" means—

(i) mortgage insurance provided by the Veterans Administration, the Federal Housing Administration, or the Rural Housing Administration, and

(ii) private mortgage insurance (as defined by section 2 of the Homeowners Protection Act of 1998 (12 U.S.C. 4901), as in effect on the date of the enactment of this subparagraph).

(F) SPECIAL RULES FOR PREPAID QUALIFIED MORTGAGE INSURANCE.—Any amount paid by the taxpayer for qualified mortgage insurance that is properly allocable to any mortgage the payment of which extends to periods that are after the close of the taxable year in which such amount is paid shall be chargeable to capital account and shall be treated as paid in such periods to which so allocated. No deduction shall be allowed for the unamortized balance of such account if such mortgage is satisfied before the end of its term. The preceding sentences shall not apply to amounts paid for qualified mortgage insurance provided by the Veterans Administration or the Rural Housing Administration.

* * *

[CCH Explanation at ¶220. Committee Reports at ¶15,640.]

Amendments

• **2006, Tax Relief and Health Care Act of 2006 (P.L. 109-432)**

P.L. 109-432, Division A, §419(a):

Amended Code Sec. 163(h)(3) by adding at the end a new subparagraph (E). **Effective** for amounts paid or accrued after 12-31-2006.

P.L. 109-432, Division A, §419(b):

Amended Code Sec. 163(h)(4) by adding at the end new subparagraphs (E) and (F). **Effective** for amounts paid or accrued after 12-31-2006.

(j) LIMITATION ON DEDUCTION FOR INTEREST ON CERTAIN INDEBTEDNESS.—

* * *

(8) TREATMENT OF CORPORATE PARTNERS.—Except to the extent provided by regulations, in applying this subsection to a corporation which owns (directly or indirectly) an interest in a partnership—

(A) such corporation's distributive share of interest income paid or accrued to such partnership shall be treated as interest income paid or accrued to such corporation,

(B) such corporation's distributive share of interest paid or accrued by such partnership shall be treated as interest paid or accrued by such corporation, and

(C) such corporation's share of the liabilities of such partnership shall be treated as liabilities of such corporation.

(9) REGULATIONS.—The Secretary shall prescribe such regulations as may be appropriate to carry out the purposes of this subsection, including—

(A) such regulations as may be appropriate to prevent the avoidance of the purposes of this subsection,

(B) regulations providing such adjustments in the case of corporations which are members of an affiliated group as may be appropriate to carry out the purposes of this subsection,

(C) regulations for the coordination of this subsection with section 884, *and*

(D) regulations providing for the reallocation of shares of partnership indebtedness, or distributive shares of the partnership's interest income or interest expense.

* * *

[CCH Explanation at ¶840. Committee Reports at ¶10,150.]

Amendments

• **2006, Tax Increase Prevention and Reconciliation Act of 2005 (P.L. 109-222)**

P.L. 109-222, §501(a):

Amended Code Sec. 163(j) by redesignating paragraph (8) as paragraph (9) and by inserting after paragraph (7) a new paragraph (8). **Effective** for tax years beginning on or after 5-17-2006.

P.L. 109-222, §501(b):

Amended Code Sec. 163(j)(9), as redesignated by Act Sec. 501(a), by striking "and" at the end of subparagraph (B), by striking the period at the end of subparagraph (C) and inserting ", and", and by adding at the end a new subparagraph (D). **Effective** for tax years beginning on or after 5-17-2006.

[¶5240] CODE SEC. 164. TAXES.

* * *

(b) DEFINITIONS AND SPECIAL RULES.—For purposes of this section—

* * *

(5) GENERAL SALES TAXES.—For purposes of subsection (a)—

* * *

(I) APPLICATION OF PARAGRAPH.—This paragraph shall apply to taxable years beginning after December 31, 2003, and before January 1, *2008.*

* * *

[CCH Explanation at ¶205. Committee Reports at ¶15,120.]

Amendments

• **2006, Tax Relief and Health Care Act of 2006 (P.L. 109-432)**

P.L. 109-432, Division A, §103(a):

Amended Code Sec. 164(b)(5)(I) by striking "2006" and inserting "2008". **Effective** for tax years beginning after 12-31-2005.

[¶5255] CODE SEC. 167. DEPRECIATION.

* * *

(g) DEPRECIATION UNDER INCOME FORECAST METHOD.—

* * *

(8) SPECIAL RULES FOR CERTAIN MUSICAL WORKS AND COPYRIGHTS.—

(A) IN GENERAL.—*If an election is in effect under this paragraph for any taxable year, then, notwithstanding paragraph (1), any expense which—*

(i) *is paid or incurred by the taxpayer in creating or acquiring any applicable musical property placed in service during the taxable year, and*

(ii) *is otherwise properly chargeable to capital account,*

shall be amortized ratably over the 5-year period beginning with the month in which the property was placed in service. The preceding sentence shall not apply to any expense which, without regard to this paragraph, would not be allowable as a deduction.

(B) EXCLUSIVE METHOD.—*Except as provided in this paragraph, no depreciation or amortization deduction shall be allowed with respect to any expense to which subparagraph (A) applies.*

(C) APPLICABLE MUSICAL PROPERTY.—*For purposes of this paragraph—*

(i) IN GENERAL.—*The term "applicable musical property" means any musical composition (including any accompanying words), or any copyright with respect to a musical composition, which is property to which this subsection applies without regard this paragraph.*

(ii) EXCEPTIONS.—*Such term shall not include any property—*

(I) *with respect to which expenses are treated as qualified creative expenses to which section 263A(h) applies,*

(II) *to which a simplified procedure established under section 263A(j)(2) applies, or*

(III) *which is an amortizable section 197 intangible (as defined in section 197(c)).*

(D) ELECTION.—*An election under this paragraph shall be made at such time and in such form as the Secretary may prescribe and shall apply to all applicable musical property placed in service during the taxable year for which the election applies.*

(E) TERMINATION.—*An election may not be made under this paragraph for any taxable year beginning after December 31, 2010.*

[CCH Explanation at ¶815. Committee Reports at ¶10,090.]

Amendments

• **2006, Tax Increase Prevention and Reconciliation Act of 2005 (P.L. 109-222)**

P.L. 109-222, §207(a):

Amended Code Sec. 167(g) by adding at the end a new paragraph (8). **Effective** for expenses paid or incurred with respect to property placed in service in tax years beginning after 12-31-2005.

(h) AMORTIZATION OF GEOLOGICAL AND GEOPHYSICAL EXPENDITURES.—

* * *

(5) SPECIAL RULE FOR MAJOR INTEGRATED OIL COMPANIES.—

(A) IN GENERAL.—In the case of a major integrated oil company, paragraphs (1) and (4) shall be applied by substituting "5-year" for "24 month".

(B) MAJOR INTEGRATED OIL COMPANY.—For purposes of this paragraph, the term "major integrated oil company" means, with respect to any taxable year, a producer of crude oil—

(i) which has an average daily worldwide production of crude oil of at least 500,000 barrels for the taxable year,

(ii) which had gross receipts in excess of $1,000,000,000 for its last taxable year ending during calendar year 2005, and

(iii) to which subsection (c) of section 613A does not apply by reason of paragraph (4) of section 613A(d), determined—

(I) by substituting "15 percent" for "5 percent" each place it occurs in paragraph (3) of section 613A(d), and

(II) without regard to whether subsection (c) of section 613A does not apply by reason of paragraph (2) of section 613A(d).

For purposes of clauses (i) and (ii), all persons treated as a single employer under subsections (a) and (b) of section 52 shall be treated as 1 person and, in case of a short taxable year, the rule under section 448(c)(3)(B) shall apply.

* * *

[CCH Explanation at ¶ 820. Committee Reports at ¶ 10,170.]
Amendments
• **2006, Tax Increase Prevention and Reconciliation Act of 2005 (P.L. 109-222)**

P.L. 109-222, § 503(a):

Amended Code Sec. 167(h) by adding at the end a new paragraph (5). **Effective** for amounts paid or incurred after 5-17-2006.

[¶ 5265] CODE SEC. 168. ACCELERATED COST RECOVERY SYSTEM.

* * *

(e) CLASSIFICATION OF PROPERTY.—For purposes of this section—

* * *

(3) CLASSIFICATION OF CERTAIN PROPERTY.—

* * *

(E) 15-YEAR PROPERTY.—The term "15-year property" includes—

(i) any municipal wastewater treatment plant,

(ii) any telephone distribution plant and comparable equipment used for 2-way exchange of voice and data communications,

(iii) any section 1250 property which is a retail motor fuels outlet (whether or not food or other convenience items are sold at the outlet),

(iv) any qualified leasehold improvement property placed in service before January 1, *2008,*

(v) any qualified restaurant property placed in service before January 1, *2008,*

(vi) initial clearing and grading land improvements with respect to gas utility property,

(vii) any section 1245 property (as defined in section 1245(a)(3)) used in the transmission at 69 or more kilovolts of electricity for sale and the original use of which commences with the taxpayer after April 11, 2005, and

(viii) any natural gas distribution line the original use of which commences with the taxpayer after April 11, 2005, and which is placed in service before January 1, 2011.

* * *

[CCH Explanation at ¶ 305. Committee Reports at ¶ 15,220.]
Amendments
- **2006, Tax Relief and Health Care Act of 2006 (P.L. 109-432)**

P.L. 109-432, Division A, § 113(a):

Amended Code Sec. 168(e)(3)(E)(iv)-(v) by striking "2006" and inserting "2008". **Effective** for property placed in service after 12-31-2005.

(j) PROPERTY ON INDIAN RESERVATIONS.—

* * *

(8) TERMINATION.—This subsection shall not apply to property placed in service after December 31, *2007.*

* * *

[CCH Explanation at ¶ 320. Committee Reports at ¶ 15,210.]
Amendments
- **2006, Tax Relief and Health Care Act of 2006 (P.L. 109-432)**

P.L. 109-432, Division A, § 112(a):

Amended Code Sec. 168(j)(8) by striking "2005" and inserting "2007". **Effective** for property placed in service after 12-31-2005.

(l) SPECIAL ALLOWANCE FOR CELLULOSIC BIOMASS ETHANOL PLANT PROPERTY.—

(1) ADDITIONAL ALLOWANCE.—In the case of any qualified cellulosic biomass ethanol plant property—

(A) the depreciation deduction provided by section 167(a) for the taxable year in which such property is placed in service shall include an allowance equal to 50 percent of the adjusted basis of such property, and

(B) the adjusted basis of such property shall be reduced by the amount of such deduction before computing the amount otherwise allowable as a depreciation deduction under this chapter for such taxable year and any subsequent taxable year.

(2) QUALIFIED CELLULOSIC BIOMASS ETHANOL PLANT PROPERTY.—The term "qualified cellulosic biomass ethanol plant property" means property of a character subject to the allowance for depreciation—

(A) which is used in the United States solely to produce cellulosic biomass ethanol,

(B) the original use of which commences with the taxpayer after the date of the enactment of this subsection,

(C) which is acquired by the taxpayer by purchase (as defined in section 179(d)) after the date of the enactment of this subsection, but only if no written binding contract for the acquisition was in effect on or before the date of the enactment of this subsection, and

(D) which is placed in service by the taxpayer before January 1, 2013.

(3) CELLULOSIC BIOMASS ETHANOL.—For purposes of this subsection, the term "cellulosic biomass ethanol" means ethanol produced by enzymatic hydrolysis of any lignocellulosic or hemicellulosic matter that is available on a renewable or recurring basis.

(4) EXCEPTIONS.—

(A) ALTERNATIVE DEPRECIATION PROPERTY.—Such term shall not include any property described in section 168(k)(2)(D)(i).

(B) TAX-EXEMPT BOND-FINANCED PROPERTY.—Such term shall not include any property any portion of which is financed with the proceeds of any obligation the interest on which is exempt from tax under section 103.

(C) ELECTION OUT.—If a taxpayer makes an election under this subparagraph with respect to any class of property for any taxable year, this subsection shall not apply to all property in such class placed in service during such taxable year.

(5) SPECIAL RULES.—For purposes of this subsection, rules similar to the rules of subparagraph (E) of section 168(k)(2) shall apply, except that such subparagraph shall be applied—

(A) by substituting "the date of the enactment of subsection (l)" for "September 10, 2001" each place it appears therein,

(B) by substituting "January 1, 2013" for "January 1, 2005" in clause (i) thereof, and

(C) by substituting "qualified cellulosic biomass ethanol plant property" for "qualified property" in clause (iv) thereof.

(6) ALLOWANCE AGAINST ALTERNATIVE MINIMUM TAX.—For purposes of this subsection, rules similar to the rules of section 168(k)(2)(G) shall apply.

(7) RECAPTURE.—For purposes of this subsection, rules similar to the rules under section 179(d)(10) shall apply with respect to any qualified cellulosic biomass ethanol plant property which ceases to be qualified cellulosic biomass ethanol plant property.

(8) DENIAL OF DOUBLE BENEFIT.—Paragraph (1) shall not apply to any qualified cellulosic biomass ethanol plant property with respect to which an election has been made under section 179C (relating to election to expense certain refineries).

[CCH Explanation at ¶323. Committee Reports at ¶15,430.]
Amendments
• 2006, Tax Relief and Health Care Act of 2006 (P.L. 109-432)

P.L. 109-432, Division A, §209(a):

Amended Code Sec. 168 by adding at the end a new subsection (l). **Effective** for property placed in service after 12-20-2006 in tax years ending after such date.

[¶5280] CODE SEC. 170. CHARITABLE, ETC., CONTRIBUTIONS AND GIFTS.
* * *

(e) CERTAIN CONTRIBUTIONS OF ORDINARY INCOME AND CAPITAL GAIN PROPERTY.—

(1) GENERAL RULE.—The amount of any charitable contribution of property otherwise taken into account under this section shall be reduced by the sum of—

(A) the amount of gain which would not have been long-term capital gain (determined without regard to section 1221(b)(3)) if the property contributed had been sold by the taxpayer at its fair market value (determined at the time of such contribution), and

* * *

(4) SPECIAL RULE FOR CONTRIBUTIONS OF SCIENTIFIC PROPERTY USED FOR RESEARCH.—

* * *

(B) QUALIFIED RESEARCH CONTRIBUTIONS.—For purposes of this paragraph, the term "qualified research contribution" means a charitable contribution by a corporation of tangible personal property described in paragraph (1) of section 1221(a), but only if—

(i) the contribution is to an organization described in subparagraph (A) or subparagraph (B) of section 41(e)(6),

(ii) the property is constructed or assembled by the taxpayer,

(iii) the contribution is made not later than 2 years after the date the construction or assembly of the property is substantially completed,

(iv) the original use of the property is by the donee,

(v) the property is scientific equipment or apparatus substantially all of the use of which by the donee is for research or experimentation (within the meaning of section 174), or for research training, in the United States in physical or biological sciences,

(vi) the property is not transferred by the donee in exchange for money, other property, or services, and

(vii) the taxpayer receives from the donee a written statement representing that its use and disposition of the property will be in accordance with the provisions of clauses (v) and (vi).

* * *

(6) SPECIAL RULE FOR CONTRIBUTIONS OF COMPUTER TECHNOLOGY AND EQUIPMENT FOR EDUCATIONAL PURPOSES.—

* * *

(B) QUALIFIED COMPUTER CONTRIBUTION.—For purposes of this paragraph, the term "qualified computer contribution" means a charitable contribution by a corporation of any computer technology or equipment, but only if—

(i) the contribution is to—

(I) an educational organization described in subsection (b)(1)(A)(ii),

(II) an entity described in section 501(c)(3) and exempt from tax under section 501(a) (other than an entity described in subclause (I)) that is organized primarily for purposes of supporting elementary and secondary education, or

(III) a public library (within the meaning of section 213(2)(A) of the Library Services and Technology Act (20 U.S.C. 9122(2)(A)), as in effect on the date of the enactment of the Community Renewal Tax Relief Act of 2000), established and maintained by an entity described in subsection (c)(1),

(ii) the contribution is made not later than 3 years after the date the taxpayer acquired the property (or in the case of property constructed *or assembled* by the taxpayer, the date the construction *or assembling* of the property is substantially completed),

(iii) the original use of the property is by the donor or the donee,

(iv) substantially all of the use of the property by the donee is for use within the United States for educational purposes that are related to the purpose or function of the donee,

(v) the property is not transferred by the donee in exchange for money, other property, or services, except for shipping, installation and transfer costs,

(vi) the property will fit productively into the donee's education plan,

(vii) the donee's use and disposition of the property will be in accordance with the provisions of clauses (iv) and (v), and

(viii) the property meets such standards, if any, as the Secretary may prescribe by regulation to assure that the property meets minimum functionality and suitability standards for educational purposes.

* * *

(D) DONATIONS OF PROPERTY REACQUIRED BY MANUFACTURER.—In the case of property which is reacquired by the person who constructed *or assembled* the property—

(i) subparagraph (B)(ii) shall be applied to a contribution of such property by such person by taking into account the date that the original construction *or assembly* of the property was substantially completed, and

(ii) subparagraph (B)(iii) shall not apply to such contribution.

* * *

(G) TERMINATION.—This paragraph shall not apply to any contribution made during any taxable year beginning after December 31, *2007*.

* * *

[CCH Explanation at ¶ 240 and ¶ 355. Committee Reports at ¶ 10,060, ¶ 15,250 and ¶ 15,570.]

Amendments

- **2006, Tax Relief and Health Care Act of 2006 (P.L. 109-432)**

P.L. 109-432, Division A, § 116(a)(1):

Amended Code Sec. 170(e)(6)(G) by striking "2005" and inserting "2007". **Effective** for contributions made in tax years beginning after 12-31-2005.

P.L. 109-432, Division A, § 116(b)(1)(A):

Amended Code Sec. 170(e)(4)(B)(ii) by inserting "or assembled" after "constructed". **Effective** for tax years beginning after 12-31-2005.

P.L. 109-432, Division A, § 116(b)(1)(B):

Amended Code Sec. 170(e)(4)(B)(iii) by inserting "or assembly" after "construction". **Effective** for tax years beginning after 12-31-2005.

P.L. 109-432, Division A, § 116(b)(2)(A):

Amended Code Sec. 170(e)(6)(B)(ii) by inserting "or assembled" after "constructed" and "or assembling" after

"construction". **Effective** for tax years beginning after 12-31-2005.

P.L. 109-432, Division A, § 116(b)(2)(B):

Amended Code Sec. 170(e)(6)(D) by inserting "or assembled" after "constructed" and "or assembly" after "construction". **Effective** for tax years beginning after 12-31-2005.

- **2006, Tax Increase Prevention and Reconciliation Act of 2005 (P.L. 109-222)**

P.L. 109-222, § 204(b):

Amended Code Sec. 170(e)(1)(A) by inserting "(determined without regard to section 1221(b)(3))" after "long-term capital gain". **Effective** for sales and exchanges in tax years beginning after 5-17-2006.

[¶ 5305] CODE SEC. 179. ELECTION TO EXPENSE CERTAIN DEPRECIABLE BUSINESS ASSETS.

* * *

(b) LIMITATIONS.—

(1) DOLLAR LIMITATION.—The aggregate cost which may be taken into account under subsection (a) for any taxable year shall not exceed $25,000 ($100,000 in the case of taxable years beginning after 2002 and before *2010*).

(2) REDUCTION IN LIMITATION.—The limitation under paragraph (1) for any taxable year shall be reduced (but not below zero) by the amount by which the cost of section 179 property placed in service during such taxable year exceeds $200,000 ($400,000 in the case of taxable years beginning after 2002 and before *2010*).

* * *

(5) INFLATION ADJUSTMENTS.—

(A) IN GENERAL.—In the case of any taxable year beginning in a calendar year after 2003 and before *2010*, the $100,000 and $400,000 amounts in paragraphs (1) and (2) shall each be increased by an amount equal to—

(i) such dollar amount, multiplied by

(ii) the cost-of-living adjustment determined under section 1(f)(3) for the calendar year in which the taxable year begins, by substituting "calendar year 2002" for "calendar year 1992" in subparagraph (B) thereof.

* * *

[CCH Explanation at ¶ 805. Committee Reports at ¶ 10,010.]

Amendments

• 2006, Tax Increase Prevention and Reconciliation
Act of 2005 (P.L. 109-222)

P.L. 109-222, § 101:

Amended Code Sec. 179(b)(1), (b)(2) and (b)(5) by striking
"2008" and inserting "2010". **Effective** 5-17-2006.

(c) ELECTION.—

* * *

(2) ELECTION IRREVOCABLE.—Any election made under this section, and any specification contained in any such election, may not be revoked except with the consent of the Secretary. Any such election or specification with respect to any taxable year beginning after 2002 and before *2010* may be revoked by the taxpayer with respect to any property, and such revocation, once made, shall be irrevocable.

[CCH Explanation at ¶ 805. Committee Reports at ¶ 10,010.]

Amendments

• 2006, Tax Increase Prevention and Reconciliation
Act of 2005 (P.L. 109-222)

P.L. 109-222, § 101:

Amended Code Sec. 179(c)(2) by striking "2008" and inserting "2010". **Effective** 5-17-2006.

(d) DEFINITIONS AND SPECIAL RULES.—

(1) SECTION 179 PROPERTY.—For purposes of this section, the term "section 179 property" means property—

(A) which is—

* * *

(ii) computer software (as defined in section 197(e)(3)(B)) which is described in section 197(e)(3)(A)(i), to which section 167 applies, and which is placed in service in a taxable year beginning after 2002 and before *2010*,

* * *

Such term shall not include any property described in section 50(b) and shall not include air conditioning or heating units.

* * *

[CCH Explanation at ¶ 805. Committee Reports at ¶ 10,010.]

Amendments

• 2006, Tax Increase Prevention and Reconciliation
Act of 2005 (P.L. 109-222)

P.L. 109-222, § 101:

Amended Code Sec. 179(d)(1)(A)(ii) by striking "2008" and inserting "2010". **Effective** 5-17-2006.

[¶ 5310] CODE SEC. 179D. ENERGY EFFICIENT COMMERCIAL BUILDINGS DEDUCTION.

* * *

(h) TERMINATION.—This section shall not apply with respect to property placed in service after *December 31, 2008.*

[CCH Explanation at ¶335. Committee Reports at ¶15,380.]

Amendments

• 2006, Tax Relief and Health Care Act of 2006
(P.L. 109-432)

P.L. 109-432, Division A, §204:

Amended Code Sec. 179D(h) by striking "December 31, 2007" and inserting "December 31, 2008". **Effective** 12-20-2006.

[¶5315] CODE SEC. 179E. ELECTION TO EXPENSE ADVANCED MINE SAFETY EQUIPMENT.

(a) TREATMENT AS EXPENSES.—A taxpayer may elect to treat 50 percent of the cost of any qualified advanced mine safety equipment property as an expense which is not chargeable to capital account. Any cost so treated shall be allowed as a deduction for the taxable year in which the qualified advanced mine safety equipment property is placed in service.

(b) ELECTION.—

(1) IN GENERAL.—An election under this section for any taxable year shall be made on the taxpayer's return of the tax imposed by this chapter for the taxable year. Such election shall specify the advanced mine safety equipment property to which the election applies and shall be made in such manner as the Secretary may by regulations prescribe.

(2) ELECTION IRREVOCABLE.—Any election made under this section may not be revoked except with the consent of the Secretary.

(c) QUALIFIED ADVANCED MINE SAFETY EQUIPMENT PROPERTY.—For purposes of this section, the term "qualified advanced mine safety equipment property" means any advanced mine safety equipment property for use in any underground mine located in the United States—

(1) the original use of which commences with the taxpayer, and

(2) which is placed in service by the taxpayer after the date of the enactment of this section.

(d) ADVANCED MINE SAFETY EQUIPMENT PROPERTY.—For purposes of this section, the term "advanced mine safety equipment property" means any of the following:

(1) Emergency communication technology or device which is used to allow a miner to maintain constant communication with an individual who is not in the mine.

(2) Electronic identification and location device which allows an individual who is not in the mine to track at all times the movements and location of miners working in or at the mine.

(3) Emergency oxygen-generating, self-rescue device which provides oxygen for at least 90 minutes.

(4) Pre-positioned supplies of oxygen which (in combination with self-rescue devices) can be used to provide each miner on a shift, in the event of an accident or other event which traps the miner in the mine or otherwise necessitates the use of such a self-rescue device, the ability to survive for at least 48 hours.

(5) Comprehensive atmospheric monitoring system which monitors the levels of carbon monoxide, methane, and oxygen that are present in all areas of the mine and which can detect smoke in the case of a fire in a mine.

(e) COORDINATION WITH SECTION 179.—No expenditures shall be taken into account under subsection (a) with respect to the portion of the cost of any property specified in an election under section 179.

(f) REPORTING.—No deduction shall be allowed under subsection (a) to any taxpayer for any taxable year unless such taxpayer files with the Secretary a report containing such information with respect to the operation of the mines of the taxpayer as the Secretary shall require.

(g) TERMINATION.—This section shall not apply to property placed in service after December 31, 2008.

[CCH Explanation at ¶330. Committee Reports at ¶15,490.]

Amendments

• **2006, Tax Relief and Health Care Act of 2006 (P.L. 109-432)**

P.L. 109-432, Division A, §404(a):

Amended part VI of subchapter B of chapter 1 by inserting after Code Sec. 179D a new Code Sec. 179E. **Effective** for costs paid or incurred after 12-20-2006.

[¶5320] CODE SEC. 198. EXPENSING OF ENVIRONMENTAL REMEDIATION COSTS.

* * *

(d) HAZARDOUS SUBSTANCE.—For purposes of this section—

(1) IN GENERAL.—The term "hazardous substance" means—

(A) any substance which is a hazardous substance as defined in section 101(14) of the Comprehensive Environmental Response, Compensation, and Liability Act of 1980,

(B) any substance which is designated as a hazardous substance under section 102 of such Act, *and*

(C) *any petroleum product (as defined in section 4612(a)(3)).*

* * *

[CCH Explanation at ¶310. Committee Reports at ¶15,180.]

Amendments

• **2006, Tax Relief and Health Care Act of 2006 (P.L. 109-432)**

P.L. 109-432, Division A, §109(b):

Amended Code Sec. 198(d)(1) by striking "and" at the end of subparagraph (A), by striking the period at the end of subparagraph (B) and inserting ", and", and by adding at the end a new subparagraph (C). **Effective** for expenditures paid or incurred after 12-31-2005.

(h) TERMINATION.—This section shall not apply to expenditures paid or incurred after December 31, *2007.*

[CCH Explanation at ¶310. Committee Reports at ¶15,180.]

Amendments

• **2006, Tax Relief and Health Care Act of 2006 (P.L. 109-432)**

P.L. 109-432, Division A, §109(a):

Amended Code Sec. 198(h) by striking "2005" and inserting "2007". **Effective** for expenditures paid or incurred after 12-31-2005.

[¶5330] CODE SEC. 199. INCOME ATTRIBUTABLE TO DOMESTIC PRODUCTION ACTIVITIES.

(a) ALLOWANCE OF DEDUCTION.—

* * *

(2) PHASEIN.—In the case of any taxable year beginning after 2004 and before 2010, paragraph (1) shall be applied by substituting for the percentage contained therein the transition percentage determined under the following table:

For taxable years beginning in:	The transition percentage is:
2005 or 2006	3
2007, 2008, or 2009	6

[CCH Explanation at ¶810. Committee Reports at ¶10,280.]

Amendments

• **2006, Tax Increase Prevention and Reconciliation Act of 2005 (P.L. 109-222)**

P.L. 109-222, §514(b)(2):

Amended Code Sec. 199(a)(2) by striking "and subsection (d)(1)" after "paragraph (1)". **Effective** for tax years beginning after 5-17-2006.

(b) DEDUCTION LIMITED TO WAGES PAID.—

* * *

(2) W-2 WAGES.—For purposes of this section—

(A) IN GENERAL.—The term "W-2 wages" means, with respect to any person for any taxable year of such person, the sum of the amounts described in paragraphs (3) and (8) of section 6051(a) paid by such person with respect to employment of employees by such person during the calendar year ending during such taxable year.

(B) LIMITATION TO WAGES ATTRIBUTABLE TO DOMESTIC PRODUCTION.—Such term shall not include any amount which is not properly allocable to domestic production gross receipts for purposes of subsection (c)(1).

(C) RETURN REQUIREMENT.—Such term shall not include any amount which is not properly included in a return filed with the Social Security Administration on or before the 60th day after the due date (including extensions) for such return.

* * *

[CCH Explanation at ¶810. Committee Reports at ¶10,280.]

Amendments

• **2006, Tax Increase Prevention and Reconciliation Act of 2005 (P.L. 109-222)**

P.L. 109-222, §514(a):

Amended Code Sec. 199(b)(2). **Effective** for tax years beginning after 5-17-2006. Prior to amendment, Code Sec. 199(b)(2) read as follows:

(2) W-2 WAGES.—For purposes of this section, the term "W-2 wages" means, with respect to any person for any taxable year of such person, the sum of the amounts described in paragraphs (3) and (8) of section 6051(a) paid by such person with respect to employment of employees by such person during the calendar year ending during such taxable year. Such term shall not include any amount which is not properly included in a return filed with the Social Security Administration on or before the 60th day after the due date (including extensions) for such return.

(d) DEFINITIONS AND SPECIAL RULES.—

(1) APPLICATION OF SECTION TO PASS-THRU ENTITIES.—

(A) PARTNERSHIPS AND S CORPORATIONS.—In the case of a partnership or S corporation—

(i) this section shall be applied at the partner or shareholder level,

(ii) each partner or shareholder shall take into account such person's allocable share of each item described in subparagraph (A) or (B) of subsection (c)(1) (determined without regard to whether the items described in such subparagraph (A) exceed the items described in such subparagraph (B)), and

(iii) each partner or shareholder shall be treated for purposes of subsection (b) as having W-2 wages for the taxable year in an amount equal to such person's allocable share of the W-2 wages of the partnership or S corporation for the taxable year (as determined under regulations prescribed by the Secretary).

* * *

(8) TREATMENT OF ACTIVITIES IN PUERTO RICO.—

(A) IN GENERAL.—In the case of any taxpayer with gross receipts for any taxable year from sources within the Commonwealth of Puerto Rico, if all of such receipts are taxable under section 1 or 11 for such taxable year, then for purposes of determining the domestic production gross receipts of

such taxpayer for such taxable year under subsection (c)(4), the term "United States" shall include the Commonwealth of Puerto Rico.

(B) SPECIAL RULE FOR APPLYING WAGE LIMITATION.—In the case of any taxpayer described in subparagraph (A), for purposes of applying the limitation under subsection (b) for any taxable year, the determination of W-2 wages of such taxpayer shall be made without regard to any exclusion under section 3401(a)(8) for remuneration paid for services performed in Puerto Rico.

(C) TERMINATION.—This paragraph shall apply only with respect to the first 2 taxable years of the taxpayer beginning after December 31, 2005, and before January 1, 2008.

(9) REGULATIONS.—The Secretary shall prescribe such regulations as are necessary to carry out the purposes of this section, including regulations which prevent more than 1 taxpayer from being allowed a deduction under this section with respect to any activity described in subsection (c)(4)(A)(i).

[CCH Explanation at ¶345 and ¶810. Committee Reports at ¶10,280 and ¶15,470.]

Amendments

• **2006, Tax Relief and Health Care Act of 2006 (P.L. 109-432)**

P.L. 109-432, Division A, §401(a):

Amended Code Sec. 199(d) by redesignating paragraph (8) as paragraph (9) and by inserting after paragraph (7) a new paragraph (8). **Effective** for tax years beginning after 12-31-2005.

• **2006, Tax Increase Prevention and Reconciliation Act of 2005 (P.L. 109-222)**

P.L. 109-222, §514(b)(1):

Amended Code Sec. 199(d)(1)(A)(iii). **Effective** for tax years beginning after 5-17-2006. Prior to amendment, Code Sec. 199(d)(1)(A)(iii) read as follows:

(iii) each partner or shareholder shall be treated for purposes of subsection (b) as having W-2 wages for the taxable year in an amount equal to the lesser of—

(I) such person's allocable share of the W-2 wages of the partnership or S corporation for the taxable year (as determined under regulations prescribed by the Secretary), or

(II) 2 times 9 percent of so much of such person's qualified production activities income as is attributable to items allocated under clause (ii) for the taxable year.

[¶5333] CODE SEC. 220. ARCHER MSAs.

* * *

(i) LIMITATION ON NUMBER OF TAXPAYERS HAVING ARCHER MSAs.—

* * *

(2) CUT-OFF YEAR.—For purposes of paragraph (1), the term "cut-off year" means the earlier of—

(A) calendar year 2007, or

(B) the first calendar year before 2007 for which the Secretary determines under subsection (j) that the numerical limitation for such year has been exceeded.

(3) ACTIVE MSA PARTICIPANT.—For purposes of this subsection—

* * *

(B) SPECIAL RULE FOR CUT-OFF YEARS BEFORE 2007.—In the case of a cut-off year before 2007—

(i) an individual shall not be treated as an eligible individual for any month of such year or an active MSA participant under paragraph (1)(A) unless such individual is, on or before the cut-off date, covered under a high deductible health plan, and

(ii) an employer shall not be treated as an MSA-participating employer unless the employer, on or before the cut-off date, offered coverage under a high deductible health plan to any employee.

* * *

[CCH Explanation at ¶ 530. Committee Reports at ¶ 15,260.]

Amendments

• 2006, Tax Relief and Health Care Act of 2006
(P.L. 109-432)

P.L. 109-432, Division A, § 117(a):

Amended Code Sec. 220(i)(2) and (3)(B) by striking "2005" each place it appears in the text and headings [sic] and inserting "2007". **Effective** 12-20-2006.

(j) DETERMINATION OF WHETHER NUMERICAL LIMITS ARE EXCEEDED.—

* * *

(2) DETERMINATION OF WHETHER LIMIT EXCEEDED FOR 1998, 1999, 2001, 2002, *2004, 2005,* OR *2006.*—

(A) IN GENERAL.—The numerical limitation for 1998, 1999, 2001, 2002, *2004, 2005, or 2006* is exceeded if the sum of—

(i) the number of MSA returns filed on or before April 15 of such calendar year for taxable years ending with or within the preceding calendar year, plus

(ii) the Secretary's estimate (determined on the basis of the returns described in clause (i)) of the number of MSA returns for such taxable years which will be filed after such date,

exceeds 750,000 (600,000 in the case of 1998). For purposes of the preceding sentence, the term "MSA return" means any return on which any exclusion is claimed under section 106(b) or any deduction is claimed under this section.

(B) ALTERNATIVE COMPUTATION OF LIMITATION.—The numerical limitation for 1998, 1999, 2001, 2002, *2004, 2005, or 2006* is also exceeded if the sum of—

(i) 90 percent of the sum determined under subparagraph (A) for such calendar year, plus

(ii) the product of 2.5 and the number of Archer MSAs established during the portion of such year preceding July 1 (based on the reports required under paragraph (4)) for taxable years beginning in such year,

exceeds 750,000.

* * *

(4) REPORTING BY MSA TRUSTEES.—

(A) IN GENERAL.—Not later than August 1 of 1997, 1998, 1999, 2001, 2002, *2004, 2005, and 2006,* each person who is the trustee of an Archer MSA established before July 1 of such calendar year shall make a report to the Secretary (in such form and manner as the Secretary shall specify) which specifies—

(i) the number of Archer MSAs established before such July 1 (for taxable years beginning in such calendar year) of which such person is the trustee,

(ii) the name and TIN of the account holder of each such account, and

(iii) the number of such accounts which are accounts of previously uninsured individuals.

* * *

[CCH Explanation at ¶ 530. Committee Reports at ¶ 15,260.]

Amendments

• 2006, Tax Relief and Health Care Act of 2006
(P.L. 109-432)

P.L. 109-432, Division A, § 117(b)(1)(A)-(B):

Amended Code Sec. 220(j)(2) by striking "or 2004" each place it appears in the text and inserting "2004, 2005, or

2006", and by striking "OR 2004" in the heading and inserting "2004, 2005, OR 2006". **Effective** 12-20-2006.

P.L. 109-432, Division A, § 117(b)(2):

Amended Code Sec. 220(j)(4)(A) by striking "and 2004" and inserting "2004, 2005, and 2006". **Effective** 12-20-2006.

P.L. 109-432, Division A, §117(c), provides:

(c) TIME FOR FILING REPORTS, ETC.—

(1) The report required by section 220(j)(4) of the Internal Revenue Code of 1986 to be made on August 1, 2005, or August 1, 2006, as the case may be, shall be treated as timely if made before the close of the 90-day period beginning on the date of the enactment of this Act.

(2) The determination and publication required by section 220(j)(5) of such Code with respect to calendar year 2005 or calendar year 2006, as the case may be, shall be treated as timely if made before the close of the 120-day period beginning on the date of the enactment of this Act. If the determination under the preceding sentence is that 2005 or 2006 is a cut-off year under section 220(i) of such Code, the cut-off date under such section 220(i) shall be the last day of such 120-day period.

[¶5336] CODE SEC. 222. QUALIFIED TUITION AND RELATED EXPENSES.

* * *

(b) DOLLAR LIMITATIONS.—

* * *

(2) APPLICABLE DOLLAR LIMIT.—

* * *

(B) *AFTER 2003.*—In the case of *any taxable year beginning after 2003*, the applicable dollar amount shall be equal to—

(i) in the case of a taxpayer whose adjusted gross income for the taxable year does not exceed $65,000 ($130,000 in the case of a joint return), $4,000,

(ii) in the case of a taxpayer not described in clause (i) whose adjusted gross income for the taxable year does not exceed $80,000 ($160,000 in the case of a joint return), $2,000, and

(iii) in the case of any other taxpayer, zero.

* * *

[CCH Explanation at ¶210. Committee Reports at ¶15,100.]

Amendments

• **2006, Tax Relief and Health Care Act of 2006 (P.L. 109-432)**

P.L. 109-432, Division A, §101(b)(1)-(2):

Amended Code Sec. 222(b)(2)(B) by striking "a taxable year beginning in 2004 or 2005" and inserting "any taxable year beginning after 2003", and by striking "2004 AND 2005" in the heading and inserting "AFTER 2003". Effective for tax years beginning after 12-31-2005.

(e) TERMINATION.—This section shall not apply to taxable years beginning after December 31, 2007.

[CCH Explanation at ¶210. Committee Reports at ¶15,100.]

Amendments

• **2006, Tax Relief and Health Care Act of 2006 (P.L. 109-432)**

P.L. 109-432, Division A, §101(a):

Amended Code Sec. 222(e) by striking "2005" and inserting "2007". Effective for tax years beginning after 12-31-2005.

[¶5339] CODE SEC. 223. HEALTH SAVINGS ACCOUNTS.

* * *

(b) LIMITATIONS.—

* * *

(2) MONTHLY LIMITATION.—The monthly limitation for any month is $1/12$ of—

(A) in the case of an eligible individual who has self-only coverage under a high deductible health plan as of the first day of such month, *$2,250.*

(B) in the case of an eligible individual who has family coverage under a high deductible health plan as of the first day of such month, *$4,500.*

* * *

(4) COORDINATION WITH OTHER CONTRIBUTIONS.—The limitation which would (but for this paragraph) apply under this subsection to an individual for any taxable year shall be reduced (but not below zero) by the sum of—

(A) the aggregate amount paid for such taxable year to Archer MSAs of such individual,

(B) the aggregate amount contributed to health savings accounts of such individual which is excludable from the taxpayer's gross income for such taxable year under section 106(d) (and such amount shall not be allowed as a deduction under subsection (a)), *and*

(C) *the aggregate amount contributed to health savings accounts of such individual for such taxable year under section 408(d)(9) (and such amount shall not be allowed as a deduction under subsection (a)).*

Subparagraph (A) shall not apply with respect to any individual to whom paragraph (5) applies.

* * *

(8) INCREASE IN LIMIT FOR INDIVIDUALS BECOMING ELIGIBLE INDIVIDUALS AFTER THE BEGINNING OF THE YEAR.—

(A) IN GENERAL.—For purposes of computing the limitation under paragraph (1) for any taxable year, an individual who is an eligible individual during the last month of such taxable year shall be treated—

(i) as having been an eligible individual during each of the months in such taxable year, and

(ii) as having been enrolled, during each of the months such individual is treated as an eligible individual solely by reason of clause (i), in the same high deductible health plan in which the individual was enrolled for the last month of such taxable year.

(B) FAILURE TO MAINTAIN HIGH DEDUCTIBLE HEALTH PLAN COVERAGE.—

(i) IN GENERAL.—If, at any time during the testing period, the individual is not an eligible individual, then—

(I) gross income of the individual for the taxable year in which occurs the first month in the testing period for which such individual is not an eligible individual is increased by the aggregate amount of all contributions to the health savings account of the individual which could not have been made but for subparagraph (A), and

(II) the tax imposed by this chapter for any taxable year on the individual shall be increased by 10 percent of the amount of such increase.

(ii) EXCEPTION FOR DISABILITY OR DEATH.—Subclauses (I) and (II) of clause (i) shall not apply if the individual ceased to be an eligible individual by reason of the death of the individual or the individual becoming disabled (within the meaning of section 72(m)(7)).

(iii) TESTING PERIOD.—The term "testing period" means the period beginning with the last month of the taxable year referred to in subparagraph (A) and ending on the last day of the 12th month following such month.

[CCH Explanation at ¶ 510, ¶ 515 and ¶ 525. Committee Reports at ¶ 15,460.]

Amendments

• **2006, Tax Relief and Health Care Act of 2006 (P.L. 109-432)**

P.L. 109-432, Division A, § 303(a)(1)-(2):

Amended Code Sec. 223(b)(2) by striking "the lesser of—" and all that follows and inserting "$2,250." in subparagraph (A), and by striking "the lesser of—" and all that follows and inserting "$4,500." in subparagraph (B). **Effective for** tax years beginning after 12-31-2006. Prior to amendment, Code Sec. 223(b)(2) read as follows:

(2) MONTHLY LIMITATION.—The monthly limitation for any month is 1/12 of—

(A) in the case of an eligible individual who has self-only coverage under a high deductible health plan as of the first day of such month, the lesser of—

(i) the annual deductible under such coverage, or

(ii) $2,250, or

(B) in the case of an eligible individual who has family coverage under a high deductible health plan as of the first day of such month, the lesser of—

(i) the annual deductible under such coverage, or

(ii) $4,500.

P.L. 109-432, Division A, §305(a):

Amended Code Sec. 223(b) by adding at the end a new paragraph (8). **Effective** for tax years beginning after 12-31-2006.

(c) DEFINITIONS AND SPECIAL RULES.—For purposes of this section—

(1) ELIGIBLE INDIVIDUAL.—

* * *

(B) CERTAIN COVERAGE DISREGARDED.—Subparagraph (A)(ii) shall be applied without regard to—

(i) coverage for any benefit provided by permitted insurance,

(ii) coverage (whether through insurance or otherwise) for accidents, disability, dental care, vision care, or long-term care, *and*

(iii) *for taxable years beginning after December 31, 2006, coverage under a health flexible spending arrangement during any period immediately following the end of a plan year of such arrangement during which unused benefits or contributions remaining at the end of such plan year may be paid or reimbursed to plan participants for qualified benefit expenses incurred during such period if—*

(I) *the balance in such arrangement at the end of such plan year is zero, or*

(II) *the individual is making a qualified HSA distribution (as defined in section 106(e)) in an amount equal to the remaining balance in such arrangement as of the end of such plan year, in accordance with rules prescribed by the Secretary.*

* * *

[CCH Explanation at ¶505. Committee Reports at ¶15,460.]

Amendments

• **2006, Tax Relief and Health Care Act of 2006 (P.L. 109-432)**

P.L. 109-432, Division A, §302(b):

Amended Code Sec. 223(c)(1)(B) by striking "and" at the end of clause (i), by striking the period at the end of clause

P.L. 109-432, Division A, §307(b):

Amended Code Sec. 223(b)(4) by striking "and" at the end of subparagraph (A), by striking the period at the end of subparagraph (B) and inserting ", and", and by inserting after subparagraph (B) a new subparagraph (C). **Effective** for tax years beginning after 12-31-2006.

(ii) and inserting ", and", and by inserting after clause (ii) a new clause (iii). **Effective** 12-20-2006.

(d) HEALTH SAVINGS ACCOUNT.—For purposes of this section—

(1) IN GENERAL.—The term "health savings account" means a trust created or organized in the United States as a health savings account exclusively for the purpose of paying the qualified medical expenses of the account beneficiary, but only if the written governing instrument creating the trust meets the following requirements:

(A) Except in the case of a rollover contribution described in subsection (f)(5) or section 220(f)(5), no contribution will be accepted—

(i) unless it is in cash, or

(ii) to the extent such contribution, when added to previous contributions to the trust for the calendar year, exceeds the sum of—

(I) the dollar amount in effect under *subsection (b)(2)(B),* and

(II) the dollar amount in effect under subsection (b)(3)(B).

[CCH Explanation at ¶510. Committee Reports at ¶15,460.]

Amendments
- **2006, Tax Relief and Health Care Act of 2006 (P.L. 109-432)**

P.L. 109-432, Division A, §303(b):

Amended Code Sec. 223(d)(1)(A)(ii)(I) by striking "subsection (b)(2)(B)(ii)" and inserting "subsection (b)(2)(B)". **Effective** for tax years beginning after 12-31-2006.

(g) COST-OF-LIVING ADJUSTMENT.—

(1) IN GENERAL.—Each dollar amount in subsections (b)(2) and (c)(2)(A) shall be increased by an amount equal to—

(A) such dollar amount, multiplied by

(B) the cost-of-living adjustment determined under section 1(f)(3) for the calendar year in which such taxable year begins determined by substituting for "calendar year 1992" in subparagraph (B) thereof—

(i) except as provided in clause (ii), "calendar year 1997", and

(ii) in the case of each dollar amount in subsection (c)(2)(A), "calendar year 2003".

In the case of adjustments made for any taxable year beginning after 2007, section 1(f)(4) shall be applied for purposes of this paragraph by substituting "March 31" for "August 31", and the Secretary shall publish the adjusted amounts under subsections (b)(2) and (c)(2)(A) for taxable years beginning in any calendar year no later than June 1 of the preceding calendar year.

* * *

[CCH Explanation at ¶510. Committee Reports at ¶15,460.]

Amendments
- **2006, Tax Relief and Health Care Act of 2006 (P.L. 109-432)**

P.L. 109-432, Division A, §304:

Amended Code Sec. 223(g)(1) by adding at the end a new flush sentence. **Effective** 12-20-2006.

[¶5341] CODE SEC. 263. CAPITAL EXPENDITURES.

(a) GENERAL RULE.—No deduction shall be allowed for—

(1) Any amount paid out for new buildings or for permanent improvements or betterments made to increase the value of any property or estate. This paragraph shall not apply to—

* * *

(J) expenditures for which a deduction is allowed under section 179C,

(K) expenditures for which a deduction is allowed under section 179D, *or*

(L) *expenditures for which a deduction is allowed under section 179E.*

* * *

[CCH Explanation at ¶330. Committee Reports at ¶15,490.]

Amendments
- **2006, Tax Relief and Health Care Act of 2006 (P.L. 109-432)**

P.L. 109-432, Division A, §404(b)(1):

Amended Code Sec. 263(a)(1) by striking "or" at the end of subparagraph (J), by striking the period at the end of subparagraph (K) and inserting ", or", and by inserting after subparagraph (K) a new subparagraph (L). **Effective** for costs paid or incurred after 12-20-2006.

[¶5344] CODE SEC. 280C. CERTAIN EXPENSES FOR WHICH CREDITS ARE ALLOWABLE.

* * *

(e) MINE RESCUE TEAM TRAINING CREDIT.—*No deduction shall be allowed for that portion of the expenses otherwise allowable as a deduction for the taxable year which is equal to the amount of the credit determined for the taxable year under section 45N(a).*

[CCH Explanation at ¶425. Committee Reports at ¶15,500.]
Amendments
• 2006, Tax Relief and Health Care Act of 2006
(P.L. 109-432)

P.L. 109-432, Division A, §405(c):

Amended Code Sec. 280C by adding at the end a new subsection (e). **Effective** for tax years beginning after 12-31-2005.

[¶5347] CODE SEC. 312. EFFECT ON EARNINGS AND PROFITS.

* * *

(k) EFFECT OF DEPRECIATION ON EARNINGS AND PROFITS.—

* * *

(3) EXCEPTION FOR TANGIBLE PROPERTY.—

* * *

(B) TREATMENT OF AMOUNTS DEDUCTIBLE UNDER SECTION 179, 179A, 179B, 179C, *179D, or 179E.*—For purposes of computing the earnings and profits of a corporation, any amount deductible under section 179, 179A, 179B, 179C, *179D, or 179E* shall be allowed as a deduction ratably over the period of 5 taxable years (beginning with the taxable year for which such amount is deductible under section 179, 179A, 179B, 179C, *179D, or 179E,* as the case may be).

* * *

[CCH Explanation at ¶330. Committee Reports at ¶15,490.]
Amendments
• 2006, Tax Relief and Health Care Act of 2006
(P.L. 109-432)

P.L. 109-432, Division A, §404(b)(2):

Amended Code Sec. 312(k)(3)(B) by striking "or 179D" each place it appears in the heading and text thereof and inserting "179D, or 179E". **Effective** for costs paid or incurred after 12-20-2006.

[¶5355] CODE SEC. 355. DISTRIBUTION OF STOCK AND SECURITIES OF A CONTROLLED CORPORATION.

* * *

(b) REQUIREMENTS AS TO ACTIVE BUSINESS.—

* * *

(3) SPECIAL RULE RELATING TO ACTIVE BUSINESS REQUIREMENT.—

(A) IN GENERAL.—*In the case of any distribution made after the date of the enactment of this paragraph, a corporation shall be treated as meeting the requirement of paragraph (2)(A) if and only if such corporation is engaged in the active conduct of a trade or business.*

(B) AFFILIATED GROUP RULE.—*For purposes of subparagraph (A), all members of such corporation's separate affiliated group shall be treated as one corporation. For purposes of the preceding sentence, a corporation's separate affiliated group is the affiliated group which would be determined under section 1504(a) if such corporation were the common parent and section 1504(b) did not apply.*

(C) TRANSITION RULE.—*Subparagraph (A) shall not apply to any distribution pursuant to a transaction which is—*

(i) *made pursuant to an agreement which was binding on the date of the enactment of this paragraph and at all times thereafter,*

(ii) *described in a ruling request submitted to the Internal Revenue Service on or before such date, or*

(iii) *described on or before such date in a public announcement or in a filing with the Securities and Exchange Commission.*

The preceding sentence shall not apply if the distributing corporation elects not to have such sentence apply to distributions of such corporation. Any such election, once made, shall be irrevocable.

(D) SPECIAL RULE FOR CERTAIN PREENACTMENT DISTRIBUTIONS.—*For purposes of determining the continued qualification under paragraph (2)(A) of distributions made on or before the date of the enactment of this paragraph as a result of an acquisition, disposition, or other restructuring after such date, such distribution shall be treated as made on the date of such acquisition, disposition, or restructuring for purposes of applying subparagraphs (A) through (C) of this paragraph.*

* * *

[CCH Explanation at ¶360. Committee Reports at ¶10,040 and ¶15,550.]

Amendments

• **2006, Tax Relief and Health Care Act of 2006 (P.L. 109-432)**

P.L. 109-432, Division A, §410(a):

Amended Code Sec. 355(b)(3) by striking "and on or before December 31, 2010" after "this paragraph" in subparagraph (A) and after "such date" in subparagraph (D). **Effective** as if included in section 202 of the Tax Increase

Prevention and Reconciliation Act of 2005 (P.L. 109-222) [effective 5-17-2006.—CCH].

• **2006, Tax Increase Prevention and Reconciliation Act of 2005 (P.L. 109-222)**

P.L. 109-222, §202:

Amended Code Sec. 355(b) by adding at the end a new paragraph (3). **Effective** 5-17-2006.

(g) SECTION NOT TO APPLY TO DISTRIBUTIONS INVOLVING DISQUALIFIED INVESTMENT CORPORATIONS.—

(1) IN GENERAL.—*This section (and so much of section 356 as relates to this section) shall not apply to any distribution which is part of a transaction if—*

(A) *either the distributing corporation or controlled corporation is, immediately after the transaction, a disqualified investment corporation, and*

(B) *any person holds, immediately after the transaction, a 50-percent or greater interest in any disqualified investment corporation, but only if such person did not hold such an interest in such corporation immediately before the transaction.*

(2) DISQUALIFIED INVESTMENT CORPORATION.—*For purposes of this subsection—*

(A) IN GENERAL.—*The term "disqualified investment corporation" means any distributing or controlled corporation if the fair market value of the investment assets of the corporation is—*

(i) *in the case of distributions after the end of the 1-year period beginning on the date of the enactment of this subsection, ⅔ or more of the fair market value of all assets of the corporation, and*

(ii) *in the case of distributions during such 1-year period, ¾ or more of the fair market value of all assets of the corporation.*

(B) INVESTMENT ASSETS.—

(i) IN GENERAL.—*Except as otherwise provided in this subparagraph, the term "investment assets" means—*

(I) *cash,*

(II) *any stock or securities in a corporation,*

(III) *any interest in a partnership,*

(IV) *any debt instrument or other evidence of indebtedness,*

(V) *any option, forward or futures contract, notional principal contract, or derivative,*

(VI) *foreign currency, or*

(VII) *any similar asset.*

(ii) EXCEPTION FOR ASSETS USED IN ACTIVE CONDUCT OF CERTAIN FINANCIAL TRADES OR BUSINESSES.—*Such term shall not include any asset which is held for use in the active and regular conduct of—*

(I) a lending or finance business (within the meaning of section 954(h)(4)),

(II) a banking business through a bank (as defined in section 581), a domestic building and loan association (within the meaning of section 7701(a)(19)), or any similar institution specified by the Secretary, or

(III) an insurance business if the conduct of the business is licensed, authorized, or regulated by an applicable insurance regulatory body.

This clause shall only apply with respect to any business if substantially all of the income of the business is derived from persons who are not related (within the meaning of section 267(b) or 707(b)(1)) to the person conducting the business.

(iii) EXCEPTION FOR SECURITIES MARKED TO MARKET.—*Such term shall not include any security (as defined in section 475(c)(2)) which is held by a dealer in securities and to which section 475(a) applies.*

(iv) STOCK OR SECURITIES IN A 20-PERCENT CONTROLLED ENTITY.—

(I) IN GENERAL.—*Such term shall not include any stock and securities in, or any asset described in subclause (IV) or (V) of clause (i) issued by, a corporation which is a 20-percent controlled entity with respect to the distributing or controlled corporation.*

(II) LOOK-THRU RULE.—*The distributing or controlled corporation shall, for purposes of applying this subsection, be treated as owning its ratable share of the assets of any 20-percent controlled entity.*

(III) 20-PERCENT CONTROLLED ENTITY.—*For purposes of this clause, the term "20-percent controlled entity" means, with respect to any distributing or controlled corporation, any corporation with respect to which the distributing or controlled corporation owns directly or indirectly stock meeting the requirements of section 1504(a)(2), except that such section shall be applied by substituting "20 percent" for "80 percent" and without regard to stock described in section 1504(a)(4).*

(v) INTERESTS IN CERTAIN PARTNERSHIPS.—

(I) IN GENERAL.—*Such term shall not include any interest in a partnership, or any debt instrument or other evidence of indebtedness, issued by the partnership, if 1 or more of the trades or businesses of the partnership are (or, without regard to the 5-year requirement under subsection (b)(2)(B), would be) taken into account by the distributing or controlled corporation, as the case may be, in determining whether the requirements of subsection (b) are met with respect to the distribution.*

(II) LOOK-THRU RULE.—*The distributing or controlled corporation shall, for purposes of applying this subsection, be treated as owning its ratable share of the assets of any partnership described in subclause (I).*

(3) 50-PERCENT OR GREATER INTEREST.—*For purposes of this subsection—*

(A) IN GENERAL.—*The term "50-percent or greater interest" has the meaning given such term by subsection (d)(4).*

(B) ATTRIBUTION RULES.—*The rules of section 318 shall apply for purposes of determining ownership of stock for purposes of this paragraph.*

(4) TRANSACTION.—*For purposes of this subsection, the term "transaction" includes a series of transactions.*

(5) REGULATIONS.—*The Secretary shall prescribe such regulations as may be necessary to carry out, or prevent the avoidance of, the purposes of this subsection, including regulations—*

(A) to carry out, or prevent the avoidance of, the purposes of this subsection in cases involving—

(i) the use of related persons, intermediaries, pass-thru entities, options, or other arrangements, and

(ii) the treatment of assets unrelated to the trade or business of a corporation as investment assets if, prior to the distribution, investment assets were used to acquire such unrelated assets,

(B) which in appropriate cases exclude from the application of this subsection a distribution which does not have the character of a redemption which would be treated as a sale or exchange under section 302, and

(C) which modify the application of the attribution rules applied for purposes of this subsection.

[CCH Explanation at ¶ 830. Committee Reports at ¶ 10,210.]

Amendments

• **2006, Tax Increase Prevention and Reconciliation Act of 2005 (P.L. 109-222)**

P.L. 109-222, § 507(a):

Amended Code Sec. 355 by adding at the end a new subsection (g). Effective generally for distributions after 5-17-2006. For a transition rule, see Act Sec. 507(b)(2), below.

P.L. 109-222, § 507(b)(2), provides:

(2) TRANSITION RULE.—The amendments made by this section shall not apply to any distribution pursuant to a transaction which is—

(A) made pursuant to an agreement which was binding on such date of enactment and at all times thereafter,

(B) described in a ruling request submitted to the Internal Revenue Service on or before such date, or

(C) described on or before such date in a public announcement or in a filing with the Securities and Exchange Commission.

[¶ 5370] CODE SEC. 408. INDIVIDUAL RETIREMENT ACCOUNTS.

* * *

(d) TAX TREATMENT OF DISTRIBUTIONS.—

* * *

(9) DISTRIBUTION FOR HEALTH SAVINGS ACCOUNT FUNDING.—

(A) IN GENERAL.—In the case of an individual who is an eligible individual (as defined in section 223(c)) and who elects the application of this paragraph for a taxable year, gross income of the individual for the taxable year does not include a qualified HSA funding distribution to the extent such distribution is otherwise includible in gross income.

(B) QUALIFIED HSA FUNDING DISTRIBUTION.—For purposes of this paragraph, the term "qualified HSA funding distribution" means a distribution from an individual retirement plan (other than a plan described in subsection (k) or (p)) of the employee to the extent that such distribution is contributed to the health savings account of the individual in a direct trustee-to-trustee transfer.

(C) LIMITATIONS.—

(i) MAXIMUM DOLLAR LIMITATION.—The amount excluded from gross income by subparagraph (A) shall not exceed the excess of—

(I) the annual limitation under section 223(b) computed on the basis of the type of coverage under the high deductible health plan covering the individual at the time of the qualified HSA funding distribution, over

(II) in the case of a distribution described in clause (ii)(II), the amount of the earlier qualified HSA funding distribution.

(ii) ONE-TIME TRANSFER.—

(I) IN GENERAL.—Except as provided in subclause (II), an individual may make an election under subparagraph (A) only for one qualified HSA funding distribution during the lifetime of the individual. Such an election, once made, shall be irrevocable.

(II) CONVERSION FROM SELF-ONLY TO FAMILY COVERAGE.—If a qualified HSA funding distribution is made during a month in a taxable year during which an individual has self-only coverage under a high deductible health plan as of the first day of the month, the individual may elect to make an additional qualified HSA funding distribution during a

subsequent month in such taxable year during which the individual has family coverage under a high deductible health plan as of the first day of the subsequent month.

*(D) F*AILURE TO MAINTAIN HIGH DEDUCTIBLE HEALTH PLAN COVERAGE.—

*(i) I*N GENERAL.—*If, at any time during the testing period, the individual is not an eligible individual, then the aggregate amount of all contributions to the health savings account of the individual made under subparagraph (A)—*

(I) shall be includible in the gross income of the individual for the taxable year in which occurs the first month in the testing period for which such individual is not an eligible individual, and

(II) the tax imposed by this chapter for any taxable year on the individual shall be increased by 10 percent of the amount which is so includible.

*(ii) E*XCEPTION FOR DISABILITY OR DEATH.—*Subclauses (I) and (II) of clause (i) shall not apply if the individual ceased to be an eligible individual by reason of the death of the individual or the individual becoming disabled (within the meaning of section 72(m)(7)).*

*(iii) T*ESTING PERIOD.—*The term "testing period" means the period beginning with the month in which the qualified HSA funding distribution is contributed to a health savings account and ending on the last day of the 12th month following such month.*

*(E) A*PPLICATION OF SECTION 72.—*Notwithstanding section 72, in determining the extent to which an amount is treated as otherwise includible in gross income for purposes of subparagraph (A), the aggregate amount distributed from an individual retirement plan shall be treated as includible in gross income to the extent that such amount does not exceed the aggregate amount which would have been so includible if all amounts from all individual retirement plans were distributed. Proper adjustments shall be made in applying section 72 to other distributions in such taxable year and subsequent taxable years.*

* * *

[CCH Explanation at ¶525. Committee Reports at ¶15,460.]
Amendments
• **2006, Tax Relief and Health Care Act of 2006 (P.L. 109-432)**

P.L. 109-432, Division A, §307(a):

Amended Code Sec. 408(d) by adding at the end a new paragraph (9). **Effective** for tax years beginning after 12-31-2006.

[¶5380] CODE SEC. 408A. ROTH IRAS.

* * *

(c) TREATMENT OF CONTRIBUTIONS.—

* * *

(3) LIMITS BASED ON MODIFIED ADJUSTED GROSS INCOME.—

* * *

⇶→ *Caution: Code Sec. 408A(c)(3)(B), below, was stricken by P.L. 109-222, applicable to tax years beginning after December 31, 2009.*

(B) ROLLOVER FROM ELIGIBLE RETIREMENT PLAN.—A taxpayer shall not be allowed to make a qualified rollover contribution to a Roth IRA from an an [sic] eligible retirement plan (as defined by section 402(c)(8)(B)) other than a Roth IRA during any taxable year if, for the taxable year of the distribution to which such contribution relates—

(i) the taxpayer's adjusted gross income exceeds $100,000, or

(ii) the taxpayer is a married individual filing a separate return.

⟫→ *Caution: Former Code Sec. 408A(c)(3)(C) was amended and redesignated as Code Sec.*
408A(c)(3)(B), below, by P.L. 109-222, applicable to tax years beginning after December 31, 2009.

(B) Definitions.—For purposes of this paragraph—

(i) adjusted gross income shall be determined in the same manner as under section 219(g)(3), *except that any amount included in gross income under subsection (d)(3) shall not be taken into account, and*

(ii) the applicable dollar amount is—

(I) in the case of a taxpayer filing a joint return, $150,000,

(II) in the case of any other taxpayer (other than a married individual filing a separate return), $95,000, and

(III) in the case of a married individual filing a separate return, zero.

⟫→ *Caution: Former Code Sec. 408A(c)(3)(D) was redesignated as Code Sec. 408A(c)(3)(C), below, by*
P.L. 109-222, applicable to tax years beginning after December 31, 2009.

(C) Marital Status.—Section 219(g)(4) shall apply for purposes of this paragraph.

* * *

[CCH Explanation at ¶705. Committee Reports at ¶10,260.]

Amendments

• **2006, Tax Increase Prevention and Reconciliation Act of 2005 (P.L. 109-222)**

P.L. 109-222, §512(a)(1):

Amended Code Sec. 408A(c)(3) by striking subparagraph (B) and redesignating subparagraphs (C) and (D) as subparagraphs (B) and (C), respectively. **Effective** for tax years beginning after 12-31-2009. Prior to being stricken, Code Sec. 408A(c)(3)(B) read as follows:

(B) Rollover from eligible retirement plan.—A taxpayer shall not be allowed to make a qualified rollover contribution to a Roth IRA from an an [sic] eligible retirement plan (as defined by section 402(c)(8)(B)) other than a Roth IRA during any taxable year if, for the taxable year of the distribution to which such contribution relates—

(i) the taxpayer's adjusted gross income exceeds $100,000, or

(ii) the taxpayer is a married individual filing a separate return.

P.L. 109-222, §512(a)(2):

Amended Code Sec. 408A(c)(3)(B)(i), as redesignated by Act Sec. 512(a)(1), by striking "except that—" and all that follows and inserting "except that any amount included in gross income under subsection (d)(3) shall not be taken into account, and". **Effective** for tax years beginning after 12-31-2009. Prior to being amended, Code Sec. 408A(c)(3)(B)(i) read as follows:

(i) adjusted gross income shall be determined in the same manner as under section 219(g)(3), except that—

(I) any amount included in gross income under subsection (d)(3) shall not be taken into account; and

(II) any amount included in gross income by reason of a required distribution under a provision described in paragraph (5) shall not be taken into account for purposes of subparagraph (B)(i), and

(d) Distribution Rules.—For purposes of this title—

* * *

(3) Rollovers from an eligible retirement plan other than a Roth IRA.—

(A) In general.—Notwithstanding sections 402(c), 403(b)(8), 408(d)(3), and 457(e)(16), in the case of any distribution to which this paragraph applies—

(i) there shall be included in gross income any amount which would be includible were it not part of a qualified rollover contribution,

(ii) section 72(t) shall not apply, and

⟫→ *Caution: Code Sec. 408A(d)(3)(A)(iii), below, as amended by P.L. 109-222, applies to tax years*
beginning after December 31, 2009.

(iii) *unless the taxpayer elects not to have this clause apply, any amount required to be included in gross income for any taxable year beginning in 2010 by reason of this paragraph shall be so included ratably over the 2-taxable-year period beginning with the first taxable year beginning in 2011.*

Any election under clause (iii) for any distributions during a taxable year may not be changed after the due date for such taxable year.

* * *

⋙→ *Caution: Code Sec. 408A(d)(3)(E), below, as amended by P.L. 109-222, applies to tax years beginning after December 31, 2009.*

(E) SPECIAL RULES FOR CONTRIBUTIONS TO WHICH 2-YEAR AVERAGING APPLIES.—In the case of a qualified rollover contribution to a Roth IRA of a distribution to which subparagraph (A)(iii) applied, the following rules shall apply:

　　(i) ACCELERATION OF INCLUSION.—

　　　　(I) IN GENERAL.—*The amount otherwise required to be included in gross income for any taxable year beginning in 2010 or the first taxable year in the 2-year period under subparagraph (A)(iii) shall be increased by the aggregate distributions from Roth IRAs for such taxable year which are allocable under paragraph (4) to the portion of such qualified rollover contribution required to be included in gross income under subparagraph (A)(i).*

　　　　(II) LIMITATION ON AGGREGATE AMOUNT INCLUDED.—*The amount required to be included in gross income for any taxable year under subparagraph (A)(iii) shall not exceed the aggregate amount required to be included in gross income under subparagraph (A)(iii) for all taxable years in the 2-year period (without regard to subclause (I)) reduced by amounts included for all preceding taxable years.*

* * *

[CCH Explanation at ¶705. Committee Reports at ¶10,260.]

Amendments

• **2006, Tax Increase Prevention and Reconciliation Act of 2005 (P.L. 109-222)**

P.L. 109-222, § 512(b)(1):

Amended Code Sec. 408A(d)(3)(A)(iii). **Effective** for tax years beginning after 12-31-2009. Prior to amendment, Code Sec. 408A(d)(3)(A)(iii) read as follows:

(iii) unless the taxpayer elects not to have this clause apply for any taxable year, any amount required to be included in gross income for such taxable year by reason of this paragraph for any distribution before January 1, 1999, shall be so included ratably over the 4-taxable year period beginning with such taxable year.

P.L. 109-222, § 512(b)(2)(A):

Amended Code Sec. 408A(d)(3)(E)(i). **Effective** for tax years beginning after 12-31-2009. Prior to amendment, Code Sec. 408A(d)(3)(E)(i) read as follows:

(i) ACCELERATION OF INCLUSION.—

(I) IN GENERAL.—The amount required to be included in gross income for each of the first 3 taxable years in the 4-year period under subparagraph (A)(iii) shall be increased by the aggregate distributions from Roth IRAs for such taxable year which are allocable under paragraph (4) to the portion of such qualified rollover contribution required to be included in gross income under subparagraph (A)(i).

(II) LIMITATION ON AGGREGATE AMOUNT INCLUDED.—The amount required to be included in gross income for any taxable year under subparagraph (A)(iii) shall not exceed the aggregate amount required to be included in gross income under subparagraph (A)(iii) for all taxable years in the 4-year period (without regard to subclause (I)) reduced by amounts included for all preceding taxable years.

P.L. 109-222, § 512(b)(2)(B):

Amended the heading for Code Sec. 408A(d)(3)(E) by striking "4-YEAR" and inserting "2-YEAR". **Effective** for tax years beginning after 12-31-2009.

[¶5405] CODE SEC. 468B. SPECIAL RULES FOR DESIGNATED SETTLEMENT FUNDS.

* * *

(g) CLARIFICATION OF TAXATION OF CERTAIN FUNDS.—

　　(1) IN GENERAL.—*Except as provided in paragraph (2), nothing in any provision of law shall be construed as providing that an escrow account, settlement fund, or similar fund is not subject to current income tax. The Secretary shall prescribe regulations providing for the taxation of any such account or fund whether as a grantor trust or otherwise.*

　　(2) EXEMPTION FROM TAX FOR CERTAIN SETTLEMENT FUNDS.—*An escrow account, settlement fund, or similar fund shall be treated as beneficially owned by the United States and shall be exempt from taxation under this subtitle if—*

　　　　(A) *it is established pursuant to a consent decree entered by a judge of a United States District Court,*

(B) it is created for the receipt of settlement payments as directed by a government entity for the sole purpose of resolving or satisfying one or more claims asserting liability under the Comprehensive Environmental Response, Compensation, and Liability Act of 1980,

(C) the authority and control over the expenditure of funds therein (including the expenditure of contributions thereto and any net earnings thereon) is with such government entity, and

(D) upon termination, any remaining funds will be disbursed to such government entity for use in accordance with applicable law.

For purposes of this paragraph, the term "government entity" means the United States, any State or political subdivision thereof, the District of Columbia, any possession of the United States, and any agency or instrumentality of any of the foregoing.

(3) [Stricken.]

[CCH Explanation at ¶375. Committee Reports at ¶10,030 and ¶15,540.]

Amendments

• **2006, Tax Relief and Health Care Act of 2006 (P.L. 109-432)**

P.L. 109-432, Division A, §409(a):

Amended Code Sec. 468B(g) by striking paragraph (3). **Effective** as if included in section 201 of the Tax Increase Prevention and Reconciliation Act of 2005 (P.L. 109-222) [effective for accounts and funds established after 5-17-2006.—CCH]. Prior to being stricken, Code Sec. 468B(g)(3) read as follows:

(3) TERMINATION.—Paragraph (2) shall not apply to accounts and funds established after December 31, 2010.

• **2006, Tax Increase Prevention and Reconciliation Act of 2005 (P.L. 109-222)**

P.L. 109-222, §201(a):

Amended Code Sec. 468B(g). **Effective** for accounts and funds established after 5-17-2006. Prior to amendment, Code Sec. 468B(g) read as follows:

(g) CLARIFICATION OF TAXATION OF CERTAIN FUNDS.—Nothing in any provision of law shall be construed as providing that an escrow account, settlement fund, or similar fund is not subject to current income tax. The Secretary shall prescribe regulations providing for the taxation of any such account or fund whether as a grantor trust or otherwise.

[¶5410] CODE SEC. 613A. LIMITATIONS ON PERCENTAGE DEPLETION IN CASE OF OIL AND GAS WELLS.

* * *

(c) EXEMPTION FOR INDEPENDENT PRODUCERS AND ROYALTY OWNERS.—

* * *

(6) OIL AND NATURAL GAS PRODUCED FROM MARGINAL PROPERTIES.—

* * *

(H) TEMPORARY SUSPENSION OF TAXABLE INCOME LIMIT WITH RESPECT TO MARGINAL PRODUCTION.—The second sentence of subsection (a) of section 613 shall not apply to so much of the allowance for depletion as is determined under subparagraph (A) for any taxable year beginning after December 31, 1997, and before January 1, *2008.*

* * *

[CCH Explanation at ¶325. Committee Reports at ¶15,270.]

Amendments

• **2006, Tax Relief and Health Care Act of 2006 (P.L. 109-432)**

P.L. 109-432, Division A, §118(a):

Amended Code Sec. 613A(c)(6)(H) by striking "2006" and inserting "2008". **Effective** for tax years beginning after 12-31-2005.

[¶5420] CODE SEC. 664. CHARITABLE REMAINDER TRUSTS.

* * *

(c) TAXATION OF TRUSTS.—

(1) INCOME TAX.—A charitable remainder annuity trust and a charitable remainder unitrust shall, for any taxable year, not be subject to any tax imposed by this subtitle.

(2) EXCISE TAX.—

(A) IN GENERAL.—In the case of a charitable remainder annuity trust or a charitable remainder unitrust which has unrelated business taxable income (within the meaning of section 512, determined as if part III of subchapter F applied to such trust) for a taxable year, there is hereby imposed on such trust or unitrust an excise tax equal to the amount of such unrelated business taxable income.

(B) CERTAIN RULES TO APPLY.—The tax imposed by subparagraph (A) shall be treated as imposed by chapter 42 for purposes of this title other than subchapter E of chapter 42.

(C) TAX COURT PROCEEDINGS.—For purposes of this paragraph, the references in section 6212(c)(1) to section 4940 shall be deemed to include references to this paragraph.

* * *

[CCH Explanation at ¶ 680. Committee Reports at ¶ 15,690.]

Amendments

• 2006, Tax Relief and Health Care Act of 2006 (P.L. 109-432)

P.L. 109-432, Division A, § 424(a):

Amended Code Sec. 664(c). **Effective** for tax years beginning after 12-31-2006. Prior to amendment, Code Sec. 664(c) read as follows:

(c) EXEMPTION FROM INCOME TAXES.—A charitable remainder annuity trust and a charitable remainder unitrust shall, for any taxable year, not be subject to any tax imposed by this subtitle, unless such trust, for such year, has unrelated business taxable income (within the meaning of section 512, determined as if part III of subchapter F applied to such trust).

[¶ 5430] CODE SEC. 852. TAXATION OF REGULATED INVESTMENT COMPANIES AND THEIR SHAREHOLDERS.

* * *

(b) METHOD OF TAXATION OF COMPANIES AND SHAREHOLDERS.—

* * *

(3) CAPITAL GAINS.—

* * *

(E) CERTAIN DISTRIBUTIONS.—In the case of a distribution to which section 897 does not apply by reason of the second sentence of section 897(h)(1), the amount of such distribution which would be included in computing long-term capital gains for the shareholder under subparagraph (B) or (D) (without regard to this subparagraph)—

(i) shall not be included in computing such shareholder's long-term capital gains, and

(ii) shall be included in such shareholder's gross income as a dividend from the regulated investment company.

* * *

[CCH Explanation at ¶ 1020. Committee Reports at ¶ 10,190.]

Amendments

• 2006, Tax Increase Prevention and Reconciliation Act of 2005 (P.L. 109-222)

P.L. 109-222, § 505(c)(1):

Amended Code Sec. 852(b)(3) by adding at the end a new subparagraph (E). **Effective** for tax years of qualified invest-

ment entities beginning after 12-31-2005, except that no amount shall be required to be withheld under Code Sec. 1441, 1442, or 1445 with respect to any distribution before 5-17-2006 if such amount was not otherwise required to be withheld under any such section as in effect before such amendments.

[¶ 5455] CODE SEC. 871. TAX ON NONRESIDENT ALIEN INDIVIDUALS.

* * *

(k) EXEMPTION FOR CERTAIN DIVIDENDS OF REGULATED INVESTMENT COMPANIES.—

* * *

(2) SHORT-TERM CAPITAL GAIN DIVIDENDS.—

* * *

(E) Certain Distributions.—In the case of a distribution to which section 897 does not apply by reason of the second sentence of section 897(h)(1), the amount which would be treated as a short-term capital gain dividend to the shareholder (without regard to this subparagraph)—

(i) shall not be treated as a short-term capital gain dividend, and

(ii) shall be included in such shareholder's gross income as a dividend from the regulated investment company.

* * *

[CCH Explanation at ¶ 1020. Committee Reports at ¶ 10,190.]

Amendments

• **2006, Tax Increase Prevention and Reconciliation Act of 2005 (P.L. 109-222)**

P.L. 109-222, § 505(c)(2):

Amended Code Sec. 871(k)(2) by adding at the end a new subparagraph (E). **Effective** for tax years of qualified invest-

ment entities beginning after 12-31-2005, except that no amount shall be required to be withheld under Code Sec. 1441, 1442, or 1445 with respect to any distribution before 5-17-2006 if such amount was not otherwise required to be withheld under any such section as in effect before such amendments.

[¶ 5480] CODE SEC. 897. DISPOSITION OF INVESTMENT IN UNITED STATES REAL PROPERTY.

* * *

(h) Special Rules for Certain Investment Entities.—For purposes of this section—

(1) Look-through of distributions.—Any distribution by a qualified investment entity to *a nonresident alien individual, a foreign corporation, or other qualified investment entity* shall, to the extent attributable to gain from sales or exchanges by the qualified investment entity of United States real property interests, be treated as gain recognized by *such nonresident alien individual, foreign corporation, or other qualified investment entity* from the sale or exchange of a United States real property interest. *Notwithstanding the preceding sentence, any distribution by a qualified investment entity to a nonresident alien individual or a foreign corporation with respect to any class of stock which is regularly traded on an established securities market located in the United States shall not be treated as gain recognized from the sale or exchange of a United States real property interest if such individual or corporation did not own more than 5 percent of such class of stock at any time during the 1-year period ending on the date of such distribution.*

* * *

(4) Definitions.—

(A) Qualified investment entity.—

(i) In general.—The term "qualified investment entity" means—

(I) any real estate investment trust, and

(II) any regulated investment company *which is a United States real property holding corporation or which would be a United States real property holding corporation if the exceptions provided in subsections (c)(3) and (h)(2) did not apply to interests in any real estate investment trust or regulated investment company.*

(ii) Termination.—*Clause (i)(II) shall not apply after December 31, 2007. Notwithstanding the preceding sentence, an entity described in clause (i)(II) shall be treated as a qualified investment entity for purposes of applying paragraphs (1) and (5) and section 1445 with respect to any distribution by the entity to a nonresident alien individual or a foreign corporation which is attributable directly or indirectly to a distribution to the entity from a real estate investment trust.*

* * *

(5) Treatment of certain wash sale transactions.—

(A) In general.—*If an interest in a domestically controlled qualified investment entity is disposed of in an applicable wash sale transaction, the taxpayer shall, for purposes of this section, be treated as having gain from the sale or exchange of a United States real property interest in an* amount equal to the portion of the distribution described in subparagraph (B) with respect to such interest which, but for the disposition, would have been treated by the taxpayer as gain from the sale or exchange of a United States real property interest under paragraph (1).

(B) APPLICABLE WASH SALES TRANSACTION.—For purposes of this paragraph—

(i) IN GENERAL.—The term "applicable wash sales transaction" means any transaction (or series of transactions) under which a nonresident alien individual, foreign corporation, or qualified investment entity—

(I) disposes of an interest in a domestically controlled qualified investment entity during the 30-day period preceding the ex-dividend date of a distribution which is to be made with respect to the interest and any portion of which, but for the disposition, would have been treated by the taxpayer as gain from the sale or exchange of a United States real property interest under paragraph (1), and

(II) acquires, or enters into a contract or option to acquire, a substantially identical interest in such entity during the 61-day period beginning with the 1st day of the 30-day period described in subclause (I).

For purposes of subclause (II), a nonresident alien individual, foreign corporation, or qualified investment entity shall be treated as having acquired any interest acquired by a person related (within the meaning of section 267(b) or 707(b)(1)) to the individual, corporation, or entity, and any interest which such person has entered into any contract or option to acquire.

(ii) APPLICATION TO SUBSTITUTE DIVIDEND AND SIMILAR PAYMENTS.—Subparagraph (A) shall apply to—

(I) any substitute dividend payment (within the meaning of section 861), or

(II) any other similar payment specified in regulations which the Secretary determines necessary to prevent avoidance of the purposes of this paragraph.

The portion of any such payment treated by the taxpayer as gain from the sale or exchange of a United States real property interest under subparagraph (A) by reason of this clause shall be equal to the portion of the distribution such payment is in lieu of which would have been so treated but for the transaction giving rise to such payment.

(iii) EXCEPTION WHERE DISTRIBUTION ACTUALLY RECEIVED.—A transaction shall not be treated as an applicable wash sales transaction if the nonresident alien individual, foreign corporation, or qualified investment entity receives the distribution described in clause (i)(I) with respect to either the interest which was disposed of, or acquired, in the transaction.

(iv) EXCEPTION FOR CERTAIN PUBLICLY TRADED STOCK.—A transaction shall not be treated as an applicable wash sales transaction if it involves the disposition of any class of stock in a qualified investment entity which is regularly traded on an established securities market within the United States but only if the nonresident alien individual, foreign corporation, or qualified investment entity did not own more than 5 percent of such class of stock at any time during the 1-year period ending on the date of the distribution described in clause (i)(I).

* * *

[CCH Explanation at ¶1015, ¶1020 and ¶1025. Committee Reports at ¶10,180 and ¶10,190.]

Amendments

• 2006, Tax Increase Prevention and Reconciliation Act of 2005 (P.L. 109-222)

P.L. 109-222, §504(a):

Amended Code Sec. 897(h)(4)(A)(i)(II) by inserting "which is a United States real property holding corporation or which would be a United States real property holding corporation if the exceptions provided in subsections (c)(3) and (h)(2) did not apply to interests in any real estate investment trust or regulated investment company" after "regulated investment company". **Effective** as if included in the provisions of section 411 of the American Jobs Creation

Act of 2004 (P.L. 108-357) to which it relates [effective after 12-31-2004.—CCH].

P.L. 109-222, §505(a)(1)(A)-(C):

Amended Code Sec. 897(h)(1) by striking "a nonresident alien individual or a foreign corporation" in the first sentence and inserting "a nonresident alien individual, a foreign corporation, or other qualified investment entity", by striking "such nonresident alien individual or foreign corporation" in the first sentence and inserting "such nonresident alien individual, foreign corporation, or other qualified investment entity", and by striking the second sentence and inserting a new sentence. **Effective** for tax years of qualified investment entities beginning after 12-31-2005, except that no amount shall be required to be withheld under Code Sec. 1441, 1442, or 1445 with respect to any distribution before 5-17-2006 if such amount was not otherwise required to be withheld under any such section as in effect before such amendments. Prior to being stricken, the second sentence of Code Sec. 897(h)(1) read as follows:

Notwithstanding the preceding sentence, any distribution by a real estate investment trust with respect to any class of stock which is regularly traded on an established securities market located in the United States shall not be treated as gain recognized from the sale or exchange of a United States real property interest if the shareholder did not own more than 5 percent of such class of stock at any time during the 1-year period ending on the date of the distribution.

P.L. 109-222, § 505(a)(2):

Amended Code Sec. 897(h)(4)(A)(ii) by adding at the end a new sentence. **Effective** for tax years of qualified invest-

ment entities beginning after 12-31-2005, except that no amount shall be required to be withheld under Code Sec. 1441, 1442, or 1445 with respect to any distribution before 5-17-2006 if such amount was not otherwise required to be withheld under any such section as in effect before such amendments.

P.L. 109-222, § 506(a):

Amended Code Sec. 897(h) by adding at the end a new paragraph (5). **Effective** for tax years beginning after 12-31-2005, except that such amendment shall not apply to any distribution, or substitute dividend payment, occurring before the date that is 30 days after 5-17-2006.

[¶ 5505] CODE SEC. 911. CITIZENS OR RESIDENTS OF THE UNITED STATES LIVING ABROAD.

* * *

(b) FOREIGN EARNED INCOME.—

* * *

(2) LIMITATION ON FOREIGN EARNED INCOME.—

* * *

(D) EXCLUSION AMOUNT.—

(i) IN GENERAL.—The exclusion amount for any calendar year is the exclusion amount determined in accordance with the following table (as adjusted by clause (ii)):

For calendar year—	The exclusion amount is—
1998	$72,000
1999	74,000
2000	76,000
2001	78,000
2002 and thereafter	80,000

(ii) INFLATION ADJUSTMENT.—In the case of any taxable year beginning in a calendar year after *2005*, the $80,000 amount in clause (i) shall be increased by an amount equal to the product of—

(I) such dollar amount, and

(II) the cost-of-living adjustment determined under section 1(f)(3) for the calendar year in which the taxable year begins, determined by substituting "*2004*" for "1992" in subparagraph (B) thereof.

If any increase determined under the preceding sentence is not a multiple of $100, such increase shall be rounded to the next lowest multiple of $100.

[CCH Explanation at ¶ 1005. Committee Reports at ¶ 10,290.]

Amendments

• **2006, Tax Increase Prevention and Reconciliation Act of 2005 (P.L. 109-222)**

P.L. 109-222, § 515(a)(1)-(2):

Amended Code Sec. 911(b)(2)(D)(ii) by striking "2007" and inserting "2005", and by striking "2006" in subclause

(II) and inserting "2004". **Effective** for tax years beginning after 12-31-2005.

(c) HOUSING COST AMOUNT.—For purposes of this section—

(1) IN GENERAL.—The term "housing cost amount" means an amount equal to the excess of—

(A) the housing expenses of an individual for the taxable year *to the extent such expenses do not exceed the amount determined under paragraph (2)*, over

(B) an amount equal to the product of—

(i) *16 percent of the amount (computed on a daily basis) in effect under subsection (b)(2)(D) for the calendar year in which such taxable year begins, multiplied by*

(ii) the number of days of such taxable year within the applicable period described in subparagraph (A) or (B) of subsection (d)(1).

(2) LIMITATION.—

(A) IN GENERAL.—The amount determined under this paragraph is an amount equal to the product of—

(i) 30 percent (adjusted as may be provided under subparagraph (B)) of the amount (computed on a daily basis) in effect under subsection (b)(2)(D) for the calendar year in which the taxable year of the individual begins, multiplied by

(ii) the number of days of such taxable year within the applicable period described in subparagraph (A) or (B) of subsection (d)(1).

(B) REGULATIONS.—The Secretary may issue regulations or other guidance providing for the adjustment of the percentage under subparagraph (A)(i) on the basis of geographic differences in housing costs relative to housing costs in the United States.

(3) HOUSING EXPENSES.—

* * *

(4) SPECIAL RULES WHERE HOUSING EXPENSES NOT PROVIDED BY EMPLOYER.—

* * *

[CCH Explanation at ¶1005. Committee Reports at ¶10,290.]

Amendments

● **2006, Tax Increase Prevention and Reconciliation Act of 2005 (P.L. 109-222)**

P.L. 109-222, §515(b)(1):

Amended Code Sec. 911(c)(1)(B)(i). **Effective** for tax years beginning after 12-31-2005. Prior to amendment, Code Sec. 911(c)(1)(B)(i) read as follows:

(i) 16 percent of the salary (computed on a daily basis) of an employee of the United States who is compensated at a rate equal to the annual rate paid for step 1 of grade GS-14, multiplied by

P.L. 109-222, §515(b)(2)(A):

Amended Code Sec. 911(c)(1)(A) by inserting "to the extent such expenses do not exceed the amount determined under paragraph (2)" after "the taxable year". **Effective** for tax years beginning after 12-31-2005.

P.L. 109-222, §515(b)(2)(B):

Amended Code Sec. 911(c) by redesignating paragraphs (2) and (3) as paragraphs (3) and (4), respectively, and by inserting after paragraph (1) a new paragraph (2). **Effective** for tax years beginning after 12-31-2005.

(d) DEFINITIONS AND SPECIAL RULES.—For purposes of this section—

* * *

(4) WAIVER OF PERIOD OF STAY IN FOREIGN COUNTRY.—Notwithstanding paragraph (1), an individual who—

(A) is a bona fide resident of, or is present in, a foreign country for any period,

(B) leaves such foreign country after August 31, 1978—

(i) during any period during which the Secretary determines, after consultation with the Secretary of State or his delegate, that individuals were required to leave such foreign country because of war, civil unrest, or similar adverse conditions in such foreign country which precluded the normal conduct of business by such individuals, and

(ii) before meeting the requirements of such paragraph (1), and

(C) establishes to the satisfaction of the Secretary that such individual could reasonably have been expected to have met such requirements but for the conditions referred to in clause (i) of subparagraph (B),

shall be treated as a qualified individual with respect to the period described in subparagraph (A) during which he was a bona fide resident of, or was present in, the foreign country, and in applying subsections (b)(2)(A), *(c)(1)(B)(ii), and (c)(2)(A)(ii)* with respect to such individual, only the days within such period shall be taken into account.

* * *

(7) AGGREGATE BENEFIT CANNOT EXCEED FOREIGN EARNED INCOME.—The sum of the amount excluded under subsection (a) and the amount deducted under *subsection (c)(4)(A)* for the taxable year shall not exceed the individual's foreign earned income for such year.

* * *

[CCH Explanation at ¶1005. Committee Reports at ¶10,290.]

Amendments

• **2006, Tax Increase Prevention and Reconciliation Act of 2005 (P.L. 109-222)**

P.L. 109-222, § 515(b)(2)(C)(i):

Amended Code Sec. 911(d)(4) by striking "and (c)(1)(B)(ii)" and inserting ", (c)(1)(B)(ii), and (c)(2)(A)(ii)". **Effective** for tax years beginning after 12-31-2005.

P.L. 109-222, § 515(b)(2)(C)(ii):

Amended Code Sec. 911(d)(7) by striking "subsection (c)(3)" and inserting "subsection (c)(4)". **Effective** for tax years beginning after 12-31-2005.

(f) DETERMINATION OF TAX LIABILITY ON NONEXCLUDED AMOUNTS.—For purposes of this chapter, if any amount is excluded from the gross income of a taxpayer under subsection (a) for any taxable year, then, notwithstanding section 1 or 55—

(1) the tax imposed by section 1 on the taxpayer for such taxable year shall be equal to the excess (if any) of—

(A) the tax which would be imposed by section 1 for the taxable year if the taxpayer's taxable income were increased by the amount excluded under subsection (a) for the taxable year, over

(B) the tax which would be imposed by section 1 for the taxable year if the taxpayer's taxable income were equal to the amount excluded under subsection (a) for the taxable year, and

(2) the tentative minimum tax under section 55 for such taxable year shall be equal to the excess (if any) of—

(A) the amount which would be such tentative minimum tax for the taxable year if the taxpayer's taxable excess were increased by the amount excluded under subsection (a) for the taxable year, over

(B) the amount which would be such tentative minimum tax for the taxable year if the taxpayer's taxable excess were equal to the amount excluded under subsection (a) for the taxable year.

For purposes of this subsection, the amount excluded under subsection (a) shall be reduced by the aggregate amount of any deductions or exclusions disallowed under subsection (d)(6) with respect to such excluded amount.

[CCH Explanation at ¶1010. Committee Reports at ¶10,290.]

Amendments

• **2006, Tax Increase Prevention and Reconciliation Act of 2005 (P.L. 109-222)**

P.L. 109-222, § 515(c):

Amended Code Sec. 911 by redesignating subsection (f) as subsection (g) and by inserting after subsection (e) a new subsection (f). **Effective** for tax years beginning after 12-31-2005.

(g) CROSS REFERENCES.—

For administrative and penal provisions relating to the exclusions provided for in this section, see sections 6001, 6011, 6012(c), and the other provisions of subtitle F.

[CCH Explanation at ¶1010. Committee Reports at ¶10,290.]

Amendments

• **2006, Tax Increase Prevention and Reconciliation Act of 2005 (P.L. 109-222)**

P.L. 109-222, §515(c):

Amended Code Sec. 911 by redesignating subsection (f) as subsection (g). **Effective** for tax years beginning after 12-31-2005.

[¶5530] CODE SEC. 953. INSURANCE INCOME.

* * *

(e) EXEMPT INSURANCE INCOME.—For purposes of this section—

* * *

(10) APPLICATION.—This subsection and section 954(i) shall apply only to taxable years of a foreign corporation beginning after December 31, 1998, and before *January 1, 2009*, and to taxable years of United States shareholders with or within which any such taxable year of such foreign corporation ends. If this subsection does not apply to a taxable year of a foreign corporation beginning after *December 31, 2008* (and taxable years of United States shareholders ending with or within such taxable year), then, notwithstanding the preceding sentence, subsection (a) shall be applied to such taxable years in the same manner as it would if the taxable year of the foreign corporation began in 1998.

* * *

[CCH Explanation at ¶1030 and ¶1035. Committee Reports at ¶10,022.]

Amendments

• **2006, Tax Increase Prevention and Reconciliation Act of 2005 (P.L. 109-222)**

P.L. 109-222, §103(a)(1)(A)-(B):

Amended Code Sec. 953(e)(10) by striking "January 1, 2007" and inserting "January 1, 2009", and by striking "De-cember 31, 2006" and inserting "December 31, 2008". **Effec-tive** 5-17-2006.

[¶5555] CODE SEC. 954. FOREIGN BASE COMPANY INCOME.

* * *

(c) FOREIGN PERSONAL HOLDING COMPANY INCOME.—

* * *

(6) LOOK-THRU RULE FOR RELATED CONTROLLED FOREIGN CORPORATIONS.—

(A) IN GENERAL.—For purposes of this subsection, dividends, interest, rents, and royalties received or accrued from a controlled foreign corporation which is a related person shall not be treated as foreign personal holding company income to the extent attributable or properly allocable (determined under rules similar to the rules of subparagraphs (C) and (D) of section 904(d)(3)) to income of the related person which is neither subpart F income nor income treated as effectively connected with the conduct of a trade or business in the United States. For purposes of this subparagraph, interest shall include factoring income which is treated as income equivalent to interest for purposes of paragraph (1)(E). The Secretary shall prescribe such regulations as may be necessary or appropriate to carry out this paragraph, including such regulations as may be necessary or appropriate to prevent the abuse of the purposes of this paragraph.

(B) APPLICATION.—Subparagraph (A) shall apply to taxable years of foreign corporations beginning after December 31, 2005, and before January 1, 2009, and to taxable years of United States shareholders with or within which such taxable years of foreign corporations end.

* * *

[CCH Explanation at ¶365. Committee Reports at ¶10,027 and ¶15,710.]

Amendments

● **2006, Tax Relief and Health Care Act of 2006 (P.L. 109-432)**

P.L. 109-432, Division A, §426(a)(1)(A):

Amended the first sentence of Code Sec. 954(c)(6)(A) by striking "which is not subpart F income" and inserting "which is neither subpart F income nor income treated as effectively connected with the conduct of a trade or business in the United States". Effective as if included in section 103(b) of the Tax Increase Prevention and Reconciliation Act of 2005 (P.L. 109-222) [effective for tax years of foreign corporations beginning after 12-31-2005, and to tax years of United States shareholders with or within which such tax years of foreign corporations end.—CCH].

P.L. 109-432, Division A, §426(a)(1)(B):

Amended Code Sec. 954(c)(6)(A) by striking the last sentence and inserting a new sentence. Effective as if included in section 103(b) of the Tax Increase Prevention and Recon-

ciliation Act of 2005 (P.L. 109-222) [effective for tax years of foreign corporations beginning after 12-31-2005, and to tax years of United States shareholders with or within which such tax years of foreign corporations end.—CCH]. Prior to being stricken, the last sentence of Code Sec. 954(c)(6)(A) read as follows:

The Secretary shall prescribe such regulations as may be appropriate to prevent the abuse of the purposes of this paragraph.

● **2006, Tax Increase Prevention and Reconciliation Act of 2005 (P.L. 109-222)**

P.L. 109-222, §103(b)(1):

Amended Code Sec. 954(c) by adding at the end a new paragraph (6). Effective for tax years of foreign corporations beginning after 12-31-2005, and to tax years of United States shareholders with or within which such tax years of foreign corporations end.

(h) SPECIAL RULE FOR INCOME DERIVED IN THE ACTIVE CONDUCT OF BANKING, FINANCING, OR SIMILAR BUSINESSES.—

* * *

(9) APPLICATION.—This subsection, subsection (c)(2)(C)(ii), and the last sentence of subsection (e)(2) shall apply only to taxable years of a foreign corporation beginning after December 31, 1998, and before *January 1, 2009*, and to taxable years of United States shareholders with or within which any such taxable year of such foreign corporation ends.

* * *

[CCH Explanation at ¶1035. Committee Reports at ¶10,022.]

Amendments

● **2006, Tax Increase Prevention and Reconciliation Act of 2005 (P.L. 109-222)**

P.L. 109-222, §103(a)(2):

Amended Code Sec. 954(h)(9) by striking "January 1, 2007" and inserting "January 1, 2009". Effective 5-17-2006.

[¶5565] CODE SEC. 1043. SALE OF PROPERTY TO COMPLY WITH CONFLICT-OF-INTEREST REQUIREMENTS.

* * *

(b) DEFINITIONS.—For purposes of this section—

(1) ELIGIBLE PERSON.—The term "eligible person" means—

(A) an officer or employee of the executive branch, *or a judicial officer*, of the Federal Government, but does not mean a special Government employee as defined in section 202 of title 18, United States Code, and

(B) any spouse or minor or dependent child whose ownership of any property is attributable under any statute, regulation, rule, *judicial canon*, or executive order referred to in paragraph (2) to a person referred to in subparagraph (A).

(2) CERTIFICATE OF DIVESTITURE.—The term "certificate of divestiture" means any written determination—

(A) that states that divestiture of specific property is reasonably necessary to comply with any Federal conflict of interest statute, regulation, rule, *judicial canon*, or executive order (including section 208 of title 18, United States Code), or requested by a congressional committee as a condition of confirmation,

(B) that has been issued by the President or the Director of the Office of Government Ethics, *in the case of executive branch officers or employees, or by the Judicial Conference of the United States (or its designee), in the case of judicial officers,* and

(C) that identifies the specific property to be divested.

* * *

(5) SPECIAL RULE FOR TRUSTS.—For purposes of this section, the trustee of a trust shall be treated as an eligible person with respect to property which is held in the trust if—

(A) any person referred to in paragraph (1)(A) has a beneficial interest in the principal or income of the trust, or

(B) any person referred to in paragraph (1)(B) has a beneficial interest in the principal or income of the trust and such interest is attributable under any statute, regulation, rule, *judicial canon,* or executive order referred to in paragraph (2) to a person referred to in paragraph (1)(A).

(6) JUDICIAL OFFICER.—*The term "judicial officer" means the Chief Justice of the United States, the Associate Justices of the Supreme Court, and the judges of the United States courts of appeals, United States district courts, including the district courts in Guam, the Northern Mariana Islands, and the Virgin Islands, Court of Appeals for the Federal Circuit, Court of International Trade, Tax Court, Court of Federal Claims, Court of Appeals for Veterans Claims, United States Court of Appeals for the Armed Forces, and any court created by Act of Congress, the judges of which are entitled to hold office during good behavior.*

* * *

[CCH Explanation at ¶ 255. Committee Reports at ¶ 15,630.]

Amendments

• **2006, Tax Relief and Health Care Act of 2006 (P.L. 109-432)**

P.L. 109-432, Division A, § 418(a)(1)(A)-(B):

Amended Code Sec. 1043(b)(1) by inserting ", or a judicial officer," after "an officer or employee of the executive branch" in subparagraph (A); and by inserting "judicial canon," after "any statute, regulation, rule," in subparagraph (B). **Effective** for sales after 12-20-2006.

P.L. 109-432, Division A, § 418(a)(2)(A)-(B):

Amended Code Sec. 1043(b)(2) by inserting "judicial canon," after "any Federal conflict of interest statute, regulation, rule," in subparagraph (A); and by inserting "in the

case of executive branch officers or employees, or by the Judicial Conference of the United States (or its designee), in the case of judicial officers," after "the Director of the Office of Government Ethics," in subparagraph (B). **Effective** for sales after 12-20-2006.

P.L. 109-432, Division A, § 418(a)(3):

Amended Code Sec. 1043(b)(5)(B) by inserting "judicial canon," after "any statute, regulation, rule,". **Effective** for sales after 12-20-2006.

P.L. 109-432, Division A, § 418(b):

Amended Code Sec. 1043(b) by adding at the end a new paragraph (6). **Effective** for sales after 12-20-2006.

[¶ 5580] CODE SEC. 1221. CAPITAL ASSET DEFINED.

* * *

(b) DEFINITIONS AND SPECIAL RULES.—

* * *

(3) *SALE OR EXCHANGE OF SELF-CREATED MUSICAL WORKS.*—*At the election of the taxpayer, paragraphs (1) and (3) of subsection (a) shall not apply to musical compositions or copyrights in musical works sold or exchanged by a taxpayer described in subsection (a)(3).*

(4) REGULATIONS.—The Secretary shall prescribe such regulations as are appropriate to carry out the purposes of paragraph (6) and (7) of subsection (a) in the case of transactions involving related parties.

* * *

[CCH Explanation at ¶240. Committee Reports at ¶10,060 and ¶15,570.]

Amendments

• **2006, Tax Relief and Health Care Act of 2006 (P.L. 109-432)**

P.L. 109-432, Division A, §412(a):

Amended Code Sec. 1221(b)(3) by striking "before January 1, 2011," before "by a taxpayer". **Effective** as if included in section 204 of the Tax Increase Prevention and Reconciliation Act of 2005 (P.L. 109-222) [**effective** for sales and exchanges in tax years beginning after 5-17-2006.—CCH].

• **2006, Tax Increase Prevention and Reconciliation Act of 2005 (P.L. 109-222)**

P.L. 109-222, §204(a):

Amended Code Sec. 1221(b) by redesignating paragraph (3) as paragraph (4) and by inserting after paragraph (2) a new paragraph (3). **Effective** for sales and exchanges in tax years beginning after 5-17-2006.

[¶5590] CODE SEC. 1245. GAIN FROM DISPOSITIONS OF CERTAIN DEPRECIABLE PROPERTY.

(a) GENERAL RULE.—

* * *

(2) RECOMPUTED BASIS.—For purposes of this section—

* * *

(C) CERTAIN DEDUCTIONS TREATED AS AMORTIZATION.—Any deduction allowable under section 179, 179A, 179B, 179C, 179D, *179E,* 181, 190, 193, or 194 shall be treated as if it were a deduction allowable for amortization.

(3) SECTION 1245 PROPERTY.—For purposes of this section, the term "section 1245 property" means any property which is or has been property of a character subject to the allowance for depreciation provided in section 167 and is either—

* * *

(C) so much of any real property (other than any property described in subparagraph B)) which has an adjusted basis in which there are reflected adjustments for amortization under section 169, 179, 179A, 179B, 179C, 179D, *179E,* 185, 188 (as in effect before its repeal by the Revenue Reconciliation Act of 1990), 190, 193, or 194,

* * *

[CCH Explanation at ¶330. Committee Reports at ¶15,490.]

Amendments

• **2006, Tax Relief and Health Care Act of 2006 (P.L. 109-432)**

P.L. 109-432, Division A, §404(b)(3):

Amended Code Sec. 1245(a)(2)(C) and (3)(C) by inserting "179E," after "179D,". **Effective** for costs paid or incurred after 12-20-2006.

[¶5605] CODE SEC. 1355. DEFINITIONS AND SPECIAL RULES.

(a) DEFINITIONS.—For purposes of this subchapter—

* * *

(4) QUALIFYING VESSEL.—The term "qualifying vessel" means a self-propelled (or a combination self-propelled and non-self-propelled) United States flag vessel of not less than *6,000* deadweight tons used exclusively in the United States foreign trade during the period that the election under this subchapter is in effect.

* * *

[CCH Explanation at ¶ 370. Committee Reports at ¶ 10,070 and ¶ 15,580.]

Amendments

• **2006, Tax Relief and Health Care Act of 2006 (P.L. 109-432)**

P.L. 109-432, Division A, § 413(a):

Amended Code Sec. 1355(a)(4) by striking "10,000 (6,000, in the case of taxable years beginning after December 31, 2005, and ending before January 1, 2011)" and inserting "6,000". **Effective** as if included in section 205 of the Tax Increase Prevention and Reconciliation Act of 2005 (P.L. 109-222) [**effective for tax years beginning after** 12-31-2005.—CCH].

• **2006, Tax Increase Prevention and Reconciliation Act of 2005 (P.L. 109-222)**

P.L. 109-222, § 205(a):

Amended Code Sec. 1355(a)(4) by inserting "(6,000, in the case of taxable years beginning after December 31, 2005, and ending before January 1, 2011)" after "10,000". **Effective for** tax years beginning after 12-31-2005.

(g) GREAT LAKES DOMESTIC SHIPPING TO NOT DISQUALIFY VESSEL.—

(1) IN GENERAL.—If the electing corporation elects (at such time and in such manner as the Secretary may require) to apply this subsection for any taxable year to any qualifying vessel which is used in qualified zone domestic trade during the taxable year—

(A) solely for purposes of subsection (a)(4), such use shall be treated as use in United States foreign trade (and not as use in United States domestic trade), and

(B) subsection (f) shall not apply with respect to such vessel for such taxable year.

(2) EFFECT OF TEMPORARILY OPERATING VESSEL IN UNITED STATES DOMESTIC TRADE.—In the case of a qualifying vessel to which this subsection applies—

(A) IN GENERAL.—An electing corporation shall be treated as using such vessel in qualified zone domestic trade during any period of temporary use in the United States domestic trade (other than qualified zone domestic trade) if the electing corporation gives timely notice to the Secretary stating—

(i) that it temporarily operates or has operated in the United States domestic trade (other than qualified zone domestic trade) a qualifying vessel which had been used in the United States foreign trade or qualified zone domestic trade, and

(ii) its intention to resume operation of the vessel in the United States foreign trade or qualified zone domestic trade.

(B) NOTICE.—Notice shall be deemed timely if given not later than the due date (including extensions) for the corporation's tax return for the taxable year in which the temporary cessation begins.

(C) PERIOD DISREGARD IN EFFECT.—The period of temporary use under subparagraph (A) continues until the earlier of the date of which—

(i) the electing corporation abandons its intention to resume operations of the vessel in the United States foreign trade or qualified zone domestic trade, or

(ii) the electing corporation resumes operation of the vessel in the United States foreign trade or qualified zone domestic trade.

(D) NO DISREGARD IF DOMESTIC TRADE USE EXCEEDS 30 DAYS.—Subparagraph (A) shall not apply to any qualifying vessel which is operated in the United States domestic trade (other than qualified zone domestic trade) for more than 30 days during the taxable year.

(3) ALLOCATION OF INCOME AND DEDUCTIONS TO QUALIFYING SHIPPING ACTIVITIES.—In the case of a qualifying vessel to which this subsection applies, the Secretary shall prescribe rules for the proper allocation of income, expenses, losses, and deductions between the qualified shipping activities and the other activities of such vessel.

(4) QUALIFIED ZONE DOMESTIC TRADE.—For purposes of this subsection—

(A) IN GENERAL.—The term "qualified zone domestic trade" means the transportation of goods or passengers between places in the qualified zone if such transportation is in the United States domestic trade.

(B) QUALIFIED ZONE.—The term "qualified zone" means the Great Lakes Waterway and the St. Lawrence Seaway.

Code Sec. 1355(g)(4)(B)   **¶5605**

[CCH Explanation at ¶370. Committee Reports at ¶15,600.]

Amendments

• **2006, Tax Relief and Health Care Act of 2006 (P.L. 109-432)**

P.L. 109-432, Division A, §415(a):

Amended Code Sec. 1355 by redesignating subsection (g) as subsection (h) and by inserting after subsection (f) a new

subsection (g). **Effective** for tax years beginning after 12-20-2006.

(h) REGULATIONS.—The Secretary shall prescribe such regulations as may be necessary or appropriate to carry out the purposes of this section.

[CCH Explanation at ¶370. Committee Reports at ¶15,600.]

Amendments

• **2006, Tax Relief and Health Care Act of 2006 (P.L. 109-432)**

P.L. 109-432, Division A, §415(a):

Amended Code Sec. 1355 by redesignating subsection (g) as subsection (h). **Effective** for tax years beginning after 12-20-2006.

[¶5608] CODE SEC. 1397E. CREDIT TO HOLDERS OF QUALIFIED ZONE ACADEMY BONDS.

* * *

(d) QUALIFIED ZONE ACADEMY BOND.—For purposes of this section—

(1) IN GENERAL.—The term "qualified zone academy bond" means any bond issued as part of an issue if—

(A) 95 percent or more of the proceeds of such issue are to be used for a qualified purpose with respect to a qualified zone academy established by an eligible local education agency,

(B) the bond is issued by a State or local government within the jurisdiction of which such academy is located,

(C) the issuer—

(i) designates such bond for purposes of this section,

(ii) certifies that it has written assurances that the private business contribution requirement of paragraph (2) will be met with respect to such academy, and

(iii) certifies that it has the written approval of the eligible local education agency for such bond issuance,

(D) the term of each bond which is part of such issue does not exceed the maximum term permitted under paragraph (3), *and*

(E) the issue meets the requirements of subsections (f), (g), and (h).

* * *

[CCH Explanation at ¶605. Committee Reports at ¶15,160.]

Amendments

• **2006, Tax Relief and Health Care Act of 2006 (P.L. 109-432)**

P.L. 109-432, Division A, §107(b)(1)(A):

Amended Code Sec. 1397E(d)(1) by striking "and" at the end of subparagraph (C)(iii), by striking the period at the

end of subparagraph (D) and inserting ", and", and by adding at the end a new subparagraph (E). **Effective** for obligations issued after 12-20-2006 pursuant to allocations of the national zone academy bond limitation for calendar years after 2005.

(e) LIMITATION ON AMOUNT OF BONDS DESIGNATED.—

(1) NATIONAL LIMITATION.—There is a national zone academy bond limitation for each calendar year. Such limitation is $400,000,000 for 1998, 1999, 2000, 2001, 2002, 2003, 2004, *2005, 2006, and 2007*, and, except as provided in paragraph (4), zero thereafter.

* * *

[CCH Explanation at ¶ 605. Committee Reports at ¶ 15,160.]

Amendments
• **2006, Tax Relief and Health Care Act of 2006 (P.L. 109-432)**

P.L. 109-432, Division A, § 107(a):

Amended Code Sec. 1397E(e)(1) by striking "and 2005" and inserting "2005, 2006, and 2007". Effective for obligations issued after 12-31-2005.

(f) SPECIAL RULES RELATING TO EXPENDITURES.—

(1) IN GENERAL.—An issue shall be treated as meeting the requirements of this subsection if, as of the date of issuance, the issuer reasonably expects—

(A) at least 95 percent of the proceeds from the sale of the issue are to be spent for 1 or more qualified purposes with respect to qualified zone academies within the 5-year period beginning on the date of issuance of the qualified zone academy bond,

(B) a binding commitment with a third party to spend at least 10 percent of the proceeds from the sale of the issue will be incurred within the 6-month period beginning on the date of issuance of the qualified zone academy bond, and

(C) such purposes will be completed with due diligence and the proceeds from the sale of the issue will be spent with due diligence.

(2) EXTENSION OF PERIOD.—Upon submission of a request prior to the expiration of the period described in paragraph (1)(A), the Secretary may extend such period if the issuer establishes that the failure to satisfy the 5-year requirement is due to reasonable cause and the related purposes will continue to proceed with due diligence.

(3) FAILURE TO SPEND REQUIRED AMOUNT OF BOND PROCEEDS WITHIN 5 YEARS.—To the extent that less than 95 percent of the proceeds of such issue are expended by the close of the 5-year period beginning on the date of issuance (or if an extension has been obtained under paragraph (2), by the close of the extended period), the issuer shall redeem all of the nonqualified bonds within 90 days after the end of such period. For purposes of this paragraph, the amount of the nonqualified bonds required to be redeemed shall be determined in the same manner as under section 142.

[CCH Explanation at ¶ 605. Committee Reports at ¶ 15,160.]

Amendments
• **2006, Tax Relief and Health Care Act of 2006 (P.L. 109-432)**

P.L. 109-432, Division A, § 107(b)(1)(B):

Amended Code Sec. 1397E by redesignating subsections (f), (g), (h), and (i) as subsections (i), (j), (k), and (l), respec- tively, and by inserting after subsection (e) new subsections (f), (g), and (h). Effective for obligations issued after 12-20-2006 pursuant to allocations of the national zone academy bond limitation for calendar years after 2005.

(g) SPECIAL RULES RELATING TO ARBITRAGE.—An issue shall be treated as meeting the requirements of this subsection if the issuer satisfies the arbitrage requirements of section 148 with respect to proceeds of the issue.

[CCH Explanation at ¶ 605. Committee Reports at ¶ 15,160.]

Amendments
• **2006, Tax Relief and Health Care Act of 2006 (P.L. 109-432)**

P.L. 109-432, Division A, § 107(b)(1)(B):

Amended Code Sec. 1397E by redesignating subsections (f), (g), (h), and (i) as subsections (i), (j), (k), and (l), respec- tively, and by inserting after subsection (f) a new subsection (g). Effective for obligations issued after 12-20-2006 pursuant to allocations of the national zone academy bond limitation for calendar years after 2005.

(h) REPORTING.—Issuers of qualified academy zone bonds shall submit reports similar to the reports required under section 149(e).

[CCH Explanation at ¶605. Committee Reports at ¶15,160.]

Amendments

• 2006, Tax Relief and Health Care Act of 2006
(P.L. 109-432)

P.L. 109-432, Division A, §107(b)(1)(B):

Amended Code Sec. 1397E by redesignating subsections
(f), (g), (h), and (i) as subsections (i), (j), (k), and (l), respec-

tively, and by inserting after subsection (g) a new subsection
(h). **Effective** for obligations issued after 12-20-2006 pursuant to allocations of the national zone academy bond limitation for calendar years after 2005.

(*i*) OTHER DEFINITIONS.—For purposes of this section—

(1) CREDIT ALLOWANCE DATE.—The term "credit allowance date" means, with respect to any issue, the last day of the 1-year period beginning on the date of issuance of such issue and the last day of each successive 1-year period thereafter.

(2) BOND.—The term "bond" includes any obligation.

(3) STATE.—The term "State" includes the District of Columbia and any possession of the United States.

[CCH Explanation at ¶605. Committee Reports at ¶15,160.]

Amendments

• 2006, Tax Relief and Health Care Act of 2006
(P.L. 109-432)

P.L. 109-432, Division A, §107(b)(1)(B):

Amended Code Sec. 1397E by redesignating subsection (f)
as subsection (i). **Effective** for obligations issued after

12-20-2006 pursuant to allocations of the national zone academy bond limitation for calendar years after 2005.

(*j*) CREDIT INCLUDED IN GROSS INCOME.—Gross income includes the amount of the credit allowed to the taxpayer under this section (determined without regard to subsection (c)).

[CCH Explanation at ¶605. Committee Reports at ¶15,160.]

Amendments

• 2006, Tax Relief and Health Care Act of 2006
(P.L. 109-432)

P.L. 109-432, Division A, §107(b)(1)(B):

Amended Code Sec. 1397E by redesignating subsection
(g) as subsection (j). **Effective** for obligations issued after

12-20-2006 pursuant to allocations of the national zone academy bond limitation for calendar years after 2005.

(*k*) CREDIT TREATED AS NONREFUNDABLE BONDHOLDER CREDIT.—For purposes of this title, the credit allowed by this section shall be treated as a credit allowable under subpart H of part IV of subchapter A of this chapter.

[CCH Explanation at ¶605. Committee Reports at ¶15,160.]

Amendments

• 2006, Tax Relief and Health Care Act of 2006
(P.L. 109-432)

P.L. 109-432, Division A, §107(b)(1)(B):

Amended Code Sec. 1397E by redesignating subsection
(h) as subsection (k). **Effective** for obligations issued after

12-20-2006 pursuant to allocations of the national zone academy bond limitation for calendar years after 2005.

(*l*) S CORPORATIONS.—In the case of a qualified zone academy bond held by an S corporation which is an eligible taxpayer—

(1) each shareholder shall take into account such shareholder's pro rata share of the credit, and

(2) no basis adjustments to the stock of the corporation shall be made under section 1367 on account of this section.

[CCH Explanation at ¶ 605. Committee Reports at ¶ 15,160.]

Amendments

• **2006, Tax Relief and Health Care Act of 2006 (P.L. 109-432)**

P.L. 109-432, Division A, § 107(b)(1)(B):

Amended Code Sec. 1397E by redesignating subsection (i) as subsection (l). **Effective** for obligations issued after 12-20-2006 pursuant to allocations of the national zone academy bond limitation for calendar years after 2005.

[¶ 5611] CODE SEC. 1400. ESTABLISHMENT OF DC ZONE.

* * *

(f) TIME FOR WHICH DESIGNATION APPLICABLE.—

(1) IN GENERAL.—The designation made by subsection (a) shall apply for the period beginning on January 1, 1998, and ending on December 31, *2007.*

(2) COORDINATION WITH DC ENTERPRISE COMMUNITY DESIGNATED UNDER SUBCHAPTER U.—The designation under subchapter U of the census tracts referred to in subsection (b)(1) as an enterprise community shall terminate on December 31, *2007.*

[CCH Explanation at ¶ 340. Committee Reports at ¶ 15,190.]

Amendments

• **2006, Tax Relief and Health Care Act of 2006 (P.L. 109-432)**

P.L. 109-432, Division A, § 110(a)(1):

Amended Code Sec. 1400(f) by striking "2005" both places it appears and inserting "2007". **Effective** for periods beginning after 12-31-2005.

[¶ 5614] CODE SEC. 1400A. TAX-EXEMPT ECONOMIC DEVELOPMENT BONDS.

* * *

(b) PERIOD OF APPLICABILITY.—This section shall apply to bonds issued during the period beginning on January 1, 1998, and ending on December 31, *2007.*

[CCH Explanation at ¶ 340. Committee Reports at ¶ 15,190.]

Amendments

• **2006, Tax Relief and Health Care Act of 2006 (P.L. 109-432)**

P.L. 109-432, Division A, § 110(b)(1):

Amended Code Sec. 1400A(b) by striking "2005" and inserting "2007". **Effective** for bonds issued after 12-31-2005.

[¶ 5617] CODE SEC. 1400B. ZERO PERCENT CAPITAL GAINS RATE.

* * *

(b) DC ZONE ASSET.—For purposes of this section—

* * *

(2) DC ZONE BUSINESS STOCK.—

(A) IN GENERAL.—The term "DC Zone business stock" means any stock in a domestic corporation which is originally issued after December 31, 1997, if—

(i) such stock is acquired by the taxpayer, before January 1, *2008,* at its original issue (directly or through an underwriter) solely in exchange for cash,

* * *

(3) DC ZONE PARTNERSHIP INTEREST.—The term "DC Zone partnership interest" means any capital or profits interest in a domestic partnership which is originally issued after December 31, 1997, if—

(A) such interest is acquired by the taxpayer, before January 1, *2008*, from the partnership solely in exchange for cash,

* * *

(4) DC ZONE BUSINESS PROPERTY.—

(A) IN GENERAL.—The term "DC Zone business property" means tangible property if—

(i) such property was acquired by the taxpayer by purchase (as defined in section 179(d)(2)) after December 31, 1997, and before January 1, *2008*,

* * *

(B) SPECIAL RULE FOR BUILDINGS WHICH ARE SUBSTANTIALLY IMPROVED.—

(i) IN GENERAL.—The requirements of clauses (i) and (ii) of subparagraph (A) shall be treated as met with respect to—

(I) property which is substantially improved by the taxpayer before January 1, *2008*, and

* * *

[CCH Explanation at ¶ 340. Committee Reports at ¶ 15,190.]
Amendments
• **2006, Tax Relief and Health Care Act of 2006 (P.L. 109-432)**

P.L. 109-432, Division A, § 110(c)(1):

Amended Code Sec. 1400B(b) by striking "2006" each place it appears and inserting "2008". **Effective** for acquisitions after 12-31-2005.

(e) OTHER DEFINITIONS AND SPECIAL RULES.—For purposes of this section—

* * *

(2) GAIN BEFORE 1998 OR AFTER *2012* NOT QUALIFIED.—The term "qualified capital gain" shall not include any gain attributable to periods before January 1, 1998, or after December 31, *2012*.

* * *

[CCH Explanation at ¶ 340. Committee Reports at ¶ 15,190.]
Amendments
• **2006, Tax Relief and Health Care Act of 2006 (P.L. 109-432)**

P.L. 109-432, Division A, § 110(c)(2)(A)(i)-(ii):

Amended Code Sec. 1400B(e)(2) by striking "2010" and inserting "2012", and by striking "2010" in the heading thereof and inserting "2012". **Effective** 12-20-2006.

(g) SALES AND EXCHANGES OF INTERESTS IN PARTNERSHIPS AND S CORPORATIONS WHICH ARE DC ZONE BUSINESSES.—In the case of the sale or exchange of an interest in a partnership, or of stock in an S corporation, which was a DC Zone business during substantially all of the period the taxpayer held such interest or stock, the amount of qualified capital gain shall be determined without regard to—

* * *

(2) any gain attributable to periods before January 1, 1998, or after December 31, *2012*.

[CCH Explanation at ¶ 340. Committee Reports at ¶ 15,190.]
Amendments
• **2006, Tax Relief and Health Care Act of 2006 (P.L. 109-432)**

P.L. 109-432, Division A, § 110(c)(2)(B):

Amended Code Sec. 1400B(g)(2) by striking "2010" and inserting "2012". **Effective** 12-20-2006.

[¶ 5620] CODE SEC. 1400C. FIRST-TIME HOMEBUYER CREDIT FOR DISTRICT OF COLUMBIA.

* * *

(i) APPLICATION OF SECTION.—This section shall apply to property purchased after August 4, 1997, and before January 1, *2008*.

[CCH Explanation at ¶ 340. Committee Reports at ¶ 15,190.]
Amendments
• **2006, Tax Relief and Health Care Act of 2006 (P.L. 109-432)**

P.L. 109-432, Division A, § 110(d)(1):

Amended Code Sec. 1400C(i) by striking "2006" and inserting "2008". **Effective** for property purchased after 12-31-2005.

[¶ 5623] CODE SEC. 1400F. RENEWAL COMMUNITY CAPITAL GAIN.

* * *

(d) CERTAIN RULES TO APPLY.—For purposes of this section, rules similar to the rules of paragraphs (5), (6), and (7) of subsection (b), and subsections (f) and (g), of section 1400B shall apply; except that for such purposes section 1400B(g)(2) shall be applied by substituting "January 1, 2002" for "January 1, 1998" and "December 31, 2014" for "December 31, *2012*".

[CCH Explanation at ¶ 340. Committee Reports at ¶ 15,190.]
Amendments
• **2006, Tax Relief and Health Care Act of 2006 (P.L. 109-432)**

P.L. 109-432, Division A, § 110(c)(2)(C):

Amended Code Sec. 1400F(d) by striking "2010" and inserting "2012". **Effective** 12-20-2006.

[¶ 5626] CODE SEC. 1400N. TAX BENEFITS FOR GULF OPPORTUNITY ZONE.

* * *

(d) SPECIAL ALLOWANCE FOR CERTAIN PROPERTY ACQUIRED ON OR AFTER AUGUST 28, 2005.—

* * *

(6) EXTENSION FOR CERTAIN PROPERTY.—

(A) IN GENERAL.—In the case of any specified Gulf Opportunity Zone extension property, paragraph (2)(A) shall be applied without regard to clause (v) thereof.

(B) SPECIFIED GULF OPPORTUNITY ZONE EXTENSION PROPERTY.—For purposes of this paragraph, the term "specified Gulf Opportunity Zone extension property" means property—

(i) substantially all of the use of which is in one or more specified portions of the GO Zone, and

(ii) which is—

(I) nonresidential real property or residential rental property which is placed in service by the taxpayer on or before December 31, 2010, or

(II) in the case of a taxpayer who places a building described in subclause (I) in service on or before December 31, 2010, property described in section 168(k)(2)(A)(i) if substantially all of the use of such property is in such building and such property is placed in service by the taxpayer not later than 90 days after such building is placed in service.

(C) SPECIFIED PORTIONS OF THE GO ZONE.—For purposes of this paragraph, the term "specified portions of the GO Zone" means those portions of the GO Zone which are in any county or parish which is identified by the Secretary as being a county or parish in which hurricanes occurring during

2005 damaged (in the aggregate) more than 60 percent of the housing units in such county or parish which were occupied (determined according to the 2000 Census).

(D) ONLY PRE-JANUARY 1, 2010, BASIS OF REAL PROPERTY ELIGIBLE FOR ADDITIONAL ALLOWANCE.— *In the case of property which is qualified Gulf Opportunity Zone property solely by reason of subparagraph (B)(ii)(I), paragraph (1) shall apply only to the extent of the adjusted basis thereof attributable to manufacture, construction, or production before January 1, 2010.*

[CCH Explanation at ¶315. Committee Reports at ¶15,290.]

Amendments

• **2006, Tax Relief and Health Care Act of 2006 (P.L. 109-432)**

P.L. 109-432, Division A, §120(a):

Amended Code Sec. 1400N(d) by adding at the end a new paragraph (6). **Effective** as if included in section 101 of the

Gulf Opportunity Zone Act of 2005 (P.L. 109-135) **[effective** for tax years ending on or after 8-28-2005.—CCH].

(e) INCREASE IN EXPENSING UNDER SECTION 179.—

* * *

(2) QUALIFIED SECTION 179 GULF OPPORTUNITY ZONE PROPERTY.—For purposes of this subsection, the term "qualified section 179 Gulf Opportunity Zone property" means section 179 property (as defined in section 179(d)) which is qualified Gulf Opportunity Zone property (as defined in subsection (d)(2) *without regard to subsection (d)(6)*).

* * *

[CCH Explanation at ¶315. Committee Reports at ¶15,290.]

Amendments

• **2006, Tax Relief and Health Care Act of 2006 (P.L. 109-432)**

P.L. 109-432, Division A, §120(b):

Amended Code Sec. 1400N(e)(2) by inserting "without regard to subsection (d)(6)" after "subsection (d)(2)". **Effec-**

tive as if included in section 101 of the Gulf Opportunity Zone Act of 2005 (P.L. 109-135) **[effective for tax years** ending on or after 8-28-2005.—CCH].

(l) CREDIT TO HOLDERS OF GULF TAX CREDIT BONDS.—

* * *

(7) OTHER DEFINITIONS AND SPECIAL RULES.—For purposes of this subsection—

* * *

(B) PARTNERSHIP; S CORPORATION; AND OTHER PASS-THRU ENTITIES.—

* * *

(ii) NO BASIS ADJUSTMENT.—In the case of a bond held by a partnership or an S corporation, rules similar to the rules under *section 1397E(l)* shall apply.

* * *

[CCH Explanation at ¶605. Committee Reports at ¶15,160.]

Amendments

• **2006, Tax Relief and Health Care Act of 2006 (P.L. 109-432)**

P.L. 109-432, Division A, §107(b)(2):

Amended Code Sec. 1400N(l)(7)(B)(ii) by striking "section 1397E(i)" and inserting "section 1397E(l)". **Effective** for obli-

gations issued after 12-20-2006 pursuant to allocations of the national zone academy bond limitation for calendar years after 2005.

[¶ 5630] CODE SEC. 1445. WITHHOLDING OF TAX ON DISPOSITIONS OF UNITED STATES REAL PROPERTY INTERESTS.

* * *

(b) EXEMPTIONS.—

* * *

(8) APPLICABLE WASH SALES TRANSACTIONS.—No person shall be required to deduct and withhold any amount under subsection (a) with respect to a disposition which is treated as a disposition of a United States real property interest solely by reason of section 897(h)(5).

* * *

[CCH Explanation at ¶ 1025. Committee Reports at ¶ 10,190.]

Amendments

• **2006, Tax Increase Prevention and Reconciliation Act of 2005 (P.L. 109-222)**

P.L. 109-222, § 506(b):

Amended Code Sec. 1445(b) by adding at the end a new paragraph (8). **Effective** for tax years beginning after 12-31-2005, except that such amendment shall not apply to any distribution, or substitute dividend payment, occurring before the date that is 30 days after 5-17-2006.

(e) SPECIAL RULES RELATING TO DISTRIBUTIONS, ETC., BY CORPORATIONS, PARTNERSHIPS, TRUSTS, OR ESTATES.—

* * *

(6) DISTRIBUTIONS BY REGULATED INVESTMENT COMPANIES AND REAL ESTATE INVESTMENT TRUSTS.—If any portion of a distribution from a qualified investment entity (as defined in section 897(h)(4)) to a nonresident alien individual or a foreign corporation is treated under section 897(h)(1) as gain realized by such individual or corporation from the sale or exchange of a United States real property interest, the qualified investment entity shall deduct and withhold under subsection (a) a tax equal to 35 percent (or, to the extent provided in regulations, 15 percent (20 percent in the case of taxable years beginning after December 31, 2010)) of the amount so treated.

(7) REGULATIONS.—The Secretary shall prescribe such regulations as may be necessary to carry out the purposes of this subsection, including regulations providing for exceptions from provisions of this subsection and regulations for the application of this subsection in the case of payments through 1 or more entities.

* * *

[CCH Explanation at ¶ 1020. Committee Reports at ¶ 10,190.]

Amendments

• **2006, Tax Increase Prevention and Reconciliation Act of 2005 (P.L. 109-222)**

P.L. 109-222, § 505(b):

Amended Code Sec. 1445(e) by redesignating paragraph (6) as paragraph (7) and by inserting after paragraph (5) a new paragraph (6). **Effective** for tax years of qualified investment entities beginning after 12-31-2005, except that no amount shall be required to be withheld under Code Sec. 1441, 1442, or 1445 with respect to any distribution before 5-17-2006 if such amount was not otherwise required to be withheld under any such section as in effect before such amendments.

[¶ 5655] CODE SEC. 3402. INCOME TAX COLLECTED AT SOURCE.

* * *

»»→ *Caution: Code Sec. 3402(t), below, as added by P.L. 109-222, applies to payments made after December 31, 2010.*

(t) EXTENSION OF WITHHOLDING TO CERTAIN PAYMENTS MADE BY GOVERNMENT ENTITIES.—

(1) GENERAL RULE.—The Government of the United States, every State, every political subdivision thereof, and every instrumentality of the foregoing (including multi-State agencies) making any payment to any person providing any property or services (including any payment made in connection with a government voucher or certificate program which functions as a payment for property or services) shall deduct and withhold from such payment a tax in an amount equal to 3 percent of such payment.

(2) PROPERTY AND SERVICES SUBJECT TO WITHHOLDING.—Paragraph (1) shall not apply to any payment—

(A) except as provided in subparagraph (B), which is subject to withholding under any other provision of this chapter or chapter 3,

(B) which is subject to withholding under section 3406 and from which amounts are being withheld under such section,

(C) of interest,

(D) for real property,

(E) to any governmental entity subject to the requirements of paragraph (1), any tax-exempt entity, or any foreign government,

(F) made pursuant to a classified or confidential contract described in section 6050M(e)(3),

(G) made by a political subdivision of a State (or any instrumentality thereof) which makes less than $100,000,000 of such payments annually,

(H) which is in connection with a public assistance or public welfare program for which eligibility is determined by a needs or income test, and

(I) to any government employee not otherwise excludable with respect to their services as an employee.

(3) COORDINATION WITH OTHER SECTIONS.—For purposes of sections 3403 and 3404 and for purposes of so much of subtitle F (except section 7205) as relates to this chapter, payments to any person for property or services which are subject to withholding shall be treated as if such payments were wages paid by an employer to an employee.

[CCH Explanation at ¶1125. Committee Reports at ¶10,250.]

Amendments
• **2006, Tax Increase Prevention and Reconciliation Act of 2005 (P.L. 109-222)**

P.L. 109-222, §511(a):

Amended Code Sec. 3402 by adding at the end a new subsection (t). **Effective** for payments made after 12-31-2010.

[¶5660] CODE SEC. 4041. IMPOSITION OF TAX.

* * *

(b) EXEMPTION FOR OFF-HIGHWAY BUSINESS USE; REDUCTION IN TAX FOR QUALIFIED METHANOL AND ETHANOL FUEL.—

* * *

(2) QUALIFIED METHANOL AND ETHANOL FUEL.—

* * *

(B) *QUALIFIED METHANOL AND ETHANOL FUEL PRODUCED FROM COAL.*—The term "qualified methanol or ethanol fuel" means any liquid at least 85 percent of which consists of methanol, ethanol, or other alcohol produced from coal (including peat).

(C) APPLICABLE BLENDER RATE.—For purposes of subparagraph (A)(i), the applicable blender rate is—

(i) except as provided in clause (ii), 5.4 cents, and

(ii) for sales or uses during calendar years 2001 through *2008*, ¹/₁₀ of the blender amount applicable under section 40(h)(2) for the calendar year in which the sale or use occurs.

(D) TERMINATION.—On and after *January 1, 2009,* subparagraph (A) shall not apply.

* * *

[CCH Explanation at ¶ 665. Committee Reports at ¶ 15,420.]

Amendments

• **2006, Tax Relief and Health Care Act of 2006 (P.L. 109-432)**

P.L. 109-432, Division A, § 208(a):

Amended Code Sec. 4041(b)(2)(D) by striking "October 1, 2007" and inserting "January 1, 2009". **Effective** 12-20-2006.

P.L. 109-432, Division A, § 208(b):

Amended Code Sec. 4041(b)(2)(C)(ii) by striking "2007" and inserting "2008". **Effective** 12-20-2006.

P.L. 109-432, Division A, § 208(c):

Amended the heading for Code Sec. 4041(b)(2)(B). **Effective** 12-20-2006. Prior to amendment, the heading for Code Sec. 4041(b)(2)(B) read as follows:

QUALIFIED METHANOL OR ETHANOL FUEL

[¶ 5665] CODE SEC. 4082. EXEMPTIONS FOR DIESEL FUEL AND KEROSENE.

* * *

(d) ADDITIONAL EXCEPTIONS TO DYEING REQUIREMENTS FOR KEROSENE.—

* * *

(2) WHOLESALE DISTRIBUTORS.—To the extent provided in regulations, subsection (a)(2) shall not apply to kerosene received by a wholesale distributor of kerosene if such distributor—

(A) is registered under section 4101 with respect to the tax imposed by section 4081 on kerosene, and

(B) sells kerosene exclusively to ultimate vendors described in *section 6427(l)(5)(B)* with respect to kerosene.

* * *

[CCH Explanation at ¶ 670. Committee Reports at ¶ 15,650.]

Amendments

• **2006, Tax Relief and Health Care Act of 2006 (P.L. 109-432)**

P.L. 109-432, Division A, § 420(b)(2):

Amended Code Sec. 4082(d)(2)(B) by striking "section 6427(l)(6)(B)" and inserting "section 6427(l)(5)(B)". **Effective**

generally for kerosene sold after 9-30-2005. For special rules, see Act Sec. 420(c)(2) and (d) in the amendment notes following Code Sec. 6427(l).

[¶ 5670] CODE SEC. 4132. DEFINITIONS AND SPECIAL RULES.

(a) DEFINITIONS RELATING TO TAXABLE VACCINES.—For purposes of this subchapter—

(1) TAXABLE VACCINE.—The term "taxable vaccine" means any of the following vaccines which are manufactured or produced in the United States or entered into the United States for consumption, use, or warehousing:

* * *

(O) *Any meningococcal vaccine.*

(P) *Any vaccine against the human papillomavirus.*

* * *

[CCH Explanation at ¶ 685. Committee Reports at ¶ 15,530.]

Amendments

• **2006, Tax Relief and Health Care Act of 2006 (P.L. 109-432)**

P.L. 109-432, Division A, § 408(a):

Amended Code Sec. 4132(a)(1) by adding at the end a new subparagraph (O). For the **effective** date, see Act Sec. 408(c), below.

P.L. 109-432, Division A, § 408(b):

Amended Code Sec. 4132(a)(1), as amended by Act Sec. 408(a), by adding at the end a new subparagraph (P). For the **effective** date, see Act Sec. 408(c), below.

P.L. 109-432, Division A, § 408(c), provides:

(c) EFFECTIVE DATE.—

(1) SALES, ETC.—The amendments made by this section shall apply to sales and uses on or after the first day of the first month which begins more than 4 weeks after the date of the enactment of this Act.

(2) DELIVERIES.—For purposes of paragraph (1) and section 4131 of the Internal Revenue Code of 1986, in the case of sales on or before the effective date described in such paragraph for which delivery is made after such date, the delivery date shall be considered the sale date.

[¶ 5680] *CODE SEC. 4965. EXCISE TAX ON CERTAIN TAX-EXEMPT ENTITIES ENTERING INTO PROHIBITED TAX SHELTER TRANSACTIONS.*

(a) BEING A PARTY TO AND APPROVAL OF PROHIBITED TRANSACTIONS.—

(1) TAX-EXEMPT ENTITY.—

(A) IN GENERAL.—*If a transaction is a prohibited tax shelter transaction at the time any tax-exempt entity described in paragraph (1), (2), or (3) of subsection (c) becomes a party to the transaction, such entity shall pay a tax for the taxable year in which the entity becomes such a party and any subsequent taxable year in the amount determined under subsection (b)(1).*

(B) POST-TRANSACTION DETERMINATION.—*If any tax-exempt entity described in paragraph (1), (2), or (3) of subsection (c) is a party to a subsequently listed transaction at any time during a taxable year, such entity shall pay a tax for such taxable year in the amount determined under subsection (b)(1).*

(2) ENTITY MANAGER.—*If any entity manager of a tax-exempt entity approves such entity as (or otherwise causes such entity to be) a party to a prohibited tax shelter transaction at any time during the taxable year and knows or has reason to know that the transaction is a prohibited tax shelter transaction, such manager shall pay a tax for such taxable year in the amount determined under subsection (b)(2).*

(b) AMOUNT OF TAX.—

(1) ENTITY.—*In the case of a tax-exempt entity—*

(A) IN GENERAL.—*Except as provided in subparagraph (B), the amount of the tax imposed under subsection (a)(1) with respect to any transaction for a taxable year shall be an amount equal to the product of the highest rate of tax under section 11, and the greater of—*

(i) *the entity's net income (after taking into account any tax imposed by this subtitle (other than by this section) with respect to such transaction) for such taxable year which—*

(I) *in the case of a prohibited tax shelter transaction (other than a subsequently listed transaction), is attributable to such transaction, or*

(II) *in the case of a subsequently listed transaction, is attributable to such transaction and which is properly allocable to the period beginning on the later of the date such transaction is identified by guidance as a listed transaction by the Secretary or the first day of the taxable year, or*

(ii) *75 percent of the proceeds received by the entity for the taxable year which—*

(I) *in the case of a prohibited tax shelter transaction (other than a subsequently listed transaction), are attributable to such transaction, or*

(II) *in the case of a subsequently listed transaction, are attributable to such transaction and which are properly allocable to the period beginning on the later of the date such transaction is identified by guidance as a listed transaction by the Secretary or the first day of the taxable year.*

(B) INCREASE IN TAX FOR CERTAIN KNOWING TRANSACTIONS.—*In the case of a tax-exempt entity which knew, or had reason to know, a transaction was a prohibited tax shelter transaction at the time the entity became a party to the transaction, the amount of the tax imposed under subsection (a)(1)(A) with respect to any transaction for a taxable year shall be the greater of—*

(i) *100 percent of the entity's net income (after taking into account any tax imposed by this subtitle (other than by this section) with respect to the prohibited tax shelter transaction) for such taxable year which is attributable to the prohibited tax shelter transaction, or*

(ii) *75 percent of the proceeds received by the entity for the taxable year which are attributable to the prohibited tax shelter transaction.*

This subparagraph shall not apply to any prohibited tax shelter transaction to which a tax-exempt entity became a party on or before the date of the enactment of this section.

(2) ENTITY MANAGER.—*In the case of each entity manager, the amount of the tax imposed under subsection (a)(2) shall be $20,000 for each approval (or other act causing participation) described in subsection (a)(2).*

(c) TAX-EXEMPT ENTITY.—*For purposes of this section, the term "tax-exempt entity" means an entity which is—*

(1) *described in section 501(c) or 501(d),*

(2) *described in section 170(c) (other than the United States),*

(3) *an Indian tribal government (within the meaning of section 7701(a)(40)),*

(4) *described in paragraph (1), (2), or (3) of section 4979(e),*

(5) *a program described in section 529,*

(6) *an eligible deferred compensation plan described in section 457(b) which is maintained by an employer described in section 4457(e)(1)(A), or*

(7) *an arrangement described in section 4973(a).*

(d) ENTITY MANAGER.—*For purposes of this section, the term "entity manager" means—*

(1) *in the case of an entity described in paragraph (1), (2), or (3) of subsection (c)—*

(A) *the person with authority or responsibility similar to that exercised by an officer, director, or trustee of an organization, and*

(B) *with respect to any act, the person having authority or responsibility with respect to such act, and*

(2) *in the case of an entity described in paragraph (4), (5), (6), or (7) of subsection (c), the person who approves or otherwise causes the entity to be a party to the prohibited tax shelter transaction.*

(e) PROHIBITED TAX SHELTER TRANSACTION; SUBSEQUENTLY LISTED TRANSACTION.—*For purposes of this section—*

(1) PROHIBITED TAX SHELTER TRANSACTION.—

(A) IN GENERAL.—*The term "prohibited tax shelter transaction" means—*

(i) *any listed transaction, and*

(ii) *any prohibited reportable transaction.*

(B) LISTED TRANSACTION.—*The term "listed transaction" has the meaning given such term by section 6707A(c)(2).*

(C) PROHIBITED REPORTABLE TRANSACTION.—*The term "prohibited reportable transaction" means any confidential transaction or any transaction with contractual protection (as defined under regulations prescribed by the Secretary) which is a reportable transaction (as defined in section 6707A(c)(1)).*

(2) SUBSEQUENTLY LISTED TRANSACTION.—*The term "subsequently listed transaction" means any transaction to which a tax-exempt entity is a party and which is determined by the Secretary to be a listed transaction at any time after the entity has become a party to the transaction. Such term shall not include a transaction which is a prohibited reportable transaction at the time the entity became a party to the transaction.*

(f) REGULATORY AUTHORITY.—*The Secretary is authorized to promulgate regulations which provide guidance regarding the determination of the allocation of net income or proceeds of a tax-exempt entity attributable to a transaction to various periods, including before and after the listing of the transaction or the date which is 90 days after the date of the enactment of this section.*

(g) COORDINATION WITH OTHER TAXES AND PENALTIES.—*The tax imposed by this section is in addition to any other tax, addition to tax, or penalty imposed under this title.*

[CCH Explanation at ¶1130. Committee Reports at ¶10,300.]

Amendments

• **2006, Tax Increase Prevention and Reconciliation Act of 2005 (P.L. 109-222)**

P.L. 109-222, §516(a)(1):

Amended chapter 42 by adding at the end a new subchapter F (Code Sec. 4965). **Effective** for tax years ending

after 5-17-2006, with respect to transactions before, on, or after such date, except that no tax under Code Sec. 4965(a), as added by Act Sec. 516, shall apply with respect to income or proceeds that are properly allocable to any period ending on or before the date which is 90 days after 5-17-2006.

[¶5690] CODE SEC. 4980G. FAILURE OF EMPLOYER TO MAKE COMPARABLE HEALTH SAVINGS ACCOUNT CONTRIBUTIONS.

* * *

(d) EXCEPTION.—For purposes of applying section 4980E to a contribution to a health savings account of an employee who is not a highly compensated employee (as defined in section 414(q)), highly compensated employees shall not be treated as comparable participating employees.

[CCH Explanation at ¶520. Committee Reports at ¶15,460.]

Amendments

• **2006, Tax Relief and Health Care Act of 2006 (P.L. 109-432)**

P.L. 109-432, Division A, §306(a):

Amended Code Sec. 4980G by adding at the end a new subsection (d). **Effective** for tax years beginning after 12-31-2006.

[¶5695] CODE SEC. 5382. CELLAR TREATMENT OF NATURAL WINE.

(a) PROPER CELLAR TREATMENT.—

(1) IN GENERAL.—Proper cellar treatment of natural wine constitutes—

(A) subject to paragraph (2), those practices and procedures in the United States, whether historical or newly developed, of using various methods and materials to *correct or stabilize* the wine, or the fruit juice from which it is made, so as to produce a finished product acceptable in good commercial practice in accordance with regulations prescribed by the Secretary; and

* * *

Amendments

• **2006, Tax Relief and Health Care Act of 2006 (P.L. 109-432)**

P.L. 109-432, Division D, §3007:

Amended Code Sec. 5382(a)(1)(A) by striking "stabilize" and inserting "correct or stabilize". **Effective** 12-20-2006.

[¶5700] CODE SEC. 5388. DESIGNATION OF WINES.

* * *

(c) USE OF SEMI-GENERIC DESIGNATIONS.—

* * *

(3) SPECIAL RULE FOR USE OF CERTAIN SEMIGENERIC DESIGNATIONS.—

(A) IN GENERAL.—In the case of any wine to which this paragraph applies—

(i) paragraph (1) shall not apply,

(ii) in the case of wine of the European Community, designations referred to in subparagraph (C)(i) may be used for such wine only if the requirement of subparagraph (B)(ii) is met, and

(iii) in the case [of] any other wine bearing a brand name, or brand name and fanciful name, semi-generic designations may be used for such wine only if the requirements of clauses (i), (ii), and (iii) of subparagraph (B) are met.

(B) REQUIREMENTS.—

(i) The requirement of this clause is met if there appears in direct conjunction with the semi-generic designation an appropriate appellation of origin disclosing the origin of the wine.

(ii) The requirement of this clause is met if the wine conforms to the standard of identity, if any, for such wine contained in the regulations under this section or, if there is no such standard, to the trade understanding of such class or type.

(iii) The requirement of this clause is met if the person, or its successor in interest, using the semi-generic designation held a Certificate of Label Approval or Certificate of Exemption from Label Approval issued by the Secretary for a wine label bearing such brand name, or brand name and fanciful name, before March 10, 2006, on which such semi-generic designation appeared.

(C) WINES TO WHICH PARAGRAPH APPLIES.—

(i) IN GENERAL.—Except as provided in clause (ii), this paragraph shall apply to any grape wine which is designated as Burgundy, Claret, Chablis, Champagne, Chianti, Malaga, Marsala, Madeira, Moselle, Port, Retsina, Rhine Wine or Hock, Sauterne, Haut Sauterne, Sherry, or Tokay.

(ii) EXCEPTION.—This paragraph shall not apply to wine which—

(I) contains less than 7 percent or more than 24 percent alcohol by volume,

(II) is intended for sale outside the United States, or

(III) does not bear a brand name.

Amendments

● **2006, Tax Relief and Health Care Act of 2006 (P.L. 109-432)**

P.L. 109-432, Division A, § 422(a):

Amended Code Sec. 5388(c) by adding at the end a new paragraph (3). **Effective** for wine imported or bottled in the United States on or after 12-20-2006.

[¶ 5702] CODE SEC. 5754. RESTRICTION ON IMPORTATION OF PREVIOUSLY EXPORTED TOBACCO PRODUCTS.

* * *

(c) CROSS REFERENCES.—

(1) For exception to this section for personal use, see *section 5761(d).*

* * *

[CCH Explanation at ¶ 345. Committee Reports at ¶ 15,470.]

Amendments

● **2006, Tax Relief and Health Care Act of 2006 (P.L. 109-432)**

P.L. 109-432, Division C, § 401(f)(2)(B):

Amended Code Sec. 5754(c)(1) by striking "section 5761(c)" and inserting "section 5761(d)". **Effective** with re-spect to goods entered, or withdrawn from warehouse for consumption, on or after the 15th day after 12-20-2006.

[¶ 5704] CODE SEC. 5761. CIVIL PENALTIES.

* * *

(c) SALE OF TOBACCO PRODUCTS AND CIGARETTE PAPERS AND TUBES FOR EXPORT.—Except as provided in subsections (b) and (d) of section 5704—

(1) every person who sells, relands, or receives within the jurisdiction of the United States any tobacco products or cigarette papers or tubes which have been labeled or shipped for exportation under this chapter,

(2) every person who sells or receives such relanded tobacco products or cigarette papers or tubes, and

(3) every person who aids or abets in such selling, relanding, or receiving,

shall, in addition to the tax and any other penalty provided in this title, be liable for a penalty equal to the greater of $1,000 or 5 times the amount of the tax imposed by this chapter. All tobacco products and cigarette papers and tubes relanded within the jurisdiction of the United States shall be forfeited to the United States and destroyed. All vessels, vehicles, and aircraft used in such relanding or in removing such products, papers, and tubes from the place where relanded, shall be forfeited to the United States.

[CCH Explanation at ¶ 341. Committee Reports at ¶ 15,470.]

Amendments

• **2006, Tax Relief and Health Care Act of 2006 (P.L. 109-432)**

P.L. 109-432, Division C, § 401(f)(2)(A):

Amended Code Sec. 5761(c) by striking the last two sentences. **Effective** with respect to goods entered, or withdrawn from warehouse for consumption, on or after the 15th day after 12-20-2006. Prior to being stricken, the last two of sentences of Code Sec. 5761(c) read as follows:

This subsection and section 5754 shall not apply to any person who relands or receives tobacco products in the quantity allowed entry free of tax and duty under chapter 98 of the Harmonized Tariff Schedule of the United States, and such person may voluntarily relinquish to the Secretary at the time of entry any excess of such quantity without incurring the penalty under this subsection. No quantity of tobacco products other than the quantity referred to in the preceding sentence may be relanded or received as a personal use quantity.

(d) PERSONAL USE QUANTITIES.—

(1) IN GENERAL.—No quantity of tobacco products other than the quantity referred to in paragraph (2) may be relanded or received as a personal use quantity.

(2) EXCEPTION FOR PERSONAL USE QUANTITY.—Subsection (c) and section 5754 shall not apply to any person who relands or receives tobacco products in the quantity allowed entry free of tax and duty under chapter 98 of the Harmonized Tariff Schedule of the United States, and such person may voluntarily relinquish to the Secretary at the time of entry any excess of such quantity without incurring the penalty under subsection (c).

(3) SPECIAL RULE FOR DELIVERY SALES.—

(A) IN GENERAL.—Paragraph (2) shall not apply to any tobacco product sold in connection with a delivery sale.

(B) DELIVERY SALE.—For purposes of subparagraph (A), the term "delivery sale" means any sale of a tobacco product to a consumer if—

(i) the consumer submits the order for such sale by means of a telephone or other method of voice transmission, the mail, or the Internet or other online service, or the seller is otherwise not in the physical presence of the buyer when the request for purchase or order is made, or

(ii) the tobacco product is delivered by use of a common carrier, private delivery service, or the mail, or the seller is not in the physical presence of the buyer when the buyer obtains personal possession of the tobacco product.

[CCH Explanation at ¶ 345. Committee Reports at ¶ 15,470.]

Amendments

• **2006, Tax Relief and Health Care Act of 2006 (P.L. 109-432)**

P.L. 109-432, Division C, § 401(f)(1):

Amended Code Sec. 5761 by redesignating subsections (d) and (e) as subsections (e) and (f), respectively, and inserting

after subsection (c) a new subsection (d). **Effective** with respect to goods entered, or withdrawn from warehouse for consumption, on or after the 15th day after 12-20-2006.

(e) APPLICABILITY OF SECTION 6665.—The penalties imposed by subsections (b) and (c) shall be assessed, collected, and paid in the same manner as taxes, as provided in section 6665(a).

[CCH Explanation at ¶345. Committee Reports at ¶15,470.]

Amendments

• **2006, Tax Relief and Health Care Act of 2006 (P.L. 109-432)**

P.L. 109-432, Division C, §401(f)(1):

Amended Code Sec. 5761 by redesignating subsection (d) as subsection (e). **Effective** with respect to goods entered, or

withdrawn from warehouse for consumption, on or after the 15th day after 12-20-2006.

(f) CROSS REFERENCES.—

For penalty for failure to make deposits or for overstatement of deposits, see section 6656.

[CCH Explanation at ¶345. Committee Reports at ¶15,470.]

Amendments

• **2006, Tax Relief and Health Care Act of 2006 (P.L. 109-432)**

P.L. 109-432, Division C, §401(f)(1):

Amended Code Sec. 5761 by redesignating subsection (e) as subsection (f). **Effective** with respect to goods entered, or

withdrawn from warehouse for consumption, on or after the 15th day after 12-20-2006.

[¶5705] CODE SEC. 6011. GENERAL REQUIREMENT OF RETURN, STATEMENT, OR LIST.

* * *

(g) DISCLOSURE OF REPORTABLE TRANSACTION TO TAX-EXEMPT ENTITY.—*Any taxable party to a prohibited tax shelter transaction (as defined in section 4965(e)(1)) shall by statement disclose to any tax-exempt entity (as defined in section 4965(c)) which is a party to such transaction that such transaction is such a prohibited tax shelter transaction.*

[CCH Explanation at ¶1130. Committee Reports at ¶10,300.]

Amendments

• **2006, Tax Increase Prevention and Reconciliation Act of 2005 (P.L. 109-222)**

P.L. 109-222, §516(b)(2):

Amended Code Sec. 6011 by redesignating subsection (g) as subsection (h) and by inserting after subsection (f) a new

subsection (g). **Effective** for disclosures the due date for which are after 5-17-2006.

(h) INCOME, ESTATE, AND GIFT TAXES.—For requirement that returns of income, estate, and gift taxes be made whether or not there is tax liability, see subparts B and C.

[CCH Explanation at ¶1130. Committee Reports at ¶10,300.]

Amendments

• **2006, Tax Increase Prevention and Reconciliation Act of 2005 (P.L. 109-222)**

P.L. 109-222, §516(b)(2):

Amended Code Sec. 6011 by redesignating subsection (g) as subsection (h). **Effective** for disclosures the due date for which are after 5-17-2006.

[¶5720] CODE SEC. 6015. RELIEF FROM JOINT AND SEVERAL LIABILITY ON JOINT RETURN.

* * *

(e) PETITION FOR REVIEW BY TAX COURT.—

(1) IN GENERAL.—In the case of an individual against whom a deficiency has been asserted and who elects to have subsection (b) or (c) apply, *or in the case of an individual who requests equitable relief under subsection (f)* —

(A) IN GENERAL.—In addition to any other remedy provided by law, the individual may petition the Tax Court (and the Tax Court shall have jurisdiction) to determine the appropriate relief available to the individual under this section if such petition is filed—

(i) at any time after the earlier of—

(I) the date the Secretary mails, by certified or registered mail to the taxpayer's last known address, notice of the Secretary's final determination of relief available to the individual, or

(II) the date which is 6 months after the date such election is filed *or request is made* with the Secretary, and

(ii) not later than the close of the 90th day after the date described in clause (i)(I).

(B) RESTRICTIONS APPLICABLE TO COLLECTION OF ASSESSMENT.—

(i) IN GENERAL.—Except as otherwise provided in section 6851 or 6861, no levy or proceeding in court shall be made, begun, or prosecuted against the individual making an election under subsection (b) or (c) *or requesting equitable relief under subsection (f)* for collection of any assessment to which such election *or request* relates until the close of the 90th day referred to in subparagraph (A)(ii), or, if a petition has been filed with the Tax Court under subparagraph (A), until the decision of the Tax Court has become final. Rules similar to the rules of section 7485 shall apply with respect to the collection of such assessment.

(ii) AUTHORITY TO ENJOIN COLLECTION ACTIONS.—Notwithstanding the provisions of section 7421(a), the beginning of such levy or proceeding during the time the prohibition under clause (i) is in force may be enjoined by a proceeding in the proper court, including the Tax Court. The Tax Court shall have no jurisdiction under this subparagraph to enjoin any action or proceeding unless a timely petition has been filed under subparagraph (A) and then only in respect of the amount of the assessment to which the election under subsection (b) or (c) relates *or to which the request under subsection (f) relates.*

* * *

(4) NOTICE TO OTHER SPOUSE.—The Tax Court shall establish rules which provide the individual filing a joint return but not making the election under subsection (b) or (c) *or the request for equitable relief under subsection (f)* with adequate notice and an opportunity to become a party to a proceeding under either such subsection.

(5) WAIVER.—An individual who elects the application of subsection (b) or (c) *or who requests equitable relief under subsection (f)* (and who agrees with the Secretary's determination of relief) may waive in writing at any time the restrictions in paragraph (1)(B) with respect to collection of the outstanding assessment (whether or not a notice of the Secretary's final determination of relief has been mailed).

* * *

[CCH Explanation at ¶ 660. Committee Reports at ¶ 15,530.]

Amendments

• **2006, Tax Relief and Health Care Act of 2006 (P.L. 109-432)**

P.L. 109-432, Division C, § 408(a):

Amended Code Sec. 6015(e)(1) by inserting ", or in the case of an individual who requests equitable relief under subsection (f)" after "who elects to have subsection (b) or (c) apply". **Effective** with respect to liability for taxes arising or remaining unpaid on or after 12-20-2006.

P.L. 109-432, Division C, § 408(b)(1):

Amended Code Sec. 6015(e)(1)(A)(i)(II) by inserting "or request is made" after "election is filed". **Effective** with respect to liability for taxes arising or remaining unpaid on or after 12-20-2006.

P.L. 109-432, Division C, § 408(b)(2)(A)-(B):

Amended Code Sec. 6015(e)(1)(B)(i) by inserting "or requesting equitable relief under subsection (f)" after "making an election under subsection (b) or (c)", and by inserting "or request" after "to which such election". **Effective** with respect to liability for taxes arising or remaining unpaid on or after 12-20-2006.

P.L. 109-432, Division C, § 408(b)(3):

Amended Code Sec. 6015(e)(1)(B)(ii) by inserting "or to which the request under subsection (f) relates" after "to which the election under subsection (b) or (c) relates". **Effective** with respect to liability for taxes arising or remaining unpaid on or after 12-20-2006.

P.L. 109-432, Division C, §408(b)(4):

Amended Code Sec. 6015(e)(4) by inserting "or the request for equitable relief under subsection (f)" after "the election under subsection (b) or (c)". **Effective** with respect to liability for taxes arising or remaining unpaid on or after 12-20-2006.

P.L. 109-432, Division C, §408(b)(5):

Amended Code Sec. 6015(e)(5) by inserting "or who requests equitable relief under subsection (f)" after "who elects the application of subsection (b) or (c)". **Effective** with respect to liability for taxes arising or remaining unpaid on or after 12-20-2006.

(g) CREDITS AND REFUNDS.—

* * *

(2) RES JUDICATA.—In the case of any election under subsection (b) or (c) *or of any request for equitable relief under subsection (f)*, if a decision of a court in any prior proceeding for the same taxable year has become final, such decision shall be conclusive except with respect to the qualification of the individual for relief which was not an issue in such proceeding. The exception contained in the preceding sentence shall not apply if the court determines that the individual participated meaningfully in such prior proceeding.

* * *

[CCH Explanation at ¶660. Committee Reports at ¶15,530.]

Amendments

• **2006, Tax Relief and Health Care Act of 2006 (P.L. 109-432)**

P.L. 109-432, Division C, §408(b)(6):

Amended Code Sec. 6015(g)(2) by inserting "or of any request for equitable relief under subsection (f)" after "any

election under subsection (b) or (c)". **Effective** with respect to liability for taxes arising or remaining unpaid on or after 12-20-2006.

(h) REGULATIONS.—The Secretary shall prescribe such regulations as are necessary to carry out the provisions of this section, including—

* * *

(2) regulations providing the opportunity for an individual to have notice of, and an opportunity to participate in, any administrative proceeding with respect to an election made under subsection (b) or (c) *or a request for equitable relief made under subsection (f)* by the other individual filing the joint return.

[CCH Explanation at ¶660. Committee Reports at ¶15,530.]

Amendments

• **2006, Tax Relief and Health Care Act of 2006 (P.L. 109-432)**

P.L. 109-432, Division C, §408(b)(7):

Amended Code Sec. 6015(h)(2) by inserting "or a request for equitable relief made under subsection (f)" after "with

respect to an election made under subsection (b) or (c)". **Effective** with respect to liability for taxes arising or remaining unpaid on or after 12-20-2006.

[¶5730] CODE SEC. 6033. RETURNS BY EXEMPT ORGANIZATIONS.

(a) ORGANIZATIONS REQUIRED TO FILE.—

(1) IN GENERAL.—Except as provided in *paragraph (3)*, every organization exempt from taxation under section 501(a) shall file an annual return, stating specifically the items of gross income, receipts, and disbursements, and such other information for the purpose of carrying out the internal revenue laws as the Secretary may by forms or regulations prescribe, and shall keep such records, render under oath such statements, make such other returns, and comply with such rules and regulations as the Secretary may from time to time prescribe; except that, in the discretion of the Secretary, any organization described in section 401(a) may be relieved from stating in its return any information which is reported in returns filed by the employer which established such organization.

(2) *BEING A PARTY TO CERTAIN REPORTABLE TRANSACTIONS.—Every tax-exempt entity described in section 4965(c) shall file (in such form and manner and at such time as determined by the Secretary) a disclosure of—*

(A) such entity's being a party to any prohibited tax shelter transaction (as defined in section 4965(e)), and

(B) the identity of any other party to such transaction which is known by such tax-exempt entity.

(3) EXCEPTIONS FROM FILING.—

* * *

[CCH Explanation at ¶1130. Committee Reports at ¶10,300.]

Amendments

• **2006, Tax Increase Prevention and Reconciliation Act of 2005 (P.L. 109-222)**

P.L. 109-222, §516(b)(1)(A):

Amended Code Sec. 6033(a) by redesignating paragraph (2) as paragraph (3) and by inserting after paragraph (1) a new paragraph (2). **Effective** for disclosures the due date[s] for which are after 5-17-2006.

P.L. 109-222, §516(b)(1)(B):

Amended Code Sec. 6033(a)(1) by striking "paragraph (2)" and inserting "paragraph (3)". **Effective** for disclosures the due date[s] for which are after 5-17-2006.

[¶5740] CODE SEC. 6039. *RETURNS* REQUIRED IN CONNECTION WITH CERTAIN OPTIONS.

(a) *REQUIREMENT OF REPORTING.*—Every corporation—

(1) which in any calendar year transfers to any person a share of stock pursuant to such person's exercise of an incentive stock option, or

(2) which in any calendar year records (or has by its agent recorded) a transfer of the legal title of a share of stock acquired by the transferor pursuant to his exercise of an option described in section 423(c) (relating to special rule where option price is between 85 percent and 100 percent of value of stock),

shall, for such calendar year, make a return at such time and in such manner, and setting forth such information, as the Secretary may by regulations prescribe.

[CCH Explanation at ¶630. Committee Reports at ¶15,480.]

Amendments

• **2006, Tax Relief and Health Care Act of 2006 (P.L. 109-432)**

P.L. 109-432, Division A, §403(a):

Amended so much of Code Sec. 6039(a) as follows paragraph (2). **Effective** for calendar years beginning after 12-20-2006. Prior to amendment, so much of Code Sec. 6039(a) as followed paragraph (2) read as follows:

shall (on or before January 31 of the following calendar year) furnish to such person a written statement in such manner and setting forth such information as the Secretary may by regulations prescribe.

P.L. 109-432, Division A, §403(c)(3):

Amended the heading of Code Sec. 6039 by striking "Information" and inserting "Returns". **Effective** for calendar years beginning after 12-20-2006.

P.L. 109-432, Division A, §403(c)(4):

Amended the heading of Code Sec. 6039(a) by striking "FURNISHING OF INFORMATION" and inserting "REQUIREMENT OF REPORTING". **Effective** for calendar years beginning after 12-20-2006.

(b) STATEMENTS TO BE FURNISHED TO PERSONS WITH RESPECT TO WHOM INFORMATION IS REPORTED.— *Every corporation making a return under subsection (a) shall furnish to each person whose name is set forth in such return a written statement setting forth such information as the Secretary may by regulations prescribe. The written statement required under the preceding sentence shall be furnished to such person on or before January 31 of the year following the calendar year for which the return under subsection (a) was made.*

[CCH Explanation at ¶630. Committee Reports at ¶15,480.]

Amendments

• **2006, Tax Relief and Health Care Act of 2006 (P.L. 109-432)**

P.L. 109-432, Division A, §403(b):

Amended Code Sec. 6039 by redesignating subsections (b) and (c) as subsections (c) and (d), respectively, and by inserting after subsection (a) a new subsection (b). **Effective** for calendar years beginning after 12-20-2006.

(c) SPECIAL RULES.—For purposes of this section—

(1) TREATMENT BY EMPLOYER TO BE DETERMINATIVE.—Any option which the corporation treats as an incentive stock option or an option granted under an employee stock purchase plan shall be deemed to be such an option.

(2) SUBSECTION (a)(2) APPLIES ONLY TO FIRST TRANSFER DESCRIBED THEREIN.—A statement is required by reason of a transfer described in subsection (a)(2) of a share only with respect to the first transfer of such share by the person who exercised the option.

(3) IDENTIFICATION OF STOCK.—Any corporation which transfers any share of stock pursuant to the exercise of any option described in subsection (a)(2) shall identify such stock in a manner adequate to carry out the purposes of this section.

[CCH Explanation at ¶ 630. Committee Reports at ¶ 15,480.]
Amendments
• **2006, Tax Relief and Health Care Act of 2006**
(P.L. 109-432)

P.L. 109-432, Division A, § 403(b):

Amended Code Sec. 6039 by redesignating subsection (b) as subsection (c). **Effective** for calendar years beginning after 12-20-2006.

(d) CROSS REFERENCES.—

For definition of—

(1) the term "incentive stock option", see section 422(b), and

(2) the term "employee stock purchase plan" see section 423(b).

[CCH Explanation at ¶ 630. Committee Reports at ¶ 15,480.]
Amendments
• **2006, Tax Relief and Health Care Act of 2006**
(P.L. 109-432)

P.L. 109-432, Division A, § 403(b):

Amended Code Sec. 6039 by redesignating subsection (c) as subsection (d). **Effective** for calendar years beginning after 12-20-2006.

[¶ 5755] CODE SEC. 6049. RETURNS REGARDING PAYMENTS OF INTEREST.

* * *

(b) INTEREST DEFINED.—

* * *

(2) EXCEPTIONS.—For purposes of subsection (a), the term "interest" does not include—

(A) interest on any obligation issued by a natural person,

(B) except to the extent otherwise provided in regulations—

(i) any amount paid to any person described in paragraph (4), or

(ii) any amount described in paragraph (5), and

(C) except to the extent otherwise provided in regulations, any amount not described in *subparagraph (B)* of this paragraph which is income from sources outside the United States or which is paid by—

(i) a foreign government or international organization or any agency or instrumentality thereof.

(ii) a foreign central bank of issue.

(iii) a foreign corporation not engaged in a trade or business in the United States,

(iv) a foreign corporation, the interest payments of which would be exempt from withholding under subchapter A of chapter 3 if paid to a person who is not a United States person, or

(v) a partnership not engaged in a trade or business in the United States and composed in whole of nonresident alien individuals and persons described in clause (i), (ii), or (iii).

* * *

[CCH Explanation at ¶1105. Committee Reports at ¶10,160.]

Amendments

• 2006, Tax Increase Prevention and Reconciliation Act of 2005 (P.L. 109-222)

P.L. 109-222, §502(a):

Amended Code Sec. 6049(b)(2) by striking subparagraph (B) and by redesignating subparagraphs (C) and (D) as subparagraphs (B) and (C), respectively. **Effective** for interest paid after 12-31-2005. Prior to being stricken, Code Sec. 6049(b)(2)(B) read as follows:

(B) interest on any obligation if such interest is exempt from tax under section 103(a) or if such interest is exempt from tax (without regard to the identity of the holder) under any other provision of this title,

P.L. 109-222, §502(b):

Amended Code Sec. 6049(b)(2)(C), as redesignated by Act Sec. 502(a), by striking "subparagraph (C)" and inserting "subparagraph (B)". **Effective** for interest paid after 12-31-2005.

[¶5765] CODE SEC. 6050H. RETURNS RELATING TO MORTGAGE INTEREST RECEIVED IN TRADE OR BUSINESS FROM INDIVIDUALS.

* * *

(h) RETURNS RELATING TO MORTGAGE INSURANCE PREMIUMS.—

(1) IN GENERAL.—The Secretary may prescribe, by regulations, that any person who, in the course of a trade or business, receives from any individual premiums for mortgage insurance aggregating $600 or more for any calendar year, shall make a return with respect to each such individual. Such return shall be in such form, shall be made at such time, and shall contain such information as the Secretary may prescribe.

(2) STATEMENT TO BE FURNISHED TO INDIVIDUALS WITH RESPECT TO WHOM INFORMATION IS REQUIRED.— Every person required to make a return under paragraph (1) shall furnish to each individual with respect to whom a return is made a written statement showing such information as the Secretary may prescribe. Such written statement shall be furnished on or before January 31 of the year following the calendar year for which the return under paragraph (1) was required to be made.

(3) SPECIAL RULES.—For purposes of this subsection—

(A) rules similar to the rules of subsection (c) shall apply, and

(B) the term "mortgage insurance" means—

(i) mortgage insurance provided by the Veterans Administration, the Federal Housing Administration, or the Rural Housing Administration, and

(ii) private mortgage insurance (as defined by section 2 of the Homeowners Protection Act of 1998 (12 U.S.C. 4901), as in effect on the date of the enactment of this subsection).

[CCH Explanation at ¶220. Committee Reports at ¶15,640.]

Amendments

• 2006, Tax Relief and Health Care Act of 2006 (P.L. 109-432)

P.L. 109-432, Division A, §419(c):

Amended Code Sec. 6050H by adding at the end a new subsection (h). **Effective** for amounts paid or accrued after 12-31-2006.

[¶5770] CODE SEC. 6103. CONFIDENTIALITY AND DISCLOSURE OF RETURNS AND RETURN INFORMATION.

* * *

(b) DEFINITIONS.—For purposes of this section—

* * *

(5) STATE.—

(A) IN GENERAL.—The term "State" means—

(i) any of the 50 States, the District of Columbia, the Commonwealth of Puerto Rico, the Virgin Islands, the Canal Zone, Guam, American Samoa, and the Commonwealth of the Northern Mariana Islands,

(ii) for purposes of subsections (a)(2), (b)(4), (d)(1), (h)(4), and (p), any municipality—

(I) with a population in excess of 250,000 (as determined under the most recent decennial United States census data available),

(II) which imposes a tax on income or wages, and

(III) with which the Secretary (in his sole discretion) has entered into an agreement regarding disclosure, and

(iii) for purposes of subsections (a)(2), (b)(4), (d)(1), (h)(4), and (p), any governmental entity—

(I) which is formed and operated by a qualified group of municipalities, and

(II) with which the Secretary (in his sole discretion) has entered into an agreement regarding disclosure.

(B) REGIONAL INCOME TAX AGENCIES.—For purposes of subparagraph (A)(iii)—

(i) QUALIFIED GROUP OF MUNICIPALITIES.—The term "qualified group of municipalities" means, with respect to any governmental entity, 2 or more municipalities—

(I) each of which imposes a tax on income or wages,

(II) each of which, under the authority of a State statute, administers the laws relating to the imposition of such taxes through such entity, and

(III) which collectively have a population in excess of 250,000 (as determined under the most recent decennial United States census data available).

(ii) REFERENCES TO STATE LAW, ETC.—For purposes of applying subparagraph (A)(iii) to the subsections referred to in such subparagraph, any reference in such subsections to State law, proceedings, or tax returns shall be treated as references to the law, proceedings, or tax returns, as the case may be, of the municipalities which form and operate the governmental entity referred to in such subparagraph.

(iii) DISCLOSURE TO CONTRACTORS AND OTHER AGENTS.—Notwithstanding any other provision of this section, no return or return information shall be disclosed to any contractor or other agent of a governmental entity referred to in subparagraph (A)(iii) unless such entity, to the satisfaction of the Secretary—

(I) has requirements in effect which require each such contractor or other agent which would have access to returns or return information to provide safeguards (within the meaning of subsection (p)(4)) to protect the confidentiality of such returns or return information,

(II) agrees to conduct an on-site review every 3 years (or a mid-point review in the case of contracts or agreements of less than 3 years in duration) of each contractor or other agent to determine compliance with such requirements,

(III) submits the findings of the most recent review conducted under subclause (II) to the Secretary as part of the report required by subsection (p)(4)(E), and

(IV) certifies to the Secretary for the most recent annual period that such contractor or other agent is in compliance with all such requirements.

The certification required by subclause (IV) shall include the name and address of each contractor and other agent, a description of the contract or agreement with such contractor or other agent, and the duration of such contract or agreement. The requirements of this clause shall not apply to disclosures pursuant to subsection (n) for purposes of Federal tax administration and a rule similar to the rule of subsection (p)(8)(B) shall apply for purposes of this clause.

* * *

[CCH Explanation at ¶635. Committee Reports at ¶15,660.]

Amendments

• **2006, Tax Relief and Health Care Act of 2006 (P.L. 109-432)**

P.L. 109-432, Division A, §421(a):

Amended Code Sec. 6103(b)(5). **Effective** for disclosures made after 12-31-2006. Prior to amendment, Code Sec. 6103(b)(5) read as follows:

(5) STATE.—The term "State" means—

(A) any of the 50 States, the District of Columbia, the Commonwealth of Puerto Rico, the Virgin Islands, the Canal Zone, Guam, American Samoa, and the Commonwealth of the Northern Mariana Islands, and

(B) for purposes of subsections (a)(2), (b)(4), (d)(1), (h)(4), and (p) any municipality—

(i) with a population in excess of 250,000 (as determined under the most recent decennial United States census data available),

(ii) which imposes a tax on income or wages, and

(iii) with which the Secretary (in his sole discretion) has entered into an agreement regarding disclosure.

(d) DISCLOSURE TO STATE TAX OFFICIALS AND STATE AND LOCAL LAW ENFORCEMENT AGENCIES.—

* * *

(5) DISCLOSURE FOR COMBINED EMPLOYMENT TAX REPORTING.—

* * *

(B) TERMINATION.—The Secretary may not make any disclosure under this paragraph after December 31, *2007.*

(6) *LIMITATION ON DISCLOSURE REGARDING REGIONAL INCOME TAX AGENCIES TREATED AS STATES.—For purposes of paragraph (1), inspection by or disclosure to an entity described in subsection (b)(5)(A)(iii) shall be for the purpose of, and only to the extent necessary in, the administration of the laws of the member municipalities in such entity relating to the imposition of a tax on income or wages. Such entity may not redisclose any return or return information received pursuant to paragraph (1) to any such member municipality.*

* * *

[CCH Explanation at ¶635. Committee Reports at ¶15,310 and ¶15,660.]

Amendments

• **2006, Tax Relief and Health Care Act of 2006 (P.L. 109-432)**

P.L. 109-432, Division A, §122(a)(1):

Amended Code Sec. 6103(d)(5)(B) by striking "2006" and inserting "2007". **Effective** for disclosures after 12-31-2006.

P.L. 109-432, Division A, §421(b):

Amended Code Sec. 6103(d) by adding at the end a new paragraph (6). **Effective** for disclosures made after 12-31-2006.

(i) DISCLOSURE TO FEDERAL OFFICERS OR EMPLOYEES FOR ADMINISTRATION OF FEDERAL LAWS NOT RELATING TO TAX ADMINISTRATION.—

* * *

(3) DISCLOSURE OF RETURN INFORMATION TO APPRISE APPROPRIATE OFFICIALS OF CRIMINAL OR TERRORIST ACTIVITIES OR EMERGENCY CIRCUMSTANCES.—

* * *

(C) TERRORIST ACTIVITIES, ETC.—

* * *

(iv) TERMINATION.—No disclosure may be made under this subparagraph after December 31, *2007.*

* * *

(7) DISCLOSURE UPON REQUEST OF INFORMATION RELATING TO TERRORIST ACTIVITIES, ETC.—

* * *

(E) TERMINATION.—No disclosure may be made under this paragraph after December 31, *2007.*

* * *

[CCH Explanation at ¶635. Committee Reports at ¶15,320.]
Amendments
- **2006, Tax Relief and Health Care Act of 2006 (P.L. 109-432)**

P.L. 109-432, Division A, §122(b)(1):

Amended Code Sec. 6103(i)(3)(C)(iv) and (i)(7)(E) by striking "2006" and inserting "2007". **Effective** for disclosures after 12-31-2006.

(1) DISCLOSURE OF RETURNS AND RETURN INFORMATION FOR PURPOSES OTHER THAN TAX ADMINISTRATION.—

* * *

(13) DISCLOSURE OF RETURN INFORMATION TO CARRY OUT INCOME CONTINGENT REPAYMENT OF STUDENT LOANS.—

* * *

(D) TERMINATION.—This paragraph shall not apply to any request made after December 31, *2007.*

* * *

[CCH Explanation at ¶635. Committee Reports at ¶15,330.]
Amendments
- **2006, Tax Relief and Health Care Act of 2006 (P.L. 109-432)**

P.L. 109-432, Division A, §122(c)(1):

Amended Code Sec. 6103(l)(13)(D) by striking "2006" and inserting "2007". **Effective** for requests made after 12-31-2006.

[¶5780] CODE SEC. 6159. AGREEMENTS FOR PAYMENT OF TAX LIABILITY IN INSTALLMENTS.

* * *

(f) CROSS REFERENCE.—

For rights to administrative review and appeal, see *section 7122(e).*

[CCH Explanation at ¶1140. Committee Reports at ¶10,230.]
Amendments
- **2006, Tax Increase Prevention and Reconciliation Act of 2005 (P.L. 109-222)**

P.L. 109-222, §509(c):

Amended Code Sec. 6159(f) by striking "section 7122(d)" and inserting "section 7122(e)". **Effective** for offers-in-compromise submitted on and after the date which is 60 days after 5-17-2006.

[¶5785] CODE SEC. 6211. DEFINITION OF A DEFICIENCY.

* * *

(b) RULES FOR APPLICATION OF SUBSECTION (a).—For purposes of this section—

* * *

(4) For purposes of subsection (a)—

(A) any excess of the sum of the credits allowable under sections 24(d), 32, 34, *and 53(e)* over the tax imposed by subtitle A (determined without regard to such credits), and

(B) any excess of the sum of such credits as shown by the taxpayer on his return over the amount shown as the tax by the taxpayer on such return (determined without regard to such credits),

shall be taken into account as negative amounts of tax.

* * *

[CCH Explanation at ¶235. Committee Reports at ¶15,480.]

Amendments

• 2006, Tax Relief and Health Care Act of 2006
(P.L. 109-432)

P.L. 109-432, Division A, §402(b)(1):

Amended Code Sec. 6211(b)(4)(A) by striking "and 34"
and inserting "34, and 53(e)". **Effective** for tax years beginning after 12-20-2006.

[¶5790] CODE SEC. 6320. NOTICE AND OPPORTUNITY FOR HEARING UPON FILING OF NOTICE OF LIEN.

* * *

(b) RIGHT TO FAIR HEARING.—

>>>→ *Caution: Code Sec. 6320(b)(1), below, as amended by P.L. 109-432, §407(c)(1), applies to submissions made and issues raised after the date on which the Secretary first prescribes a list under Code Sec. 6702(c), as amended by P.L. 109-432, §407(a).*

(1) IN GENERAL.—If the person requests a hearing *in writing under subsection (a)(3)(B) and states the grounds for the requested hearing,* such hearing shall be held by the Internal Revenue Service Office of Appeals.

* * *

[CCH Explanation at ¶640. Committee Reports at ¶15,520.]

Amendments

• 2006, Tax Relief and Health Care Act of 2006
(P.L. 109-432)

P.L. 109-432, Division A, §407(c)(1):

Amended Code Sec. 6320(b)(1) by striking "under subsection (a)(3)(B)" and inserting "in writing under subsection
(a)(3)(B) and states the grounds for the requested hearing".
Effective for submissions made and issues raised after the
date on which the Secretary first prescribes a list under
Code Sec. 6702(c), as amended by Act Sec. 407(a).

>>>→ *Caution: Code Sec. 6320(c), below, as amended by P.L. 109-432, §407(c)(2), applies to submissions made and issues raised after the date on which the Secretary first prescribes a list under Code Sec. 6702(c), as amended by P.L. 109-432, §407(a).*

(c) CONDUCT OF HEARING; REVIEW; SUSPENSIONS.—For purposes of this section, subsections (c), (d) (other than paragraph (2)(B) thereof), *(e), and (g)* of section 6330 shall apply.

[CCH Explanation at ¶640. Committee Reports at ¶15,520.]

Amendments

• 2006, Tax Relief and Health Care Act of 2006
(P.L. 109-432)

P.L. 109-432, Division A, §407(c)(2):

Amended Code Sec. 6320(c) by striking "and (e)" and
inserting "(e), and (g)". **Effective** for submissions made and
issues raised after the date on which the Secretary first
prescribes a list under Code Sec. 6702(c), as amended by Act
Sec. 407(a).

[¶5795] CODE SEC. 6330. NOTICE AND OPPORTUNITY FOR HEARING BEFORE LEVY.

* * *

(b) Right to Fair Hearing.—

>>→ *Caution: Code Sec. 6330(b)(1), below, as amended by P.L. 109-432, §407(b)(3), applies to submissions made and issues raised after the date on which the Secretary first prescribes a list under Code Sec. 6702(c), as amended by P.L. 109-432, §407(a).*

(1) In general.—If the person requests a hearing *in writing under subsection (a)(3)(B) and states the grounds for the requested hearing,* such hearing shall be held by the Internal Revenue Service Office of Appeals.

* * *

[CCH Explanation at ¶640. Committee Reports at ¶15,520.]

Amendments

• **2006, Tax Relief and Health Care Act of 2006 (P.L. 109-432)**

P.L. 109-432, Division A, §407(b)(3):

Amended Code Sec. 6330(b)(1) by striking "under subsection (a)(3)(B)" and inserting "in writing under subsection

(a)(3)(B) and states the grounds for the requested hearing". Effective for submissions made and issues raised after the date on which the Secretary first prescribes a list under Code Sec. 6702(c), as amended by Act Sec. 407(a).

(c) Matters Considered at Hearing.—In the case of any hearing conducted under this section—

* * *

(4) Certain issues precluded.—An issue may not be raised at the hearing if—

(A)(i) the issue was raised and considered at a previous hearing under section 6320 or in any other previous administrative or judicial proceeding; and

(ii) the person seeking to raise the issue participated meaningfully in such hearing or proceeding; or

>>→ *Caution: Code Sec. 6330(c)(4)(B), below, as added by P.L. 109-432, §407(b)(2)(D), applies to submissions made and issues raised after the date on which the Secretary first prescribes a list under Code Sec. 6702(c), as amended by P.L. 109-432, §407(a).*

(B) the issue meets the requirement of clause (i) or (ii) of section 6702(b)(2)(A).

This paragraph shall not apply to any issue with respect to which subsection (d)(2)(B) applies.

* * *

[CCH Explanation at ¶640. Committee Reports at ¶15,520.]

Amendments

• **2006, Tax Relief and Health Care Act of 2006 (P.L. 109-432)**

P.L. 109-432, Division A, §407(b)(2)(A)-(D):

Amended Code Sec. 6330(c)(4) by striking "(A)" and inserting "(A)(i)"; by striking "(B)" and inserting "(ii)"; by

striking the period at the end of the first sentence [of subparagraph (A)(ii), as so redesignated] and inserting "; or"; and by inserting after subparagraph (A)(ii) (as so redesignated) a new subparagraph (B). Effective for submissions made and issues raised after the date on which the Secretary first prescribes a list under Code Sec. 6702(c), as amended by Act Sec. 407(a).

>>→ *Caution: Code Sec. 6330(g), below, as added by P.L. 109-432, §407(b)(1), applies to submissions made and issues raised after the date on which the Secretary first prescribes a list under Code Sec. 6702(c), as amended by P.L. 109-432, §407(a).*

(g) Frivolous Requests for Hearing, etc.—*Notwithstanding any other provision of this section, if the Secretary determines that any portion of a request for a hearing under this section or section 6320 meets the requirement of clause (i) or (ii) of section 6702(b)(2)(A), then the Secretary may treat such portion as if it were never submitted and such portion shall not be subject to any further administrative or judicial review.*

[CCH Explanation at ¶640. Committee Reports at ¶15,520.]

Amendments

• **2006, Tax Relief and Health Care Act of 2006 (P.L. 109-432)**

P.L. 109-432, Division A, §407(b)(1):

Amended Code Sec. 6330 by adding at the end a new subsection (g). **Effective** for submissions made and issues raised after the date on which the Secretary first prescribes a list under Code Sec. 6702(c), as amended by Act Sec. 407(a).

[¶5800] CODE SEC. 6427. FUELS NOT USED FOR TAXABLE PURPOSES.

* * *

(i) TIME FOR FILING CLAIMS; PERIOD COVERED.—

* * *

(4) SPECIAL RULE FOR VENDOR REFUNDS.—

(A) IN GENERAL.—A claim may be filed under subsections (b)(4) and *paragraph (4)(C) or (5)* of subsection (l) by any person with respect to fuel sold by such person for any period—

(i) for which $200 or more ($100 or more in the case of kerosene) is payable under *paragraph (4)(C) or (5)* of subsection (l), and

(ii) which is not less than 1 week.

Notwithstanding subsection (l)(1), paragraph (3)(B) shall apply to claims filed under subsections (b)(4), *(l)(4)(C)(ii), and (l)(5).*

* * *

[CCH Explanation at ¶670. Committee Reports at ¶15,650.]

Amendments

• **2006, Tax Relief and Health Care Act of 2006 (P.L. 109-432)**

P.L. 109-432, Division A, §420(b)(3)(A)-(B):

Amended Code Sec. 6427(i)(4)(A) by striking "paragraph (4)(B), (5), or (6)" each place it appears and inserting "para-graph (4)(C) or (5)", and by striking "(l)(5), and (l)(6)" and inserting "(l)(4)(C)(ii), and (l)(5)". **Effective** generally for kerosene sold after 9-30-2005. For special rules, see Act Sec. 420(c)(2) and (d) in the amendment notes following Code Sec. 6427(l).

(l) NONTAXABLE USES OF DIESEL FUEL AND KEROSENE.—

(1) IN GENERAL.—Except as otherwise provided in this subsection and in subsection (k), if any diesel fuel or kerosene on which tax has been imposed by section 4041 or 4081 is used by any person in a nontaxable use, the Secretary shall pay (without interest) to the ultimate purchaser of such fuel an amount equal to the aggregate amount of tax imposed on such fuel under section 4041 or 4081, as the case may be, reduced by any payment made to the ultimate vendor under *paragraph (4)(C)(i).*

* * *

(4) REFUNDS FOR KEROSENE USED IN AVIATION.—

(A) KEROSENE USED IN COMMERCIAL AVIATION.—In the case of kerosene used in commercial aviation (as defined in section 4083(b)) (other than supplies for vessels or aircraft within the meaning of section 4221(d)(3)), paragraph (1) shall not apply to so much of the tax imposed by section 4041 or 4081, as the case may be, as is attributable to—

(i) the Leaking Underground Storage Tank Trust Fund financing rate imposed by such section, and

(ii) so much of the rate of tax specified in section 4041(c) or 4081(a)(2)(A)(iii), as the case may be, as does not exceed 4.3 cents per gallon.

(B) KEROSENE USED IN NONCOMMERCIAL AVIATION.—In the case of kerosene used in aviation that is not commercial aviation (as so defined) (other than any use which is exempt from the tax imposed by section 4041(c) other than by reason of a prior imposition of tax), paragraph (1) shall not apply to—

(i) any tax imposed by subsection (c) or (d)(2) of section 4041, and

(ii) so much of the tax imposed by section 4081 as is attributable to—

(I) the Leaking Underground Storage Tank Trust Fund financing rate imposed by such section, and

(II) so much of the rate of tax specified in section 4081(a)(2)(A)(iii) as does not exceed the rate specified in section 4081(a)(2)(C)(ii).

(C) PAYMENTS TO ULTIMATE, REGISTERED VENDOR.—

(i) IN GENERAL.—With respect to any kerosene used in aviation (other than kerosene described in clause (ii) or kerosene to which paragraph (5) applies), if the ultimate purchaser of such kerosene waives (at such time and in such form and manner as the Secretary shall prescribe) the right to payment under paragraph (1) and assigns such right to the ultimate vendor, then the Secretary shall pay the amount which would be paid under paragraph (1) to such ultimate vendor, but only if such ultimate vendor—

(I) is registered under section 4101, and

(II) meets the requirements of subparagraph (A), (B), or (D) of section 6416(a)(1).

(ii) PAYMENTS FOR KEROSENE USED IN NONCOMMERCIAL AVIATION.—The amount which would be paid under paragraph (1) with respect to any kerosene to which subparagraph (B) applies shall be paid only to the ultimate vendor of such kerosene. A payment shall be made to such vendor if such vendor—

(I) is registered under section 4101, and

(II) meets the requirements of subparagraph (A), (B), or (D) of section 6416(a)(1).

(5) REGISTERED VENDORS TO ADMINISTER CLAIMS FOR REFUND OF DIESEL FUEL OR KEROSENE SOLD TO STATE AND LOCAL GOVERNMENTS.—

* * *

[CCH Explanation at ¶670. Committee Reports at ¶15,650.]

Amendments

• **2006, Tax Relief and Health Care Act of 2006 (P.L. 109-432)**

P.L. 109-432, Division A, §420(a):

Amended Code Sec. 6427(l)(4). **Effective** generally for kerosene sold after 9-30-2005. For special rules, see Act Sec. 420(c)(2) and (d), below. Prior to amendment, Code Sec. 6427(l)(4) read as follows:

(4) REFUNDS FOR KEROSENE USED IN COMMERCIAL AVIATION.—

(A) NO REFUND OF CERTAIN TAXES ON FUEL USED IN COMMERCIAL AVIATION.—In the case of kerosene used in commercial aviation (as defined in section 4083(b)) (other than supplies for vessels or aircraft within the meaning of section 4221(d)(3)), paragraph (1) shall not apply to so much of the tax imposed by section 4081 as is attributable to—

(i) the Leaking Underground Storage Tank Trust Fund financing rate imposed by such section, and

(ii) so much of the rate of tax specified in section 4081(a)(2)[A](iii) as does not exceed 4.3 cents per gallon.

(B) PAYMENT TO ULTIMATE, REGISTERED VENDOR.—With respect to kerosene used in commercial aviation as described in subparagraph (A), if the ultimate purchaser of such kerosene waives (at such time and in such form and manner as the Secretary shall prescribe) the right to payment under paragraph (1) and assigns such right to the ultimate vendor, then the Secretary shall pay the amount which would be paid under paragraph (1) to such ultimate vendor, but only if such ultimate vendor—

(i) is registered under section 4101, and

(ii) meets the requirements of subparagraph (A), (B), or (D) of section 6416(a)(1).

P.L. 109-432, Division A, §420(b)(1):

Amended Code Sec. 6427(l) by striking paragraph (5) and by redesignating paragraph (6) as paragraph (5). **Effective** generally for kerosene sold after 9-30-2005. For special rules, see Act Sec. 420(c)(2) and (d), below. Prior to being stricken, Code Sec. 6427(l)(5) read as follows:

(5) REFUNDS FOR KEROSENE USED IN NONCOMMERCIAL AVIATION.—

(A) IN GENERAL.—In the case of kerosene used in aviation not described in paragraph (4)(A) (other than any use which is exempt from the tax imposed by section 4041(c) other than by reason of a prior imposition of tax), paragraph (1) shall not apply to so much of the tax imposed by section 4081 as is attributable to—

(i) the Leaking Underground Storage Tank Trust Fund financing rate imposed by such section, and

(ii) so much of the rate of tax specified in section 4081(a)(2)(A)(iii) as does not exceed the rate specified in section 4081(a)(2)(C)(ii).

(B) PAYMENT TO ULTIMATE, REGISTERED VENDOR.—The amount which would be paid under paragraph (1) with respect to any kerosene shall be paid only to the ultimate vendor of such kerosene. A payment shall be made to such vendor if such vendor—

(i) is registered under section 4101, and

(ii) meets the requirements of subparagraph (A), (B), or (D) of section 6416(a)(1).

P.L. 109-432, Division A, §420(b)(4):

Amended Code Sec. 6427(l)(1) by striking "paragraph (4)(B)" and inserting "paragraph (4)(C)(i)". **Effective** generally for kerosene sold after 9-30-2005. For special rules, see Act Sec. 420(c)(2) and (d), below.

P.L. 109-432, Division A, § 420(c)(2) and (d), provide:

(c) EFFECTIVE DATE.—

* * *

(2) SPECIAL RULE FOR PENDING CLAIMS.—In the case of kerosene sold for use in aviation (other than kerosene to which section 6427(l)(4)(C)(ii) of the Internal Revenue Code of 1986 (as added by subsection (a)) applies or kerosene to which section 6427(l)(5) of such Code (as redesignated by subsection (b)) applies) after September 30, 2005, and before the date of the enactment of this Act, the ultimate purchaser shall be treated as having waived the right to payment under section 6427(l)(1) of such Code and as having assigned such right to the ultimate vendor if such ultimate vendor has met the requirements of subparagraph (A), (B), or (D) of section 6416(a)(1) of such Code.

(d) SPECIAL RULE FOR KEROSENE USED IN AVIATION ON A FARM FOR FARMING PURPOSES.—

(1) REFUNDS FOR PURCHASES AFTER DECEMBER 31, 2004, AND BEFORE OCTOBER 1, 2005.—The Secretary of the Treasury shall pay to the ultimate purchaser of any kerosene which is used in aviation on a farm for farming purposes and which was purchased after December 31, 2004, and before October 1, 2005, an amount equal to the aggregate amount of tax imposed on such fuel under section 4041 or 4081 of the Internal Revenue Code of 1986, as the case may be, reduced by any payment to the ultimate vendor under section 6427(l)(5)(C) of such Code (as in effect on the day before the date of the enactment of the Safe, Accountable, Flexible, Efficient Transportation Equity Act: a Legacy for Users).

(2) USE ON A FARM FOR FARMING PURPOSES.—For purposes of paragraph (1), kerosene shall be treated as used on a farm for farming purposes if such kerosene is used for farming purposes (within the meaning of section 6420(c)(3) of the Internal Revenue Code of 1986) in carrying on a trade or business on a farm situated in the United States. For purposes of the preceding sentence, rules similar to the rules of section 6420(c)(4) of such Code shall apply.

(3) TIME FOR FILING CLAIMS.—No claim shall be allowed under paragraph (1) unless the ultimate purchaser files such claim before the date that is 3 months after the date of the enactment of this Act.

(4) NO DOUBLE BENEFIT.—No amount shall be paid under paragraph (1) or section 6427(l) of the Internal Revenue Code of 1986 with respect to any kerosene described in paragraph (1) to the extent that such amount is in excess of the tax imposed on such kerosene under section 4041 or 4081 of such Code, as the case may be.

(5) APPLICABLE LAWS.—For purposes of this subsection, rules similar to the rules of section 6427(j) of the Internal Revenue Code of 1986 shall apply.

[¶ 5805] CODE SEC. 6652. FAILURE TO FILE CERTAIN INFORMATION RETURNS, REGISTRATION STATEMENTS, ETC.

* * *

(c) RETURNS BY EXEMPT ORGANIZATIONS AND BY CERTAIN TRUSTS.—

(1) ANNUAL RETURNS UNDER SECTION *6033(a)(1)* OR 6012(a)(6).—

(A) PENALTY ON ORGANIZATION.—In the case of—

(i) a failure to file a return required under section *6033(a)(1)* (relating to returns by exempt organizations) or section 6012(a)(6) (relating to returns by political organizations) on the date and in the manner prescribed therefor (determined with regard to any extension of time for filing), or

(ii) a failure to include any of the information required to be shown on a return filed under section *6033(a)(1)* or section 6012(a)(6) or to show the correct information,

there shall be paid by the exempt organization $20 for each day during which such failure continues. The maximum penalty under this subparagraph on failures with respect to any 1 return shall not exceed the lesser of $10,000 or 5 percent of the gross receipts of the organization for the year. In the case of an organization having gross receipts exceeding $1,000,000 for any year, with respect to the return required under section *6033(a)(1)* or section 6012(a)(6) for such year, the first sentence of this subparagraph shall be applied by substituting "$100" for "$20" and, in lieu of applying the second sentence of this subparagraph, the maximum penalty under this subparagraph shall not exceed $50,000.

* * *

(3) *DISCLOSURE UNDER SECTION 6033(a)(2).—*

(A) PENALTY ON ENTITIES.—In the case of a failure to file a disclosure required under section 6033(a)(2), there shall be paid by the tax-exempt entity (the entity manager in the case of a tax-exempt entity described in paragraph (4), (5), (6), or (7) of section 4965(c)) $100 for each day during which such failure continues. The maximum penalty under this subparagraph on failures with respect to any 1 disclosure shall not exceed $50,000.

(B) WRITTEN DEMAND.—

(i) IN GENERAL.—*The Secretary may make a written demand on any entity or manager subject to penalty under subparagraph (A) specifying therein a reasonable future date by which the disclosure shall be filed for purposes of this subparagraph.*

(ii) FAILURE TO COMPLY WITH DEMAND.—*If any entity or manager fails to comply with any demand under clause (i) on or before the date specified in such demand, there shall be paid by such entity or manager failing to so comply $100 for each day after the expiration of the time specified in such demand during which such failure continues. The maximum penalty imposed under this subparagraph on all entities and managers for failures with respect to any 1 disclosure shall not exceed $10,000.*

(C) DEFINITIONS.—*Any term used in this section which is also used in section 4965 shall have the meaning given such term under section 4965.*

(4) REASONABLE CAUSE EXCEPTION.—No penalty shall be imposed under this subsection with respect to any failure if it is shown that such failure is due to reasonable cause.

(5) OTHER SPECIAL RULES.—

(A) TREATMENT AS TAX.—Any penalty imposed under this subsection shall be paid on notice and demand of the Secretary and in the same manner as tax.

(B) JOINT AND SEVERAL LIABILITY.—If more than 1 person is liable under this subsection for any penalty with respect to any failure, all such persons shall be jointly and severally liable with respect to such failure.

(C) PERSON.—For purposes of this subsection, the term "person" means any officer, director, trustee, employee, or other individual who is under a duty to perform the act in respect of which the violation occurs.

* * *

[CCH Explanation at ¶1130. Committee Reports at ¶10,300.]

Amendments

● **2006, Tax Increase Prevention and Reconciliation Act of 2005 (P.L. 109-222)**

P.L. 109-222, §516(c)(1):

Amended Code Sec. 6652(c) by redesignating paragraphs (3) and (4) as paragraphs (4) and (5), respectively, and by inserting after paragraph (2) a new paragraph (3). **Effective** for disclosures the due date for which are after 5-17-2006.

P.L. 109-222, §516(c)(2):

Amended Code Sec. 6652(c)(1) by striking "6033" each place it appears in the text and heading thereof and inserting "6033(a)(1)". **Effective** for disclosures the due date for which are after 5-17-2006.

➤➤➤ *Caution: Code Sec. 6702, as amended by P.L. 109-432, §407(a), applies to submissions made and issues raised after the date on which the Secretary first prescribes a list under Code Sec. 6702(c), as amended by P.L. 109-432, §407(a).*

[¶5810] CODE SEC. 6702. FRIVOLOUS TAX SUBMISSIONS.

(a) CIVIL PENALTY FOR FRIVOLOUS TAX RETURNS.—*A person shall pay a penalty of $5,000 if—*

(1) such person files what purports to be a return of a tax imposed by this title but which—

(A) does not contain information on which the substantial correctness of the self-assessment may be judged, or

(B) contains information that on its face indicates that the self-assessment is substantially incorrect, and

(2) the conduct referred to in paragraph (1)—

(A) is based on a position which the Secretary has identified as frivolous under subsection (c), or

(B) reflects a desire to delay or impede the administration of Federal tax laws.

(b) CIVIL PENALTY FOR SPECIFIED FRIVOLOUS SUBMISSIONS.—

(1) IMPOSITION OF PENALTY.—*Except as provided in paragraph (3), any person who submits a specified frivolous submission shall pay a penalty of $5,000.*

(2) SPECIFIED FRIVOLOUS SUBMISSION.—*For purposes of this section—*

(A) SPECIFIED FRIVOLOUS SUBMISSION.—*The term "specified frivolous submission" means a specified submission if any portion of such submission—*

(i) is based on a position which the Secretary has identified as frivolous under subsection (c), or

(ii) reflects a desire to delay or impede the administration of Federal tax laws.

(B) SPECIFIED SUBMISSION.—*The term "specified submission" means—*

(i) a request for a hearing under—

(I) section 6320 (relating to notice and opportunity for hearing upon filing of notice of lien), or

(II) section 6330 (relating to notice and opportunity for hearing before levy), and

(ii) an application under—

(I) section 6159 (relating to agreements for payment of tax liability in installments),

(II) section 7122 (relating to compromises), or

(III) section 7811 (relating to taxpayer assistance orders).

(3) OPPORTUNITY TO WITHDRAW SUBMISSION.—*If the Secretary provides a person with notice that a submission is a specified frivolous submission and such person withdraws such submission within 30 days after such notice, the penalty imposed under paragraph (1) shall not apply with respect to such submission.*

(c) LISTING OF FRIVOLOUS POSITIONS.—*The Secretary shall prescribe (and periodically revise) a list of positions which the Secretary has identified as being frivolous for purposes of this subsection. The Secretary shall not include in such list any position that the Secretary determines meets the requirement of section 6662(d)(2)(B)(ii)(II).*

(d) REDUCTION OF PENALTY.—*The Secretary may reduce the amount of any penalty imposed under this section if the Secretary determines that such reduction would promote compliance with and administration of the Federal tax laws.*

(e) PENALTIES IN ADDITION TO OTHER PENALTIES.—*The penalties imposed by this section shall be in addition to any other penalty provided by law.*

[CCH Explanation at ¶ 640. Committee Reports at ¶ 15,520.]

Amendments

• **2006, Tax Relief and Health Care Act of 2006 (P.L. 109-432)**

P.L. 109-432, Division A, § 407(a):

Amended Code Sec. 6702. **Effective** for submissions made and issues raised after the date on which the Secretary first prescribes a list under Code Sec. 6702(c), as amended by Act Sec. 407(a). Prior to amendment, Code Sec. 6702 read as follows:

SEC. 6702. FRIVOLOUS INCOME TAX RETURN.

(a) CIVIL PENALTY.—If—

(1) any individual files what purports to be a return of the tax imposed by subtitle A but which—

(A) does not contain information on which the substantial correctness of the self-assessment may be judged, or

(B) contains information that on its face indicates that the self-assessment is substantially incorrect; and

(2) the conduct referred to in paragraph (1) is due to—

(A) a position which is frivolous, or

(B) a desire (which appears on the purported return) to delay or impede the administration of Federal income tax laws,

then such individual shall pay a penalty of $500.

(b) PENALTY IN ADDITION TO OTHER PENALTIES.—The penalty imposed by subsection (a) shall be in addition to any other penalty provided by law.

[¶ 5820] CODE SEC. 6724. WAIVER; DEFINITIONS AND SPECIAL RULES.

* * *

(d) DEFINITIONS.—For purposes of this part—

(1) INFORMATION RETURN.—The term "information return" means—

* * *

(B) any return required by—

(i) section 6041A(a) or (b) (relating to returns of direct sellers),

(ii) section 6043A(a) (relating to returns relating to taxable mergers and acquisitions),

(iii) section 6045(a) or (d) (relating to returns of brokers),

(iv) section 6050H(a) (relating to mortgage interest received in trade or business from individuals),

(v) section 6050I(a) or (g)(1) (relating to cash received in trade or business, etc.),

(vi) section 6050J(a) (relating to foreclosures and abandonments of security),

(vii) section 6050K(a) (relating to exchanges of certain partnership interests),

(viii) section 6050L(a) (relating to returns relating to certain dispositions of donated property),

(ix) section 6050P (relating to returns relating to the cancellation of indebtedness by certain financial entities),

(x) section 6050Q (relating to certain long-term care benefits),

(xi) section 6050S (relating to returns relating to payments for qualified tuition and related expenses),

(xii) section 6050T (relating to returns relating to credit for health insurance costs of eligible individuals),

(xiii) section 6052(a) (relating to reporting payment of wages in the form of group-life insurance),

(xiv) section 6050V (relating to returns relating to applicable insurance contracts in which certain exempt organizations hold interests),

(xv) section 6053(c)(1) (relating to reporting with respect to certain tips),

(xvi) subsection (b) or (e) of section 1060 (relating to reporting requirements of transferors and transferees in certain asset acquisitions),

(xvii) section 4101(d) (relating to information reporting with respect to fuels taxes),

(xviii) subparagraph (C) of section 338(h)(10) (relating to information required to be furnished to the Secretary in case of elective recognition of gain or loss),

(xix) section 264(f)(5)(A)(iv) (relating to reporting with respect to certain life insurance and annuity contracts),

(xx) section 6050U (relating to charges or payments for qualified long-term care insurance contracts under combined arrangements), *or*

(xix)[(xxi)] section 6039(a) (relating to returns required with respect to certain options), and

* * *

(2) PAYEE STATEMENT.—The term "payee statement" means any statement required to be furnished under—

* * *

(B) *section 6039(b) (relating to information required in connection with certain options),*

* * *

[CCH Explanation at ¶630. Committee Reports at ¶15,480.]

<table>
<tr><td>

Amendments

• **2006, Tax Relief and Health Care Act of 2006 (P.L. 109-432)**

P.L. 109-432, Division A, §403(c)(1):

Amended Code Sec. 6724(d)(1)(B) by striking "or" at the end of clause (xvii)[(xix)], by striking "and" at the end of clause (xviii)[(xx)] and inserting "or", and by adding at the

</td><td>

end a new clause (xix)[(xxi)]. **Effective** for calendar years beginning after 12-20-2006.

P.L. 109-432, Division A, §403(c)(2):

Amended Code Sec. 6724(d)(2)(B) by striking "section 6039(a)" and inserting "section 6039(b)". **Effective** for calendar years beginning after 12-20-2006.

</td></tr>
</table>

[¶5830] CODE SEC. 7122. COMPROMISES.

* * *

(c) RULES FOR SUBMISSION OF OFFERS-IN-COMPROMISE.—

   (1) PARTIAL PAYMENT REQUIRED WITH SUBMISSION.—

      (A) LUMP-SUM OFFERS.—

         (i) IN GENERAL.—The submission of any lump-sum offer-in-compromise shall be accompanied by the payment of 20 percent of the amount of such offer.

         (ii) LUMP-SUM OFFER-IN-COMPROMISE.—For purposes of this section, the term "lump-sum offer-in-compromise" means any offer of payments made in 5 or fewer installments.

      (B) PERIODIC PAYMENT OFFERS.—

         (i) IN GENERAL.—The submission of any periodic payment offer-in-compromise shall be accompanied by the payment of the amount of the first proposed installment.

         (ii) FAILURE TO MAKE INSTALLMENT DURING PENDENCY OF OFFER.—Any failure to make an installment (other than the first installment) due under such offer-in-compromise during the period such offer is being evaluated by the Secretary may be treated by the Secretary as a withdrawal of such offer-in-compromise.

   (2) RULES OF APPLICATION.—

      (A) USE OF PAYMENT.—The application of any payment made under this subsection to the assessed tax or other amounts imposed under this title with respect to such tax may be specified by the taxpayer.

      (B) APPLICATION OF USER FEE.—In the case of any assessed tax or other amounts imposed under this title with respect to such tax which is the subject of an offer-in-compromise to which this subsection applies, such tax or other amounts shall be reduced by any user fee imposed under this title with respect to such offer-in-compromise.

      (C) WAIVER AUTHORITY.—The Secretary may issue regulations waiving any payment required under paragraph (1) in a manner consistent with the practices established in accordance with the requirements under subsection (d)(3).

[CCH Explanation at ¶1140. Committee Reports at ¶10,230.]

<table>
<tr><td>

Amendments

• **2006, Tax Increase Prevention and Reconciliation Act of 2005 (P.L. 109-222)**

P.L. 109-222, §509(a):

Amended Code Sec. 7122 by redesignating subsections (c) and (d) as subsections (d) and (e), respectively, and by

</td><td>

inserting after subsection (b) a new subsection (c). **Effective** for offers-in-compromise submitted on and after the date which is 60 days after 5-17-2006.

</td></tr>
</table>

(d) STANDARDS FOR EVALUATION OF OFFERS.—

* * *

   (3) SPECIAL RULES RELATING TO TREATMENT OF OFFERS.—The guidelines under paragraph (1) shall provide that—

(A) an officer or employee of the Internal Revenue Service shall not reject an offer-in-compromise from a low-income taxpayer solely on the basis of the amount of the offer,

(B) in the case of an offer-in-compromise which relates only to issues of liability of the taxpayer—

(i) such offer shall not be rejected solely because the Secretary is unable to locate the taxpayer's return or return information for verification of such liability; and

(ii) the taxpayer shall not be required to provide a financial statement, *and*

(C) any offer-in-compromise which does not meet the requirements of subparagraph (A)(i) or (B)(i), as the case may be, of subsection (c)(1) may be returned to the taxpayer as unprocessable.

[CCH Explanation at ¶1140. Committee Reports at ¶10,230.]
Amendments

• **2006, Tax Increase Prevention and Reconciliation Act of 2005 (P.L. 109-222)**

P.L. 109-222, §509(a):

Amended Code Sec. 7122 by redesignating subsection (c) as subsection (d). **Effective** for offers-in-compromise submitted on and after the date which is 60 days after 5-17-2006.

P.L. 109-222, §509(b)(1):

Amended Code Sec. 7122(d)(3), as redesignated by Act Sec. 509(a), by striking "; and" at the end of subparagraph (A) and inserting a comma, by striking the period at the end of subparagraph (B) and inserting ", and", and by adding at the end a new subparagraph (C). **Effective** for offers-in-compromise submitted on and after the date which is 60 days after 5-17-2006.

(e) ADMINISTRATIVE REVIEW.—The Secretary shall establish procedures—

(1) for an independent administrative review of any rejection of a proposed offer-in-compromise or installment agreement made by a taxpayer under this section or section 6159 before such rejection is communicated to the taxpayer; and

(2) which allow a taxpayer to appeal any rejection of such offer or agreement to the Internal Revenue Service Office of Appeals.

[CCH Explanation at ¶1140. Committee Reports at ¶10,230.]
Amendments

• **2006, Tax Increase Prevention and Reconciliation Act of 2005 (P.L. 109-222)**

P.L. 109-222, §509(a):

Amended Code Sec. 7122 by redesignating subsection (d) as subsection (e). **Effective** for offers-in-compromise submitted on and after the date which is 60 days after 5-17-2006.

(f) DEEMED ACCEPTANCE OF OFFER NOT REJECTED WITHIN CERTAIN PERIOD.—*Any offer-in-compromise submitted under this section shall be deemed to be accepted by the Secretary if such offer is not rejected by the Secretary before the date which is 24 months after the date of the submission of such offer. For purposes of the preceding sentence, any period during which any tax liability which is the subject of such offer-in-compromise is in dispute in any judicial proceeding shall not be taken into account in determining the expiration of the 24-month period.*

[CCH Explanation at ¶1140. Committee Reports at ¶10,230.]
Amendments

• **2006, Tax Increase Prevention and Reconciliation Act of 2005 (P.L. 109-222)**

P.L. 109-222, §509(b)(2):

Amended Code Sec. 7122, as amended by Act Sec. 509(a), by adding at the end a new subsection (f). **Effective** for offers-in-compromise submitted on and after the date which is 60 days after 5-17-2006.

➤➤➤ *Caution: Code Sec. 7122(f)[(g)], below, as added by P.L. 109-432, §407(d), applies to submissions made and issues raised after the date on which the Secretary first prescribes a list under Code Sec. 6702(c), as amended by P.L. 109-432, §407(a).*

(f)[(g)] FRIVOLOUS SUBMISSIONS, ETC.—*Notwithstanding any other provision of this section, if the Secretary determines that any portion of an application for an offer-in-compromise or installment agreement submitted under this section or section 6159 meets the requirement of clause (i) or (ii) of section 6702(b)(2)(A),*

then the Secretary may treat such portion as if it were never submitted and such portion shall not be subject to any further administrative or judicial review.

[CCH Explanation at ¶640. Committee Reports at ¶15,520.]

Amendments

• **2006, Tax Relief and Health Care Act of 2006 (P.L. 109-432)**

P.L. 109-432, Division A, §407(d):

Amended Code Sec. 7122 by adding at the end a new subsection (f)[(g)]. **Effective** for submissions made and is-

sues raised after the date on which the Secretary first prescribes a list under Code Sec. 6702(c), as amended by Act Sec. 407(a).

[¶5835] CODE SEC. 7443A. SPECIAL TRIAL JUDGES.

* * *

(b) PROCEEDINGS WHICH MAY BE ASSIGNED TO SPECIAL TRIAL JUDGES.—The chief judge may assign—

    (1) any declaratory judgment proceeding,

    (2) any proceeding under section 7463,

    (3) any proceeding where neither the amount of the deficiency placed in dispute (within the meaning of section 7463) nor the amount of any claimed overpayment exceeds $50,000,

    (4) any proceeding under section 6320 or 6330,

    (5) any proceeding under section 7436(c),

    (6) any proceeding under section 7623(b)(4), and

    (7) any other proceeding which the chief judge may designate,

to be heard by the special trial judges of the court.

[CCH Explanation at ¶650. Committee Reports at ¶15,510.]

Amendments

• **2006, Tax Relief and Health Care Act of 2006 (P.L. 109-432)**

P.L. 109-432, Division A, §406(a)(2)(A):

Amended Code Sec. 7443A(b) by striking "and" at the end of paragraph (5), by redesignating paragraph (6) as

paragraph (7), and by inserting after paragraph (5) a new paragraph (6). **Effective** for information provided on or after 12-20-2006.

(c) AUTHORITY TO MAKE COURT DECISIONS.—The court may authorize a special trial judge to make the decision of the court with respect to any proceeding described in paragraph (1), (2), (3), (4), *(5), or (6)* of subsection (b), subject to such conditions and review as the court may provide.

[CCH Explanation at ¶650. Committee Reports at ¶15,510.]

Amendments

• **2006, Tax Relief and Health Care Act of 2006 (P.L. 109-432)**

P.L. 109-432, Division A, §406(a)(2)(B):

Amended Code Sec. 7443A(c) by striking "or (5)" and inserting "(5), or (6)". **Effective** for information provided on or after 12-20-2006.

[¶5840] CODE SEC. 7608. AUTHORITY OF INTERNAL REVENUE ENFORCEMENT OFFICERS.

* * *

(c) RULES RELATING TO UNDERCOVER OPERATIONS.—

* * *

    (6) APPLICATION OF SECTION.—The provisions of this subsection—

        (A) shall apply after November 17, 1988, and before January 1, 1990, and

(B) shall apply after the date of the enactment of this paragraph and before January 1, *2008.*

All amounts expended pursuant to this subsection during the period described in subparagraph (B) shall be recovered to the extent possible, and deposited in the Treasury of the United States as miscellaneous receipts, before January 1, *2008.*

* * *

[CCH Explanation at ¶ 645. Committee Reports at ¶ 15,300.]

Amendments
- **2006, Tax Relief and Health Care Act of 2006 (P.L. 109-432)**

P.L. 109-432, Division A, § 121:

Amended Code Sec. 7608(c)(6) by striking "2007" both places it appears and inserting "2008". **Effective** 12-20-2006.

[¶ 5845] CODE SEC. 7623. EXPENSES OF DETECTION OF UNDERPAYMENTS AND FRAUD, ETC.

(a) IN GENERAL.—*The Secretary*, under regulations prescribed by the Secretary, is authorized to pay such sums as he deems necessary for—

(1) detecting underpayments of tax, *or*

(2) detecting and bringing to trial and punishment persons guilty of violating the internal revenue laws or conniving at the same,

in cases where such expenses are not otherwise provided for by law. Any amount payable under the preceding sentence shall be paid from the proceeds of amounts collected by reason of the information provided, and any amount so collected shall be available for such payments.

[CCH Explanation at ¶ 650. Committee Reports at ¶ 15,510.]

Amendments
- **2006, Tax Relief and Health Care Act of 2006 (P.L. 109-432)**

P.L. 109-432, Division A, § 406(a)(1)(A)-(C):

Amended Code Sec. 7623 by striking "The Secretary" and inserting "(a) IN GENERAL.—The Secretary", by striking "and" at the end of paragraph (1) and inserting "or", and by striking "(other than interest)" following "paid from the proceeds of amounts". **Effective** for information provided on or after 12-20-2006.

(b) AWARDS TO WHISTLEBLOWERS.—

(1) IN GENERAL.—*If the Secretary proceeds with any administrative or judicial action described in subsection (a) based on information brought to the Secretary's attention by an individual, such individual shall, subject to paragraph (2), receive as an award at least 15 percent but not more than 30 percent of the collected proceeds (including penalties, interest, additions to tax, and additional amounts) resulting from the action (including any related actions) or from any settlement in response to such action. The determination of the amount of such award by the Whistleblower Office shall depend upon the extent to which the individual substantially contributed to such action.*

(2) AWARD IN CASE OF LESS SUBSTANTIAL CONTRIBUTION.—

(A) IN GENERAL.—*In the event the action described in paragraph (1) is one which the Whistleblower Office determines to be based principally on disclosures of specific allegations (other than information provided by the individual described in paragraph (1)) resulting from a judicial or administrative hearing, from a governmental report, hearing, audit, or investigation, or from the news media, the Whistleblower Office may award such sums as it considers appropriate, but in no case more than 10 percent of the collected proceeds (including penalties, interest, additions to tax, and additional amounts) resulting from the action (including any related actions) or from any settlement in response to such action, taking into account the significance of the individual's information and the role of such individual and any legal representative of such individual in contributing to such action.*

Code Sec. 7623(b)(2)(A) **¶5845**

(B) Nonapplication of Paragraph Where Individual Is Original Source of Information.— *Subparagraph (A) shall not apply if the information resulting in the initiation of the action described in paragraph (1) was originally provided by the individual described in paragraph (1).*

(3) Reduction in or Denial of Award.—*If the Whistleblower Office determines that the claim for an award under paragraph (1) or (2) is brought by an individual who planned and initiated the actions that led to the underpayment of tax or actions described in subsection (a)(2), then the Whistleblower Office may appropriately reduce such award. If such individual is convicted of criminal conduct arising from the role described in the preceding sentence, the Whistleblower Office shall deny any award.*

(4) Appeal of Award Determination.—*Any determination regarding an award under paragraph (1), (2), or (3) may, within 30 days of such determination, be appealed to the Tax Court (and the Tax Court shall have jurisdiction with respect to such matter).*

(5) Application of This Subsection.—*This subsection shall apply with respect to any action—*

(A) *against any taxpayer, but in the case of any individual, only if such individual's gross income exceeds $200,000 for any taxable year subject to such action, and*

(B) *if the tax, penalties, interest, additions to tax, and additional amounts in dispute exceed $2,000,000.*

(6) Additional Rules.—

(A) No Contract Necessary.—*No contract with the Internal Revenue Service is necessary for any individual to receive an award under this subsection.*

(B) Representation.—*Any individual described in paragraph (1) or (2) may be represented by counsel.*

(C) Submission of Information.—*No award may be made under this subsection based on information submitted to the Secretary unless such information is submitted under penalty of perjury.*

[CCH Explanation at ¶ 650. Committee Reports at ¶ 15,510.]

Amendments

• **2006, Tax Relief and Health Care Act of 2006 (P.L. 109-432)**

P.L. 109-432, Division A, § 406(a)(1)(A)-(D):

Amended Code Sec. 7623 by striking "The Secretary" and inserting "(a) In General.—The Secretary", by striking

"and" at the end of paragraph (1) and inserting "or", by striking "(other than interest)" following "paid from the proceeds of amounts", and by adding at the end a new subsection (b). **Effective** for information provided on or after 12-20-2006.

[¶ 5850] CODE SEC. 7652. SHIPMENTS TO THE UNITED STATES.

* * *

(f) Limitation on Cover Over of Tax on Distilled Spirits.—For purposes of this section, with respect to taxes imposed under section 5001 or this section on distilled spirits, the amount covered into the treasuries of Puerto Rico and the Virgin Islands shall not exceed the lesser of the rate of—

(1) $10.50 ($13.25 in the case of distilled spirits brought into the United States after June 30, 1999, and before January 1, *2008*), or

* * *

[CCH Explanation at ¶ 690. Committee Reports at ¶ 15,230.]

Amendments

• **2006, Tax Relief and Health Care Act of 2006 (P.L. 109-432)**

P.L. 109-432, Division A, § 114(a):

Amended Code Sec. 7652(f)(1) by striking "2006" and inserting "2008". **Effective** for articles brought into the United States after 12-31-2005.

[¶5855] CODE SEC. 7872. TREATMENT OF LOANS WITH BELOW-MARKET INTEREST RATES.

* * *

(g) Exception for Certain Loans to Qualified Continuing Care Facilities.—

* * *

(6) Suspension of application.—Paragraph (1) shall not apply for any calendar year to which subsection (h) applies.

[CCH Explanation at ¶245. Committee Reports at ¶10,110.]

Amendments

• 2006, Tax Increase Prevention and Reconciliation Act of 2005 (P.L. 109-222)

P.L. 109-222, §209(b)(1):

Amended Code Sec. 7872(g) by adding at the end a new paragraph (6). **Effective** for calendar years beginning after 12-31-2005, with respect to loans made before, on, or after such date.

(h) Exception for Loans to Qualified Continuing Care Facilities.—

(1) In general.—This section shall not apply for any calendar year to any below-market loan owed by a facility which on the last day of such year is a qualified continuing care facility, if such loan was made pursuant to a continuing care contract and if the lender (or the lender's spouse) attains age 62 before the close of such year.

(2) Continuing care contract.—For purposes of this section, the term "continuing care contract" means a written contract between an individual and a qualified continuing care facility under which—

(A) the individual or individual's spouse may use a qualified continuing care facility for their life or lives,

(B) the individual or individual's spouse will be provided with housing, as appropriate for the health of such individual or individual's spouse—

(i) in an independent living unit (which has additional available facilities outside such unit for the provision of meals and other personal care), and

(ii) in an assisted living facility or a nursing facility, as is available in the continuing care facility, and

(C) the individual or individual's spouse will be provided assisted living or nursing care as the health of such individual or individual's spouse requires, and as is available in the continuing care facility.

The Secretary shall issue guidance which limits such term to contracts which provide only facilities, care, and services described in this paragraph.

(3) Qualified continuing care facility.—

(A) In general.—For purposes of this section, the term "qualified continuing care facility" means 1 or more facilities—

(i) which are designed to provide services under continuing care contracts,

(ii) which include an independent living unit, plus an assisted living or nursing facility, or both, and

(iii) substantially all of the independent living unit residents of which are covered by continuing care contracts.

(B) Nursing homes excluded.—The term "qualified continuing care facility" shall not include any facility which is of a type which is traditionally considered a nursing home.

(4) [Stricken.]

[CCH Explanation at ¶245 and ¶735. Committee Reports at ¶10,110 and ¶15,700.]

Amendments

• 2006, Tax Relief and Health Care Act of 2006 (P.L. 109-432)

P.L. 109-432, Division A, §425(a):

Amended Code Sec. 7872(h) by striking paragraph (4). **Effective** as if included in section 209 of the Tax Increase Prevention and Reconciliation Act of 2005 (P.L. 109-222) [**effective** for calendar years beginning after 12-31-2005, with respect to loans made before, on, or after such date.— CCH]. Prior to being stricken, Code Sec. 7872(h)(4) read as follows:

(4) TERMINATION.—This subsection shall not apply to any calendar year after 2010.

• 2006, Tax Increase Prevention and Reconciliation Act of 2005 (P.L. 109-222)

P.L. 109-222, §209(a):

Amended Code Sec. 7872 by redesignating subsection (h) as subsection (i) and inserting after subsection (g) a new subsection (h). **Effective** for calendar years beginning after 12-31-2005, with respect to loans made before, on, or after such date.

(i) REGULATIONS.—

(1) IN GENERAL.—The Secretary shall prescribe such regulations as may be necessary or appropriate to carry out the purposes of this section, including—

(A) regulations providing that where, by reason of varying rates of interest, conditional interest payments, waivers of interest, disposition of the lender's or borrower's interest in the loan, or other circumstances, the provisions of this section do not carry out the purposes of this section, adjustments to the provisions of this section will be made to the extent necessary to carry out the purposes of this section,

(B) regulations for the purpose of assuring that the positions of the borrower and lender are consistent as to the application (or nonapplication) of this section, and

(C) regulations exempting from the application of this section any class of transactions the interest arrangements of which have no significant effect on any Federal tax liability of the lender or the borrower.

(2) ESTATE TAX COORDINATION.—Under regulations prescribed by the Secretary, any loan which is made with donative intent and which is a term loan shall be taken into account for purposes of chapter 11 in a manner consistent with the provisions of subsection (b).

[CCH Explanation at ¶245. Committee Reports at ¶10,110.]

Amendments

• 2006, Tax Increase Prevention and Reconciliation Act of 2005 (P.L. 109-222)

P.L. 109-222, §209(a):

Amended Code Sec. 7872 by redesignating subsection (h) as subsection (i). **Effective** for calendar years beginning

after 12-31-2005, with respect to loans made before, on, or after such date.

[¶5860] CODE SEC. 9502. AIRPORT AND AIRWAY TRUST FUND.

* * *

(d) EXPENDITURES FROM AIRPORT AND AIRWAY TRUST FUND.—

* * *

(2) TRANSFERS FROM AIRPORT AND AIRWAY TRUST FUND ON ACCOUNT OF CERTAIN REFUNDS.—The Secretary of the Treasury shall pay from time to time from the Airport and Airway Trust Fund into the general fund of the Treasury amounts equivalent to the amounts paid after August 31, 1982, in respect of fuel used in aircraft, under section 6420 (relating to amounts paid in respect of gasoline used on farms), 6421 (relating to amounts paid in respect of gasoline used for certain nonhighway purposes), or 6427 (relating to fuels not used for taxable purposes) (other than subsection (l)(4) thereof).

(3) TRANSFERS FROM THE AIRPORT AND AIRWAY TRUST FUND ON ACCOUNT OF CERTAIN SECTION 34 CREDITS.—The Secretary of the Treasury shall pay from time to time from the Airport and Airway Trust Fund into the general fund of the Treasury amounts equivalent to the credits allowed under section 34 (other than payments made by reason of paragraph (4) of section 6427(l)) with respect to fuel used after August 31, 1982. Such amounts shall be transferred on the basis of estimates by

the Secretary of the Treasury, and proper adjustments shall be made in amounts subsequently transferred to the extent prior estimates were in excess of or less than the credits allowed.

* * *

[CCH Explanation at ¶670. Committee Reports at ¶15,650.]

Amendments

• **2006, Tax Relief and Health Care Act of 2006 (P.L. 109-432)**

P.L. 109-432, Division A, §420(b)(5)(A)-(B):

Amended Code Sec. 9502(d) by striking "and (l)(5)" following "subsection (l)(4)" in paragraph (2), and by striking "or (5)" following "paragraph (4)" in paragraph (3). **Effective** for kerosene sold after 9-30-2005. For special rules, see Act Sec. 420(c)(2) and (d), below.

P.L. 109-432, Division A, §420(c)(2) and (d), provide:

(c) EFFECTIVE DATE.—

* * *

(2) SPECIAL RULE FOR PENDING CLAIMS.—In the case of kerosene sold for use in aviation (other than kerosene to which section 6427(l)(4)(C)(ii) of the Internal Revenue Code of 1986 (as added by subsection (a)) applies or kerosene to which section 6427(l)(5) of such Code (as redesignated by subsection (b)) applies) after September 30, 2005, and before December 20, 2006, the ultimate purchaser shall be treated as having waived the right to payment under section 6427(l)(1) of such Code and as having assigned such right to the ultimate vendor if such ultimate vendor has met the requirements of subparagraph (A), (B), or (D) of section 6416(a)(1) of such Code.

(d) SPECIAL RULE FOR KEROSENE USED IN AVIATION ON A FARM FOR FARMING PURPOSES.—

(1) REFUNDS FOR PURCHASES AFTER DECEMBER 31, 2004, AND BEFORE OCTOBER 1, 2005.—The Secretary of the Treasury shall pay to the ultimate purchaser of any kerosene which is used in aviation on a farm for farming purposes and which was purchased after December 31, 2004, and before October 1, 2005, an amount equal to the aggregate amount of tax imposed on such fuel under section 4041 or 4081 of the Internal Revenue Code of 1986, as the case may be, reduced by any payment to the ultimate vendor under section 6427(l)(5)(C) of such Code (as in effect on the day before the date of the enactment of the Safe, Accountable, Flexible, Efficient Transportation Equity Act: a Legacy for Users).

(2) USE ON A FARM FOR FARMING PURPOSES.—For purposes of paragraph (1), kerosene shall be treated as used on a farm for farming purposes if such kerosene is used for farming purposes (within the meaning of section 6420(c)(3) of the Internal Revenue Code of 1986) in carrying on a trade or business on a farm situated in the United States. For purposes of the preceding sentence, rules similar to the rules of section 6420(c)(4) of such Code shall apply.

(3) TIME FOR FILING CLAIMS.—No claim shall be allowed under paragraph (1) unless the ultimate purchaser files such claim before the date that is 3 months after the date of the enactment of this Act.

(4) NO DOUBLE BENEFIT.—No amount shall be paid under paragraph (1) or section 6427(l) of the Internal Revenue Code of 1986 with respect to any kerosene described in paragraph (1) to the extent that such amount is in excess of the tax imposed on such kerosene under section 4041 or 4081 of such Code, as the case may be.

(5) APPLICABLE LAWS.—For purposes of this subsection, rules similar to the rules of section 6427(j) of the Internal Revenue Code of 1986 shall apply.

[¶5865] CODE SEC. 9503. HIGHWAY TRUST FUND.

* * *

(c) EXPENDITURES FROM HIGHWAY TRUST FUND.—

* * *

(7)[(6)] TRANSFERS FROM THE TRUST FUND FOR CERTAIN AVIATION FUEL TAXES.—The Secretary shall pay at least monthly from the Highway Trust Fund into the Airport and Airway Trust Fund amounts (as determined by the Secretary) equivalent to the taxes received on or after October 1, 2005, and before October 1, 2011, under section 4081 with respect to so much of the rate of tax as does not exceed—

(A) *4.3 cents per gallon of kerosene subject to section 6427(l)(4)(A) with respect to which a payment has been made by the Secretary under section 6427(l), and*

(B) *21.8 cents per gallon of kerosene subject to section 6427(l)(4)(B) with respect to which a payment has been made by the Secretary under section 6427(l).*

Transfers under the preceding sentence shall be made on the basis of estimates by the Secretary, and proper adjustments shall be made in the amounts subsequently transferred to the extent prior estimates were in excess of or less than the amounts required to be transferred. Any amount allowed as a credit under section 34 by reason of paragraph (4) of section 6427(l) shall be treated for purposes of subparagraphs (A) and (B) as a payment made by the Secretary under such paragraph.

* * *

[CCH Explanation at ¶670. Committee Reports at ¶15,650.]

Amendments

• **2006, Tax Relief and Health Care Act of 2006 (P.L. 109-432)**

P.L. 109-432, Division A, §420(b)(6)(A)-(B):

Amended Code Sec. 9503(c)(7)[(6)] by amending subparagraphs (A) and (B), and by striking "or (5)" following "paragraph (4)" in the matter following subparagraph (B). **Effective** for kerosene sold after 9-30-2005. For special rules,

see Act Sec. 420(c)(2) and (d) in the amendment notes following Code Sec. 9502(d). Prior to amendment, Code Sec. 9503(c)(7)[(6)](A)-(B) read as follows:

(A) 4.3 cents per gallon of kerosene with respect to which a payment has been made by the Secretary under section 6427(l)(4), and

(B) 21.8 cents per gallon of kerosene with respect to which a payment has been made by the Secretary under section 6427(l)(5).

[¶5870] CODE SEC. 9508. LEAKING UNDERGROUND STORAGE TANK TRUST FUND.

* * *

(c) EXPENDITURES.—Amounts in the Leaking Underground Storage Tank Trust Fund shall be available, as provided in appropriation Acts, only for purposes of making expenditures to carry out *sections 9003(h), 9003(i), 9003(j), 9004(f), 9005(c), 9010, 9011, 9012, and 9013* of the Solid Waste Disposal Act as in effect on the date of the enactment of the *Public Law 109-168.*

* * *

[CCH Explanation at ¶675. Committee Reports at ¶15,440.]

Amendments

• **2006, Tax Relief and Health Care Act of 2006 (P.L. 109-432)**

P.L. 109-432, Division A, §210(a)(1)-(2):

Amended Code Sec. 9508(c) by striking "section 9003(h)" and inserting "sections 9003(h), 9003(i), 9003(j), 9004(f),

9005(c), 9010, 9011, 9012, and 9013", and by striking "Superfund Amendments and Reauthorization Act of 1986" and inserting "Public Law 109-168". **Effective** 12-20-2006.

[¶5875] CODE SEC. 9701. DEFINITIONS OF GENERAL APPLICABILITY.

* * *

(c) TERMS RELATING TO OPERATORS.—For purposes of this section—

* * *

(8) SUCCESSOR IN INTEREST.—

(A) SAFE HARBOR.—The term "successor in interest" shall not include any person who—

(i) is an unrelated person to an eligible seller described in subparagraph (C); and

(ii) purchases for fair market value assets, or all of the stock, of a related person to such seller, in a bona fide, arm's-length sale.

(B) UNRELATED PERSON.—The term "unrelated person" means a purchaser who does not bear a relationship to the eligible seller described in section 267(b).

(C) ELIGIBLE SELLER.—For purposes of this paragraph, the term "eligible seller" means an assigned operator described in section 9704(j)(2) or a related person to such assigned operator.

* * *

Amendments

• **2006, Tax Relief and Health Care Act of 2006 (P.L. 109-432)**

P.L. 109-432, Division C, §211(d):

Amended Code Sec. 9701(c) by adding at the end a new paragraph (8). **Effective** for transactions after 12-20-2006.

[¶5880] CODE SEC. 9702. ESTABLISHMENT OF THE UNITED MINE WORKERS OF AMERICA COMBINED BENEFIT FUND.

* * *

(b) BOARD OF TRUSTEES.—

(1) IN GENERAL.—For purposes of subsection (a), the board of trustees for the Combined Fund shall be appointed as follows:

(A) 2 individuals who represent employers in the coal mining industry shall be designated by the BCOA;

(B) 2 individuals designated by the United Mine Workers of America; and

(C) 3 individuals selected by the individuals appointed under subparagraphs (A) and (B).

(2) SUCCESSOR TRUSTEES.—Any successor trustee shall be appointed in the same manner as the trustee being succeeded. The plan establishing the Combined Fund shall provide for the removal of trustees.

(3) SPECIAL RULE.—If the BCOA ceases to exist, any trustee or successor under paragraph (1)(A) shall be designated by the 3 employers who were members of the BCOA on the enactment date and who have been assigned the greatest number of eligible beneficiaries under section 9706.

* * *

Amendments

● 2006, Tax Relief and Health Care Act of 2006 (P.L. 109-432)

P.L. 109-432, Division C, §213(a):

Amended Code Sec. 9702(b). **Effective 12-20-2006.** Prior to amendment, Code Sec. 9702(b) read as follows:

(b) BOARD OF TRUSTEES.—

(1) IN GENERAL.—For purposes of subsection (a), the board of trustees for the Combined Fund shall be appointed as follows:

(A) one individual who represents employers in the coal mining industry shall be designated by the BCOA;

(B) one individual shall be designated by the three employers, other than 1988 agreement operators, who have been assigned the greatest number of eligible beneficiaries under section 9706;

(C) two individuals designated by the United Mine Workers of America; and

(D) three persons selected by the persons appointed under subparagraphs (A), (B), and (C).

(2) SUCCESSOR TRUSTEES.—Any successor trustee shall be appointed in the same manner as the trustee being succeeded. The plan establishing the Combined Fund shall provide for the removal of trustees.

(3) SPECIAL RULES.—

(A) BCOA.—If the BCOA ceases to exist, any trustee or successor under paragraph (1)(A) shall be designated by the 3 employers who were members of the BCOA on the enactment date and who have been assigned the greatest number of eligible beneficiaries under section 9706.

(B) FORMER SIGNATORIES.—The initial trustee under paragraph (1)(B) shall be designated by the 3 employers, other than 1988 agreement operators, which the records of the 1950 UMWA Benefit Plan and 1974 UMWA Benefit Plan indicate have the greatest number of eligible beneficiaries as of the enactment date, and such trustee and any successor shall serve until November 1, 1993.

[¶5885] CODE SEC. 9704. LIABILITY OF ASSIGNED OPERATORS.

* * *

(d) UNASSIGNED BENEFICIARIES PREMIUM.—

(1) PLAN YEARS ENDING ON OR BEFORE SEPTEMBER 30, 2006.—For plan years ending on or before September 30, 2006, the unassigned beneficiaries premium for any assigned operator shall be equal to the applicable percentage of the product of the per beneficiary premium for the plan year multiplied by the number of eligible beneficiaries who are not assigned under section 9706 to any person for such plan year.

(2) PLAN YEARS BEGINNING ON OR AFTER OCTOBER 1, 2006.—

(A) IN GENERAL.—For plan years beginning on or after October 1, 2006, subject to subparagraph (B), there shall be no unassigned beneficiaries premium, and benefit costs with respect to eligible beneficiaries who are not assigned under section 9706 to any person for any such plan year shall be paid from amounts transferred under section 9705(b).

(B) INADEQUATE TRANSFERS.—If, for any plan year beginning on or after October 1, 2006, the amounts transferred under section 9705(b) are less than the amounts required to be transferred to the Combined Fund under subsection (h)(2)(A) or (i) of section 402 of the Surface Mining Control and Reclamation Act of 1977 (30 U.S.C. 1232)), then the unassigned beneficiaries premium for any assigned operator shall be equal to the operator's applicable percentage of the amount required to be so transferred which was not so transferred.

Code Sec. 9704(d)(2)(B) ¶5885

(e) PREMIUM ACCOUNTS; ADJUSTMENTS.—

(1) ACCOUNTS.—The trustees of the Combined Fund shall establish and maintain 3 separate accounts for each of the premiums described in subsections (b), (c), and (d). Such accounts shall be credited with the premiums received *and amounts transferred under section 9705(b)* and debited with expenditures allocable to such premiums.

* * *

(3) SHORTFALLS AND SURPLUSES.—

(A) IN GENERAL.—Except as provided in subparagraph (B), if, for any plan year, there is a shortfall or surplus in any premium account, the premium for the following plan year for each assigned operator shall be proportionately reduced or increased, whichever is applicable, by the amount of such shortfall or surplus. *Amounts credited to an account from amounts transferred under section 9705(b) shall not be taken into account in determining whether there is a surplus in the account for purposes of this paragraph.*

* * *

(f) APPLICABLE PERCENTAGE.—For purposes of this section—

* * *

(2) ANNUAL ADJUSTMENTS.—In the case of any plan year beginning on or after October 1, 1994, the applicable percentage for any assigned operator shall be redetermined under paragraph (1) by making the following changes to the assignments as of October 1, 1993:

* * *

(C) *In the case of plan years beginning on or after October 1, 2007, the total number of assigned eligible beneficiaries shall be reduced by the eligible beneficiaries whose assignments have been revoked under section 9706(h).*

* * *

(j) PREPAYMENT OF PREMIUM LIABILITY.—

(1) IN GENERAL.—If—

(A) *a payment meeting the requirements of paragraph (3) is made to the Combined Fund by or on behalf of—*

(i) *any assigned operator to which this subsection applies, or*

(ii) *any related person to any assigned operator described in clause (i), and*

(d) UNASSIGNED BENEFICIARIES PREMIUM.—The unassigned beneficiaries premium for any plan year for any assigned operator shall be equal to the applicable percentage of the product of the per beneficiary premium for the plan year multiplied by the number of eligible beneficiaries who are not assigned under section 9706 to any person for such plan year.

(B) the common parent of the controlled group of corporations described in paragraph (2)(B) is jointly and severally liable for any premium under this section which (but for this subsection) would be required to be paid by the assigned operator or related person,

then such common parent (and no other person) shall be liable for such premium.

(2) ASSIGNED OPERATORS TO WHICH SUBSECTION APPLIES.—

(A) IN GENERAL.—This subsection shall apply to any assigned operator if—

(i) the assigned operator (or a related person to the assigned operator)—

(I) made contributions to the 1950 UMWA Benefit Plan and the 1974 UMWA Benefit Plan for employment during the period covered by the 1988 agreement; and

(II) is not a 1988 agreement operator,

(ii) the assigned operator (and all related persons to the assigned operator) are not actively engaged in the production of coal as of July 1, 2005, and

(iii) the assigned operator was, as of July 20, 1992, a member of a controlled group of corporations described in subparagraph (B).

(B) CONTROLLED GROUP OF CORPORATIONS.—A controlled group of corporations is described in this subparagraph if the common parent of such group is a corporation the shares of which are publicly traded on a United States exchange.

(C) COORDINATION WITH REPEAL OF ASSIGNMENTS.—A person shall not fail to be treated as an assigned operator to which this subsection applies solely because the person ceases to be an assigned operator by reason of section 9706(h)(1) if the person otherwise meets the requirements of this subsection and is liable for the payment of premiums under section 9706(h)(3).

(D) CONTROLLED GROUP.—For purposes of this subsection, the term "controlled group of corporations" has the meaning given such term by section 52(a).

(3) REQUIREMENTS.—A payment meets the requirements of this paragraph if—

(A) the amount of the payment is not less than the present value of the total premium liability under this chapter with respect to the Combined Fund of the assigned operators or related persons described in paragraph (1) or their assignees, as determined by the operator's or related person's enrolled actuary (as defined in section 7701(a)(35)) using actuarial methods and assumptions each of which is reasonable and which are reasonable in the aggregate, as determined by such enrolled actuary;

(B) such enrolled actuary files with the Secretary of Labor a signed actuarial report containing—

(i) the date of the actuarial valuation applicable to the report; and

(ii) a statement by the enrolled actuary signing the report that, to the best of the actuary's knowledge, the report is complete and accurate and that in the actuary's opinion the actuarial assumptions used are in the aggregate reasonably related to the experience of the operator and to reasonable expectations; and

(C) 90 calendar days have elapsed after the report required by subparagraph (B) is filed with the Secretary of Labor, and the Secretary of Labor has not notified the assigned operator in writing that the requirements of this paragraph have not been satisfied.

(4) USE OF PREPAYMENT.—The Combined Fund shall—

(A) establish and maintain an account for each assigned operator or related person by, or on whose behalf, a payment described in paragraph (3) was made,

(B) credit such account with such payment (and any earnings thereon), and

(C) use all amounts in such account exclusively to pay premiums that would (but for this subsection) be required to be paid by the assigned operator.

Upon termination of the obligations for the premium liability of any assigned operator or related person for which such account is maintained, all funds remaining in such account (and earnings thereon) shall be refunded to such person as may be designated by the common parent described in paragraph (1)(B).

Amendments

• **2006, Tax Relief and Health Care Act of 2006 (P.L. 109-432)**

P.L. 109-432, Division C, § 211(a):

Amended Code Sec. 9704 by adding at the end a new subsection (j). **Effective** 12-20-2006.

[¶ 5890] CODE SEC. 9705. TRANSFERS.

* * *

(b) TRANSFERS.—

(1) IN GENERAL.—The Combined Fund shall include any amount transferred to the Fund under *subsections (h) and (i) of section 402* of the Surface Mining Control and Reclamation Act of 1977 (30 U.S.C. 1323(h)).

(2) USE OF FUNDS.—*Any amount transferred under paragraph (1) for any fiscal year shall be used to pay benefits and administrative costs of beneficiaries of the Combined Fund or for such other purposes as are specifically provided in the Acts described in paragraph (1).*

Amendments

• **2006, Tax Relief and Health Care Act of 2006 (P.L. 109-432)**

P.L. 109-432, Division C, § 212(a)(1)(A)-(C):

Amended Code Sec. 9705(b) by striking "section 402(h)" and inserting "subsections (h) and (i) of section 402" in paragraph (1); by striking paragraph (2) and inserting a new paragraph (2); and by striking "FROM ABANDONED MINE REC-

LAMATION FUND" following "TRANSFERS" in the heading thereof. **Effective** for plan years of the Combined Fund beginning after 9-30-2006. Prior to being stricken, Code Sec. 9705(b)(2) read as follows:

(2) USE OF FUNDS.—Any amount transferred under paragraph (1) for any fiscal year shall be used to proportionately reduce the unassigned beneficiary premium under section 9704(a)(3) of each assigned operator for the plan year in which transferred.

[¶ 5895] CODE SEC. 9706. ASSIGNMENT OF ELIGIBLE BENEFICIARIES.

* * *

(h) ASSIGNMENTS AS OF OCTOBER 1, 2007.—

(1) IN GENERAL.—*Subject to the premium obligation set forth in paragraph (3), the Commissioner of Social Security shall—*

(A) *revoke all assignments to persons other than 1988 agreement operators for purposes of assessing premiums for plan years beginning on and after October 1, 2007; and*

(B) *make no further assignments to persons other than 1988 agreement operators, except that no individual who becomes an unassigned beneficiary by reason of subparagraph (A) may be assigned to a 1988 agreement operator.*

(2) REASSIGNMENT UPON PURCHASE.—*This subsection shall not be construed to prohibit the reassignment under subsection (b)(2) of an eligible beneficiary.*

(3) LIABILITY OF PERSONS DURING THREE FISCAL YEARS BEGINNING ON AND AFTER OCTOBER 1, 2007.—*In the case of each of the fiscal years beginning on October 1, 2007, 2008, and 2009, each person other than a 1988 agreement operator shall pay to the Combined Fund the following percentage of the amount of annual premiums that such person would otherwise be required to pay under section 9704(a), determined on the basis of assignments in effect without regard to the revocation of assignments under paragraph (1)(A):*

(A) *For the fiscal year beginning on October 1, 2007, 55 percent.*

(B) *For the fiscal year beginning on October 1, 2008, 40 percent.*

(C) *For the fiscal year beginning on October 1, 2009, 15 percent.*

Amendments

• **2006, Tax Relief and Health Care Act of 2006 (P.L. 109-432)**

P.L. 109-432, Division C, § 212(a)(3):

Amended Code Sec. 9706 by adding at the end a new subsection (h). **Effective** for plan years of the Combined Fund beginning after 9-30-2006.

[¶5900] CODE SEC. 9707. FAILURE TO PAY PREMIUM.

(a) FAILURES TO PAY.—

(1) PREMIUMS FOR ELIGIBLE BENEFICIARIES.—There is hereby imposed a penalty on the failure of any assigned operator to pay any premium required to be paid under section 9704 with respect to any eligible beneficiary.

(2) CONTRIBUTIONS REQUIRED UNDER THE MINING LAWS.—There is hereby imposed a penalty on the failure of any person to make a contribution required under section 402(h)(5)(B)(ii) of the Surface Mining Control and Reclamation Act of 1977 to a plan referred to in section 402(h)(2)(C) of such Act. For purposes of applying this section, each such required monthly contribution for the hours worked of any individual shall be treated as if it were a premium required to be paid under section 9704 with respect to an eligible beneficiary.

* * *

Amendments

● **2006, Tax Relief and Health Care Act of 2006 (P.L. 109-432)**

P.L. 109-432, Division C, §213(b)(1):

Amended Code Sec. 9707(a). **Effective** 12-20-2006. Prior to amendment, Code Sec. 9707(a) read as follows:

(a) GENERAL RULE.—There is hereby imposed a penalty on the failure of any assigned operator to pay any premium required to be paid under section 9704 with respect to any eligible beneficiary.

[¶5905] CODE SEC. 9711. CONTINUED OBLIGATIONS OF INDIVIDUAL EMPLOYER PLANS.

* * *

(c) JOINT AND SEVERAL LIABILITY OF RELATED PERSONS.—

(1) IN GENERAL.—Except as provided in paragraph (2), each related person of a last signatory operator to which subsection (a) or (b) applies shall be jointly and severally liable with the last signatory operator for the provision of health care coverage described in subsection (a) or (b).

(2) LIABILITY LIMITED IF SECURITY PROVIDED.—If—

(A) security meeting the requirements of paragraph (3) is provided by or on behalf of—

(i) any last signatory operator which is an assigned operator described in section 9704(j)(2), or

(ii) any related person to any last signatory operator described in clause (i), and

(B) the common parent of the controlled group of corporations described in section 9704(j)(2)(B) is jointly and severally liable for the provision of health care under this section which, but for this paragraph, would be required to be provided by the last signatory operator or related person,

then, as of the date the security is provided, such common parent (and no other person) shall be liable for the provision of health care under this section which the last signatory operator or related person would otherwise be required to provide. Security may be provided under this paragraph without regard to whether a payment was made under section 9704(j).

(3) SECURITY.—Security meets the requirements of this paragraph if—

(A) the security—

(i) is in the form of a bond, letter of credit, or cash escrow,

(ii) is provided to the trustees of the 1992 UMWA Benefit Plan solely for the purpose of paying premiums for beneficiaries who would be described in section 9712(b)(2)(B) if the requirements of this section were not met by the last signatory operator, and

(iii) is in an amount equal to 1 year of liability of the last signatory operator under this section, determined by using the average cost of such operator's liability during the prior 3 calendar years;

(B) the security is in addition to any other security required under any other provision of this title; and

(C) the security remains in place for 5 years.

(4) REFUNDS OF SECURITY.—*The remaining amount of any security provided under this subsection (and earnings thereon) shall be refunded to the last signatory operator as of the earlier of—*

(A) the termination of the obligations of the last signatory operator under this section, or

(B) the end of the 5-year period described in paragraph (4)(C).

* * *

Amendments

• **2006, Tax Relief and Health Care Act of 2006 (P.L. 109-432)**

P.L. 109-432, Division C, §211(b):

Amended Code Sec. 9711(c). **Effective** 12-20-2006. Prior to amendment, Code Sec. 9711(c) read as follows:

(c) JOINT AND SEVERAL LIABILITY OF RELATED PERSONS.—Each related person of a last signatory operator to which subsection (a) or (b) applies shall be jointly and severally liable with the last signatory operator for the provision of health care coverage described in subsection (a) or (b).

[¶5910] CODE SEC. 9712. ESTABLISHMENT AND COVERAGE OF 1992 UMWA BENEFIT PLAN

(a) CREATION OF PLAN.—

* * *

(3) TRANSFERS UNDER OTHER FEDERAL STATUTES.—

(A) IN GENERAL.—*The 1992 UMWA Benefit Plan shall include any amount transferred to the plan under subsections (h) and (i) of section 402 of the Surface Mining Control and Reclamation Act of 1977 (30 U.S.C. 1232).*

(B) USE OF FUNDS.—*Any amount transferred under subparagraph (A) for any fiscal year shall be used to provide the health benefits described in subsection (c) with respect to any beneficiary for whom no monthly per beneficiary premium is paid pursuant to paragraph (1)(A) or (3) of subsection (d).*

(4) SPECIAL RULE FOR 1993 PLAN.—

(A) IN GENERAL.—*The plan described in section 402(h)(2)(C) of the Surface Mining Control and Reclamation Act of 1977 (30 U.S.C. 1232(h)(2)(C)) shall include any amount transferred to the plan under subsections (h) and (i) of the Surface Mining Control and Reclamation Act of 1977 (30 U.S.C. 1232).*

(B) USE OF FUNDS.—*Any amount transferred under subparagraph (A) for any fiscal year shall be used to provide the health benefits described in section 402(h)(2)(C)(i) of the Surface Mining Control and Reclamation Act of 1977 (30 U.S.C. 1232(h)(2)(C)(i)) to individuals described in section 402(h)(2)(C) of such Act (30 U.S.C. 1232(h)(2)(C)).*

* * *

Amendments

• **2006, Tax Relief and Health Care Act of 2006 (P.L. 109-432)**

P.L. 109-432, Division C, §212(b)(1):

Amended Code Sec. 9712(a) by adding at the end new paragraphs (3) and (4). **Effective** 12-20-2006.

(d) GUARANTEE OF BENEFITS.—

➤➤➤ *Caution: Code Sec. 9712(d)(1)-(3), below, as amended by P.L. 109-432, applies to fiscal years beginning on or after October 1, 2010.*

(1) IN GENERAL.—*All 1988 last signatory operators shall be responsible for financing the benefits described in subsection (c) by meeting the following requirements in accordance with the contribution requirements established in the 1992 UMWA Benefit Plan:*

(A) The payment of a monthly per beneficiary premium by each 1988 last signatory operator for each eligible beneficiary of such operator who is described in subsection (b)(2) and who is receiving benefits under the 1992 UMWA Benefit Plan.

(B) The provision of a security (in the form of a bond, letter of credit, or cash escrow) in an amount equal to a portion of the projected future cost to the 1992 UMWA Benefit Plan of providing health benefits for eligible and potentially eligible beneficiaries attributable to the 1988 last signatory operator.

(C) If the amounts transferred under subsection (a)(3) are less than the amounts required to be transferred to the 1992 UMWA Benefit Plan under subsections (h) and (i) of section 402 of the Surface Mining Control and Reclamation Act of 1977 (30 U.S.C. 1232), the payment of an additional backstop premium by each 1988 last signatory operator which is equal to such operator's share of the amounts required to be so transferred but which were not so transferred, determined on the basis of the number of eligible and potentially eligible beneficiaries attributable to the operator.

(2) ADJUSTMENTS.—The 1992 UMWA Benefit Plan shall provide for—

(A) annual adjustments of the per beneficiary premium to cover changes in the cost of providing benefits to eligible beneficiaries, and

(B) adjustments as necessary to the annual *backstop* premium to reflect changes in the cost of providing benefits to eligible beneficiaries for whom per beneficiary premiums are not paid.

(3) ADDITIONAL LIABILITY.—Any last signatory operator who is not a 1988 last signatory operator shall pay the monthly per beneficiary premium under *paragraph (1)(A)* for each eligible beneficiary described in such paragraph attributable to that operator.

(4) JOINT AND SEVERAL LIABILITY.—A 1988 last signatory operator or last signatory operator described in paragraph (3), and any related person to any such operator, shall be jointly and severally liable with such operator for any amount required to be paid by such operator under this section. *The provisions of section 9711(c)(2) shall apply to any last signatory operator described in such section (without regard to whether security is provided under such section, a payment is made under section 9704(j), or both) and if security meeting the requirements of section 9711(c)(3) is provided, the common parent described in section 9711(c)(2)(B) shall be exclusively responsible for any liability for premiums under this section which, but for this sentence, would be required to be paid by the last signatory operator or any related person.*

* * *

Amendments

• **2006, Tax Relief and Health Care Act of 2006 (P.L. 109-432)**

P.L. 109-432, Division C, §211(c):

Amended Code Sec. 9712(d)(4) by adding at the end a new sentence. **Effective** 12-20-2006.

P.L. 109-432, Division C, §212(b)(2)(A):

Amended Code Sec. 9712(d)(1). **Effective** for fiscal years beginning on or after 10-1-2010. Prior to amendment, Code Sec. 9712(d)(1) read as follows:

(1) IN GENERAL.—All 1988 last signatory operators shall be responsible for financing the benefits described in subsection (c), in accordance with contribution requirements established in the 1992 UMWA Benefit Plan. Such contribution requirements, which shall be applied uniformly to each 1988 last signatory operator, on the basis of the number of eligible and potentially eligible beneficiaries attributable to each operator, shall include:

(A) the payment of an annual prefunding premium for all eligible and potentially eligible beneficiaries attributable to a 1988 last signatory operator,

(B) the payment of a monthly per beneficiary premium by each 1988 last signatory operator for each eligible beneficiary of such operator who is described in subsection (b)(2) and who is receiving benefits under the 1992 UMWA Benefit Plan, and

(C) the provision of security (in the form of a bond, letter of credit or cash escrow) in an amount equal to a portion of the projected future cost to the 1992 UMWA Benefit Plan of providing health benefits for eligible and potentially eligible beneficiaries attributable to the 1988 last signatory operator. If a 1988 last signatory operator is unable to provide the security required, the 1992 UMWA Benefit Plan shall require the operator to pay an annual prefunding premium that is greater than the premium otherwise applicable.

P.L. 109-432, Division C, §212(b)(2)(B)(i)-(ii):

Amended Code Sec. 9712(d) by striking "prefunding" and inserting "backstop" in paragraph (2)(B), and by striking "paragraph (1)(B)" and inserting "paragraph (1)(A)" in paragraph (3). **Effective** for fiscal years beginning on or after 10-1-2010.

[¶ 5915] CODE SEC. 9721. CIVIL ENFORCEMENT.

The provisions of section 4301 of the Employee Retirement Income Security Act of 1974 shall apply, in the same manner as any claim arising out of an obligation to pay withdrawal liability under subtitle E of title IV of such Act, to any claim—

(1) arising out of an obligation to pay any amount required to be paid by this chapter; or

(2) arising out of an obligation to pay any amount required by section 402(h)(5)(B)(ii) of the Surface Mining Control and Reclamation Act of 1977 (30 U.S.C. 1232(h)(5)(B)(ii)).

Amendments

• **2006, Tax Relief and Health Care Act of 2006 (P.L. 109-432)**

P.L. 109-432, Division C, § 213(b)(2):

Amended Code Sec. 9721. **Effective** 12-20-2006. Prior to amendment, Code Sec. 9721 read as follows:

SEC. 9721. CIVIL ENFORCEMENT.

The provisions of section 4301 of the Employee Retirement Income Security Act of 1974 shall apply to any claim arising out of an obligation to pay any amount required to be paid by this chapter in the same manner as any claim arising out of an obligation to pay withdrawal liability under subtitle E of title IV of such Act. For purposes of the preceding sentence, a signatory operator and related persons shall be treated in the same manner as employers.

[¶ 5920] CODE SEC. 9812. PARITY IN THE APPLICATION OF CERTAIN LIMITS TO MENTAL HEALTH BENEFITS.

* * *

(f) APPLICATION OF SECTION.—This section shall not apply to benefits for services furnished—

* * *

(3) after December 31, 2007.

[CCH Explanation at ¶ 535. Committee Reports at ¶ 15,240.]

Amendments

• **2006, Tax Relief and Health Care Act of 2006 (P.L. 109-432)**

P.L. 109-432, Division A, § 115(a):

Amended Code Sec. 9812(f)(3) by striking "2006" and inserting "2007". **Effective** 12-20-2006.

Act Sections Not Amending Code Sections

TAX INCREASE PREVENTION AND RECONCILIATION ACT OF 2005

[¶7005] ACT SEC. 1. SHORT TITLE, ETC.

(a) SHORT TITLE.—This Act may be cited as the "Tax Increase Prevention and Reconciliation Act of 2005".

(b) AMENDMENT OF 1986 CODE.—Except as otherwise expressly provided, whenever in this Act an amendment or repeal is expressed in terms of an amendment to, or repeal of, a section or other provision, the reference shall be considered to be made to a section or other provision of the Internal Revenue Code of 1986.

* * *

TITLE I—EXTENSION AND MODIFICATION OF CERTAIN PROVISIONS
* * *

[¶7010] ACT SEC. 102. CAPITAL GAINS AND DIVIDENDS RATES.

Section 303 of the Jobs and Growth Tax Relief Reconciliation Act of 2003 is amended by striking "December 31, 2008" and inserting "December 31, 2010".

• • *JOBS AND GROWTH ACT OF 2003 ACT SEC. 303 AS AMENDED*————————

ACT SEC. 303. SUNSET OF TITLE.

All provisions of, and amendments made by, this title shall not apply to taxable years beginning after *December 31, 2010*, and the Internal Revenue Code of 1986 shall be applied and administered to such years as if such provisions and amendments had never been enacted.

* * *

[CCH Explanations at ¶405, ¶910, ¶915, ¶920 and ¶925. Committee Reports at ¶10,020.]

TITLE II—OTHER PROVISIONS
* * *

[¶7015] ACT SEC. 206. MODIFICATION OF SPECIAL ARBITRAGE RULE FOR CERTAIN FUNDS.

In the case of bonds issued after the date of the enactment of this Act and before August 31, 2009—

(1) the requirement of paragraph (1) of section 648 of the Deficit Reduction Act of 1984 (98 Stat. 941) shall be treated as met with respect to the securities or obligations referred to in such section if such securities or obligations are held in a fund the annual distributions from which cannot exceed 7 percent of the average fair market value of the assets held in such fund except to the extent distributions are necessary to pay debt service on the bond issue, and

(2) paragraph (3) of such section shall be applied by substituting "distributions from" for "the investment earnings of" both places it appears.

* * *

[CCH Explanation at ¶1120. Committee Reports at ¶10,080.]

TITLE IV—CORPORATE ESTIMATED TAX PROVISIONS

[¶7020] ACT SEC. 401. TIME FOR PAYMENT OF CORPORATE ESTIMATED TAXES.

Notwithstanding section 6655 of the Internal Revenue Code of 1986—

(1) in the case of a corporation with assets of not less than $1,000,000,000 (determined as of the end of the preceding taxable year)—

(A) the amount of any required installment of corporate estimated tax which is otherwise due in July, August, or September of 2006 shall be 105 percent of such amount,

(B) the amount of any required installment of corporate estimated tax which is otherwise due in July, August, or September of 2012 shall be 106.25 percent of such amount,

(C) the amount of any required installment of corporate estimated tax which is otherwise due in July, August, or September of 2013 shall be 100.75 percent of such amount, and

(D) the amount of the next required installment after an installment referred to in subparagraph (A), (B), or (C) shall be appropriately reduced to reflect the amount of the increase by reason of such subparagraph,

(2) 20.5 percent of the amount of any required installment of corporate estimated tax which is otherwise due in September 2010 shall not be due until October 1, 2010, and

(3) 27.5 percent of the amount of any required installment of corporate estimated tax which is otherwise due in September 2011 shall not be due until October 1, 2011.

[CCH Explanation at ¶835. Committee Reports at ¶10,140.]

TITLE V—REVENUE OFFSET PROVISIONS
* * *

[¶7025] ACT SEC. 513. REPEAL OF FSC/ETI BINDING CONTRACT RELIEF.

(a) FSC PROVISIONS.—Paragraph (1) of section 5(c) of the FSC Repeal and Extraterritorial Income Exclusion Act of 2000 is amended by striking "which occurs—" and all that follows and inserting "which occurs before January 1, 2002.".

• • *FSC REPEAL ACT OF 2000 ACT SEC. 5(c)(1) BEFORE AMENDMENT*——————

ACT SEC. 5. EFFECTIVE DATE.
* * *

(c) TRANSITION PERIOD FOR EXISTING FOREIGN SALES CORPORATIONS.—

(1) IN GENERAL.—In the case of a FSC (as so defined) in existence on September 30, 2000, and at all times thereafter, the amendments made by this Act shall not apply to any transaction in the ordinary course of trade or business involving a FSC which occurs—

(A) before January 1, 2002; or

(B) after December 31, 2001, pursuant to a binding contract—

(i) which is between the FSC (or any related person) and any person which is not a related person; and

(ii) which is in effect on September 30, 2000, and at all times thereafter.

For purposes of this paragraph, a binding contract shall include a purchase option, renewal option, or replacement option which is included in such contract and which is enforceable against the seller or lessor.

(b) ETI PROVISIONS.—Section 101 of the American Jobs Creation Act of 2004 is amended by striking subsection (f).

• • *AJCA OF 2004 ACT SEC. 101(f) BEFORE AMENDMENT*————————————

ACT SEC. 101. REPEAL OF EXCLUSION FOR EXTRATERRITORIAL INCOME.

* * *

(f) BINDING CONTRACTS.—The amendments made by this section shall not apply to any transaction in the ordinary course of a trade or business which occurs pursuant to a binding contract—

(1) which is between the taxpayer and a person who is not a related person (as defined in section 943(b)(3) of such Code, as in effect on the day before the date of the enactment of this Act), and

(2) which is in effect on September 17, 2003, and at all times thereafter.

For purposes of this subsection, a binding contract shall include a purchase option, renewal option, or replacement option which is included in such contract and which is enforceable against the seller or lessor.

————————————

(c) EFFECTIVE DATE.—The amendments made by this section shall apply to taxable years beginning after the date of the enactment of this Act.

* * *

[CCH Explanation at ¶ 1045. Committee Reports at ¶ 10,270.]

TAX RELIEF AND HEALTH CARE ACT OF 2006

[¶ 7030] ACT SEC. 1. SHORT TITLE, ETC.

(a) SHORT TITLE.—This Act may be cited as the "Tax Relief and Health Care Act of 2006".

* * *

DIVISION A—EXTENSION AND EXPANSION OF CERTAIN TAX RELIEF PROVISIONS, AND OTHER TAX PROVISIONS

[¶ 7035] ACT SEC. 100. REFERENCE.

Except as otherwise expressly provided, whenever in this division an amendment or repeal is expressed in terms of an amendment to, or repeal of, a section or other provision, the reference shall be considered to be made to a section or other provision of the Internal Revenue Code of 1986.

TITLE I—EXTENSION AND MODIFICATION OF CERTAIN PROVISIONS

* * *

[¶ 7040] ACT SEC. 115. PARITY IN APPLICATION OF CERTAIN LIMITS TO MENTAL HEALTH BENEFITS.

* * *

(b) AMENDMENT TO THE EMPLOYEE RETIREMENT INCOME SECURITY ACT OF 1974.—Section 712(f) of the Employee Retirement Income Security Act of 1974 (29 U.S.C. 1185a(f)) is amended by striking "2006" and inserting "2007".

(c) AMENDMENT TO THE PUBLIC HEALTH SERVICE ACT.—Section 2705(f) of the Public Health Service Act (42 U.S.C. 300gg-5(f)) is amended by striking "2006" and inserting "2007".

* * *

[CCH Explanation at ¶540. Committee Reports at ¶15,240.]

[¶7045] ACT SEC. 117. AVAILABILITY OF MEDICAL SAVINGS ACCOUNTS.

* * *

(c) TIME FOR FILING REPORTS, ETC.—

(1) The report required by section 220(j)(4) of the Internal Revenue Code of 1986 to be made on August 1, 2005, or August 1, 2006, as the case may be, shall be treated as timely if made before the close of the 90-day period beginning on the date of the enactment of this Act.

(2) The determination and publication required by section 220(j)(5) of such Code with respect to calendar year 2005 or calendar year 2006, as the case may be, shall be treated as timely if made before the close of the 120-day period beginning on the date of the enactment of this Act. If the determination under the preceding sentence is that 2005 or 2006 is a cut-off year under section 220(i) of such Code, the cut-off date under such section 220(i) shall be the last day of such 120-day period.

* * *

[CCH Explanation at ¶535. Committee Reports at ¶10,260.]

[¶7050] ACT SEC. 119. AMERICAN SAMOA ECONOMIC DEVELOPMENT CREDIT.

(a) IN GENERAL.—For purposes of section 30A of the Internal Revenue Code of 1986, a domestic corporation shall be treated as a qualified domestic corporation to which such section applies if such corporation—

(1) is an existing credit claimant with respect to American Samoa, and

(2) elected the application of section 936 of the Internal Revenue Code of 1986 for its last taxable year beginning before January 1, 2006.

(b) SPECIAL RULES FOR APPLICATION OF SECTION.—The following rules shall apply in applying section 30A of the Internal Revenue Code of 1986 for purposes of this section:

(1) AMOUNT OF CREDIT.—Notwithstanding section 30A(a)(1) of such Code, the amount of the credit determined under section 30A(a)(1) of such Code for any taxable year shall be the amount determined under section 30A(d) of such Code, except that section 30A(d) shall be applied without regard to paragraph (3) thereof.

(2) SEPARATE APPLICATION.—In applying section 30A(a)(3) of such Code in the case of a corporation treated as a qualified domestic corporation by reason of this section, section 30A of such Code (and so much of section 936 of such Code as relates to such section 30A) shall be applied separately with respect to American Samoa.

(3) FOREIGN TAX CREDIT ALLOWED.—Notwithstanding section 30A(e) of such Code, the provisions of section 936(c) of such Code shall not apply with respect to the credit allowed by reason of this section.

(c) DEFINITIONS.—For purposes of this section, any term which is used in this section which is also used in section 30A or 936 of such Code shall have the same meaning given such term by such section 30A or 936.

(d) APPLICATION OF SECTION.—Notwithstanding section 30A(h) or section 936(j) of such Code, this section (and so much of section 30A and section 936 of such Code as relates to this section) shall apply to the first two taxable years of a corporation to which subsection (a) applies which begin after December 31, 2005, and before January 1, 2008.

* * *

[CCH Explanation at ¶435. Committee Reports at ¶15,280.]

[¶7055] ACT SEC. 123. SPECIAL RULE FOR ELECTIONS UNDER EXPIRED PROVISIONS.

(a) RESEARCH CREDIT ELECTIONS.—In the case of any taxable year ending after December 31, 2005, and before the date of the enactment of this Act, any election under section 41(c)(4) or section

280C(c)(3)(C) of the Internal Revenue Code of 1986 shall be treated as having been timely made for such taxable year if such election is made not later than the later of April 15, 2007, or such time as the Secretary of the Treasury, or his designee, may specify. Such election shall be made in the manner prescribed by such Secretary or designee.

(b) OTHER ELECTIONS.—Except as otherwise provided by such Secretary or designee, a rule similar to the rule of subsection (a) shall apply with respect to elections under any other expired provision of the Internal Revenue Code of 1986 the applicability of which is extended by reason of the amendments made by this title.

[CCH Explanation at ¶405. Committee Reports at ¶15,340.]

TITLE II—ENERGY TAX PROVISIONS
* * *

[¶7060] ACT SEC. 210. EXPENDITURES PERMITTED FROM THE LEAKING UNDERGROUND STORAGE TANK TRUST FUND.
* * *

(b) CONFORMING AMENDMENTS.—Section 9014(2) of the Solid Waste Disposal Act is amended by striking "Fund, notwithstanding section 9508(c)(1) of the Internal Revenue Code of 1986" and inserting "Fund".

(c) EFFECTIVE DATE.—The amendments made by this section shall take effect on the date of the enactment of this Act.
* * *

[CCH Explanation at ¶675. Committee Reports at ¶15,440.]

TITLE IV—OTHER PROVISIONS
* * *

[¶7065] ACT SEC. 402. CREDIT FOR PRIOR YEAR MINIMUM TAX LIABILITY MADE REFUNDABLE AFTER PERIOD OF YEARS.
* * *

(b) CONFORMING AMENDMENTS.—
* * *

(2) Paragraph (2) of section 1324(b) of title 31, United States Code, is amended by inserting "or 53(e)" after "section 35".

(c) EFFECTIVE DATE.—The amendments made by this section shall apply to taxable years beginning after the date of the enactment of this Act.
* * *

[CCH Explanation at ¶235. Committee Reports at ¶15,480.]

[¶7070] ACT SEC. 406. WHISTLEBLOWER REFORMS.
* * *

(b) WHISTLEBLOWER OFFICE.—

(1) IN GENERAL.—Not later than the date which is 12 months after the date of the enactment of this Act, the Secretary of the Treasury shall issue guidance for the operation of a whistleblower program to be administered in the Internal Revenue Service by an office to be known as the "Whistleblower Office" which—

(A) shall at all times operate at the direction of the Commissioner of Internal Revenue and coordinate and consult with other divisions in the Internal Revenue Service as directed by the Commissioner of Internal Revenue,

(B) shall analyze information received from any individual described in section 7623(b) of the Internal Revenue Code of 1986 and either investigate the matter itself or assign it to the appropriate Internal Revenue Service office, and

(C) in its sole discretion, may ask for additional assistance from such individual or any legal representative of such individual.

(2) REQUEST FOR ASSISTANCE.—The guidance issued under paragraph (1) shall specify that any assistance requested under paragraph (1)(C) shall be under the direction and control of the Whistleblower Office or the office assigned to investigate the matter under paragraph (1)(A). No individual or legal representative whose assistance is so requested may by reason of such request represent himself or herself as an employee of the Federal Government.

(c) REPORT BY SECRETARY.—The Secretary of the Treasury shall each year conduct a study and report to Congress on the use of section 7623 of the Internal Revenue Code of 1986, including—

(1) an analysis of the use of such section during the preceding year and the results of such use, and

(2) any legislative or administrative recommendations regarding the provisions of such section and its application.

(d) EFFECTIVE DATE.—The amendments made by subsection (a) shall apply to information provided on or after the date of the enactment of this Act.

* * *

[CCH Explanation at ¶ 650. Committee Reports at ¶ 15,510.]

[¶ 7075] ACT SEC. 414. MODIFICATION OF SPECIAL ARBITRAGE RULE FOR CERTAIN FUNDS MADE PERMANENT.

(a) IN GENERAL.—Section 206 of the Tax Increase Prevention and Reconciliation Act of 2005 is amended by striking "and before August 31, 2009".

• • TIPRA OF 2005 ACT SEC. 206 BEFORE AMENDMENT———————————————

ACT SEC. 206. MODIFICATION OF SPECIAL ARBITRAGE RULE FOR CERTAIN FUNDS.

In the case of bonds issued after the date of the enactment of this Act and before August 31, 2009—

(1) the requirement of paragraph (1) of section 648 of the Deficit Reduction Act of 1984 (98 Stat. 941) shall be treated as met with respect to the securities or obligations referred to in such section if such securities or obligations are held in a fund the annual distributions from which cannot exceed 7 percent of the average fair market value of the assets held in such fund except to the extent distributions are necessary to pay debt service on the bond issue, and

(2) paragraph (3) of such section shall be applied by substituting "distributions from" for "the investment earnings of" both places it appears.

(b) EFFECTIVE DATE.—The amendment made by this section shall take effect as if included in section 206 of the Tax Increase Prevention and Reconciliation Act of 2005.

* * *

[CCH Explanation at ¶ 615. Committee Reports at ¶ 15,590.]

[¶ 7080] ACT SEC. 420. MODIFICATION OF REFUNDS FOR KEROSENE USED IN AVIATION.

* * *

(d) SPECIAL RULE FOR KEROSENE USED IN AVIATION ON A FARM FOR FARMING PURPOSES.—

(1) REFUNDS FOR PURCHASES AFTER DECEMBER 31, 2004, AND BEFORE OCTOBER 1, 2005.—The Secretary of the Treasury shall pay to the ultimate purchaser of any kerosene which is used in aviation on a farm for farming purposes and which was purchased after December 31, 2004, and before October 1, 2005, an amount equal to the aggregate amount of tax imposed on such fuel

under section 4041 or 4081 of the Internal Revenue Code of 1986, as the case may be, reduced by any payment to the ultimate vendor under section 6427(l)(5)(C) of such Code (as in effect on the day before the date of the enactment of the Safe, Accountable, Flexible, Efficient Transportation Equity Act: a Legacy for Users).

(2) USE ON A FARM FOR FARMING PURPOSES.—For purposes of paragraph (1), kerosene shall be treated as used on a farm for farming purposes if such kerosene is used for farming purposes (within the meaning of section 6420(c)(3) of the Internal Revenue Code of 1986) in carrying on a trade or business on a farm situated in the United States. For purposes of the preceding sentence, rules similar to the rules of section 6420(c)(4) of such Code shall apply.

(3) TIME FOR FILING CLAIMS.—No claim shall be allowed under paragraph (1) unless the ultimate purchaser files such claim before the date that is 3 months after the date of the enactment of this Act.

(4) NO DOUBLE BENEFIT.—No amount shall be paid under paragraph (1) or section 6427(l) of the Internal Revenue Code of 1986 with respect to any kerosene described in paragraph (1) to the extent that such amount is in excess of the tax imposed on such kerosene under section 4041 or 4081 of such Code, as the case may be.

(5) APPLICABLE LAWS.—For purposes of this subsection, rules similar to the rules of section 6427(j) of the Internal Revenue Code of 1986 shall apply.

* * *

[CCH Explanation at ¶670. Committee Reports at ¶15,650.]

[¶7085] SEC. 426. TECHNICAL CORRECTIONS.

* * *

(b) TECHNICAL CORRECTION REGARDING AUTHORITY TO EXERCISE REASONABLE CAUSE AND GOOD FAITH EXCEPTION.—

(1) IN GENERAL.—Section 903(d)(2)(B)(iii) of the American Jobs Creation Act of 2004, as amended by section 303(a) of the Gulf Opportunity Zone Act of 2005, is amended by inserting "or the Secretary's delegate" after "the Secretary of the Treasury".

• • *AJCA OF 2004 ACT SEC. 903(d)(2)(B)(iii) [as amended by P.L. 109-135, §303(a)] AS AMENDED*

ACT SEC. 903. FREEZE OF PROVISIONS REGARDING SUSPENSION OF INTEREST WHERE SECRETARY FAILS TO CONTACT TAXPAYER.

(d) EFFECTIVE DATES.—

* * *

(2) EXCEPTION FOR REPORTABLE OR LISTED TRANSACTIONS.—

* * *

(B) SPECIAL RULE FOR CERTAIN LISTED AND REPORTABLE TRANSACTIONS.—

* * *

(iii) TAXPAYERS ACTING IN GOOD FAITH.—The Secretary of the Treasury *or the Secretary's delegate* may except from the application of clause (i) any transaction in which the taxpayer has acted reasonably and in good faith.

(2) EFFECTIVE DATE.—The amendment made by this subsection shall take effect as if included in the provisions of the American Jobs Creation Act of 2004 to which it relates.

* * *

[CCH Explanation at ¶655. Committee Reports at ¶15,710.]

DIVISION C—OTHER PROVISIONS
* * *

TITLE IV—OTHER PROVISIONS
* * *

[¶7090] ACT SEC. 403. WITHDRAWAL OF CERTAIN FEDERAL LAND AND INTERESTS IN CERTAIN FEDERAL LAND FROM LOCATION, ENTRY, AND PATENT UNDER THE MINING LAWS AND DISPOSITION UNDER THE MINERAL AND GEOTHERMAL LEASING LAWS.

(a) DEFINITIONS.—In this section:

(1) BUREAU OF LAND MANAGEMENT LAND.—The term "Bureau of Land Management land" means the Bureau of Land Management land and any federally-owned minerals located south of the Blackfeet Indian Reservation and east of the Lewis and Clark National Forest to the eastern edge of R. 8 W., beginning in T. 29 N. down to and including T. 19 N. and all of T. 18 N., R. 7 W.

(2) ELIGIBLE FEDERAL LAND.—The term "eligible Federal land" means the Bureau of Land Management land and the Forest Service land, as generally depicted on the map.

(3) FOREST SERVICE LAND.—The term "Forest Service land" means—

(A) the Forest Service land and any federally-owned minerals located in the Rocky Mountain Division of the Lewis and Clark National Forest, including the approximately 356,111 acres of land made unavailable for leasing by the August 28, 1997, Record of Decision for the Lewis and Clark National Forest Oil and Gas Leasing Environmental Impact Statement and that is located from T. 31 N. to T. 16 N. and R. 13 W. to R. 7 W.; and

(B) the Forest Service land and any federally-owned minerals located within the Badger Two Medicine area of the Flathead National Forest, including—

(i) the land located in T. 29 N. from the western edge of R. 16 W. to the eastern edge of R. 13 W.; and

(ii) the land located in T. 28 N., Rs. 13 and 14 W.

(4) MAP.—The term "map" means the map entitled "Rocky Mountain Front Mineral Withdrawal Area" and dated December 31, 2006.

(b) WITHDRAWAL.—

(1) IN GENERAL.—Subject to valid existing rights, the eligible Federal land (including any interest in the eligible Federal land) is withdrawn from—

(A) all forms of location, entry, and patent under the mining laws; and

(B) disposition under all laws relating to mineral and geothermal leasing.

(2) AVAILABILITY OF MAP.—The map shall be on file and available for inspection in the Office of the Chief of the Forest Service.

(c) TAX INCENTIVE FOR SALE OF EXISTING MINERAL AND GEOTHERMAL RIGHTS TO TAX-EXEMPT ENTITIES.—

(1) EXCLUSION.—For purposes of the Internal Revenue Code of 1986, gross income shall not include 25 percent of the qualifying gain from a conservation sale of a qualifying mineral or geothermal interest.

(2) QUALIFYING GAIN.—For purposes of this subsection, the term "qualifying gain" means any gain which would be recognized as long-term capital gain under such Code.

(3) CONSERVATION SALE.—For purposes of this subsection, the term "conservation sale" means a sale which meets the following requirements:

(A) TRANSFEREE IS AN ELIGIBLE ENTITY.—The transferee of the qualifying mineral or geothermal interest is an eligible entity.

(B) Q<small>UALIFYING</small> L<small>ETTER</small> <small>OF</small> I<small>NTENT</small> R<small>EQUIRED</small>.—At the time of the sale, such transferee provides the taxpayer with a qualifying letter of intent.

(C) N<small>ONAPPLICATION</small> <small>TO</small> <small>CERTAIN</small> S<small>ALES</small>.—The sale is not made pursuant to an order of condemnation or eminent domain.

(4) Q<small>UALIFYING</small> M<small>INERAL</small> <small>OR</small> G<small>EOTHERMAL</small> I<small>NTEREST</small>.—For purposes of this subsection—

(A) I<small>N</small> G<small>ENERAL</small>.—The term "qualifying mineral or geothermal interest" means an interest in any mineral or geothermal deposit located on eligible Federal land which constitutes a taxpayer's entire interest in such deposit.

(B) E<small>NTIRE</small> I<small>NTEREST</small>.—For purposes of subparagraph (A)—

(i) an interest in any mineral or geothermal deposit is not a taxpayer's entire interest if such interest in such mineral or geothermal deposit was divided in order to avoid the requirements of such subparagraph or section 170(f)(3)(A) of such Code, and

(ii) a taxpayer's entire interest in such deposit does not fail to satisfy such subparagraph solely because the taxpayer has retained an interest in other deposits, even if the other deposits are contiguous with such certain deposit and were acquired by the taxpayer along with such certain deposit in a single conveyance.

(5) O<small>THER</small> D<small>EFINITIONS</small>.—For purposes of this subsection—

(A) E<small>LIGIBLE</small> E<small>NTITY</small>.—The term "eligible entity" means—

(i) a governmental unit referred to in section 170(c)(1) of such Code, or an agency or department thereof operated primarily for 1 or more of the conservation purposes specified in clause (i), (ii), or (iii) of section 170(h)(4)(A) of such Code, or

(ii) an entity which is—

(I) described in section 170(b)(1)(A)(vi) or section 170(h)(3)(B) of such Code, and

(II) organized and at all times operated primarily for 1 or more of the conservation purposes specified in clause (i), (ii), or (iii) of section 170(h)(4)(A) of such Code.

(B) Q<small>UALIFYING</small> L<small>ETTER</small> <small>OF</small> I<small>NTENT</small>.—The term "qualifying letter of intent" means a written letter of intent which includes the following statement: "The transferee's intent is that this acquisition will serve 1 or more of the conservation purposes specified in clause (i), (ii), or (iii) of section 170(h)(4)(A) of the Internal Revenue Code of 1986, that the transferee's use of the deposits so acquired will be consistent with section 170(h)(5) of such Code, and that the use of the deposits will continue to be consistent with such section, even if ownership or possession of such deposits is subsequently transferred to another person.".

(6) T<small>AX</small> <small>ON</small> S<small>UBSEQUENT</small> T<small>RANSFERS</small>.—

(A) I<small>N</small> G<small>ENERAL</small>.—A tax is hereby imposed on any subsequent transfer by an eligible entity of ownership or possession, whether by sale, exchange, or lease, of an interest acquired directly or indirectly in—

(i) a conservation sale described in paragraph (1), or

(ii) a transfer described in clause (i), (ii), or (iii) of subparagraph (D).

(B) A<small>MOUNT</small> <small>OF</small> T<small>AX</small>.—The amount of tax imposed by subparagraph (A) on any transfer shall be equal to the sum of—

(i) 20 percent of the fair market value (determined at the time of the transfer) of the interest the ownership or possession of which is transferred, plus

(ii) the product of—

(I) the highest rate of tax specified in section 11 of such Code, times

(II) any gain or income realized by the transferor as a result of the transfer.

(C) L<small>IABILITY</small>.—The tax imposed by subparagraph (A) shall be paid by the transferor.

(D) R<small>ELIEF</small> <small>FROM</small> L<small>IABILITY</small>.—The person (otherwise liable for any tax imposed by subparagraph (A)) shall be relieved of liability for the tax imposed by subparagraph (A) with respect to any transfer if—

(i) the transferee is an eligible entity which provides such person, at the time of transfer, a qualifying letter of intent,

(ii) in any case where the transferee is not an eligible entity, it is established to the satisfaction of the Secretary of the Treasury, that the transfer of ownership or possession, as the case may be, will be consistent with section 170(h)(5) of such Code, and the transferee provides such person, at the time of transfer, a qualifying letter of intent, or

(iii) tax has previously been paid under this paragraph as a result of a prior transfer of ownership or possession of the same interest.

(E) ADMINISTRATIVE PROVISIONS.—For purposes of subtitle F of such Code, the taxes imposed by this paragraph shall be treated as excise taxes with respect to which the deficiency procedures of such subtitle apply.

(7) REPORTING.—The Secretary of the Treasury may require such reporting as may be necessary or appropriate to further the purpose under this subsection that any conservation use be in perpetuity.

(d) EFFECTIVE DATES.—

(1) MORATORIUM.—Subsection (b) shall take effect on the date of the enactment of this Act.

(2) TAX INCENTIVE.—Subsection (c) shall apply to sales occurring on or after the date of the enactment of this Act.

* * *

[CCH Explanation at ¶ 358. Committee Reports at ¶ 15,720.]

Committee Reports

Tax Increase Prevention and Reconciliation Act of 2005

¶10,001 Introduction

The Conference Committee Report accompanying the Tax Increase Prevention and Reconciliation Act of 2005 (P.L. 109-222) explains the intent of Congress regarding the provisions in the Act. At the end of the Conference Report text, references are provided to corresponding explanations and Code provisions. Subscribers to the electronic version can link from these references to the corresponding material. *The pertinent sections of the Conference Report appear in Act Section order beginning at ¶10,010.*

¶10,005 Background

The Tax Increase Prevention and Reconciliation Act of 2005 (H.R. 4297) was introduced in the House of Representatives on November 10, 2005. The House Committee on Ways and Means amended and reported favorably on H.R. 4297 on November 17, 2005 (H.R. REP. NO. 109-304). The bill passed the House on December 8, 2005, by a vote of 234 to 197. The Senate passed H.R. 4297 with an amendment on February 2, 2006, by a vote of 66 to 31.

On February 8, 2006, the House disagreed to the Senate Amendment to H.R. 4297 and requested a conference. A conference report on H.R. 4297 was filed on May 9, 2006 (H.R. CONF. REP. NO. 109-455). The House agreed to the conference report on May 10, 2006, by a vote of 244 to 185. On May 11, the Senate agreed to the conference report by a vote of 54-44.

The following material is the official wording of the conference report accompanying H.R. 4297, The Tax Increase Prevention and Reconciliation Act of 2005, as released on May 9, 2006. Headings have been added for the reader's convenience. Omissions of text are indicated by asterisks (* * *). References are to the following reports:

• The Tax Relief Extension Reconciliation Act of 2005 (H.R. 4297), House Ways and Means Committee Report, as reported on November 17, 2005, is referred to as House Committee Report (H.R. REP. NO. 109-304).

• The Conference Committee Report on the Tax Increase Prevention and Reconciliation Act of 2005, as released on May 9, 2006, is referred to as Conference Committee Report (H.R. CONF. REP. NO. 109-455).

President Bush signed the Tax Increase Prevention and Reconciliation Act of 2005 (P.L. 109-222) on May 17, 2006.

[¶10,010] Act Sec. 101. Extension of increased expensing for small business

House Committee Report (H.R. REP. NO. 109-304)

[Code Sec. 179]

Present Law

In lieu of depreciation, a taxpayer with a sufficiently small amount of annual investment may elect to deduct (or "expense") such costs. Present law provides that the maximum amount a taxpayer may expense, for taxable years beginning in 2003 through 2007, is $100,000 of the cost of qualifying property placed in service for the taxable year.[29] In general, qualifying property is defined as depreciable tangible personal property that is purchased for use in the active conduct of a trade or business. Off-the-shelf computer software placed in service in taxable years beginning before 2008 is treated as qualifying property. The $100,000 amount is reduced (but not below zero) by the amount by which the cost of qualifying property placed in service during the taxable year exceeds $400,000. The $100,000 and $400,000 amounts are indexed for inflation for taxable years beginning after 2003 and before 2008.

The amount eligible to be expensed for a taxable year may not exceed the taxable income for a taxable year that is derived from the active conduct of a trade or business (determined without regard to this provision). Any amount that is not allowed as a deduction because of the taxable income limitation may be carried forward to succeeding taxable years (subject to similar limitations). No general business credit under section 38 is allowed with respect to any amount for which a deduction is allowed under section 179. An expensing election is made under rules prescribed by the Secretary.[30]

For taxable years beginning in 2008 and thereafter (or before 2003), the following rules apply. A taxpayer with a sufficiently small amount of annual investment may elect to deduct up to $25,000 of the cost of qualifying property placed in service for the taxable year. The $25,000 amount is reduced (but not below zero) by the amount by which the cost of qualifying property placed in service during the taxable year exceeds $200,000. The $25,000 and $200,000 amounts are not indexed. In general, qualifying property is defined as depreciable tangible personal property that is purchased for use in the active conduct of a trade or business (not including off-the-shelf computer software). An expensing election may be revoked only with consent of the Commissioner.[31]

Reasons for Change

The Committee believes that section 179 expensing provides two important benefits for small businesses. First, it lowers the cost of capital for property used in a trade or business. With a lower cost of capital, the Committee believes small businesses will invest in more equipment and employ more workers. Second, it eliminates depreciation recordkeeping requirements with respect to expensed property. In 2004, Congress acted to increase the value of these benefits and to increase the number of taxpayers eligible for taxable years through 2007. The Committee believes that the changes to section 179 expensing will continue to provide important benefits if extended, and the bill therefore extends these changes for an additional two years.

Explanation of Provision

The provision extends for two years the increased amount that a taxpayer may deduct and the other section 179 rules applicable in taxable years beginning before 2008. Thus, under the provision, these present-law rules continue in effect for taxable years beginning after 2007 and before 2010.

Effective Date

The provision is effective for taxable years beginning after 2007 and before 2010.

---

[29] Additional section 179 incentives are provided with respect to a qualified property used by a business in the New York Liberty Zone (sec. 1400L(f)), an empowerment zone (sec. 1397A), or a renewal community (sec. 1400J).

[30] Sec. 179(c)(1). Under Treas. Reg. sec. 179-5, applicable to property placed in service in taxable years beginning after 2002 and before 2008, a taxpayer is permitted to make

or revoke an election under section 179 without the consent of the Commissioner on an amended Federal tax return for that taxable year. This amended return must be filed within the time prescribed by law for filing an amended return for the taxable year. T.D. 9209, July 12, 2005.

[31] Sec. 179(c)(2).

Conference Committee Report (H.R. CONF. REP. NO. 109-455)

Senate Amendment	Conference Agreement
The Senate amendment provision is the same as the House bill.	The conference agreement includes the provision in the House bill and the Senate amendment.

[Law at ¶5305. CCH Explanation at ¶805.]

[¶10,020] Act Sec. 102. Reduced rates for capital gains and dividends of individuals

House Committee Report (H.R. REP. NO. 109-304)

[Code Sec. 1(h)]

Present Law

Capital gains

In general

In general, gain or loss reflected in the value of an asset is not recognized for income tax purposes until a taxpayer disposes of the asset. On the sale or exchange of a capital asset, any gain generally is included in income. Any net capital gain of an individual is taxed at maximum rates lower than the rates applicable to ordinary income. Net capital gain is the excess of the net long-term capital gain for the taxable year over the net short-term capital loss for the year. Gain or loss is treated as long-term if the asset is held for more than one year.

Capital losses generally are deductible in full against capital gains. In addition, individual taxpayers may deduct capital losses against up to $3,000 of ordinary income in each year. Any remaining unused capital losses may be carried forward indefinitely to another taxable year.

A capital asset generally means any property except (1) inventory, stock in trade, or property held primarily for sale to customers in the ordinary course of the taxpayer's trade or business, (2) depreciable or real property used in the taxpayer's trade or business, (3) specified literary or artistic property, (4) business accounts or notes receivable, (5) certain U.S. publications, (6) certain commodity derivative financial instruments, (7) hedging transactions, and (8) business supplies. In addition, the net gain from the disposition of certain property used in the taxpayer's trade or business is treated as long-term capital gain. Gain from the disposition of depreciable personal property is not treated as capital gain to the extent of all previous depreciation allowances. Gain from the disposition of depreciable real property is generally not treated as capital gain to the extent of the depreciation

allowances in excess of the allowances that would have been available under the straightline method of depreciation.

Tax rates before 2009

Under present law, for taxable years beginning before January 1, 2009, the maximum rate of tax on the adjusted net capital gain of an individual is 15 percent. Any adjusted net capital gain which otherwise would be taxed at a 10- or 15-percent rate is taxed at a five-percent rate (zero for taxable years beginning after 2007). These rates apply for purposes of both the regular tax and the alternative minimum tax.

Under present law, the "adjusted net capital gain" of an individual is the net capital gain reduced (but not below zero) by the sum of the 28-percent rate gain and the unrecaptured section 1250 gain. The net capital gain is reduced by the amount of gain that the individual treats as investment income for purposes of determining the investment interest limitation under section 163(d).

The term "28-percent rate gain" means the amount of net gain attributable to long-term capital gains and losses from the sale or exchange of collectibles (as defined in section 408(m) without regard to paragraph (3) thereof), an amount of gain equal to the amount of gain excluded from gross income under section 1202 (relating to certain small business stock), the net short-term capital loss for the taxable year, and any long-term capital loss carryover to the taxable year.

"Unrecaptured section 1250 gain" means any long-term capital gain from the sale or exchange of section 1250 property (i.e., depreciable real estate) held more than one year to the extent of the gain that would have been treated as ordinary income if section 1250 applied to all depreciation, reduced by the net loss (if any) attributable to the items taken into account in computing 28-percent rate gain. The amount of unrecaptured section 1250 gain (before the reduction for the net loss) attributable to the disposition of property to which section 1231 (relating to certain property used in a trade or business) applies may not exceed the net section 1231 gain for the year.

An individual's unrecaptured section 1250 gain is taxed at a maximum rate of 25 percent, and the 28-percent rate gain is taxed at a maximum rate of 28 percent. Any amount of unrecaptured section 1250 gain or 28-percent rate gain otherwise taxed at a 10- or 15-percent rate is taxed at the otherwise applicable rate.

Tax rates after 2008

For taxable years beginning after December 31, 2008, the maximum rate of tax on the adjusted net capital gain of an individual is 20 percent. Any adjusted net capital gain which otherwise would be taxed at a 10- or 15-percent rate is taxed at a 10-percent rate.

In addition, any gain from the sale or exchange of property held more than five years that would otherwise have been taxed at the 10-percent rate is taxed at an eight-percent rate. Any gain from the sale or exchange of property held more than five years and the holding period for which began after December 31, 2000, that would otherwise have been taxed at a 20-percent rate is taxed at an 18-percent rate.

The tax rates on 28-percent gain and unrecaptured section 1250 gain are the same as for taxable years beginning before 2009.

Dividends

In general

A dividend is the distribution of property made by a corporation to its shareholders out of its after-tax earnings and profits.

Tax rates before 2009

Under present law, dividends received by an individual from domestic corporations and qualified foreign corporations are taxed at the same rates that apply to capital gains. This treatment applies for purposes of both the regular tax and the alternative minimum tax. Thus, for taxable years beginning before 2009, dividends received by an individual are taxed at rates of five (zero for taxable years beginning after 2007) and 15 percent.

If a shareholder does not hold a share of stock for more than 60 days during the 121-day period beginning 60 days before the exdividend date (as measured under section 246(c)), dividends received on the stock are not eligible for the reduced rates. Also, the reduced rates are not available for dividends to the extent that the taxpayer is obligated to make related payments with respect to positions in substantially similar or related property.

Qualified dividend income includes otherwise qualified dividends received from qualified foreign corporations. The term "qualified foreign corporation" includes a foreign corporation that is eligible for the benefits of a comprehensive income tax treaty with the United States which the Treasury Department determines to be satisfactory and which includes an exchange of information program. In addition, a foreign corporation is treated as a qualified foreign corporation with respect to any dividend paid by the corporation with respect to stock that is readily tradable on an established securities market in the United States.

Dividends received from a corporation that is a passive foreign investment company (as defined in section 1297) in either the taxable year of the distribution, or the preceding taxable year, are not qualified dividends.

Special rules apply in determining a taxpayer's foreign tax credit limitation under section 904 in the case of qualified dividend income. For these purposes, rules similar to the rules of section 904(b)(2)(B) concerning adjustments to the foreign tax credit limitation to reflect any capital gain rate differential will apply to any qualified dividend income.

If a taxpayer receives an extraordinary dividend (within the meaning of section 1059(c)) eligible for the reduced rates with respect to any share of stock, any loss on the sale of the stock is treated as a long-term capital loss to the extent of the dividend.

A dividend is treated as investment income for purposes of determining the amount of deductible investment interest only if the taxpayer elects to treat the dividend as not eligible for the reduced rates.

The amount of dividends qualifying for reduced rates that may be paid by a regulated investment company ("RIC") for any taxable year in which the qualified dividend income received by the company is less than 95 percent of its gross income (as specially computed) may not exceed the sum of (i) the qualified dividend income of the RIC for the taxable year and (ii) the amount of earnings and profits accumulated in a non-RIC taxable year that were distributed by the RIC during the taxable year.

The amount of dividends qualifying for reduced rates that may be paid by a real estate investment trust ("REIT") for any taxable year may not exceed the sum of (i) the qualified dividend income of the REIT for the taxable year, (ii) an amount equal to the excess of the income subject to the taxes imposed by section 857(b)(1) and the regulations prescribed under section 337(d) for the preceding taxable year over the amount of these taxes for the preceding taxable year, and (iii) the amount of earnings and profits accumulated in a non-REIT taxable year that were distributed by the REIT during the taxable year.

The reduced rates do not apply to dividends received from an organization that was exempt from tax under section 501 or was a tax-exempt farmers' cooperative in either the taxable year of the distribution or the preceding taxable year; dividends received from a mutual savings bank that received a deduction under section 591; or deductible dividends paid on employer securities.[27]

Tax rates after 2008

For taxable years beginning after 2008, dividends received by an individual are taxed as ordinary income at rates of up to 35 percent.

Reasons for Change

The Committee believes that the lower capital gain and dividend rates have had a positive effect on the economy and should be extended to continue to promote economic growth by increasing the after-tax return to saving and investment. The Committee further believes that the extension will encourage the payment of dividends by corporations.

Explanation of Provision

The bill extends for two years the present-law provisions relating to lower capital gain and dividend tax rates (through taxable years beginning on or before December 31, 2010).

Effective Date

The provision applies to taxable years beginning after December 31, 2008.

Conference Committee Report (H.R. CONF. REP. NO. 109-455)

Senate Amendment

No provision.

[Law at ¶7010. CCH Explanation at ¶905, ¶910, ¶915, ¶920 and ¶925.]

Conference Agreement

The conference agreement includes the House bill provision.

[¶10,022] Act Sec. 103(a). Subpart F exception for active financing

House Committee Report (H.R. REP. NO. 109-304)

[Code Secs. 953 and 954]

Present Law

Under the subpart F rules, 10-percent U.S. shareholders of a controlled foreign corporation ("CFC") are subject to U.S. tax currently on certain income earned by the CFC, whether or not such income is distributed to the shareholders. The income subject to current inclusion under the subpart F rules includes, among other things, insurance income and foreign base company in-

come. Foreign base company income includes, among other things, foreign personal holding company income and foreign base company services income (i.e., income derived from services performed for or on behalf of a related person outside the country in which the CFC is organized).

Foreign personal holding company income generally consists of the following: (1) dividends, interest, royalties, rents, and annuities; (2)

---

[27] In addition, for taxable years beginning before 2009, amounts treated as ordinary income on the disposition of certain preferred stock (sec. 306) are treated as dividends for purposes of applying the reduced rates; the tax rate for the

accumulated earnings tax (sec. 531) and the personal holding company tax (sec. 541) is reduced to 15 percent; and the collapsible corporation rules (sec. 341) are repealed.

net gains from the sale or exchange of (a) property that gives rise to the preceding types of income, (b) property that does not give rise to income, and (c) interests in trusts, partnerships, and REMICs; (3) net gains from commodities transactions; (4) net gains from certain foreign currency transactions; (5) income that is equivalent to interest; (6) income from notional principal contracts; (7) payments in lieu of dividends; and (8) amounts received under personal service contracts.

Insurance income subject to current inclusion under the subpart F rules includes any income of a CFC attributable to the issuing or reinsuring of any insurance or annuity contract in connection with risks located in a country other than the CFC's country of organization. Subpart F insurance income also includes income attributable to an insurance contract in connection with risks located within the CFC's country of organization, as the result of an arrangement under which another corporation receives a substantially equal amount of consideration for insurance of other country risks. Investment income of a CFC that is allocable to any insurance or annuity contract related to risks located outside the CFC's country of organization is taxable as subpart F insurance income.[22]

Temporary exceptions from foreign personal holding company income, foreign base company services income, and insurance income apply for subpart F purposes for certain income that is derived in the active conduct of a banking, financing, or similar business, or in the conduct of an insurance business (so-called "active financing income").[23]

With respect to income derived in the active conduct of a banking, financing, or similar business, a CFC is required to be predominantly engaged in such business and to conduct substantial activity with respect to such business in order to qualify for the exceptions. In addition, certain nexus requirements apply, which provide that income derived by a CFC or a qualified business unit ("QBU") of a CFC from transactions with customers is eligible for the exceptions if, among other things, substantially all of the activities in connection with such transactions are conducted directly by the CFC or QBU in its home country, and such income is treated

as earned by the CFC or QBU in its home country for purposes of such country's tax laws. Moreover, the exceptions apply to income derived from certain cross border transactions, provided that certain requirements are met. Additional exceptions from foreign personal holding company income apply for certain income derived by a securities dealer within the meaning of section 475 and for gain from the sale of active financing assets.

In the case of insurance, in addition to a temporary exception from foreign personal holding company income for certain income of a qualifying insurance company with respect to risks located within the CFC's country of creation or organization, certain temporary exceptions from insurance income and from foreign personal holding company income apply for certain income of a qualifying branch of a qualifying insurance company with respect to risks located within the home country of the branch, provided certain requirements are met under each of the exceptions. Further, additional temporary exceptions from insurance income and from foreign personal holding company income apply for certain income of certain CFCs or branches with respect to risks located in a country other than the United States, provided that the requirements for these exceptions are met.

In the case of a life insurance or annuity contract, reserves for such contracts are determined as follows for purposes of these provisions. The reserves equal the greater of: (1) the net surrender value of the contract (as defined in section 807(e)(1)(A)), including in the case of pension plan contracts; or (2) the amount determined by applying the tax reserve method that would apply if the qualifying life insurance company were subject to tax under Subchapter L of the Code, with the following modifications. First, there is substituted for the applicable Federal interest rate an interest rate determined for the functional currency of the qualifying insurance company's home country, calculated (except as provided by the Treasury Secretary in order to address insufficient data and similar problems) in the same manner as the mid-term applicable Federal interest rate (within the meaning of section 1274(d)). Second, there is substituted for the prevailing State assumed rate the highest assumed interest rate permitted to be used for

---

[22] Prop. Treas. Reg. sec. 1.953-1(a).

[23] Temporary exceptions from the subpart F provisions for certain active financing income applied only for taxable years beginning in 1998. Those exceptions were modified and extended for one year, applicable only for taxable years beginning in 1999. The Tax Relief Extension Act of 1999

(Pub. L. No. 106-170) clarified and extended the temporary exceptions for two years, applicable only for taxable years beginning after 1999 and before 2002. The Job Creation and Worker Assistance Act of 2002 (Pub. L. No. 107-147) modified and extended the temporary exceptions for five years, for taxable years beginning after 2001 and before 2007.

purposes of determining statement reserves in the foreign country for the contract. Third, in lieu of U.S. mortality and morbidity tables, mortality and morbidity tables are applied that reasonably reflect the current mortality and morbidity risks in the foreign country. Fourth, the Treasury Secretary may provide that the interest rate and mortality and morbidity tables of a qualifying insurance company may be used for one or more of its branches when appropriate. In no event may the reserve for any contract at any time exceed the foreign statement reserve for the contract, reduced by any catastrophe, equalization, or deficiency reserve or any similar reserve.

Present law permits a taxpayer in certain circumstances, subject to approval by the IRS through the ruling process or in published guidance, to establish that the reserve of a life insurance company for life insurance and annuity contracts is the amount taken into account in determining the foreign statement reserve for the contract (reduced by catastrophe, equalization, or deficiency reserve or any similar reserve). IRS approval is to be based on whether the method, the interest rate, the mortality and morbidity assumptions, and any other factors taken into account in determining foreign statement reserves (taken together or separately) provide an appropriate means of measuring income for Federal income tax purposes. In seeking a ruling, the taxpayer is required to provide the IRS with necessary and appropriate information as to the method, interest rate, mortality and morbidity assumptions and other assumptions under the foreign reserve rules so that a comparison can be made to the reserve amount determined by applying the tax reserve method that would apply if the qualifying insurance company were subject to tax under Subchapter L of the Code (with the

modifications provided under present law for purposes of these exceptions). The IRS also may issue published guidance indicating its approval. Present law continues to apply with respect to reserves for any life insurance or annuity contract for which the IRS has not approved the use of the foreign statement reserve. An IRS ruling request under this provision is subject to the present-law provisions relating to IRS user fees.

Reasons for Change

In the Taxpayer Relief Act of 1997, one-year temporary exceptions from foreign personal holding company income were enacted for income from the active conduct of an insurance, banking, financing, or similar business.[24] In 1998, 1999, and 2002, the provisions were extended, and in some cases, modified.[25] The Committee believes that it is appropriate to extend the temporary provisions, as modified by the previous legislation, for an additional two years.

Explanation of Provision

The provision extends for two years (for taxable years beginning before 2009) the present-law temporary exceptions from subpart F foreign personal holding company income, foreign base company services income, and insurance income for certain income that is derived in the active conduct of a banking, financing, or similar business, or in the conduct of an insurance business.

Effective Date

The provision is effective for taxable years of foreign corporations beginning after December 31, 2006, and before January 1, 2009, and for taxable years of U.S. shareholders with or within which such taxable years of such foreign corporations end.

Conference Committee Report (H.R. CONF. REP. NO. 109-455)

Senate Amendment

No provision.

Conference Agreement

The conference agreement includes the House bill provision.

[Law at ¶5530 and ¶5555. CCH Explanation at ¶1030 and ¶1035.]

---

[24] The President canceled this provision in 1997 pursuant to the Line Item Veto Act. On June 25, 1998, the Supreme Court held that the cancellation procedures set forth in the Line Item Veto Act are unconstitutional. *Clinton* v. *City of New York*, 524 U.S. 417 (1998).

[25] The Tax and Trade Relief Extension Act of 1998, Division J, Making Omnibus Consolidated and Emergency Supplemental Appropriations for Fiscal Year 1999, Pub. L. No. 105-277, sec. 1005 (1998), provided a one-year extension, with modifications. The Tax Relief Extension Act of 1999, Pub.L. No. 106-170, sec. 503 (1999), provided an additional

two-year extension, with a clarification. The Job Creation and Worker Assistance Act of 2002 (Pub. L. No. 107-147, sec. 614) provided an additional five-year extension and provided that in certain circumstances an insurance company may establish reserves taking into account foreign statement reserves. The House bill, H.R. 3090, the "Economic Security and Recovery Act of 2001," had provided for a permanent extension (H. R. Rep. No. 107-251 at 50 (2001)), while the Senate bill, the "Economic Recovery and Assistance for American Workers Act of 2001," had provided for a one-year extension. See S. Prt. No. 107-49 at 58-60 (2001).

[¶10,027] Act Sec. 103(b). Look-through treatment of payments between related controlled foreign corporations under foreign personal holding company income rules

House Committee Report (H.R. REP. NO. 109-304)

[Code Sec. 954(c)]

Present Law

In general, the rules of subpart F (secs. 951-964) require U.S. shareholders with a 10-percent or greater interest in a controlled foreign corporation ("CFC") to include certain income of the CFC (referred to as "subpart F income") on a current basis for U.S. tax purposes, regardless of whether the income is distributed to the shareholders.

. Subpart F income includes foreign base company income. One category of foreign base company income is foreign personal holding company income. For subpart F purposes, foreign personal holding company income generally includes dividends, interest, rents, and royalties, among other types of income. However, foreign personal holding company income does not include dividends and interest received by a CFC from a related corporation organized and operating in the same foreign country in which the CFC is organized, or rents and royalties received by a CFC from a related corporation for the use of property within the country in which the CFC is organized. Interest, rent, and royalty payments do not qualify for this exclusion to the extent that such payments reduce the subpart F income of the payor.

Reasons for Change

Most countries allow their companies to redeploy active foreign earnings with no additional tax burden. The Committee believes that this provision will make U.S. companies and U.S. workers more competitive with respect to such countries. By allowing U.S. companies to reinvest their active foreign earnings where they are most needed without incurring the immediate additional tax that companies based in many other countries never incur, the Committee believes that the provision will enable U.S. companies to make more sales overseas, and thus produce more goods in the United States.

Explanation of Provision

Under the provision, for taxable years beginning after 2005 and before 2009, dividends, interest,[26] rents, and royalties received by one CFC from a related CFC are not treated as foreign personal holding company income to the extent attributable or properly allocable to non-subpart-F income of the payor. For this purpose, a related CFC is a CFC that controls or is controlled by the other CFC, or a CFC that is controlled by the same person or persons that control the other CFC. Ownership of more than 50 percent of the CFC's stock (by vote or value) constitutes control for these purposes.

Effective Date

The provision is effective for taxable years of foreign corporations beginning after December 31, 2005 but before January 1, 2009, and for taxable years of U.S. shareholders with or within which such taxable years of such foreign corporations end.

Conference Committee Report (H.R. CONF. REP. NO. 109-455)

Senate Amendment

No provision.

Conference Agreement

The conference agreement includes the House bill provision.

[Law at ¶5555. CCH Explanation at ¶365.]

---

[26] Interest for this purpose includes factoring income which is treated as equivalent to interest under sec. 954(c)(1)(E).

[¶10,030] Act Sec. 201. Taxation of certain settlement funds

House Committee Report (H.R. REP. NO. 109-304)

[Code Sec. 468B]

Present Law

Present law provides that if a taxpayer makes a payment to a designated settlement fund pursuant to a court order, the deduction timing rules that require economic performance generally are deemed to be met as the payments are made by the taxpayer to the fund. A designated settlement fund means a fund which: is established pursuant to a court order; extinguishes completely the taxpayer's tort liability arising out of personal injury, death or property damage; is administered by persons a majority of whom are independent of the taxpayer; and under the terms of the fund the taxpayer (or any related person) may not hold any beneficial interest in the income or corpus of the fund.

Generally, a designated or qualified settlement fund is taxed as a separate entity at the maximum trust rate on its modified income. Modified income is generally gross income less deductions for administrative costs and other incidental expenses incurred in connection with the operation of the settlement fund.

The cleanup of hazardous waste sites is sometimes funded by environmental "settlement funds" or escrow accounts. These escrow accounts are established in consent decrees between the Environmental Protection Agency ("EPA") and the settling parties under the jurisdiction of a Federal district court. The EPA uses these accounts to resolve claims against private parties under Comprehensive Environmental Response, Compensation and Liability Act of 1980 ("CERCLA").

Present law provides that nothing in any provision of law is to be construed as providing that an escrow account, settlement fund, or similar fund is not subject to current income tax.

Reasons for Change

The Committee believes that environmental escrow accounts established under court consent decrees are essential for the EPA to resolve or satisfy claims under the CERCLA. The tax treatment of these settlement funds may prevent taxpayers from entering into prompt settlements with the EPA for the cleanup of Superfund hazardous waste sites and reduce the ultimate amount of funds available for the sites' cleanup. Because these settlement funds are controlled by the government and, upon termination, any remaining funds belong to the government, the Committee believes it is appropriate to establish that these funds are to be treated as beneficially owned by the United States.

Explanation of Provision

The provision provides that certain settlement funds established in consent decrees for the sole purpose of resolving claims under CERCLA are to be treated as beneficially owned by the United States government and therefore, not subject to Federal income tax.

To qualify the settlement fund must be: (1) established pursuant to a consent decree entered by a judge of a United States District Court; (2) created for the receipt of settlement payments for the sole purpose of resolving claims under CERCLA; (3) controlled (in terms of expenditures of contributions and earnings thereon) by the government or an agency or instrumentality thereof; and (4) upon termination, any remaining funds will be disbursed to such government entity and used in accordance with applicable law. For purposes of the provision, a government entity means the United States, any State of political subdivision thereof, the District of Columbia, any possession of the United States, and any agency or instrumentality of the foregoing.

The provision does not apply to accounts or funds established after December 31, 2010.

Effective Date

The provision is effective for accounts and funds established after the date of enactment.

Conference Committee Report (H.R. CONF. REP. NO. 109-455)

Senate Amendment

No provision.

Conference Agreement

The conference agreement includes the House bill provision.

[Law at ¶5405. CCH Explanation at ¶375.]

Act Sec. 201 ¶10,030

[¶10,040] Act Sec. 202. Modifications to rules relating to taxation of distributions of stock and securities of a controlled corporation

House Committee Report (H.R. REP. No. 109-304)

[Code Sec. 355(b)(3)]

Present Law

A corporation generally is required to recognize gain on the distribution of property (including stock of a subsidiary) to its shareholders as if such property had been sold for its fair market value. An exception to this rule applies if the distribution of the stock of a controlled corporation satisfies the requirements of section 355 of the Code. To qualify for tax-free treatment under section 355, both the distributing corporation and the controlled corporation must be engaged immediately after the distribution in the active conduct of a trade or business that has been conducted for at least five years and was not acquired in a taxable transaction during that period.[32] For this purpose, a corporation is engaged in the active conduct of a trade or business only if (1) the corporation is directly engaged in the active conduct of a trade or business, or (2) the corporation is not directly engaged in an active business, but substantially all of its assets consist of stock and securities of a corporation it controls that is engaged in the active conduct of a trade or business.[33]

In determining whether a corporation is directly engaged in an active trade or business that satisfies the requirement, old IRS guidelines for advance ruling purposes required that the value of the gross assets of the trade or business being relied on must ordinarily constitute at least five percent of the total fair market value of the gross assets of the corporation directly conducting the trade or business.[34] More recently, the IRS has suspended this specific rule in connection with its general administrative practice of moving IRS resources away from advance rulings on factual aspects of section 355 transactions in general.[35]

If the distributing or controlled corporation is not directly engaged in an active trade or business, then the IRS takes the position that the "substantially all" test requires that at least 90 percent of the fair market value of the corporation's gross assets consist of stock and securities of a controlled corporation that is engaged in the active conduct of a trade or business.[36]

Reasons for Change

Prior to a spin-off under section 355 of the Code, corporate groups that have conducted business in separate corporate entities often must undergo elaborate restructurings to place active businesses in the proper entities to satisfy the five-year active business requirement. If the top-tier corporation of a chain that is being spun off or retained is a holding company, then the requirements regarding the activities of its subsidiaries are more stringent than if the top-tier corporation itself engaged in some active business. The Committee believes that it is appropriate to simplify planning for corporate groups that use a holding company structure to engage in distributions that qualify for tax-free treatment under section 355.

Explanation of Provision

Under the bill, the active business test is determined by reference to the relevant affiliated group. For the distributing corporation, the relevant affiliated group consists of the distributing corporation as the common parent and all corporations affiliated with the distributing corporation through stock ownership described in section 1504(a)(1)(B) (regardless of whether the corporations are includible corporations under section 1504(b)), immediately after the distribution. The relevant affiliated group for a controlled corporation is determined in a similar manner (with the controlled corporation as the common parent).

---

[32] Section 355(b).
[33] Section 355(b)(2)(A).
[34] Rev. Proc. 2003-3, sec. 4.01(30), 2003-1 I.R.B. 113.

[35] Rev. Proc. 2003-48, 2003-29 I.R.B. 86.
[36] Rev. Proc. 96-30, sec. 4.03(5), 1996-1 C.B. 696; Rev. Proc. 77-37, sec. 3.04, 1977-2 C.B. 568.

Conference Committee Report (H.R. Conf. Rep. No. 109-455)

Senate Amendment

The Senate amendment provision is the same as the House bill with respect to the House bill provision described above, except for the date on which that provision sunsets.[49]

* * *

Conference Agreement

The conference agreement includes the House bill and the Senate amendment with modifications.

With respect to the provision that applies the active business test by reference to the relevant affiliated group, the conference agreement provision is the same as the House bill and the Senate amendment except for the date on which the conference agreement provision sunsets.[50]

* * *

Effective Date

The starting effective date of the provision that applies the active business test by reference to the relevant affiliated group is the same as that of the House bill and the Senate amendment provisions. The conference agreement changes the date on which the provision sunsets so that the provision does not apply for distributions (or for acquisitions, dispositions, or other restructurings as relating to continuing qualification of pre-effective date distributions) occurring after December 31, 2010.

* * *

[Law at ¶ 5355. CCH Explanation at ¶ 360.]

[¶ 10,050] Act Sec. 203. Qualified veteran's mortgage bonds

House Committee Report (H.R. Rep. No. 109-304)

[Code Sec. 143]

Present Law

Qualified veterans' mortgage bonds are private activity bonds the proceeds of which are used to make mortgage loans to certain veterans. Authority to issue qualified veterans' mortgage bonds is limited to States that had issued such bonds before June 22, 1984. Qualified veterans' mortgage bonds are not subject to the State volume limitations generally applicable to private activity bonds. Instead, annual issuance in each State is subject to a State volume limitation based on the volume of such bonds issued by the State before June 22, 1984. The five States eligible to issue these bonds are Alaska, California, Oregon, Texas, and Wisconsin. Loans financed with qualified veterans' mortgage bonds can be made only with respect to principal residences and can not be made to acquire or replace existing mortgages. Mortgage loans made with the proceeds of these bonds can be made only to veterans who served on active duty before 1977 and who applied for the financing before the date 30 years after the last date on which such veteran left active service (the "eligibility period").

Reasons for Change

The Committee believes that the qualified veterans' mortgage bond program should be expanded to more recent veterans including potentially the men and women serving on active duty today. The Committee also believes that such an expansion requires modified volume limits for these bonds.

Explanation of Provision

The bill repeals the requirement that veterans receiving loans financed with veterans' bonds must have served before 1977. It also reduces the eligibility period to 25 years (rather than 30 years) following release from the military service. The bill provides new State volume limits for these bonds for the five eligible States. In 2010, the new annual limit on the total volume of veterans' bonds is $25 million for Alaska, $66.25 million for California, $25 million for Oregon, $53.75 million for Texas, and $25 million for Wisconsin. These volume limits are phased-in over the four-year period immediately preceding 2010 by allowing the applicable percentage of

---

[49] See "Effective date" for the Senate Amendment, *infra.*

[50] See "Effective date" of the conference agreement provision, *infra.*

the 2010 volume limits. The following table provides those percentages.

Calendar year:	Applicable percentage is:
2006	20 percent
2007	40 percent
2008	60 percent
2009	80 percent

The volume limits are zero for 2011 and each year thereafter. Unused allocation cannot be carried forward to subsequent years.

Effective Date

The provision generally applies to bonds issued after December 31, 2005.

Conference Committee Report (H.R. CONF. REP. NO. 109-455)

Senate Amendment

No provision.

Conference Agreement

The conference agreement includes the House bill with the following modifications. The conference agreement does not amend present law as it relates to qualified veterans' mortgage bonds issued by the States of California and Texas. In the case of qualified veterans' mortgage bonds issued by the States of Alaska, Oregon, and Wisconsin, (1) the requirement that veterans must have served before 1977 is repealed and (2) the eligibility period for applying for a loan following release from the military service is reduced from 30 years to 25 years.

In addition, the annual issuance of qualified veterans' mortgage bonds in the States of Alaska, Oregon and Wisconsin is subject to new State volume limitations which are phased in between the years 2006 and 2010. The State volume limit in these States for any calendar year after 2010 is zero.

Effective Date

The provision expanding the definition of eligible veterans applies to bonds issued on or after date of enactment. The provision amending State volume limitations applies to allocations of volume limitation made after April 5, 2006.

[Law at ¶ 5130. CCH Explanation at ¶ 620.]

[¶ 10,060] Act Sec. 204. Capital gains treatment for certain self-created musical works

House Committee Report (H.R. REP. NO. 109-304)

[Code Sec. 1221]

Present Law

Capital gains

The maximum tax rate on the net capital gain income of an individual is 15 percent for taxable years beginning in 2005. By contrast, the maximum tax rate on an individual's ordinary income is 35 percent. The reduced 15-percent rate generally is available for gain from the sale or exchange of a capital asset for which the taxpayer has satisfied a holding-period requirement. Capital assets generally include all property held by a taxpayer with certain specified exclusions.

An exclusion from the definition of a capital asset applies to inventory property or property held by a taxpayer primarily for sale to customers in the ordinary course of the taxpayer's trade or business. Another exclusion from capital asset status applies to copyrights, literary, musical, or artistic compositions, letters or memoranda, or similar property held by a taxpayer whose personal efforts created the property (or held by a taxpayer whose basis in the property is determined by reference to the basis of the taxpayer whose personal efforts created the property). Consequently, when a taxpayer that owns copyrights in, for example, books, songs, or paintings that the taxpayer created (or when a taxpayer to which the copyrights have been transferred by the works' creator in a substituted basis transaction) sells the copyrights, gain from the sale is treated as ordinary income, not capital gain.

Charitable contributions

A taxpayer generally is allowed a deduction for the fair market value of property contributed to a charity. If a taxpayer makes a contribution of property that would have generated ordinary income (or short-term capital gain), the taxpayer's charitable contribution deduction generally is limited to the property's adjusted basis.

Reasons for Change

The Committee believes it is appropriate to allow taxpayers to treat as capital gain the income from a sale or exchange of musical compositions or copyrights in musical works the taxpayer created.

Explanation of Provision

The provision provides that at the election of a taxpayer, the sale or exchange before January 1, 2011 of musical compositions or copyrights in musical works created by the taxpayer's personal efforts (or having a basis determined by reference to the basis in the hands of the tax-payer whose personal efforts created the compositions or copyrights) is treated as the sale or exchange of a capital asset. The provision does not change the present law limitation on a tax-payer's charitable deduction for the contribution of such compositions or copyrights.

Effective Date

The provision is effective for sales or exchanges in taxable years beginning after the date of enactment.

Conference Committee Report (H.R. CONF. REP. NO. 109-455)

Senate Amendment

No provision.

Conference Agreement

The conference agreement includes the House bill provision.

[Law at ¶5280 and ¶5580. CCH Explanation at ¶240.]

[¶10,070] Act Sec. 205. Decrease minimum vessel tonnage limit to 6,000 deadweight tons

House Committee Report (H.R. REP. NO. 109-304)

[Code Sec. 1355]

Present Law

The United States employs a "worldwide" tax system, under which domestic corporations generally are taxed on all income, including income from shipping operations, whether derived in the United States or abroad. In order to mitigate double taxation, a foreign tax credit for income taxes paid to foreign countries is provided to reduce or eliminate the U.S. tax owed on such income, subject to certain limitations.

Generally, the United States taxes foreign corporations only on income that has a sufficient nexus to the United States. Thus, a foreign corporation is generally subject to U.S. tax only on income, including income from shipping operations, which is "effectively connected" with the conduct of a trade or business in the United States (sec. 882). Such "effectively connected income" generally is taxed in the same manner and at the same rates as the income of a U.S. corporation.

The United States imposes a four percent tax on the amount of a foreign corporation's U.S. source gross transportation income (sec. 887).

Transportation income includes income from the use (or hiring or leasing for use) of a vessel and income from services directly related to the use of a vessel. Fifty percent of the transportation income attributable to transportation that either begins or ends (but not both) in the United States is treated as U.S. source gross transportation income. The tax does not apply, however, to U.S. source gross transportation income that is treated as income effectively connected with the conduct of a U.S. trade or business. U.S. source gross transportation income is not treated as effectively connected income unless (1) the taxpayer has a fixed place of business in the United States involved in earning the income, and (2) substantially all the income is attributable to regularly scheduled transportation.

The tax imposed by section 882 or 887 on income from shipping operations may be limited by an applicable U.S. income tax treaty or by an exemption of a foreign corporation's international shipping operations income in instances where a foreign country grants an equivalent exemption (sec. 883).

Notwithstanding the general rules described above, the American Jobs Creation Act of 2004

("AJCA")[38] generally allows corporations that are qualifying vessel operators[39] to elect a "tonnage tax" in lieu of the corporate income tax on taxable income from certain shipping activities. Accordingly, an electing corporation's gross income does not include its income from qualifying shipping activities (and items of loss, deduction, or credit are disallowed with respect to such excluded income), and electing corporations are only subject to tax on these activities at the maximum corporate income tax rate on their notional shipping income, which is based on the net tonnage of the corporation's qualifying vessels.[40] No deductions are allowed against the notional shipping income of an electing corporation, and no credit is allowed against the notional tax imposed under the tonnage tax regime. In addition, special deferral rules apply to the gain on the sale of a qualifying vessel, if such vessel is replaced during a limited replacement period.

Generally, a "qualifying vessel" is defined as a self-propelled (or a combination of self-propelled and non-self-propelled) U.S.-flag vessel of not less than 10,000 deadweight tons[41] that is used exclusively in the U.S. foreign trade.

Reasons for Change

The Committee believes that the tonnage tax regime provides operators of qualifying U.S.-flag vessels in the U.S. foreign trade the opportunity to be competitive with their tax-advantaged foreign competitors. However, there are a number of U.S.-flag vessels that are operated in the U.S. foreign trade but which do not qualify for tonnage tax treatment because their carrying capacity is less than 10,000 deadweight tons. The Committee believes that the expansion of the tonnage tax regime to smaller vessels will permit the operators of such vessels to be competitive with their foreign competitors as well as with their larger U.S.-flag competitors.

Explanation of Provision

The provision expands the definition of "qualifying vessel" to include self-propelled (or a combination of self-propelled and non-self-propelled) U.S. flag vessels of not less than 6,000 deadweight tons used exclusively in the United States foreign trade. The modified definition applies for taxable years beginning after December 31, 2005 and ending before January 1, 2011.

Effective Date

The provision applies to taxable years beginning after December 31, 2005 and ending before January 1, 2011.

Conference Committee Report (H.R. Conf. Rep. No. 109-455)

Senate Amendment

No provision.

Conference Agreement

The conference agreement includes the provision in the House bill.

[Law at ¶ 5605. CCH Explanation at ¶ 370.]

---

[38] Pub. L. No. 108-357, sec. 248. The tonnage tax regime is effective for taxable years beginning after the date of enactment of AJCA (October 22, 2004).

[39] Generally, a qualifying vessel operator is a corporation that (1) operates one or more qualifying vessels and (2) meets certain requirements with respect to its shipping activities.

[40] An electing corporation's notional shipping income for the taxable year is the product of the following amounts for each of the qualifying vessels it operates: (1) the daily notional shipping income from the operation of the qualifying vessel, and (2) the number of days during the taxable year that the electing corporation operated such vessel as a qualifying vessel in the United States foreign trade. The daily notional shipping income from the operation of a qualifying vessel is (1) 40 cents for each 100 tons of so much of the net

tonnage of the vessel as does not exceed 25,000 net tons, and (2) 20 cents for each 100 tons of so much of the net tonnage of the vessel as exceeds 25,000 net tons. "United States foreign trade" means the transportation of goods or passengers between a place in the United States and a foreign place or between foreign places. The temporary use in the United States domestic trade (i.e., the transportation of goods or passengers between places in the United States) of any qualifying vessel or the temporary ceasing to use a qualifying vessel may be disregarded, under special rules.

[41] Deadweight measures the lifting capacity of a ship expressed in long tons (2,240 lbs.), including cargo, crew, and consumables such as fuel, lube oil, drinking water, and stores. It is the difference between the number of tons of water a vessel displaces without such items on board and the number of tons it displaces when fully loaded.

[¶ 10,080] Act Sec. 206. Modification of special arbitrage rule for certain funds

House Committee Report (H.R. REP. NO. 109-304)

[Act Sec. 206]

Present Law

In general, present-law tax-exempt bond arbitrage restrictions provide that interest on a State or local government bond is not eligible for tax-exemption if the proceeds are invested, directly or indirectly, in materially higher yielding investments or if the debt service on the bond is secured by or paid from (directly or indirectly) such investments. An exception to the arbitrage restrictions, enacted in 1984, provides that the pledge of income from investments in the Texas Permanent University Fund (the "Fund") as security for a limited amount of tax-exempt bonds will not cause interest on those bonds to be taxable. The terms of this exception are limited to State constitutional or statutory restrictions continuously in effect since October 9, 1969. In addition, the exception only applies to an amount of tax-exempt bonds that does not exceed 20 percent of the value of the Fund.

The Fund consists of certain State lands that were set aside for the benefit of higher education, the income from mineral rights to these lands, and certain other earnings on Fund assets. The Texas constitution directs that monies held in the Fund are to be invested in interest-bearing obligations and other securities. Income from the Fund is apportioned between two university systems operated by the State. Tax-exempt bonds issued by the university systems to finance buildings and other permanent improvements were secured by and payable from the income of the Fund.

Prior to 1999, the constitution did not permit the expenditure or mortgage of the Fund for any purpose. In 1999, the State constitutional rules governing the Fund were modified with regard to the manner in which amounts in the Fund are distributed for the benefit of the two university systems. The State constitutional amendments allow for the possibility that in the event investment earnings are less than annual debt service on the bonds some of the debt service could be considered as having been paid with the Fund corpus. The 1984 exception refers only to bonds secured by investment earnings on securities or obligations held by the Fund. Despite the constitutional amendments, the IRS has agreed to continue to apply the 1984 exception to the Fund through August 31, 2007, if clarifying legislation is introduced in the 109th Congress prior to August 31, 2005. Clarifying legislation was introduced in the 109th Congress on May 26, 2005.[42]

Reasons for Change

The Committee understands that the State constitutional amendments have the effect of permitting the Fund to make annual distributions in a manner similar to standard university endowment funds, rather than tying distributions to annual income performance, which can create a variable pattern of distributions. The Committee does not believe that the Fund should lose the benefits of the 1984 exception from the tax-exempt bond arbitrage restrictions by adopting a more modern approach to the management of Fund distributions.

Explanation of Provision

The provision affirms and extends the IRS agreement through August 31, 2009. The 1984 exception is conformed to the State constitutional amendments to permit its continued applicability to bonds of the two university systems. The limitation on the aggregate amount of bonds which may benefit from the exception is not modified, and remains at 20 percent. The provision sunsets after August 31, 2009.

Effective Date

The provision is effective on the date of enactment.

Conference Committee Report (H.R. CONF. REP. NO. 109-455)

Conference Agreement

The conference agreement includes the House bill provision.

[Law at ¶ 7015. CCH Explanation at ¶ 1120.]

---

[42] H.R. 2661.

[¶10,090] Act Sec. 207. Amortization of expenses incurred in creating or acquiring music or music copyrights

Conference Committee Report (H.R. Conf. Rep. No. 109-455)

[Code Secs. 167(g) and 263A]

Present Law

A taxpayer is allowed to recover, through annual depreciation deductions, the cost of certain property used in a trade or business or for the production of income. Section 167(g) provides that the cost of motion picture films, sound recordings, copyrights, books, patents, and other property specified in regulations is eligible to be recovered using the income forecast method of depreciation.

Under the income forecast method, the depreciation deduction with respect to eligible property for a taxable year is determined by multiplying the adjusted basis of the property by a fraction, the numerator of which is the income generated by the property during the year, and the denominator of which is the total forecasted or estimated income expected to be generated prior to the close of the tenth taxable year after the year the property was placed in service. Any costs that are not recovered by the end of the tenth taxable year after the property was placed in service may be taken into account as depreciation in such year.

The adjusted basis of property that may be taken into account under the income forecast method includes only amounts that satisfy the economic performance standard of section 461(h) (except in the case of certain participations and residuals). In addition, taxpayers that claim depreciation deductions under the income forecast method are required to pay (or receive) interest based on a recalculation of depreciation under a "look-back" method.

The "look-back" method is applied in any "recomputation year" by (1) comparing depreciation deductions that had been claimed in prior periods to depreciation deductions that would have been claimed had the taxpayer used actual, rather than estimated, total income from the property; (2) determining the hypothetical overpayment or underpayment of tax based on this recalculated depreciation; and (3) applying the overpayment rate of section 6621 of the Code. Except as provided in Treasury regulations, a "recomputation year" is the third and tenth taxable year after the taxable year the property was placed in service, unless the actual income from the property for each taxable year ending with or before the close of such years was within 10 percent of the estimated income from the property for such years.

A special rule is provided under Treasury guidance in the case of certain authors and other taxpayers, with respect to their capitalization of costs under section 263A and with respect to the recovery or amortization of such costs. Specifically, IRS Notice 88-62 (1988-1 C.B. 548) provides an elective safe harbor under which eligible taxpayers capitalize qualified created costs incurred during the taxable year and amortize 50 percent of the costs in the taxable year incurred, and 25 percent in each of the two successive taxable years. Under the Notice, qualified creative costs generally are those incurred by a self-employed individual in the production of creative properties (such as films, sound recordings, musical and dance compositions including accompanying words, and other similar properties), provided the personal efforts of the individual predominantly create the properties. An eligible taxpayer is an individual, and also a corporation or partnership, substantially all of which is owned by one qualified employee owner (an individual and family members).

House Bill

No provision.

Senate Amendment

The Senate amendment provides that if any expense is paid or incurred by the taxpayer in creating or acquiring any musical composition (including accompanying words) or any copyright with respect to a musical composition that is required to be capitalized, then the income forecast method does not apply to such expenses, but rather, the expenses are amortized over a five-year period. The five-year period is the period beginning with the month in which the composition or copyright was acquired (or if created, the five-taxable-year period beginning with the taxable year in which the expenses were paid or incurred).

The provision does not apply to certain expenses. The expenses to which it does not apply are expenses: (1) that are qualified creative expenses under section 263A(h); (2) to which a simplified procedure established under section 263A(j)(2) applies; (3) that are an amortizable section 197 intangible; or (4) that, without regard to this provision, would not be allowable as a deduction.

Conference Agreement

The conference agreement includes the Senate amendment provision with the following modifications. Under the conference agreement, the five-year amortization period is elective for the taxable year. Thus, a taxpayer that places in service any musical composition or copyright with respect to a musical composition in a taxable year may elect to apply the provision with respect to all musical compositions and musical composition copyrights placed in service in that taxable year. An eligible taxpayer that does not make the election may recover the costs under any method allowable under present law, including the income forecast method.

Under the conference agreement, the election may be made for any taxable year which begins before January 1, 2011.

In addition, the conference agreement provides that the five-year amortization period begins in the month the property is placed in service.

Effective Date

The conference agreement is effective for expenses paid or incurred with respect to property placed in service in taxable years beginning after December 31, 2005 and before January 1, 2011.

[Law at ¶ 5255. CCH Explanation at ¶ 815.]

[¶ 10,100] Act Sec. 208. Capital expenditure limitation for qualified small issue bonds

Conference Committee Report (H.R. CONF. REP. NO. 109-455)

[Code Sec. 144(a)(4)]

Present Law

Qualified small-issue bonds are tax-exempt State and local government bonds used to finance private business manufacturing facilities (including certain directly related and ancillary facilities) or the acquisition of land and equipment by certain farmers. In both instances, these bonds are subject to limits on the amount of financing that may be provided, both for a single borrowing and in the aggregate. In general, no more than $1 million of small-issue bond financing may be outstanding at any time for property of a business (including related parties) located in the same municipality or county. Generally, this $1 million limit may be increased to $10 million if all other capital expenditures of the business in the same municipality or county are counted toward the limit over a six-year period that begins three years before the issue date of the bonds and ends three years after such date. Outstanding aggregate borrowing is limited to $40 million per borrower (including related parties) regardless of where the property is located.

For bonds issued after September 30, 2009, the Code permits up to $10 million of capital expenditures to be disregarded, in effect increasing from $10 million to $20 million the maximum

allowable amount of total capital expenditures by an eligible business in the same municipality or county.[339] However, no more than $10 million of bond financing may be outstanding at any time for property of an eligible business (including related parties) located in the same municipality or county. Other limits (e.g., the $40 million per borrower limit) also continue to apply.

House Bill

No provision.

Senate Amendment

The provision accelerates the application of the $20 million capital expenditure limitation from bonds issued after September 30, 2009, to bonds issued after December 31, 2006.

Effective Date

The provision is effective on the date of enactment for bonds issued after December 31, 2006.

Conference Agreement

The conference agreement includes the Senate amendment provision.

[Law at ¶ 5155. CCH Explanation at ¶ 1110.]

---

[339] Sec. 144(a)(4)(G) as added by sec. 340(a) of the American Jobs Creation Act of 2004, Pub. L. No. 108-357 (2004).

[¶10,110] Act Sec. 209. Modification of treatment of loans to qualified continuing care facilities

Conference Committee Report (H.R. CONF. REP. NO. 109-455)

[Code Sec. 7872(g)]

Present Law

Present law provides generally that certain loans that bear interest at a below-market rate are treated as loans bearing interest at the market rate, accompanied by imputed payments characterized in accordance with the substance of the transaction (for example, as a gift, compensation, a dividend, or interest).[342]

An exception to this imputation rule is provided for any calendar year for a below-market loan made by a lender to a qualified continuing care facility pursuant to a continuing care contract, if the lender or the lender's spouse attains age 65 before the close of the calendar year.[343]

The exception applies only to the extent the aggregate outstanding loans by the lender (and spouse) to any qualified continuing care facility do not exceed $163,300 (for 2006).[344]

For this purpose, a continuing care contract means a written contract between an individual and a qualified continuing care facility under which: (1) the individual or the individual's spouse may use a qualified continuing care facility for their life or lives; (2) the individual or the individual's spouse will first reside in a separate, independent living unit with additional facilities outside such unit for the providing of meals and other personal care and will not require long-term nursing care, and then will be provided long-term and skilled nursing care as the health of the individual or the individual's spouse requires; and (3) no additional substantial payment is required if the individual or the individual's spouse requires increased personal care services or long-term and skilled nursing care.

For this purpose, a qualified continuing care facility means one or more facilities that are designed to provide services under continuing care contracts, and substantially all of the residents of which are covered by continuing care contracts. A facility is not treated as a qualified continuing care facility unless substantially all facilities that are used to provide services required to be provided under a continuing care contract are

owned or operated by the borrower. For these purposes, a nursing home is not a qualified continuing care facility.

House Bill

No provision.

Senate Amendment

The Senate amendment provision modifies the present-law exception under section 7872(g) relating to loans to continuing care facilities by eliminating the dollar cap on aggregate outstanding loans and making other modifications.

The Senate amendment provision provides an exception to the imputation rule of section 7872 for any calendar year for any below-market loan owed by a facility which on the last day of the year is a qualified continuing care facility, if the loan was made pursuant to a continuing care contract and if the lender or the lender's spouse attains age 62 before the close of the year.

For this purpose, a continuing care contract means a written contract between an individual and a qualified continuing care facility under which: (1) the individual or the individual's spouse may use a qualified continuing care facility for their life or lives; (2) the individual or the individual's spouse will be provided with housing in an independent living unit (which has additional available facilities outside such unit for the provision of meals and other personal care), an assisted living facility or nursing facility, as is available in the continuing care facility, as appropriate for the health of the individual or the individual's spouse; and (3) the individual or the individual's spouse will be provided assisted living or nursing care as the health of the individual or the individual's spouse requires, and as is available in the continuing care facility.

For this purpose, a qualified continuing care facility means one or more facilities: (1) that are designed to provide services under continuing care contracts; (2) that include an independent living unit, plus an assisted living or nursing facility, or both; and (3) substantially all of the independent living unit residents of which are covered by continuing care contracts. For these

---

[342] Sec. 7872.
[343] Sec. 7872(g).

[344] Rev. Rul. 2005-75, 2005-49 I.R.B. 1073.

purposes, a nursing home is not a qualified continuing care facility.

Conference Agreement

The conference agreement includes the Senate amendment provision, with modifications. The conference agreement provision provides that a continuing care contract is a written contract between an individual and a qualified continuing care facility under which: (1) the individual or the individual's spouse may use a qualified continuing care facility for their life or lives; (2) the individual or the individual's spouse will be provided with housing, as appropriate for the health of such individual or individual's spouse, (i) in an independent living unit (which has additional available facilities outside such unit for the provision of meals and other personal care), and (ii) in an assisted living facility or a nursing facility, as is available in the continuing care facility; and (3) the individual or the individual's spouse will be provided assisted living or nursing care as the health of the individual or the individual's spouse requires, and as is available in the continuing care facility. The Secretary is required to issue guidance that limits the term "continuing care contract" to contracts that provide only facilities, care, and services described in the preceding sentence.

For purposes of defining the terms "continuing care contract" and "qualified continuing care facility" under the conference agreement provision, the term "assisted living facility" is intended to mean a facility at which assistance is provided (1) with activities of daily living (such as eating, toileting, transferring, bathing, dressing, and continence) or (2) in cases of cognitive impairment, to protect the health or safety of an individual. The term "nursing facility" is intended to mean a facility that offers care requiring the utilization of licensed nursing staff.

Effective Date

The conference agreement provision is generally effective for calendar years beginning after December 31, 2005, with respect to loans made before, on, or after such date. The conference agreement provision does not apply to any calendar year after 2010. Thus, the conference agreement provision does not apply with respect to interest imputed after December 31, 2010. After such date, the law as in effect prior to enactment applies.

[Law at ¶5105 and ¶5855. CCH Explanation at ¶245.]

[¶10,120] Act Sec. 301. Extend and increase alternative minimum tax exemption amount for individuals

Conference Committee Report (H.R. CONF. REP. NO. 109-455)

[Code Sec. 55(d)]

Present Law

Present law imposes an alternative minimum tax. The alternative minimum tax is the amount by which the tentative minimum tax exceeds the regular income tax. An individual's tentative minimum tax is the sum of (1) 26 percent of so much of the taxable excess as does not exceed $175,000 ($87,500 in the case of a married individual filing a separate return) and (2) 28 percent of the remaining taxable excess. The taxable excess is so much of the alternative minimum taxable income ("AMTI") as exceeds the exemption amount. The maximum tax rates on net capital gain and dividends used in computing the regular tax are used in computing the tentative minimum tax. AMTI is the individual's taxable income adjusted to take account of specified preferences and adjustments.

The exemption amount is: (1) $45,000 ($58,000 for taxable years beginning before 2006)

in the case of married individuals filing a joint return and surviving spouses; (2) $33,750 ($40,250 for taxable years beginning before 2006) in the case of unmarried individuals other than surviving spouses; (3) $22,500 ($29,000 for taxable years beginning before 2006) in the case of married individuals filing a separate return; and (4) $22,500 in the case of estates and trusts. The exemption amount is phased out by an amount equal to 25 percent of the amount by which the individual's AMTI exceeds (1) $150,000 in the case of married individuals filing a joint return and surviving spouses, (2) $112,500 in the case of unmarried individuals other than surviving spouses, and (3) $75,000 in the case of married individuals filing separate returns, estates, and trusts. These amounts are not indexed for inflation.

House Bill

No provision.

Senate Amendment

Under the Senate amendment, for taxable years beginning in 2006, the exemption amounts are increased to: (1) $62,550 in the case of married individuals filing a joint return and surviving spouses; (2) $42,500 in the case of unmarried individuals other than surviving spouses; and (3) $31,275 in the case of married individuals filing a separate return.

Conference Agreement

The conference agreement includes the provision in the Senate amendment.

Effective Date

The provision applies to taxable years beginning after December 31, 2005.

[Law at ¶5080. CCH Explanation at ¶720.]

[¶10,130] Act Sec. 302. Allowance of nonrefundable personal credits against regular and alternative minimum tax liability

House Committee Report (H.R. REP. NO. 109-304)

[Code Sec. 26(a)(2)]

Present Law

Present law provides for certain nonrefundable personal tax credits (i.e., the dependent care credit, the credit for the elderly and disabled, the adoption credit, the child tax credit, the credit for interest on certain home mortgages, the HOPE Scholarship and Lifetime Learning credits, the credit for savers, the credit for certain nonbusiness energy property, the credit for residential energy efficient property, and the D.C. first-time homebuyer credit).

For taxable years beginning in 2005, the nonrefundable personal credits are allowed to the extent of the full amount of the individual's regular tax and alternative minimum tax.

For taxable years beginning after 2005, the nonrefundable personal credits (other than the adoption credit, child credit and saver's credit) are allowed only to the extent that the individual's regular income tax liability exceeds the individual's tentative minimum tax, determined without regard to the minimum tax foreign tax credit. The adoption credit, child credit, and saver's credit are allowed to the full extent of the individual's regular tax and alternative minimum tax.

The alternative minimum tax is the amount by which the tentative minimum tax exceeds the regular income tax. An individual's tentative minimum tax is the sum of (1) 26 percent of so much of the taxable excess as does not exceed $175,000 ($87,500 in the case of a married individual filing a separate return) and (2) 28 percent of the remaining taxable excess. The taxable excess is so much of the alternative minimum taxable income ("AMTI") as exceeds the exemption amount. The maximum tax rates on net capital gain and dividends used in computing the regular tax are used in computing the tentative minimum tax. AMTI is the individual's taxable income adjusted to take account of specified preferences and adjustments.

The exemption amount is: (1) $45,000 ($58,000 for taxable years beginning before 2006) in the case of married individuals filing a joint return and surviving spouses; (2) $33,750 ($40,250 for taxable years beginning before 2006) in the case of other unmarried individuals; (3) $22,500 ($29,000 for taxable years beginning before 2006) in the case of married individuals filing a separate return; and (4) $22,500 in the case of an estate or trust. The exemption amount is phased out by an amount equal to 25 percent of the amount by which the individual's AMTI exceeds (1) $150,000 in the case of married individuals filing a joint return and surviving spouses, (2) $112,500 in the case of other unmarried individuals, and (3) $75,000 in the case of married individuals filing separate returns, an estate, or a trust. These amounts are not indexed for inflation.

Reasons for Change

The Committee believes that the nonrefundable personal credits should be useable without limitation by reason of the alternative minimum tax.

Explanation of Provision

The provision extends for one year the present-law provision allowing nonrefundable personal credits to the full extent of the individual's regular tax and alternative minimum tax (through taxable years beginning on or before December 31, 2006).

Effective Date

The provision applies to taxable years beginning after December 31, 2005.

Conference Committee Report (H.R. CONF. REP. NO. 109-455)

Senate Amendment

The Senate amendment extends for two years the present-law provision allowing nonrefundable personal credits to the full extent of the individual's regular tax and alternative minimum tax (through taxable years beginning on or before December 31, 2007).

The provision also applies to the personal credits for alternative motor vehicles, and alternative motor vehicle refueling property.

Conference Agreement

The conference agreement includes the House bill provision.

[Law at ¶ 5030. CCH Explanation at ¶ 725.]

[¶ 10,140] Act Sec. 401. Corporate estimated tax provisions

Conference Committee Report (H.R. CONF. REP. NO. 109-455)

[Act Sec. 401]

Present Law

In general, corporations are required to make quarterly estimated tax payments of their income tax liability. For a corporation whose taxable year is a calendar year, these estimated tax payments must be made by April 15, June 15, September 15, and December 15.

House Bill

No provision.

Senate Amendment

No provision.

Conference Agreement

In case of a corporation with assets of at least $1 billion, payments due in July, August, and September, 2006, shall be increased to 105 percent of the payment otherwise due and the next required payment shall be reduced accordingly.

In case of a corporation with assets of at least $1 billion, the payments due in July, Au-

gust, and September, 2012, shall be increased to 106.25 percent of the payment otherwise due and the next required payment shall be reduced accordingly.

In case of a corporation with assets of at least $1 billion, the payments due in July, August, and September, 2013, shall be increased to 100.75 percent of the payment otherwise due and the next required payment shall be reduced accordingly.

With respect to corporate estimated tax payments due on September 15, 2010, 20.5 percent shall not be due until October 1, 2010.

With respect to corporate estimated tax payments due on September 15, 2011, 27.5 percent shall not be due until October 1, 2011.

Effective Date

The provision is effective on the date of enactment.

[Law at ¶ 7020. CCH Explanation at ¶ 835.]

[¶ 10,150] Act Sec. 501. Application of earnings stripping rules to partners which are corporations

Conference Committee Report (H.R. CONF. REP. NO. 109-455)

[Code Sec. 163(j)]

Present Law

Present law provides rules to limit the ability of U.S. corporations to reduce the U.S. tax on

their U.S.-source income through earnings stripping transactions. Section 163(j) specifically addresses earnings stripping involving interest payments, by limiting the deductibility of interest paid to certain related parties ("disqualified interest"),[442] if the payor's debt-equity ratio exceeds 1.5 to 1 and the payor's net interest expense exceeds 50 percent of its "adjusted taxable income" (generally taxable income computed without regard to deductions for net interest expense, net operating losses, and depreciation, amortization, and depletion). Disallowed interest amounts can be carried forward indefinitely. In addition, excess limitation (i.e., any excess of the 50-percent limit over a company's net interest expense for a given year) can be carried forward three years.

Proposed Treasury regulations provide that a partner's proportionate share of partnership liabilities is treated as liabilities incurred directly by the partner, for purposes of applying the earnings stripping limitation to interest payments by a corporate partner of a partnership.[443] The proposed Treasury regulations provide that interest paid or accrued to a partnership is treated as paid or accrued to the partners of the partnership in proportion to each partner's distributive share of the partnership's interest income for the taxable year.[444] In addition, the proposed Treasury regulations provide that interest expense paid or accrued by a partnership is treated as paid or accrued by the partners of the partnership in proportion to each partner's distributive share of the partnership's interest expense.[445]

House Bill

No provision.

Senate Amendment

The Senate amendment provision codifies the approach of the proposed Treasury regula-

tions by providing that, except to the extent provided by regulations, in the case of a corporation that owns, directly or indirectly, an interest in a partnership, the corporation's share of partnership liabilities is treated as liabilities of the corporation for purposes of applying the earnings stripping rules to the corporation. The provision provides that the corporation's distributive share of interest income of the partnership, and of interest expense of the partnership, is treated as interest income or interest expense of the corporation.

The provision provides Treasury regulatory authority to reallocate shares of partnership debt, or distributive shares of the partnership's interest income or interest expense, as may be appropriate to carry out the purposes of the provision. For example, it is not intended that the application of the earnings stripping rules to corporations with direct or indirect interests in partnerships be circumvented through the use of allocations of partnership interest income or expense (or partnership liabilities) to or away from partners.

Effective Date

The provision is effective for taxable years beginning on or after the date of enactment.

Conference Agreement

The conference agreement includes the Senate amendment provision.

[Law at ¶ 5230. CCH Explanation at ¶ 840.]

[¶ 10,160] Act Sec. 502. Amend information reporting requirements to include interest on tax-exempt bonds

Conference Committee Report (H.R. CONF. REP. NO. 109-455)

[Code Sec. 6049(b)]

Present Law

Tax-exempt bonds

Generally, gross income does not include interest on State or local bonds.[476] State and local bonds are classified generally as either governmental bonds or private activity bonds. Govern-

mental bonds are bonds the proceeds of which are primarily used to finance governmental facilities or the debt is repaid with governmental funds. Private activity bonds are bonds in which the State or local government serves as a conduit providing financing to nongovernmental persons (e.g., private businesses or individuals). The exclusion from income for State and local bonds

---

[442] This interest also may include interest paid to unrelated parties in certain cases in which a related party guarantees the debt.

[443] Prop. Treas. Reg. sec. 1.163(j)-3(b)(3).

[444] Prop. Treas. Reg. sec. 1.163(j)-2(e)(4).

[445] Prop. Treas. reg. sec. 1.163(j)-2(e)(5).

[476] Sec. 103.

does not apply to private activity bonds, unless the bonds are issued for certain purposes ("qualified private activity bonds") permitted by the Code.[477]

Tax-exempt interest reporting by taxpayers

The Code provides that every person required to file a return must report the amount of tax-exempt interest received or accrued during any taxable year.[478] There are a number of reasons why the amount of tax-exempt interest received is relevant to determining tax liability despite the general exclusion from income. For example, the interest income from qualified private activity bonds (other than qualified 501(c)(3) bonds) issued after August 7, 1986, is a preference item for purposes of calculating the alternative minimum tax ("AMT").[479] Tax-exempt interest also is relevant for determining eligibility for the earned income credit (the "EIC")[480] and the amount of Social Security benefits includable in gross income.[481] Moreover, determining includable Social Security benefits is necessary for calculating either adjusted or modified adjusted gross income under several Code sections.[482]

Information reporting by payors

The Code generally requires every person who makes payments of interest aggregating $10 or more or receives payments of interest as a nominee and who makes payments aggregating $10 or more to file an information return setting forth the amount of interest payments for the calendar year and the name, address, and TIN[483] of the person to whom interest is paid.[484] Treasury regulations prescribe the form and manner for filing interest payment information returns. Penalties are imposed for failures to file interest payment information returns or payee statements.[485] Treasury Regulations also impose recordkeeping requirements on any person required to file information returns.[486] The Code excludes interest paid on tax-exempt bonds from interest reporting requirements.[487]

House Bill

No provision.

Senate Amendment

The provision eliminates the exception from information reporting requirements for interest paid on tax-exempt bonds.

Effective Date

The provision is effective for interest paid on tax-exempt bonds after December 31, 2005.

Conference Agreement

The conference agreement includes the Senate amendment provision.

[Law at ¶5755. CCH Explanation at ¶1105.]

[¶10,170] Act Sec. 503. Amortization of geological and geophysical expenditures

Conference Committee Report (H.R. CONF. REP. NO. 109-455)

[Code Sec. 167(h)]

Present Law

Geological and geophysical expenditures ("G&G costs") are costs incurred by a taxpayer for the purpose of obtaining and accumulating data that will serve as the basis for the acquisition and retention of mineral properties by taxpayers exploring for minerals. G&G costs incurred in connection with oil and gas exploration in the United States may be amortized over two years.[493] In the case of abandoned property, remaining basis may not be recovered in the year of abandonment of a property as all basis is recovered over the two-year amortization period.

House Bill

No provision.

---

[477] Secs. 103(b)(1) and 141.
[478] Sec. 6012(d).
[479] Sec. 57(a)(5). Special rules apply to exclude refundings of bonds issued before August 8, 1986, and certain bonds issued before September 1, 1986.
[480] Sec. 32(i).
[481] Sec. 86.
[482] See Secs. 135, 219, and 221.

[483] The taxpayer's identification number, generally, for individuals is the taxpayer's social security number. Sec. 7701(a)(41).
[484] Sec. 6049.
[485] Secs. 6721 and 6722.
[486] Treas. Reg. sec. 1.6001-1(a).
[487] Sec. 6049.
[493] Sec. 167(h).

Senate Amendment

The provision repeals the two-year amortization period with respect to G&G costs paid or incurred by certain large integrated oil companies, defined to include integrated oil companies (as defined in section 291(b)(4) of the Code) that have an average daily worldwide production of crude oil of at least 500,000 barrels. Thus, affected oil companies are required to capitalize their G&G costs associated with successful exploration projects that result in the acquisition of property. Such companies can recover any G&G costs associated with abandoned property in the year of abandonment.

Effective Date

The provision is effective for G&G costs paid or incurred in taxable years beginning after August 8, 2005.

Conference Agreement

The conference agreement extends the two-year amortization period for G&G costs to five years for certain major integrated oil companies. Under the conference agreement, the five-year amortization rule for G&G costs applies only to integrated oil companies that have an average daily worldwide production of crude oil of at least 500,000 barrels for the taxable year, gross receipts in excess of $1 billion in the last taxable year ending during calendar year 2005, and an ownership interest in a crude oil refiner of 15 percent or more.

Effective Date

The provision applies to amounts paid or incurred after the date of enactment.

[Law at ¶ 5255. CCH Explanation at ¶ 820.]

[¶ 10,180]   Act Sec. 504. Application of Foreign Investment in Real Property Tax Act ("FIRPTA") to regulated investment companies ("RICs")

Conference Committee Report (H.R. Conf. Rep. No. 109-455)

[Code Sec. 897]

In general

A nonresident alien individual or foreign corporation is taxable on its taxable income which is effectively connected with the conduct of a trade or business within the United States, at the income tax rates applicable to U. S. persons. A nonresident alien individual is taxed (at a 30-percent rate) on gains, derived from sources within the United States, from the sale or exchange of capital assets if the individual is present in the United States for 183 days or more during the taxable year.

In addition, the Foreign Investment in Real Property Tax Act (FIRPTA)[497] generally treats a nonresident alien individual or foreign corporation's gain or loss from the disposition of a U.S. real property interest (USRPI) as income that is effectively connected with a U.S. trade or business, and thus taxable at the income tax rates applicable to U.S. persons, including the rates for net capital gain. A foreign investor subject to tax on this income is required to file a U.S. income tax return under the normal rules relating to receipt of income effectively connected with a U.S. trade or business.

The payor of FIRPTA effectively connected income to a foreign person is generally required to withhold U.S. tax from the payment. Withholding is generally 10 percent of the sales price in the case of a direct sale by the foreign person of a USRPI, and 35 percent of the amount of a distribution to a foreign person of proceeds attributable to such sales from an entity such as a partnership.[498] The foreign person can request a refund with its U.S. tax return, if appropriate based on that person's total U.S. effectively connected income and deductions (if any) for the taxable year.

---

[497] FIRPTA is codified in section 897 of the Code.

[498] Sec. 1445 and Treasury regulations thereunder. The Treasury department is authorized to issue regulations that would reduce the 35 percent withholding on distributions to 15 percent during the time that the maximum income tax rate on dividends and capital gains of U.S. persons is 15 percent.

Section 1445 statutorily requires the 10 percent withholding by the purchaser of a USRPI and the 35 percent

withholding (or less if directed by Treasury) on certain distributions by partnerships, trusts, and estates, among other situations. Treasury regulations prescribe the 35 percent withholding requirement for distributions by REITs to foreign shareholders. Treas. Reg. sec. 1.1445-8. No regulations have been issued relating specifically to RIC distributions, which first became subject to FIRPTA in 2005.

USRPIs include interests in real property located in the United States or the U.S. Virgin Islands, and stock of a domestic U.S. real property holding company (USRPHC), generally defined as any corporation, unless the taxpayer established that the fair market value of its U.S. real property interests is less than 50 percent of the combined fair market value of all its real property interests (U.S. and worldwide) and of all its assets used or held for use in a trade or business.[499] However, any class of stock that is regularly traded on an established securities market located in the U.S. is treated as a U.S. real property interest only if the seller held more than 5 percent of the stock at any time during the 5-year period ending on the date of disposition of the stock.[500]

Special rules for certain investment entities

Real estate investment trusts and regulated investment companies are generally passive investment entities. They are organized as U.S. domestic entities and are taxed as U.S. domestic corporations. However, because of their special status, they are entitled to deduct amounts distributed to shareholders and, in some cases, to allow the shareholders to characterize these amounts based on the type of income the REIT or RIC received. Among numerous other requirements for qualification as a REIT or RIC, the entity is required to distribute to shareholders at least 90 percent its income (excluding net capital gain) annually.[501] A REIT or RIC may designate a capital gain dividend to its shareholders, who then treat the amount designated as capital gain.[502] A REIT or RIC is taxed at regular corporate rates on undistributed income; but the combination of the requirement to distribute income other than net capital gain, plus the ability to declare a capital gain dividend and avoid corporate level tax on such income, can result in little, if any, corporate level tax paid by a REIT or RIC. Instead, the shareholder-level tax on distributions is the principal tax paid with respect to income of these entities. The requirements for REIT eligibility include primary investment in real estate assets (which assets can include mortgages). The requirements for RIC eligibility include primary investment in stocks

and securities (which can include stock of REITs or of other RICs).

FIRPTA contains special rules for real estate investment trusts (REITs) and regulated investment companies (RICs).[503]

Stock of a "domestically controlled" REIT is not a USRPI. The term "domestically controlled" is defined to mean that less than 50 percent in value of the REIT has been owned by non-U.S. shareholders during the 5-year period ending on the date of disposition.[504] For 2005, 2006, and 2007, a similar exception applies to RIC stock. Thus, stock of a domestically controlled REIT or RIC can be sold without FIRPTA consequences. This exception applies regardless of whether the sale of stock is made directly by a foreign person, or by a REIT or RIC whose distributions to foreign persons of gain attributable to the sale of USRPI's would be subject to FIRPTA as described below.

A distribution by a REIT to a foreign shareholder, to the extent attributable to gain from the REIT's sale or exchange of USRPIs, is generally treated as FIRPTA gain to the shareholder. An exception enacted in 2004 applies if the distribution is made on a class of REIT stock that is regularly traded on an established securities market located in the United States and the foreign shareholder has not held more than 5 percent of the class of stock at any time during the one-year period ending on the date of the distribution.[505] Where the exception applies, the distribution to the foreign shareholder is treated as the distribution of an ordinary dividend (rather than as a capital gain dividend), subject to 30-percent (or lower treaty rate) withholding.[506]

Prior to 2005, distributions by RICs to foreign shareholders, to the extent attributable to the RIC's sale or exchange of USRPIs, were not treated as FIRPTA gain. If distributions were attributable to long-term capital gains, the RIC could designate the distributions as long-term capital gain dividends that would not be subject to any tax to the foreign shareholder, rather than as a regular dividends subject to 30-percent (or lower treaty rate) withholding.[507] For 2005, 2006, and 2007, RICs are subject to the rule that had applied to REITs prior to 2005, i.e., any distribu-

---

[499] Sec. 897(c)(2).

[500] Sec. 897(c)(3).

[501] Secs. 852(a)(1) and 852(b)(2)(A); 857(a)(1).

[502] Secs. 852(b)(3); 857(b)(3).

[503] Sec. 897(h).

[504] Sec. 897(h)(2) and (h)(4)(B).

[505] This exception, effective beginning in 2005, was added by section 418 of the American Jobs Creation Act of 2004 ("AJCA"), Pub. L. No. 108-357, and modified by section 403(p) of the Tax Technical Corrections Act of 2005.

[506] Sec. 857(b)(3)(F).

[507] Sec. 852(b)(3)(C); Treas. Reg. sec. 1.1441-3(c)(2)(D).

tion to a foreign shareholder attributable to gain from the RIC's sale of a USRPI is characterized as FIRPTA gain, without any exceptions.[508]

House Bill

No provision.

Senate Amendment

The Senate amendment provision provides that distributions by a RIC to foreign shareholders of amounts attributable to the sale of USRPIs are not treated as FIRPTA income unless the RIC itself is a U.S. real property holding corporation (i.e. 50 percent or more of its value is represented by its U.S. real property interests, including investments in U.S. real property holding corporations). In determining whether a RIC is a real property holding company for this purpose, a special rule applies that requires the RIC to include as U.S. real property interests its holdings of RIC or REIT stock if such RIC or REIT is a U.S. real property holding corporation, even if such

stock is regularly traded on an established securities market and even if the RIC owns less than 5 percent of such stock. Another special rule requires the RIC to include as U.S. real property interests its interests in any domestically controlled RIC or REIT that is a U.S. real property holding corporation.

Effective Date

The provision applies to distributions with respect to taxable years beginning after December 31, 2004.

Conference Agreement

The conference agreement includes the Senate amendment provision with a clarification to the effective date. Under the clarification, the provision takes effect as if included in the provisions of section 411 of the American Jobs Creation Act of 2004 to which it relates.

[Law at ¶5480. CCH Explanation at ¶1015.]

[¶10,190] Act Secs. 505 and 506. Treatment of REIT and RIC distributions attributable to FIRPTA gains

Conference Committee Report (H.R. CONF. REP. NO. 109-455)

[Code Secs. 852, 871 and 897]

Present Law

General treatment of U.S.-source income of foreign investors

Fixed and determinable annual and periodic income

The United States generally imposes a flat 30-percent tax, collected by withholding, on the gross amount of U.S.-source investment income payments, such as interest, dividends, rents, royalties and similar types of fixed and determinable annual and periodical income, to nonresident alien individuals and foreign corporations ("foreign persons").[509] Under treaties, the United States may reduce or eliminate such taxes.

Dividends

Even taking into account U.S. treaties, the tax on a dividend generally is not entirely eliminated. Instead, U.S.-source portfolio investment dividends received by foreign persons generally are subject to U.S. withholding tax at a rate of at least 15 percent.

Interest

Although payments of U.S.-source interest that is not effectively connected with a U.S. trade or business generally are subject to the 30-percent withholding tax, there are exceptions to that rule. For example, interest from certain deposits with banks and other financial institutions is exempt from tax.[510] Original issue discount on obligations maturing in 183 days or less from the

---

[508] This requirement for RICs was added by section 411 of the American Jobs Creation Act of 2004 ("AJCA"), in connection with the enactment of other rules that allow RICs to identify certain types of distributions to foreign shareholders, attributable to the RIC's receipt of short-term capital gains or interest income, as distributions to such shareholders of such short-term gains or interest income and thus not taxed to the foreign shareholders, rather than as regular dividends that would be subject to withholding.

See Secs. 871(k), 881(e), 1441(c)(12) and 1442(a). All these rules are scheduled to expire at the end of 2007, as is the rule subjecting to FIRPTA all distributions of RIC gain attributable to sales of U.S. real property interests and the rule excepting from FIRPTA a foreign person's sale of stock of a "domestically controlled" RIC.

[509] Secs. 871(a), 881, 1441, and 1442.

[510] Secs. 871(i)(2)(A) and 881(d).

date of original issue (without regard to the period held by the taxpayer) is also exempt from tax.[511] An additional exception is provided for certain interest paid on portfolio obligations.[512] Such "portfolio interest" generally is defined as any U.S.-source interest (including original issue discount), not effectively connected with the conduct of a U.S. trade or business, (i) on an obligation that satisfies certain registration requirements or specified exceptions thereto (i.e., the obligation is "foreign targeted"), and (ii) that is not received by a 10-percent shareholder.[513] With respect to a registered obligation, a statement that the beneficial owner is not a U.S. person is required.[514] This exception is not available for any interest received either by a bank on a loan extended in the ordinary course of its business (except in the case of interest paid on an obligation of the United States), or by a controlled foreign corporation from a related person.[515] Moreover, this exception is not available for certain contingent interest payments.[516] For 2005, 2006 and 2007, a regulated investment company ("RIC") may designate certain distributions to foreign shareholders that are attributable to the RIC's qualified interest income as non-taxable interest distributions to such foreign persons.[517]

Capital gains

A foreign person generally is not subject to U.S. tax on capital gain, including gain realized on the disposition of stock or securities issued by a U.S. person, unless the gain is effectively connected with the conduct of a trade or business in the United States or such person is an individual present in the United States for a period or periods aggregating 183 days or more during the taxable year.[518] A regulated investment company (RIC) can generally designate dividends to foreign persons that are attributable to the RIC's long term capital gain as a long-term gain dividends that are not subject to withholding.[519] For 2005, 2006 and 2007, RICs may also designate short-term capital gain dividends.[520]

For the years 2005, 2006 and 2007, RIC capital gain dividends that are attributable to the sale of U.S. real property interests (which can include stock of companies that are U.S. real property holding companies) are subject to special rules described below.

Real estate investment trusts (REITs) can also designate long-term capital gain dividends to shareholders; but when made to a foreign person such distributions attributable to the sale of U.S. real property interests are also subject to the special rules described below.

Foreign Investment in Real Property Tax Act ("FIRPTA")

Unlike most other U.S. source capital gains, which are generally not taxed to a foreign investor, the Foreign Investment in Real Property Tax Act of 1980 (FIRPTA) subjects gain or loss of a foreign person from the disposition of a U.S. real property interest (USRPI) to tax as if the taxpayer were engaged in a trade or business within the United States and the gain or loss were effectively connected with such trade or business.[521] In addition to an interest in real property located in the United States or the Virgin Islands, USRPIs include (among other things) any interest in a domestic corporation unless the taxpayer establishes that the corporation was not, during a five-year period ending on the date of the disposition of the interest, a U.S. real property holding corporation (which is defined generally to mean any corporation the fair market value of whose U.S. real property interests equals or exceeds 50 percent of the sum of the fair market values of its real property interests and any other of its assets used or held for use in a trade or business).

Distributions by a REIT to its foreign shareholders attributable to the sale of USRPI's are generally treated as income from the sale of USRPIs.[522] Treasury regulations require the REIT to withhold at 35 percent on such a distribution.[523] However, there is an exception for distributions by a REIT with respect to stock of the REIT that is regularly traded on an established securities market located in the U.S., to a foreign shareholder that has not held more than 5 percent of the stock of the REIT for the one year period ending with the date of the distribu-

---

[511] Sec. 871(g).

[512] Secs. 871(h) and 881(c).

[513] Secs. 871(h)(3) and 881(c)(3).

[514] Secs. 871(h)(2), (5) and 881(c)(2).

[515] Sec. 881(c)(3).

[516] Secs. 871(h)(4) and 881(c)(4).

[517] This interest distribution rule was added by section 411 of the American Jobs Creation Act of 2004 ("AJCA"), Pub. L. No. 108-357.

[518] Secs. 871(a)(2) and 881.

[519] Treas. Reg. sec. 1.1441-3(c)(2)(D).

[520] This short-term gain distribution rule was added by section 411 of AJCA.

[521] Sec. 897.

[522] Sec. 897(h)(1).

[523] Treas. Reg. sec. 1.1445-8.

tion.[524] In such cases, the REIT and the shareholder treat the distribution to a foreign shareholder as the distribution of an ordinary dividend,[525] subject to the 30-percent (or lower treaty rate) withholding applicable to dividends.

For 2005, 2006, and 2007, any RIC distribution to a foreign shareholder attributable to the sale of USRPIs is treated as FIRPTA income, without any exceptions.[526] However, no Treasury regulations have been issued addressing withholding obligations with respect to such distributions.

A more complete description of the provisions of FIRPTA and the special rules under FIRPTA that apply to RICs and REITs is contained under "Present Law" for the provision "Application of Foreign Investors in Real Property Tax Act (FIRPTA) to Regulated Investment Companies (RICS)."

Although the law thus provides rules for taxing foreign persons under FIRPTA on distributions of gain from the sale of USRPIs by RICs or REITs, some taxpayers may be taking the position that if a foreign person invests in a RIC or REIT that, in turn, invests in a lower-tier RIC or REIT that is the entity that disposes of USRPIs and distributes the proceeds, then the proceeds from such disposition by the lower-tier RIC or REIT cease to be FIRPTA income when distributed to the upper-tier RIC or REIT (which is not itself a foreign person), and can thereafter be distributed by that latter entity to its foreign shareholders as non-FIRPTA income of such RIC or REIT, rather than continuing to be categorized as FIRPTA income. Furthermore, RICs may take the position that in the absence of regulations or a specific statutory rule addressing the withholding rules for FIRPTA capital gain that is treated

as effectively connected with a U.S. trade or business, such gain should be considered capital gain for which no withholding is required.

In addition, some foreign persons may be attempting to avoid FIRPTA tax on a distribution from a RIC or a REIT, by selling the RIC or REIT stock shortly before the distribution and buying back the stock shortly after the distribution. If the stock is not a U.S. real property interest in the hands of the foreign seller, that person would take the position that the gain on the sale of the stock is capital gain not subject to U.S. tax. Stock of a RIC or REIT that is "domestically controlled" is not a U.S. real property interest.[527]

If the stock is a USRPI in the hands of the foreign person, the transferee generally is required to withhold 10 percent of the gross sales price under general FIRPTA withholding rules.[528]

House Bill

No provision.

Senate Amendment

The first part of the Senate amendment provision requires any distribution that is made by a RIC or a REIT that would otherwise be subject to FIRPTA because the distribution is attributable to the disposition of a U.S. real property interest (USRPI) to retain its character as FIRPTA income when distributed to any other RIC or REIT, and to be treated as if it were from the disposition of a USRPI by that other RIC or REIT. Under the provision, a RIC continues to be subject to FIRPTA, even after December 31, 2007, in any case in which a REIT makes a distribution to the RIC that is attributable to gain from the sale of U.S. real property interests.

---

[524] Sec. 897(h)(1)(second sentence).
[525] Sec. 857(b)(3)(F).
[526] Sec. 897(h)(1)
[527] Sec. 897(g)(3). A RIC or REIT is "domestically controlled" if less than 50 percent in value of the entity's stock is held by foreign persons. RIC stock ceases to be eligible for this exception as of the end of 2007. Distributions by a domestically controlled RIC or REIT, if attributable to the sale of U.S. real property interests, are not exempt from FIRPTA by reason of such domestic control. A foreign person that would be subject to FIRPTA on receipt of a distribution from such an entity might sell its stock before the distribution and repurchase stock after the distribution in an attempt to avoid FIRPTA consequences.

Under a different exception from FIRPTA, applicable to stock of all entities, neither RIC nor REIT stock is a U.S. real property interest if the RIC or REIT stock is regularly traded on an established securities market located in the United States and if the stock sale is made by a foreign shareholder that has not owned more than five percent of the stock

during the five years ending with the date of the sale. Sec. 897(c)(3). Distributions by a REIT to a foreign person, attributable to the sale of U.S. real property interests, are also not subject to FIRPTA if made with respect to stock that is regularly traded on an established securities market located in the United States and made to a foreign person that has not held more than five percent of the REIT stock for the one-year period ending on the date of distribution. (Sec. 897 (h)(1), second sentence.) Thus, any foreign shareholder of such a regularly traded REIT that would be exempt from FIRPTA on a sale of the REIT stock immediately before a distribution would also generally be exempt from FIRPTA on a distribution from the REIT if such shareholder held the stock through the date of the distribution, due to the holding period requirements. Distributions that are not subject to FIRPTA under this five percent exception are recharacterized as ordinary dividends and thus would normally be subject to ordinary dividend withholding rules. Secs. 857(b)(3)(F) and 1441.
[528] Secs. 1445(a) and 1445(e).

The second part of the Senate amendment provision provides that a distribution by a RIC to a foreign shareholder, or to a RIC or REIT shareholder, attributable to sales of USRPIs is not treated as gain from the sale of a USRPI by that shareholder if the distribution is made with respect to a class of RIC stock that is regularly traded on an established securities market[529] located in the U.S. and if such shareholder did not hold more than 5 percent of such stock of within the one year period ending on the date of the distribution. Such distributions instead are treated as dividend distributions.[530]

The third part of the Senate amendment provision requires a foreign person that disposes of stock of a RIC or REIT during the 30-day period preceding a distribution on that stock that would have been treated as a distribution from the disposition of a USRPI, that acquires an identical stock interest during the 60 day period beginning the first day of such 30-day period preceding the distribution, and that does not in fact receive the distribution in a manner that subjects the person to tax under FIRPTA, to pay FIRPTA tax on an amount equal to the amount of the distribution that was not taxed under FIRPTA as a result of the disposition. A foreign person is treated as having acquired any interest acquired by any person treated as related to that foreign first person under section 465(b)(3)(C).[531]

This third part of the Senate amendment provision applies only in the case of a shareholder that would have been treated as receiving FIRPTA income on the distribution if that shareholder had in fact received the distribution, but that would not have been treated as receiving FIRPTA income if the form of the disposition transaction were respected. This category of persons consists of persons that are shareholders in a domestically controlled RIC or REIT (since sales of shares of such an entity are not subject to FIRPTA tax), but does not include a person who sells stock that is regularly traded on an established securities market located in the U.S. and

who did not own more than five percent of such stock during the one year period ending on the date of the distribution (since such a person would not have been subject to FIRPTA tax under present law for REITs and under the second part of the Senate amendment provision for RICs, *supra.*, if that person had received the dividend instead of disposing of the stock).

Notwithstanding the recharacterization of the disposition as involving a FIRPTA distribution to the foreign person, no withholding on disposition proceeds to the foreign person on the disposition of such stock would be required. No inference is intended as to what situations under present law would or would not be respected as dispositions.

Conference Agreement

The conference agreement includes the Senate amendment provision with modifications and clarifications.

The conference agreement provides that the second part of the Senate amendment provision, treating certain distributions attributable to sales of U.S. real property interests as dividends subject to dividend withholding, applies when the distribution is made to a foreign shareholder of a RIC or REIT, but does not apply when the distribution is made to another RIC or a REIT. In such cases, the character of the distribution as FIRPTA gain is retained and must be tracked by the recipient RIC or REIT, but the distribution itself does not become dividend income in the hands of such RIC or REIT. Therefore, such recipient RIC or REIT can in turn distribute amounts attributable to that distribution (attributable to the sale of USRPIs) to its U.S shareholders as capital gain. However, if any recipient RIC or REIT in turn distributes to a foreign shareholder amounts that are attributable to a sale by a lower tier RIC or REIT of USRPIs, such amounts distributed to a foreign shareholder shall be treated as FIRPTA gain or as dividend income, accord-

---

[529] It is intended that the rules generally applicable for this purpose under section 897 also apply under the provision in determining whether a class of interests is regularly traded on an established securities market located in the United Sates. For example, at the present time the rules currently in force for this purpose include Temp. Reg. sec. 1.897-9T(d)(2).

[530] The provision treats such distributions as ordinary dividend distributions rather than as distributions of long term capital gain. This rule is the same as the present law rule for publicly traded REITs making a distribution to a foreign shareholder. In addition, under the immediately preceding provision (sec. 464) of the Senate amendment, for the years 2005, 2006 and 2007 that RICs are subject to FIRPTA, a RIC can make distributions from sales of USRPIs

to shareholders who do not meet this rule, and such distributions will be treated not as dividends but as non-taxable long- or short-term capital gain, if so designated by the RIC, as long as the RIC itself is not a USRPHC after applying the special rules for counting the RIC's ownership of REIT or other RIC stock.

[531] These relationships generally include persons that are engaged in trades or businesses under common control (generally, a more than 50 percent relationship) and also include persons that have a more than 10 percent relationship, such as (for example) a corporation and an individual owning more than 10 percent of the corporation; or a corporation and a partnership if the same persons own more than 10 percent of the interests in each.

ing to whether or not such distribution to such foreign shareholder qualifies for dividend treatment.

The conference agreement amends section 1445 so that it explicitly requires withholding on RIC and REIT distributions to foreign persons, attributable to the sale of USRPIs, at 35 percent, or, to the extent provided by regulations, at 15 percent.[532]

The conference agreement clarifies that the treatment of a RIC as a qualified investment entity continues after December 2007 with respect to a RIC that receives a distribution from a REIT, not only for purposes of the distribution rules, including withholding on distributions to foreign shareholders, but also for purposes of the new "wash sale" rules of the provision.

The conference agreement modifies the new "wash sale" rule. The period within which the basic "wash-sale" rule applies is changed from 60 days to 61 days.[533] The definition of "applicable wash sales transaction" is expanded to cover not only situations in which the taxpayer acquires a substantially identical interest, but also situations in which the taxpayer enters into a contract or option to acquire such an interest. The related party rule is also modified to apply the 50-percent relationship test under section 267(b) and 707(b)(1) rather than a 10-percent test.

In addition, treatment of a foreign shareholder of a RIC or REIT as if it had received a FIRPTA distribution that is treated as U.S. effectively connected income is extended to transactions that meet the definition of "substitute

dividend payments" provided for purposes of section 861 and that would be properly treated by the foreign taxpayer as receipt of a distribution of FIRPTA gain if the distribution from the RIC or REIT had itself been received by the taxpayer, but that, by virtue of the substitute dividend payment, is not so treated but for the provision,[534] as well as to other similar arrangements to which Treasury may extend the rules.

Effective Date

The first part of the conference agreement provision, relating to distributions generally, applies to distributions with respect to taxable years of RICs and REITs beginning after December 31, 2005, except that no withholding is required under sections 1441, 1442, or 1445 with respect to any distribution before the date of enactment if such amount was not otherwise required to be withheld under any such section as in affect before the amendments made by the conference agreement.

The second part of the conference agreement, relating to the "wash sale" and substitute dividend payment transactions, is applicable to distributions and substitute dividend payments occurring on or after the 30th day following the date of enactment.

No inference is intended regarding the treatment under present law of any transactions addressed by the conference agreement.

[Law at ¶5430, ¶5455, ¶5480 and ¶5630. CCH Explanation at ¶1020 and ¶1025.]

---

[532] This provision is similar to present law section 1445(c)(1). The regulatory authority to reduce the withholding to 15 percent sunsets in accordance with the same sunset that applies to section 1445(c)(1), at the time that the present law maximum 15 percent rate on dividends is scheduled to sunset.

Treasury regulations under section 1445 already impose FIRPTA withholding on REITs under present law. Treasury has not yet written regulations applicable to RICs. No inference is intended regarding the existing Treasury regulations in force under section 1445 with respect to REITs

[533] Thus the period includes the 30 days before and the 30 days after the ex-dividend date, in addition to the ex-dividend date itself.

[534] The conference agreement adopts the definition of "substitute dividend payment" used for purposes of section 861, which definition applies to determine substitute dividend payments under the conference agreement provision, even though the recipient may not be an individual and even though the underlying payment would not have been

treated as a dividend to the recipient but as a distribution of FIRPTA gain. Treasury regulations section 1.861-3(a)(6) defines a "substitute dividend payment" as a payment, made to the transferor of a security in a securities lending transaction or a sale-repurchase transaction, of an amount equivalent to a dividend distribution which the owner of the transferred security is entitled to receive during the term of the transaction. The regulation applies to amounts received or accrued by the taxpayer. The regulation defines a securities lending transaction as a transfer of one or more securities that is described in section 1058(a) or a substantially similar transaction. The regulation defines a sale-repurchase transaction as an agreement under which a person transfers a security in exchange for cash and simultaneously agrees to receive substantially identical securities from the transferee in the future in exchange for cash. Under the regulation, a "substitute dividend payment" is generally sourced and in many instances characterized in the same manner as the underlying distribution with respect to the transferred security.

[¶10,210] Act Sec. 507. Modifications to rules relating to taxation of distributions of stock and securities of a controlled corporation

Conference Committee Report (H.R. CONF. REP. NO. 109-455)

[Code Sec. 355]

Present Law

A corporation generally is required to recognize gain on the distribution of property (including stock of a subsidiary) to its shareholders as if the corporation had sold such property for its fair market value. In addition, the shareholders receiving the distributed property are ordinarily treated as receiving a dividend of the value of the distribution (to the extent of the distributing corporation's earnings and profits), or capital gain in the case of a stock buyback that significantly reduces the shareholder's interest in the parent corporation.

An exception to these rules applies if the distribution of the stock of a controlled corporation satisfies the requirements of section 355 of the Code. If all the requirements are satisfied, there is no tax to the distributing corporation or to the shareholders on the distribution.

One requirement to qualify for tax-free treatment under section 355 is that both the distributing corporation and the controlled corporation must be engaged immediately after the distribution in the active conduct of a trade or business that has been conducted for at least five years and was not acquired in a taxable transaction during that period (the "active business test").[40] For this purpose, a corporation is engaged in the active conduct of a trade or business only if (1) the corporation is directly engaged in the active conduct of a trade or business, or (2) the corporation is not directly engaged in an active business, but substantially all its assets consist of stock and securities of one or more corporations that it controls that are engaged in the active conduct of a trade or business.[41]

In determining whether a corporation is directly engaged in an active trade or business that satisfies the requirement, old IRS guidelines for

advance ruling purposes required that the value of the gross assets of the trade or business being relied on must ordinarily constitute at least five percent of the total fair market value of the gross assets of the corporation directly conducting the trade or business.[42] More recently, the IRS has suspended this specific rule in connection with its general administrative practice of moving IRS resources away from advance rulings on factual aspects of section 355 transactions in general.[43]

If the distributing or controlled corporation is not directly engaged in an active trade or business, then the IRS takes the position that the "substantially all" test as applied to that corporation requires that at least 90 percent of the fair market value of the corporation's gross assets consist of stock and securities of a controlled corporation that is engaged in the active conduct of a trade or business.[44]

In determining whether assets are part of a five-year qualifying active business, assets acquired more recently than five years prior to the distribution, in a taxable transaction, are permitted to qualify as five-year "active business" assets if they are considered to have been acquired as part of an expansion of an existing business that does so qualify.[45]

When a corporation holds an interest in a partnership, IRS revenue rulings have allowed an active business of the partnership to count as an active business of a corporate partner in certain circumstances. One such case involved a situation in which the corporation owned at least 20 percent of the partnership, was actively engaged in management of the partnership, and the partnership itself had an active business.[46]

In addition to its active business requirements, section 355 does not apply to any transaction that is a "device" for the distribution of earnings and profits to a shareholder without the

---

[40] Section 355(b).

[41] Section 355(b)(2)(A). The IRS takes the position that the statutory test requires that at least 90 percent of the fair market value of the corporation's gross assets consist of stock and securities of a controlled corporation that is engaged in the active conduct of a trade or business. Rev. Proc. 96-30, sec. 4.03(5), 1996-1 C.B. 696; Rev. Proc. 77-37, sec. 3.04, 1977-2 C.B. 568.

[42] Rev. Proc. 2003-3, sec. 4.01(30), 2003-1 I.R.B. 113.

[43] Rev. Proc. 2003-48, 2003-29 I.R.B. 86.

[44] Rev. Proc. 96-30, sec. 4.03(5), 1996-1 C.B. 696; Rev. Proc. 77-37, sec. 3.04, 1977-2 C.B. 568.

[45] Treas. Reg. sec. 1.355-3(b)(ii).

[46] Rev. Rul. 92-17, 1002-1 C.B. 142; see also, Rev. Rul. 2002-49, 2002-2 C.B. 50.

payment of tax on a dividend. A transaction is ordinarily not considered a "device" to avoid dividend tax if the distribution would have been treated by the shareholder as a redemption that was a sale or exchange of its stock, rather than as a dividend, if section 355 had not applied.[47]

* * *

Senate Amendment

* * *

In addition, the Senate amendment contains another provision that denies section 355 treatment if either the distributing or distributed corporation is a disqualified investment corporation immediately after the transaction (including any series of related transactions) and any person that did not hold 50 percent or more of the voting power or value of stock of such distributing or controlled corporation immediately before the transaction does hold a such a 50 percent or greater interest immediately after such transaction. The attribution rules of section 318 apply for purposes of this determination.

A disqualified investment corporation is any distributing or controlled corporation if the fair market value of the investment assets of the corporation is 75 percent or more of the fair market value of all assets of the corporation. Except as otherwise provided, the term "investment assets" for this purpose means (i) cash, (ii) any stock or securities in a corporation, (iii) any interest in a partnership, (iv) any debt instrument or other evidence of indebtedness; (v) any option, forward or futures contract, notional principal contract, or derivative; (vi) foreign currency, or (vii) any similar asset.

The term "investment assets" does not include any asset which is held for use in the active and regular conduct of (i) a lending or finance business (as defined in section 954(h)(4)); (ii) a banking business through a bank (as defined in section 581), a domestic building and loan association (within the meaning of section 7701(a)(19), or any similar institution specified by the Secretary; or (iii) an insurance business if the conduct of the business is licensed, authorized, or regulated by an applicable insurance regulatory body. These exceptions only apply with respect to any business if substantially all the income of the business is derived from persons who are not related (within the meaning of section 267(b) or 707(b)(1) to the person conducting the business.

The term "investment assets" also does not include any security (as defined in section 475(c)(2)) which is held by a dealer in securities and to which section 475(a) applies.

The term "investment assets" also does not include any stock or securities in, or any debt instrument, evidence of indebtedness, option, forward or futures contract, notional principal contract, or derivative issued by, a corporation which is a 25-percent controlled entity with respect to the distributing or controlled corporation. Instead, the distributing or controlled corporation is treated as owning its ratable share of the assets of any 25-percent controlled entity.

The term 25-percent controlled entity means any corporation with respect to which the corporation in question (distributing or controlled) owns directly or indirectly stock possessing at least 25 percent of voting power and value, excluding stock that is not entitled to vote, is limited and preferred as to dividends and does not participate in corporate growth to any significant extent, has redemption and liquidation rights which do not exceed the issue price of such stock (except for a reasonable redemption or liquidation premium), and is not convertible into another class of stock.

The term "investment assets" also does not include any interest in a partnership, or any debt instrument or other evidence of indebtedness issued by the partnership, if one or more trades or businesses of the partnership are, (or without regard to the 5-year requirement of section 355(b)(2)(B), would be) taken into account by the distributing or controlled corporation, as the case may be, in determining whether the active business test of section 355 is met by such corporation.

The Treasury department shall provide regulations as may be necessary to carry out, or prevent the avoidance of, the purposes of the provision, including regulations in cases involving related persons, intermediaries, pass-through entities, or other arrangements; and the treatment of assets unrelated to the trade or business of a corporation as investment assets if, prior to the distribution, investment assets were used to acquire such assets. Regulations may also in appropriate cases exclude from the application of the provision a distribution which does not have the character of a redemption and which would be treated as a sale or exchange under section 302, and may modify the application of the attribution rules.

---

[47] Treas, Reg, sec, 1.355-2(d)(5)(iv).

Conference Agreement

The conference agreement includes the House bill and the Senate amendment with modifications.

* * *

With respect to the provision that affects transactions involving disqualified investment corporations, the conference agreement reduces the percentage of investment assets of a corporation that will cause such corporation to be a disqualified investment corporation, from 75 percent (three-quarters) to two-thirds of the fair market value of the corporation's assets, for distributions occurring after one year after the date of enactment.

The conference agreement also reduces from 25 percent to 20 percent the percentage stock ownership in a corporation that will cause such ownership to be disregarded as an investment asset itself, instead requiring "look-through" to the ratable share of the underlying assets of such corporation attributable to such stock ownership.

The conferees wish to clarify that the disqualified investment corporation provision applies when a person directly or indirectly holds 50 percent of either the vote or the value of a company immediately following a distribution, and such person did not hold such 50 percent interest directly or indirectly prior to the distribution. As one example, the provision applies if a person that held 50 percent or more of the vote,

but not of the value, of a distributing corporation immediately prior to a transaction in which a controlled corporation that was 100 percent owned by that distributing corporation is distributed, directly or indirectly holds 50 percent of the value of either the distributing or controlled corporation immediately following such transaction.

The conferees further wish to clarify that the enumeration in subsection 355(g)(5)(A) through (C) of specific situations that Treasury regulations may address is not intended to restrict or limit any other situations that Treasury may address under the general authority of new section 355(g)(5) to carry out, or prevent the avoidance of, the purposes of the disqualified investment corporation provision.

Effective Date

* * *

The effective date of the provision that affects transactions involving disqualified investment corporations is the same as that of the Senate amendment provision, except for the conference agreement reduction in the amount of investment assets of a corporation that will cause it to be a disqualified investment corporation, from three-quarters to two thirds of the fair market value of all assets of the corporation. The two-thirds test applies for distributions occurring after one year after the date of enactment.

[Law at ¶5355. CCH Explanation at ¶830.]

[¶10,220] Act Sec. 508. Impose loan and redemption requirements on pooled financing bonds

Conference Committee Report (H.R. Conf. Rep. No. 109-455)

[Code Sec. 149]

Present Law

In general

Interest on bonds issued by State and local governments generally is excluded from gross income for Federal income tax purposes if the proceeds of such bonds are used to finance direct activities of governmental units or if such bonds are repaid with revenues of governmental units. These bonds are called "governmental bonds." Interest on State or local government bonds issued to finance activities of private persons is taxable unless a specific exception applies. These bonds are called "private activity bonds." The

exclusion from income for State and local bonds does not apply to private activity bonds, unless the bonds are issued for certain permitted purposes. In addition, the Code imposes qualification requirements that apply to all State and local bonds. Arbitrage restrictions, for example, limit the ability of issuers to profit from investment of tax-exempt bond proceeds. The Code also imposes requirements that only apply to specific types of bond issues. For instance, pooled financing bonds (defined below) are not tax-exempt unless the issuer meets certain requirements regarding the expected use of proceeds.

Pooled financing bond restrictions

State or local governments also issue bonds to provide financing for the benefit of a third party (a "conduit borrower"). Pooled financing bonds are bond issues that are used to make or finance loans to two or more conduit borrowers, unless the conduit loans are to be used to finance a single project.[469] The Code imposes several requirements on pooled financing bonds if more than $5 million of proceeds are expected to be used to make loans to conduit borrowers. For purposes of these rules, a pooled financing bond does not include certain private activity bonds.[470]

A pooled financing bond is not tax-exempt unless the issuer reasonably expects that at least 95 percent of the net proceeds will be lent to ultimate borrowers by the end of the third year after the date of issue. The term "net proceeds" is defined to mean the proceeds of the issue less the following amounts: 1) proceeds used to finance issuance costs; 2) proceeds necessary to pay interest on the bonds during a three-year period; and 3) amounts in reasonably required reserves.[471]

An issuer's past experience regarding loan origination is a criterion upon which the reasonableness of the issuer's expectations can be based. As an additional requirement for tax exemption, all legal and underwriting costs associated with the issuance of pooled financing bonds may not be contingent and must be substantially paid within 180 days of the date of issuance.

Arbitrage restrictions on tax-exempt bonds

To prevent the issuance of more Federally subsidized tax-exempt bonds than necessary; the tax exemption for State and local bonds does not apply to any arbitrage bond.[472] An arbitrage bond is defined as any bond that is part of an issue if any proceeds of the issue are reasonably expected to be used (or intentionally are used) to acquire higher yielding investments or to replace funds that are used to acquire higher yielding investments. In general, arbitrage profits may be earned only during specified periods (e.g., defined "temporary periods") before funds are needed for the purpose of the borrowing or on specified types of investments (e.g., "reasonably required reserve or replacement funds"). Subject to limited exceptions, investment profits that are earned during these periods or on such investments must be rebated to the Federal Government ("arbitrage rebate").

The Code contains several exceptions to the arbitrage rebate requirement, including an exception for bonds issued by small governments (the "small issuer exception"). For this purpose, small governments are defined as general purpose governmental units that issue no more than $5 million of tax-exempt governmental bonds in a calendar year.[473]

Pooled financing bonds are subject to the arbitrage restrictions that apply to all tax-exempt bonds, including arbitrage rebate. Under certain circumstances, however, small governments may issue pooled financing bonds without those bonds counting towards the determination of whether the issuer qualifies for the small issuer exception to arbitrage rebate. In the case of a pooled financing bond where the ultimate borrowers are governmental units with general taxing powers not subordinate to the issuer of the pooled bond, the pooled bond does not count against the issuer's $5 million limitation, provided the issuer is not a borrower from the pooled bond.[474] However, the issuer of the pooled financing bond remains subject to the arbitrage rebate requirement for unloaned proceeds.[475]

House Bill

No provision.

Senate Amendment

In general

The provision imposes new requirements on pooled financing bonds as a condition of tax-exemption. First, the provision imposes a written loan commitment requirement to restrict the issuance of pooled bonds where potential borrowers have not been identified ("blind pools"). Second, in addition to the current three-year expectations requirement, the issuer must reasonably expect that at least 50 percent of the net proceeds of the pooled bond will be lent to bor-

---

[469] Treas. Reg. sec. 1.150-1(b).

[470] Sec. 149(f)(4)(B).

[471] Sec. 149(f)(2)(C).

[472] Secs. 103(a) and (b)(2).

[473] The $5 million limit is increased to $15 million if at least $10 million of the bonds are used to finance public schools.

[474] Sec. 148(f)(4)(D)(ii)(II).

[475] Treas. Reg. sec. 1.148-8(d)(1).

rowers one year after the date of issue. Third, the provision requires the redemption of outstanding bonds with proceeds that are not loaned to borrowers within the expected loan origination periods. Finally, the provision eliminates the rule allowing an issuer of pooled financing bonds to disregard the pooled bonds for purposes of determining whether the issuer qualifies for the small issuer exception to rebate.

Borrower identification

Under the provision, interest on a pooled financing bond is tax exempt only if the issuer obtains written commitments with ultimate borrowers for loans equal to at least 50 percent of the net proceeds of the pooled bond prior to issuance. The loan commitment requirement does not apply to bonds issued by States (or an integral part of a State) to provide loans to subordinate governmental units or State entities created to provide financing for water-infrastructure projects through the federally-sponsored State revolving fund program.

Loan origination expectations

The provision imposes new reasonable expectations requirements for loan originations. The issuer must expect that at least 50 percent of the net proceeds of a pooled financing bond will be lent to ultimate borrowers one year after the date of issue. This is in addition to the present-law requirement that at least 95 percent of the net proceeds will be lent to ultimate borrowers by the end of the third year after the date of issue.

Redemption requirement

Under the provision, if bond proceeds are not loaned to borrowers within prescribed periods, outstanding bonds equal to the amount of proceeds that were not loaned within the required period must be redeemed with 90 days. The bond redemption requirement applies with respect to proceeds that are unloaned as of expiration of the one-year and three-year loan origination periods. For example, if an amount equal to 45 percent of the net proceeds of an issue are used to make loans to ultimate borrowers as of one year after the bonds are issued, an amount equal to five percent of the net proceeds of the issue is no longer available for lending and must be used to redeem bonds within the following six-month period. Similarly, if only 85 percent of

the net proceeds of the issue are used to make qualifying loans (or to redeem bonds) as of three years after the bonds are issued, 10 percent of the remaining net proceeds is no longer available for lending and must be used to redeem bonds within the following six months.

Small issuer exception

The provision eliminates the rule disregarding pooled financing bonds from the issuer's $5,000,000 annual limitation for purposes of the small issuer exception to arbitrage rebate.

Effective Date

The provision is effective for bonds issued after the date of enactment.

Conference Agreement

The conference agreement includes the Senate amendment provision, with the following modifications.

Under the conference agreement, issuers of pooled financing bonds must reasonably expect that at least 30 percent of the net proceeds of such bonds will be loaned to ultimate borrowers one year after the date of issue. The present-law requirement that issuers must reasonably expect to loan at least 95 percent of the net proceeds of a pooled financing bond to ultimate borrowers three years after the date of issue is unchanged. Bond proceeds that are not loaned to borrowers as required under the one- and three-year rules must be used to redeem outstanding bonds within 90 days of the expiration of such one- and three-year periods.

The conference agreement requires issuers of pooled financing bonds to obtain, prior to issuance, written commitments from borrowers equal to at least 30 percent of the net proceeds of the pooled financing bond. The conference agreement includes the Senate amendment's exception to the written loan commitment requirement. Thus, the loan commitment requirement does not apply to pooled financing bonds issued by States (or an integral part of a State) to provide loans to subordinate governmental units or State entities created to provide financing for water-infrastructure projects through the federally-sponsored State revolving fund program.

[Law at ¶ 5055, ¶ 5180 and ¶ 5205. CCH Explanation at ¶ 1135.]

[¶10,230] Act Sec. 509. Partial payments required with submissions of offers-in-compromise

Conference Committee Report (H.R. CONF. REP. NO. 109-455)

[Code Sec. 7122]

Present Law

The IRS has the authority to compromise any civil or criminal case arising under the internal revenue laws.[401] In general, taxpayers initiate this process by making an offer-in-compromise, which is an offer by the taxpayer to settle an outstanding tax liability for less than the total amount due. The IRS currently imposes a user fee of $150 on most offers, payable upon submission of the offer to the IRS. Taxpayers may justify their offers on the basis of doubt as to collectibility or liability or on the basis of effective tax administration. In general, enforcement action is suspended during the period that the IRS evaluates an offer. In some instances, it may take the IRS 12 to 18 months to evaluate an offer.[402] Taxpayers are permitted (but not required) to make a deposit with their offer; if the offer is rejected, the deposit is generally returned to the taxpayer. There are two general categories[403] of offers-in-compromise, lump-sum offers and periodic payment offers. Taxpayers making lump-sum offers propose to make one lump-sum payment of a specified dollar amount in settlement of their outstanding liability. Taxpayers making periodic payment offers propose to make a series of payments over time (either short-term or long-term) in settlement of their outstanding liability.

House Bill

No provision.

Senate Amendment

The provision requires a taxpayer to make partial payments to the IRS while the taxpayer's offer is being considered by the IRS. For lump-sum offers, taxpayers must make a down payment of 20 percent of the amount of the offer with any application. For purposes of this provision, a lump-sum offer includes single payments as well as payments made in five or fewer installments. For periodic payment offers, the provision requires the taxpayer to comply with the taxpayer's own proposed payment schedule while the offer is being considered. Offers submitted to the IRS that do not comport with these payment requirements are returned to the taxpayer as unprocessable and immediate enforcement action is permitted. The provision eliminates the user fee requirement for offers submitted with the appropriate partial payment.

The provision also provides that an offer is deemed accepted if the IRS does not make a decision with respect to the offer within two years from the date the offer was submitted.

The Senate amendment authorizes the Secretary to issue regulations providing exceptions to the partial payment requirements in the case of offers from certain low-income taxpayers and offers based on doubt as to liability.

Effective Date

The provision is effective for offers-in-compromise submitted on and after the date which is 60 days after the date of enactment.

Conference Agreement

The conference agreement includes the Senate amendment provision, with the following modifications. Under the conference agreement, any user fee imposed by the IRS for participation in the offer-in-compromise program must be submitted with the appropriate partial payment. The user fee is applied to the taxpayer's outstanding tax liability. In addition, under the conference agreement, offers submitted to the IRS that do not comport with the payment requirements may be returned to the taxpayer as unprocessable.

[Law at ¶5780 and ¶5830. CCH Explanation at ¶1140.]

---

[401] Sec. 7122.

[402] *Olsen v. United States*, 326 F. Supp. 2d 184 (D. Mass. 2004).

[403] The IRS categorizes payment plans with more specificity, which is generally not significant for purposes of the provision. See Form 656, Offer in Compromise, page 6 of instruction booklet (revised July 2004).

[¶10,240] Act Sec. 510. Increase in age of minor children whose unearned income is taxed as if parent's income

Conference Committee Report (H.R. Conf. Rep. No. 109-455)

[Code Sec. 1(g)]

Present Law

Filing requirements for children

A single unmarried individual eligible to be claimed as a dependent on another taxpayer's return generally must file an individual income tax return if he or she has: (1) earned income only over $5,150 (for 2006); (2) unearned income only over the minimum standard deduction amount for dependents ($850 in 2006); or (3) both earned income and unearned income totaling more than the smaller of (a) $5,150 (for 2006) or (b) the larger of (i) $850 (for 2006), or (ii) earned income plus $300.[455] Thus, if a dependent child has less than $850 in gross income, the child does not have to file an individual income tax return for 2006.[456]

A child who cannot be claimed as a dependent on another person's tax return is subject to the generally applicable filing requirements. Such a child generally must file a return if the individual's gross income exceeds the sum of the standard deduction and the personal exemption amount ($3,300 for 2006).

Taxation of unearned income under section 1(g)

Special rules (generally referred to as the "kiddie tax") apply to the unearned income of a child who is under age 14.[457] The kiddie tax applies if: (1) the child has not reached the age of 14 by the close of the taxable year; (2) the child's unearned income was more than $1,700 (for 2006); and (3) the child is required to file a return for the year. The kiddie tax applies regardless of whether the child may be claimed as a dependent on the parent's return.

For these purposes, unearned income is income other than wages, salaries, professional fees, or other amounts received as compensation for personal services actually rendered.[458] For children under age 14, net unearned income (for 2006, generally unearned income over $1,700) is taxed at the parent's rate if the parent's rate is higher than the child's rate. The remainder of a child's taxable income (i.e., earned income, plus unearned income up to $1,700 (for 2006), less the child's standard deduction) is taxed at the child's rates, regardless of whether the kiddie tax applies to the child. In general, a child is eligible to use the preferential tax rates for qualified dividends and capital gains.[459]

The kiddie tax is calculated by computing the "allocable parental tax." This involves adding the net unearned income of the child to the parent's income and then applying the parent's tax rate. A child's "net unearned income" is the child's unearned income less the sum of (1) the minimum standard deduction allowed to dependents ($850 for 2006), and (2) the greater of (a) such minimum standard deduction amount or (b) the amount of allowable itemized deductions that are directly connected with the production of the unearned income.[460] A child's net unearned income cannot exceed the child's taxable income.

The allocable parental tax equals the hypothetical increase in tax to the parent that results from adding the child's net unearned income to the parent's taxable income. If the child has net capital gains or qualified dividends, these items are allocated to the parent's hypothetical taxable income according to the ratio of net unearned income to the child's total unearned income. If a parent has more than one child subject to the kiddie tax, the net unearned income of all children is combined, and a single kiddie tax is calculated. Each child is then allocated a proportionate share of the hypothetical increase, based upon the child's net unearned income relative to the aggregate net unearned income of all of the parent's children subject to the tax.

---

[455] Sec. 6012(a)(1)(C). Other filing requirements apply to dependents who are married, elderly, or blind. See, Internal Revenue Service, Publication 929, *Tax Rules for Children and Dependents*, at 2, Table 1 (2005).

[456] A taxpayer generally need not file a return if he or she has gross income in an amount less than the standard deduction (and, if allowable to the taxpayer, the personal exemption amount). An individual who may be claimed as a dependent of another taxpayer is not eligible to claim the dependency exemption relating to that individual. Sec.

151(d)(2). For taxable years beginning in 2006, the standard deduction amount for an individual who may be claimed as a dependent by another taxpayer may not exceed the greater of $850 or the sum of $300 and the individual's earned income.

[457] Sec. 1(g).

[458] Sec. 1(g)(4) and sec. 911(d)(2).

[459] Sec. 1(h).

[460] Sec. 1(g)(4).

Special rules apply to determine which parent's tax return and rate is used to calculate the kiddie tax. If the parents file a joint return, the allocable parental tax is calculated using the income reported on the joint return. In the case of parents who are married but file separate returns, the allocable parental tax is calculated using the income of the parent with the greater amount of taxable income. In the case of unmarried parents, the child's custodial parent is the parent whose taxable income is taken into account in determining the child's liability. If the custodial parent has remarried, the stepparent is treated as the child's other parent. Thus, if the custodial parent and stepparent file a joint return, the kiddie tax is calculated using that joint return. If the custodial parent and stepparent file separate returns, the return of the one with the greater taxable income is used. If the parents are unmarried but lived together all year, the return of the parent with the greater taxable income is used.[461]

Unless the parent elects to include the child's income on the parent's return (as described below) the child files a separate return to report the child's income.[462] In this case, items on the parent's return are not affected by the child's income. The total tax due from a child is the greater of:

1. the sum of (a) the tax payable by the child on the child's earned income and unearned income up to $1,700 (for 2006), plus (b) the allocable parental tax on the child's unearned income, or

2. the tax on the child's income without regard to the kiddie tax provisions.

Parental election to include child's dividends and interest on parent's return

Under certain circumstances, a parent may elect to report a child's dividends and interest on the parent's return. If the election is made, the child is treated as having no income for the year and the child does not have to file a return. The parent makes the election on Form 8814, Parents' Election to Report Child's Interest and Dividends. The requirements for the parent's election are that:

1. the child has gross income only from interest and dividends (including capital gains distributions and Alaska Permanent Fund Dividends);[463]

2. such income is more than the minimum standard deduction amount for dependents ($850 in 2006) and less than 10 times that amount ($8500 in 2006);

3. no estimated tax payments for the year were made in the child's name and taxpayer identification number;

4. no backup withholding occurred; and

5. the child is required to file a return if the parent does not make the election.

Only the parent whose return must be used when calculating the kiddie tax may make the election. The parent includes in income the child's gross income in excess of twice the minimum standard deduction amount for dependents (i.e., the child's gross income in excess of $1,700 for 2007). This amount is taxed at the parent's rate. The parent also must report an additional tax liability equal to the lesser of: (1) $85 (in 2006), or (2) 10 percent of the child's gross income exceeding the child's standard deduction ($850 in 2006).

Including the child's income on the parent's return can affect the parent's deductions and credits that are based on adjusted gross income, as well as income-based phaseouts, limitations, and floors.[464] In addition, certain deductions that the child would have been entitled to take on his or her own return are lost.[465] Further, if the child received tax-exempt interest from a private activity bond, that item is considered a tax preference of the parent for alternative minimum tax purposes.[466]

Taxation of compensation for services under section 1(g)

Compensation for a child's services is considered the gross income of the child, not the parent, even if the compensation is not received or retained by the child (e.g. is the parent's income under local law).[467] If the child's income tax is not paid, however, an assessment against

---

[461] Sec. 1(g)(5); Internal Revenue Service, Publication 929, *Tax Rules for Children and Dependents*, at 6 (2005).

[462] The child must attach to the return Form 8615, Tax for Children Under Age 14 With Investment Income of More Than $1,700 (2006).

[463] Internal Revenue Service, Publication 929, *Tax Rules for Children and Dependents*, at 6 (2005).

[464] Internal Revenue Service, Publication 929, *Tax Rules for Children and Dependents*, at 7 (2005).

[465] Internal Revenue Service, Publication 929, *Tax Rules for Children and Dependents*, at 7 (2005).

[466] Sec. 1(g)(7)(B).

[467] Sec. 73(a).

the child will be considered as also made against the parent to the extent the assessment is attributable to amounts received for the child's services.[468]

House Bill

No provision.

Senate Amendment

The provision increases the age to which the kiddie tax provisions apply from under 14 to under 18 years of age. The provision also creates an exception to the kiddie tax for distributions from certain qualified disability trusts, defined by cross-reference to sections 1917 and 1614(a)(3) of the Social Security Act.

Effective Date

The provision applies to taxable years beginning after December 31, 2005.

Conference Agreement

The conference agreement includes the Senate amendment provision with one modification. This modification provides that the kiddie tax does not apply to a child who is married and files a joint return for the taxable year.

[Law at ¶5005. CCH Explanation at ¶710.]

[¶10,250] Act Sec. 511. Imposition of withholding on certain payments made by government entities

Conference Committee Report (H.R. CONF. REP. NO. 109-455)

[Code Sec. 3402]

Present Law

Withholding requirements

Employers are required to withhold income tax on wages paid to employees, including wages and salaries of employees or elected officials of Federal, State, and local government units. Withholding rates vary depending on the amount of wages paid, the length of the payroll period, and the number of withholding allowances claimed by the employee.

Certain non-wage payments also are subject to mandatory or voluntary withholding. For example:

• Employers are required to withhold FICA and Railroad Retirement taxes from wages paid to their employees. Withholding rates are generally uniform.

• Payors of pensions are required to withhold from payments made to payees, unless the payee elects no withholding.[540] Withholding from periodic payments is at variable rates, parallel to income tax withholding from wages, whereas withholding from nonperiodic payments is at a flat 10-percent rate.

• A variety of payments (such as interest and dividends) are subject to backup withhold-

ing if the payee has not provided a valid taxpayer identification number (TIN). Withholding is at a flat rate based on the fourth lowest rate of tax applicable to single taxpayers.

• Certain gambling proceeds are subject to withholding. Withholding is at a flat rate based on the third lowest rate of tax applicable to single taxpayers.

• Voluntary withholding applies to certain Federal payments, such as Social Security payments. Withholding is at rates specified by Treasury regulations.

• Voluntary withholding applies to unemployment compensation benefits. Withholding is at a flat 10-percent rate.

• Foreign taxpayers are generally subject to withholding on certain U.S.-source income which is not effectively connected with the conduct of a U.S. trade or business. Withholding is at a flat 30-percent rate (14-percent for certain items of income).

Many payments, including payments made by government entities, are not subject to withholding under present law. For example, no tax is generally withheld from payments made to workers who are not classified as employees (i.e., independent contractors).

---

[468] Sec. 6201(c).

[540] Withholding at a rate of 20 percent is required in the case of an eligible rollover distribution that is not directly rolled over.

Information reporting

Present law imposes numerous information reporting requirements that enable the Internal Revenue Service ("IRS") to verify the correctness of taxpayers' returns. For example, every person engaged in a trade or business generally is required to file information returns for each calendar year for payments of $600 or more made in the course of the payor's trade or business. Special information reporting requirements exist for employers required to deduct and withhold tax from employees' income. In addition, any service recipient engaged in a trade or business and paying for services is required to make a return according to regulations when the aggregate of payments is $600 or more. Government entities are specifically required to make an information return, reporting certain payments to corporations as well as individuals. Moreover, the head of every Federal executive agency that enters into certain contracts must file an information return reporting the contractor's name, address, TIN, date of contract action, amount to be paid to the contractor, and any other information required by Forms 8596 (Information Return for Federal Contracts) and 8596A (Quarterly Transmittal of Information Returns for Federal Contracts).

House Bill

No provision.

Senate Amendment

No provision.

Conference Agreement

The conference agreement requires withholding on certain payments to persons providing property or services made by the Government of the United States, every State, every political subdivision thereof, and every instrumentality of the foregoing (including multi-State agencies). The withholding requirement applies regardless of whether the government entity making such payment is the recipient of the property or services. Political subdivisions of States (or any instrumentality thereof) with less than $100 million of annual expenditures for property or services that would otherwise be subject to withholding under this provision are exempt from the withholding requirement.

The rate of withholding is three percent on all payments regardless of whether the payments are for property or services. Payments subject to withholding under the provision include any payment made in connection with a government voucher or certificate program which functions as a payment for property or services. For example, payments to a commodity producer under a government commodity support program are subject to the withholding requirement. The provision imposes information reporting requirements on the payments that are subject to withholding under the provision.

The provision does not apply to any payments made through a Federal, State, or local government public assistance or public welfare program for which eligibility is determined by a needs or income test. For example, payments under government programs providing food vouchers or medical assistance to low-income individuals are not subject to withholding under the provision. However, payments under government programs to provide health care or other services that are not based on the needs or income of the recipients are subject to withholding, including programs where eligibility is based on the age of the beneficiary.

The provision does not apply to payments of wages or to any other payment with respect to which mandatory (e.g., U.S.-source income of foreign taxpayers) or voluntary (e.g., unemployment benefits) withholding applies under present law. The provision does not exclude payments that are potentially subject to backup withholding under section 3406. If, however, payments are actually being withheld under backup withholding, withholding under the provision does not apply.

The provision also does not apply to the following: payments of interest; payments for real property; payments to tax-exempt entities or foreign governments; intra-governmental payments; payments made pursuant to a classified or confidential contract (as defined in section 6050M(e)(3)); and payments to government employees that are not otherwise excludable from the new withholding provision with respect to the employees' services as an employees.

Effective Date

The provision applies to payments made after December 31, 2010.

[Law at ¶ 5655. CCH Explanation at ¶ 1125.]

[¶10,260] Act Sec. 512. Eliminate income limitations on Roth IRA conversions

Conference Committee Report (H.R. CONF. REP. NO. 109-455)

[Code Sec. 408A]

Present Law

There are two general types of individual retirement arrangements ("IRAs"): traditional IRAs and Roth IRAs. The total amount that an individual may contribute to one or more IRAs for a year is generally limited to the lesser of: (1) a dollar amount ($4,000 for 2006); and (2) the amount of the individual's compensation that is includible in gross income for the year. In the case of an individual who has attained age 50 before the end of the year, the dollar amount is increased by an additional amount ($1,000 for 2006). In the case of a married couple, contributions can be made up to the dollar limit for each spouse if the combined compensation of the spouses that is includible in gross income is at least equal to the contributed amount. IRA contributions in excess of the applicable limit are generally subject to an excise tax of six percent per year until withdrawn.

Contributions to a traditional IRA may or may not be deductible. The extent to which contributions to a traditional IRA are deductible depends on whether or not the individual (or the individual's spouse) is an active participant in an employer-sponsored retirement plan and the taxpayer's AGI. An individual may deduct his or her contributions to a traditional IRA if neither the individual nor the individual's spouse is an active participant in an employer-sponsored retirement plan. If an individual or the individual's spouse is an active participant in an employer-sponsored retirement plan, the deduction is phased out for taxpayers with AGI over certain levels. To the extent an individual does not or cannot make deductible contributions, the individual may make nondeductible contributions to a traditional IRA, subject to the maximum contribution limit. Distributions from a traditional IRA are includible in gross income to the extent not attributable to a return of nondeductible contributions.

Individuals with adjusted gross income ("AGI") below certain levels may make contributions to a Roth IRA (up to the maximum IRA contribution limit). The maximum Roth IRA contribution is phased out between $150,000 to $160,000 of AGI in the case of married taxpayers filing a joint return and between $95,000 to $105,000 in the case of all other returns (except a

separate return of a married individual).[541] Contributions to a Roth IRA are not deductible. Qualified distributions from a Roth IRA are excludable from gross income. Distributions from a Roth IRA that are not qualified distributions are includible in gross income to the extent attributable to earnings. In general, a qualified distribution is a distribution that is made on or after the individual attains age 59-1/2, death, or disability or which is a qualified special purpose distribution. A distribution is not a qualified distribution if it is made within the five-taxable year period beginning with the taxable year for which an individual first made a contribution to a Roth IRA.

A taxpayer with AGI of $100,000 or less may convert all or a portion of a traditional IRA to a Roth IRA.[542] The amount converted is treated as a distribution from the traditional IRA for income tax purposes, except that the 10-percent additional tax on early withdrawals does not apply.

In the case of a distribution from a Roth IRA that is not a qualified distribution, certain ordering rules apply in determining the amount of the distribution that is includible in income. For this purpose, a distribution that is not a qualified distribution is treated as made in the following order: (1) regular Roth IRA contributions; (2) conversion contributions (on a first in, first out basis); and (3) earnings. To the extent a distribution is treated as made from a conversion contribution, it is treated as made first from the portion, if any, of the conversion contribution that was required to be included in income as a result of the conversion.

Includible amounts withdrawn from a traditional IRA or a Roth IRA before attainment of age 59-1/2, death, or disability are subject to an additional 10-percent early withdrawal tax, unless an exception applies.

House Bill

No provision.

Senate Amendment

No provision.

Conference Agreement

The conference agreement eliminates the income limits on conversions of traditional IRAs to

---

[541] In the case of a married taxpayer filing a separate return, the phaseout range is $0 to $10,000 of AGI.

[542] Married taxpayers filing a separate return may not convert amounts in a traditional IRA into a Roth IRA.

Roth IRAs.[543] Thus, taxpayers may make such conversions without regard to their AGI.

For conversions occurring in 2010, unless a taxpayer elects otherwise, the amount includible in gross income as a result of the conversion is included ratably in 2011 and 2012. That is, unless a taxpayer elects otherwise, none of the amount includible in gross income as a result of a conversion occurring in 2010 is included in income in 2010, and half of the income resulting from the conversion is includible in gross income in 2011 and half in 2012. However, income inclusion is accelerated if converted amounts are distributed before 2012.[544] In that case, the amount included in income in the year of the distribution is increased by the amount distributed, and the amount included in income in 2012 (or 2011 and 2012 in the case of a distribution in 2010) is lesser of: (1) half of the amount includible in income as a result of the conversion; and (2) the remaining portion of such amount not already included in income. The following example illustrates the application of the accelerated inclusion rule.

Example.—Taxpayer A has a traditional IRA with a value of $100, consisting of deductible contributions and earnings. A does not have a Roth IRA. A converts the traditional IRA to a Roth IRA in 2010, and, as a result of the conversion, $100 is includible in gross income. Unless A elects otherwise, $50 of the income resulting from the conversion is included in income in 2011 and $50 in 2012. Later in 2010, A takes a $20 distribution, which is not a qualified distribution and all of which, under the ordering rules, is attributable to amounts includible in gross income as a result of the conversion. Under the accelerated inclusion rule, $20 is included in income in 2010. The amount included in income in 2011 is the lesser of (1) $50 (half of the income resulting from the conversion) or (2) $70 (the remaining income from the conversion), or $50. The amount included in income in 2012 is the lesser of (1) $50 (half of the income resulting from the conversion) or (2) $30 (the remaining income from the conversion, i.e., $100 – $70 ($20 included in income in 2010 and $50 included in income in 2011)), or $30.

Effective Date

The provision is effective for taxable years beginning after December 31, 2009.

[Law at ¶ 5380. CCH Explanation at ¶ 705.]

[¶ 10,270] Act Sec. 513. Repeal of FSC/ETI binding contract relief

Conference Committee Report (H.R. Conf. Rep. No. 109-455)

[Act Sec. 513]

Prior and Present Law

For most of the last two decades, the United States provided export-related tax benefits under the foreign sales corporation ("FSC") regime. In 2000, the World Trade Organization ("WTO") held that the FSC regime constituted a prohibited export subsidy under the relevant trade agreements. In response to this WTO finding, the United States repealed the FSC rules and enacted a new regime, under the FSC Repeal and Extraterritorial Income ("ETI") Exclusion Act of 2000. Transition rules delayed the repeal of the FSC rules and the effective date of ETI for transactions in the ordinary course of a trade or business occurring before January 1, 2002, or after December 31, 2001 pursuant to a binding contract between the taxpayer and an unrelated person which was in effect on September 30, 2000 and at all times thereafter (the "FSC binding contract relief").[545] In 2002, the WTO held that the ETI regime also constituted a prohibited export subsidy.

In general, under the ETI regime, an exclusion from gross income applied with respect to "extraterritorial income," which was a taxpayer's gross income attributable to "foreign trading gross receipts." This income was eligible for the exclusion to the extent that it was "qualifying foreign trade income." Qualifying foreign trade

---

[543] Under the conference agreement, married taxpayers filing a separate return may convert amounts in a traditional IRA into a Roth IRA.

[544] Whether a distribution consists of converted amounts is determined under the present-law ordering rules.

[545] An election was provided, however, under which taxpayers could adopt ETI at an earlier date for transactions after September 30, 2000. This election allowed the ETI rules to apply to transactions after September 30, 2000, including transactions occurring pursuant to pre-existing binding contracts.

income was the amount of gross income that, if excluded, would result in a reduction of taxable income by the greatest of: (1) 1.2 percent of the foreign trading gross receipts derived by the taxpayer from the transaction; (2) 15 percent of the "foreign trade income" derived by the taxpayer from the transaction;[546] or (3) 30 percent of the "foreign sale and leasing income" derived by the taxpayer from the transaction.[547]

Foreign trading gross receipts were gross receipts derived from certain activities in connection with "qualifying foreign trade property" with respect to which certain economic processes had taken place outside of the United States. Specifically, the gross receipts must have been: (1) from the sale, exchange, or other disposition of qualifying foreign trade property; (2) from the lease or rental of qualifying foreign trade property for use by the lessee outside the United States; (3) for services which were related and subsidiary to the sale, exchange, disposition, lease, or rental of qualifying foreign trade property (as described above); (4) for engineering or architectural services for construction projects located outside the United States; or (5) for the performance of certain managerial services for unrelated persons. A taxpayer could elect to treat gross receipts from a transaction as not being foreign trading gross receipts. As a result of such an election, a taxpayer could use any related foreign tax credits in lieu of the exclusion.

Qualifying foreign trade property generally was property manufactured, produced, grown, or extracted within or outside the United States that was held primarily for sale, lease, or rental in the ordinary course of a trade or business for direct use, consumption, or disposition outside the United States. No more than 50 percent of the fair market value of such property could be attributable to the sum of: (1) the fair market value of articles manufactured outside the United States; and (2) the direct costs of labor performed outside the United States. With respect to property that was manufactured outside the United States, certain rules were provided to ensure consistent U.S. tax treatment with respect to manufacturers.

The American Jobs Creation Act of 2004 ("AJCA") repealed the ETI exclusion,[548] generally effective for transactions after December 31, 2004. AJCA provides a general transition rule under which taxpayers retain 100 percent of their ETI benefits for transactions prior to 2005, 80 percent of their otherwise-applicable ETI benefits for transactions during 2005, and 60 percent of their otherwise-applicable ETI benefits for transactions during 2006.

In addition to the general transition rule, AJCA provides that the ETI exclusion provisions remain in effect for transactions in the ordinary course of a trade or business if such transactions are pursuant to a binding contract[549] between the taxpayer and an unrelated person and such contract is in effect on September 17, 2003, and at all times thereafter (the "ETI binding contract relief").

In early 2006, the WTO Appellate Body held that the ETI general transition rule and the FSC and ETI binding contract relief measures are prohibited export subsidies.

House Bill

No provision.

Senate Amendment

No provision.

Conference Agreement

The conference agreement repeals both the FSC binding contract relief and the ETI binding contract relief. The general transition rule remains in effect.

Effective date

The provision is effective for taxable years beginning after date of enactment.

[Law at ¶7025. CCH Explanation at ¶1045.]

---

[546] "Foreign trade income" was the taxable income of the taxpayer (determined without regard to the exclusion of qualifying foreign trade income) attributable to foreign trading gross receipts.

[547] "Foreign sale and leasing income" was the amount of the taxpayer's foreign trade income (with respect to a transaction) that was properly allocable to activities constituting foreign economic processes. Foreign sale and leasing income also included foreign trade income derived by the taxpayer in connection with the lease or rental of qualifying foreign trade property for use by the lessee outside the United States.

[548] Pub. L. No. 108-357, sec. 101. In addition, foreign corporations that elected to be treated for all Federal tax purposes as domestic corporations in order to facilitate the claiming of ETI benefits were allowed to revoke such elections within one year of the date of enactment of the repeal without recognition of gain or loss, subject to anti-abuse rules.

[549] This rule also applies to a purchase option, renewal option, or replacement option that is included in such contract. For this purpose, a replacement option is considered enforceable against a lessor notwithstanding the fact that a lessor retained approval of the replacement lessee.

[¶10,280] Act Sec. 514. Modification of wage limit for purposes of domestic production activities deduction

Conference Committee Report (H.R. Conf. Rep. No. 109-455)

[Code Sec. 199]

Present Law

In general

Present law provides a deduction from taxable income (or, in the case of an individual, adjusted gross income) that is equal to a portion of the taxpayer's qualified production activities income. For taxable years beginning after 2009, the deduction is nine percent of such income. For taxable years beginning in 2005 and 2006, the deduction is three percent of income and, for taxable years beginning in 2007, 2008 and 2009, the deduction is six percent of income. However, the deduction for a taxable year is limited to 50 percent of the wages paid by the taxpayer during the calendar year that ends in such taxable year.[550]

Qualified production activities income

In general, "qualified production activities income" is equal to domestic production gross receipts (defined by section 199(c)(4)), reduced by the sum of: (1) the costs of goods sold that are allocable to such receipts; and (2) other expenses, losses, or deductions which are properly allocable to such receipts.

Application of wage limitation to passthrough entities

For purposes of applying the wage limitation, a shareholder, partner, or similar person who is allocated components of qualified production activities income from a passthrough entity also is treated as having been allocated wages from such entity in an amount that is equal to the lesser of: (1) such person's allocable share of wages, as determined under regulations prescribed by the Secretary; or (2) twice the qualified production activities income that actually is allocated to such person for the taxable year.

House Bill

No provision.

Senate Amendment

No provision.

Conference Agreement

Under the conference agreement, the wage limitation is modified such that taxpayers may only include amounts which are properly allocable to domestic production gross receipts.[551] Thus, the wage limitation is 50 percent of those wages which are deducted in arriving at qualified production activities income.

In addition, the conference agreement repeals the special limitation on wages treated as allocated to partners or shareholders of passthrough entities. Accordingly, for purposes of the wage limitation, a shareholder, partner, or similar person who is allocated components of qualified production activities income from a passthrough entity is treated as having been allocated wages from such entity in an amount that is equal to such person's allocable share of wages as determined under regulations prescribed by the Secretary, even if such amount is more than twice the qualified production activities income that actually is allocated to such person for the taxable year. The shareholder, partner, or similar person will then include in its wage limitation only those wages which are deducted in arriving at qualified production activities income.

Effective date

The conference agreement is effective with respect to taxable years beginning after the date of enactment.

[Law at ¶5330. CCH Explanation at ¶810.]

---

[550] For purposes of the provision, "wages" include the sum of the amounts of wages as defined in section 3401(a) and elective deferrals that the taxpayer properly reports to the Social Security Administration with respect to the employment of employees of the taxpayer during the calendar year ending during the taxpayer's taxable year. Elective deferrals include elective deferrals as defined in section 402(g)(3), amounts deferred under section 457, and, for taxable years beginning after December 31, 2005, designated Roth contributions (as defined in section 402A).

[551] As under present law, the Secretary shall provide rules for the proper allocation of items (including wages) in determining qualified production activities income. Section 199(c)(2).

[¶10,290] Act Sec. 515. Modification of exclusion for citizens living abroad

Conference Committee Report (H.R. CONF. REP. NO. 109-455)

[Code Sec. 911]

Present Law

In general

U.S. citizens generally are subject to U.S. income tax on all their income, whether derived in the United States or elsewhere. A U.S. citizen who earns income in a foreign country also may be taxed on that income by the foreign country. The United States generally cedes the primary right to tax a U.S. citizen's non-U.S. source income to the foreign country in which the income is derived. This concession is effected by the allowance of a credit against the U.S. income tax imposed on foreign-source income for foreign taxes paid on that income. The amount of the credit for foreign income tax paid on foreign-source income generally is limited to the amount of U.S. tax otherwise owed on that income. Accordingly, if the amount of foreign tax paid on foreign-source income is less than the amount of U.S. tax owed on that income, a foreign tax credit generally is allowed in an amount not exceeding the amount of the foreign tax, and a residual U.S. tax liability remains.

A U.S. citizen or resident living abroad may be eligible to exclude from U.S. taxable income certain foreign earned income and foreign housing costs.[552] This exclusion applies regardless of whether any foreign tax is paid on the foreign earned income or housing costs. To qualify for these exclusions, an individual (a "qualified individual") must have his or her tax home in a foreign country and must be either (1) a U.S. citizen[553] who is a bona fide resident of a foreign country or countries for an uninterrupted period that includes an entire taxable year, or (2) a U.S. citizen or resident present in a foreign country or countries for at least 330 full days in any 12-consecutive-month period.

Exclusion for compensation

The foreign earned income exclusion generally is available for a qualified individual's non-U.S. source earned income attributable to per-

sonal services performed by that individual during the period of foreign residence or presence described above. The maximum exclusion amount for any calendar year is $80,000 in 2002 through 2007 and is indexed for inflation after 2007.

Exclusion for housing costs

A qualified individual is allowed an exclusion from gross income (or, as described below, a deduction) for certain foreign housing costs paid or incurred by or on behalf of the individual. The amount of this housing cost exclusion is equal to the excess of a taxpayer's "housing expenses" over a base housing amount. The term "housing expenses" means the reasonable expenses paid or incurred during the taxable year for a taxpayer's housing (and, if they live with the taxpayer, for the housing of the taxpayer's spouse and dependents) in a foreign country. The term includes expenses attributable to housing such as utilities and insurance, but it does not include separately deductible interest and taxes. If the taxpayer maintains a second household outside the United States for a spouse or dependents who do not reside with the taxpayer because of dangerous, unhealthful, or otherwise adverse living conditions, the housing expenses of the second household also are eligible for exclusion. The base housing amount above which costs are eligible for exclusion in a taxable year is 16 percent of the annual salary (computed on a daily basis) of a grade GS-14, step 1, U.S. government employee, multiplied by the number of days of foreign residence or presence (as described above) in the taxable year. For 2006 this salary is $77,793; the current base housing amount therefore is $12,447 (assuming the taxpayer is a bona fide resident of or is present in a foreign country every day during the year).

To the extent otherwise excludable housing costs are not paid or reimbursed by a taxpayer's employer, these costs generally are allowed as a deduction in computing adjusted gross income.

---

[552] Sec. 911.

[553] Generally, only U.S. citizens may qualify under the bona fide residence test. A U.S. resident alien who is a citizen of a country with which the United States has a tax

treaty may, however, qualify for the section 911 exclusions under the bona fide residence test by application of a non-discrimination provision of the treaty.

Exclusion limitation amounts

The combined foreign earned income exclusion and housing cost exclusion (including the amount of any deductible housing costs) may not exceed the taxpayer's total foreign earned income for the taxable year. The taxpayer's foreign tax credit is reduced by the amount of the credit that is attributable to excluded income.

Tax brackets

A taxpayer with excludable income under section 911 is subject to tax on the taxpayer's other income, after deductions, starting in the lowest tax rate bracket.

House Bill

No provision.

Senate Amendment

No provision.

Conference Agreement

Exclusion for compensation

The conference agreement provision adjusts for inflation the maximum amount of the foreign earned income exclusion in taxable years beginning in calendar years after 2005 (rather than, as under present law, after 2007). The limitation in 2006 therefore is $82,400.[554]

Exclusion for housing costs

Under the conference agreement, the base housing amount used in calculating the foreign housing cost exclusion in a taxable year is 16 percent of the amount (computed on a daily basis) of the foreign earned income exclusion limitation (instead of the present law 16 percent of the grade GS-14, step 1 amount), multiplied by the number of days of foreign residence or presence (as previously described) in that year.

Reasonable foreign housing expenses in excess of the base housing amount remain excluded from gross income (or, if paid by the taxpayer, are deductible) under the conference agreement, but the amount of the exclusion is limited to 30 percent of the maximum amount of a taxpayer's foreign earned income exclusion.[555] The Secretary is given authority to issue regulations or other guidance providing for the adjustment of this 30-percent housing cost limitation based on geographic differences in housing costs relative to housing costs in the United States. The conferees intend that the Secretary be permitted to use publicly available data, such as the Quarterly Report Indexes published by the U.S. Department of State or any other information deemed reliable by the Secretary, in making adjustments. The conferees also intend that the Secretary may adjust the 30-percent amount upward or downward. The conferees intend that the Secretary make adjustments annually.

Under the 30-percent rule described above, the maximum amount of the foreign housing cost exclusion in 2006 is (assuming foreign residence or presence on all days in the year) $11,536 (= ($82,400 × 30 percent) – ($82,400 × 16 percent)).[556]

Tax brackets

Under the conference agreement, if an individual excludes an amount from income under section 911, any income in excess of the exclusion amount determined under section 911 is taxed (under the regular tax and alternative minimum tax) by applying to that income the tax rates that would have been applicable had the individual not elected the section 911 exclusion. For example, an individual with $80,000 of foreign earned income that is excluded under section 911 and with $20,000 in other taxable income (after deductions) would be subject to tax on that $20,000 at the rate or rates applicable to taxable income in the range of $80,000 to $100,000.

Effective Date

The conference agreement provision is effective for taxable years beginning after December 31, 2005.

[Law at ¶ 5505. CCH Explanation at ¶ 1005 and ¶ 1010.]

---

[554] This $82,400 amount is calculated under section 911(b)(2)(D)(ii), as amended by the conference agreement provision, using current U.S. Bureau of Labor Statistics ("BLS") Consumer Price Index data.

[555] In certain programs including grant-making to subsidize rents, the U.S. Department of Housing and Urban Development considers maximum affordable housing costs to be 30 percent of a household's income. See, e.g., United States Housing Act of 1937, 42 U.S.C. sec. 1437a(a)(1)(A), as amended.

[556] The $11,536 amount is based on a calculation under section 911(b)(2)(D)(ii), as amended by the conference agreement, using the BLS data described above.

[¶10,300] Act Sec. 516. Tax involvement of accommodation parties in tax-shelter transactions

Conference Committee Report (H.R. Conf. Rep. No. 109-455)

[Code Secs. 6011, 6033, 6652 and New Code Sec. 4965]

Present Law

Disclosure of listed and other reportable transactions by taxpayers

Present law provides that a taxpayer that participates in a reportable transaction (including a listed transaction) and that is required to file a tax return must attach to its return a disclosure statement in the form prescribed by the Secretary.[97] For this purpose, the term taxpayer includes any person, including an individual, trust, estate, partnership, association, company, or corporation.[98]

Under present Treasury regulations, a reportable transaction includes a listed transaction and five other categories of transactions: (1) confidential transactions, which are transactions offered to a taxpayer under conditions of confidentiality and for which the taxpayer has paid an advisor a minimum fee; (2) transactions with contractual protection, which include transactions for which the taxpayer or a related party has the right to a full or partial refund of fees if all or part of the intended tax consequences from the transaction are not sustained, or for which fees are contingent on the taxpayer's realization of tax benefits from the transaction; (3) loss transactions, which are transactions resulting in the taxpayer claiming a loss under section 165 that exceeds certain thresholds, depending upon the type of taxpayer; (4) transactions with a significant book-tax difference; and (5) transactions involving a brief asset holding period.[99] A listed transaction means a reportable transaction which is the same as, or substantially similar to, a transaction specifically identified by the Secretary as a tax avoidance transaction for purposes of section 6011 (relating to the filing of returns and statements), and identified by notice, regulation, or other form of published guidance as a listed transaction.[100] The fact that a transaction is a reportable transaction does not affect the legal determination of whether the taxpayer's treatment of the transaction is proper.[101] Present law authorizes the Secretary to define a reportable transaction on the basis of such transaction being of a type which the Secretary determines as having a potential for tax avoidance or evasion.[102]

Treasury regulations provide guidance regarding the determination of when a taxpayer participates in a transaction for these purposes.[103] A taxpayer has participated in a listed transaction if the taxpayer's tax return reflects tax consequences or a tax strategy described in the published guidance that lists the transaction, or if the taxpayer knows or has reason to know that the taxpayer's tax benefits are derived directly or indirectly from tax consequences or a tax strategy described in published guidance that lists a transaction. A taxpayer has participated in a confidential transaction if the taxpayer's tax return reflects a tax benefit from the transaction and the taxpayer's disclosure of the tax treatment or tax structure of the transaction is limited under conditions of confidentiality. A taxpayer has participated in a transaction with contractual protection if the taxpayer's tax return reflects a tax benefit from the transaction, and the taxpayer has the right to the full or partial refund of fees or the fees are contingent.

Present law provides a penalty for any person who fails to include on any return or statement any required information with respect to a reportable transaction.[104] The penalty applies without regard to whether the transaction ultimately results in an understatement of tax, and applies in addition to any other penalty that may be imposed.

The penalty for failing to disclose a reportable transaction is $10,000 in the case of a natural person and $50,000 in any other case. The amount is increased to $100,000 and $200,000, respectively, if the failure is with respect to a listed transaction. The penalty cannot be waived with respect to a listed transaction. As to reportable transactions, the IRS Commissioner may rescind all or a portion of the penalty if rescission would promote compliance with the tax laws and effective tax administration.

Disclosure of listed and other reportable transactions by material advisors

Present law requires each material advisor with respect to any reportable transaction (in-

---

[97] Treas. Reg. sec. 1.6011-4(a).
[98] Sec. 7701(a)(1); Treas. Reg. sec. 1.6011-4(c)(1).
[99] Treas. Reg. sec. 1.6011-4(b). In Notice 2006-6 (January 6, 2006), the Service indicated that it was removing transactions with a significant book-tax difference from the categories of reportable transactions.
[100] Sec. 6707A(c)(2); Treas. Reg. sec. 1.6011-4(b)(2).
[101] Treas. Reg. sec. 1.6011-4(a).
[102] Sec. 6707A(c)(1).
[103] Treas. Reg. sec. 1.6011-4(c)(3).
[104] Sec. 6707A.

cluding any listed transaction) to timely file an information return with the Secretary (in such form and manner as the Secretary may prescribe).[105] The information return must include (1) information identifying and describing the transaction, (2) information describing any potential tax benefits expected to result from the transaction, and (3) such other information as the Secretary may prescribe. The return must be filed by the date specified by the Secretary.

A "material advisor" means any person (1) who provides material aid, assistance, or advice with respect to organizing, managing, promoting, selling, implementing, insuring, or carrying out any reportable transaction, and (2) who directly or indirectly derives gross income in excess of $250,000 ($50,000 in the case of a reportable transaction substantially all of the tax benefits from which are provided to natural persons) or such other amount as may be prescribed by the Secretary for such advice or assistance.[106]

The Secretary may prescribe regulations which provide (1) that only one material advisor is required to file an information return in cases in which two or more material advisors would otherwise be required to file information returns with respect to a particular reportable transaction, (2) exemptions from the requirements of this section, and (3) other rules as may be necessary or appropriate to carry out the purposes of this section.[107]

Present law imposes a penalty on any material advisor who fails to timely file an information return, or who files a false or incomplete information return, with respect to a reportable transaction (including a listed transaction).[108] The amount of the penalty is $50,000. If the penalty is with respect to a listed transaction, the amount of the penalty is increased to the greater of (1) $200,000, or (2) 50 percent of the gross income derived by such person with respect to aid, assistance, or advice which is provided with respect to the transaction before the date the information return that includes the transaction is filed. An intentional failure or act by a material advisor with respect to the requirement to disclose a listed transaction increases the penalty to 75 percent of the gross income derived from the transaction.

The penalty cannot be waived with respect to a listed transaction. As to reportable transactions, the IRS Commissioner can rescind all or a portion of the penalty if rescission would promote compliance with the tax laws and effective tax administration.

House Bill

No provision.

Senate Amendment

In general

In general, under the provision, certain tax-exempt entities are subject to penalties for being a party to a prohibited tax shelter transaction. A prohibited tax shelter transaction is a transaction that the Secretary determines is a listed transaction (as defined in section 6707A(c)(2)) or a prohibited transaction. A prohibited reportable transaction is a confidential transaction or a transaction with contractual protection (as defined by the Secretary in regulations) which is a reportable transaction as defined in sec. 6707A(c)(1). Under the provision, a tax-exempt entity is an entity that is described in section 501(c), 501(d), or 170(c) (not including the United States), Indian tribal governments, and tax qualified pension plans, individual retirement arrangements ("IRAs"), and similar tax-favored savings arrangements (such as Coverdell education savings accounts, health savings accounts, and qualified tuition plans).

Entity level tax

Under the provision, if a tax-exempt entity is a party at any time to a transaction during a taxable year and knows or has reason to know that the transaction is a prohibited tax shelter transaction, the entity is subject to a tax for such year equal to the greater of (1) 100 percent of the entity's net income (after taking into account any tax imposed with respect to the transaction) for such year that is attributable to the transaction or (2) 75 percent of the proceeds received by the entity that are attributable to the transaction.

In addition, if a transaction is not a listed transaction at the time a tax-exempt entity enters into the transaction (and is not otherwise a prohibited tax shelter transaction), but the transaction subsequently is determined by the Secretary to be a listed transaction (a "subsequently listed transaction"), the entity must pay each taxable year an excise tax at the highest unrelated business taxable income rate times the greater of (1) the entity's net income (after taking into account any tax imposed) that is attributable to the subsequently listed transaction and that is properly

---

[105] Sec. 6707(a), as added by the American Jobs Creation Act of 2004, Pub. L. No. 108-357, sec. 816(a).

[106] Sec. 6707(b)(1).

[107] Sec. 6707(c).

[108] Sec. 6707(b).

allocable to the period beginning on the later of the date such transaction is listed by the Secretary or the first day of the taxable year or (2) 75 percent of the proceeds received by the entity that are attributable to the subsequently listed transaction and that are properly allocable to the period beginning on the later of the date such transaction is listed by the Secretary or the first day of the taxable year. The Secretary has the authority to promulgate regulations that provide guidance regarding the determination of the allocation of net income of a tax-exempt entity that is attributable to a transaction to various periods, including before and after the listing of the transaction or the date which is 90 days after the date of enactment of the provision.

The entity level tax does not apply if the entity's participation is not willful and is due to reasonable cause, except that the willful and reasonable cause exception does not apply to the tax imposed for subsequently listed transactions. The entity level taxes do not apply to tax qualified pension plans, IRAs, and similar tax-favored savings arrangements (such as Coverdell education savings accounts, health savings accounts, and qualified tuition plans).

Disclosure of participation in prohibited tax shelter transactions

The provision requires that a taxable party to a prohibited tax shelter transaction disclose to the tax-exempt entity that the transaction is a prohibited tax shelter transaction. Failure to make such disclosure is subject to the present-law penalty for failure to include reportable transaction information under section 6707A. Thus, the penalty is $10,000 in the case of a natural person or $50,000 in any other case, except that if the transaction is a listed transaction, the penalty is $100,000 in the case of a natural person and $200,000 in any other case.[109]

The provision requires disclosure by a tax-exempt entity to the IRS of each participation in a prohibited tax shelter transaction and disclosure of other known parties to the transaction. The penalty for failure to disclose is imposed on the entity (or entity manager, in the case of qualified pension plans and similar tax favored retirement arrangements) at $100 per day the failure continues, not to exceed $50,000. If any person fails to comply with a demand on the tax-exempt

entity by the Secretary for disclosure, such person or persons shall pay a penalty of $100 per day (beginning on the date of the failure to comply) not to exceed $10,000 per prohibited tax shelter transaction. As under present-law section 6652, no penalty is imposed with respect to any failure if it is shown that the failure is due to reasonable cause.

Penalty on entity managers

A tax of $20,000 is imposed on an entity manager that approves or otherwise causes a tax-exempt entity to be a party to a prohibited tax shelter transaction at any time during the taxable year, knowing or with reason to know that the transaction is a prohibited tax shelter transaction. An entity manager is defined as a person with authority or responsibility similar to that exercised by an officer, director, or trustee of an organization, except: (1) in the case of an entity described in section 501(c)(3) or (c)(4) (other than a private foundation), an entity manager is an organization manager as defined in section 4958(f)(2); and (2) in the case of a private foundation, an entity manager is a foundation manager as defined in section 4946(b). The reasonable cause (or no willful participation) exception applies to this tax.

Conference Agreement

The conference agreement includes the Senate amendment provision, with modifications.

The conference agreement does not include the provision that the entity level or entity manager tax does not apply if the entity's participation is not willful and is due to reasonable cause.

In addition, the conference agreement adds a tax in the event that a tax-exempt entity becomes a party to a prohibited tax shelter transaction without knowing or having reason to know that the transaction is a prohibited tax shelter transaction. In that case, the tax-exempt entity is subject to a tax in the taxable year the entity becomes a party and any subsequent taxable year of the highest unrelated business taxable income rate times the greater of (1) the entity's net income (after taking into account any tax imposed with respect to the transaction) for such year that is attributable to the transaction or (2) 75 percent of the proceeds received by the entity

---

[109] The IRS Commissioner may rescind all or any portion of any such penalty if the violation is with respect to a prohibited tax shelter transaction other than a listed transac-

tion and doing so would promote compliance with the requirements of the Code and effective tax administration. See sec. 6707A(d).

that are attributable to the transaction for such year.[110]

The conference agreement clarifies that the entity level tax rate that applies if the entity knows or has reason to know that a transaction is a prohibited tax shelter transaction does not apply to subsequently listed transactions.

The conference agreement modifies the definition of an entity manager to provide that: (1) in the case of tax qualified pension plans, IRAs, and similar tax-favored savings arrangements (such as Coverdell education savings accounts, health savings accounts, and qualified tuition plans) an entity manager is the person that approves or otherwise causes the entity to be a party to a prohibited tax shelter transaction, and (2) in all other cases the entity manager is the person with authority or responsibility similar to that exercised by an officer, director, or trustee of an organization, and with respect to any act, the person having authority or responsibility with respect to such act.

In the case of a qualified pension plan, IRA, or similar tax-favored savings arrangement (such as a Coverdell education savings account, health savings account, or qualified tuition plan), the conferees intend that, in general, a person who decides that assets of the plan, IRA, or other savings arrangement are to be invested in a prohibited tax shelter transaction is the entity manager under the provision. Except in the case of a fully self-directed plan or other savings arrangement with respect to which a participant or beneficiary decides to invest in the prohibited tax shelter transaction, a participant or beneficiary generally is not an entity manager under the provision. Thus, for example, a participant or beneficiary is not an entity manager merely by reason of choosing among pre-selected investment options (as is typically the case if a qualified retirement plan provides for participant-directed investments).[111] Similarly, if an individual has an IRA and may choose among various mutual funds offered by the IRA trustee, but has no control over the investments held in the mutual funds, the individual is not an entity manager under the provision.

Under the provision, certain taxes are imposed if the entity or entity manager knows or has reason to know that a transaction is a prohibited tax shelter transaction. In general, the conferees intend that in order for an entity or entity manager to have reason to know that a transac-

tion is a prohibited tax shelter transaction, the entity or entity manager must have knowledge of sufficient facts that would lead a reasonable person to conclude that the transaction is a prohibited tax shelter transaction. If there is justifiable reliance on a reasoned written opinion of legal counsel (including in-house counsel) or of an independent accountant with expertise in tax matters, after making full disclosure of relevant facts about a transaction to such counsel or accountant, that a transaction is not a prohibited tax shelter transaction, then absent knowledge of facts not considered in the reasoned written opinion that would lead a reasonable person to conclude that the transaction is a prohibited tax shelter transaction, the reason to know standard is not met.

Not obtaining a reasoned written opinion of legal counsel does not alone indicate whether a person has reason to know. However, if a transaction is extraordinary for the entity, promises a return for the organization that is exceptional considering the amount invested by, the participation of, or the absence of risk to the organization, or the transaction is of significant size, either in an absolute sense or relative to the receipts of the entity, then, in general, the presence of such factors may indicate that the entity or entity manager has a responsibility to inquire further about whether a transaction is a prohibited tax shelter transaction, or, absent such inquiry, that the reason to know standard is satisfied. For example, if a tax-exempt entity's investment in a transaction is $1,000, and the entity is promised or expects to receive $10,000 in the near term, in general, the rate of return would be considered exceptional and the entity should make inquiries with respect to the transaction. As another example, if a tax-exempt entity's expected income from a transaction is greater than five percent of the entity's annual receipts, or is in excess of $1,000,000, and the entity fails to make appropriate inquiries with respect to its participation in such transaction, such failure is a factor tending to show that the reason to know standard is met. Appropriate inquiries need not involve obtaining a reasoned written opinion. In general, if a transaction does not present the factors described above and the organization is small (measured by receipts and assets) and described in section 501(c)(3), it is expected that the reason to know standard will not be met.

---

[110] The conference agreement clarifies that in all cases the 75 percent of proceeds received by the entity that are attributable to the transaction are with respect to the taxable year.

[111] Depending on the circumstances, the person who is responsible for determining the pre-selected investment options may be an entity manager under the provision.

In general, the conferees intend that in determining whether a tax-exempt entity is a "party" to a prohibited tax shelter transaction all the facts and circumstances should be taken into account. Absence of a written agreement is not determinative. Certain indirect involvement in a prohibited tax shelter transaction would not result in an entity being considered a party to the transaction. For example, investment by a tax-exempt entity in a mutual fund that in turn invests in or participates in a prohibited tax shelter transaction does not, in general, make the tax-exempt entity a party to such transaction, absent facts or circumstances that indicate that the purpose of the tax exempt entity's investment in the mutual fund was specifically to participate in such a transaction. However, whether a tax-exempt entity is a party to such a transaction will be informed by whether the entity or entity manager knew or had reason to know that an investment of the entity would be used in a prohibited tax shelter transaction. Presence of such knowledge or reason to know may indicate that that the purpose of the investment was to participate in the prohibited tax shelter transaction and that the tax-exempt entity is a party to such transaction.

The conference agreement clarifies that a subsequently listed transaction means any transaction to which a tax-exempt entity is a party and which is determined by the Secretary to be a listed transaction at any time after the entity has "become a party to" the transaction, and not, as under the Senate amendment, when the entity "entered into" the transaction. The conference agreement provides that a subsequently listed transaction does not include a transaction that is a prohibited reportable transaction. The conference agreement provides that the Secretary has the authority to allocate proceeds as well as income of a tax-exempt entity to various periods. The conference agreement also provides that the disclosure by tax-exempt entities to the Internal Revenue Service required under the provision is based on an entity's being a party to a prohibited tax shelter transaction and not, as under the Senate amendment, on an entity's "participation" in a prohibited tax shelter transaction. The conference agreement further provides that the Secretary may make a demand for disclosure on any entity manager subject to the tax, as well as on any tax exempt entity, and also provides that such managers and entities and not, as under the Senate amendment, "persons" are subject to the penalty for failure to comply with the demand.

Effective Date

In general, the provision is effective for taxable years ending after the date of enactment, with respect to transactions before, on, or after such date, except that no tax shall apply with respect to income or proceeds that are properly allocable to any period ending on or before the date that is 90 days after the date of enactment. The tax on certain knowing transactions does not apply to any prohibited tax shelter transaction to which a tax-exempt entity became a party on or before the date of enactment. The disclosure provisions apply to disclosures the due date for which are after the date of enactment.

[Law at ¶5680, ¶5705, ¶5730 and ¶5805. CCH Explanation at ¶1130.]

Committee Reports

Tax Relief and Health Care Act of 2006

¶15,001 Introduction

The Joint Committee on Taxation, Technical Explanation of H.R. 6408, The "Tax Relief and Health Care Act of 2006," as Introduced in the House on December 7, 2006 (JCX-50-06), explains the intent of Congress regarding the provisions in the Tax Relief and Health Care Act of 2006 (P.L. 109-432). There was no Conference Report issued for this Act. The Technical Explanation from the Joint Committee on Taxation is included in this section to aid the reader's understanding, but may not be cited as an official House, Senate, or Conference Committee Report accompanying the 2006 Extenders Act. At the end of each section of the Technical Explanation, references are provided to corresponding explanations and Code provisions. Subscribers to the electronic version can link from these references to the corresponding material.*The pertinent sections of the Technical Explanation appear in Act Section order beginning at ¶15,100.*

¶15,005 Background

The Tax Relief and Health Care Act of 2006 is the result of three bills. The untitled H.R. 6111, as introduced in the House on September 19, 2006, would have amended the Internal Revenue Code of 1986 to provide for Tax Court review of claims for equitable innocent spouse relief. H.R. 6111 was passed with an amendment by voice vote on December 5 and sent to the Senate. The Senate passed the bill with an amendment on December 7. On that same day, H.R. 6408, the Tax Relief and Health Care Act of 2006, was introduced in the House. Its stated purpose was to amend the Internal Revenue Code to extend expiring provisions.

The provisions of H.R. 6408 were incorporated into H.R. 6111 and agreed to by the House on December 8 by a vote of 367 to 45. The Senate agreed to the House amendment to the Senate amendment by a vote of 79 to 9 on December 9.

The text of a third bill, H.R. 6406, which would modify rates of duty and make technical amendments to trade laws, was later appended to the engrossed House amendment to the Senate amendment of H.R. 6111. The President signed the final bill on December 20, 2006.

[¶15,100] Act Sec. 101. Above-the-line deduction for higher education expenses

Joint Committee Taxation (J.C.T. REP. NO. JCX-50-06)

[Code Sec. 222]

Present Law

An individual is allowed an above-the-line deduction for qualified tuition and related expenses for higher education paid by the individual during the taxable year. Qualified tuition and related expenses include tuition and fees required for the enrollment or attendance of the taxpayer, the taxpayer's spouse, or any dependent of the taxpayer with respect to whom the taxpayer may claim a personal exemption, at an eligible institution of higher education for courses of instruction of such individual at such institution. Charges and fees associated with meals, lodging, insurance, transportation, and similar personal, living, or family expenses are not eligible for the deduction. The expenses of education involving sports, games, or hobbies are not qualified tuition and related expenses unless this education is part of the student's degree program.

The amount of qualified tuition and related expenses must be reduced by certain scholarships, educational assistance allowances, and other amounts paid for the benefit of such individual, and by the amount of such expenses taken into account for purposes of determining any exclusion from gross income of: (1) income from certain United States Savings Bonds used to pay higher education tuition and fees; and (2) income from a Coverdell education savings account. Additionally, such expenses must be reduced by the earnings portion (but not the return of principal) of distributions from a qualified tuition program if an exclusion under section 529 is claimed with respect to expenses otherwise deductible under section 222. No deduction is allowed for any expense for which a deduction is otherwise allowed or with respect to an individual for whom a Hope credit or Lifetime Learning credit is elected for such taxable year.

The expenses must be in connection with enrollment at an institution of higher education during the taxable year, or with an academic term beginning during the taxable year or during the first three months of the next taxable year. The deduction is not available for tuition and related expenses paid for elementary or secondary education.

For taxable years beginning in 2004 and 2005, the maximum deduction is $4,000 for an individual whose adjusted gross income for the taxable year does not exceed $65,000 ($130,000 in the case of a joint return), or $2,000 for other individuals whose adjusted gross income does not exceed $80,000 ($160,000 in the case of a joint return). No deduction is allowed for an individual whose adjusted gross income exceeds the relevant adjusted gross income limitations, for a married individual who does not file a joint return, or for an individual with respect to whom a personal exemption deduction may be claimed by another taxpayer for the taxable year. The deduction is not available for taxable years beginning after December 31, 2005.

Explanation of Provision

The provision extends the tuition deduction for two years, through December 31, 2007.

Effective Date

The provision is effective for taxable years beginning after December 31, 2005.

[Law at ¶5336. CCH Explanation at ¶210.]

[¶15,110] Act Sec. 102. Extension and modification of the new markets tax credit

Joint Committee Taxation (J.C.T. REP. NO. JCX-50-06)

[Code Sec. 45D]

Present Law

Section 45D provides a new markets tax credit for qualified equity investments made to acquire stock in a corporation, or a capital interest in a partnership, that is a qualified community development entity ("CDE").[4] The amount of the credit allowable to the investor (either the original purchaser or a subsequent holder) is (1) a five-percent credit for the year in which the equity interest is purchased from the CDE and for each of the following two years, and (2) a six-percent credit for each of the following four years. The credit is determined by applying the applicable percentage (five or six percent) to the amount paid to the CDE for the investment at its original issue, and is available for a taxable year to the taxpayer who holds the qualified equity investment on the date of the initial investment or on the respective anniversary date that occurs during the taxable year. The credit is recaptured if at any time during the seven-year period that begins on the date of the original issue of the investment the entity ceases to be a qualified CDE, the proceeds of the investment cease to be used as required, or the equity investment is redeemed.

A qualified CDE is any domestic corporation or partnership: (1) whose primary mission is serving or providing investment capital for low-income communities or low-income persons; (2) that maintains accountability to residents of low-income communities by their representation on any governing board of or any advisory board to the CDE; and (3) that is certified by the Secretary as being a qualified CDE. A qualified equity investment means stock (other than nonqualified preferred stock as defined in sec. 351(g)(2)) in a corporation or a capital interest in a partnership that is acquired directly from a CDE for cash, and includes an investment of a subsequent purchaser if such investment was a qualified equity investment in the hands of the prior holder. Substantially all of the investment proceeds must be used by the CDE to make qualified low-income community investments. For this purpose, qualified low-income community investments include: (1) capital or equity investments in, or loans to, qualified active low-income community businesses; (2) certain financial counseling and other services to businesses and residents in low-income communities; (3) the purchase from another CDE of any loan made by such entity that is a qualified low-income community investment; or (4) an equity investment in, or loan to, another CDE.

A "low-income community" is a population census tract with either (1) a poverty rate of at least 20 percent or (2) median family income which does not exceed 80 percent of the greater of metropolitan area median family income or statewide median family income (for a non-metropolitan census tract, does not exceed 80 percent of statewide median family income). In the case of a population census tract located within a high migration rural county, low-income is defined by reference to 85 percent (rather than 80 percent) of statewide median family income. For this purpose, a high migration rural county is any county that, during the 20-year period ending with the year in which the most recent census was conducted, has a net out-migration of inhabitants from the county of at least 10 percent of the population of the county at the beginning of such period.

The Secretary has the authority to designate "targeted populations" as low-income communities for purposes of the new markets tax credit. For this purpose, a "targeted population" is defined by reference to section 103(20) of the Riegle Community Development and Regulatory Improvement Act of 1994 (12 U.S.C. 4702(20)) to mean individuals, or an identifiable group of individuals, including an Indian tribe, who (A) are low-income persons; or (B) otherwise lack adequate access to loans or equity investments. Under such Act, "low-income" means (1) for a targeted population within a metropolitan area, less than 80 percent of the area median family income; and (2) for a targeted population within a non-metropolitan area, less than the greater of 80 percent of the area median family income or 80 percent of the statewide non-metropolitan area median family income.[5] Under such Act, a targeted population is not required to be within any census tract. In addition, a population census tract with a population of less than 2,000 is treated as a low-income community for purposes of the credit if such tract is within an empowerment zone, the designation of which is in effect under section 1391, and is contiguous to one or more low-income communities.

A qualified active low-income community business is defined as a business that satisfies, with respect to a taxable year, the following requirements: (1) at least 50 percent of the total gross income of the business is derived from the active conduct of trade or business activities in any low-income community; (2) a substantial portion of the tangible property of such business is used in a low-income community; (3) a substantial portion of the services performed for such business by its employees is performed in a low-income community; and (4) less than five percent of the average of the aggregate unadjusted bases of the property of such business is

---

[4] Section 45D was added by section 121(a) of the Community Renewal Tax Relief Act of 2000, Pub. L. No. 106-554 (December 21, 2000).

[5] 12 U.S.C. 4702(17) defines "low-income" for purposes of 12 U.S.C. 4702(20).

attributable to certain financial property or to certain collectibles.

The maximum annual amount of qualified equity investments is capped at $2.0 billion per year for calendar years 2004 and 2005, and at $3.5 billion per year for calendar years 2006 and 2007.

Explanation of Provision

The provision extends the new markets tax credit through 2008, permitting up to $3.5 billion

in qualified equity investments for that calendar year. The provision also requires that the Secretary prescribe regulations to ensure that non-metropolitan counties receive a proportional allocation of qualified equity investments.

Effective Date

The provision is effective on the date of enactment.

[Law at ¶5044. CCH Explanation at ¶415.]

[¶15,120] Act Sec. 103. Deduction of state and local general sales taxes

Joint Committee Taxation (J.C.T. Rep. No. JCX-50-06)

[Code Sec. 164]

Present Law

For purposes of determining regular tax liability, an itemized deduction is permitted for certain State and local taxes paid, including individual income taxes, real property taxes, and personal property taxes. The itemized deduction is not permitted for purposes of determining a taxpayer's alternative minimum taxable income. For taxable years beginning in 2004 and 2005, at the election of the taxpayer, an itemized deduction may be taken for State and local general sales taxes in lieu of the itemized deduction provided under present law for State and local income taxes. As is the case for State and local income taxes, the itemized deduction for State and local general sales taxes is not permitted for purposes of determining a taxpayer's alternative minimum taxable income. Taxpayers have two options with respect to the determination of the sales tax deduction amount. Taxpayers may deduct the total amount of general State and local sales taxes paid by accumulating receipts showing general sales taxes paid. Alternatively, taxpayers may use tables created by the Secretary of the Treasury that show the allowable deduction. The tables are based on average consumption by taxpayers on a State-by-State basis taking into account number of dependents, modified adjusted gross income and rates of State and local general sales taxation. Taxpayers who live in more than one jurisdiction during the tax year are required to pro-rate the table amounts based on the time they live in each jurisdiction. Taxpayers who use the tables created by the Secretary may, in addition to the table amounts, deduct eligible general sales taxes paid with respect to the purchase of motor vehicles, boats

and other items specified by the Secretary. Sales taxes for items that may be added to the tables are not reflected in the tables themselves.

The term "general sales tax" means a tax imposed at one rate with respect to the sale at retail of a broad range of classes of items. However, in the case of items of food, clothing, medical supplies, and motor vehicles, the fact that the tax does not apply with respect to some or all of such items is not taken into account in determining whether the tax applies with respect to a broad range of classes of items, and the fact that the rate of tax applicable with respect to some or all of such items is lower than the general rate of tax is not taken into account in determining whether the tax is imposed at one rate. Except in the case of a lower rate of tax applicable with respect to food, clothing, medical supplies, or motor vehicles, no deduction is allowed for any general sales tax imposed with respect to an item at a rate other than the general rate of tax. However, in the case of motor vehicles, if the rate of tax exceeds the general rate, such excess shall be disregarded and the general rate is treated as the rate of tax.

A compensating use tax with respect to an item is treated as a general sales tax, provided such tax is complementary to a general sales tax and a deduction for sales taxes is allowable with respect to items sold at retail in the taxing jurisdiction that are similar to such item.

Explanation of Provision

The present-law provision allowing taxpayers to elect to deduct State and local sales taxes in lieu of State and local income taxes is extended for two years (through December 31, 2007).

Effective Date   [Law at ¶ 5240. CCH Explanation at ¶ 205.]

Effective Date

The provision applies to taxable years beginning after December 31, 2005.

[¶ 15,130] Act Sec. 104. Extension and modification of the research credit

Joint Committee Taxation (J.C.T. REP. NO. JCX-50-06)

[Code Sec. 41]

Present Law

General rule

Prior to January 1, 2006, a taxpayer could claim a research credit equal to 20 percent of the amount by which the taxpayer's qualified research expenses for a taxable year exceeded its base amount for that year.[6] Thus, the research credit was generally available with respect to incremental increases in qualified research.

A 20-percent research tax credit was also available with respect to the excess of (1) 100 percent of corporate cash expenses (including grants or contributions) paid for basic research conducted by universities (and certain nonprofit scientific research organizations) over (2) the sum of (a) the greater of two minimum basic research floors plus (b) an amount reflecting any decrease in nonresearch giving to universities by the corporation as compared to such giving during a fixed-base period, as adjusted for inflation. This separate credit computation was commonly referred to as the university basic research credit (see sec. 41(e)).

Finally, a research credit was available for a taxpayer's expenditures on research undertaken by an energy research consortium. This separate credit computation was commonly referred to as the energy research credit. Unlike the other research credits, the energy research credit applied to all qualified expenditures, not just those in excess of a base amount.

The research credit, including the university basic research credit and the energy research credit, expired on December 31, 2005.

Computation of allowable credit

Except for energy research payments and certain university basic research payments made by corporations, the research tax credit applied only to the extent that the taxpayer's qualified research expenses for the current taxable year exceeded its base amount. The base amount for the current year generally was computed by multiplying the taxpayer's fixed-base percentage by the average amount of the taxpayer's gross receipts for the four preceding years. If a taxpayer both incurred qualified research expenses and had gross receipts during each of at least three years from 1984 through 1988, its fixed-base percentage was the ratio that its total qualified research expenses for the 1984-1988 period bore to its total gross receipts for that period (subject to a maximum fixed-base percentage of 16 percent). All other taxpayers (so-called start-up firms) were assigned a fixed-base percentage of three percent.[7]

In computing the credit, a taxpayer's base amount could not be less than 50 percent of its current-year qualified research expenses.

To prevent artificial increases in research expenditures by shifting expenditures among commonly controlled or otherwise related entities, a special aggregation rule provided that all members of the same controlled group of corporations were treated as a single taxpayer (sec. 41(f)(1)). Under regulations prescribed by the Secretary, special rules applied for computing the credit when a major portion of a trade or business (or unit thereof) changed hands, under which qualified research expenses and gross receipts for periods prior to the change of owner-

---

[6] Sec. 41.

[7] The Small Business Job Protection Act of 1996 expanded the definition of start-up firms under section 41(c)(3)(B)(i) to include any firm if the first taxable year in which such firm had both gross receipts and qualified research expenses began after 1983. A special rule (enacted in 1993) was designed to gradually recompute a start-up firm's fixed-base percentage based on its actual research experience. Under this special rule, a start-up firm would be assigned a fixed-base percentage of three percent for each of its first five taxable years after 1993 in which it incurs qualified research

expenses. In the event that the research credit is extended beyond its expiration date, a start-up firm's fixed-base percentage for its sixth through tenth taxable years after 1993 in which it incurs qualified research expenses will be a phased-in ratio based on its actual research experience. For all subsequent taxable years, the taxpayer's fixed-base percentage will be its actual ratio of qualified research expenses to gross receipts for any five years selected by the taxpayer from its fifth through tenth taxable years after 1993 (sec. 41(c)(3)(B)).

ship of a trade or business were treated as transferred with the trade or business that gave rise to those expenses and receipts for purposes of recomputing a taxpayer's fixed-base percentage (sec. 41(f)(3)).

Alternative incremental research credit regime

Taxpayers were allowed to elect an alternative incremental research credit regime.[8] If a taxpayer elected to be subject to this alternative regime, the taxpayer was assigned a three-tiered fixed-base percentage (that was lower than the fixed-base percentage otherwise applicable) and the credit rate likewise was reduced. Under the alternative incremental credit regime, a credit rate of 2.65 percent applied to the extent that a taxpayer's current-year research expenses exceeded a base amount computed by using a fixed-base percentage of one percent (i.e., the base amount equaled one percent of the taxpayer's average gross receipts for the four preceding years) but did not exceed a base amount computed by using a fixed-base percentage of 1.5 percent. A credit rate of 3.2 percent applied to the extent that a taxpayer's current-year research expenses exceeded a base amount computed by using a fixed-base percentage of 1.5 percent but did not exceed a base amount computed by using a fixed-base percentage of two percent. A credit rate of 3.75 percent applied to the extent that a taxpayer's current-year research expenses exceeded a base amount computed by using a fixed-base percentage of two percent. An election to be subject to this alternative incremental credit regime could be made for any taxable year beginning after June 30, 1996, and such an election applied to that taxable year and all subsequent years unless revoked with the consent of the Secretary of the Treasury.

Eligible expenses

Qualified research expenses eligible for the research tax credit consisted of: (1) in-house expenses of the taxpayer for wages and supplies attributable to qualified research; (2) certain time-sharing costs for computer use in qualified research; and (3) 65 percent of amounts paid or incurred by the taxpayer to certain other persons for qualified research conducted on the taxpayer's behalf (so-called contract research ex-

penses).[9] Notwithstanding the limitation for contract research expenses, qualified research expenses included 100 percent of amounts paid or incurred by the taxpayer to an eligible small business, university, or Federal laboratory for qualified energy research.

To be eligible for the credit, the research did not only have to satisfy the requirements of present-law section 174 (described below) but also had to be undertaken for the purpose of discovering information that is technological in nature, the application of which was intended to be useful in the development of a new or improved business component of the taxpayer, and substantially all of the activities of which had to constitute elements of a process of experimentation for functional aspects, performance, reliability, or quality of a business component. Research did not qualify for the credit if substantially all of the activities related to style, taste, cosmetic, or seasonal design factors (sec. 41(d)(3)). In addition, research did not qualify for the credit: (1) if conducted after the beginning of commercial production of the business component; (2) if related to the adaptation of an existing business component to a particular customer's requirements; (3) if related to the duplication of an existing business component from a physical examination of the component itself or certain other information; or (4) if related to certain efficiency surveys, management function or technique, market research, market testing, or market development, routine data collection or routine quality control (sec. 41(d)(4)). Research did not qualify for the credit if it was conducted outside the United States, Puerto Rico, or any U.S. possession.

Relation to deduction

Under section 174, taxpayers may elect to deduct currently the amount of certain research or experimental expenditures paid or incurred in connection with a trade or business, notwithstanding the general rule that business expenses to develop or create an asset that has a useful life extending beyond the current year must be capitalized.[10] While the research credit was in effect, however, deductions allowed to a taxpayer under section 174 (or any other section) were reduced by an amount equal to 100 percent of

---

[8] Sec. 41(c)(4).

[9] Under a special rule, 75 percent of amounts paid to a research consortium for qualified research were treated as qualified research expenses eligible for the research credit (rather than 65 percent under the general rule under section 41(b)(3) governing contract research expenses) if (1) such research consortium was a tax-exempt organization that is described in section 501(c)(3) (other than a private founda-

tion) or section 501(c)(6) and was organized and operated primarily to conduct scientific research, and (2) such qualified research was conducted by the consortium on behalf of the taxpayer and one or more persons not related to the taxpayer. Sec. 41(b)(3)(C).

[10] Taxpayers may elect 10-year amortization of certain research expenditures allowable as a deduction under section 174(a). Secs. 174(f)(2) and 59(e).

the taxpayer's research tax credit determined for the taxable year (Sec. 280C(c)). Taxpayers could alternatively elect to claim a reduced research tax credit amount (13 percent) under section 41 in lieu of reducing deductions otherwise allowed (sec. 280C(c)(3)).

Explanation of Provision

The provision extends the research credit two years (for amounts paid or incurred after December 31, 2005, and before January 1, 2008).

The provision also modifies the research credit for taxable years ending after December 31, 2006, subject to the general termination provision applicable to the credit.

The provision increases the rates of the alternative incremental credit: (1) a credit rate of three percent (rather than 2.65 percent) applies to the extent that a taxpayer's current-year research expenses exceed a base amount computed by using a fixed-base percentage of one percent (i.e., the base amount equals one percent of the taxpayer's average gross receipts for the four preceding years) but do not exceed a base amount computed by using a fixed-base percentage of 1.5 percent; (2) a credit rate of four percent (rather than 3.2 percent) applies to the extent that a taxpayer's current-year research expenses exceed a base amount computed by using a fixed-base percentage of 1.5 percent but do not exceed a base amount computed by using a fixed-base percentage of two percent; and (3) a credit rate of five percent (rather than 3.75 percent) applies to the extent that a taxpayer's current-year research expenses exceed a base amount computed by using a fixed-base percentage of two percent.

The provision also creates, at the election of the taxpayer, an alternative simplified credit for qualified research expenses. The alternative simplified research is equal to 12 percent of qualified research expenses that exceed 50 percent of the average qualified research expenses for the three preceding taxable years. The rate is reduced to 6 percent if a taxpayer has no qualified research expenses in any one of the three preceding taxable years.

An election to use the alternative simplified credit applies to all succeeding taxable years unless revoked with the consent of the Secretary. An election to use the alternative simplified credit may not be made for any taxable year for which an election to use the alternative incremental credit is in effect. A transition rule applies which permits a taxpayer to elect to use the alternative simplified credit in lieu of the alternative incremental credit if such election is made during the taxable year which includes January 1, 2007. The transition rule only applies to the taxable year which includes that date.

Effective Date

The extension of the research credit applies to amounts paid or incurred after December 31, 2005. The modification of the alternative incremental credit and the addition of the alternative simplified credit are effective for taxable years ending after December 31, 2006.

Special transitional rules apply to fiscal year 2006-2007 taxpayers. In the case of a taxpayer electing the alternative incremental credit, the amount of the credit is the sum of (1) the credit calculated as if it were extended but not modified multiplied by a fraction the numerator of which is the number of days in the taxable year before January 1, 2007, and the denominator of which is the total number of days in the taxable year and (2) the credit calculated under the provision as amended multiplied by a fraction the numerator of which is the number of days in the taxable year after December 31, 2006, and the denominator of which is the total number of days in the taxable year.

In the case of a taxpayer electing the new alternative simplified credit, the amount of the credit under section 41(a)(1) for the taxable year is the sum of (1) the credit that would be determined under section 41(a)(1) (including the alternative incremental credit for a taxpayer electing that credit) if it were extended but not modified multiplied by a fraction the numerator of which is the number of days in the taxable year before January 1, 2007, and the denominator of which is the total number of days in the taxable year and (2) the alternative simplified credit determined for the year multiplied by a fraction the numerator of which is the number of days in the taxable year after December 31, 2006, and the denominator of which is the total number of days in the taxable year.

[Law at ¶5036 and ¶5042. CCH Explanation at ¶405.]

[¶15,140] Act Sec. 105. Work opportunity tax credit and welfare-to-work tax credit

Joint Committee Taxation (J.C.T. Rep. No. JCX-50-06)

[Code Secs. 51 and 51A]

Present Law

Work opportunity tax credit

Targeted groups eligible for the credit

The work opportunity tax credit is available on an elective basis for employers hiring individuals from one or more of eight targeted groups. The eight targeted groups are: (1) certain families eligible to receive benefits under the Temporary Assistance for Needy Families Program; (2) high-risk youth; (3) qualified ex-felons; (4) vocational rehabilitation referrals; (5) qualified summer youth employees; (6) qualified veterans; (7) families receiving food stamps; and (8) persons receiving certain Supplemental Security Income (SSI) benefits.

A high-risk youth is an individual aged 18 but not aged 25 on the hiring date who is certified by a designated local agency as having a principal place of abode within an empowerment zone, enterprise community, or renewal community. The credit is not available if such youth's principal place of abode ceases to be within an empowerment zone, enterprise community, or renewal community.

A qualified ex-felon is an individual certified by a designated local agency as: (1) having been convicted of a felony under State or Federal law; (2) being a member of an economically disadvantaged family; and (3) having a hiring date within one year of release from prison or conviction.

A food stamp recipient is an individual aged 18 but not aged 25 on the hiring date certified by a designated local agency as being a member of a family either currently or recently receiving assistance under an eligible food stamp program.

Qualified wages

Generally, qualified wages are defined as cash wages paid by the employer to a member of a targeted group. The employer's deduction for wages is reduced by the amount of the credit.

Calculation of the credit

The credit equals 40 percent (25 percent for employment of 400 hours or less) of qualified first-year wages. Generally, qualified first-year wages are qualified wages (not in excess of $6,000) attributable to service rendered by a member of a targeted group during the one-year period beginning with the day the individual began work for the employer. Therefore, the maximum credit per employee is $2,400 (40 percent of the first $6,000 of qualified first-year wages). With respect to qualified summer youth employees, the maximum credit is $1,200 (40 percent of the first $3,000 of qualified first-year wages).

Certification rules

An individual is not treated as a member of a targeted group unless: (1) on or before the day on which an individual begins work for an employer, the employer has received a certification from a designated local agency that such individual is a member of a targeted group; or (2) on or before the day an individual is offered employment with the employer, a pre-screening notice is completed by the employer with respect to such individual, and not later than the 21st day after the individual begins work for the employer, the employer submits such notice, signed by the employer and the individual under penalties of perjury, to the designated local agency as part of a written request for certification.

Minimum employment period

No credit is allowed for qualified wages paid to employees who work less than 120 hours in the first year of employment.

Coordination of the work opportunity tax credit and the welfare-to-work tax credit

An employer cannot claim the work opportunity tax credit with respect to wages of any employee on which the employer claims the welfare-to-work tax credit.

Other rules

The work opportunity tax credit is not allowed for wages paid to a relative or dependent of the taxpayer. Similarly wages paid to replacement workers during a strike or lockout are not eligible for the work opportunity tax credit. Wages paid to any employee during any period for which the employer received on-the-job training program payments with respect to that employee are not eligible for the work opportunity tax credit. The work opportunity tax credit generally is not allowed for wages paid to individuals who had previously been employed by the employer. In addition, many other technical rules apply.

Expiration

The work opportunity tax credit is not available for individuals who begin work for an employer after December 31, 2005.

Welfare-to-work tax credit

Targeted group eligible for the credit

The welfare-to-work tax credit is available on an elective basis to employers of qualified long-term family assistance recipients. Qualified long-term family assistance recipients are: (1) members of a family that have received family assistance for at least 18 consecutive months ending on the hiring date; (2) members of a family that have received such family assistance for a total of at least 18 months (whether or not consecutive) after August 5, 1997 (the date of enactment of the welfare-to-work tax credit) if they are hired within 2 years after the date that the 18-month total is reached; and (3) members of a family who are no longer eligible for family assistance because of either Federal or State time limits, if they are hired within 2 years after the Federal or State time limits made the family ineligible for family assistance.

Qualified wages

Qualified wages for purposes of the welfare-to-work tax credit are defined more broadly than the work opportunity tax credit. Unlike the definition of wages for the work opportunity tax credit which includes simply cash wages, the definition of wages for the welfare-to-work tax credit includes cash wages paid to an employee plus amounts paid by the employer for: (1) educational assistance excludable under a section 127 program (or that would be excludable but for the expiration of sec. 127); (2) health plan coverage for the employee, but not more than the applicable premium defined under section 4980B(f)(4); and (3) dependent care assistance excludable under section 129. The employer's deduction for wages is reduced by the amount of the credit.

Calculation of the credit

The welfare-to-work tax credit is available on an elective basis to employers of qualified long-term family assistance recipients during the first two years of employment. The maximum credit is 35 percent of the first $10,000 of qualified first-year wages and 50 percent of the first $10,000 of qualified second-year wages. Qualified first-year wages are defined as qualified wages (not in excess of $10,000) attributable to service rendered by a member of the targeted

group during the one-year period beginning with the day the individual began work for the employer. Qualified second-year wages are defined as qualified wages (not in excess of $10,000) attributable to service rendered by a member of the targeted group during the one-year period beginning immediately after the first year of that individual's employment for the employer. The maximum credit is $8,500 per qualified employee.

Certification rules

An individual is not treated as a member of the targeted group unless: (1) on or before the day on which an individual begins work for an employer, the employer has received a certification from a designated local agency that such individual is a member of the targeted group; or (2) on or before the day an individual is offered employment with the employer, a pre-screening notice is completed by the employer with respect to such individual, and not later than the 21st day after the individual begins work for the employer, the employer submits such notice, signed by the employer and the individual under penalties of perjury, to the designated local agency as part of a written request for certification.

Minimum employment period

No credit is allowed for qualified wages paid to a member of the targeted group unless the number they work is at least 400 hours or 180 days in the first year of employment.

Coordination of the work opportunity tax credit and the welfare-to-work tax credit

An employer cannot claim the work opportunity tax credit with respect to wages of any employee on which the employer claims the welfare-to-work tax credit.

Other rules

The welfare-to-work tax credit incorporates directly or by reference many of these other rules contained on the work opportunity tax credit.

Expiration

The welfare-to-work credit is not available for individuals who begin work for an employer after December 31, 2005.

Explanation of Provision

First year of extension

The provision extends the work opportunity tax credit and welfare-to-work tax credits for one year without modification, respectively (for qualified individuals who begin work for an employer after December 31, 2005 and before January 1, 2007).

Second year of extension

In general

The provision then combines and extends the two credits for a second year (for qualified individuals who begin work for an employer after December 31, 2006 and before January 1, 2008).

Targeted groups eligible for the combined credit

The combined credit is available on an elective basis for employers hiring individuals from one or more of all nine targeted groups. The nine targeted groups are the present-law eight groups with the addition of the welfare-to-work credit/long-term family assistance recipient as the ninth targeted group.

The provision repeals the requirement that a qualified ex-felon be an individual certified as a member of an economically disadvantaged family.

The provision raises the age limit for the food stamp recipient category to include individuals aged 18 but not aged 40 on the hiring date.

Qualified wages

Qualified first-year wages for the eight work opportunity tax credit categories remain capped at $6,000 ($3,000 for qualified summer youth employees). No credit is allowed for second-year wages. In the case of long-term family assistance recipients, the cap is $10,000 for both qualified first-year wages and qualified second-year wages. The combined credit follows the work opportunity tax credit definition of wages which does not include amounts paid by the employer for: (1) educational assistance excludable under a section 127 program (or that would be excludable but for the expiration of sec. 127); (2) health plan coverage for the employee, but not more than the applicable premium defined under section 4980B(f)(4); and (3) dependent care assistance excludable under section 129. For all targeted groups, the employer's deduction for wages is reduced by the amount of the credit.

Calculation of the credit

First-year wages.-For the eight work opportunity tax credit categories, the credit equals 40

percent (25 percent for employment of 400 hours or less) of qualified first-year wages. Generally, qualified first-year wages are qualified wages (not in excess of $6,000) attributable to service rendered by a member of a targeted group during the one-year period beginning with the day the individual began work for the employer. Therefore, the maximum credit per employee for members of any of the eight work opportunity tax credit targeted groups generally is $2,400 (40 percent of the first $6,000 of qualified first-year wages). With respect to qualified summer youth employees, the maximum credit remains $1,200 (40 percent of the first $3,000 of qualified first-year wages). For the welfare-to-work/long-term family assistance recipients, the maximum credit equals $4,000 per employee (40 percent of $10,000 of wages).

Second year wages.-In the case of long-term family assistance recipients the maximum credit is $5,000 (50 percent of the first $10,000 of qualified second-year wages).

Certification rules

The provision changes the present-law 21-day requirement to 28 days.

Minimum employment period

No credit is allowed for qualified wages paid to employees who work less than 120 hours in the first year of employment.

Coordination of the work opportunity tax credit and the welfare-to-work tax credit

Coordination is no longer necessary once the two credits are combined.

Effective Date

Generally, the extension of the credits is effective for wages paid or incurred to a qualified individual who begins work for an employer after December 31, 2005, and before January 1, 2008. The consolidation of the credits and other modifications are effective for wages paid or incurred to a qualified individual who begins work for an employer after December 31, 2006, and before January 1, 2008.

[Law at ¶5052 and ¶5053. CCH Explanation at ¶410.]

[¶15,150] Act Sec. 106. Election to treat combat pay as earned income for purposes of the earned income credit

Joint Committee Taxation (J.C.T. REP. No. JCX-50-06)

[Code Sec. 32]

Present Law

In general

Subject to certain limitations, military compensation earned by members of the Armed Forces while serving in a combat zone may be excluded from gross income. In addition, for up to two years following service in a combat zone, military personnel may also exclude compensation earned while hospitalized from wounds, disease, or injuries incurred while serving in the zone.

Child credit

Combat pay that is otherwise excluded from gross income under section 112 is treated as earned income which is taken into account in computing taxable income for purposes of calculating the refundable portion of the child credit.

Earned income credit

Any taxpayer may elect to treat combat pay that is otherwise excluded from gross income under section 112 as earned income for purposes of the earned income credit. This election is available with respect to any taxable year ending after the date of enactment and before January 1, 2007.

Explanation of Provision

The provision extends for one year (through December 31, 2007) the availability of the election to treat combat pay that is otherwise excluded from gross income under section 112 as earned income for purposes of the earned income credit.

Effective Date

The provision is effective in taxable years beginning after December 31, 2006.

[Law at ¶5032. CCH Explanation at ¶225.]

[¶15,160] Act Sec. 107. Extension and modification of qualified zone academy bonds

Joint Committee Taxation (J.C.T. REP. No. JCX-50-06)

[Code Sec. 1397E]

Present Law

Tax-exempt bonds

Interest on State and local governmental bonds generally is excluded from gross income for Federal income tax purposes if the proceeds of the bonds are used to finance direct activities of these governmental units or if the bonds are repaid with revenues of these governmental units. Activities that can be financed with these tax-exempt bonds include the financing of public schools.

An issuer must file with the IRS certain information in order for a bond issue to be tax-exempt.[11] Generally, this information return is required to be filed no later the 15th day of the second month after the close of the calendar quarter in which the bonds were issued.

Qualified zone academy bonds

As an alternative to traditional tax-exempt bonds, the Code permits three types of tax-credit bonds. States and local governments have the authority to issue qualified zone academy bonds ("QZABS"), clean renewable energy bonds ("CREBS"), and "Gulf tax credit bonds."[12] In lieu of tax-exempt interest, these bonds entitle eligible holders to a tax credit.

QZABs are defined as any bond issued by a State or local government, provided that: (1) at least 95 percent of the proceeds are used for the purpose of renovating, providing equipment to, developing course materials for use at, or train-

---

[11] Sec. 149(e).

[12] Secs. 1397E, 54, and 1400N(l), respectively.

ing teachers and other school personnel in a "qualified zone academy" ("qualified zone academy property") and (2) private entities have promised to contribute to the qualified zone academy certain equipment, technical assistance or training, employee services, or other property or services with a value equal to at least 10 percent of the bond proceeds.

A school is a "qualified zone academy" if: (1) the school is a public school that provides education and training below the college level, (2) the school operates a special academic program in cooperation with businesses to enhance the academic curriculum and increase graduation and employment rates, and (3) either (a) the school is located in an empowerment zone or enterprise community designated under the Code or (b) it is reasonably expected that at least 35 percent of the students at the school will be eligible for free or reduced-cost lunches under the school lunch program established under the National School Lunch Act.

A total of $400 million of QZABs may be issued annually in calendar years 1998 through 2005. The $400 million aggregate bond cap is allocated each year to the States according to their respective populations of individuals below the poverty line. Each State, in turn, allocates the issuance authority to qualified zone academies within such State.

Financial institutions (banks, insurance companies, and corporations in the business of lending money) are the only taxpayers eligible to hold QZABs. An eligible taxpayer holding a QZAB on the credit allowance date is entitled to a credit. The credit is an amount equal to a credit rate multiplied by the face amount of the bond. The credit is includable in gross income (as if it were a taxable interest payment on the bond), and may be claimed against regular income tax and AMT liability.

The Treasury Department sets the credit rate on QZABs at a rate estimated to allow issuance of the bonds without discount and without interest cost to the issuer. The maximum term of the bond is determined by the Treasury Department, so that the present value of the obligation to repay the bond is 50 percent of the face value of the bond.

Issuers of QZABs are not required to report issuance of such bonds to the IRS under present law.

Arbitrage restrictions on tax-exempt bonds

To prevent States and local governments from issuing more tax-exempt bonds than is necessary for the activity being financed or from issuing such bonds earlier than needed for the purpose of the borrowing, the income exclusion for interest paid on States and local bonds does not apply to any arbitrage bond.[13] An arbitrage bond is defined as any bond that is part of an issue if any proceeds of the issue are reasonably expected to be used (or intentionally are used) to acquire higher yielding investments or to replace funds that are used to acquire higher yielding investments.[14] In general, arbitrage profits may be earned only during specified periods (e.g., defined "temporary periods" before funds are needed for the purpose of the borrowing) or on specified types of investments (e.g., "reasonably required reserve or replacement funds"). Subject to limited exceptions, profits that are earned during these periods or on such investments must be rebated to the Federal government. Under present law, the arbitrage rules apply to CREBs and Gulf tax credit bonds, but do not apply to QZABs.

Explanation of Provision

The provision extends the present-law provision for two years (through December 31, 2007).

In addition, the provision imposes the arbitrage requirements of section 148 that apply to interest-bearing tax-exempt bonds to QZABs. Principles under section 148 and the regulations thereunder shall apply for purposes of determining the yield restriction and arbitrage rebate requirements applicable to QZABs. For example, for arbitrage purposes, the yield on an issue of QZABs is computed by taking into account all payments of interest, if any, on such bonds, i.e., whether the bonds are issued at par, premium, or discount. However, for purposes of determining yield, the amount of the credit allowed to a taxpayer holding QZABs is not treated as interest, although such credit amount is treated as interest income to the taxpayer.

The provision also imposes new spending requirements for QZABs. An issuer of QZABs must reasonably expect to and actually spend 95 percent or more of the proceeds of such bonds on qualified zone academy property within the

---

[13] Sec. 103(b)(2).   [14] Sec. 148.

five-year period that begins on the date of issuance. To the extent less than 95 percent of the proceeds are used to finance qualified zone academy property during the five-year spending period, bonds will continue to qualify as QZABs if unspent proceeds are used within 90 days from the end of such five-year period to redeem any nonqualified bonds. For these purposes, the amount of nonqualified bonds is to be determined in the same manner as Treasury regulations under section 142. The provision provides that the five-year spending period may be extended by the Secretary if the issuer establishes that the failure to meet the spending requirement is due to reasonable cause and the related purposes for issuing the bonds will continue to proceed with due diligence.

Finally, issuers of QZABs are required to report issuance to the IRS in a manner similar to the information returns required for tax-exempt bonds.

Effective Date

The provision extending issuance authority is effective for obligations issued after December 31, 2005. The provisions imposing arbitrage restrictions, reporting requirements, and spending requirements apply to obligations issued after the date of enactment with respect to allocations of the annual aggregate bond cap for calendar years after 2005.

[Law at ¶5055, ¶5608 and ¶5626. CCH Explanation at ¶605.]

[¶15,170] Act Sec. 108. Above-the-line deduction for certain expenses of elementary and secondary school teachers

Joint Committee Taxation (J.C.T. REP. No. JCX-50-06)

[Code Sec. 62]

Present Law

In general, ordinary and necessary business expenses are deductible (sec. 162). However, in general, unreimbursed employee business expenses are deductible only as an itemized deduction and only to the extent that the individual's total miscellaneous deductions (including employee business expenses) exceed two percent of adjusted gross income. An individual's otherwise allowable itemized deductions may be further limited by the overall limitation on itemized deductions, which reduces itemized deductions for taxpayers with adjusted gross income in excess of $150,500 (for 2006).[15] In addition, miscellaneous itemized deductions are not allowable under the alternative minimum tax.

Certain expenses of eligible educators are allowed an above-the-line deduction. Specifically, for taxable years beginning after December 31, 2001, and prior to January 1, 2006, an above-the-line deduction is allowed for up to $250 annually of expenses paid or incurred by an eligible educator for books, supplies (other than nonathletic supplies for courses of instruction in health or physical education), computer equipment (including related software and services) and other equipment, and supplementary materials used by the eligible educator in the class-

room. To be eligible for this deduction, the expenses must be otherwise deductible under 162 as a trade or business expense. A deduction is allowed only to the extent the amount of expenses exceeds the amount excludable from income under section 135 (relating to education savings bonds), 529(c)(1) (relating to qualified tuition programs), and section 530(d)(2) (relating to Coverdell education savings accounts).

An eligible educator is a kindergarten through grade 12 teacher, instructor, counselor, principal, or aide in a school for at least 900 hours during a school year. A school means any school which provides elementary education or secondary education, as determined under State law.

The above-the-line deduction for eligible educators is not allowed for taxable years beginning after December 31, 2005.

Explanation of Provision

The present-law provision is extended for two years, through December 31, 2007.

Effective Date

The provision is effective for expenses paid or incurred in taxable years beginning after December 31, 2005.

[Law at ¶5085. CCH Explanation at ¶215.]

---

[15] The adjusted income threshold is $75,250 in the case of a married individual filing a separate return (for 2006). For 2007, the adjusted income threshold is $156,400 ($78,200 for a married individual filing a separate return).

[¶15,180] Act Sec. 109. Extension and expansion to petroleum products of expensing for environmental remediation costs

Joint Committee Taxation (J.C.T. REP. No. JCX-50-06)

[Code Sec. 198]

Present Law

Present law allows a deduction for ordinary and necessary expenses paid or incurred in carrying on any trade or business.[16] Treasury regulations provide that the cost of incidental repairs that neither materially add to the value of property nor appreciably prolong its life, but keep it in an ordinarily efficient operating condition, may be deducted currently as a business expense. Section 263(a)(1) limits the scope of section 162 by prohibiting a current deduction for certain capital expenditures. Treasury regulations define "capital expenditures" as amounts paid or incurred to materially add to the value, or substantially prolong the useful life, of property owned by the taxpayer, or to adapt property to a new or different use. Amounts paid for repairs and maintenance do not constitute capital expenditures. The determination of whether an expense is deductible or capitalizable is based on the facts and circumstances of each case.

Taxpayers may elect to treat certain environmental remediation expenditures that would otherwise be chargeable to capital account as deductible in the year paid or incurred.[17] The deduction applies for both regular and alternative minimum tax purposes. The expenditure must be incurred in connection with the abatement or control of hazardous substances at a qualified contaminated site. In general, any expenditure for the acquisition of depreciable property used in connection with the abatement or control of hazardous substances at a qualified contaminated site does not constitute a qualified environmental remediation expenditure. However, depreciation deductions allowable for such property, which would otherwise be allocated to the site under the principles set forth in *Commissioner v. Idaho Power Co.*[18] and section 263A, are treated as qualified environmental remediation expenditures.

A "qualified contaminated site" (a so-called "brownfield") generally is any property that is held for use in a trade or business, for the production of income, or as inventory and is certified by the appropriate State environmental agency to be an area at or on which there has been a release (or threat of release) or disposal of a hazardous substance. Both urban and rural property may qualify. However, sites that are identified on the national priorities list under the Comprehensive Environmental Response, Compensation, and Liability Act of 1980 ("CERCLA")[19] cannot qualify as targeted areas. Hazardous substances generally are defined by reference to sections 101(14) and 102 of CERCLA, subject to additional limitations applicable to asbestos and similar substances within buildings, certain naturally occurring substances such as radon, and certain other substances released into drinking water supplies due to deterioration through ordinary use. Petroleum products generally are not regarded as hazardous substances for purposes of section 198 (except for purposes of determining qualified environmental remediation expenditures in the "Gulf Opportunity Zone" under section 1400N(g), as described below).[20]

In the case of property to which a qualified environmental remediation expenditure otherwise would have been capitalized, any deduction allowed under section 198 is treated as a depreciation deduction and the property is treated as section 1245 property. Thus, deductions for qualified environmental remediation expenditures are subject to recapture as ordinary income upon a sale or other disposition of the property. In addition, sections 280B (demolition of structures) and 468 (special rules for mining and solid waste reclamation and closing costs) do not apply to amounts that are treated as expenses under this provision.

Eligible expenditures are those paid or incurred before January 1, 2006.

Under section 1400N(g), the above provisions apply to expenditures paid or incurred to abate contamination at qualified contaminated

---

[16] Sec. 162.
[17] Sec. 198.
[18] 418 U.S. 1 (1974).
[19] Pub. L. No. 96-510 (1980).
[20] Section 101(14) of CERCLA specifically excludes "petroleum, including crude oil or any fraction thereof which is

not otherwise specifically listed or designated as a hazardous substance under subparagraphs (A) through (F) of this paragraph," from the definition of "hazardous substance."

sites in the Gulf Opportunity Zone (defined as that portion of the Hurricane Katrina Disaster Area determined by the President to warrant individual or individual and public assistance from the Federal government under the Robert T. Stafford Disaster Relief and Emergency Assistance Act by reason of Hurricane Katrina) before January 1, 2008; in addition, within the Gulf Opportunity Zone section 1400N(g) broadens the definition of hazardous substance to include petroleum products (defined by reference to section 4612(a)(3)).

Explanation of Provision

The provision extends for two years the present-law provisions relating to environmental remediation expenditures (through December 31, 2007).

In addition, the provision expands the definition of hazardous substance to include petroleum products. Under the provision, petroleum products are defined by reference to section 4612(a)(3), and thus include crude oil, crude oil condensates and natural gasoline.[21]

Effective Date

The provision applies to expenditures paid or incurred after December 31, 2005, and before January 1, 2008.

[Law at ¶ 5320. CCH Explanation at ¶ 310.]

[¶ 15,190] Act Sec. 110. Tax incentives for investment in the District of Columbia

Joint Committee Taxation (J.C.T. REP. No. JCX-50-06)

[Code Secs. 1400, 1400A, 1400B and 1400C]

Present Law

In general

The Taxpayer Relief Act of 1997 designated certain economically depressed census tracts within the District of Columbia as the District of Columbia Enterprise Zone (the "D.C. Zone"), within which businesses and individual residents are eligible for special tax incentives. The census tracts that compose the D.C. Zone are (1) all census tracts that presently are part of the D.C. enterprise community designated under section 1391 (i.e., portions of Anacostia, Mt. Pleasant, Chinatown, and the easternmost part of the District), and (2) all additional census tracts within the District of Columbia where the poverty rate is not less than 20 percent. The D.C. Zone designation remains in effect for the period from January 1, 1998, through December 31, 2005. In general, the tax incentives available in connection with the D.C. Zone are a 20-percent wage credit, an additional $35,000 of section 179 expensing for qualified zone property, expanded tax-exempt financing for certain zone facilities, and a zero-percent capital gains rate from the sale of certain qualified D.C. zone assets.

Wage credit

A 20-percent wage credit is available to employers for the first $15,000 of qualified wages paid to each employee (i.e., a maximum credit of $3,000 with respect to each qualified employee) who (1) is a resident of the D.C. Zone, and (2) performs substantially all employment services within the D.C. Zone in a trade or business of the employer.

Wages paid to a qualified employee who earns more than $15,000 are eligible for the wage credit (although only the first $15,000 of wages is eligible for the credit). The wage credit is available with respect to a qualified full-time or part-time employee (employed for at least 90 days), regardless of the number of other employees who work for the employer. In general, any taxable business carrying out activities in the D.C. Zone may claim the wage credit, regardless of whether the employer meets the definition of a "D.C. Zone business."[22]

An employer's deduction otherwise allowed for wages paid is reduced by the amount of wage credit claimed for that taxable year.[23] Wages are not to be taken into account for purposes of the wage credit if taken into account in

---

[21] The present law exceptions for sites on the national priorities list under CERCLA, and for substances with respect to which a removal or remediation is not permitted under section 104 of CERCLA by reason of subsection (a)(3) thereof, would continue to apply to all hazardous substances (including petroleum products).

[22] However, the wage credit is not available for wages paid in connection with certain business activities described

in section 144(c)(6)(B) or certain farming activities. In addition, wages are not eligible for the wage credit if paid to (1) a person who owns more than five percent of the stock (or capital or profits interests) of the employer, (2) certain relatives of the employer, or (3) if the employer is a corporation or partnership, certain relatives of a person who owns more than 50 percent of the business.

[23] Sec. 280C(a).

determining the employer's work opportunity tax credit under section 51 or the welfare-to-work credit under section 51A.[24] In addition, the $15,000 cap is reduced by any wages taken into account in computing the work opportunity tax credit or the welfare-to-work credit.[25] The wage credit may be used to offset up to 25 percent of alternative minimum tax liability.[26]

Section 179 expensing

In general, a D.C. Zone business is allowed an additional $35,000 of section 179 expensing for qualifying property placed in service by a D.C. Zone business.[27] The section 179 expensing allowed to a taxpayer is phased out by the amount by which 50 percent of the cost of qualified zone property placed in service during the year by the taxpayer exceeds $200,000 ($400,000 for taxable years beginning after 2002 and before 2010). The term "qualified zone property" is defined as depreciable tangible property (including buildings), provided that (1) the property is acquired by the taxpayer (from an unrelated party) after the designation took effect, (2) the original use of the property in the D.C. Zone commences with the taxpayer, and (3) substantially all of the use of the property is in the D.C. Zone in the active conduct of a trade or business by the taxpayer.[28] Special rules are provided in the case of property that is substantially renovated by the taxpayer.

Tax-exempt financing

A qualified D.C. Zone business is permitted to borrow proceeds from tax-exempt qualified enterprise zone facility bonds (as defined in section 1394) issued by the District of Columbia.[29] Such bonds are subject to the District of Columbia's annual private activity bond volume limitation. Generally, qualified enterprise zone facility bonds for the District of Columbia are bonds 95 percent or more of the net proceeds of which are used to finance certain facilities within the D.C. Zone. The aggregate face amount of all outstanding qualified enterprise zone facility bonds per qualified D.C. Zone business may not exceed $15 million and may be issued only while the D.C. Zone designation is in effect.

Zero-percent capital gains

A zero-percent capital gains rate applies to capital gains from the sale of certain qualified D.C. Zone assets held for more than five years.[30] In general, a qualified "D.C. Zone asset" means stock or partnership interests held in, or tangible property held by, a D.C. Zone business. For purposes of the zero-percent capital gains rate, the D.C. Enterprise Zone is defined to include all census tracts within the District of Columbia where the poverty rate is not less than 10 percent.

In general, gain eligible for the zero-percent tax rate means gain from the sale or exchange of a qualified D.C. Zone asset that is (1) a capital asset or property used in the trade or business as defined in section 1231(b), and (2) acquired before January 1, 2006. Gain that is attributable to real property, or to intangible assets, qualifies for the zero-percent rate, provided that such real property or intangible asset is an integral part of a qualified D.C. Zone business.[31] However, no gain attributable to periods before January 1, 1998, and after December 31, 2010, is qualified capital gain.

District of Columbia homebuyer tax credit

First-time homebuyers of a principal residence in the District of Columbia are eligible for a nonrefundable tax credit of up to $5,000 of the amount of the purchase price. The $5,000 maximum credit applies both to individuals and married couples. Married individuals filing separately can claim a maximum credit of $2,500 each. The credit phases out for individual taxpayers with adjusted gross income between $70,000 and $90,000 ($110,000-$130,000 for joint filers). For purposes of eligibility, "first-time homebuyer" means any individual if such individual did not have a present ownership interest in a principal residence in the District of Columbia in the one-year period ending on the date of the purchase of the residence to which the credit applies. The credit expired for purchases after December 31, 2005.[32]

Explanation of Provision

The provision extends the designation of the D.C. Zone for two years (through December 31, 2007), thus extending the wage credit and section 179 expensing for two years.

The provision extends the tax-exempt financing authority for two years, applying to

---

[24] Secs. 1400H(a), 1396(c)(3)(A) and 51A(d)(2).

[25] Secs. 1400H(a), 1396(c)(3)(B) and 51A(d)(2).

[26] Sec. 38(c)(2).

[27] Sec. 1397A.

[28] Sec. 1397D.

[29] Sec. 1400A.

[30] Sec. 1400B.

[31] However, sole proprietorships and other taxpayers selling assets directly cannot claim the zero-percent rate on capital gain from the sale of any intangible property (i.e., the integrally related test does not apply).

[32] Sec. 1400C(i).

bonds issued during the period beginning on January 1, 1998, and ending on December 31, 2007.

The provision extends the zero-percent capital gains rate applicable to capital gains from the sale of certain qualified D.C. Zone assets for two years.

The provision extends the first-time homebuyer credit for two years, through December 31, 2007.

Effective Date

The provision is effective for periods beginning after, bonds issued after, acquisitions after, and property purchased after December 31, 2005.

[Law at ¶5611, ¶5614, ¶5617, ¶5620 and ¶5623. CCH Explanation at ¶340.]

[¶15,200] Act Sec. 111. Indian employment tax credit

Joint Committee Taxation (J.C.T. Rep. No. JCX-50-06)

[Code Sec. 45A]

Present Law

In general, a credit against income tax liability is allowed to employers for the first $20,000 of qualified wages and qualified employee health insurance costs paid or incurred by the employer with respect to certain employees (sec. 45A). The credit is equal to 20 percent of the excess of eligible employee qualified wages and health insurance costs during the current year over the amount of such wages and costs incurred by the employer during 1993. The credit is an incremental credit, such that an employer's current-year qualified wages and qualified employee health insurance costs (up to $20,000 per employee) are eligible for the credit only to the extent that the sum of such costs exceeds the sum of comparable costs paid during 1993. No deduction is allowed for the portion of the wages equal to the amount of the credit.

Qualified wages means wages paid or incurred by an employer for services performed by a qualified employee. A qualified employee means any employee who is an enrolled member of an Indian tribe or the spouse of an enrolled member of an Indian tribe, who performs substantially all of the services within an Indian reservation, and whose principal place of abode while performing such services is on or near the reservation in which the services are performed. An "Indian reservation" is a reservation as defined in section 3(d) of the Indian Financing Act of 1974 or section 4(1) of the Indian Child Welfare Act of 1978. For purposes of the preceding sentence, section 3(d) is applied by treating "former Indian reservations in Oklahoma" as including only lands that are (1) within the jurisdictional area of an Oklahoma Indian tribe as determined by the Secretary of the Interior,

and (2) recognized by such Secretary as an area eligible for trust land status under 25 C.F.R. Part 151 (as in effect on August 5, 1997).

An employee is not treated as a qualified employee for any taxable year of the employer if the total amount of wages paid or incurred by the employer with respect to such employee during the taxable year exceeds an amount determined at an annual rate of $30,000 (which after adjusted for inflation after 1993 is currently $35,000). In addition, an employee will not be treated as a qualified employee under certain specific circumstances, such as where the employee is related to the employer (in the case of an individual employer) or to one of the employer's shareholders, partners, or grantors. Similarly, an employee will not be treated as a qualified employee where the employee has more than a 5 percent ownership interest in the employer. Finally, an employee will not be considered a qualified employee to the extent the employee's services relate to gaming activities or are performed in a building housing such activities.

The wage credit is available for wages paid or incurred on or after January 1, 1994, in taxable years that begin before January 1, 2006.

Explanation of Provision

The provision extends for two years the present-law employment credit provision (through taxable years beginning on or before December 31, 2007).

Effective Date

The provision is effective for taxable years beginning after December 31, 2005.

[Law at ¶5040. CCH Explanation at ¶420.]

[¶15,210] Act Sec. 112. Accelerated depreciation for business property on Indian reservations

Joint Committee Taxation (J.C.T. REP. NO. JCX-50-06)

[Code Sec. 168]

Present Law

With respect to certain property used in connection with the conduct of a trade or business within an Indian reservation, depreciation deductions under section 168(j) are determined using the following recovery periods:

3-year property	2 years
5-year property	3 years
7-year property	4 years
10-year property	6 years
15-year property	9 years
20-year property	12 years
Nonresidential real property	22 years

"Qualified Indian reservation property" eligible for accelerated depreciation includes property which is (1) used by the taxpayer predominantly in the active conduct of a trade or business within an Indian reservation, (2) not used or located outside the reservation on a regular basis, (3) not acquired (directly or indirectly) by the taxpayer from a person who is related to the taxpayer (within the meaning of section 465(b)(3)(C)), and (4) described in the recovery-period table above. In addition, property is not "qualified Indian reservation property" if it is placed in service for purposes of conducting gaming activities. Certain "qualified infrastructure property" may be eligible for the accelerated depreciation even if located outside an Indian reservation, provided that the purpose of such property is to connect with qualified infrastructure property located within the reservation (e.g., roads, power lines, water systems, railroad spurs, and communications facilities).

An "Indian reservation" means a reservation as defined in section 3(d) of the Indian Financing Act of 1974 or section 4(1) of the Indian Child Welfare Act of 1978. For purposes of the preceding sentence, section 3(d) is applied by treating "former Indian reservations in Oklahoma" as including only lands that are (1) within the jurisdictional area of an Oklahoma Indian tribe as determined by the Secretary of the Interior, and (2) recognized by such Secretary as an area eligible for trust land status under 25 C.F.R. Part 151 (as in effect on August 5, 1997).

The depreciation deduction allowed for regular tax purposes is also allowed for purposes of the alternative minimum tax. The accelerated depreciation for Indian reservation property is available with respect to property placed in service on or after January 1, 1994, and before January 1, 2006.

Explanation of Provision

The provision extends for two years the present-law incentive relating to depreciation of qualified Indian reservation property (to apply to property placed in service through December 31, 2007).

Effective Date

The provision applies to property placed in service after December 31, 2005.

[Law at ¶5265. CCH Explanation at ¶320.]

[¶15,220] Act Sec. 113. Fifteen-year straight-line cost recovery for qualified leasehold improvements and qualified restaurant property

Joint Committee Taxation (J.C.T. REP. NO. JCX-50-06)

[Code Sec. 168]

Present Law

In general

A taxpayer generally must capitalize the cost of property used in a trade or business and recover such cost over time through annual deductions for depreciation or amortization. Tangible property generally is depreciated under the modified accelerated cost recovery system ("MACRS"), which determines depreciation by applying specific recovery periods, placed-in-service conventions, and depreciation methods to the cost of various types of depreciable property (sec. 168). The cost of nonresidential real property is recovered using the straight-line method of depreciation and a recovery period of 39 years. Nonresidential real property is subject to the mid-month placed-in-service convention. Under the mid-month convention, the depreciation allowance for the first year property is placed in service is based on the number of months the property was in service, and property placed in service at any time during a month is treated as having been placed in service in the middle of the month.

Depreciation of leasehold improvements

Generally, depreciation allowances for improvements made on leased property are determined under MACRS, even if the MACRS recovery period assigned to the property is longer than the term of the lease. This rule applies regardless of whether the lessor or the lessee places the leasehold improvements in service. If a leasehold improvement constitutes an addition or improvement to nonresidential real property already placed in service, the improvement generally is depreciated using the straight-line method over a 39-year recovery period, beginning in the month the addition or improvement was placed in service. However, exceptions exist for certain qualified leasehold improvements and certain qualified restaurant property.

Qualified leasehold improvement property

Section 168(e)(3)(E)(iv) provides a statutory 15-year recovery period for qualified leasehold improvement property placed in service before January 1, 2006. Qualified leasehold improvement property is recovered using the straight-line method. Leasehold improvements placed in service in 2006 and later are subject to the general rules described above.

Qualified leasehold improvement property is any improvement to an interior portion of a building that is nonresidential real property, provided certain requirements are met. The improvement must be made under or pursuant to a lease either by the lessee (or sublessee), or by the lessor, of that portion of the building to be occupied exclusively by the lessee (or sublessee). The improvement must be placed in service more than three years after the date the building was first placed in service. Qualified leasehold improvement property does not include any improvement for which the expenditure is attributable to the enlargement of the building, any elevator or escalator, any structural component benefiting a common area, or the internal structural framework of the building. However, if a lessor makes an improvement that qualifies as qualified leasehold improvement property, such improvement does not qualify as qualified leasehold improvement property to any subsequent owner of such improvement. An exception to the rule applies in the case of death and certain transfers of property that qualify for nonrecognition treatment.

Qualified restaurant property

Section 168(e)(3)(E)(v) provides a statutory 15-year recovery period for qualified restaurant property placed in service before January 1, 2006. For purposes of the provision, qualified restaurant property means any improvement to a building if such improvement is placed in service more than three years after the date such building was first placed in service and more than 50 percent of the building's square footage is devoted to the preparation of, and seating for on-premises consumption of, prepared meals. Qualified restaurant property is recovered using the straight-line method.

Explanation of Provision

The present-law provisions are extended for two years (through December 31, 2007).

Effective Date

The provision applies to property placed in service after December 31, 2005.

[Law at ¶5265. CCH Explanation at ¶305.]

[¶15,230] Act Sec. 114. Suspend limitation on rate of rum excise tax cover over to Puerto Rico and Virgin Islands

Joint Committee Taxation (J.C.T. REP. NO. JCX-50-06)

[Code Sec. 7652]

Present Law

A $13.50 per proof gallon[33] excise tax is imposed on distilled spirits produced in or imported (or brought) into the United States.[34] The excise tax does not apply to distilled spirits that are exported from the United States, including exports to U.S. possessions (e.g., Puerto Rico and the Virgin Islands).[35]

The Code provides for cover over (payment) to Puerto Rico and the Virgin Islands of the excise tax imposed on rum imported (or brought) into the United States, without regard to the country of origin.[36] The amount of the cover over is limited under Code section 7652(f) to $10.50 per proof gallon ($13.25 per proof gallon during the period July 1, 1999 through December 31, 2005).

Tax amounts attributable to shipments to the United States of rum produced in Puerto Rico are covered over to Puerto Rico. Tax amounts attributable to shipments to the United States of rum produced in the Virgin Islands are covered over to the Virgin Islands. Tax amounts attributable to shipments to the United States of rum produced in neither Puerto Rico nor the Virgin Islands are divided and covered over to the two possessions under a formula.[37] Amounts covered over to Puerto Rico and the Virgin Islands are deposited into the treasuries of the two possessions for use as those possessions determine.[38] All of the amounts covered over are subject to the limitation.

Explanation of Provision

The provision temporarily suspends the $10.50 per proof gallon limitation on the amount of excise taxes on rum covered over to Puerto Rico and the Virgin Islands. Under the provision, the cover over amount of $13.25 per proof gallon is extended for rum brought into the United States after December 31, 2005 and before January 1, 2008. After December 31, 2007, the cover over amount reverts to $10.50 per proof gallon.

Effective Date

The changes in the cover over rate are effective for articles brought into the United States after December 31, 2005.

[Law at ¶5850. CCH Explanation at ¶690.]

[¶15,240] Act Sec. 115. Parity in the application of certain limits to mental health benefits

Joint Committee Taxation (J.C.T. REP. NO. JCX-50-06)

[Code Sec. 9812(f)(3)]

Present Law

The Code, the Employee Retirement Income Security Act of 1974 ("ERISA") and the Public Health Service Act ("PHSA") contain provisions under which group health plans that provide both medical and surgical benefits and mental health benefits cannot impose aggregate lifetime or annual dollar limits on mental health benefits that are not imposed on substantially all medical and surgical benefits ("mental health parity requirements"). In the case of a group health plan which provides benefits for mental health, the

---

[33] A proof gallon is a liquid gallon consisting of 50 percent alcohol. *See* sec. 5002(a)(10) and (11).

[34] Sec. 5001(a)(1).

[35] Secs. 5062(b), 7653(b) and (c).

[36] Secs. 7652(a)(3), (b)(3), and (e)(1). One percent of the amount of excise tax collected from imports into the United

States of articles produced in the Virgin Islands is retained by the United States under section 7652(b)(3).

[37] Sec. 7652(e)(2).

[38] Secs. 7652(a)(3), (b)(3), and (e)(1).

mental health parity requirements do not affect the terms and conditions (including cost sharing, limits on numbers of visits or days of coverage, and requirements relating to medical necessity) relating to the amount, duration, or scope of mental health benefits under the plan, except as specifically provided in regard to parity in the imposition of aggregate lifetime limits and annual limits.

The Code imposes an excise tax on group health plans which fail to meet the mental health parity requirements. The excise tax is equal to $100 per day during the period of noncompliance and is generally imposed on the employer sponsoring the plan if the plan fails to meet the requirements. The maximum tax that can be imposed during a taxable year cannot exceed the lesser of 10 percent of the employer's group health plan expenses for the prior year or $500,000. No tax is imposed if the Secretary determines that the employer did not know, and in exercising reasonable diligence would not have known, that the failure existed.

The mental health parity requirements do not apply to group health plans of small employ-

ers nor do they apply if their application results in an increase in the cost under a group health plan of at least one percent. Further, the mental health parity requirements do not require group health plans to provide mental health benefits.

The Code, ERISA and PHSA mental health parity requirements are scheduled to expire with respect to benefits for services furnished after December 31, 2006.

Explanation of Provision

The provision extends the present-law Code excise tax for failure to comply with the mental health parity requirements through December 31, 2007. It also extends the ERISA and PHSA requirements through December 31, 2007.

Effective Date

The provision is effective on the date of enactment.

[Law at ¶5920 and ¶7040. CCH Explanation at ¶535.]

[¶15,250] Act Sec. 116. Expand charitable contribution allowed for scientific property used for research and expand and extend the charitable contribution allowed computer technology and equipment

Joint Committee Taxation (J.C.T. REP. No. JCX-50-06)

[Code Sec. 170]

Present Law

In the case of a charitable contribution of inventory or other ordinary-income or short-term capital gain property, the amount of the charitable deduction generally is limited to the taxpayer's basis in the property. In the case of a charitable contribution of tangible personal property, the deduction is limited to the taxpayer's basis in such property if the use by the recipient charitable organization is unrelated to the organization's tax-exempt purpose. In cases involving contributions to a private foundation (other than certain private operating foundations), the amount of the deduction is limited to the taxpayer's basis in the property.[39]

Under present law, a taxpayer's deduction for charitable contributions of scientific property used for research and for contributions of computer technology and equipment generally is

limited to the taxpayer's basis (typically, cost) in the property. However, certain corporations may claim a deduction in excess of basis for a "qualified research contribution" or a "qualified computer contribution."[40] This enhanced deduction is equal to the lesser of (1) basis plus one-half of the item's appreciation (i.e., basis plus one half of fair market value in excess of basis) or (2) two times basis. The enhanced deduction for qualified computer contributions expired for any contribution made during any taxable year beginning after December 31, 2005.

A qualified research contribution means a charitable contribution of inventory that is tangible personal property. The contribution must be to a qualified educational or scientific organization and be made not later than two years after construction of the property is substantially completed. The original use of the property must be by the donee, and be used substantially for research or experimentation, or for research train-

---

[39] Sec. 170(e)(1).

[40] Secs. 170(e)(4) and 170(e)(6).

ing, in the U.S. in the physical or biological sciences. The property must be scientific equipment or apparatus, constructed by the taxpayer, and may not be transferred by the donee in exchange for money, other property, or services. The donee must provide the taxpayer with a written statement representing that it will use the property in accordance with the conditions for the deduction. For purposes of the enhanced deduction, property is considered constructed by the taxpayer only if the cost of the parts used in the construction of the property (other than parts manufactured by the taxpayer or a related person) do not exceed 50 percent of the taxpayer's basis in the property.

A qualified computer contribution means a charitable contribution of any computer technology or equipment, which meets standards of functionality and suitability as established by the Secretary of the Treasury. The contribution must be to certain educational organizations or public libraries and made not later than three years after the taxpayer acquired the property or, if the taxpayer constructed the property, not later than the date construction of the property is substantially completed.[41] The original use of the property must be by the donor or the donee,[42] and in the case of the donee, must be used substantially for educational purposes related to the function or purpose of the donee. The property must fit productively into the donee's education plan. The donee may not transfer the property in ex-

change for money, other property, or services, except for shipping, installation, and transfer costs. To determine whether property is constructed by the taxpayer, the rules applicable to qualified research contributions apply. Contributions may be made to private foundations under certain conditions.[43]

Explanation of Provision

The provision extends the present-law provision relating to the enhanced deduction for computer technology and equipment for two years to apply to contributions made during any taxable year beginning after December 31, 2005, and before January 1, 2008.

Under the provision, property assembled by the taxpayer, in addition to property constructed by the taxpayer, is eligible for either the enhanced deduction relating to computer technology and equipment or to scientific property used for research. It is not intended that old or used components assembled by the taxpayer into scientific property or computer technology or equipment are eligible for the enhanced deduction.

Effective Date

The provision is effective for taxable years beginning after December 31, 2005.

[Law at ¶5280. CCH Explanation at ¶355.]

[¶15,260] Act Sec. 117. Availability of Archer medical savings accounts

Joint Committee Taxation (J.C.T. REP. No. JCX-50-06)

[Code Sec. 220]

Present Law

Archer medical savings accounts

In general

Within limits, contributions to an Archer medical savings account ("Archer MSA") are deductible in determining adjusted gross income if made by an eligible individual and are excludable from gross income and wages for employ-

ment tax purposes if made by the employer of an eligible individual. Earnings on amounts in an Archer MSA are not currently taxable. Distributions from an Archer MSA for medical expenses are not includible in gross income. Distributions not used for medical expenses are includible in gross income. In addition, distributions not used for medical expenses are subject to an additional 15-percent tax unless the distribution is made after age 65, death, or disability.

---

[41] If the taxpayer constructed the property and reacquired such property, the contribution must be within three years of the date the original construction was substantially completed. Sec. 170(e)(6)(D)(i).

[42] This requirement does not apply if the property was reacquired by the manufacturer and contributed. Sec. 170(e)(6)(D)(ii).

[43] Sec. 170(e)(6)(C).

Eligible individuals

Archer MSAs are available to employees covered under an employer-sponsored high deductible plan of a small employer and self-employed individuals covered under a high deductible health plan. An employer is a small employer if it employed, on average, no more than 50 employees on business days during either the preceding or the second preceding year. An individual is not eligible for an Archer MSA if he or she is covered under any other health plan in addition to the high deductible plan.

Tax treatment of and limits on contributions

Individual contributions to an Archer MSA are deductible (within limits) in determining adjusted gross income (i.e., "above-the-line"). In addition, employer contributions are excludable from gross income and wages for employment tax purposes (within the same limits), except that this exclusion does not apply to contributions made through a cafeteria plan. In the case of an employee, contributions can be made to an Archer MSA either by the individual or by the individual's employer.

The maximum annual contribution that can be made to an Archer MSA for a year is 65 percent of the deductible under the high deductible plan in the case of individual coverage and 75 percent of the deductible in the case of family coverage.

Definition of high deductible plan

A high deductible plan is a health plan with an annual deductible of at least $1,800 and no more than $2,700 in the case of individual coverage and at least $3,650 and no more than $5,450 in the case of family coverage (for 2006). In addition, the maximum out-of-pocket expenses with respect to allowed costs (including the deductible) must be no more than $3,650 in the case of individual coverage and no more than $6,650 in the case of family coverage (for 2006). A plan does not fail to qualify as a high deductible plan merely because it does not have a deductible for preventive care as required by State law. A plan does not qualify as a high deductible health plan if substantially all of the coverage under the plan is for certain permitted coverage. In the case of a self-insured plan, the plan must in fact be insurance (e.g., there must be appropriate risk shifting) and not merely a reimbursement arrangement.

Cap on taxpayers utilizing Archer MSAs and expiration of pilot program

The number of taxpayers benefiting annually from an Archer MSA contribution is limited to a threshold level (generally 750,000 taxpayers). The number of Archer MSAs established has not exceeded the threshold level.

After 2005, no new contributions may be made to Archer MSAs except by or on behalf of individuals who previously made (or had made on their behalf) Archer MSA contributions and employees who are employed by a participating employer.

Trustees of Archer MSAs are generally required to make reports to the Treasury by August 1 regarding Archer MSAs established by July 1 of that year. If the threshold level is reached in a year, the Secretary is required to make and publish such determination by October 1 of such year.

Health savings accounts

Health savings accounts ("HSAs") were enacted by the Medicare Prescription Drug, Improvement, and Modernization Act of 2003. Like Archer MSAs, an HSA is a tax-exempt trust or custodial account to which tax-deductible contributions may be made by individuals with a high deductible health plan. HSAs provide tax benefits similar to, but more favorable than, those provide by Archer MSAs. HSAs were established on a permanent basis.

Explanation of Provision

The provision extends for two years the present-law Archer MSA provisions (through December 31, 2007).

The report required by Archer MSA trustees to be made on August 1, 2005, or August 1, 2006, (as the case may be) is treated as timely filed if made before the close of the 90-day period beginning on the date of enactment. The determination and publication with respect to calendar year 2005 or 2006 whether the threshold level has been exceeded is treated as timely if made before the close of the 120-day period beginning on the date of enactment. If it is determined that 2005 or 2006 is a cut-off year, the cut-off date is the last date of such 120-day period.

Effective Date

The provision is effective on the date of enactment.

[Law at ¶5333 and ¶7045. CCH Explanation at ¶530.]

[¶15,270] Act Sec. 118. Taxable income limit on percentage depletion for oil and natural gas produced from marginal properties

Joint Committee Taxation (J.C.T. Rep. No. JCX-50-06)

[Code Sec. 613A]

Present Law

The Code permits taxpayers to recover their investments in oil and gas wells through depletion deductions. Two methods of depletion are currently allowable under the Code: (1) the cost depletion method, and (2) the percentage depletion method. Under the cost depletion method, the taxpayer deducts that portion of the adjusted basis of the depletable property which is equal to the ratio of units sold from that property during the taxable year to the number of units remaining as of the end of taxable year plus the number of units sold during the taxable year. Thus, the amount recovered under cost depletion may never exceed the taxpayer's basis in the property.

The Code generally limits the percentage depletion method for oil and gas properties to independent producers and royalty owners. Generally, under the percentage depletion method, 15 percent of the taxpayer's gross income from an oil- or gas-producing property is allowed as a deduction in each taxable year. The amount deducted generally may not exceed 100 percent of the taxable income from that property in any year. For marginal production, the 100-percent taxable income limitation has been

suspended for taxable years beginning after December 31, 1997, and before January 1, 2006.

Marginal production is defined as domestic crude oil and natural gas production from stripper well property or from property substantially all of the production from which during the calendar year is heavy oil. Stripper well property is property from which the average daily production is 15 barrel equivalents or less, determined by dividing the average daily production of domestic crude oil and domestic natural gas from producing wells on the property for the calendar year by the number of wells. Heavy oil is domestic crude oil with a weighted average gravity of 20 degrees API or less (corrected to 60 degrees Fahrenheit).

Explanation of Provision

The provision extends for two years the present-law taxable income limitation suspension provision for marginal production (through taxable years beginning on or before December 31, 2007).

Effective Date

The provision applies to taxable years beginning after December 31, 2005.

[Law at ¶5410. CCH Explanation at ¶325.]

[¶15,280] Act Sec. 119. Economic development credit with respect to American Samoa

Joint Committee Taxation (J.C.T. Rep. No. JCX-50-06)

[Act Sec. 119]

Present Law

In general

Certain domestic corporations with business operations in the U.S. possessions are eligible for the possession tax credit.[44] This credit offsets the U.S. tax imposed on certain income related to operations in the U.S. possessions.[45] For pur-

poses of the credit, possessions include, among other places, American Samoa. Subject to certain limitations described below, the amount of the possession tax credit allowed to any domestic corporation equals the portion of that corporation's U.S. tax that is attributable to the corporation's non-U.S. source taxable income from (1) the active conduct of a trade or business within a U.S. possession, (2) the sale or exchange of sub-

---

[44] Secs. 27(b), 936.

[45] Domestic corporations with activities in Puerto Rico are eligible for the section 30A economic activity credit. That credit is calculated under the rules set forth in section 936.

stantially all of the assets that were used in such a trade or business, or (3) certain possessions investment.[46] No deduction or foreign tax credit is allowed for any possessions or foreign tax paid or accrued with respect to taxable income that is taken into account in computing the credit under section 936.[47] The section 936 credit expires for taxable years beginning after December 31, 2005.

To qualify for the possession tax credit for a taxable year, a domestic corporation must satisfy two conditions. First, the corporation must derive at least 80 percent of its gross income for the three-year period immediately preceding the close of the taxable year from sources within a possession. Second, the corporation must derive at least 75 percent of its gross income for that same period from the active conduct of a possession business.

The possession tax credit is available only to a corporation that qualifies as an existing credit claimant. The determination of whether a corporation is an existing credit claimant is made separately for each possession. The possession tax credit is computed separately for each possession with respect to which the corporation is an existing credit claimant, and the credit is subject to either an economic activity-based limitation or an income-based limit.

Qualification as existing credit claimant

A corporation is an existing credit claimant with respect to a possession if (1) the corporation was engaged in the active conduct of a trade or business within the possession on October 13, 1995, and (2) the corporation elected the benefits of the possession tax credit in an election in effect for its taxable year that included October 13, 1995.[48] A corporation that adds a substantial new line of business (other than in a qualifying acquisition of all the assets of a trade or business of an existing credit claimant) ceases to be an existing credit claimant as of the close of the taxable year ending before the date on which that new line of business is added.

Economic activity-based limit

Under the economic activity-based limit, the amount of the credit determined under the rules described above may not exceed an amount equal to the sum of (1) 60 percent of the tax-payer's qualified possession wages and allocable employee fringe benefit expenses, (2) 15 percent of depreciation allowances with respect to short-life qualified tangible property, plus 40 percent of depreciation allowances with respect to medium-life qualified tangible property, plus 65 percent of depreciation allowances with respect to long-life qualified tangible property, and (3) in certain cases, a portion of the taxpayer's possession income taxes.

Income-based limit

As an alternative to the economic activity-based limit, a taxpayer may elect to apply a limit equal to the applicable percentage of the credit that would otherwise be allowable with respect to possession business income; the applicable percentage currently is 40 percent.

Repeal and phase out

In 1996, the section 936 credit was repealed for new claimants for taxable years beginning after 1995 and was phased out for existing credit claimants over a period including taxable years beginning before 2006. The amount of the available credit during the phase-out period generally is reduced by special limitation rules. These phase-out period limitation rules do not apply to the credit available to existing credit claimants for income from activities in Guam, American Samoa, and the Northern Mariana Islands. As described previously, the section 936 credit is repealed for all possessions, including Guam, American Samoa, and the Northern Mariana Islands, for all taxable years beginning after 2005.

Explanation of Provision

Under the provision, a domestic corporation that is an existing credit claimant with respect to American Samoa and that elected the application of section 936 for its last taxable year beginning before January 1, 2006 is allowed, for two taxable years, a credit based on the economic activity-based limitation rules described above. The credit is not part of the Code but is computed based on the rules secs. 30A and 936.

The amount of the credit allowed to a qualifying domestic corporation under the provision is equal to the sum of the amounts used in computing the corporation's economic activity-based limitation (described above in the present

---

[46] Under phase-out rules described below, investment only in Guam, American Samoa, and the Northern Mariana Islands (and not in other possessions) now may give rise to income eligible for the section 936 credit.

[47] Sec. 936(c).

[48] A corporation will qualify as an existing credit claimant if it acquired all the assets of a trade or business of a corporation that (1) actively conducted that trade or business in a possession on October 13, 1995, and (2) had elected the benefits of the possession tax credit in an election in effect for the taxable year that included October 13, 1995.

law section) with respect to American Samoa, except that no credit is allowed for the amount of any American Samoa income taxes. Thus, for any qualifying corporation the amount of the credit equals the sum of (1) 60 percent of the corporation's qualified American Samoa wages and allocable employee fringe benefit expenses and (2) 15 percent of the corporation's depreciation allowances with respect to short-life qualified American Samoa tangible property, plus 40 percent of the corporation's depreciation allowances with respect to medium-life qualified American Samoa tangible property, plus 65 percent of the corporation's depreciation allowances with respect to long-life qualified American Samoa tangible property.

The present-law section 936(c) rule denying a credit or deduction for any possessions or foreign tax paid with respect to taxable income taken into account in computing the credit under section 936 does not apply with respect to the credit allowed by the provision.

The two-year credit allowed by the provision is intended to provide additional time for the development of a comprehensive, long-term economic policy toward American Samoa. It is expected that in developing a long-term policy, non-tax policy alternatives should be carefully considered. It is expected that long-term policy toward the possessions should take into account the unique circumstances in each possession.

Effective Date

The provision is effective for the first two taxable years of a corporation which begin after December 31, 2005, and before January 1, 2008.

[Law at ¶7050. CCH Explanation at ¶435.]

[¶15,290] Act Sec. 120. Extension of placed-in-service deadline for certain Gulf Opportunity Zone property

Joint Committee Taxation (J.C.T. REP. No. JCX-50-06)

[Code Sec. 1400N]

Present Law

In general

A taxpayer is allowed to recover, through annual depreciation deductions, the cost of certain property used in a trade or business or for the production of income. The amount of the depreciation deduction allowed with respect to tangible property for a taxable year is determined under the modified accelerated cost recovery system ("MACRS"). Under MACRS, different types of property generally are assigned applicable recovery periods and depreciation methods. The recovery periods applicable to most tangible personal property (generally tangible property other than residential rental property and nonresidential real property) range from 3 to 25 years. The depreciation methods generally applicable to tangible personal property are the 200-percent and 150-percent declining balance methods, switching to the straight-line method for the taxable year in which the depreciation deduction would be maximized.

Gulf Opportunity Zone property

Present law provides an additional first-year depreciation deduction equal to 50 percent of the adjusted basis of qualified Gulf Opportunity Zone[49] property. In order to qualify, property generally must be placed in service on or before December 31, 2007 (December 31, 2008 in the case of nonresidential real property and residential rental property).

The additional first-year depreciation deduction is allowed for both regular tax and alternative minimum tax purposes for the taxable year in which the property is placed in service. The additional first-year depreciation deduction is subject to the general rules regarding whether an item is deductible under section 162 or subject to capitalization under section 263 or section 263A. The basis of the property and the depreciation allowances in the year of purchase and later years are appropriately adjusted to reflect the additional first-year depreciation deduction. In addition, the provision provides that there is no adjustment to the allowable amount of deprecia-

---

[49] The "Gulf Opportunity Zone" is defined as that portion of the Hurricane Katrina Disaster Area determined by the President to warrant individual or individual and public assistance from the Federal government under the Robert T. Stafford Disaster Relief and Emergency Assistance Act by reason of Hurricane Katrina. The term "Hurricane Katrina disaster area" means an area with respect to which a major disaster has been declared by the President before September 14, 2005, under section 401 of the Robert T. Stafford Disaster Relief and Emergency Assistance Act by reason of Hurricane Katrina.

tion for purposes of computing a taxpayer's alternative minimum taxable income with respect to property to which the provision applies. A taxpayer is allowed to elect out of the additional first-year depreciation for any class of property for any taxable year.

In order for property to qualify for the additional first-year depreciation deduction, it must meet all of the following requirements. First, the property must be property (1) to which the general rules of the Modified Accelerated Cost Recovery System ("MACRS") apply with an applicable recovery period of 20 years or less, (2) computer software other than computer software covered by section 197, (3) water utility property (as defined in section 168(e)(5)), (4) certain leasehold improvement property, or (5) certain nonresidential real property and residential rental property. Second, substantially all of the use of such property must be in the Gulf Opportunity Zone and in the active conduct of a trade or business by the taxpayer in the Gulf Opportunity Zone. Third, the original use of the property in the Gulf Opportunity Zone must commence with the taxpayer on or after August 28, 2005. (Thus, used property may constitute qualified property so long as it has not previously been used within the Gulf Opportunity Zone. In addition, it is intended that additional capital expenditures incurred to recondition or rebuild property the original use of which in the Gulf Opportunity Zone began with the taxpayer would satisfy the "original use" requirement. See Treasury Regulation 1.48-2 Example 5.) Finally, the property must be acquired by purchase (as defined under section 179(d)) by the taxpayer on or after August 28, 2005 and placed in service on or before December 31, 2007. For qualifying nonresidential real property and residential rental property, the property must be placed in service on or before December 31, 2008, in lieu of December 31, 2007. Property does not qualify if a binding written contract for the acquisition of such property was in effect before August 28, 2005. However, property is not precluded from qualifying for the additional first-year depreciation merely because a binding written contract to acquire a component of the property is in effect prior to August 28, 2005.

Property that is manufactured, constructed, or produced by the taxpayer for use by the taxpayer qualifies if the taxpayer begins the manufacture, construction, or production of the

property on or after August 28, 2005, and the property is placed in service on or before December 31, 2007 (and all other requirements are met). In the case of qualified nonresidential real property and residential rental property, the property must be placed in service on or before December 31, 2008. Property that is manufactured, constructed, or produced for the taxpayer by another person under a contract that is entered into prior to the manufacture, construction, or production of the property is considered to be manufactured, constructed, or produced by the taxpayer.

Under a special rule, property any portion of which is financed with the proceeds of a tax-exempt obligation under section 103 is not eligible for the additional first-year depreciation deduction. Recapture rules apply under the provision if the property ceases to be qualified Gulf Opportunity Zone property.

Explanation of Provision

The provision extends the placed-in-service deadline for specified Gulf Opportunity Zone extension property to qualify for the additional first-year depreciation deduction.[50] Specified Gulf Opportunity Zone extension property is defined as property substantially all the use of which is in one or more specified portions of the Gulf Opportunity Zone and which is either: (1) nonresidential real property or residential rental property which is placed in service by the taxpayer on or before December 31, 2010, or (2) in the case of a taxpayer who places in service a building described in (1), property described in section 168(k)(2)(A)(i)[51] if substantially all the use of such property is in such building and such property is placed in service within 90 days of the date the building is placed in service. However, in the case of nonresidential real property or residential rental property, only the adjusted basis of such property attributable to manufacture, construction, or production before January 1, 2010 ("progress expenditures") is eligible for the additional first-year depreciation.

The specified portions of the Gulf Opportunity Zone are defined as those portions of the Gulf Opportunity Zone which are in a county or parish which is identified by the Secretary of the Treasury (or his delegate) as being a county or parish in which hurricanes occurring in 2005 damaged (in the aggregate) more than 60 percent

---

[50] The extension of the placed-in-service deadline does not apply for purposes of the increased section 179 expensing limit available to Gulf Opportunity Zone property.

[51] Generally, property described in section 168(k)(2)(A)(i) is (1) property to which the general rules of the Modified

Accelerated Cost Recovery System ("MACRS") apply with an applicable recovery period of 20 years or less, (2) computer software other than computer software covered by section 197, (3) water utility property (as defined in section 168(e)(5)), or (4) certain leasehold improvement property.

of the housing units in such county or parish which were occupied (determined according to the 2000 Census.)[52]

Effective Date

The provision applies as if included in section 101 of the Gulf Opportunity Zone Act of 2005[53] ("GOZA"). Section 101 of GOZA is effective for property placed in service on or after August 28, 2005, in taxable years ending on or after such date.

[Law at ¶ 5626. CCH Explanation at ¶ 315.]

[¶ 15,300] Act Sec. 121. Authority for undercover operations

Joint Committee Taxation (J.C.T. REP. NO. JCX-50-06)

[Code Sec. 7608]

Present Law

IRS undercover operations are exempt from the otherwise applicable statutory restrictions controlling the use of government funds (which generally provide that all receipts must be deposited in the general fund of the Treasury and all expenses paid out of appropriated funds). In general, the exemption permits the IRS to use proceeds from an undercover operation to pay additional expenses incurred in the undercover operation. The IRS is required to conduct a detailed financial audit of large undercover operations in which the IRS is using proceeds from such operations and to provide an annual audit report to the Congress on all such large undercover operations.

The provision was originally enacted in The Anti-Drug Abuse Act of 1988. The exemption originally expired on December 31, 1989, and was extended by the Comprehensive Crime Control Act of 1990 to December 31, 1991. There followed a gap of approximately four and a half years during which the provision had lapsed. In the Taxpayer Bill of Rights II, the authority to use proceeds from undercover operations was extended for five years, through 2000. The Community Renewal Tax Relief Act of 2000 extended the authority of the IRS to use proceeds from undercover operations for an additional five years, through 2005. The Gulf Opportunity Zone Act of 2005 extended the authority through December 31, 2006.

Explanation of Provision

The provision extends for one year the present-law authority of the IRS to use proceeds from undercover operations to pay additional expenses incurred in conducting undercover operations (through December 31, 2007).

Effective Date

The provision is effective on the date of enactment.

[Law at ¶ 5840. CCH Explanation at ¶ 645.]

[¶ 15,310] Act Sec. 122(a). Disclosure of tax information to facilitate combined employment tax reporting

Joint Committee Taxation (J.C.T. REP. NO. JCX-50-06)

[Code Sec. 6103]

Present Law

Traditionally, Federal tax forms are filed with the Federal government and State tax forms are filed with individual States. This necessitates duplication of items common to both returns. The Code permits the IRS to disclose taxpayer identity information and signatures to any agency, body, or commission of any State for the purpose of carrying out with such agency, body or commission a combined Federal and State employment tax reporting program approved by the Secretary.[54] The Federal disclosure restrictions, safeguard requirements, and criminal penalties for unauthorized disclosure and

---

[52] The Office of the Federal Coordinator for Gulf Coast Rebuilding at the Department of Homeland Security, in cooperation with the Federal Emergency Management Agency, the Small Business Administration, and the Department of Housing and Urban Development, compiled data to assess the full extent of housing damage due to 2005 Hurricanes Katrina, Rita, and Wilma. The data was published on February 12, 2006 and is available at www.dhs.gov/ xlibrary/assets/ GulfCoast_HousingDamageEstimates_021206.pdf (last accessed December 5, 2006). It is intended that the Secretary or his delegate will make use of this data in identifying counties and parishes which qualify under the provision.

[53] Pub. L. No. 109-135 (2005).

[54] Sec. 6103(d)(5).

unauthorized inspection do not apply with respect to disclosures or inspections made pursuant to this authority. This provision expires after December 31, 2006.

Separately, under section 6103(c), the IRS may disclose a taxpayer's return or return information to such person or persons as the taxpayer may designate in a request for or consent to such disclosure. Pursuant to Treasury regulations, a taxpayer's participation in a combined return filing program between the IRS and a State agency, body or commission constitutes a consent to the disclosure by the IRS to the State agency of taxpayer identity information, signature and items of common data contained on the return.[55] No disclosures may be made under this authority unless there are provisions of State law protecting the confidentiality of such items of common data.

Explanation of Provision

The provision extends for one year the present-law authority under section 6103(d)(5) for the combined employment tax reporting program (through December 31, 2007).

Effective Date

The provision applies to disclosures after December 31, 2006.

[**Law at ¶5770. CCH Explanation at ¶635.**]

[¶15,320] Act Sec. 122(b). Disclosure of return information regarding terrorist activities

Joint Committee Taxation (J.C.T. REP. No. JCX-50-06)

[Code Sec. 6103]

Present Law

In general

Section 6103 provides that returns and return information may not be disclosed by the IRS, other Federal employees, State employees, and certain others having access to the information except as provided in the Internal Revenue Code. Section 6103 contains a number of exceptions to this general rule of nondisclosure that authorize disclosure in specifically identified circumstances (including nontax criminal investigations) when certain conditions are satisfied.

Among the disclosures permitted under the Code is disclosure of returns and return information for purposes of investigating terrorist incidents, threats, or activities, and for analyzing intelligence concerning terrorist incidents, threats, or activities. The term "terrorist incident, threat, or activity" is statutorily defined to mean an incident, threat, or activity involving an act of domestic terrorism or international terrorism.[56] In general, returns and taxpayer return information must be obtained pursuant to an ex parte court order. Return information, other than taxpayer return information, generally is available upon a written request meeting specific requirements. The IRS also is permitted to make limited disclosures of such information on its own initiative to the appropriate Federal law enforcement agency.

No disclosures may be made under these provisions after December 31, 2006. The procedures applicable to these provisions are described in detail below.

Disclosure of returns and return information - by ex parte court order

Ex parte court orders sought by Federal law enforcement and Federal intelligence agencies

The Code permits, pursuant to an ex parte court order, the disclosure of returns and return information (including taxpayer return information) to certain officers and employees of a Federal law enforcement agency or Federal intelligence agency. These officers and employees are required to be personally and directly engaged in any investigation of, response to, or analysis of intelligence and counterintelligence information concerning any terrorist incident, threat, or activity. These officers and employees are permitted to use this information solely for their use in the investigation, response, or analysis, and in any judicial, administrative, or grand jury proceeding, pertaining to any such terrorist incident, threat, or activity.

The Attorney General, Deputy Attorney General, Associate Attorney General, an Assis-

---

[55] Treas. Reg. sec. 301.6103(c)-1(d)(2).

[56] Sec. 6103(b)(11). For this purpose, "domestic terrorism" is defined in 18 U.S.C. Sec. 2331(5) and "international terrorism" is defined in 18 U.S.C. sec. 2331.

tant Attorney General, or a United States attorney, may authorize the application for the ex parte court order to be submitted to a Federal district court judge or magistrate. The Federal district court judge or magistrate would grant the order if based on the facts submitted he or she determines that: (1) there is reasonable cause to believe, based upon information believed to be reliable, that the return or return information may be relevant to a matter relating to such terrorist incident, threat, or activity; and (2) the return or return information is sought exclusively for the use in a Federal investigation, analysis, or proceeding concerning any terrorist incident, threat, or activity.

Special rule for ex parte court ordered disclosure initiated by the IRS

If the Secretary possesses returns or return information that may be related to a terrorist incident, threat, or activity, the Secretary may on his own initiative, authorize an application for an ex parte court order to permit disclosure to Federal law enforcement. In order to grant the order, the Federal district court judge or magistrate must determine that there is reasonable cause to believe, based upon information believed to be reliable, that the return or return information may be relevant to a matter relating to such terrorist incident, threat, or activity. The information may be disclosed only to the extent necessary to apprise the appropriate Federal law enforcement agency responsible for investigating or responding to a terrorist incident, threat, or activity and for officers and employees of that agency to investigate or respond to such terrorist incident, threat, or activity. Further, use of the information is limited to use in a Federal investigation, analysis, or proceeding concerning a terrorist incident, threat, or activity. Because the Department of Justice represents the Secretary in Federal district court, the Secretary is permitted to disclose returns and return information to the Department of Justice as necessary and solely for the purpose of obtaining the special IRS ex parte court order.

Disclosure of return information other than by ex parte court order

Disclosure by the IRS without a request

The Code permits the IRS to disclose return information, other than taxpayer return information, related to a terrorist incident, threat, or activity to the extent necessary to apprise the head of the appropriate Federal law enforcement agency responsible for investigating or responding to such terrorist incident, threat, or activity. The IRS on its own initiative and without a written request may make this disclosure. The

head of the Federal law enforcement agency may disclose information to officers and employees of such agency to the extent necessary to investigate or respond to such terrorist incident, threat, or activity. A taxpayer's identity is not treated as return information supplied by the taxpayer or his or her representative.

Disclosure upon written request of a Federal law enforcement agency

The Code permits the IRS to disclose return information, other than taxpayer return information, to officers and employees of Federal law enforcement upon a written request satisfying certain requirements. The request must: (1) be made by the head of the Federal law enforcement agency (or his delegate) involved in the response to or investigation of terrorist incidents, threats, or activities, and (2) set forth the specific reason or reasons why such disclosure may be relevant to a terrorist incident, threat, or activity. The information is to be disclosed to officers and employees of the Federal law enforcement agency who would be personally and directly involved in the response to or investigation of terrorist incidents, threats, or activities. The information is to be used by such officers and employees solely for such response or investigation.

The Code permits the redisclosure by a Federal law enforcement agency to officers and employees of State and local law enforcement personally and directly engaged in the response to or investigation of the terrorist incident, threat, or activity. The State or local law enforcement agency must be part of an investigative or response team with the Federal law enforcement agency for these disclosures to be made.

Disclosure upon request from the Departments of Justice or Treasury for intelligence analysis of terrorist activity

Upon written request satisfying certain requirements discussed below, the IRS is to disclose return information (other than taxpayer return information) to officers and employees of the Department of Justice, Department of Treasury, and other Federal intelligence agencies, who are personally and directly engaged in the collection or analysis of intelligence and counterintelligence or investigation concerning terrorist incidents, threats, or activities. Use of the information is limited to use by such officers and employees in such investigation, collection, or analysis.

The written request is to set forth the specific reasons why the information to be disclosed is relevant to a terrorist incident, threat, or activity. The request is to be made by an individual who is: (1) an officer or employee of the Department of Justice or the Department of Treasury, (2) appointed by the President with the advice and consent of the Senate, and (3) responsible for the collection, and analysis of intelligence and counterintelligence information concerning terrorist incidents, threats, or activities. The Director of the United States Secret Service also is an authorized requester under the Act.

Explanation of Provision

The provision extends for one year the present-law terrorist activity disclosure provisions (through December 31, 2007).

Effective Date

The provision applies to disclosures after December 31, 2006.

[Law at ¶5770. CCH Explanation at ¶635.]

[¶15,330] Act Sec. 122(c). Disclosure of return information to carry out income contingent repayment of student loans

Joint Committee Taxation (J.C.T. REP. No. JCX-50-06)

[Code Sec. 6103]

Present Law

Present law prohibits the disclosure of returns and return information, except to the extent specifically authorized by the Code. An exception is provided for disclosure to the Department of Education (but not to contractors thereof) of a taxpayer's filing status, adjusted gross income and identity information (i.e., name, mailing address, taxpayer identifying number) to establish an appropriate repayment amount for an applicable student loan. The disclosure authority for the income-contingent loan repayment program is scheduled to expire after December 31, 2006.

The Department of Education utilizes contractors for the income-contingent loan verification program. The specific disclosure exception for the program does not permit disclosure of return information to contractors. As a result, the Department of Education obtains return information from the Internal Revenue Service by taxpayer consent (under section 6103(c)), rather than under the specific exception for the income-contingent loan verification program (sec. 6103(l)(13)).

Explanation of Provision

The provision extends for one year the present-law authority to disclose return information for purposes of the income-contingent loan repayment program (through December 31, 2007).

Effective Date

The provision applies to requests made after December 31, 2006.

[Law at ¶5770. CCH Explanation at ¶635.]

[¶15,340] Act Sec. 123. Special rule for elections under expired provisions

Joint Committee Taxation (J.C.T. REP. No. JCX-50-06)

[Act Sec. 123]

Present Law

Under present law, various elections under provisions of the Code must be made by a certain date and in a certain manner. For example, the election under section 280C(c)(3) of a reduced credit for increasing research expenditures must be made not later than the time for filing a return (including extensions).

Explanation of Provision

The provision provides that, in the case of any taxable year which ends after December 31, 2005 and before the date of enactment of the bill, an election under section 41(c)(4), 280C(c)(3)(C), or any other expired provision of the Code which is extended by the bill is treated as timely if made not later than April 15, 2007, or such other time as the Secretary or his designee provide. The election shall be made in the manner prescribed by the Secretary or his designee.

Effective Date

The provision is effective on the date of enactment.

[Law at ¶7055. CCH Explanation at ¶405, ¶410, ¶415 and ¶420.]

[¶15,350] Act Sec. 201. Extension of placed-in-service date for tax credit for electricity produced at wind, closed-loop biomass, open-loop biomass, geothermal energy, small irrigation power, landfill gas, trash combustion, or qualified hydropower facilities

Joint Committee Taxation (J.C.T. REP. NO. JCX-50-06)

[Code Sec. 45]

Present Law

In general

An income tax credit is allowed for the production of electricity at qualified facilities using qualified energy resources (sec. 45). Qualified energy resources comprise wind, closed-loop biomass, open-loop biomass, geothermal, energy, solar energy, small irrigation power, municipal solid waste, and qualified hydropower production. Qualified facilities are, generally, facilities that generate electricity using qualified energy resources. To be eligible for the credit, electricity produced from qualified energy resources at qualified facilities must be sold by the taxpayer to an unrelated person. In addition to the electricity production credit, an income tax credit is allowed for the production of refined coal and Indian coal at qualified facilities.

Credit amounts and credit period

In general

The base amount of the credit is 1.5 cents per kilowatt-hour (indexed annually for inflation) of electricity produced. The amount of the credit is 1.9 cents per kilowatt-hour for 2006. A taxpayer may generally claim a credit during the 10-year period commencing with the date the qualified facility is placed in service. The credit is reduced for grants, tax-exempt bonds, subsidized energy financing, and other credits.

The amount of credit a taxpayer may claim is phased out as the market price of electricity (or refined coal in the case of the refined coal production credit) exceeds certain threshold levels. The electricity production credit is reduced over a 3 cent phase-out range to the extent the annual average contract price per kilowatt hour of electricity sold in the prior year from the same qualified energy resource exceeds 8 cents (adjusted for inflation). The refined coal credit is reduced over an $8.75 phase-out range as the reference price of the fuel used as feedstock for the refined coal exceeds the reference price for such fuel in 2002 (adjusted for inflation).

Reduced credit amounts and credit periods

Generally, in the case of open-loop biomass facilities (including agricultural livestock waste nutrient facilities), geothermal energy facilities, solar energy facilities, small irrigation power facilities, landfill gas facilities, and trash combustion facilities, the 10-year credit period is reduced to five years commencing on the date the facility was originally placed in service, for qualified facilities placed in service before August 8, 2005. However, for qualified open-loop biomass facilities (other than a facility described in sec. 45(d)(3)(A)(i) that uses agricultural livestock waste nutrients) placed in service before October 22, 2004, the five-year period commences on January 1, 2005. In the case of a closed-loop biomass facility modified to co-fire with coal, to co-fire with other biomass, or to co-fire with coal and other biomass, the credit period begins no earlier than October 22, 2004.

In the case of open-loop biomass facilities (including agricultural livestock waste nutrient facilities), small irrigation power facilities, landfill gas facilities, trash combustion facilities, and qualified hydropower facilities the otherwise allowable credit amount is 0.75 cent per kilowatt-hour, indexed for inflation measured after 1992 (currently 0.9 cents per kilowatt-hour for 2006).

Credit applicable to refined coal

The amount of the credit for refined coal is $4.375 per ton (also indexed for inflation after 1992 and equaling $5.679 per ton for 2006).

Credit applicable to Indian coal

A credit is available for the sale of Indian coal to an unrelated third part from a qualified facility for a seven-year period beginning on January 1, 2006, and before January 1, 2013. The amount of the credit for Indian coal is $1.50 per ton for the first four years of the seven-year period and $2.00 per ton for the last three years of the seven-year period. Beginning in calendar years after 2006, the credit amounts are indexed annually for inflation using 2005 as the base year.

Other limitations on credit claimants and credit amounts

In general, in order to claim the credit, a taxpayer must own the qualified facility and sell the electricity produced by the facility (or refined coal or Indian coal, with respect to those credits) to an unrelated party. A lessee or operator may claim the credit in lieu of the owner of the qualifying facility in the case of qualifying open-loop biomass facilities and in the case of a closed-loop biomass facilities modified to co-fire with coal, to co-fire with other biomass, or to co-fire with coal and other biomass. In the case of a poultry waste facility, the taxpayer may claim the credit as a lessee or operator of a facility owned by a governmental unit.

For all qualifying facilities, other than closed-loop biomass facilities modified to co-fire with coal, to co-fire with other biomass, or to co-fire with coal and other biomass, the amount of credit a taxpayer may claim is reduced by reason of grants, tax-exempt bonds, subsidized energy financing, and other credits, but the reduction cannot exceed 50 percent of the otherwise allowable credit. In the case of closed-loop biomass facilities modified to co-fire with coal, to co-fire with other biomass, or to co-fire with coal and other biomass, there is no reduction in credit by reason of grants, tax-exempt bonds, subsidized energy financing, and other credits.

The credit for electricity produced from renewable sources is a component of the general business credit (sec. 38(b)(8)). Generally, the general business credit for any taxable year may not exceed the amount by which the taxpayer's net income tax exceeds the greater of the tentative minimum tax or so much of the net regular tax liability as exceeds $25,000. Excess credits may be carried back one year and forward up to 20 years.

A taxpayer's tentative minimum tax is treated as being zero for purposes of determining the tax liability limitation with respect to the section 45 credit for electricity produced from a facility (placed in service after October 22, 2004) during the first four years of production beginning on the date the facility is placed in service.

Qualified facilities

Wind energy facility

A wind energy facility is a facility that uses wind to produce electricity. To be a qualified facility, a wind energy facility must be placed in service after December 31, 1993, and before January 1, 2008.

Closed-loop biomass facility

A closed-loop biomass facility is a facility that uses any organic material from a plant which is planted exclusively for the purpose of being used at a qualifying facility to produce electricity. In addition, a facility can be a closed-loop biomass facility if it is a facility that is modified to use closed-loop biomass to co-fire with coal, with other biomass, or with both coal and other biomass, but only if the modification is approved under the Biomass Power for Rural Development Programs or is part of a pilot project of the Commodity Credit Corporation.

To be a qualified facility, a closed-loop biomass facility must be placed in service after December 31, 1992, and before January 1, 2008. In the case of a facility using closed-loop biomass but also co-firing the closed-loop biomass with coal, other biomass, or coal and other biomass, a qualified facility must be originally placed in service and modified to co-fire the closed-loop biomass at any time before January 1, 2008.

Open-loop biomass (including agricultural livestock waste nutrients) facility

An open-loop biomass facility is a facility that uses open-loop biomass to produce electricity. For purposes of the credit, open-loop biomass is defined as (1) any agricultural livestock waste nutrients or (2) any solid, nonhazardous, cellulosic waste material or any lignin material that is segregated from other waste materials and which is derived from:

- forest-related resources, including mill and harvesting residues, precommercial thinnings, slash, and brush;

- solid wood waste materials, including waste pallets, crates, dunnage, manufacturing and construction wood wastes, landscape or right-of-way tree trimming; or

- agricultural sources, including orchard tree crops, vineyard, grain, legumes, sugar, and other crop by-products or residues.

Agricultural livestock waste nutrients are defined as agricultural livestock manure and litter, including bedding material for the disposition of manure. Wood waste materials do not qualify as open-loop biomass to the extent they are pressure treated, chemically treated, or painted. In addition, municipal solid waste, gas derived from the biodegradation of solid waste, and paper which is commonly recycled do not qualify as open-loop biomass. Open-loop biomass does not include closed-loop biomass or any biomass burned in conjunction with fossil fuel (co-firing) beyond such fossil fuel required for start up and flame stabilization.

In the case of an open-loop biomass facility that uses agricultural livestock waste nutrients, a qualified facility is one that was originally placed in service after October 22, 2004, and before January 1, 2008, and has a nameplate capacity rating which is not less than 150 kilowatts. In the case of any other open-loop biomass facility, a qualified facility is one that was originally placed in service before January 1, 2008.

Geothermal facility

A geothermal facility is a facility that uses geothermal energy to produce electricity. Geothermal energy is energy derived from a geothermal deposit which is a geothermal reservoir consisting of natural heat which is stored in rocks or in an aqueous liquid or vapor (whether or not under pressure). To be a qualified facility, a geothermal facility must be placed in service after October 22, 2004 and before January 1, 2008.

Solar facility

A solar facility is a facility that uses solar energy to produce electricity. To be a qualified facility, a solar facility must be placed in service after October 22, 2004 and before January 1, 2006.

Small irrigation facility

A small irrigation power facility is a facility that generates electric power through an irrigation system canal or ditch without any dam or impoundment of water. The installed capacity of a qualified facility must be not less than 150 kilowatts but less than five megawatts. To be a qualified facility, a small irrigation facility must be originally placed in service after October 22, 2004 and before January 1, 2008.

Landfill gas facility

A landfill gas facility is a facility that uses landfill gas to produce electricity. Landfill gas is defined as methane gas derived from the biodegradation of municipal solid waste. To be a qualified facility, a landfill gas facility must be placed in service after October 22, 2004 and before January 1, 2008.

Trash combustion facility

Trash combustion facilities are facilities that burn municipal solid waste (garbage) to produce steam to drive a turbine for the production of electricity. To be a qualified facility, a trash combustion facility must be placed in service after October 22, 2004 and before January 1, 2008. A qualified trash combustion facility includes a new unit, placed in service after October 22,

2004, that increases electricity production capacity at an existing trash combustion facility. A new unit generally would include a new burner/boiler and turbine. The new unit may share certain common equipment, such as trash handling equipment, with other pre-existing units at the same facility. Electricity produced at a new unit of an existing facility qualifies for the production credit only to the extent of the increased amount of electricity produced at the entire facility.

Hydropower facility

A qualifying hydropower facility is (1) a facility that produced hydroelectric power (a hydroelectric dam) prior to August 8, 2005, at which efficiency improvements or additions to capacity have been made after such date and before January 1, 2009, that enable the taxpayer to produce incremental hydropower or (2) a facility placed in service before August 8, 2005, that did not produce hydroelectric power (a nonhydroelectric dam) on such date, and to which turbines or other electricity generating equipment have been added such date and before January 1, 2009.

At an existing hydroelectric facility, the taxpayer may only claim credit for the production of incremental hydroelectric power. Incremental hydroelectric power for any taxable year is equal to the percentage of average annual hydroelectric power produced at the facility attributable to the efficiency improvement or additions of capacity determined by using the same water flow information used to determine an historic average annual hydroelectric power production baseline for that facility. The Federal Energy Regulatory Commission will certify the baseline power production of the facility and the percentage increase due to the efficiency and capacity improvements.

At a nonhydroelectric dam, the facility must be licensed by the Federal Energy Regulatory Commission and meet all other applicable environmental, licensing, and regulatory requirements and the turbines or other generating devices must be added to the facility after August 8, 2005 and before January 1, 2009. In addition there must not be any enlargement of the diversion structure, or construction or enlargement of a bypass channel, or the impoundment or any withholding of additional water from the natural stream channel.

Refined coal facility

A qualifying refined coal facility is a facility producing refined coal that is placed in service after October 22, 2004 and before January 1, 2009.

Refined coal is a qualifying liquid, gaseous, or solid synthetic fuel produced from coal (including lignite) or high-carbon fly ash, including such fuel used as a feedstock. A qualifying fuel is a fuel that when burned emits 20 percent less nitrogen oxides and either SO2 or mercury than the burning of feedstock coal or comparable coal predominantly available in the marketplace as of January 1, 2003, and if the fuel sells at prices at least 50 percent greater than the prices of the feedstock coal or comparable coal. In addition, to be qualified refined coal the fuel must be sold by the taxpayer with the reasonable expectation that it will be used for the primary purpose of producing steam.

Indian coal facility

A qualified Indian coal facility is a facility which is placed in service before January 1, 2009, that produces coal from reserves that on June 14, 2005, were owned by a Federally recognized tribe of Indians or were held in trust by the United States for a tribe or its members.

Summary of credit rate and credit period by facility type

Table 1.-Summary of Section 45 Credit for Electricity Produced from Certain Renewable Resources, for Refined Coal, and for Indian Coal

Eligible electricity production or coal production activity	Credit amount for 2006 (cents per kilowatt-hour; dollars per ton)	Credit period for facilities placed in service on or before August 8, 2005 (years from placed-in-service date)	Credit period facilities placed in service after August 8, 2005 (years from placed-in-service date)
Wind	1.900	10	10
Closed-loop biomass	1.900	10 [1]	10 [1]
Open-loop biomass	0.900	5 [2]	10
(including agricultural livestock waste nutrient facilities)			
Geothermal	1.900	5	10
Solar	1.900	5	10
Small irrigation power	0.900	5	10
Municipal solid waste	0.900	5	10
(including landfill gas facilities and trash combustion facilities)			
Qualified hydropower	0.900	N/A	10
Refined Coal	5.679	10	10
Indian Coal	1.500	7 [3]	7 [3]

[1] In the case of certain co-firing closed-loop facilities, the credit period begins no earlier than October 22, 2004.
[2] For certain facilities placed in service before October 22, 2004, the 5-year credit period commences on January 1, 2005.
[3] For Indian coal, the credit period begins for coal sold after January 1, 2006.

For eligible pre-existing facilities and other facilities placed in service prior to January 1, 2005, the credit period commences on January 1, 2005. In the case of certain co-firing closed-loop facilities, the credit period begins no earlier than October 22, 2004. For Indian coal, the credit period begins for coal sold after January 1, 2006, for facilities placed-in-service before January 1, 2009.

Taxation of cooperatives and their patrons

For Federal income tax purposes, a cooperative generally computes its income as if it were a taxable corporation, with one exception-the co-operative may exclude from its taxable income distributions of patronage dividends. Generally, cooperatives that are subject to the cooperative tax rules of subchapter T of the Code[57] are permitted a deduction for patronage dividends from their taxable income only to the extent of net income that is derived from transactions with patrons who are members of the cooperative.[58] The availability of such deductions from taxable income has the effect of allowing the cooperative to be treated like a conduit with respect to profits derived from transactions with patrons who are members of the cooperative. For taxable years

[57] Sec. 1381, et seq.

[58] Sec. 1382.

ending on or before August 8, 2005, cooperatives may not pass any portion of the income tax credit for electricity production through to their patrons.

For taxable years ending after August 8, 2005, eligible cooperatives may elect to pass any portion of the credit through to their patrons. An eligible cooperative is defined as a cooperative organization that is owned more than 50 percent by agricultural producers or entities owned by agricultural producers. The credit may be apportioned among patrons eligible to share in patronage dividends on the basis of the quantity or value of business done with or for such patrons for the taxable year. The election must be made on a timely filed return for the taxable year, and once made, is irrevocable for such taxable year. The amount of the credit apportioned to patrons is not included in the organization's credit for the taxable year of the organization. The amount of the credit apportioned to a patron is included in the taxable year the patron with or within which the taxable year of the organization ends. If the amount of the credit for any taxable year is less than the amount of the credit shown on the cooperative's return for such taxable year, an amount equal to the excess of the reduction in the credit over the amount not apportioned to patrons for the taxable year is treated as an increase in the cooperative's tax. The increase is not treated as tax imposed for purposes of determining the amount of any tax credit.

Explanation of Provision

The provision extends through December 31, 2008, the period during which certain facilities may be placed in service as qualified facilities for purposes of the electricity production credit. The placed-in-service date extension applies for all qualified facilities, except for qualified solar, refined coal, and Indian coal facilities.

Effective Date

The provision is effective for facilities placed in service after December 31, 2007.

[Law at ¶5038. CCH Explanation at ¶450.]

[¶15,360] Act Sec. 202. Extension and expansion of clean renewable energy bonds

Joint Committee Taxation (J.C.T. Rep. No. JCX-50-06)

[Code Sec. 54]

Present law

Tax-exempt bonds

Interest on State and local governmental bonds generally is excluded from gross income for Federal income tax purposes if the proceeds of the bonds are used to finance direct activities of these governmental units or if the bonds are repaid with revenues of the governmental units. Activities that can be financed with these tax-exempt bonds include the financing of electric power facilities (i.e., generation, transmission, distribution, and retailing).

Interest on State or local government bonds to finance activities of private persons ("private activity bonds") is taxable unless a specific exception is contained in the Code (or in a non-Code provision of a revenue Act). The term "private person" generally includes the Federal government and all other individuals and entities other than States or local governments. The Code includes exceptions permitting States or local governments to act as conduits providing tax-exempt financing for certain private activities. In most cases, the aggregate volume of these tax-exempt private activity bonds is restricted by annual aggregate volume limits imposed on bonds issued by issuers within each State. For calendar year 2006, these annual volume limits, which are indexed for inflation, equal $80 per resident of the State, or $246.6 million, if greater.

The tax exemption for State and local bonds also does not apply to any arbitrage bond.[59] An arbitrage bond is defined as any bond that is part of an issue if any proceeds of the issue are reasonably expected to be used (or intentionally are used) to acquire higher yielding investments or to replace funds that are used to acquire higher yielding investments.[60] In general, arbitrage profits may be earned only during specified periods (e.g., defined "temporary periods") before funds are needed for the purpose of the borrowing or on specified types of investments (e.g., "reasonably required reserve or replacement funds"). Subject to limited exceptions, investment profits that are earned during these

---

[59] Secs. 103(a) and (b)(2).

[60] Sec. 148.

periods or on such investments must be rebated to the Federal government.

An issuer must file with the IRS certain information about the bonds issued by them in order for that bond issue to be tax-exempt.[61] Generally, this information return is required to be filed no later the 15th day of the second month after the close of the calendar quarter in which the bonds were issued.

Clean renewable energy bonds

As an alternative to traditional tax-exempt bonds, States and local governments may issue clean renewable energy bonds ("CREBs"). CREBs are defined as any bond issued by a qualified issuer if, in addition to the requirements discussed below, 95 percent or more of the proceeds of such bonds are used to finance capital expenditures incurred by qualified borrowers for facilities that qualify for the tax credit under section 45 (other than Indian coal production facilities), without regard to the placed-in-service date requirements of that section. The term "qualified issuers" includes (1) governmental bodies (including Indian tribal governments); (2) mutual or cooperative electric companies (described in section 501(c)(12) or section 1381(a)(2)(C), or a not-for-profit electric utility which has received a loan or guarantee under the Rural Electrification Act); and (3) clean energy bond lenders. The term "qualified borrower" includes a governmental body (including an Indian tribal government) and a mutual or cooperative electric company.

In addition, Notice 2006-7 provides that projects that may be financed with CREBs include any facility owned by a qualified borrower that is functionally related and subordinate (as determined under Treas. Reg. sec. 1.103-8(a)(3)) to any qualified facility described in sections 45(d)(1) through (d)(9) (determined without regard to any placed in service date) and owned by such qualified borrower.

Unlike tax-exempt bonds, CREBs are not interest-bearing obligations. Rather, the taxpayer holding CREBs on a credit allowance date is entitled to a tax credit. The amount of the credit is determined by multiplying the bond's credit rate by the face amount on the holder's bond. The credit rate on the bonds is determined by the Secretary and is to be a rate that permits issuance of CREBs without discount and interest cost to the qualified issuer. The credit accrues quarterly and is includible in gross income (as if it were an interest payment on the bond), and can be claimed against regular income tax liability and alternative minimum tax liability.

CREBs are subject to a maximum maturity limitation. The maximum maturity is the term which the Secretary estimates will result in the present value of the obligation to repay the principal on a CREBs being equal to 50 percent of the face amount of such bond. In addition, the Code requires level amortization of CREBs during the period such bonds are outstanding.

CREBs also are subject to the arbitrage requirements of section 148 that apply to traditional tax-exempt bonds. Principles under section 148 and the regulations thereunder apply for purposes of determining the yield restriction and arbitrage rebate requirements applicable to CREBs.

To qualify as CREBs, the qualified issuer must reasonably expect to and actually spend 95 percent or more of the proceeds of such bonds on qualified projects within the five-year period that begins on the date of issuance. To the extent less than 95 percent of the proceeds are used to finance qualified projects during the five-year spending period, bonds will continue to qualify as CREBs if unspent proceeds are used within 90 days from the end of such five-year period to redeem any "nonqualified bonds." The five-year spending period may be extended by the Secretary upon the qualified issuer's request demonstrating that the failure to satisfy the five-year requirement is due to reasonable cause and the projects will continue to proceed with due diligence.

Issuers of CREBs are required to report issuance to the IRS in a manner similar to the information returns required for tax-exempt bonds. There is a national CREB limitation of $800 million. CREBs must be issued before January 1, 2008. Under present law, no more than $500 million of CREBs authority may be allocated to projects for governmental bodies.

Explanation of Provision

The provision authorizes an additional $400 million of CREBs that may be issued and extends the authority to issue such bonds through December 31, 2008. It is expected that the additional authority will be allocated through a new application process similar to that set forth in Notice 2005-98, 2005-52 I.R.B 1211.

In addition to increasing the national limitation on the amount of CREBs, the provision increases the maximum amount of CREBs that

---

[61] Sec. 149(e).

may be allocated to qualified projects of governmental bodies to $750 million.

The provision provides an extension of the CREBs program, but it is expected that Congress will review the efficacy of the program, including the efficacy of imposing limitations on allocations to projects for governmental bodies, before granting additional extensions.

Effective Date

The provision authorizing an additional $400 million of CREBs and extending the author-ity to issue such bonds through December 31, 2008, is effective for bonds issued after December 31, 2006. The provision increasing the maximum amount of CREBs that may be allocated to qualified projects of governmental bodies is effective for allocations or reallocations after December 31, 2006.

[Law at ¶5055. CCH Explanation at ¶625.]

[¶15,370] Act Sec. 203. Modification of advanced coal credit with respect to subbituminous coal

Joint Committee Taxation (J.C.T. REP. NO. JCX-50-06)

[Code Sec. 48A]

Present Law

An investment tax credit is available for investments in certain qualifying advanced coal projects (sec. 48A). The credit amount is 20 percent for investments in qualifying projects that use integrated gasification combined cycle ("IGCC"). The credit amount is 15 percent for investments in qualifying projects that use other advanced coal-based electricity generation technologies.

To qualify, an advanced coal project must be located in the United States and use an advanced coal-based generation technology to power a new electric generation unit or to retrofit or re-power an existing unit. An electric generation unit using an advanced coal-based technology must be designed to achieve a 99 percent reduction in sulfur dioxide and a 90 percent reduction in mercury, as well as to limit emissions of nitrous oxide and particulate matter.

The fuel input for a qualifying project, when completed, must use at least 75 percent coal. The project, consisting of one or more electric generation units at one site, must have a nameplate generating capacity of at least 400 megawatts, and the taxpayer must provide evidence that a majority of the output of the project is reasonably expected to be acquired or utilized.

Credits are available only for projects certified by the Secretary of Treasury, in consultation with the Secretary of Energy. Certifications are issued using a competitive bidding process. The Secretary of Treasury must establish a certification program no later than 180 days after August 8, 2005, and each project application must be submitted during the three-year period begin-ning on the date such certification program is established.

The Secretary of Treasury may allocate $800 million of credits to IGCC projects and $500 million to projects using other advanced coal-based electricity generation technologies. Qualified projects must be economically feasible and use the appropriate clean coal technologies. With respect to IGCC projects, credit-eligible investments include only investments in property associated with the gasification of coal, including any coal handling and gas separation equipment. Thus, investments in equipment that could operate by drawing fuel directly from a natural gas pipeline do not qualify for the credit.

In determining which projects to certify that use IGCC technology, the Secretary must allocate power generation capacity in relatively equal amounts to projects that use bituminous coal, subbituminous coal, and lignite as primary feedstock. In addition, the Secretary must give high priority to projects which include greenhouse gas capture capability, increased by-product utilization, and other benefits.

Explanation of Provision

The provision modifies one of the performance requirements necessary for an electric generation unit to be treated as using advanced coal-based generation technology. Under the provision, the performance requirement relating to the removal of sulfur dioxide is changed so that an electric generation unit designed to use subbituminous coal can meet the standard if it is designed either to remove 99 percent of the sulfur dioxide or to achieve an emission limit of 0.04 pounds of sulfur dioxide per million British thermal units on a 30-day average.

Effective Date

The provision is effective for advanced coal project certification applications submitted after October 2, 2006.

[Law at ¶5051. CCH Explanation at ¶455.]

[¶15,380] Act Sec. 204. Extension of energy efficient commercial buildings deduction

Joint Committee Taxation (J.C.T. Rep. No. JCX-50-06)

[Code Sec. 179D]

Present Law

In general

Code section 179D provides a deduction equal to energy-efficient commercial building property expenditures made by the taxpayer. Energy-efficient commercial building property expenditures is defined as property (1) which is installed on or in any building located in the United States that is within the scope of Standard 90.1-2001 of the American Society of Heating, Refrigerating, and Air Conditioning Engineers and the Illuminating Engineering Society of North America ("ASHRAE/IESNA"), (2) which is installed as part of (i) the interior lighting systems, (ii) the heating, cooling, ventilation, and hot water systems, or (iii) the building envelope, and (3) which is certified as being installed as part of a plan designed to reduce the total annual energy and power costs with respect to the interior lighting systems, heating, cooling, ventilation, and hot water systems of the building by 50 percent or more in comparison to a reference building which meets the minimum requirements of Standard 90.1-2001 (as in effect on April 2, 2003). The deduction is limited to an amount equal to $1.80 per square foot of the property for which such expenditures are made. The deduction is allowed in the year in which the property is placed in service.

Certain certification requirements must be met in order to qualify for the deduction. The Secretary, in consultation with the Secretary of Energy, will promulgate regulations that describe methods of calculating and verifying energy and power costs using qualified computer software based on the provisions of the 2005 California Nonresidential Alternative Calculation Method Approval Manual or, in the case of residential property, the 2005 California Residential Alternative Calculation Method Approval Manual.

The Secretary is required to prescribe procedures for the inspection and testing for compliance of buildings that are comparable, given the difference between commercial and residential buildings, to the requirements in the Mortgage Industry National Accreditation Procedures for Home Energy Rating Systems. Individuals qualified to determine compliance are only those recognized by one or more organizations certified by the Secretary for such purposes.

For energy-efficient commercial building property expenditures made by a public entity, such as public schools, the Secretary is required to promulgate regulations that allow the deduction to be allocated to the person primarily responsible for designing the property in lieu of the public entity.

If a deduction is allowed under this provision, the basis of the property is reduced by the amount of the deduction.

Partial allowance of deduction

In the case of a building that does not meet the overall building requirement of a 50-percent energy savings, a partial deduction is allowed with respect to each separate building system that comprises energy efficient property and which is certified by a qualified professional as meeting or exceeding the applicable system-specific savings targets established by the Secretary of the Treasury. The applicable system-specific savings targets to be established by the Secretary are those that would result in a total annual energy savings with respect to the whole building of 50 percent, if each of the separate systems met the system specific target. The separate building systems are (1) the interior lighting system, (2) the heating, cooling, ventilation and hot water systems, and (3) the building envelope. The maximum allowable deduction is $0.60 per square foot for each separate system.

In the case of system-specific partial deductions, in general no deduction is allowed until the Secretary establishes system-specific targets. However, in the case of lighting system retrofits, until such time as the Secretary issues final regulations, the system-specific energy savings target for the lighting system is deemed to be met by a reduction in Lighting Power Density of 40 percent (50 percent in the case of a warehouse) of the minimum requirements in Table 9.3.1.1 or Table 9.3.1.2 of ASHRAE/IESNA Standard 90.1-2001. Also, in the case of a lighting system that reduces lighting power density by 25 percent, a partial deduction of 30 cents per square foot is allowed. A pro-rated partial deduction is allowed in the case of a lighting system that reduces lighting power density between 25 percent and 40 percent. Certain lighting level and lighting control requirements must also be met in order to qualify for the partial lighting deductions.

The deduction is effective for property placed in service after December 31, 2005 and prior to January 1, 2008.

[¶15,390] Act Sec. 205. Extension of energy efficient new homes credit

Joint Committee Taxation (J.C.T. REP. NO. JCX-50-06)

[Code Sec. 45L]

Present Law

Code section 45L provides a credit to an eligible contractor for the construction of a qualified new energy-efficient home. To qualify as a new energy-efficient home, the home must be: (1) a dwelling located in the United States, (2) substantially completed after August 8, 2005, and (3) certified in accordance with guidance prescribed by the Secretary to have a projected level of annual heating and cooling energy consumption that meets the standards for either a 30-percent or 50-percent reduction in energy usage, compared to a comparable dwelling constructed in accordance with the standards of chapter 4 of the 2003 International Energy Conservation Code as in effect (including supplements) on August 8, 2005, and any applicable Federal minimum efficiency standards for equipment. With respect to homes that meet the 30-percent standard, one-third of such 30 percent savings must come from the building envelope, and with respect to homes that meet the 50-percent standard, one-fifth of such 50 percent savings must come from the building envelope.

Manufactured homes that conform to Federal manufactured home construction and safety standards are eligible for the credit provided all the criteria for the credit are met. The eligible contractor is the person who constructed the home, or in the case of a manufactured home, the producer of such home.

The credit equals $1,000 in the case of a new home that meets the 30 percent standard and $2,000 in the case of a new home that meets the 50 percent standard. Only manufactured homes are eligible for the $1,000 credit.

In lieu of meeting the standards of chapter 4 of the 2003 International Energy Conservation Code, manufactured homes certified by a method prescribed by the Administrator of the Environmental Protection Agency under the Energy Star Labeled Homes program are eligible for the $1,000 credit provided criteria (1) and (2), above, are met.

The credit is part of the general business credit. No credits attributable to qualified new energy efficient homes can be carried back to any taxable year ending on or before the effective date of the credit.

The credit applies to homes whose construction is substantially completed after December 31, 2005, and which are purchased after December 31, 2005 and prior to January 1, 2008.

Explanation of Provision

The provision extends the credit to homes whose construction is substantially completed after December 31, 2005, and which are purchased after December 31, 2005 and prior to January 1, 2009.

Explanation of Provision

The provision extends the deduction to property placed in service prior to January 1, 2009.

Effective Date

The provision is effective on the date of enactment.

[Law at ¶5310. CCH Explanation at ¶335.]

Effective Date

The provision is effective on the date of enactment.

[Law at ¶5048. CCH Explanation at ¶445.]

[¶15,400] Act Sec. 206. Extension of credit for residential energy efficient property

Joint Committee Taxation (J.C.T. REP. NO. JCX-50-06)

[Code Sec. 25D]

Present Law

Code section 25D provides a personal tax credit for the purchase of qualified photovoltaic property and qualified solar water heating property that is used exclusively for purposes other than heating swimming pools and hot tubs. The credit is equal to 30 percent of qualifying expenditures, with a maximum credit for each of these systems of property of $2,000. Section 25D also provides a 30 percent credit for the purchase of qualified fuel cell power plants. The credit for any fuel cell may not exceed $500 for each 0.5 kilowatt of capacity.

Qualifying solar water heating property means an expenditure for property to heat water for use in a dwelling unit located in the United States and used as a residence if at least half of the energy used by such property for such purpose is derived from the sun. Qualified photovoltaic property is property that uses solar energy to generate electricity for use in a dwelling unit. A qualified fuel cell power plant is an integrated system comprised of a fuel cell stack assembly and associated balance of plant components that (1) converts a fuel into electricity using electrochemical means, (2) has an electricity-only generation efficiency of greater than 30 percent. The qualified fuel cell power plant must be installed on or in connection with a dwelling unit located in the United States and used by the taxpayer as a principal residence.

The credit is nonrefundable, and the depreciable basis of the property is reduced by the amount of the credit. Expenditures for labor costs allocable to onsite preparation, assembly, or original installation of property eligible for the credit are eligible expenditures.

Certain equipment safety requirements need to be met to qualify for the credit. Special proration rules apply in the case of jointly owned property, condominiums, and tenant-stockholders in cooperative housing corporations. If less than 80 percent of the property is used for non-business purposes, only that portion of expenditures that is used for nonbusiness purposes is taken into account.

The credit applies to property placed in service after December 31, 2005 and prior to January 1, 2008.

Explanation Provision

The provision extends the credit to property placed in service after December 31, 2005 and prior to January 1, 2009. The provision also clarifies that all property, not just photovoltaic property, that uses solar energy to generate electricity for use in a dwelling unit is qualifying property.

Effective Date

The provision is effective on the date of enactment.

[Law at ¶5010. CCH Explanation at ¶230.]

[¶15,410] Act Sec. 207. Extension of business solar and fuel cell energy credit

Joint Committee Taxation (J.C.T. REP. NO. JCX-50-06)

[Code Sec. 48]

Present Law

In general

A nonrefundable, 10-percent business energy credit is allowed for the cost of new property that is equipment (1) that uses solar energy to generate electricity, to heat or cool a structure, or to provide solar process heat, or (2) used to produce, distribute, or use energy derived from a geothermal deposit, but only, in the case of electricity generated by geothermal power, up to the

electric transmission stage. Property used to generate energy for the purposes of heating a swimming pool is not eligible solar energy property.

The business energy tax credits are components of the general business credit (sec. 38(b)(1)). The business energy tax credits, when combined with all other components of the general business credit, generally may not exceed for any taxable year the excess of the taxpayer's net income tax over the greater of (1) 25 percent of so much of the net regular tax liability as exceeds $25,000 or (2) the tentative minimum tax. An unused general business credit generally may be carried back one year and carried forward 20 years (sec. 39).

In general, property that is public utility property is not eligible for the credit. This rule is waived in the case of telecommunication companies' purchases of fuel cell and microturbine property.

The credit is nonrefundable. The taxpayer's basis in the property is reduced by the amount of the credit claimed.

Special rules for solar energy property

The credit for solar energy property is increased to 30 percent in the case of periods after December 31, 2005 and prior to January 1, 2008. Additionally, equipment that uses fiber-optic distributed sunlight to illuminate the inside of a structure is solar energy property eligible for the 30-percent credit.

Fuel cells and microturbines

The business energy credit also applies for the purchase of qualified fuel cell power plants, but only for periods after December 31, 2005 and prior to January 1, 2008. The credit rate is 30 percent. A qualified fuel cell power plant is an integrated system composed of a fuel cell stack assembly and associated balance of plant components that (1) converts a fuel into electricity using electrochemical means, (2) has an electricity-only generation efficiency of greater than 30 percent. The credit may not exceed $500 for each 0.5 kilowatt of capacity.

The business energy credit also applies for the purchase of qualifying stationary microturbine power plants, but only for periods

after December 31, 2005 and prior to January 1, 2008. The credit is limited to the lesser of 10 percent of the basis of the property or $200 for each kilowatt of capacity.

A qualified stationary microturbine power plant is an integrated system comprised of a gas turbine engine, a combustor, a recuperator or regenerator, a generator or alternator, and associated balance of plant components that converts a fuel into electricity and thermal energy. Such system also includes all secondary components located between the existing infrastructure for fuel delivery and the existing infrastructure for power distribution, including equipment and controls for meeting relevant power standards, such as voltage, frequency and power factors. Such system must have an electricity-only generation efficiency of not less that 26 percent at International Standard Organization conditions and a capacity of less than 2,000 kilowatts.

Additionally, for purposes of the fuel cell and microturbine credits, and only in the case of telecommunications companies, the general present-law section 48 restriction that would otherwise prohibit telecommunication companies from claiming the new credit due to their status as public utilities is waived.

Explanation of Provision

The provision extends the present law credit at current credit rates through December 31, 2008.

Effective Date

The provision is effective on the date of enactment.

[Law at ¶5050. CCH Explanation at ¶440.]

[¶15,420] Act Sec. 208. Special rule for qualified methanol and ethanol fuel produced from coal

Joint Committee Taxation (J.C.T. Rep. No. JCX-50-06)

[Code Sec. 4041]

Present Law

The term "qualified methanol or ethanol fuel" means any liquid at least 85 percent of which consists of methanol, ethanol or other alcohol produced from coal (including peat). Qualified methanol or ethanol fuel is taxed at a reduced rate. Qualified methanol is taxed at 12.35 cents per gallon. Qualified ethanol is taxed at 13.25 cents per gallon. These reduced rates expire after September 30, 2007.

Explanation of Provision

The provision extends the reduced rates for qualified methanol or ethanol fuel through December 31, 2008.

Effective Date

The provision is effective on the date of enactment.

[Law at ¶5660. CCH Explanation at ¶665.]

[¶15,430] Act Sec. 209. Special depreciation allowance for cellulosic biomass ethanol plant property

Joint Committee Taxation (J.C.T. REP. NO. JCX-50-06)

[New Code Sec. 168(l)]

Present Law

A taxpayer is allowed to recover, through annual depreciation deductions, the cost of certain property used in a trade or business or for the production of income. The amount of the depreciation deduction allowed with respect to tangible property for a taxable year is determined under the modified accelerated cost recovery system ("MACRS"). Under MACRS, different types of property generally are assigned applicable recovery periods and depreciation methods. The recovery periods applicable to most tangible personal property (generally tangible property other than residential rental property and nonresidential real property) range from 3 to 25 years. The depreciation methods generally applicable to tangible personal property are the 200-percent and 150-percent declining balance methods, switching to the straight-line method for the taxable year in which the depreciation deduction would be maximized.

In lieu of depreciation, a taxpayer with a sufficiently small amount of annual investment may elect to deduct (or "expense") such costs (sec. 179). Present law provides that the maximum amount a taxpayer may expense, for taxable years beginning in 2003 through 2009, is $100,000 of the cost of qualifying property placed in service for the taxable year. The $100,000 amount is reduced (but not below zero) by the amount by which the cost of qualifying property placed in service during the taxable year exceeds $400,000. The $100,000 and $400,000 amounts are indexed for inflation for taxable years beginning after 2003 and before 2010. In general, under section 179, qualifying property is defined as depreciable tangible personal property that is purchased for use in the active conduct of a trade or business. Additional section 179 incentives are provided with respect to a qualified property used by a business in the New York Liberty Zone (sec. 1400L(f)), an empowerment zone (sec. 1397A), a renewal community (sec. 1400J), or the Gulf Opportunity Zone (section 1400N). Recapture rules generally apply with respect to property that ceases to be qualified property.

Section 179C provides a temporary election to expense 50 percent of the cost of qualified refinery property. Qualified refinery property generally includes assets, located in the United States, used in the refining of liquid fuels: (1) with respect to the construction of which there is a binding construction contract before January 1, 2008; (2) which are placed in service before January 1, 2012; (3) which increase the output capacity of an existing refinery by at least five percent or increase the percentage of total throughput attributable to qualified fuels (as defined in section 45K(c)) such that it equals or exceeds 25 percent; and (4) which meet all applicable environmental laws in effect when the property is placed in service.

For purposes of section 179C, the term "refinery" refers to facilities the primary purpose of which is the processing of crude oil (whether or not previously refined) or qualified fuels as defined in section 45K(c). The limitation of section 45K(d) requiring domestic production of qualified fuels is not applicable with respect to the definition of refinery under this provision; thus, otherwise qualifying refinery property is eligible even if the primary purpose of the refinery is the processing of oil produced from shale and tar sands outside the United States. The term refinery would include a facility which processes coal or biomass via gas into liquid fuel.

Explanation of Provision

The provision allows an additional first-year depreciation deduction equal to 50 percent of the adjusted basis of qualified cellulosic biomass ethanol plant property. In order to qualify, the property generally must be placed in service before January 1, 2013.

Qualified cellulosic biomass ethanol plant property means property used in the U.S. solely to produce cellulosic biomass ethanol. For this purpose, cellulosic biomass ethanol means ethanol derived from any lignocellulosic or hemicellulosic matter that is available on a renewable or recurring basis. For example, lignocellulosic or hemicellulosic matter that is available on a renewable or recurring basis includes bagasse (from sugar cane), corn stalks, and switchgrass.

The additional first-year depreciation deduction is allowed for both regular tax and alternative minimum tax purposes for the taxable year in which the property is placed in service. The additional first-year depreciation deduction is subject to the general rules regarding whether an item is deductible under section 162 or subject to capitalization under section 263 or section 263A. The basis of the property and the depreciation allowances in the year of purchase and later years are appropriately adjusted to reflect the additional first-year depreciation deduction. In addition, the provision provides that there is no adjustment to the allowable amount of depreciation for purposes of computing a taxpayer's alternative minimum taxable income with respect to property to which the provision applies. A taxpayer is allowed to elect out of the additional first-year depreciation for any class of property for any taxable year.

In order for property to qualify for the additional first-year depreciation deduction, it must meet the following requirements. The original use of the property must commence with the taxpayer on or after the date of enactment of the provision. The property must be acquired by purchase (as defined under section 179(d)) by the taxpayer after the date of enactment and placed in service before January 1, 2013. Property does not qualify if a binding written contract for the acquisition of such property was in effect on or before the date of enactment.

Property that is manufactured, constructed, or produced by the taxpayer for use by the taxpayer qualifies if the taxpayer begins the manufacture, construction, or production of the property after the date of enactment, and the property is placed in service before January 1, 2013 (and all other requirements are met). Property that is manufactured, constructed, or produced for the taxpayer by another person under a contract that is entered into prior to the manufacture, construction, or production of the property is considered to be manufactured, constructed, or produced by the taxpayer.

Property any portion of which is financed with the proceeds of a tax-exempt obligation under section 103 is not eligible for the additional first-year depreciation deduction. Recapture rules apply under the provision if the property ceases to be qualified cellulosic biomass ethanol plant property.

Property with respect to which the taxpayer has elected 50 percent expensing under section 179C is not eligible for the additional first-year depreciation deduction under the provision.

Effective Date

The provision applies to property placed in service after the date of enactment, in taxable years ending after such date.

[Law at ¶5265. CCH Explanation at ¶323.]

[¶15,440] Act Sec. 210. Expenditures permitted from the Leaking Underground Storage Tank Trust Fund

Joint Committee Taxation (J.C.T. REP. No. JCX-50-06)

[Code Sec. 9508]

Present Law

Internal Revenue Code provisions

Section 1362 of the Energy Policy Act of 2005[62] extended the 0.1 cent per-gallon Leaking Underground Storage Tank ("LUST") Trust Fund tax until October 1, 2011. Under section 9508 of the Internal Revenue Code (the "Code"), the LUST Trust Fund is available only for purposes specified in section 9003(h) of the Solid Waste Disposal Act as in effect on the date of enactment of the Superfund Amendments and Reauthorization Act of 1986.[63]

All expenditures from the LUST Trust Fund must be authorized by the Code. In the event of an expenditure from the LUST Trust Fund that is not authorized by the Code, the Code provides that no amounts may be appropriated to the LUST Trust Fund on or after the date of such expenditure. An exception to this rule is provided to allow for the liquidation of contracts entered into in accordance with the Code before October 1, 2011. The determination of whether an expenditure is permitted is to be made without regard to (1) any provision of law that is not contained or referenced in the Code or in a revenue Act, and (2) whether such provision of law is a subsequently enacted provision or directly or indirectly seeks to waive the application of the Code restriction. This provision became effective on August 10, 2005.[64]

---

[62] Pub. L. No. 109-58.

[63] Sec. 9508(c).

[64] Sec. 9508(e). This provision was added to the Code by section 11147 of the Safe, Accountable, Flexible, Efficient Transportation Equity Act: A Legacy for Users (Pub. L. No. 109-59).

Underground Storage Tank Compliance Act of 2005

Sections 1521 through 1533 of the Energy Policy Act of 2005 (also known as the "Underground Storage Tank Compliance Act of 2005") broadened the uses of the LUST Trust Fund and authorizes States and the Environmental Protection Agency ("EPA") to use funds appropriated from the LUST Trust Fund to address methyl tertiary butyl ether ("MTBE") leaks.[65]

Section 1522 directs EPA to allot at least 80 percent of the funds made available from the LUST Trust Fund to the States for the LUST cleanup program (section 9004 of the Solid Waste Disposal Act). It also requires EPA or States to conduct compliance inspections of underground storage tanks every three years (sec. 1523 (section 9005(c) of the Solid Waste Disposal Act)); adds operator training requirements (sec. 1524 (section 9010 of the Solid Waste Disposal Act)); and authorizes EPA and States to use LUST Trust Fund money to respond to tank leaks involving oxygenated fuel additives (e.g., MTBE and ethanol) (sec. 1525 (section 9003(h) of the Solid Waste Disposal Act)). Section 1526 authorizes EPA and States to use LUST Trust Fund money to conduct inspections and enforce tank release prevention and detection requirements (sections 9011 and 9003(j) of the Solid Waste Disposal Act). The Act also prohibits fuel delivery to ineligible tanks (sec. 1527 (section 9012 of the Solid Waste Disposal Act)); and requires EPA, with Indian tribes, to develop and implement a strategy to address releases on tribal lands (sec. 1529 (section 9013 of the Solid Waste Disposal Act)).

Sec. 1530 (section 9003(i) of the Solid Waste Disposal Act) requires States to do one of the following to protect groundwater: (1) require that new tanks are secondarily contained and monitored for leaks if the tank is within 1,000 feet of a community water system or potable well; or (2) require that underground storage tank manufacturers and installers maintain evidence of financial responsibility to pay for corrective actions. It also requires that persons installing underground storage tank systems are certified or licensed, or that their underground

storage tank system installation is certified by a professional engineer or inspected and approved by the State, or is compliant with a code of practice or other method that is no less protective of human health and the environment.

Sec. 1531 (section 9014 of the Solid Waste Disposal Act) authorized to be appropriated from the LUST Trust Fund, for each of FY2005 through FY2009, $200 million for cleaning up leaks from petroleum tanks generally, and another $200 million for responding to tank leaks involving MTBE or other oxygenated fuel additives (e.g., other ethers and ethanol). This section further authorizes to be appropriated from the LUST Trust Fund, for each of FY2005 through FY2009, $155 million for EPA and States to carry out and enforce the underground storage tank leak prevention and detection requirements added by the Act and the LUST cleanup program.[66]

These provisions became effective on the date of enactment (August 8, 2005).

Public Law No. 109-168 made certain technical corrections to the Solid Waste Disposal Act as amended by the Energy Policy Act of 2005 with respect to the regulation of underground storage tanks and government-owned tanks. It also adjusted and extended the authorization for appropriations to cover fiscal year 2006 through fiscal year 2011.

Although the Underground Storage Tank Compliance Act of 2005 and Public Law No. 109-168 amended the Solid Waste Disposal Act, neither Act made conforming amendments to section 9508 of the Code.

Explanation of Provision

The provision updates the permitted expenditure purposes of Code section 9508(c) to include the purposes added by the Energy Policy Act of 2005. Specifically, the provision authorizes LUST Trust Fund amounts to be used to carry out the following provisions of the Solid Waste Disposal Act (as in effect on January 10, 2006, the date of enactment of Pub. L. No. 109-168):

---

[65] The description that follows is taken primarily from Congressional Research Service, *Energy Policy Act of 2005: Summary and Analysis of Enacted Provisions* (March 8, 2006).

[66] Section 9014 provides in pertinent part: There are authorized to be appropriated to the Administrator the following amounts: ...

(2) From the Trust Fund, notwithstanding section 9508(c)(1) of the Internal Revenue Code of 1986:

(A) to carry out section 9003(h) (except section 9003(h)(12) $200,000,000 for each of fiscal years 2005 through 2009;

(B) to carry out section 9003(h)(12), $200,000,000 for each of fiscal years 2005 through 2009;

(C) to carry out sections 9003(i), 9004(f), and 9005(c) $100,000,000 for each of fiscal years 2005 through 2009, and

(D) to carry out sections 9010, 9011, 9012, and 9013 $55,000,000 for each of fiscal years 2005 through 2009.

- section 9003(i) (relating to measures to protect ground water);

- section 9003(j) (relating to compliance of government-owned tanks);

- section 9004(f) (relating to 80 percent distribution requirement for State enforcement efforts);

- section 9005(c) (relating to inspection of underground storage tanks);

- section 9010 (relating to operator training);

- section 9011 (relating to funds for release prevention and compliance);

- section 9012 (relating to the delivery prohibition for ineligible tanks/guidance/compliance); and

- section 9013 (relating to strategy for addressing tanks on tribal lands).

The Code continues to authorize the use of amounts in the LUST Trust Fund to carry out the purposes of section 9003(h) of the Solid Waste Disposal Act (as in effect on January 10, 2006, the date of enactment of Pub. L. No. 109-168).

Effective Date

The provision is effective on the date of enactment.

[Law at ¶5870 and ¶7060. CCH Explanation at ¶675.]

[¶15,450] Act Sec. 211. Modification of credit for fuel from a non-conventional source

Joint Committee Taxation (J.C.T. REP. No. JCX-50-06)

[Code Sec. 45K]

Present Law

Certain fuels produced from "non-conventional sources" and sold to unrelated parties are eligible for an income tax credit equal to $3 (generally adjusted for inflation)[67] per barrel or Btu oil barrel equivalent ("non-conventional source fuel credit").[68] Qualified fuels must be produced within the United States.

Qualified fuels include:

- oil produced from shale and tar sands;

- gas produced from geopressured brine, Devonian shale, coal seams, tight formations, or biomass; and

- liquid, gaseous, or solid synthetic fuels produced from coal (including lignite).

Generally, the non-conventional source fuel credit has expired, except for certain biomass gas and synthetic fuels sold before January 1, 2008, and produced at facilities placed in service after December 31, 1992, and before July 1, 1998.

The non-conventional source fuel credit provision also includes a credit for coke or coke gas produced at qualified facilities during a four-year period beginning on the later of January 1, 2006, or the date the facility was placed in service. For purposes of the coke production credit, qualified facilities are facilities placed in service before January 1, 1993, or after June 30, 1998, and before January 1, 2010. The amount of credit-eligible coke produced at any one facility may not exceed an average barrel-of-oil equivalent of 4,000 barrels per day.

The non-conventional source fuel credit is reduced (but not below zero) over a $6 (inflation-adjusted) phase-out period as the reference price for oil exceeds $23.50 per barrel (also adjusted for inflation). The reference price is the Secretary's estimate of the annual average wellhead price per barrel for all domestic crude oil. The credit did not phase-out for 2005 because the reference price for that year of $50.26 did not exceed the inflation adjusted threshold of $51.35. Beginning with taxable years ending after December 31, 2005, the non-conventional source fuel credit is part of the general business credit (sec. 38).

Explanation of Provision

The provision repeals the phase-out limitation for coke and coke gas otherwise eligible for a credit under section 45K(g). The provision also clarifies that qualifying facilities producing coke and coke gas under section 45K(g) do not in-

---

[67] The inflation adjustment is generally calculated using 1979 as the base year. Generally, the value of the credit for fuel produced in 2005 was $6.79 per barrel-of-oil equivalent produced, which is approximately $1.20 per thousand cubic feet of natural gas. In the case of fuel sold after 2005, the credit for coke or coke gas is indexed for inflation using 2004 as the base year instead of 1979.

[68] Sec. 29 (for tax years ending before 2006); sec. 45K (for tax years ending after 2005).

clude facilities that produce petroleum-based coke or coke gas. The provision does not modify the existing 4,000 barrel-of-oil equivalent per day limitation.

Effective Date

The provision is effective as if included in section 1321 of the Energy Policy Act of 2005.

[Law at ¶ 5047. CCH Explanation at ¶ 460.]

[¶ 15,460] Act Secs. 301 through 307. Provisions relating to health savings accounts

Joint Committee Taxation (J.C.T. REP. NO. JCX-50-06)

[Code Sec. 223]

Present Law

Health savings accounts

In general

Individuals with a high deductible health plan (and no other health plan other than a plan that provides certain permitted coverage) may establish a health savings account ("HSA"). In general, HSAs provide tax-favored treatment for current medical expenses as well as the ability to save on a tax-favored basis for future medical expenses. In general, HSAs are tax-exempt trusts or custodial accounts created exclusively to pay for the qualified medical expenses of the account holder and his or her spouse and dependents.

Within limits, contributions to an HSA made by or on behalf of an eligible individual are deductible by the individual. Contributions to an HSA are excludable from income and employment taxes if made by the employer. Earnings on amounts in HSAs are not taxable. Distributions from an HSA for qualified medical expenses are not includible in gross income. Distributions from an HSA that are not used for qualified medical expenses are includible in gross income and are subject to an additional tax of 10 percent. The 10-percent additional tax does not apply if the distribution is made after death, disability, or the individual attains the age of Medicare eligibility (i.e., age 65).

Eligible individuals

Eligible individuals for HSAs are individuals who are covered by a high deductible health plan and no other health plan that is not a high deductible health plan and which provides coverage for any benefit which is covered under the high deductible health plan. After an individual has attained age 65 and becomes enrolled in Medicare benefits, contributions cannot be made to an HSA.[69] Eligible individuals do not include individuals who may be claimed as a dependent on another person's tax return.

An individual with other coverage in addition to a high deductible health plan is still eligible for an HSA if such other coverage is certain permitted insurance or permitted coverage. Permitted insurance is: (1) insurance if substantially all of the coverage provided under such insurance relates to (a) liabilities incurred under worker's compensation law, (b) tort liabilities, (c) liabilities relating to ownership or use of property (e.g., auto insurance), or (d) such other similar liabilities as the Secretary of Treasury may prescribe by regulations; (2) insurance for a specified disease or illness; and (3) insurance that provides a fixed payment for hospitalization. Permitted coverage is coverage (whether provided through insurance or otherwise) for accidents, disability, dental care, vision care, or long-term care.

A high deductible health plan is a health plan that, for 2007, has a deductible that is at least $1,100 for self-only coverage or $2,200 for family coverage and that has an out-of-pocket expense limit that is no more than $5,500 in the case of self-only coverage and $11,000 in the case of family coverage.[70] Out-of-pocket expenses include deductibles, co-payments, and other amounts (other than premiums) that the individ-

---

[69] Sec. 223(b)(7), as interpreted by Notice 2004-2, 2004-2 I.R.B. 269, corrected by Announcement 2004-67, 2004-36 I.R.B. 459.

[70] The limits are indexed for inflation. For 2006, a high deductible plan is a health plan that has a deductible that is at least $1,050 for self-only coverage or $2,100 for family coverage and that has an out-of-pocket expense limit that is

no more than $5,250 in the case of self-only coverage and $10,500 in the case of family coverage. The family coverage limits always will be twice the self-only coverage limits (as indexed for inflation). In the case of the plan using a network of providers, the plan does not fail to be a high deductible health plan (if it would otherwise meet the requirements of a high deductible health plan) solely because

ual must pay for covered benefits under the plan. A plan is not a high deductible health plan if substantially all of the coverage is for permitted coverage or coverage that may be provided by permitted insurance, as described above. A plan does not fail to be a high deductible health plan by reason of failing to have a deductible for preventive care.

Health flexible spending arrangement ("FSAs") and health reimbursement arrangements ("HRAs") are health plans that constitute other coverage under the HSA rules. These arrangements are discussed in more detail, below. An individual who is covered by a high deductible health plan and a health FSA or HRA generally is not eligible to make contributions to an HSA. An individual is eligible to make contributions to an HSA if the health FSA or HRA is: (1) a limited purpose health FSA or HRA; (2) a suspended HRA; (3) a post-deductible health FSA or HRA; or (4) a retirement HRA.[71]

Tax treatment of and limits on contributions

Contributions to an HSA by or on behalf of an eligible individual are deductible (within limits) in determining adjusted gross income (i.e., "above-the-line") of the individual. In addition, employer contributions to HSAs (including salary reduction contributions made through a cafeteria plan) are excludable from gross income and wages for employment tax purposes. In the case of an employee, contributions to an HSA may be made by both the individual and the individual's employer. All contributions are aggregated for purposes of the maximum annual contribution limit. Contributions to Archer MSAs reduce the annual contribution limit for HSAs.

The maximum aggregate annual contribution that can be made to an HSA is the lesser of (1) 100 percent of the annual deductible under the high deductible health plan, or (2) (for 2007) $2,850 in the case of self-only coverage and $5,650 in the case of family coverage.[72] The annual contribution limit is the sum of the limits determined separately for each month, based on the individual's status and health plan coverage as of the first day of the month. The annual contribution limits are increased for individuals who have attained age 55 by the end of the taxable year. In the case of policyholders and covered spouses who are age 55 or older, the HSA annual contribution limit is greater than the otherwise applicable limit by $700 in 2006, $800 in 2007, $900 in 2008, and $1,000 in 2009 and thereafter. As in determining the general annual contribution limit, the increase in the annual contribution limit for individuals who have attained age 55 is also determined on a monthly basis. As previously discussed, contributions, including catch-up contributions, cannot be made once an individual is enrolled in Medicare.

In the case of individuals who are married to each other and either spouse has family coverage, both spouses are treated as having only the family coverage with the lowest annual deductible. The annual contribution limit (without regard to the catch-up contribution amounts) is divided equally between the spouses unless they agree on a different division (after reduction for amounts paid from any Archer MSA of the spouses).

An excise tax applies to contributions in excess of the maximum contribution amount for the HSA. The excise tax generally is equal to six percent of the cumulative amount of excess contributions that are not distributed from the HSA.

Amounts can be rolled over into an HSA from another HSA or from an Archer MSA.

Comparable contributions

If an employer makes contributions to employees' HSAs, the employer must make available comparable contributions on behalf of all employees with comparable coverage during the same period. Contributions are considered comparable if they are either of the same amount or the same percentage of the deductible under the plan. If employer contributions do not satisfy the comparability rule during a period, then the employer is subject to an excise tax equal to 35 percent of the aggregate amount contributed by the employer to HSAs for that period. The com-

---

(Footnote Continued)

the out-of-pocket expense limit for services provided outside of the network exceeds the out-of-pocket expense limits. In addition, such plan's deductible for out-of-network services is not taken into account in determining the annual contribution limit (i.e., the deductible for services within the network is used for such purpose).

[71] Rev. Rul. 2004-45, 2004-22 I.R.B. 1. A limited purpose health FSA pays or reimburses benefits for permitted coverage and a limited purpose HRA pays or reimburses benefits for permitted insurance or permitted coverage. A limited purpose health FSA or HRA may also pay or reimburse preventive care benefits. A suspended HRA does not pay medical expense incurred during a suspension period except for preventive care, permitted insurance and permitted coverage. A post-deductible health FSA or HRA does not pay or reimburse any medical expenses incurred before the minimum annual deductible under the HSA rules is satisfied. A retirement HSA pays or reimburses only medical expenses incurred after retirement.

[72] These amounts are indexed for inflation. For 2006, the dollar limits are $2,700 in the case of self-only coverage and $5,450 in the case of family coverage.

parability rule does not apply to contributions made through a cafeteria plan.

Taxation of distributions

Distributions from an HSA for qualified medical expenses of the individual and his or her spouse or dependents generally are excludable from gross income. In general, amounts in an HSA can be used for qualified medical expenses even if the individual is not currently eligible for contributions to the HSA.

Qualified medical expenses generally are defined as under section 213(d) and include expenses for diagnosis, cure, mitigation, treatment, or prevention of disease. Qualified medical expenses do not include expenses for insurance other than for (1) long-term care insurance, (2) premiums for health coverage during any period of continuation coverage required by Federal law, (3) premiums for health care coverage while an individual is receiving unemployment compensation under Federal or State law, or (4) in the case of an account beneficiary who has attained the age of Medicare eligibility, health insurance premiums for Medicare, other than premiums for Medigap policies. Such qualified health insurance premiums include, for example, Medicare Part A and Part B premiums, Medicare HMO premiums, and the employee share of premiums for employer-sponsored health insurance including employer-sponsored retiree health insurance. Whether the expenses are qualified medical expenses is determined as of the time the expenses were incurred.

For purposes of determining the itemized deduction for medical expenses, distributions from an HSA for qualified medical expenses are not treated as expenses paid for medical care under section 213. Distributions from an HSA that are not for qualified medical expenses are includible in gross income. Distributions includible in gross income also are subject to an additional 10-percent tax unless made after death, disability, or the individual attains the age of Medicare eligibility (i.e., age 65).

Reporting requirements

Employer contributions are required to be reported on the employee's Form W-2. Trustees of HSAs may be required to report to the Secretary of the Treasury amounts with respect to contributions, distributions, the return of excess contributions, and other matters as determined appropriate by the Secretary. In addition, the Secretary may require providers of high deducti-

ble health plans to make reports to the Secretary and to account beneficiaries as the Secretary determines appropriate.

Health flexible spending arrangements and health reimbursement arrangements

Arrangements commonly used by employers to reimburse medical expenses of their employees (and their spouses and dependents) include health flexible spending arrangements ("FSAs") and health reimbursement accounts ("HRAs"). Health FSAs typically are funded on a salary reduction basis, meaning that employees are given the option to reduce current compensation and instead have the compensation used to reimburse the employee for medical expenses. If the health FSA meets certain requirements, then the compensation that is forgone is not includible in gross income or wages and reimbursements for medical care from the health FSA are excludable from gross income and wages. Health FSAs are subject to the general requirements relating to cafeteria plans, including a requirement that a cafeteria plan generally may not provide deferred compensation.[73] This requirement often is referred to as the "use-it-or-lose-it-rule." Until May of 2005, this requirement was interpreted to mean that amounts available from a health FSA as of the end of a plan year must be forfeited by the employee. In May 2005, the Treasury Department issued a notice that allows a grace period not to exceed two and one-half months immediately following the end of the plan year during which unused amounts may be used.[74] An individual participating in a health FSA that allows reimbursements during a grace period is generally not eligible to make contributions to the HSA until the first month following the end of the grace period even if the individual's health FSA has no unused benefits as of the end of the prior plan year.[75] Health FSAs are subject to certain other requirements, including rules that require that the FSA have certain characteristics similar to insurance.

HRAs operate in a manner similar to health FSAs, in that they are an employer-maintained arrangement that reimburses employees for medical expenses. Some of the rules applicable to HRAs and health FSAs are similar, e.g., the amounts in the arrangements can only be used to reimburse medical expenses and not for other purposes. Some of the rules are different. For example, HRAs cannot be funded on a salary reduction basis and the use-it-or-lose-it rule does not apply. Thus, amounts remaining at the end

---

[73] Sec. 125(d)(2).

[74] Notice 2005-42, 2005-23 I.R.B. 1204.

[75] Notice 2005-86, 2005-49 I.R.B. 1075.

of the year may be carried forward to be used to reimburse medical expenses in the next year.[76] Reimbursements for insurance covering medical care expenses are allowable reimbursements under an HRA, but not under a health FSA.

As mentioned above, subject to certain limited exceptions, health FSAs and HRAs constitute other coverage under the HSA rules.

Explanation of Provision

Allow rollovers from health FSAs and HRAs into HSAs for a limited time

The provision allows certain amounts in a health FSA or HRA to be distributed from the health FSA or HRA and contributed through a direct transfer to an HSA without violating the otherwise applicable requirements for such arrangements. The amount that can be distributed from a health FSA or HRA and contributed to an HSA may not exceed an amount equal to the lesser of (1) the balance in the health FSA or HRA as of September 21, 2006 or (2) the balance in the health FSA or HRA as of the date of the distribution. The balance in the health FSA or HRA as of any date is determined on a cash basis (i.e., expenses incurred that have not been reimbursed as of the date the determination is made are not taken into account). Amounts contributed to an HSA under the provision are excludable from gross income and wages for employment tax purposes, are not taken into account in applying the maximum deduction limitation for other HSA contributions, and are not deductible. Contributions must be made directly to the HSA before January 1, 2012. The provision is limited to one distribution with respect to each health FSA or HRA of the individual.

The provision is designed to assist individuals in transferring from another type of health plan to a high deductible health plan. Thus, if an individual for whom a contribution is made under the provision does not remain an eligible individual during the testing period, the amount of the contribution is includible in gross income of the individual. An exception applies if the employee ceases to be an eligible individual by reason of death or disability. The testing period is the period beginning with the month of the contribution and ending on the last day of the 12th month following such month. The amount is includible for the taxable year of the first day during the testing period that the individual is not an eligible individual. A 10-percent additional tax also applies to the amount includible.

A modified comparability rule applies with respect to contributions under the provision. If the employer makes available to any employee the ability to make contributions to the HSA from distributions from a health FSA or HRA under the provision, all employees who are covered under a high deductible plan of the employer must be allowed to make such distributions and contributions. The present-law excise tax applies if this requirement is not met.

For example, suppose the balance in a health FSA as of September 21, 2006, is $2,000 and the balance in the account as January 1, 2008 is $3,000. Under the provision, a health FSA will not be considered to violate applicable rules if, as of January 1, 2008, an amount not to exceed $2,000 is distributed from the health FSA and contributed to an HSA of the individual. The $2,000 distribution would not be includible in income, and the subsequent contribution would not be deductible and would not count against the annual maximum tax deductible contribution that can be made to the HSA. If the individual ceases to be an eligible individual as of June 1, 2008, the $2,000 contribution amount is included in gross income and subject to a 10-percent additional tax. If instead the distribution and contribution are made as of June 30, 2008, when the balance in the health FSA is $1,500, the amount of the distribution and contribution is limited to $1,500.

The present law rule that an individual is not an eligible individual if the individual has coverage under a general purpose health FSA or HRA continues to apply. Thus, for example, if the health FSA or HRA from which the contribution is made is a general purpose health FSA or HRA and the individual remains eligible under such arrangement after the distribution and contribution, the individual is not an eligible individual.

Certain FSA coverage treated as disregarded coverage

The provision provides that, for taxable years beginning after December 31, 2006, in certain cases, coverage under a health flexible spending arrangement ("FSA") during the period immediately following the end of a plan year during which unused benefits or contributions remaining at the end of such plan year may

---

[76] Guidance with respect to HRAs, including the interaction of FSAs and HRAs in the case an individual is covered under both, is provided in Notice 2002-45, 2002-2 C.B. 93.

be paid or reimbursed to plan participants for qualified expenses is disregarded coverage. Such coverage is disregarded if (1) the balance in the health FSA at the end of the plan year is zero, or (2) in accordance with rules prescribed by the Secretary of Treasury, the entire remaining balance in the health FSA at the end of the plan year is contributed to an HSA as provided under another provision of the bill.[77]

Thus, for example, if as of December 31, 2006, a participant's health FSA balance is zero, coverage under the health FSA during the period from January 1, 2007, until March 15, 2007 (i.e., the "grace period") is disregarded in determining if tax deductible contributions can be made to an HSA for that period. Similarly, if the entire balance in an individual's health FSA as of December 31, 2006, is distributed and contributed to an HSA (as under another provision of the bill) coverage during the health FSA grace period is disregarded.

It is intended that the Secretary will provide guidance under the provision with respect to the timing of health FSA distributions contributed to an HSA in order to facilitate such rollovers and the establishment of HSAs in connection with high deductible plans. For example, it is intended that the Secretary would provide rules under which coverage is disregarded if, before the end of a year, an individual elects high deductible plan coverage and to contribute any remaining FSA balance to an HSA in accordance with the provision even if the trustee-to-trustee transfer cannot be completed until the following plan year. Similar rules apply for the general provision allowing amounts from a health FSA or HRA to be contributed to an HSA in order to facilitate such contributions at the beginning of an employee's first year of HSA eligibility.

The provision does not modify the permitted health FSA grace period allowed under existing Treasury guidance.

Repeal of annual plan deductible limitation on HSA contribution limitation

The provision modifies the limit on the annual deductible contributions that can be made to an HSA so that the maximum deductible contribution is not limited to the annual deductible under the high deductible health plan. Thus, under the provision, the maximum aggregate annual contribution that can be made to an HSA is $2,850 (for 2007) in the case of self-only coverage and $5,650 (for 2007) in the case of family coverage.

Earlier indexing of cost of living adjustments

Under the provision, in the case of adjustments made for any taxable year beginning after 2007, the Consumer Price Index for a calendar year is determined as of the close of the 12-month period ending on March 31 of the calendar year (rather than August 31 as under present law) for the purpose of making cost-of-living adjustments for the HSA dollar amounts that are indexed for inflation (i.e., the contribution limits and the high-deductible health plan requirements). The provision also requires the Secretary of Treasury to publish the adjusted amounts for a year no later than June 1 of the preceding calendar year.

Allow full contribution for months preceding month that taxpayer is an eligible individual

In general, the provision allows individuals who become covered under a high deductible plan in a month other than January to make the full deductible HSA contribution for the year. Under the provision, an individual who is an eligible individual during the last month of a taxable year is treated as having been an eligible individual during every month during the taxable year for purposes of computing the amount that may be contributed to the HSA for the year. Thus, such individual is allowed to make contributions for months before the individual was enrolled in a high deductible health plan. For the months preceding the last month of the taxable year that the individual is treated as an eligible individual solely by reason of the provision, the individual is treated as having been enrolled in the same high deductible health plan in which the individual was enrolled during the last month of the taxable year.

If an individual makes contributions under the provision and does not remain an eligible individual during the testing period, the amount of the contributions attributable to months preceding the month in which the individual was an eligible individual which could not have been made but for the provision are includible in gross income. An exception applies if the employee ceases to be an eligible individual by reason of death or disability. The testing period is the period beginning with the last month of the taxable year and ending on the last day of the 12th month following such month. The amount is includible for the taxable year of the first day during the testing period that the indi-

---

[77] The amount that can be contributed is limited to the balance in the health FSA as of September 21, 2006.

vidual is not an eligible individual. A 10-percent additional tax also applies to the amount includible.

For example, suppose individual "A" enrolls in high deductible plan "H" in December of 2007 and is otherwise an eligible individual in that month. A was not an eligible individual in any other month in 2007. A may make HSA contributions as if she had been enrolled in plan H for all of 2007. If A ceases to be an eligible individual (e.g., if she ceases to be covered under the high deductible health plan) in June 2008, an amount equal to the HSA deduction attributable to treating A as an eligible individual for January through November 2007 is included in income in 2008. In addition, a 10-percent additional tax applies to the amount includible.

Modify employer comparable contribution requirements for contributions made to nonhighly compensated employees

The provision provides an exception to the comparable contribution requirements which allows employers to make larger HSA contributions for nonhighly compensated employees than for highly compensated employees. Highly compensated employees are defined as under section 414(q) and include any employee who was (1) a five-percent owner at any time during the year or the preceding year; or (2) for the preceding year, (A) had compensation from the employer in excess of $100,000[78] (for 2007) and (B) if elected by the employer, was in the group consisting of the top-20 percent of employees when ranked based on compensation. Nonhighly compensated employees are employees not included in the definition of highly compensated employee under section 414(q).

The comparable contribution rules continue to apply to the contributions made to nonhighly compensated employees so that the employer must make available comparable contributions on behalf of all nonhighly compensated employees with comparable coverage during the same period.

For example, an employer is permitted to make a $1,000 contribution to the HSA of each nonhighly compensated employee for a year without making contributions to the HSA of each highly compensated employee.

One-time rollovers from IRAs into HSAs

The provision allows a one-time contribution to an HSA of amounts distributed from an

individual retirement arrangement ("IRA"). The contribution must be made in a direct trustee-to-trustee transfer. Amounts distributed from an IRA under the provision are not includible in income to the extent that the distribution would otherwise be includible in income. In addition, such distributions are not subject to the 10-percent additional tax on early distributions.

In determining the extent to which amounts distributed from the IRA would otherwise be includible in income, the aggregate amount distributed from the IRA is treated as includible in income to the extent of the aggregate amount which would have been includible if all amounts were distributed from all IRAs of the same type (i.e., in the case of a traditional IRA, there is no pro-rata distribution of basis). As under present law, this rule is applied separately to Roth IRAs and other IRAs.

The amount that can be distributed from the IRA and contributed to an HSA is limited to the otherwise maximum deductible contribution amount to the HSA computed on the basis of the type of coverage under the high deductible health plan at the time of the contribution. The amount that can otherwise be contributed to the HSA for the year of the contribution from the IRA is reduced by the amount contributed from the IRA. No deduction is allowed for the amount contributed from an IRA to an HSA.

Under the provision, only one distribution and contribution may be made during the lifetime of the individual, except that if a distribution and contribution are made during a month in which an individual has self-only coverage as of the first day of the month, an additional distribution and contribution may be made during a subsequent month within the taxable year in which the individual has family coverage. The limit applies to the combination of both contributions.

If the individual does not remain an eligible individual during the testing period, the amount of the distribution and contribution is includible in gross income of the individual. An exception applies if the employee ceases to be an eligible individual by reason of death or disability. The testing period is the period beginning with the month of the contribution and ending on the last day of the 12th month following such month. The amount is includible for the taxable year of the first day during the testing period that the individual is not an eligible individual. A 10-percent additional tax also applies to the amount includible.

---

[78] This amount is indexed for inflation.

The provision does not apply to simplified employee pensions ("SEPs") or to SIMPLE retirement accounts.

Effective Date

The provision allowing rollovers from heath FSAs and HRAs into HSAs is effective for distributions and contributions on or after the date of enactment and before January 1, 2012. The provision disregarding certain FSA coverage is effective after the date of enactment with respect to coverage for taxable years beginning after December 31, 2006. The provision repealing the annual plan limitation on the HSA contribution limitation is effective for taxable years beginning after December 31, 2006. The provision relating to cost-of-living adjustments is effective for adjustments made for taxable years beginning after 2007. The provision allowing contributions for months preceding the month that the taxpayer is an eligible individual is effective for taxable years beginning after December 31, 2006. The provision modifying the comparability rule is effective for taxable years beginning after December 31, 2006. The provision allowing one-time rollovers from an IRA into an HSA is effective for taxable years beginning after December 31, 2006.

[**Law at ¶5090, ¶5339, ¶5370 and ¶5690. CCH Explanation at ¶505, ¶510, ¶515, ¶520 and ¶525.**]

[¶15,470] Act Sec. 401. Deduction allowable with respect to income attributable to domestic production activities in Puerto Rico

Joint Committee Taxation (J.C.T. REP. NO. JCX-50-06)

[Code Sec. 199]

Present Law

In general

Present law provides a deduction from taxable income (or, in the case of an individual, adjusted gross income) that is equal to a portion of the taxpayer's qualified production activities income. For taxable years beginning after 2009, the deduction is nine percent of such income. For taxable years beginning in 2005 and 2006, the deduction is three percent of income and, for taxable years beginning in 2007, 2008 and 2009, the deduction is six percent of income. For taxpayers subject to the 35-percent corporate income tax rate, the 9-percent deduction effectively reduces the corporate income tax rate to just under 32 percent on qualified production activities income.

Qualified production activities income

In general, "qualified production activities income" is equal to domestic production gross receipts (defined by section 199(c)(4)), reduced by the sum of: (1) the costs of goods sold that are allocable to such receipts; and (2) other expenses, losses, or deductions which are properly allocable to such receipts.

Domestic production gross receipts

"Domestic production gross receipts" generally are gross receipts of a taxpayer that are derived from: (1) any sale, exchange or other disposition, or any lease, rental or license, of qualifying production property[79] that was manufactured, produced, grown or extracted by the taxpayer in whole or in significant part within the United States; (2) any sale, exchange or other disposition, or any lease, rental or license, of qualified film[80] produced by the taxpayer; (3) any sale, exchange or other disposition of electricity, natural gas, or potable water produced by the taxpayer in the United States; (4) construction activities performed in the United States; or (5) engineering or architectural services performed in the United States for construction projects located in the United States.

For purposes of section 199, the United States does not include Puerto Rico or other U.S. possessions.[81]

---

[79] "Qualifying production property" generally includes any tangible personal property, computer software, or sound recordings.

[80] "Qualified film" includes any motion picture film or videotape (including live or delayed television programming, but not including certain sexually explicit productions) if 50 percent or more of the total compensation relating to the production of such film (including compensation in the form of residuals and participations) constitutes compensation for services performed in the United States by actors, production personnel, directors, and producers.

[81] Sec. 7701(a)(9) ("the term 'United States' when used in a geographical sense includes only the States and the District of Columbia").

Wage limitation

For taxable years beginning after May 17, 2006, the amount of the deduction for a taxable year is limited to 50 percent of the wages paid by the taxpayer, and properly allocable to domestic production gross receipts, during the calendar year that ends in such taxable year.[82] Wages paid to bona fide residents of Puerto Rico generally are not included in the wage limitation amount.[83]

Explanation of Provision

The provision amends section 199 of the Code to include Puerto Rico within the definition of the United States for purposes of determining the domestic production gross receipts of eligible taxpayers. Under the provision, a taxpayer is allowed to treat Puerto Rico as part of the United States for purposes of section 199 (thus allowing the taxpayer to take into account

its Puerto Rico business activity for purposes of calculating its domestic production gross receipts and qualified production activities income), but only if all of the taxpayer's gross receipts from sources within Puerto Rico are currently taxable for U.S. Federal income tax purposes. Consequently, a controlled foreign corporation is not eligible for the section 199 deduction made available by the provision. In addition, any such taxpayer is also allowed to take into account wages paid to bona fide residents of Puerto Rico for purposes of calculating the 50-percent wage limitation.

Effective Date

The provision is effective for the first two taxable years beginning after December 31, 2005, and before January 1, 2008.

[Law at ¶ 5330. CCH Explanation at ¶ 345.]

[¶ 15,480]   Act Secs. 402 and 403. Alternative minimum tax credit relief for individuals; returns required for certain options

Joint Committee Taxation (J.C.T. Rep. No. JCX-50-06)

[Code Secs. 53 and 6039]

Present Law

In general

Present law imposes an alternative minimum tax ("AMT") on an individual taxpayer to the extent the taxpayer's tentative minimum tax liability exceeds his or her regular income tax liability. An individual's tentative minimum tax is the sum of (1) 26 percent of so much of the taxable excess as does not exceed $175,000 ($87,500 in the case of a married individual filing a separate return) and (2) 28 percent of the remaining taxable excess. The taxable excess is the amount by which the alternative minimum taxable income ("AMTI") exceeds an exemption amount.

An individual's AMTI is the taxpayer's taxable income increased by certain preference items and adjusted by determining the tax treatment of certain items in a manner that negates the deferral of income resulting from the regular tax treatment of those items.

The individual AMT attributable to deferral adjustments generates a minimum tax credit that is allowable to the extent the regular tax (reduced by other nonrefundable credits) exceeds the tentative minimum tax in a future taxable year. Unused minimum tax credits are carried forward indefinitely.

AMT treatment of incentive stock options

One of the adjustments in computing AMTI is the tax treatment of the exercise of an incentive stock option. An incentive stock option is an option granted by a corporation in connection with an individual's employment, so long as the option meets certain specified requirements.[84] Under the regular tax, the exercise of an incentive stock option is tax-free if the stock is not disposed of within one year of exercise of the option or within two years of the grant of the option.[85] The individual then computes the long-term capital gain or loss on the sale of the stock using the amount paid for the stock as the cost basis. If the holding period requirements are not satisfied, the individual generally takes into ac-

---

[82] For purposes of the provision, "wages" include the sum of the amounts of wages as defined in section 3401(a) and elective deferrals that the taxpayer properly reports to the Social Security Administration with respect to the employment of employees of the taxpayer during the calendar year ending during the taxpayer's taxable year. For taxable years beginning before May 18, 2006, the limitation is based

upon all wages paid by the taxpayer, rather than only wages properly allocable to domestic production gross receipts.

[83] Sec. 3401(a)(8)(C).

[84] Sec. 422.

[85] Sec. 421.

count at the exercise of the option an amount of ordinary income equal to the excess of the fair market value of the stock on the date of exercise over the amount paid for the stock. The cost basis of the stock is increased by the amount taken into account.[86]

Under the individual alternative minimum tax, the exercise of an incentive stock option is treated as the exercise of an option other than an incentive stock option. Under this treatment, generally the individual takes into account as ordinary income for purposes of computing AMTI the excess of the fair market value of the stock at the date of exercise over the amount paid for the stock.[87] When the stock is later sold, for purposes of computing capital gain or loss for purposes of AMTI, the adjusted basis of the stock includes the amount taken into account as AMTI.

The adjustment relating to incentive stock options is a deferral adjustment and therefore generates an AMT credit in the year the stock is sold.[88]

Furnishing of information

Under present law,[89] employers are required to provide to employees information regarding the transfer of stock pursuant to the exercise of an incentive stock option and to transfers of stock under an employee stock purchase plan where the option price is between 85 percent and 100 percent of the value of the stock.[90]

Explanation of Provision

Allowance of credit

Under the provision, an individual's minimum tax credit allowable for any taxable year beginning before January 1, 2013, is not less than the "AMT refundable credit amount". The "AMT refundable credit amount" is the greater of (1) the lesser of $5,000 or the long-term unused minimum tax credit, or (2) 20 percent of the long-term unused minimum tax credit. The long-term unused minimum tax credit for any taxable year means the portion of the minimum tax credit attributable to the adjusted net minimum tax for taxable years before the 3rd taxable year immediately preceding the taxable year (assum-

ing the credits are used on a first-in, first-out basis). In the case of an individual whose adjusted gross income for a taxable year exceeds the threshold amount (within the meaning of section 151(d)(3)(C)), the AMT refundable credit amount is reduced by the applicable percentage (within the meaning of section 151(d)(3)(B)). The additional credit allowable by reason of this provision is refundable.

Example.—Assume in 2010 an individual has an adjusted gross income that results in an applicable percentage of 50 percent under section 151(d)(3)(B), a regular tax of $45,000, a tentative minimum tax of $40,000, no other credits allowable, and a minimum tax credit for the taxable year (before limitation under section 53(c)) of $1.1 million of which $1 million is a long-term unused minimum tax credit.

The AMT refundable credit amount for the taxable year is $100,000 (20 percent of the $1 million long-term unused minimum tax credit reduced by an applicable percentage of 50 percent). The minimum tax credit allowable for the taxable year is $100,000 (the greater of the AMT refundable credit amount or the amount of the credit otherwise allowable). The $5,000 credit allowable without regard to this provision is nonrefundable and the additional $95,000 of credit allowable by reason of this provision is treated as a refundable credit. Thus, the taxpayer has an overpayment of $55,000 ($45,000 regular tax less $5,000 nonrefundable AMT credit less $95,000 refundable AMT credit). The $55,000 overpayment is allowed as a refund or credit to the taxpayer. The remaining $1 million minimum tax credit is carried forward to future taxable years.

If, in the above example, the adjusted gross income did not exceed the threshold amount under section 151(d)(3)(C), the AMT refundable credit amount for the taxable year would be $200,000, and the overpayment would be $155,000.

Information returns

The provision requires an employer to make an information return with the IRS, in addition to providing information to the employee, regarding the transfer of stock pursuant to exercise

---

[86] If the stock is sold at a loss before the required holding periods are met, the amount taken into account may not exceed the amount realized on the sale over the adjusted basis of the stock. If the stock is sold after the taxable year in which the option was exercised but before the required holding periods are met, the required inclusion is made in the year the stock is sold.

[87] If the stock is sold in the same taxable year the option is exercised, no adjustment in computing AMTI is required.

[88] If the stock is sold for less than the amount paid for the stock, the loss may not be allowed in full in computing AMTI by reason of the $3,000 limit on the deductibility of net capital losses. Thus, the excess of the regular tax over the tentative minimum tax may not reflect the full amount of the loss.

[89] Sec. 6039.

[90] Sec. 423(c).

of an incentive stock option, and to certain stock transfers regarding employee stock purchase plans.

Effective Date

The provision relating to the minimum tax credit applies to taxable years beginning after the date of enactment.

The provision relating to returns applies to calendar years beginning after the date of enactment.

[Law at ¶ 5054, ¶ 5740, ¶ 5785, ¶ 5820 and ¶ 7065. CCH Explanation at ¶ 235 and ¶ 630.]

[¶ 15,490] Act Sec. 404. Partial expensing for advanced mine safety equipment

Joint Committee Taxation (J.C.T. REP. NO. JCX-50-06)

[New Code Sec. 179E]

Present Law

A taxpayer generally must capitalize the cost of property used in a trade or business and recover such cost over time through annual deductions for depreciation or amortization. Tangible property generally is depreciated under the Modified Accelerated Cost Recovery System ("MACRS"), which determines depreciation by applying specific recovery periods, placed-in-service conventions, and depreciation methods to the cost of various types of depreciable property (sec. 168).

Personal property is classified under MACRS based on the property's class life unless a different classification is specifically provided in section 168. The class life applicable for personal property is the asset guideline period (midpoint class life as of January 1, 1986). Based on the property's classification, a recovery period is prescribed under MACRS. In general, there are six classes of recovery periods to which personal property can be assigned. For example, personal property that has a class life of four years or less has a recovery period of three years, whereas personal property with a class life greater than four years but less than 10 years has a recovery period of five years. The class lives and recovery periods for most property are contained in Revenue Procedure 87-56.[91]

In lieu of depreciation, a taxpayer with a sufficiently small amount of annual investment may elect to deduct (or "expense") such costs. Present law provides that the maximum amount a taxpayer may expense, for taxable years beginning in 2003 through 2009, is $100,000 of the cost of qualifying property placed in service for the taxable year. In general, qualifying property is defined as depreciable tangible personal property that is purchased for use in the active conduct of a trade or business. The $100,000 amount is reduced (but not below zero) by the amount by which the cost of qualifying property placed in service during the taxable year exceeds $400,000.

Explanation of Provision

Under the provision, a taxpayer may elect to treat 50 percent of the cost of any qualified advanced mine safety equipment property as a deduction in the taxable year in which the equipment is placed in service.

Advanced mine safety equipment property means any of the following: (1) emergency communication technology or devices used to allow a miner to maintain constant communication with an individual who is not in the mine; (2) electronic identification and location devices that allow individuals not in the mine to track at all times the movements and location of miners working in or at the mine; (3) emergency oxygen-generating, self-rescue devices that provide oxygen for at least 90 minutes; (4) pre-positioned supplies of oxygen providing each miner on a shift the ability to survive for at least 48 hours; and (5) comprehensive atmospheric monitoring systems that monitor the levels of carbon monoxide, methane and oxygen that are present in all areas of the mine and that can detect smoke in the case of a fire in a mine.

To be treated as qualified advanced mine safety equipment property under the provision, the original use of the property must have commenced with the taxpayer, and the taxpayer must have placed the property in service after the date of enactment.

The portion of the cost of any property with respect to which an expensing election under

---

[91] 1987-2 C.B. 674 (as clarified and modified by Rev. Proc. 88-22, 1988-1 C.B. 785).

section 179 is made may not be taken into account for purposes of the 50-percent deduction allowed under this provision. For Federal tax purposes, the basis of property is reduced by the portion of its cost that is taken into account for purposes of the 50-percent deduction allowed under the provision.

The provision requires the taxpayer to report information required by the Treasury Secretary with respect to the operation of mines of the taxpayer, in order for the deduction to be allowed for the taxable year.

An election made by the taxpayer under the provision may not be revoked except with the consent of the Secretary.

The provision includes a termination rule providing that it does not apply to property placed in service after December 31, 2008.

Effective Date

The provision applies to costs paid or incurred after the date of enactment, with regard to property placed in service on or before December 31, 2008.

[Law at ¶5315, ¶5341, ¶5347 and ¶5590. CCH Explanation at ¶330.]

[¶15,500] Act Sec. 405. Mine rescue team training credit

Joint Committee Taxation (J.C.T. REP. NO. JCX-50-06)

[New Code Sec. 45N]

Present Law

There is no present law credit for expenditures incurred by a taxpayer to train mine rescue workers. In general, a deduction is allowed for all ordinary and necessary expenses that are paid or incurred by the taxpayer during the taxable year in carrying on any trade or business.[92] A taxpayer that employs individuals as miners in underground mines will generally be permitted to deduct as ordinary and necessary expenses the educational expenditures such taxpayer incurs to train its employees in the principles, procedures, and techniques of mine rescue, as well as the wages paid by the taxpayer for the time its employees were engaged in such training.

Explanation of Provision

Under the provision, a taxpayer which is an eligible employer may claim a credit with respect to each qualified mine rescue team employee equal to the lesser of (1) 20 percent of the amount paid or incurred by the taxpayer during the taxable year with respect to the training program costs of such qualified mine rescue team employee (including wages of the employee while attending the program), or (2) $10,000.[93] For purposes of the provision, "wages" has the meaning given to such term by sec. 3306(b) (determined without regard to any dollar limitation contained in that section). An eligible employer is any taxpayer which employs individuals as miners in underground mines in the United States. No deduction is allowed for the amount of the expenses otherwise deductible which is equal to the amount of the credit.

A qualified mine rescue team employee is any full-time employee of the taxpayer who is a miner eligible for more than six months of a taxable year to serve as a mine rescue team member by virtue of either having completed the initial 20-hour course of instruction prescribed by the Mine Safety and Health Administration's Office of Educational Policy and Development, or receiving at least 40 hours of refresher training in such instruction.

Effective Date

The provision is effective for taxable years beginning after December 31, 2005, and before January 1, 2009.

[Law at ¶5034, ¶5049 and ¶5344. CCH Explanation at ¶425.]

---

[92] Sec. 162(a).

[93] The credit is part of the general business credit (sec. 38).

[¶ 15,510] Act Sec. 406. Whistleblower reforms

Joint Committee Taxation (J.C.T. REP. No. JCX-50-06)

[Code Sec. 7623]

Present Law

The Code authorizes the IRS to pay such sums as deemed necessary for: "(1) detecting underpayments of tax; and (2) detecting and bringing to trial and punishment persons guilty of violating the internal revenue laws or conniving at the same."[94] Amounts are paid based on a percentage of tax, fines, and penalties (but not interest) actually collected based on the information provided. For specific information that caused the investigation and resulted in recovery, the IRS administratively has set the reward in an amount not to exceed 15 percent of the amounts recovered. For information, although not specific, that nonetheless caused the investigation and was of value in the determination of tax liabilities, the reward is not to exceed 10 percent of the amount recovered. For information that caused the investigation, but had no direct relationship to the determination of tax liabilities, the reward is not to exceed one percent of the amount recovered. The reward ceiling is $10 million (for payments made after November 7, 2002), and the reward floor is $100. No reward will be paid if the recovery was so small as to call for payment of less than $100 under the above formulas. Both the ceiling and percentages can be increased with a special agreement. The Code permits the IRS to disclose return information pursuant to a contract for tax administration services.[95]

Explanation of Provision

The provision reforms the reward program for individuals who provide information regarding violations of the tax laws to the Secretary. Generally, the provision establishes a reward floor of 15 percent of the collected proceeds (including penalties, interest, additions to tax and additional amounts) if the IRS moves forward with an administrative or judicial action based on information brought to the IRS's attention by an individual. The provision caps the available reward at 30 percent of the collected proceeds. The provision permits awards of lesser amounts (but no more than 10 percent) if the action was based principally on allegations (other than information provided by the individual) resulting from a judicial or administrative hearing, government report, hearing, audit, investigation, or from the news media.

The provision requires the Secretary to issue guidance within one year of the date of enactment for the operation of a Whistleblower Office within the IRS to administer the reward program. To the extent possible, it is expected that such guidance will address the recommendations of the Treasury Inspector General for Tax Administration regarding the informant's reward program, including the recommendations to centralize management of the reward program and to reduce the processing time for claims.[96] Under the provision, the Whistleblower Office may seek assistance from the individual providing information or from his or her legal representative, and may reimburse the costs incurred by any legal representative out of the amount of the reward. To the extent the disclosure of returns or return information is required to render such assistance, the disclosure must be pursuant to an IRS tax administration contract. It is expected that such disclosures will be infrequent and will be made only when the assigned task cannot be properly or timely completed without the return information to be disclosed.

The provision also provides an above-the-line deduction for attorneys' fees and costs paid by, or on behalf of, the individual in connection with any award for providing information regarding violations of the tax laws. The amount that may be deducted above-the-line may not exceed the amount includible in the taxpayer's gross income for the taxable year on account of such award (whether by suit or agreement and whether as lump sum or periodic payments).

The provision permits an individual to appeal the amount or a denial of an award determination to the United States Tax Court (the "Tax Court") within 30 days of such determination. Under the provision, Tax Court review of an award determination may be assigned to a special trial judge.

---

[94] Sec. 7623.

[95] Sec. 6103(n).

[96] Treasury Inspector General for Tax Administration, *The Informants' Rewards Program Needs More Centralized Management Oversight*, 2006-30-092 (June 2006).

In addition, the provision requires the Secretary to conduct a study and report to Congress on the effectiveness of the whistleblower reward program and any legislative or administrative recommendations regarding the administration of the program.

Effective Date

The provision generally is effective for information provided on or after the date of enactment.

[Law at ¶5085, ¶5835, ¶5845 and ¶7070. CCH Explanation at ¶650.]

[¶15,520] Act Sec. 407. Frivolous tax submissions

Joint Committee Taxation (J.C.T. REP. NO. JCX-50-06)

[Code Sec. 6702]

Present Law

The Code provides that an individual who files a frivolous income tax return is subject to a penalty of $500 imposed by the IRS (sec. 6702). The Code also permits the Tax Court[97] to impose a penalty of up to $25,000 if a taxpayer has instituted or maintained proceedings primarily for delay or if the taxpayer's position in the proceeding is frivolous or groundless (sec. 6673(a)).

Explanation of Provision

The provision modifies the IRS-imposed penalty by increasing the amount of the penalty to up to $5,000 and by applying it to all taxpayers and to all types of Federal taxes.

The provision also modifies present law with respect to certain submissions that raise frivolous arguments or that are intended to delay or impede tax administration. The submissions to which the provision applies are requests for a collection due process hearing, installment agreements, and offers-in-compromise. First, the provision permits the IRS to disregard such requests. Second, the provision permits the IRS to impose a penalty of up to $5,000 for such requests, unless the taxpayer withdraws the request after being given an opportunity to do so.

The provision requires the IRS to publish a list of positions, arguments, requests, and submissions determined to be frivolous for purposes of these provisions.

Effective Date

The provision applies to submissions made and issues raised after the date on which the Secretary first prescribes the required list of frivolous positions.

[Law at ¶5790, ¶5795, ¶5810 and ¶5830. CCH Explanation at ¶640.]

[¶15,530] Act Sec. 408. Addition of meningococcal and human papillomavirus vaccines to the list of taxable vaccines

Joint Committee Taxation (J.C.T. REP. NO. JCX-50-06)

[Code Sec. 4132]

Present Law

A manufacturer's excise tax is imposed at the rate of 75 cents per dose[98] on the following vaccines routinely recommended for administration to children: diphtheria, pertussis, tetanus, measles, mumps, rubella, polio, HIB (haemophilus influenza type B), hepatitis A, hepatitis B, varicella (chicken pox), rotavirus gastroenteritis, streptococcus pneumoniae and trivalent vaccines against influenza. The tax applied to any vaccine that is a combination of vaccine components equals 75 cents times the number of components in the combined vaccine.

---

[97] Because in general the Tax Court is the only pre-payment forum available to taxpayers, it deals with most of the frivolous, groundless, or dilatory arguments raised in tax cases.

[98] Sec. 4131.

Amounts equal to net revenues from this excise tax are deposited in the Vaccine Injury Compensation Trust Fund to finance compensation awards under the Federal Vaccine Injury Compensation Program for individuals who suffer certain injuries following administration of the taxable vaccines. This program provides a Federal "no fault" insurance system substitute for the State-law tort and private liability insurance systems otherwise applicable to vaccine manufacturers. All persons immunized after September 30, 1988, with covered vaccines must pursue compensation under this Federal program before bringing civil tort actions under State law.

Explanation of Provision

The provision adds meningococcal vaccines and human papillomavirus vaccines to the list of taxable vaccines.

Effective Date

The provision is effective for vaccines sold or used on or after the first day of the first month beginning more than four weeks after the date of enactment.

In the case of sales on or before the effective date for which delivery is made after such date, the delivery date shall be considered the sale date.

[Law at ¶ 5670. CCH Explanation at ¶ 685.]

[¶ 15,540] Act Sec. 409. Make permanent the tax treatment of certain settlement funds

Joint Committee Taxation (J.C.T. REP. NO. JCX-50-06)

[Code Sec. 468B]

Present Law

The cleanup of hazardous waste sites is sometimes funded by environmental "settlement funds" or escrow accounts. These escrow accounts are established in consent decrees between the Environmental Protection Agency ("EPA") and the settling parties under the jurisdiction of a Federal district court. The EPA uses these accounts to resolve claims against private parties under Comprehensive Environmental Response, Compensation, and Liability Act of 1980 ("CERCLA").

Present law provides that certain settlement funds established in consent decrees for the sole purpose of resolving claims under CERCLA are to be treated as beneficially owned by the United States government and therefore, not subject to Federal income tax.

To qualify the settlement fund must be: (1) established pursuant to a consent decree entered by a judge of a United States District Court; (2) created for the receipt of settlement payments for the sole purpose of resolving claims under CERCLA; (3) controlled (in terms of expenditures of

contributions and earnings thereon) by the government or an agency or instrumentality thereof; and (4) upon termination, any remaining funds will be disbursed to such government entity and used in accordance with applicable law. For purposes of the provision, a government entity means the United States, any State of political subdivision thereof, the District of Columbia, any possession of the United States, and any agency or instrumentality of the foregoing.

The provision does not apply to accounts or funds established after December 31, 2010.

Explanation of Provision

The provision permanently extends to funds and accounts established after December 31, 2010, the treatment of certain settlement funds as beneficially owned by the United States government and therefore, not subject to Federal income tax.

Effective Date

The provision is effective as if included in section 201 of the Tax Increase Prevention and Reconciliation Act of 2005.

[Law at ¶ 5405. CCH Explanation at ¶ 375.]

[¶15,550] Act Sec. 410. Make permanent the active business rules relating to taxation of distributions of stock and securities of a controlled corporation

Joint Committee Taxation (J.C.T. REP. NO. JCX-50-06)

[Code Sec. 355]

Present Law

A corporation generally is required to recognize gain on the distribution of property (including stock of a subsidiary) to its shareholders as if the corporation had sold such property for its fair market value. In addition, the shareholders receiving the distributed property are ordinarily treated as receiving a dividend of the value of the distribution (to the extent of the distributing corporation's earnings and profits), or capital gain in the case of a stock buyback that significantly reduces the shareholder's interest in the parent corporation.

An exception to these rules applies if the distribution of the stock of a controlled corporation satisfies the requirements of section 355 of the Code. If all the requirements are satisfied, there is no tax to the distributing corporation or to the shareholders on the distribution.

One requirement to qualify for tax-free treatment under section 355 is that both the distributing corporation and the controlled corporation must be engaged immediately after the distribution in the active conduct of a trade or business that has been conducted for at least five years and was not acquired in a taxable transaction during that period (the "active business test").[99] For this purpose, prior to the enactment of the Tax Increase Prevention and Reconciliation Act of 2005, if the distributing or the controlled corporation to which the test was being applied was itself the parent of other subsidiary corporations, the determination whether such parent corporation was considered engaged in the active conduct of a trade or business was made only at that parent corporation level. The test would be satisfied only if (1) that corporation itself was directly engaged in the active conduct of a trade or business, or (2) that corporation was not directly engaged in the active conduct of a trade or business, but substantially all its assets consisted of stock and securities of one or more corporations

that it controls that are engaged in the active conduct of a trade or business.[100] Thus, different tests applied, depending upon whether the corporation being tested itself was engaged in the active conduct of a trade or business, or whether it was a holding company holding stock of other corporations that were engaged in the active conduct of a trade or business.

The Tax Increase Prevention and Reconciliation Act of 2005 provided that the active trade or business test is always determined by reference to the relevant affiliated group. For the distributing corporation, the relevant affiliated group consists of the distributing corporation as the common parent and all corporations affiliated with the distributing corporation through stock ownership described in section 1504(a)(1)(B) (regardless of whether the corporations are includible corporations under section 1504(b)), immediately after the distribution. The relevant affiliated group for a controlled corporation is determined in a similar manner (with the controlled corporation as the common parent).

The provision enacted in the Tax Increase Prevention and Reconciliation Act of 2005 applies to distributions after the date of enactment and on or before December 31, 2010, with three exceptions. The provision does not apply to distributions (1) made pursuant to an agreement which is binding on the date of enactment and at all times thereafter, (2) described in a ruling request submitted to the IRS on or before the date of enactment, or (3) described on or before the date of enactment in a public announcement or in a filing with the Securities and Exchange Commission. The distributing corporation may irrevocably elect not to have the exceptions described above apply.

The provision also applies, solely for the purpose of determining whether, after the date of enactment, there is continuing qualification under the requirements of section 355(b)(2)(A) of distributions made before such date, as a result of an acquisition, disposition, or other restructur-

---

[99] Sec. 355(b). In determining whether a corporation is engaged in an active trade or business that satisfies the requirement, old IRS guidelines for advance ruling purposes required that the value of the gross assets of the trade or business being relied on must ordinarily constitute at least five percent of the total fair market value of the gross assets of the corporation directly conducting the trade or business. Rev. Proc. 2003-3, sec. 4.01(30), 2003-1 I.R.B. 113. More recently, the IRS suspended this specific rule in connection with its general administrative practice of moving IRS resources away from advance rulings on factual aspects of

section 355 transactions in general. Rev. Proc. 2003-48, 2003-29 I.R.B. 86.

[100] Section 355(b)(2)(A). The IRS position has been that the statutory "substantially all" test has required that at least 90 percent of the fair market value of the corporation's gross assets consist of stock and securities of a controlled corporation that is engaged in the active conduct of a trade or business. Rev. Proc. 96-30, sec. 4.03(5), 1996-1 C.B. 696; Rev. Proc. 77-37, sec. 3.04, 1977-2 C.B. 568.

ing after such date on or before December 31, 2010.[101]

Explanation of Provision

The provision deletes the sunset date of December 31, 2010, for all purposes of the provision enacted in the Tax Increase Prevention and Reconciliation Act of 2005. Thus, that provision is made permanent.

Effective Date

The provision is effective as if included in section 202 of the Tax Increase Prevention and Reconciliation Act of 2005.

[Law at ¶5355. CCH Explanation at ¶360.]

[¶15,560] Act Sec. 411. Make permanent the modifications to qualified veterans' mortgage bonds

Joint Committee Taxation (J.C.T. REP. NO. JCX-50-06)

[Code Sec. 143]

Present Law

Private activity bonds are bonds that nominally are issued by States or local governments, but the proceeds of which are used (directly or indirectly) by a private person and payment of which is derived from funds of such private person. The exclusion from income for State and local bonds does not apply to private activity bonds, unless the bonds are issued for certain permitted purposes ("qualified private activity bonds"). The definition of a qualified private activity bond includes both qualified mortgage bonds and qualified veterans' mortgage bonds.

Qualified mortgage bonds are issued to make mortgage loans to qualified mortgagors for owner-occupied residences. The Code imposes several limitations on qualified mortgage bonds, including income limitations for homebuyers and purchase price limitations for the home financed with bond proceeds. In addition, qualified mortgage bonds generally cannot be used to finance a mortgage for a homebuyer who had an ownership interest in a principal residence in the three years preceding the execution of the mortgage (the "first-time homebuyer" requirement).

Qualified veterans' mortgage bonds are private activity bonds the proceeds of which are used to make mortgage loans to certain veterans. Authority to issue qualified veterans' mortgage bonds is limited to States that had issued such bonds before June 22, 1984. Qualified veterans' mortgage bonds are not subject to the State volume limitations generally applicable to private

activity bonds. Instead, annual issuance in each State is subject to a separate State volume limitation. The five States eligible to issue these bonds are Alaska, California, Oregon, Texas, and Wisconsin. Loans financed with qualified veterans' mortgage bonds can be made only with respect to principal residences and can not be made to acquire or replace existing mortgages. Under prior law, mortgage loans made with the proceeds of bonds issued by the five States could be made only to veterans who served on active duty before 1977 and who applied for the financing before the date 30 years after the last date on which such veteran left active service (the "eligibility period"). However, in the case of qualified veterans' mortgage bonds issued by the States of Alaska, Oregon, and Wisconsin, the Tax Increase Prevention and Reconciliation Act of 2005 ("TIPRA") repealed the requirement that veterans receiving loans financed with qualified veterans' mortgage bonds must have served before 1977 and reduced the eligibility period to 25 years (rather than 30 years) following release from the military service.

In addition, TIPRA provided new State volume limits for qualified veterans' mortgage bonds issued in the States of Alaska, Oregon and Wisconsin. In 2010, the new annual limit on the total volume of veterans' bonds that can be issued in each of these three States is $25 million. These volume limits are phased-in over the four-year period immediately preceding 2010 by allowing the applicable percentage of the 2010 volume limits. The following table provides those percentages.

---

[101] For example, a holding company taxpayer that had distributed a controlled corporation in a spin-off prior to the date of enactment, in which spin-off the taxpayer satisfied the "substantially all" active business stock test of prior law section 355(b)(2)(A) immediately after the distribution, would not be deemed to have failed to satisfy any require-ment that it continue that same qualified structure for any period of time after the distribution, solely because of a restructuring that occurred after the date of enactment and before January 1, 2010, and that would satisfy the requirements of new section 355(b)(2)(A).

Calendar Year:	Applicable Percentage is:
2006	20 percent
2007	40 percent
2008	60 percent
2009	80 percent

The volume limits are zero for 2011 and each year thereafter. Unused allocation cannot be carried forward to subsequent years.

Explanation of Provision

The provision makes permanent TIPRA's changes to the definition of an eligible veteran and the State volume limits for qualified veterans' mortgage bonds issued by the States of Alaska, Oregon, and Wisconsin. The total volume of veterans' bonds that can be issued in each of these three States is $25 million for 2010 and each calendar year thereafter.

Effective Date

The provision is effective as if included in section 203 of TIPRA.

[Law at ¶5130. CCH Explanation at ¶620.]

[¶15,570] Act Sec. 412. Make permanent the capital gains treatment for certain self-created musical works

Joint Committee Taxation (J.C.T. REP. No. JCX-50-06)

[Code Sec. 1221]

Present Law

Capital gains

The maximum tax rate on the net capital gain income of an individual is 15 percent for taxable years beginning in 2006. By contrast, the maximum tax rate on an individual's ordinary income is 35 percent. The reduced 15-percent rate generally is available for gain from the sale or exchange of a capital asset for which the taxpayer has satisfied a holding-period requirement. Capital assets generally include all property held by a taxpayer with certain specified exclusions.

An exclusion from the definition of a capital asset applies to inventory property or property held by a taxpayer primarily for sale to customers in the ordinary course of the taxpayer's trade or business.[102] Another exclusion from capital asset status applies to copyrights, literary, musical, or artistic compositions, letters or memoranda, or similar property held by a taxpayer whose personal efforts created the property (or held by a taxpayer whose basis in the property is determined by reference to the basis of the taxpayer whose personal efforts created the property).[103] Under a provision included in the Tax Increase Prevention and Reconciliation Act of 2005 ("TIPRA"),[104] at the election of a taxpayer, the section 1221(a)(1) and (a)(3) exclusions from capital asset status do not apply to musical compositions or copyrights in musical works sold or exchanged before January 1, 2011 by a taxpayer described in section 1221(a)(3).[105] Thus, if a taxpayer who owns musical compositions or copyrights in musical works that the taxpayer created (or if a taxpayer to which the musical compositions or copyrights have been transferred by the works' creator in a substituted basis transaction) elects the application of this provision, gain from a sale of the compositions or copyrights is treated as capital gain, not ordinary income.

Charitable contributions

A taxpayer generally is allowed a deduction for the fair market value of property contributed to a charity. If a taxpayer makes a contribution of property that would have generated ordinary income (or short-term capital gain), the taxpayer's charitable contribution deduction generally is limited to the property's adjusted basis.[106] The determination whether property would have generated ordinary income (or short-term capital gain) is made without regard to new section 1221(b)(3) described above.[107]

---

[102] Sec. 1221(a)(1).
[103] Sec. 1221(a)(3).
[104] Pub. L. No. 109-222, sec. 204(a) (2006).
[105] Sec. 1221(b)(3).

[106] Sec. 170(e)(1)(A).
[107] Sec. 170(e)(1)(A), as modified by TIPRA, Pub. L. No. 109-222, sec. 204(b) (2006).

Explanation of Provision

The provision makes permanent the availability of the section 1221(b)(3) election to treat certain sales of musical compositions or copyrights in musical works as being sales of capital assets (and therefore as generating capital gain). The provision also makes permanent the accompanying rule limiting to adjusted basis the amount of a charitable contribution deduction allowed for musical compositions or copyrights in musical works to which a taxpayer has elected the application of section 1221(b)(3).

Effective Date

The provision is effective as if included in section 204 of the Tax Increase Prevention and Reconciliation Act of 2005.

[Law at ¶ 5580. CCH Explanation at ¶ 240.]

[¶ 15,580] Act Sec. 413. Make permanent the decrease in minimum vessel tonnage limit to 6,000 deadweight tons

Joint Committee Taxation (J.C.T. Rep. No. JCX-50-06)

[Code Sec. 1355]

Present Law

The United States employs a "worldwide" tax system, under which domestic corporations generally are taxed on all income, including income from shipping operations, whether derived in the United States or abroad. In order to mitigate double taxation, a foreign tax credit for income taxes paid to foreign countries is provided to reduce or eliminate the U.S. tax owed on such income, subject to certain limitations.

Generally, the United States taxes foreign corporations only on income that has a sufficient nexus to the United States. Thus, a foreign corporation is generally subject to U.S. tax only on income, including income from shipping operations, which is "effectively connected" with the conduct of a trade or business in the United States (sec. 882). Such "effectively connected income" generally is taxed in the same manner and at the same rates as the income of a U.S. corporation.

The United States imposes a four percent tax on the amount of a foreign corporation's U.S. source gross transportation income (sec. 887). Transportation income includes income from the use (or hiring or leasing for use) of a vessel and income from services directly related to the use of a vessel. Fifty percent of the transportation income attributable to transportation that either begins or ends (but not both) in the United States is treated as U.S. source gross transportation income. The tax does not apply, however, to U.S. source gross transportation income that is treated as income effectively connected with the conduct of a U.S. trade or business. U.S. source gross transportation income is not treated as effectively connected income unless (1) the taxpayer has a fixed place of business in the United States involved in earning the income, and (2) substantially all the income is attributable to regularly scheduled transportation.

The tax imposed by section 882 or 887 on income from shipping operations may be limited by an applicable U.S. income tax treaty or by an exemption of a foreign corporation's international shipping operations income in instances where a foreign country grants an equivalent exemption (sec. 883).

Notwithstanding the general rules described above, the American Jobs Creation Act of 2004 ("AJCA")[108] generally allows corporations that are qualifying vessel operators[109] to elect a "tonnage tax" in lieu of the corporate income tax on taxable income from certain shipping activities. Accordingly, an electing corporation's gross income does not include its income from qualifying shipping activities (and items of loss, deduction, or credit are disallowed with respect to such excluded income), and electing corporations are only subject to tax on these activities at the maximum corporate income tax rate on their notional shipping income, which is based on the net tonnage of the corporation's qualifying vessels.[110] No deductions are allowed against the notional shipping income of an electing corporation, and no credit is allowed against the no-

---

[108] Pub. L. No. 108-357, sec. 248. The tonnage tax regime is effective for taxable years beginning after the date of enactment of AJCA (October 22, 2004).

[109] Generally, a qualifying vessel operator is a corporation that (1) operates one or more qualifying vessels and (2) meets certain requirements with respect to its shipping activities.

[110] An electing corporation's notional shipping income for the taxable year is the product of the following amounts for each of the qualifying vessels it operates: (1) the daily notional shipping income from the operation of the qualifying vessel, and (2) the number of days during the taxable year that the electing corporation operated such vessel as a qualifying vessel in the United States foreign trade. The

tional tax imposed under the tonnage tax regime. In addition, special deferral rules apply to the gain on the sale of a qualifying vessel, if such vessel is replaced during a limited replacement period.

Prior to the enactment of the Tax Increase Prevention and Reconciliation Act of 2005 ("TIPRA"),[111] a "qualifying vessel" was defined as a self-propelled (or a combination of self-propelled and non-self-propelled) United States flag vessel of not less than 10,000 deadweight tons[112] that is used exclusively in the United States foreign trade. TIPRA expands the definition of "qualifying vessel" to include self-propelled (or a combination of self-propelled and non-self-propelled) United States flag vessels of

not less than 6,000 deadweight tons used exclusively in the United States foreign trade. The modified definition of TIPRA applies for taxable years beginning after December 31, 2005 and ending before January 1, 2011.

Explanation of Provision

The provision makes permanent the minimum 6,000 deadweight tons threshold.

Effective Date

The provision is effective as if included in section 205 of the Tax Increase Prevention and Reconciliation Act of 2005.

[Law at ¶ 5605. CCH Explanation at ¶ 370.]

[¶ 15,590] Act Sec. 414. Make permanent the modification of special arbitrage rule for certain funds

Joint Committee Taxation (J.C.T. REP. No. JCX-50-06)

[Act Sec. 414]

Present Law

In general, present-law tax-exempt bond arbitrage restrictions provide that interest on a State or local government bond is not eligible for tax-exemption if the proceeds are invested, directly or indirectly, in materially higher yielding investments or if the debt service on the bond is secured by or paid from (directly or indirectly) such investments. An exception to the arbitrage restrictions, enacted in 1984, provides that the pledge of income from investments in the Texas Permanent University Fund (the "Fund") as security for a limited amount of tax-exempt bonds will not cause interest on those bonds to be taxable. The terms of this exception are limited to State constitutional or statutory restrictions continuously in effect since October 9, 1969. In addition, the exception only applies to an amount of tax-exempt bonds that does not exceed 20 percent of the value of the Fund.

The Fund consists of certain State lands that were set aside for the benefit of higher education, the income from mineral rights to these

lands, and certain other earnings on Fund assets. The Texas constitution directs that monies held in the Fund are to be invested in interest-bearing obligations and other securities. Income from the Fund is apportioned between two university systems operated by the State. Tax-exempt bonds issued by the university systems to finance buildings and other permanent improvements were secured by and payable from the income of the Fund.

Prior to 1999, the constitution did not permit the expenditure or mortgage of the Fund for any purpose. In 1999, the State constitutional rules governing the Fund were modified with regard to the manner in which amounts in the Fund are distributed for the benefit of the two university systems. The State constitutional amendments allow for the possibility that in the event investment earnings are less than annual debt service on the bonds some of the debt service could be considered as having been paid with the Fund corpus. The 1984 exception refers only to bonds secured by investment earnings on securities or obligations held by the Fund. Despite the constitutional amendments, the IRS has agreed to con-

---

(Footnote Continued)

daily notional shipping income from the operation of a qualifying vessel is (1) 40 cents for each 100 tons of so much of the net tonnage of the vessel as does not exceed 25,000 net tons, and (2) 20 cents for each 100 tons of so much of the net tonnage of the vessel as exceeds 25,000 net tons. "United States foreign trade" means the transportation of goods or passengers between a place in the United States and a foreign place or between foreign places. The temporary use in the United States domestic trade (i.e., the transportation of goods or passengers between places in the United States)

of any qualifying vessel or the temporary ceasing to use a qualifying vessel may be disregarded, under special rules.

[111] Pub. L. No. 109-222, sec. 205 (May 17, 2006).

[112] Deadweight measures the lifting capacity of a ship expressed in long tons (2,240 lbs.), including cargo, crew, and consumables such as fuel, lube oil, drinking water, and stores. It is the difference between the number of tons of water a vessel displaces without such items on board and the number of tons it displaces when fully loaded.

tinue to apply the 1984 exception to the Fund through August 31, 2007, if clarifying legislation is introduced in the 109th Congress prior to August 31, 2005. Clarifying legislation was introduced in the 109th Congress on May 26, 2005.[113]

The Tax Increase Prevention and Reconciliation Act of 2005 ("TIPRA") codified and extended the IRS agreement until August 31, 2009. TIPRA conformed the 1984 exception to the State constitutional amendments to permit its continued applicability to bonds of the two university systems. The limitation on the aggregate amount of bonds which may benefit from the exception

was not modified, and remains at 20 percent of the value of the Fund.

Explanation of Provision

The provision makes permanent TIPRA's changes to the Fund's arbitrage exception.

Effective Date

The provision is effective as if included in section 206 of TIPRA.

[Law at ¶7075. CCH Explanation at ¶615.]

[¶15,600] Act Sec. 415. Great Lakes domestic shipping to not disqualify vessel from tonnage tax

Joint Committee Taxation (J.C.T. Rep. No. JCX-50-06)

[Code Sec. 1355]

Present Law

The United States employs a "worldwide" tax system, under which domestic corporations generally are taxed on all income, including income from shipping operations, whether derived in the United States or abroad. In order to mitigate double taxation, a foreign tax credit for income taxes paid to foreign countries is provided to reduce or eliminate the U.S. tax owed on such income, subject to certain limitations.

Generally, the United States taxes foreign corporations only on income that has a sufficient nexus to the United States. Thus, a foreign corporation is generally subject to U.S. tax only on income, including income from shipping operations, which is "effectively connected" with the conduct of a trade or business in the United States (sec. 882). Such "effectively connected income" generally is taxed in the same manner and at the same rates as the income of a U.S. corporation.

The United States imposes a four percent tax on the amount of a foreign corporation's U.S. source gross transportation income (sec. 887). Transportation income includes income from the use (or hiring or leasing for use) of a vessel and income from services directly related to the use of a vessel. Fifty percent of the transportation income attributable to transportation that either

begins or ends (but not both) in the United States is treated as U.S. source gross transportation income. The tax does not apply, however, to U.S. source gross transportation income that is treated as income effectively connected with the conduct of a U.S. trade or business. U.S. source gross transportation income is not treated as effectively connected income unless (1) the taxpayer has a fixed place of business in the United States involved in earning the income, and (2) substantially all the income is attributable to regularly scheduled transportation.

The tax imposed by section 882 or 887 on income from shipping operations may be limited by an applicable U.S. income tax treaty or by an exemption of a foreign corporation's international shipping operations income in instances where a foreign country grants an equivalent exemption (sec. 883).

Notwithstanding the general rules described above, the American Jobs Creation Act of 2004 ("AJCA")[114] generally allows corporations that are qualifying vessel operators[115] to elect a "tonnage tax" in lieu of the corporate income tax on taxable income from certain shipping activities. Accordingly, an electing corporation's gross income does not include its income from qualifying shipping activities (and items of loss, deduction, and credit are disallowed with respect to such excluded income),[116] and electing corporations are only subject to tax on these

---

[113] H.R. 2661.

[114] Pub. L. No. 108-357, sec. 248. The tonnage tax regime is effective for taxable years beginning after the date of enactment of AJCA (October 22, 2004).

[115] Generally, a qualifying vessel operator is a corporation that (1) operates one or more qualifying vessels and (2)

meets certain requirements with respect to its shipping activities.

[116] Sec. 1357.

activities at the maximum corporate income tax rate on their notional shipping income, which is based on the net tonnage of the corporation's qualifying vessels operated in the United States foreign trade.[117] "United States foreign trade" means the transportation of goods or passengers between a place in the United States and a foreign place or between foreign places. No deductions are allowed against the notional shipping income of an electing corporation, and no credit is allowed against the notional tax imposed under the tonnage tax regime. In addition, special deferral rules apply to the gain on the sale of a qualifying vessel, if such vessel is replaced during a limited replacement period.

A "qualifying vessel" is defined as a self-propelled (or a combination of self-propelled and non-self-propelled) United States flag vessel of not less than 6,000 deadweight tons[118] that is used exclusively in the United States foreign trade. Notwithstanding the "exclusively in the United States foreign trade" requirement, the temporary use of any qualifying vessel in the United States domestic trade (i.e., the transportation of goods or passengers between places in the United States) may be disregarded, and treated as the continued use of such vessel in the United States foreign trade, if the electing corporation provides timely notice of such temporary use to the Secretary. However, if a qualifying vessel is operated in the United States domestic trade for more than 30 days during the taxable year, then no usage in the United States domestic trade during such year may be disregarded (and the vessel is thereby disqualified). The Secretary has the authority to prescribe regulations as may be necessary or appropriate to carry out the purposes of the statutory rules relating to the temporary domestic use of vessels.[119]

Explanation of Provision

Under the provision, a corporation for which a tonnage tax election is in effect ("electing corporation") may make a further election with respect to a qualifying vessel used during a taxable year in "qualified zone domestic trade."

The term "qualified zone domestic trade" means the transportation of goods or passengers between places in the "qualified zone" if such transportation is in the United States domestic trade. The transportation of goods or passengers between a U.S. port in the qualified zone and a U.S. port outside the qualified zone (in either direction) is United States domestic trade that is not qualified zone domestic trade.

The term "qualified zone" means the Great Lakes Waterway and the St. Lawrence Seaway. This area consists of the deep-draft waterways of Lake Superior, Lake Michigan, Lake Huron (including Lake St. Clair), Lake Eire, and Lake Ontario, connecting deep-draft channels, including the Detroit River, the St. Clair River, the St. Marys River, and the Welland Canal, and the waterway between the port of Sept-Iles, Quebec and Lake Ontario, including all locks, canals, and connecting and contiguous waters that are part of these deep-draft waterways.

Activities in qualified zone domestic trade are not qualifying shipping activities and, therefore, do not qualify for the tonnage tax regime. In the case of a qualifying vessel for which an election under this provision ("qualified zone domestic trade election") is in force, the Secretary is to prescribe rules for the proper allocation of income, expenses, losses, and deductions between the qualified shipping activities and the other activities of such vessel. These rules may include intra-vessel allocation rules that are different than the rules pertaining to allocations of items between qualifying vessels and other vessels.

An electing corporation making a qualified zone domestic trade election with respect to a vessel is not required to give notice to the Secretary of the use of such vessel in qualified zone domestic trade, and an otherwise qualifying vessel does not cease to be a qualifying vessel solely due to such use when such election is in effect, even if such use exceeds 30 days during the taxable year. An electing corporation making a qualified zone domestic trade election with re-

---

[117] An electing corporation's notional shipping income for the taxable year is the product of the following amounts for each of the qualifying vessels it operates: (1) the daily notional shipping income from the operation of the qualifying vessel, and (2) the number of days during the taxable year that the electing corporation operated such vessel as a qualifying vessel in the United States foreign trade. The daily notional shipping income from the operation of a qualifying vessel is (1) 40 cents for each 100 tons of so much of the net tonnage of the vessel as does not exceed 25,000 net tons, and (2) 20 cents for each 100 tons of so much of the net tonnage of the vessel as exceeds 25,000 net tons.

[118] Prior to the enactment on May 17, 2006 of Pub. L. No. 109-222, the Tax Increase Prevention and Reconciliation Act

of 2005 ("TIPRA"), "qualifying vessel" meant a self-propelled (or a combination of self-propelled and non-self-propelled) United States flag vessel of not less than 10,000 deadweight tons used exclusively in the United States foreign trade. TIPRA changed the threshold to 6,000 deadweight tons, effective for taxable years beginning after December 31, 2005 and ending before January 1, 2011. Section 1283 of this Act permanently extends the 6,000 deadweight tons threshold.

[119] Sec. 1355(g).

spect to a vessel is treated as using such vessel in qualified zone domestic trade during any period of temporary use in the United States domestic trade (other than qualified zone domestic trade) if such electing corporation gives timely notice to the Secretary stating that it temporarily operates or has operated in the United States domestic trade (other than qualified zone domestic trade) a qualifying vessel which had been used in the United States foreign trade or qualified zone domestic trade, and that it intends to resume operating such vessel in the United States foreign trade or qualified zone domestic trade. The period of such permissible temporary use of such vessel in such United States domestic trade continues until the earlier of the date on which the electing corporation abandons its intention to resume operation of the vessel in the United States foreign trade or qualified zone domestic trade, or the electing corporation resumes operation of the vessel in the United States foreign trade or qualified zone domestic trade. However, if a qualifying vessel is operated in the United States domestic trade (other than qualified zone domestic trade) for more than 30 days during the taxable year, then no usage in the United States domestic trade (other than qualified zone domestic trade) during such year may be disregarded (and the vessel is thereby disqualified). Thus, a vessel used for 120 days in the taxable year in qualified zone domestic trade and 180 days in the taxable year in the United States foreign trade is not a qualifying vessel if it is used for over 30 days in the taxable year in the United States domestic trade that is not qualified zone domestic trade.

Under the provision, the Secretary may specify the time, manner and other conditions for making, maintaining, and terminating the qualified zone domestic trade election.

Effective Date

The provision is effective for taxable years beginning after date of enactment.

[Law at ¶ 5605. CCH Explanation at ¶ 370.]

[¶ 15,610] Act Sec. 416. Expansion of the qualified mortgage bond program

Joint Committee Taxation (J.C.T. Rep. No. JCX-50-06)

[Code Sec. 143]

Present Law

Private activity bonds are bonds that nominally are issued by States or local governments, but the proceeds of which are used (directly or indirectly) by a private person and payment of which is derived from funds of such private person. The exclusion from income for State and local bonds does not apply to private activity bonds, unless the bonds are issued for certain permitted purposes ("qualified private activity bonds"). The definition of a qualified private activity bond includes both qualified mortgage bonds and qualified veterans' mortgage bonds.

Qualified mortgage bonds are issued to make mortgage loans to qualified mortgagors for owner-occupied residences. The Code imposes several limitations on qualified mortgage bonds, including income limitations for homebuyers and purchase price limitations for the home financed with bond proceeds. In addition, qualified mortgage bonds generally cannot be used to finance a mortgage for a homebuyer who had an ownership interest in a principal residence in the three years preceding the execution of the mortgage (the "first-time homebuyer" requirement).

Qualified veterans' mortgage bonds are private activity bonds the proceeds of which are used to make mortgage loans to certain veterans. Authority to issue qualified veterans' mortgage bonds is limited to States that had issued such bonds before June 22, 1984. Qualified veterans' mortgage bonds are not subject to the State volume limitations generally applicable to private activity bonds. Instead, annual issuance in each State is subject to a separate State volume limitation. The five States eligible to issue these bonds are Alaska, California, Oregon, Texas, and Wisconsin. Loans financed with qualified veterans' mortgage bonds can be made only with respect to principal residences and can not be made to acquire or replace existing mortgages. Under prior law, mortgage loans made with the proceeds of bonds issued by the five States could be made only to veterans who served on active duty before 1977 and who applied for the financing before the date 30 years after the last date on which such veteran left active service (the "eligibility period"). However, in the case of qualified veterans' mortgage bonds issued by the States of Alaska, Oregon, and Wisconsin, the Tax Increase Prevention and Reconciliation Act of 2005 ("TIPRA") repealed the requirement that veterans receiving loans financed with qualified veterans' mortgage bonds must have served before 1977 and reduced the eligibility period to 25 years (rather than 30 years) following release from the military service. In addition, TIPRA provided new State volume limits for qualified veterans' mortgage bonds issued in the States of Alaska, Oregon and Wisconsin, phased-in over a four-year period.

Explanation of Provision

Under the provision, qualified mortgage bonds may be issued to finance mortgages for veterans who served in the active military without regard to the first-time homebuyer requirement. Present-law income and purchase price limitations apply to loans to veterans financed with the proceeds of qualified mortgage bonds.

Veterans are eligible for the exception from the first-time homebuyer requirement without regard to the date they last served on active duty or the date they applied for a loan after leaving active duty. However, veterans may only use the exception one time.

Effective Date

The provision applies to bonds issued after the date of enactment and before January 1, 2008.

[Law at ¶ 5130. CCH Explanation at ¶ 610.]

[¶ 15,620] Act Sec. 417. Exclusion of gain on sale of a principal residence by a member of the intelligence community

Joint Committee Taxation (J.C.T. REP. NO. JCX-50-06)

[Code Sec. 121]

Present Law

Under present law, an individual taxpayer may exclude up to $250,000 ($500,000 if married filing a joint return) of gain realized on the sale or exchange of a principal residence. To be eligible for the exclusion, the taxpayer must have owned and used the residence as a principal residence for at least two of the five years ending on the sale or exchange. A taxpayer who fails to meet these requirements by reason of a change of place of employment, health, or, to the extent provided under regulations, unforeseen circumstances is able to exclude an amount equal to the fraction of the $250,000 ($500,000 if married filing a joint return) that is equal to the fraction of the two years that the ownership and use requirements are met.

Present law also contains special rules relating to members of the uniformed services or the Foreign Service of the United States. An individual may elect to suspend for a maximum of 10 years the five-year test period for ownership and use during certain absences due to service in the uniformed services or the Foreign Service of the United States. The uniformed services include: (1) the Armed Forces (the Army, Navy, Air Force, Marine Corps, and Coast Guard); (2) the commissioned corps of the National Oceanic and Atmospheric Administration; and (3) the commissioned corps of the Public Health Service. If the election is made, the five-year period ending on the date of the sale or exchange of a principal residence does not include any period up to 10 years during which the taxpayer or the taxpayer's spouse is on qualified official extended duty as a member of the uniformed services or in the Foreign Service of the United States. For

these purposes, qualified official extended duty is any period of extended duty while serving at a place of duty at least 50 miles away from the taxpayer's principal residence or under orders compelling residence in government furnished quarters. Extended duty is defined as any period of duty pursuant to a call or order to such duty for a period in excess of 90 days or for an indefinite period. The election may be made with respect to only one property for a suspension period.

Explanation of Provision

Under the provision, specified employees of the intelligence community may elect to suspend the running of the five-year test period during any period in which they are serving on extended duty. The term "employee of the intelligence community" means an employee of the Office of the Director of National Intelligence, the Central Intelligence Agency, the National Security Agency, the Defense Intelligence Agency, the National Geospatial-Intelligence Agency, or the National Reconnaissance Office. The term also includes employment with: (1) any other office within the Department of Defense for the collection of specialized national intelligence through reconnaissance programs; (2) any of the intelligence elements of the Army, the Navy, the Air Force, the Marine Corps, the Federal Bureau of Investigation, the Department of the Treasury, the Department of Energy, and the Coast Guard; (3) the Bureau of Intelligence and Research of the Department of State; and (4) the elements of the Department of Homeland Security concerned with the analyses of foreign intelligence information. To qualify, a specified employee must move from one duty station to another and the new duty station must be located outside of the

United States. As under present law, the five-year period may not be extended more than 10 years.

[Law at ¶ 5095. CCH Explanation at ¶ 250.]

Effective Date

The provision is effective for sales and exchanges after the date of enactment and before January 1, 2011.

[¶ 15,630] Act Sec. 418. Sale of property to comply with conflict-of interest requirements

Joint Committee Taxation (J.C.T. REP. NO. JCX-50-06)

[Code Sec. 1043]

Present Law

Present law provides special rules for deferring the recognition of gain on sales of property which are required in order to comply with certain conflict of interest requirements imposed by the Federal government. Certain executive branch Federal employees (and their spouses and minor or dependent children) who are required to divest property in order to comply with conflict of interest requirements may elect to postpone the recognition of resulting gains by investing in certain replacement property within a 60-day period. The basis of the replacement property is reduced by the amount of the gain not recognized. Permitted replacement property is limited to any obligation of the United States or any diversified investment fund approved by regulations issued by the Office of Government Ethics. The rule applies only to sales under certificates of divestiture issued by the President or the Director of the Office of Government Ethics.

Explanation of Provision

The provision extends the provision deferring recognition of gain to a judicial officer who receives a certificate of divestiture from the Judicial Conference of the United States (or its designee) regarding the divestiture of certain property reasonably necessary to comply with conflict of interest rules or the judicial canon. For purposes of this provision, a judicial officer means the Chief Justice of the United States, the Associate Justices of the Supreme Court, and the judges of the United States courts of appeals, United States district courts, including the district courts in Guam, the Northern Mariana Islands, and the Virgin Islands, Court of Appeals for the Federal Circuit, Court of International Trade, Tax Court, Court of Federal Claims, Court of Appeals for Veterans Claims, United States Court of Appeals for the Armed Forces, and any court created by Act of Congress, the judges of which are entitled to hold office during good behavior.

Effective Date

The provision applies to sales after the date of enactment.

[Law at ¶ 5565. CCH Explanation at ¶ 255.]

[¶ 15,640] Act Sec. 419. Premiums for mortgage insurance

Joint Committee Taxation (J.C.T. REP. NO. JCX-50-06)

[Code Sec. 163]

Present Law

Present law provides that qualified residence interest is deductible notwithstanding the general rule that personal interest is nondeductible (sec. 163(h)).

Qualified residence interest is interest on acquisition indebtedness and home equity indebtedness with respect to a principal and a second residence of the taxpayer. The maximum amount of home equity indebtedness is $100,000. The maximum amount of acquisition indebtedness is $1 million. Acquisition indebtedness means debt that is incurred in acquiring constructing, or substantially improving a qualified residence of the taxpayer, and that is secured by the residence. Home equity indebtedness is debt (other than acquisition indebtedness) that is secured by the taxpayer's principal or second residence, to the extent the aggregate amount of such debt does not exceed the difference between the total acquisition indebtedness with respect to the residence, and the fair market value of the residence.

Explanation of Provision

The provision provides that premiums paid or accrued for qualified mortgage insurance by a taxpayer during the taxable year in connection with acquisition indebtedness on a qualified residence of the taxpayer are treated as interest that is qualified residence interest and thus deductible. The amount allowable as a deduction under the provision is phased out ratably by 10 percent for each $1,000 by which the taxpayer's adjusted gross income exceeds $100,000 ($500 and $50,000, respectively, in the case of a married individual filing a separate return). Thus, the deduction is not allowed if the taxpayer's adjusted gross income exceeds $110,000 ($55,000 in the case of married individual filing a separate return).

For this purpose, qualified mortgage insurance means mortgage insurance provided by the Veterans Administration, the Federal Housing Administration, or the Rural Housing Administration, and private mortgage insurance (defined in section 2 of the Homeowners Protection Act of

1998 as in effect on the date of enactment of the provision).

Amounts paid for qualified mortgage insurance that are properly allocable to periods after the close of the taxable year are treated as paid in the period to which they are allocated. No deduction is allowed for the unamortized balance if the mortgage is paid before its term (except in the case of qualified mortgage insurance provided by the Department of Veterans Affairs or Rural Housing Administration).

The provision does not apply with respect to any mortgage insurance contract issued before January 1, 2007. The provision terminates for any amount paid or accrued after December 21, 2007, or properly allocable to any period after that date.

Reporting rules apply under the provision.

Effective Date

The provision is effective for amounts paid or accrued after December 31, 2006.

[Law at ¶5230 and ¶5765. CCH Explanation at ¶220.]

[¶15,650] Act Sec. 420. Modification of refunds for kerosene used in aviation

Joint Committee Taxation (J.C.T. REP. NO. JCX-50-06)

[Code Sec. 6427]

Present Law

Nontaxable uses of kerosene

In general, if kerosene on which tax has been imposed is used by any person for a nontaxable use, a refund in an amount equal to the amount of tax imposed may be obtained either by the purchaser, or in specific cases, the registered ultimate vendor of the kerosene.[120] However, the 0.1 cent per gallon representing the Leaking Underground Storage Tank Trust Fund financing rate generally is not refundable, except for exports.[121]

A nontaxable use is any use which is exempt from the tax imposed by section 4041(a)(1) other

than by reason of a prior imposition of tax.[122] Nontaxable uses of kerosene include:

- Use on a farm for farming purposes;[123]

- Use in foreign trade or trade between the United States and any of its possessions;[124]

- Use as a fuel in vessels and aircraft owned by the United States or any foreign nation and constituting equipment of the armed forces thereof;[125]

- Exclusive use of a state or local government;[126]

- Export or shipment to a possession of the United States;[127]

- Exclusive use of a nonprofit educational organization;[128]

[120] Sec. 6427(l).
[121] Sec. 6430.
[122] Sec. 6427(l)(2).
[123] Sec. 4041(f).
[124] Sec. 4041(g)(1).
[125] Id.
[126] Sec. 4041(g)(2).
[127] Sec. 4041(g)(3).
[128] Sec. 4041(g)(4).

- Use as a fuel in an aircraft museum for the procurement, care, or exhibition of aircraft of the type used for combat or transport in World War II;[129] and

- Use as a fuel in (a) helicopters engaged in the exploration for or the development or removal of hard minerals, oil, or gas and in timber (including logging) operations if the helicopters neither take off from nor land at a facility eligible for Airport Trust Fund assistance or otherwise use federal aviation services during flights or (b) any air transportation for the purpose of providing emergency medical services (1) by helicopter or (2) by a fixed-wing aircraft equipped for and exclusively dedicated on that flight to acute care emergency medical services.[130]

- Off-highway business use.

Since 4041(a) is limited to the delivery into the fuel supply tank of a diesel-powered highway vehicle or train, kerosene delivered into the fuel supply tank of aircraft is a nontaxable use for purposes of section 4041(a).

Claims for refund of kerosene used in aviation

"Commercial aviation" is the use of an aircraft in a business of transporting persons or property for compensation or hire by air, with certain exceptions.[131] All other aviation is noncommercial aviation.

For fuel not removed directly into the wing of an airplane, the Safe, Accountable, Flexible, Efficient, Transportation Equity Act: A Legacy for Users ("SAFETEA") changed the rate of taxation for aviation-grade kerosene from 21.8 cents per gallon to the general kerosene and diesel rate of 24.3 cents per gallon.[132] In order to preserve the aviation rate for fuel actually used in aviation, the 21.8 cent rate of taxation (or as the case may be, the 4.3 cent commercial aviation rate, or the nontaxable use rate) is achieved through a refund when the fuel is used in aviation (a refund of 2.5 cents for taxable noncommercial aviation, 20 cents in the case of commercial aviation, and 24.3 cents for nontaxable uses).[133] These changes became effective on October 1, 2005.

Prior to October 1, 2005, if fuel that was previously taxed was used in noncommercial aviation for a nontaxable use, generally, the ultimate purchaser of such fuel (other than for the exclusive use of a State or local government, or for use on a farm for farming purposes) could claim a refund for the tax that was paid. SAFETEA eliminated the ability of a purchaser to file for a refund with respect to fuel used in noncommercial aviation. Instead, the registered ultimate vendor is the exclusive party entitled to a refund with respect to kerosene used in noncommercial aviation.[134] An ultimate vendor is the person who sells the kerosene to an ultimate purchaser for use in noncommercial aviation. If the fuel was used for a nontaxable use, the vendor may make a claim for 24.3 cents per gallon, otherwise, the vendor is permitted to claim 2.5 cents per gallon for kerosene sold for use in noncommercial aviation.[135]

For commercial aviation, the ultimate purchaser has the option of filing a claim itself, or waiving the right to refund to its ultimate vendor, if the vendor agrees to file on behalf of the purchaser.[136]

A separate special rule also applies to kerosene sold to a State or local government, regardless of whether the kerosene was sold for aviation or other purposes.[137] In general, this rule makes the registered ultimate vendor the appropriate party for filing refund claims on behalf of a State or local government. Special rules apply for credit card sales.[138]

---

[129] Sec. 4041(h).

[130] Secs. 4041(l), 4261(f) and (g).

[131] "Commercial aviation" does not include aircraft used for skydiving, small aircraft on nonestablished lines or transportation for affiliated group members.

[132] Sec. 11161 of Pub. L. No. 109-59 (2005).

[133] Sec. 6427(l)(1), (4) and (5).

[134] Sec. 6427(l)(5)(B).

[135] Sec. 6427(l)(5)(A). Under this provision, of the 24.4 cents of tax imposed on kerosene used in taxable noncommercial aviation, the 0.1 cent for the Leaking Underground Storage Tank Trust Fund financing rate and 21.8 cents of the tax imposed on kerosene cannot be refunded. The limitations of sec. 6427(l)(5)(A) on the amount that cannot be refunded do not apply to uses exempt from tax. However, sec. 6430 prevents a refund of the Leaking Underground

Storage Tank Trust Fund financing rate in all cases except export. Sec. 6427(l)(5)(B) requires that all amounts that would have been paid to the ultimate purchaser pursuant to sec. 6427(l)(1) are to paid to the ultimate registered vendor, therefore the ultimate registered vendor is the only claimant for both nontaxable and taxable use of kerosene in noncommercial aviation.

[136] Sec. 6427(l)(4)(B).

[137] Sec. 6427(l)(6).

[138] If certain conditions are met, a registered credit card issuer may make the claim for refund in place of the ultimate vendor. If the diesel fuel or kerosene is purchased with a credit card issued to a State but the credit card issuer is not registered with the IRS (or does not meet certain other conditions) the credit card issuer must collect the amount of the tax and the State is the proper claimant.

Explanation of Provision

In general

The provision allows purchasers that use kerosene for an exempt aviation purpose (other than in the case of a State or local government) to make a claim for refund of the tax that was paid on such fuel or waive their right to claim a refund to their registered ultimate vendors. As a result, under the provision, crop-dusters, air ambulances, aircraft engaged in foreign trade and other exempt users may either make the claim for refund of the 24.3 cents per gallon themselves or waive the right to their vendors.

General noncommercial aviation use (which is entitled to a refund of 2.5 cents-per-gallon) remains an exclusive ultimate vendor rule. The rules for State and local governments also are unchanged.

Special rule for purchases of kerosene used in aviation on a farm for farming purposes

For kerosene used in aviation on a farm for farming purposes that was purchased after December 31, 2004, and before October 1, 2005, the Secretary is to pay to the ultimate purchaser (without interest) an amount equal to the aggregate amount of tax imposed on such fuel, reduced by any payments made to the ultimate vendor of such fuel. Such claims must be filed within 3 months of the date of enactment and may not duplicate claims filed under section 6427(l).

Effective Date

In general, the provision is effective for kerosene sold after September 30, 2005. For kerosene used for an exempt aviation purpose eligible for the waiver rule created by the provision, the ultimate purchaser is treated as having waived the right to payment and as having assigned such right to the ultimate vendor if the vendor meets the requirements of subparagraph (A), (B) or (D) of section 6416(a)(1). The rule of the preceding sentence applies to kerosene sold after September 30, 2005, and before the date of enactment.

The special rule for kerosene used in aviation on a farm for farming purposes is effective on the date of enactment.

[Law at ¶5665, ¶5800, ¶5860, ¶5865 and ¶7080. CCH Explanation at ¶670.]

[¶15,660] Act Sec. 421. Regional income tax agencies treated as States for purposes of confidentiality and disclosure requirements

Joint Committee Taxation (J.C.T. REP. NO. JCX-50-06)

[Code Sec. 6103]

Present Law

Generally, tax returns and return information ("tax information") is confidential and may not be disclosed unless authorized in the Code. One exception to the general rule of confidentiality is the disclosure of the tax information to States.

Tax information with respect to certain taxes is open to inspection by State agencies, bodies, commissions, or its legal representatives, charged under the laws of the State with tax administration responsibilities.[139] Such inspection is permitted only to the extent necessary for State tax administration proposes. The Code requires a written request from the head of the agency, body or commission as a prerequisite for disclosure. State officials who receive this information may redisclose it to the agency's contractors but only for State tax administration purposes.[140]

The term "State" includes the 50 States, the District of Columbia, and certain territories.[141] In addition, cities with populations in excess of 250,000 that impose a tax or income or wages and with which the IRS is entered into an agreement regarding disclosure also are treated as States.[142]

Explanation of Provision

The provision broadens the definition of "State" to include a regional income tax agency administering the tax laws of municipalities which have a collective population in excess of 250,000. Specifically, under the provision, the term "State" includes any governmental entity (1) that is formed and operated by a qualified

---

[139] Sec. 6103(d)(1).
[140] Sec. 6103(n).

[141] Sec. 6103(b)(5)(A).
[142] Sec. 6103(b)(5)(B).

group of municipalities, and (2) with which the Secretary (in his sole discretion) has entered into an agreement regarding disclosure. The term "qualified group of municipalities" means, with respect to any governmental entity, two or more municipalities: (1) each of which imposes a tax on income or wages, (2) each of which, under the authority of a State statute, administers the laws relating to the imposition of such taxes through such entity, and (3) which collectively have a population in excess of 250,000 (as determined under the most recent decennial United States census data available).

The regional income tax agency is treated as a State for purposes of applying the confidentiality and disclosure provisions for State tax officials, determining the scope of tax administration, applying the rules governing disclosures in judicial and administrative tax proceedings, and applying the safeguard procedures. Because a regional income tax agency administers the laws of its member municipalities, the provision provides that references to State law, State proceedings or State tax returns should be treated as references to the law, proceedings or tax returns of the municipalities which form and operate the regional income tax agency.

Inspection by or disclosure to an entity described above shall be only for the purpose of and to the extent necessary in the administration of the tax laws of the member municipalities in such entity relating to the imposition of a tax on income or wages. Such entity may not redisclose tax information to its member municipalities. This rule does not preclude the entity from disclosing data in a form which cannot be associated with or otherwise identify directly or indirectly a particular taxpayer.[143]

The provision requires that a regional income tax agency conduct on-site reviews every three years of all of its contractors or other agents receiving Federal returns and return information. If the duration of the contract or agreement is less than three years, a review is required at the mid-point of the contract. The purpose of the review is to assess the contractor's efforts to safeguard Federal tax information. This review is intended to cover secure storage, restricting access, computer security, and other safeguards deemed appropriate by the Secretary. Under the provision, the regional income tax agency is required to submit a report of its findings to the IRS and certify annually that such contractors and other agents are in compliance with the requirements to safeguard the confidentiality of Federal tax information. The certification is required to include the name and address of each contractor or other agent with the agency, the duration of the contract, and a description of the contract or agreement with the regional income tax agency.

This provision does not alter or affect in any way the right of the IRS to conduct safeguard reviews of regional income tax agency contractors or other agents. It also does not affect the right of the IRS to approve initially the safeguard language in the contract or agreement and the safeguards in place prior to any disclosures made in connection with such contracts or agreements.

Effective Date

The provision is effective for disclosures made after December 31, 2006.

[Law at ¶ 5770. CCH Explanation at ¶ 635.]

[¶ 15,680] Act Sec. 423. Railroad track maintenance credit

Joint Committee Taxation (J.C.T. Rep. No. JCX-50-06)

[Code Sec. 45G]

Present Law

Present law provides a 50-percent business tax credit for qualified railroad track maintenance expenditures paid or incurred by an eligible taxpayer during the taxable year. The credit is limited to the product of $3,500 times the number of miles of railroad track (1) owned or leased by an eligible taxpayer as of the close of its taxable year, and (2) assigned to the eligible

taxpayer by a Class II or Class III railroad that owns or leases such track at the close of the taxable year. Each mile of railroad track may be taken into account only once, either by the owner of such mile or by the owner's assignee, in computing the per-mile limitation. Under the provision, the credit is limited in respect of the total number of miles of track (1) owned or leased by the Class II or Class III railroad and (2) assigned to the Class II or Class III railroad for purposes of the credit.

---

[143] By definition "return information" does not include data in a form which cannot be associated with or otherwise

identify directly or indirectly a particular taxpayer (sec. 6103(b)(2)).

Qualified railroad track maintenance expenditures are defined as expenditures (whether or not otherwise chargeable to capital account) for maintaining railroad track (including roadbed, bridges, and related track structures) owned or leased as of January 1, 2005, by a Class II or Class III railroad.

An eligible taxpayer means any Class II or Class III railroad, and any person who transports property using the rail facilities of a Class II or Class III railroad or who furnishes railroad-related property or services to a Class II or Class III railroad, but only with respect to miles of railroad track assigned to such person by such railroad under the provision.

The terms Class II or Class III railroad have the meanings given by the Surface Transportation Board.

The provision applies to qualified railroad track maintenance expenditures paid or incurred during taxable years beginning after December 31, 2004, and before January 1, 2008.

Explanation of Provision

The provision modifies the definition of qualified railroad track expenditures, so that the term means gross expenditures (whether or not otherwise chargeable to capital account) for maintaining railroad track (including roadbed,

bridges, and related track structures) owned or leased as of January 1, 2005, by a Class II or Class III railroad (determined without regard to any consideration for such expenditures given by the Class II or Class III railroad which made the assignment of such track).

Thus, for example, under the provision, qualified railroad track maintenance expenditures are not reduced by the discount amount in the case of discounted freight shipping rates, the increment in a markup of the price for track materials, or by debt forgiveness or by cash payments made by the Class II or Class III railroad to the assignee as consideration for the expenditures. Consideration received directly or indirectly from persons other that the Class II or Class III railroad, however, does reduce the amount of qualified railroad track maintenance expenditures. No inference is intended under the provision as to whether or not any such consideration is or is not includable in the assignee's income for Federal tax purposes.

Effective Date

The provision is effective for expenditures paid or incurred during taxable years beginning after December 31, 2004, and before January 1, 2008.

[Law at ¶ 5046. CCH Explanation at ¶ 430.]

[¶ 15,690] Act Sec. 424. Modify tax on unrelated business taxable income of charitable remainder trusts

Joint Committee Taxation (J.C.T. REP. NO. JCX-50-06)

[Code Sec. 664]

Present Law

A charitable remainder annuity trust is a trust that is required to pay, at least annually, a fixed dollar amount of at least five percent of the initial value of the trust to a noncharity for the life of an individual or for a period of 20 years or less, with the remainder passing to charity. A charitable remainder unitrust is a trust that generally is required to pay, at least annually, a fixed percentage of at least five percent of the fair market value of the trust's assets determined at least annually to a noncharity for the life of an individual or for a period 20 years or less, with the remainder passing to charity.[145]

A trust does not qualify as a charitable remainder annuity trust if the annuity for a year is greater than 50 percent of the initial fair market

value of the trust's assets. A trust does not qualify as a charitable remainder unitrust if the percentage of assets that are required to be distributed at least annually is greater than 50 percent. A trust does not qualify as a charitable remainder annuity trust or a charitable remainder unitrust unless the value of the remainder interest in the trust is at least 10 percent of the value of the assets contributed to the trust.

Distributions from a charitable remainder annuity trust or charitable remainder unitrust are treated in the following order as: (1) ordinary income to the extent of the trust's current and previously undistributed ordinary income for the trust's year in which the distribution occurred; (2) capital gains to the extent of the trust's current capital gain and previously undistributed capital gain for the trust's year in which the distribution occurred; (3) other income (e.g.,

---

[145] Sec. 664(d).

tax-exempt income) to the extent of the trust's current and previously undistributed other income for the trust's year in which the distribution occurred; and (4) corpus.[146]

In general, distributions to the extent they are characterized as income are includible in the income of the beneficiary for the year that the annuity or unitrust amount is required to be distributed even though the annuity or unitrust amount is not distributed until after the close of the trust's taxable year.[147]

Charitable remainder annuity trusts and charitable remainder unitrusts are exempt from Federal income tax for a tax year unless the trust has any unrelated business taxable income for the year. Unrelated business taxable income includes certain debt financed income. A charitable remainder trust that loses exemption from income tax for a taxable year is taxed as a regular complex trust. As such, the trust is allowed a deduction in computing taxable income for amounts required to be distributed in a taxable

year, not to exceed the amount of the trust's distributable net income for the year.

Explanation of Provision

The provision imposes a 100-percent excise tax on the unrelated business taxable income of a charitable remainder trust. This replaces the present-law rule that takes away the income tax exemption of a charitable remainder trust for any year in which the trust has any unrelated business taxable income. Consistent with present law, the tax is treated as paid from corpus. The unrelated business taxable income is considered income of the trust for purposes of determining the character of the distribution made to the beneficiary.

Effective Date

The provision is effective for taxable years beginning after December 31, 2006.

[Law at ¶ 5420. CCH Explanation at ¶ 680.]

[¶ 15,700] Act Sec. 425. Make permanent the special rule regarding treatment of loans to qualified continuing care facilities

Joint Committee Taxation (J.C.T. REP. NO. JCX-50-06)

[Code Sec. 7872(h)]

Present Law

In general

For calendar years beginning before January 1, 2006, present law provides generally that certain loans that bear interest at a below-market rate are treated as loans bearing interest at the market rate, accompanied by imputed payments characterized in accordance with the substance of the transaction (for example, as a gift, compensation, a dividend, or interest).[148]

An exception to this imputation rule is provided for any calendar year for a below-market loan made by a lender to a qualified continuing care facility pursuant to a continuing care contract, if the lender or the lender's spouse attains age 65 before the close of the calendar year.[149]

The exception applies only to the extent the aggregate outstanding loans by the lender (and spouse) to any qualified continuing care facility do not exceed $163,300 (for 2006).[150]

For this purpose, a continuing care contract means a written contract between an individual and a qualified continuing care facility under which: (1) the individual or the individual's spouse may use a qualified continuing care facility for the life or lives of one or both individuals; (2) the individual or the individual's spouse will first reside in a separate, independent living unit with additional facilities outside such unit for the providing of meals and other personal care and will not require long-term nursing care, and then will be provided long-term and skilled nursing care as the health of the individual or the individual's spouse requires; and (3) no additional substantial payment is required if the individual or the individual's spouse requires increased personal care services or long-term and skilled nursing care.[151]

For this purpose, a qualified continuing care facility means one or more facilities that are designed to provide services under continuing care contracts, and substantially all of the residents of which are covered by continuing care contracts.

---

[146] Sec. 664(b).
[147] Treas. Reg. sec. 1.664-1(d)(4).
[148] Sec. 7872.

[149] Sec. 7872(g).
[150] Rev. Rul. 2005-75, 2005-49 I.R.B. 1073.
[151] Sec. 7872(g)(3).

A facility is not treated as a qualified continuing care facility unless substantially all facilities that are used to provide services required to be provided under a continuing care contract are owned or operated by the borrower. For these purposes, a nursing home is not a qualified continuing care facility.[152]

Special rule for calendar years beginning after 2005 and before 2011

The Tax Increase Prevention and Reconciliation Act of 2005 ("TIPRA") includes a provision modifying the exception under section 7872 relating to loans to continuing care facilities. Among other things, the modification eliminates the dollar cap on aggregate outstanding loans.[153]

Under the TIPRA provision, a continuing care contract is a written contract between an individual and a qualified continuing care facility under which: (1) the individual or the individual's spouse may use a qualified continuing care facility for the life or lives of one or both individuals; (2) the individual or the individual's spouse will be provided with housing, as appropriate for the health of such individual or individual's spouse, (i) in an independent living unit (which has additional available facilities outside such unit for the provision of meals and other personal care), and (ii) in an assisted living facility or a nursing facility, as is available in the continuing care facility; and (3) the individual or the individual's spouse will be provided assisted living or nursing care as the health of the individual or the individual's spouse requires, and as is available in the continuing care facility. The Secretary is required to issue guidance that limits the term "continuing care contract" to contracts that provide only facilities, care, and services described in the preceding sentence.[154]

For purposes of defining the terms "continuing care contract" and "qualified continuing care facility," the term "assisted living facility" is intended to mean a facility at which assistance is provided (1) with activities of daily living (such as eating, toileting, transferring, bathing, dressing, and continence) or (2) in cases of cognitive impairment, to protect the health or safety of an individual. The term "nursing facility" is intended to mean a facility that offers care requiring the utilization of licensed nursing staff.

The TIPRA modifications generally are effective for calendar years beginning after December 31, 2005, with respect to loans made before, on, or after such date. The TIPRA modifications do not apply to any calendar year after 2010. Thus, the TIPRA modifications do not apply with respect to interest imputed after December 31, 2010. After such date, the law as in effect prior to enactment applies.

Explanation of Provision

The provision makes permanent the TIPRA modifications to section 7872 regarding below-market loans to qualified continuing care facilities.

Effective Date

The provision is effective as if included in section 209 of the TIPRA.

[Law at ¶ 5855. CCH Explanation at ¶ 245.]

[¶ 15,710] Act Sec. 426. Tax technical corrections

Joint Committee Taxation (J.C.T. REP. NO. JCX-50-06)

[Act Sec. 426]

In general

The bill includes technical corrections to recently enacted tax legislation. Except as otherwise provided, the amendments made by the technical corrections contained in the bill take effect as if included in the original legislation to which each amendment relates.

Amendment Related to the Tax Increase Prevention and Reconciliation Act of 2005

Look-through treatment and regulatory authority (Act sec. 103(b)).—Under the Act, for taxable years beginning after 2005 and before 2009, dividends, interest (including factoring income which is treated as equivalent to interest under sec. 954(c)(1)(E)), rents, and royalties received by one controlled foreign corporation ("CFC") from a related CFC are not treated as foreign personal holding company income to the extent attributable or properly allocable to non-subpart F income of the payor (the "TIPRA look-through rule"). The Act further provides that the Secretary shall prescribe such regulations as are appropriate to prevent the abuse of the purposes of the rule.

---

[152] Sec. 7872(g)(4).
[153] Sec. 7872(h).

[154] Sec. 7872(h)(2).

Section 952(b) provides that subpart F income of a CFC does not include any item of income from sources within the United States which is effectively connected with the conduct by such CFC of a trade or business within the United States ("ECI") unless such item is exempt from taxation (or is subject to a reduced rate of tax) pursuant to a tax treaty. Thus, for example, a payment of interest from a CFC all of the income of which is U.S.-source ECI (and therefore not subpart F income) may receive the unintended benefit of the TIPRA look-through rule under the Act, even though the payment may be deductible for U.S. tax purposes.

The provision conforms the TIPRA look-through rule to the rule's purpose of allowing U.S. companies to redeploy their active foreign earnings (i.e., CFC earnings subject to U.S. tax deferral) without an additional tax burden in appropriate circumstances. Under the provision, in order to be excluded from foreign personal holding company income under the TIPRA look-through rule, the dividend, interest, rent, or royalty also must not be attributable or properly allocable to income of the related party payor that is treated as ECI. Thus, for example, a payment of interest made by a CFC does not qualify under the TIPRA look-through rule to the extent that the interest payment is allocated to the CFC's ECI. This is the case even if the interest payment creates or increases a net operating loss of the CFC. The rule applies to dividends, notwithstanding that dividends are not deductible.

The provision clarifies the authority of the Secretary to issue regulations under the TIPRA look-through rule, as amended by this provision. It is intended that the Secretary will prescribe regulations that are necessary or appropriate to carry out the amended TIPRA look-through rule, including, but not limited to, regulations that prevent the inappropriate use of the amended TIPRA look-through rule to strip income from the U.S. income tax base. Regulations issued pursuant to this authority may, for example, include regulations that prevent the application of the amended TIPRA look-through rule to interest deemed to arise under certain related party factoring arrangements pursuant to section 864(d), or under other transactions the net effect of which is the deduction of a payment, accrual, or loss for U.S. tax purposes without a corresponding inclusion in the subpart F income of the CFC income recipient, where such inclusion would have resulted in the absence of the amended TIPRA look-through rule.

Amendment related to the American Jobs Creation Act of 2004

Modification of effective date of exception from interest suspension rules for certain listed and reportable transactions (Act sec. 903).—Section 903 of the American Jobs Creation Act of 2004 ("AJCA"), as modified by section 303 of the Gulf Opportunity Zone Act of 2005, provides that the Secretary of the Treasury may permit interest suspension where taxpayers have acted reasonably and in good faith. For provisions that are included in the Code, section 7701(a)(11) provides that the term "Secretary of the Treasury" means the Secretary in his non-delegable capacity, and the term "Secretary" means the Secretary or his delegate. However, section 903 of AJCA (as modified) is not included in the Code. To clarify that the Secretary may delegate authority under section 903 of AJCA (as modified), the provision adds the words "or the Secretary's delegate" following the reference to the Secretary of the Treasury.

[Law at ¶5555 and ¶7085. CCH Explanation at ¶365 and ¶655.]

[¶15,720] Act Sec. 403 (Division C). Exclusion of 25 percent of capital gain for certain sales of mineral and oil leases for conservation purposes

Joint Committee Taxation (J.C.T. Rep. No. JCX-50-06)

[Act Sec. 403]

Present Law

Gain from the sale or exchange of land held more than one year generally is treated as long-term capital gain. Generally, the net capital gain of an individual is subject to a maximum tax rate of 15 percent. The net capital gain of a corporation is subject to tax at the same rate as ordinary income.

Explanation of Provision

In general

The provision provides a 25-percent exclusion from gross income of long-term capital gain from the conservation sale of a qualifying mineral or geothermal interest.[172] The conservation sale must be made to an eligible entity that intends that the acquired property be used for qualified conservation purposes in perpetuity.[173]

Qualifying interests

A qualifying mineral or geothermal interest means an interest in any mineral or geothermal deposit located on eligible Federal land which constitutes a taxpayer's entire interest in such deposit. Eligible Federal land means (1) Bureau of Land Management land and any Federally-owned minerals located south of the Blackfeet Indian Reservation and East of the Lewis and Clark national Forest to the Eastern edge of R. 8 W., beginning in T. 29 N. down to and including T. 19 N. and all of T. 18 N., R. 7 W, (2) the Forest Service land and any Federally-owned minerals located in the Rocky Mountain Division of the Lewis and Clark national Forest, including the approximately 356,111 acres of land made unavailable for leasing by the August 28, 1997, Record of Decision for the Lewis and Clark National Forest Oil and Gas Leasing Environmental Impact Statement and that is located form T. 31 N. to T. 16 N. and R. 13 W. to R. 7 W., and (3) the Forest Service land and any Federally-owned minerals located within the Badger Two Medicine area of the Flathead National Forest, including the land located in T. 29 N. from the Western edge of R. 16 W. to the Eastern edge of R. 13 W. and the land located in T. 28 N., Rs 13 and 14 W. All such land is as generally depicted on the map entitled "Rocky Mountain Front Mineral Withdrawal Area" and dated December 31, 2006. The map shall be on file and available for inspection in the Office of the Chief of the Forest Service.

An interest in property is not the entire interest of the taxpayer if such interest was divided in an attempt to avoid the requirement that the taxpayer sell the taxpayer's entire interest in the property. An interest may be considered the taxpayer's entire interest notwithstanding that the taxpayer retains an interest in other deposits, even if the other deposits are contiguous with the sold deposit and were acquired by the taxpayer along with such deposit in a single conveyance. It is intended that the partial interest rules contained in Treasury Regulations section 1.170A-7(a)(2)(i) and generally applicable to

charitable contributions of partial interests be applied similarly for purposes of this provision.

Conservation sales

A conservation sale is a sale (excluding a transfer made by order of condemnation or eminent domain) to an eligible entity, defined as a Federal, State, or local government, or an agency or department thereof or a section 501(c)(3) organization that is organized and operated primarily to meet a qualified conservation purpose. In addition, to be a conservation sale, the organization acquiring the property interest must provide the taxpayer with a written letter stating that the acquisition will serve one or more qualified conservation purposes, that the use of the deposits will be exclusively for conservation purposes, and that such use will continue in the event of a subsequent transfer of the acquired interest. A qualified conservation purpose is: (1) the preservation of land areas for outdoor recreation by, or the education of, the general public; (2) the protection of a relatively natural habitat of fish, wildlife, or plants, or similar ecosystem; or (3) the preservation of open space (including farmland and forest land) where the preservation is for the scenic enjoyment of the general public or pursuant to a clearly delineated Federal, State, or local governmental conservation policy and will yield a significant public benefit. Use of property is not considered to be exclusively for conservation purposes unless the conservation purpose is protected in perpetuity and no surface mining is permitted with respect to the property (sec. 170(h)(5)).

Protection of conservation purposes

The provision provides for the imposition of penalty excise taxes if an eligible entity fails to take steps consistent with the protection of conservation purposes. If ownership or possession of the property is transferred by a qualified organization, then: (1) a 20-percent excise tax applies to the fair market value of the property, and (2) any realized gain or income is subject to an additional excise tax imposed at the highest income tax rate applicable to C corporations. In the case of a transfer by an eligible entity to another eligible entity, the excise tax does not apply if the transferee provides the transferor at the time of the transfer a letter of intent (as

---

[172] In a non tax-related provision, the provision also provides that, subject to valid existing rights, eligible Federal land (including any interest in eligible Federal land) is withdrawn from: (1) all forms of location, entry, and patent under the mining laws; and (2) disposition under all laws relating to mineral and geothermal leasing.

[173] The exclusion is mandatory if all of the requirements of the provision are satisfied, and a taxpayer need not file an

election to take advantage of the exclusion. A taxpayer who transfers qualifying property to a qualified organization may opt out of the 25-percent exclusion by choosing not to satisfy one or more of the provision's requirements without having to file a formal election with the Secretary, such as by failing to obtain the requisite letter of intent from the qualified organization.

described above). In the case of a transfer by an eligible entity to a transferee that is not an eligible entity, the excise tax does not apply if it is established to the satisfaction of the Secretary that the transfer is exclusively for conservation purposes (as provided in section 170(h)(5)) and the transferee provides the transferor a letter of intent (as described above) at the time of the transfer. Once a transfer has been subject to the excise tax, the excise tax may not apply to any subsequent transfers. The provision provides that the Secretary may require such reporting as may be necessary or appropriate to further the purpose that any conservation use be in perpetuity.

Effective Date

The provision is effective for sales occurring on or after the date of enactment.

[Law at ¶7090. CCH Explanation at ¶358.]

¶20,001 Effective Dates

Tax Increase Prevention and Reconciliation Act of 2005

This CCH-prepared table presents the general effective dates for major law provisions added, amended or repealed by the Tax Increase Prevention and Reconcilation Act of 2005 (P.L. 109-222), enacted May 17, 2006. Entries are listed in Code Section order.

Code Sec.	Act Sec.	Act Provision Subject	Effective Date
1(g)(2)(A)	510(a)	Increase in Age of Minor Children Whose Unearned Income is Taxed as if Parent's Income	Tax years beginning after December 31, 2005
1(g)(2)(A)-(C)	510(c)	Increase in Age of Minor Children Whose Unearned Income is Taxed as if Parent's Income—Conforming Amendment	Tax years beginning after December 31, 2005
1(g)(4)(c)	510(b)	Increase in Age of Minor Children Whose Unearned Income is Taxed as if Parent's Income—Treatment of Distributions From Qualified Disability Trusts	Tax years beginning after December 31, 2005
26(a)(2)	302(a)(1)-(2)	Allowance of Nonrefundable Personal Credits Against Regular and Alternative Minimum Tax Liability	Tax years beginning after December 31, 2005
54(l)(2)	508(d)(3)	Loan and Redemption Requirements on Pooled Financing Requirements—Conforming Amendments	Bonds issued after May 17, 2006
55(d)(1)(A)	301(a)(1)	Increase in Alternative Minimum Tax Exemption Amount for 2006	Tax years beginning after December 31, 2005
55(d)(1)(B)	301(a)(2)	Increase in Alternative Minimum Tax Exemption Amount for 2006	Tax years beginning after December 31, 2005
142(d)(2)(B)	209(b)(2)	Modification of Treatment of Loans to Qualified Continuing Care Facilities—Conforming Amendments	Calendar years beginning after December 31, 2005, with respect to loans made before, on, or after such date
143(l)(3)(B)	203(b)(1)(A)-(C)	Veterans' Mortgage Bonds—Revision of State Veterans Limit	Allocations of State volume limit after April 5, 2006
143(l)(4)	203(a)(1)	Veterans' Mortgage Bonds—Expansion of Definition of Veterans Eligible for State Home Loan Programs Funded by Qualified Veterans' Mortgage Bonds	Bonds issued on or after May 17, 2006
144(a)(4)(F)	208(b)	Modification of Effective Date of Disregard of Certain Capital Expenditures for Purposes of Qualified Small Issue Bonds—Conforming Amendment	May 17, 2006

Code Sec.	Act Sec.	Act Provision Subject	Effective Date
144(a)(4)(G)	208(a)	Modification of Effective Date of Disregard of Certain Capital Expenditures for Purposes of Qualified Small Issue Bonds	May 17, 2006
148(f)(4)(D)(ii)(II)-(IV)	508(c)	Loan and Redemption Requirements on Pooled Financing Requirements—Elimination of Disregard of Pooled Bonds in Determining Eligibility for Small Issuer Exception to Arbitrage Rebate	Bonds issued after May 17, 2006
149(f)(1)	508(d)(1)	Loan and Redemption Requirements on Pooled Financing Requirements—Conforming Amendments	Bonds issued after May 17, 2006
149(f)(2)(A)	508(a)	Loan and Redemption Requirements on Pooled Financing Requirements—Strengthened Reasonable Expectation Requirement	Bonds issued after May 17, 2006
149(f)(4)-(7)	508(b)	Loan and Redemption Requirements on Pooled Financing Requirements—Written Loan Commitment and Redemption Requirements	Bonds issued after May 17, 2006
149(f)(7)(B)	508(d)(2)	Loan and Redemption Requirements on Pooled Financing Requirements—Conforming Amendments	Bonds issued after May 17, 2006
163(j)(8)-(9)	501(a)	Application of Earnings Stripping Rules to Partners Which Are Corporations	Tax years beginning on or after May 17, 2006
163(j)(9)(B)-(D)	501(b)	Application of Earnings Stripping Rules to Partners Which Are Corporations—Additional Regulatory Authority	Tax years beginning on or after May 17, 2006
167(g)(8)	207(a)	Amortization of Expenses Incurred in Creating or Acquiring Music or Music Copyrights	Expenses paid or incurred with respect to property placed in service in tax years beginning after December 31, 2005
167(h)(5)	503(a)	5-Year Amortization of Geological and Geophysical Expenditures For Certain Major Integrated Oil Companies	Amounts paid or incurred after May 17, 2006
170(e)(1)(A)	204(b)	Capital Gains Treatment for Certain Self-Created Musical Works—Limitation on Charitable Contributions	Sales and exchanges in tax years beginning after May 17, 2006
179(b)(1)	101	Increased Expensing for Small Business	May 17, 2006
179(b)(2)	101	Increased Expensing for Small Business	May 17, 2006
179(b)(5)	101	Increased Expensing for Small Business	May 17, 2006
179(c)(2)	101	Increased Expensing for Small Business	May 17, 2006
179(d)(1)(A)(ii)	101	Increased Expensing for Small Business	May 17, 2006
199(a)(2)	514(b)(2)	Only Wages Attributable to Domestic Production Taken Into Account in Determining Deduction for Domestic Production—Simplification of Rules For Determining W-2 Wages of Partners and S Corporation Shareholders—Conforming Amendment	Tax years beginning after May 17, 2006

¶20,001

Code Sec.	Act Sec.	Act Provision Subject	Effective Date
199(b)(2)	514(a)	Only Wages Attributable to Domestic Production Taken Into Account in Determining Deduction for Domestic Production	Tax years beginning after May 17, 2006
199(d)(1)(A)(iii)	514(b)(1)	Only Wages Attributable to Domestic Production Taken Into Account in Determining Deduction for Domestic Production—Simplification of Rules For Determining W-2 Wages of Partners and S Corporation Shareholders	Tax years beginning after May 17, 2006
355(b)(3)	202	Modification of Active Business Definition Under Section 355	May 17, 2006
355(g)	507(a)	Section 355 Not to Apply to Distributions Involving Disqualified Investment Companies	Distributions after May 17, 2006, generally
408A(c)(3)(B)(i)	512(a)(2)	Conversions to Roth IRAs—Repeal of Income Limitations—Conforming Amendment	Tax years beginning after December 31, 2009
408A(c)(3)(B)-(D)	512(a)(1)	Conversions to Roth IRAs—Repeal of Income Limitations	Tax years beginning after December 31, 2009
408A(d)(3)(A)(iii)	512(b)(1)	Conversions to Roth IRAs—Rollovers to a Roth IRA From an IRA Other Than a Roth IRA	Tax years beginning after December 31, 2009
408A(d)(3)(E)	512(b)(2)(B)	Conversions to Roth IRAs—Rollovers to a Roth IRA From an IRA Other Than a Roth IRA—Conforming Amendments	Tax years beginning after December 31, 2009
408A(d)(3)(E)(i)	512(b)(2)(A)	Conversions to Roth IRAs—Rollovers to a Roth IRA From an IRA Other Than a Roth IRA—Conforming Amendments	Tax years beginning after December 31, 2009
468B(g)	201(a)	Clarification of Taxation of Certain Settlement Funds	Accounts and funds established after May 17, 2006
852(b)(3)(E)	505(c)(1)	Treatment of Distributions Attributable to FIRPTA Gains—Treatment of Certain Distributions as Dividends	Tax years of qualified investment entities beginning after December 31, 2005, generally
871(k)(2)(E)	505(c)(2)	Treatment of Distributions Attributable to FIRPTA Gains—Treatment of Certain Distributions as Dividends—Conforming Amendment	Tax years of qualified investment entities beginning after December 31, 2005, generally
897(h)(1)	505(a)(1)(A)-(C)	Treatment of Distributions Attributable to FIRPTA Gains—Qualified Investment Entity	Tax years of qualified investment entities beginning after December 31, 2005, generally
897(h)(4)(A)(i)(II)	504(a)	Application of FIRPTA to Regulated Investment Companies	After December 31, 2004

Code Sec.	Act Sec.	Act Provision Subject	Effective Date
897(h)(4)(A)(ii)	505(a)(2)	Treatment of Distributions Attributable to FIRPTA Gains—Qualified Investment Entity—Exception of Termination of Application of Section 897 Rules to Regulated Investment Companies	Tax years of qualified investment entities beginning after December 31, 2005, generally
897(h)(5)	506(a)	Prevention of Avoidance of Tax on Investments of Foreign Persons in United States Real Property Through Wash Sales Transactions	Tax years beginning after December 31, 2005, except any distribution, or substitute dividend payment, occurring before the date that is 30 days after May 17, 2006
911(b)(2)(D)(ii)	515(a)(1)	Modification of Exclusion For Citizens Living Abroad—Inflation Adjustment of Foreign Earned Income Limitation	Tax years beginning after December 31, 2005
911(b)(2)(D)(ii)(II)	515(a)(2)	Modification of Exclusion For Citizens Living Abroad—Inflation Adjustment of Foreign Earned Income Limitation	Tax years beginning after December 31, 2005
911(c)(1)(A)	515(b)(2)(A)	Modification of Exclusion For Citizens Living Abroad—Modification of Housing Cost Amount—Maximum Amount of Exclusion	Tax years beginning after December 31, 2005
911(c)(1)(B)(i)	515(b)(1)	Modification of Exclusion For Citizens Living Abroad—Modification of Housing Cost Amount—Modification of Housing Cost Floor	Tax years beginning after December 31, 2005
911(c)(2)-(4)	515(b)(2)(B)	Modification of Exclusion For Citizens Living Abroad—Modification of Housing Cost Amount—Maximum Amount of Exclusion—Limitation	Tax years beginning after December 31, 2005
911(d)(4)	515(b)(2)(C)(i)	Modification of Exclusion For Citizens Living Abroad—Modification of Housing Cost Amount—Maximum Amount of Exclusion—Conforming Amendments	Tax years beginning after December 31, 2005
911(d)(7)	515(b)(2)(C)(ii)	Modification of Exclusion For Citizens Living Abroad—Modification of Housing Cost Amount—Maximum Amount of Exclusion—Conforming Amendments	Tax years beginning after December 31, 2005
911(f)-(g)	515(c)	Modification of Exclusion For Citizens Living Abroad—Rates of Tax Applicable to Nonexcluded Income	Tax years beginning after December 31, 2005
953(e)(10)	103(a)(1)(A)-(B)	Controlled Foreign Corporations—Subpart F Exception for Active Financing—Exempt Insurance Income	May 17, 2006

¶20,001

Code Sec.	Act Sec.	Act Provision Subject	Effective Date
954(c)(6)	103(b)(1)	Controlled Foreign Corporations—Look-Through Treatment of Payments Between Related Controlled Foreign Corporations Under the Foreign Personal Holding Company Rules	Tax years of foreign corporations beginning after December 31, 2005, and to tax years of United States shareholders with or within which such tax years of foreign corporations end
954(h)(9)	103(a)(2)	Controlled Foreign Corporations—Subpart F Exception for Active Financing—Exception to Treatment as Foreign Personal Holding Company Income	May 17, 2006
1221(b)(3)-(4)	204(a)	Capital Gains Treatment for Certain Self-Created Musical Works	Sales and exchanges in tax years beginning after May 17, 2006
1355(a)(4)	205(a)	Vessel Tonnage Limit	Tax years beginning after December 31, 2005
1445(b)(8)	506(b)	Prevention of Avoidance of Tax on Investments of Foreign Persons in United States Real Property Through Wash Sales Transactions—No Withholding Required	Tax years beginning after December 31, 2005, except any distribution, or substitute dividend payment, occurring before the date that is 30 days after May 17, 2006
1445(e)(6)-(7)	505(b)	Treatment of Distributions Attributable to FIRPTA Gains—Withholding on Distributions Treated as Gain From United States Real Property Interests	Tax years of qualified investment entities beginning after December 31, 2005, generally
3402(t)	511(a)	Imposition of Withholding on Certain Payments Made by Government Entities	Payments made after December 31, 2010
4965	516(a)(1)	Tax Involvement of Accomodation Parties In Tax Shelter—Imposition of Excise Tax	Tax years ending after May 17, 2006, with respect to transactions before, on, or after such date, generally
6011(g)-(h)	516(b)(2)	Tax Involvement of Accomodation Parties In Tax Shelter—Disclosure Requirements—Disclosure By Other Entities to the Tax-Exempt Entity	Disclosures the due date for which are after May 17, 2006
6033(a)(1)	516(b)(1)(B)	Tax Involvement of Accomodation Parties In Tax Shelter—Disclosure Requirements—Disclosure by Entity to the Internal Revenue Service—Conforming Amendment	Disclosures the due date for which are after May 17, 2006
6033(a)(2)-(3)	516(b)(1)(A)	Tax Involvement of Accomodation Parties In Tax Shelter—Disclosure Requirements—Disclosure by Entity to the Internal Revenue Service	Disclosures the due date for which are after May 17, 2006

¶20,001

Code Sec.	Act Sec.	Act Provision Subject	Effective Date
6049(b)(2)(B)-(D)	502(a)	Reporting of Interest on Tax-Exempt Bonds	Interest paid after December 31, 2005
6049(b)(2)(C)	502(b)	Reporting of Interest on Tax-Exempt Bonds—Conforming Amendment	Interest paid after December 31, 2005
6159(f)	509(c)	Partial Payments Required With Submission of Offers-In-Compromise—Conforming Amendment	Offers-in-compromise submitted on and after the date which is 60 days after May 17, 2006
6652(c)(1)	516(c)(2)	Tax Involvement of Accomodation Parties In Tax Shelter—Penalty for Nondisclosure—Conforming Amendment	Disclosures the due date for which are after May 17, 2006
6652(c)(3)-(5)	516(c)(1)	Tax Involvement of Accomodation Parties In Tax Shelter—Penalty for Nondisclosure	Disclosures the due date for which are after May 17, 2006
7122(c)-(e)	509(a)	Partial Payments Required With Submission of Offers-In-Compromise	Offers-in-compromise submitted on and after the date which is 60 days after May 17, 2006
7122(d)(3)(A)-(C)	509(b)(1)	Partial Payments Required With Submission of Offers-In-Compromise—Additional Rules Relating to Treatment of Offers—Unprocessable Offer if Payment Requirements Are Not Met	Offers-in-compromise submitted on and after the date which is 60 days after May 17, 2006
7122(f)	509(b)(2)	Partial Payments Required With Submission of Offers-In-Compromise—Additional Rules Relating to Treatment of Offers—Deemed Acceptance of Offer Not Rejected Within Certain Period	Offers-in-compromise submitted on and after the date which is 60 days after May 17, 2006
7872(g)(6)	209(b)(1)	Modification of Treatment of Loans to Qualified Continuing Care Facilities—Conforming Amendments	Calendar years beginning after December 31, 2005, with respect to loans made before, on, or after such date
7872(h)-(i)	209(a)	Modification of Treatment of Loans to Qualified Continuing Care Facilities	Calendar years beginning after December 31, 2005, with respect to loans made before, on, or after such date
...	102	Capital Gains and Dividend Rates	May 17, 2006
...	206	Modification of Special Arbitrage Rule For Certain Funds	May 17, 2006
...	401	Time For Payment of Corporate Estimated Taxes	May 17, 2006
...	513(a)	Repeal of FSC/ETI Binding Contract Relief—FSC Provisions	Tax years beginning after May 17, 2006
...	513(b)	Repeal of FSC/ETI Binding Contract Relief—ETI Provisions	Tax years beginning after May 17, 2006
...	516(a)(2)	Tax Involvement of Accomodation Parties In Tax Shelter—Imposition of Excise Tax—Conforming Amendment	May 17, 2006

¶20,001

¶20,005 Effective Dates

Tax Relief and Health Care Act of 2006

This CCH-prepared table presents the general effective dates for major law provisions added, amended or repealed by the Tax Relief and Health Care Act of 2006 (P.L. 109-432), enacted December 20, 2006. Entries are listed in Code Section order.

Code Sec.	Act Sec.	Act Provision Subject	Effective Date
25D(a)(1)	206(b)(1)	Credit for Residential Energy Efficient Property—Clarification of Term	December 20, 2006
25D(b)(1)(A)	206(b)(1)	Credit for Residential Energy Efficient Property—Clarification of Term	December 20, 2006
25D(d)(2)	206(b)(2)(A)-(B)	Credit for Residential Energy Efficient Property—Clarification of Term	December 20, 2006
25D(e)(4)(A)(i)	206(b)(1)	Credit for Residential Energy Efficient Property—Clarification of Term	December 20, 2006
25D(g)	206(a)	Credit for Residential Energy Efficient Property—Extension	December 20, 2006
32(c)(2)(B)(vi)(II)	106(a)	Election to Include Combat Pay as Earned Income for Purposes of Earned Income Credit	Tax years beginning after December 31, 2006
38(b)(29)-(31)	405(b)	Mine Rescue Team Training Tax Credit—Credit Made Part of General Business Credit	Tax years beginning after December 31, 2005
41(c)(4)(A)	104(b)(1)(A)-(C)	Extension and Modification of Research Credit—Increase in Rates of Alternative Incremental Credit	Tax years ending after December 31, 2006, generally
41(c)(5)-(7)	104(c)(1)	Extension and Modification of Research Credit—Alternative Simplified Credit for Qualified Research Expenses	Tax years ending after December 31, 2006, generally
41(h)(1)(B)	104(a)(1)	Extension and Modification of Research Credit—Extension	Amounts paid or incurred after December 31, 2005
45(d)	201	Credit for Electricity Produced From Certain Renewable Resources	December 20, 2006
45A(f)	111(a)	Indian Employment Tax Credit	Tax years beginning after December 31, 2005
45C(b)(1)(D)	104(a)(2)	Extension and Modification of Research Credit—Extension—Conforming Amendment	Amounts paid or incurred after December 31, 2005
45D(f)(1)(D)	102(a)	Extension and Modification of New Markets Credit—Extension	December 20, 2006
45D(i)(4)-(6)	102(b)	Extension and Modification of New Markets Credit—Regulations Regarding Non-Metropolitan Counties	December 20, 2006
45G(d)	423(a)(1)-(2)	Modification of Railroad Track Maintenance Credit	Tax years beginning after December 31, 2004

Code Sec.	Act Sec.	Act Provision Subject	Effective Date
45K(g)(1)	211(b)	Treatment of Coke and Coke Gas—Clarification of Qualifying Facility	Fuel produced and sold after December 31, 2005, in tax years ending after such date
45K(g)(2)(D)	211(a)	Treatment of Coke and Coke Gas—Nonapplication of Phaseout	Fuel produced and sold after December 31, 2005, in tax years ending after such date
45L(g)	205	Credit for New Energy Efficient Homes	December 20, 2006
45N	405(a)	Mine Rescue Team Training Tax Credit	Tax years beginning after December 31, 2005
48	207(1)-(2)	Energy Credit	December 20, 2006
48A(f)(1)	203(a)	Performance Standards for Sulfur Dioxide Removal in Advanced Coal-Based Generation Technology Units Designed to Use Subbituminous Coal	Applications for certification under Code Sec. 48A(d)(2) submitted after October 2, 2006
51(c)(4)(B)	105(a)	Work Opportunity Tax Credit and Welfare-To-Work Credit	Individuals who begin work for the employer after December 31, 2005
51(d)(1)(G)-(I)	105(e)(1)	Work Opportunity Tax Credit and Welfare-To-Work Credit—Consolidation of Work Opportunity Credit With Welfare-to-Work Credit	Individuals who begin work for the employer after December 31, 2006
51(d)(4)A)-(B)	105(b)	Work Opportunity Tax Credit and Welfare-To-Work Credit—Eligibility of Ex-Felons Determined Without Regard to Family Income	Individuals who begin work for the employer after December 31, 2006
51(d)(8)(A)(i)	105(c)	Work Opportunity Tax Credit and Welfare-To-Work Credit—Increase in Maximum Age for Eligibility of Food Stamp Recipients	Individuals who begin work for the employer after December 31, 2006
51(d)(10)-(13)	105(e)(2)	Work Opportunity Tax Credit and Welfare-To-Work Credit—Consolidation of Work Opportunity Credit With Welfare-to-Work Credit—Long-Term Family Assistance Recipient	Individuals who begin work for the employer after December 31, 2006
51(d)(12)(A)(ii)(II)	105(d)	Work Opportunity Tax Credit and Welfare-To-Work Credit—Extension of Paperwork Filing Deadline	Individuals who begin work for the employer after December 31, 2006
51(e)	105(e)(3)	Work Opportunity Tax Credit and Welfare-To-Work Credit—Consolidation of Work Opportunity Credit With Welfare-to-Work Credit—Increased Credit for Employment of Long-Term Family Assistance Recipients	Individuals who begin work for the employer after December 31, 2006
51A	105(e)(4)(A)	Work Opportunity Tax Credit and Welfare-To-Work Credit—Consolidation of Work Opportunity Credit With Welfare-to-Work Credit—Repeal of Separate Welfare-to-Work Credit	Individuals who begin work for the employer after December 31, 2006

¶20,005

Code Sec.	Act Sec.	Act Provision Subject	Effective Date
51A(f)	105(a)	Work Opportunity Tax Credit and Welfare-To-Work Credit	Individuals who begin work for the employer after December 31, 2005
53(e)	402(a)	Credit for Prior Year Minimum Tax Liability Made Refundable After Period of Years	Tax years beginning after December 20, 2006
54(f)(1)	202(a)(1)	Credit to Holders of Clean Renewable Energy Bonds	Bonds issued after December 31, 2006
54(f)(2)	202(a)(2)	Credit to Holders of Clean Renewable Energy Bonds	Allocations or reallocations after December 31, 2006
54(l)(3)(B)	107(b)(2)	Extension and Modification of Qualified Zone Academy Bonds—Special Rules Relating to Expenditures, Arbitrage, and Reporting—Conforming Amendments	Obligations issued after December 20, 2006 pursuant to allocations of the national zone academy bond limitation for calendar years after 2005
54(m)	202(a)(3)	Credit to Holders of Clean Renewable Energy Bonds	Bonds issued after December 31, 2006
62(a)(2)(D)	108(a)	Above-The-Line Deduction for Certain Expenses of Elementary and Secondary School Teachers	Tax years beginning after December 31, 2005
62(a)(21)	406(a)(3)	Whistleblower Reforms—Deduction Allowed Whether or Not Taxpayer Itemizes	Information provided on or after December 20, 2006
106(e)	302(a)	FSA and HRA Terminations to Fund HSAs	Distributions on or after December 20, 2006
121(d)(9)	417(d)	Exclusion of Gain From Sale of a Principal Residence by Certain Employees of the Intelligence Community—Conforming Amendment	Sales or exchanges after December 20, 2006 and before January 1, 2011
121(d)(9)(A)	417(a)	Exclusion of Gain From Sale of a Principal Residence by Certain Employees of the Intelligence Community	Sales or exchanges after December 20, 2006 and before January 1, 2011
121(d)(9)(C)(iv)-(v)	417(b)	Exclusion of Gain From Sale of a Principal Residence by Certain Employees of the Intelligence Community—Employee of Intelligence Community Defined	Sales or exchanges after December 20, 2006 and before January 1, 2011
121(d)(9)(C)(vi)	417(c)	Exclusion of Gain From Sale of a Principal Residence by Certain Employees of the Intelligence Community—Special Rule	Sales or exchanges after December 20, 2006 and before January 1, 2011
143(d)(2)((B)-(D)	416(a)	Use of Qualified Mortgage Bonds to Finance Residences for Veterans Without Regard to First-time Homebuyer Requirement	Bonds issued after December 20, 2006
143(l)(3)(B)(iv)	411(a)	Revision of State Veterans Limit Made Permanent	Allocations of State volume limit after April 5, 2006

Code Sec.	Act Sec.	Act Provision Subject	Effective Date
163(h)(3)(E)	419(a)	Premiums for Mortgage Insurance	Amounts paid or accrued after December 31, 2006
163(h)(4)(E)–(F)	419(b)	Premiums for Mortgage Insurance—Definition and Special Rules	Amounts paid or accrued after December 31, 2006
164(b)(5)(I)	103(a)	Election to Deduct State and Local General Sales Taxes	Tax years beginning after December 31, 2005
168(e)(3)(E)(iv)-(v)	113(a)	Fifteen-Year Straight-Line Cost Recovery for Qualified Leasehold Improvements and Qualified Restaurant Property	Property placed in service after December 31, 2005
168(j)(8)	112(a)	Accelerated Depreciation for Business Property on Indian Reservations	Property placed in service after December 31, 2005
168(l)	209(a)	Special Depreciation Allowance for Cellulosic Biomass Ethanol Plant Property	Property placed in service after December 20, 2006 in tax years ending after such date
170(e)(4)(B)(ii)	116(b)(1)(A)	Corporate Donations of Scientific Property Used for Research and of Computer Technology and Equipment—Expansion of Charitable Contribution Allowed for Scientific Property Used for Research and for Computer Technology and Equipment Used for Educational Purposes—Scientific Property Used for Research	Tax years beginning after December 31, 2005
170(e)(4)(B)(iii)	116(b)(1)(B)	Corporate Donations of Scientific Property Used for Research and of Computer Technology and Equipment—Expansion of Charitable Contribution Allowed for Scientific Property Used for Research and for Computer Technology and Equipment Used for Educational Purposes—Conforming Amendment	Tax years beginning after December 31, 2005
170(e)(6)(B)(ii)	116(b)(2)(A)	Corporate Donations of Scientific Property Used for Research and of Computer Technology and Equipment—Computer Technology and Equipment for Educational Purposes	Tax years beginning after December 31, 2005
170(e)(6)(D)	116(b)(2)(B)	Corporate Donations of Scientific Property Used for Research and of Computer Technology and Equipment—Computer Technology and Equipment for Educational Purposes—Conforming Amendment	Tax years beginning after December 31, 2005
170(e)(6)(G)	116(a)(1)	Corporate Donations of Scientific Property Used for Research and of Computer Technology and Equipment—Extension of Computer Technology and Equipment Donation	Contributions made in tax years beginning after December 31, 2005
179D(h)	204	Deduction for Energy Efficient Commercial Buildings	December 20, 2006

¶20,005

Code Sec.	Act Sec.	Act Provision Subject	Effective Date
179E	404(a)	Partial Expensing for Advanced Mine Safety Equipment	Costs paid or incurred after December 20, 2006
198(d)(1)(A)-(C)	109(b)	Extension and Expansion of Expensing of Brownsfields Remediation Costs—Expansion	Expenditures paid or incurred after December 31, 2005
198(h)	109(a)	Extension and Expansion of Expensing of Brownsfields Remediation Costs—Extension	Expenditures paid or incurred after December 31, 2005
199(d)(8)-(9)	401(a)	Deduction Allowable With Respect to Income Attributable to Domestic Production Activities in Puerto Rico	Tax years beginning after December 31, 2005
220(i)(2)	117(a)	Availability of Medical Savings Accounts	December 20, 2006
220(i)(3)(B)	117(a)	Availability of Medical Savings Accounts	December 20, 2006
220(j)(2)	117(b)(1)(A)-(B)	Availability of Medical Savings Accounts—Conforming Amendments	December 20, 2006
220(j)(4)(A)	117(b)(2)	Availability of Medical Savings Accounts—Conforming Amendments	December 20, 2006
222(b)(2)(B)	101(b)(1)-(2)	Deduction for Qualified Tuition and Related Expenses—Conforming Amendments	Tax years beginning after December 31, 2005
222(e)	101(a)	Deduction for Qualified Tuition and Related Expenses	Tax years beginning after December 31, 2005
223(b)(2)(A)	303(a)(1)	Repeal of Annual Deductible Limitation on HSA Contributions	Tax years beginning after December 31, 2006
223(b)(2)(B)	303(a)(2)	Repeal of Annual Deductible Limitation on HSA Contributions	Tax years beginning after December 31, 2006
223(b)(4)(A)-(C)	307(b)	One-Time Distribution From Individual Retirement Plans to Fund HSAs—Coordination With Limitation on Contributions to HSAs	Tax years beginning after December 31, 2006
223(b)(8)	305(a)	Contribution Limitation Not Reduced for Part-Year Coverage—Increase in Limit for Individuals Becoming Eligible Individuals After Beginning of the Year	Tax years beginning after December 31, 2006
223(c)(1)(B)(i)-(iii)	302(b)	FSA and HRA Terminations to Fund HSAs—Certain FSA Coverage Disregarded Coverage	December 20, 2006
223(d)(1)(A)(ii)(I)	303(b)	Repeal of Annual Deductible Limitation on HSA Contributions—Conforming Amendment	Tax years beginning after December 31, 2006
223(g)(1)	304	Modification of Cost-of-Living Adjustment	December 20, 2006
263(a)(1)(J)-(L)	404(b)(1)	Partial Expensing for Advanced Mine Safety Equipment—Conforming Amendments	Costs paid or incurred after December 20, 2006
280C(e)	405(c)	Mine Rescue Team Training Tax Credit—No Double Benefit	Tax years beginning after December 31, 2005
312(k)(3)(B)	404(b)(2)	Partial Expensing for Advanced Mine Safety Equipment—Conforming Amendments	Costs paid or incurred after December 20, 2006
355(b)(3)(A)	410(a)	Modification of Active Business Definition Under Section 355 Made Permanent	May 17, 2006

Code Sec.	Act Sec.	Act Provision Subject	Effective Date
355(b)(3)(D)	410(a)	Modification of Active Business Definition Under Section 355 Made Permanent	May 17, 2006
408(d)(9)	307(a)	One-Time Distribution From Individual Retirement Plans to Fund HSAs	Tax years beginning after December 31, 2006
468B(g)(3)	409(a)	Clarification of Taxation of Certain Settlement Funds Made Permanent	Accounts and funds established after May 17, 2006
613A(c)(6)(H)	118(a)	Taxable Income Limit on Percentage Depletion for Oil and Natural Gas Produced From Marginal Properties	Tax years beginning after December 31, 2005
664(c)	424(a)	Modification of Excise Tax on Unrelated Business Taxable Income of Charitable Remainder Trusts	Tax years beginning after December 31, 2006
954(c)(6)(A)	426(a)(1)(A)	Technical Corrections—Technical Corrections Relating to Look-Through Treatment of Payments Between Related Controlled Foreign Corporations Under the Foreign Personal Holding Company Rules	Tax years of foreign corporations beginning after December 31, 2005, and to tax years of United States shareholders with or within which such tax years of foreign corporations end
954(c)(6)(A)	426(a)(1)(B)	Technical Corrections—Technical Corrections Relating to Look-Through Treatment of Payments Between Related Controlled Foreign Corporations Under the Foreign Personal Holding Company Rules	Tax years of foreign corporations beginning after December 31, 2005, and to tax years of United States shareholders with or within which such tax years of foreign corporations end
1043(b)(1)(A)	418(a)(1)(A)	Sale of Property by Judicial Officers	Sales after December 20, 2006
1043(b)(1)(B)	418(a)(1)(B)	Sale of Property by Judicial Officers	Sales after December 20, 2006
1043(b)(2)(A)	418(a)(2)(A)	Sale of Property by Judicial Officers	Sales after December 20, 2006
1043(b)(2)(B)	418(a)(2)(B)	Sale of Property by Judicial Officers	Sales after December 20, 2006
1043(b)(5)(B)	418(a)(3)	Sale of Property by Judicial Officers	Sales after December 20, 2006
1043(b)(6)	418(b)	Sale of Property by Judicial Officers—Judicial Officer Defined	Sales after December 20, 2006
1221(b)(3)	412(a)	Capital Gains Treatment for Certain Self-Created Musical Works Made Permanent	Sales and exchanges in tax years beginning after May 17, 2006
1245(a)(2)(C)	404(b)(3)	Partial Expensing for Advanced Mine Safety Equipment—Conforming Amendments	Costs paid or incurred after December 20, 2006
1245(a)(3)(C)	404(b)(3)	Partial Expensing for Advanced Mine Safety Equipment—Conforming Amendments	Costs paid or incurred after December 20, 2006

¶20,005

Code Sec.	Act Sec.	Act Provision Subject	Effective Date
1355(a)(4)	413(a)	Reduction in Minimum Vessel Tonnage Which Qualifies for Tonnage Tax Made Permanent	Tax years beginning after December 31, 2005
1355(g)-(h)	415(a)	Great Lakes Domestic Shipping to Not Disqualify Vessel From Tonnage Tax	Tax years beginning after December 20, 2006
1397E(d)(1)(C)-(E)	107(b)(1)(A)	Extension and Modification of Qualified Zone Academy Bonds—Special Rules Relating to Expenditures, Arbitrage, and Reporting	Obligations issued after December 20, 2006 pursuant to allocations of the national zone academy bond limitation for calendar years after 2005
1397E(e)(1)	107(a)	Extension and Modification of Qualified Zone Academy Bonds	Obligations issued after December 31, 2005
1397E(f)-(l)	107(b)(1)(B)	Extension and Modification of Qualified Zone Academy Bonds—Special Rules Relating to Expenditures, Arbitrage, and Reporting	Obligations issued after December 20, 2006 pursuant to allocations of the national zone academy bond limitation for calendar years after 2005
1400(f)	110(a)(1)	Tax Incentives for Investment in the District of Columbia—Designation of Zone	Periods beginning after December 31, 2005
1400A(b)	110(b)(1)	Tax Incentives for Investment in the District of Columbia—Tax-Exempt Economic Development Bonds	Bonds issued after December 31, 2005
1400B(b)	110(c)(1)	Tax Incentives for Investment in the District of Columbia—Zero Percent Capital Gains Rate	Acquisitions after December 31, 2005
1400B(e)(2)	110(c)(2)(A)(i)-(ii)	Tax Incentives for Investment in the District of Columbia—Zero Percent Capital Gains Rate—Conforming Amendments	December 20, 2006
1400B(g)(2)	110(c)(2)(B)	Tax Incentives for Investment in the District of Columbia—Zero Percent Capital Gains Rate—Conforming Amendments	December 20, 2006
1400C(i)	110(d)(1)	Tax Incentives for Investment in the District of Columbia—First-Time Homebuyer Credit	Property purchased after December 31, 2005
1400F(d)	110(c)(2)(C)	Tax Incentives for Investment in the District of Columbia—Zero Percent Capital Gains Rate—Conforming Amendments	December 20, 2006
1400N(d)(6)	120(a)	Extension of Bonus Depreciation for Certain Qualified Gulf Opportunity Zone Property	Tax years ending on or after August 28, 2005, generally
1400N(e)(2)	120(b)	Extension of Bonus Depreciation for Certain Qualified Gulf Opportunity Zone Property—Extension Not Applicable to Increased Section 179 Expensing	Tax years ending on or after August 28, 2005, generally

¶20,005

Code Sec.	Act Sec.	Act Provision Subject	Effective Date
1400N(l)(7)(B)(ii)	107(b)(2)	Extension and Modification of Qualified Zone Academy Bonds—Special Rules Relating to Expenditures, Arbitrage, and Reporting—Conforming Amendments	Obligations issued after December 20, 2006 pursuant to allocations of the national zone academy bond limitation for calendar years after 2005
4041(b)(2)(B)	208(c)	Special Rule for Qualified Methanol or Ethanol Fuel—Clerical Amendment	December 20, 2006
4041(b)(2)(C)(ii)	208(b)	Special Rule for Qualified Methanol or Ethanol Fuel—Applicable Blender Rate	December 20, 2006
4041(b)(2)D	208(a)	Special Rule for Qualified Methanol or Ethanol Fuel—Extension	December 20, 2006
4082(d)(2)(B)	420(b)(2)	Modification of Refunds for Kerosene Used in Aviation—Conforming Amendments	Kerosene sold after September 30, 2005, generally
4132(a)(1)(O)	408(a)	Addition of Meningococcal and Human Papillomavirus Vaccines to List of Taxable Vaccines—Meningococcal Vaccine	Sales and uses on or after February 1, 2007, generally
4132(a)(1)(P)	408(b)	Addition of Meningococcal and Human Papillomavirus Vaccines to List of Taxable Vaccines—Human Papillomavirus Vaccine	Sales and uses on or after February 1, 2007, generally
4980G(d)	306(a)	Exception to Requirement for Employers to Make Comparable Health Savings Account Contributions	Tax years beginning after December 31, 2006
5382(a)(1)(A)	3007	Cellar Treatment of Wine	December 20, 2006
5388(c)(3)	422(a)	Designation of Wines by Semi-Generic Names	Wine imported or bottled in the United States on or after December 20, 2006
5754(c)(1)	401(f)(2)(B)	Tobacco Personal Use Quantity Exception to Not Apply to Delivery Sales—Application of Civil Penalties to Relandings of Tobacco Products Sold in a Delivery Sale—Conforming Amendments	Goods entered, or withdrawn from warehouse for consumption, on or after January 4, 2007
5761(c)	401(f)(2)(A)	Tobacco Personal Use Quantity Exception to Not Apply to Delivery Sales—Application of Civil Penalties to Relandings of Tobacco Products Sold in a Delivery Sale—Conforming Amendments	Goods entered, or withdrawn from warehouse for consumption, on or after January 4, 2007
5761(d)-(f)	401(f)(1)	Tobacco Personal Use Quantity Exception to Not Apply to Delivery Sales—Application of Civil Penalties to Relandings of Tobacco Products Sold in a Delivery Sale	Goods entered, or withdrawn from warehouse for consumption, on or after January 4, 2007
6015(e)(1)	408(a)	Tax Court Review of Requests for Equitable Relief From Joint and Several Liability	Liability for taxes arising or remaining unpaid on or after December 20, 2006

Code Sec.	Act Sec.	Act Provision Subject	Effective Date
6015(e)(1)(A)(i)(II)	408(b)(1)	Tax Court Review of Requests for Equitable Relief From Joint and Several Liability—Conforming Amendments	Liability for taxes arising or remaining unpaid on or after December 20, 2006
6015(e)(1)(B)(i)	408(b)(2)(A)-(B)	Tax Court Review of Requests for Equitable Relief From Joint and Several Liability—Conforming Amendments	Liability for taxes arising or remaining unpaid on or after December 20, 2006
6015(e)(1)(B)(ii)	408(b)(3)	Tax Court Review of Requests for Equitable Relief From Joint and Several Liability—Conforming Amendments	Liability for taxes arising or remaining unpaid on or after December 20, 2006
6015(e)(4)	408(b)(4)	Tax Court Review of Requests for Equitable Relief From Joint and Several Liability—Conforming Amendments	Liability for taxes arising or remaining unpaid on or after December 20, 2006
6015(e)(5)	408(b)(5)	Tax Court Review of Requests for Equitable Relief From Joint and Several Liability—Conforming Amendments	Liability for taxes arising or remaining unpaid on or after December 20, 2006
6015(g)(2)	408(b)(6)	Tax Court Review of Requests for Equitable Relief From Joint and Several Liability—Conforming Amendments	Liability for taxes arising or remaining unpaid on or after December 20, 2006
6015(h)(2)	408(b)(7)	Tax Court Review of Requests for Equitable Relief From Joint and Several Liability—Conforming Amendments	Liability for taxes arising or remaining unpaid on or after December 20, 2006
6039	403(c)(3)	Returns Required in Connection With Certain Options—Conforming Amendments	Calendar years beginning after December 20, 2006
6039(a)	403(a)	Returns Required in Connection With Certain Options	Calendar years beginning after December 20, 2006
6039(a)	403(c)(4)	Returns Required in Connection With Certain Options—Conforming Amendments	Calendar years beginning after December 20, 2006
6039(b)-(d)	403(b)	Returns Required in Connection With Certain Options—Statements to Persons With Respect to Whom Information is Furnished	Calendar years beginning after December 20, 2006
6050H(h)	419(c)	Premiums for Mortgage Insurance—Information Returns Relating to Mortgage Insurance Premiums	Amounts paid or accrued after December 31, 2006
6103(b)(5)	421(a)	Regional Income Tax Agencies Treated as States for Purposes of Confidentiality and Disclosure Requirements	Disclosures made after December 31, 2006
6103(d)(5)(B)	122(a)(1)	Disclosures of Certain Tax Return Information—Disclosures to Facilitate Employment Tax Reporting	Disclosures after December 31, 2006
6103(d)(6)	421(b)	Regional Income Tax Agencies Treated as States for Purposes of Confidentiality and Disclosure Requirements—Special Rules for Disclosure	Disclosures made after December 31, 2006

Code Sec.	Act Sec.	Act Provision Subject	Effective Date
6103(i)(3)(C)(iv)	122(b)(1)	Disclosures of Certain Tax Return Information—Disclosures Relating to Terrorist Activities	Disclosures after December 31, 2006
6103(i)(7)(E)	122(b)(1)	Disclosures of Certain Tax Return Information—Disclosures Relating to Terrorist Activities	Disclosures after December 31, 2006
6103(l)(13)(D)	122(c)(1)	Disclosures of Certain Tax Return Information—Disclosures Relating to Student Loans	Requests made after December 31, 2006
6211(b)(4)(A)	402(b)(1)	Credit to Prior Year Minimum Tax Liability Made Refundable After Period of Years—Conforming Amendments	Tax years beginning after December 20, 2006
6320(b)(1)	407(c)(1)	Frivolous Tax Submissions—Treatment of Frivolous Requests for Hearings Upon filing of Notice of Liens	Submissions made and issues raised after the date on which the Secretary first prescribes a list under Code Sec. 6702(c), as amended by Act Sec. 407(a)
6320(c)	407(c)(2)	Frivolous Tax Submissions—Treatment of Frivolous Requests for Hearings Upon filing of Notice of Liens	Submissions made and issues raised after the date on which the Secretary first prescribes a list under Code Sec. 6702(c), as amended by Act Sec. 407(a)
6330(b)(1)	407(b)(3)	Frivolous Tax Submissions—Treatment of Frivolous Requests for Hearings Before Levy—Statement of Grounds	Submissions made and issues raised after the date on which the Secretary first prescribes a list under Code Sec. 6702(c), as amended by Act Sec. 407(a)
6330(c)(4)	407(b)(2)(A)-(D)	Frivolous Tax Submissions—Treatment of Frivolous Requests for Hearings Before Levy—Preclusion From Raising Frivolous Issues at Hearing	Submissions made and issues raised after the date on which the Secretary first prescribes a list under Code Sec. 6702(c), as amended by Act Sec. 407(a)
6330(g)	407(b)(1)	Frivolous Tax Submissions—Treatment of Frivolous Requests for Hearings Before Levy—Frivolous Requests Disregarded	Submissions made and issues raised after the date on which the Secretary first prescribes a list under Code Sec. 6702(c), as amended by Act Sec. 407(a)
6427(i)(4)(A)	420(b)(3)(A)-(B)	Modification of Refunds for Kerosene Used in Aviation—Conforming Amendments	Kerosene sold after September 30, 2005, generally

¶20,005

Code Sec.	Act Sec.	Act Provision Subject	Effective Date
6427(l)(1)	420(b)(4)	Modification of Refunds for Kerosene Used in Aviation—Conforming Amendments	Kerosene sold after September 30, 2005, generally
6427(l)(4)	420(a)	Modification of Refunds for Kerosene Used in Aviation	Kerosene sold after September 30, 2005, generally
6427(l)(5)-(6)	420(b)(1)	Modification of Refunds for Kerosene Used in Aviation—Conforming Amendments	Kerosene sold after September 30, 2005, generally
6702	407(a)	Frivolous Tax Submissions—Civil Penalties	Submissions made and issues raised after the date on which the Secretary first prescribes a list under Code Sec. 6702(c), as amended by Act Sec. 407(a)
6724(d)(1)(B) (xvii)-(xix)	403(c)(1)	Returns Required in Connection With Certain Options—Conforming Amendments	Calendar years beginning after December 20, 2006
6724(d)(2)(B)	403(c)(2)	Returns Required in Connection With Certain Options—Conforming Amendments	Calendar years beginning after December 20, 2006
7122(f)	407(d)	Frivolous Tax Submissions—Treatment of Frivolous Applications for Offers-in-Compromise and Installment Agreements	Submissions made and issues raised after the date on which the Secretary first prescribes a list under Code Sec. 6702(c), as amended by Act Sec. 407(a)
7443A(b)(5)-(7)	406(a)(2)(A)	Whistleblower Reforms—Assignment to Special Trial Judges	Information provided on or after December 20, 2006
7443A(c)	406(a)(2)(B)	Whistleblower Reforms—Assignment to Special Trial Judges—Conforming Amendment	Information provided on or after December 20, 2006
7608(c)(6)	121	Authority for Undercover Operations	December 20, 2006
7623(a)	406(a)(1)(A)	Whistleblower Reforms—Awards to Whistleblowers	Information provided on or after December 20, 2006
7623(a)	406(a)(1)(B)	Whistleblower Reforms—Awards to Whistleblowers	Information provided on or after December 20, 2006
7623(a)	406(a)(1)(C)	Whistleblower Reforms—Awards to Whistleblowers	Information provided on or after December 20, 2006
7623(b)	406(a)(1)(D)	Whistleblower Reforms—Awards to Whistleblowers	Information provided on or after December 20, 2006
7652(f)(1)	114(a)	Cover Over of Tax on Distilled Spirits	Articles brought into the United States after December 31, 2005

¶20,005

Code Sec.	Act Sec.	Act Provision Subject	Effective Date
7872(h)(4)	425(a)	Loans to Qualified Continuing Care Facilities Made Permanent	Calendar years beginning after December 31, 2005, with respect to loans made before, on, or after such date
9502(d)(2)-(3)	420(b)(5)(A)-(B)	Modification of Refunds for Kerosene Used in Aviation—Conforming Amendments	Kerosene sold after September 30, 2005, generally
9503(c)(7)	420(b)(6)(A)-(B)	Modification of Refunds for Kerosene Used in Aviation—Conforming Amendments	Kerosene sold after September 30, 2005, generally
9508(c)	210(a)(1)-(2)	Expenditures Permitted From the Leaking Underground Storage Tank Trust Fund	December 20, 2006
9701(c)(8)	211(d)	Certain Related Persons and Successors In Interest Relieved of Liability if Premiums Paid—Successor in Interest	Transactions after December 20, 2006
9702(b)	213(a)	Other Provisions—Board of Trustees	December 20, 2006
9704(d)	212(a)(2)(A)	Transfers to Funds; Premium Relief—Combined Benefit Fund—Modifications of Premiums to Reflect Federal Transfers—Elimination of Unassigned Beneficiaries Premium	Plan years of the Combined Fund beginning after September 30, 2006
9704(e)(1)	212(a)(2)(B)(i)	Transfers to Funds; Premium Relief—Combined Benefit Fund—Modifications of Premiums to Reflect Federal Transfers—Premium Accounts—Crediting of Accounts	Plan years of the Combined Fund beginning after September 30, 2006
9704(e)(3)(A)	212(a)(2)(B)(ii)	Transfers to Funds; Premium Relief—Combined Benefit Fund—Modifications of Premiums to Reflect Federal Transfers—Premium Accounts—Surpluses Attributable to Public Funding	Plan years of the Combined Fund beginning after September 30, 2006
9704(f)(2)(c)	212(a)(2)(c)	Transfers to Funds; Premium Relief—Combined Benefit Fund—Modifications of Premiums to Reflect Federal Transfers—Applicable Percentage	Plan years of the Combined Fund beginning after September 30, 2006
9704(j)	211(a)	Certain Related Persons and Successors In Interest Relieved of Liability if Premiums Paid	December 20, 2006
9705	212(a)(1)(C)	Transfers to Funds; Premium Relief—Combined Benefit Fund—Federal Transfers	Plan years of the Combined Fund beginning after September 30, 2006
9705(b)(1)	212(a)(1)(A)	Transfers to Funds; Premium Relief—Combined Benefit Fund—Federal Transfers	Plan years of the Combined Fund beginning after September 30, 2006
9705(b)(2)	212(a)(1)(B)	Transfers to Funds; Premium Relief—Combined Benefit Fund—Federal Transfers	Plan years of the Combined Fund beginning after September 30, 2006

Code Sec.	Act Sec.	Act Provision Subject	Effective Date
9706(h)	212(a)(3)	Transfers to Funds; Premium Relief—Combined Benefit Fund—Assignments and Reassignments	Plan years of the Combined Fund beginning after September 30, 2006
9707(a)	213(b)(1)	Other Provisions—Enforcement of Obligations—Failure to Pay Premiums	December 20, 2006
9711(c)	211(b)	Certain Related Persons and Successors In Interest Relieved of Liability if Premiums Paid—Individual Employer Plans	December 20, 2006
9712(a)(3)-(4)	212(b)(1)	Transfers to Funds; Premium Relief—1992 UMWA Benefit and Other Plans—Transfers to Plans	December 20, 2006
9712(d)(1)	212(b)(2)(A)	Transfers to Funds; Premium Relief—1992 UMWA Benefit and Other Plans—Premium Adjustments	Fiscal years beginning on or after October 1, 2010
9712(d)(2)(B)	212(b)(2)(B)(i)	Transfers to Funds; Premium Relief—UMWA Benefit and Other Plans—Conforming Amendments	Fiscal years beginning on or after October 1, 2010
9712(d)(3)	212(b)(2)(B)(ii)	Transfers to Funds; Premium Relief—UMWA Benefit and Other Plans—Conforming Amendments	Fiscal years beginning on or after October 1, 2010
9712(d)(4)	211(c)	Certain Related Persons and Successors In Interest Relieved of Liability if Premiums Paid—1992 UMWA Benefit Plan	December 20, 2006
9721	213(b)(2)	Other Provisions—Enforcement of Obligations—Civil Enforcement	December 20, 2006
9812(f)(3)	115(a)	Parity in Application of Certain Limits to Mental Health Benefits—Amendment to the Internal Revenue Code 0f 1986	December 20, 2006
...	115(b)	Parity in Application of Certain Limits to Mental Health Benefits—Amendment to the Employee Retirement Income Security Act of 1974	December 20, 2006
...	115(c)	Parity in Application of Certain Limits to Mental Health Benefits—Amendment to the Public Health Service Act	December 20, 2006
...	117(c)(1)	Availability of Medical Savings Accounts—Time for Filing Reports, Etc,	December 20, 2006
...	117(c)(2)	Availability of Medical Savings Accounts—Time for Filing Reports, Etc,	December 20, 2006
...	119(a)(1)-(2)	American Samoa Economic Development Credit	Generally, first two taxable years of a corporation to which Act Sec. 119(a) applies which begin after December 31, 2005, and before January 1, 2008

Code Sec.	Act Sec.	Act Provision Subject	Effective Date
...	119(b)(1)	American Samoa Economic Development Credit—Special Rules for Application of Section—Amount of Credit	Generally, first two taxable years of a corporation to which Act Sec. 119(a) applies which begin after December 31, 2005, and before January 1, 2008
...	119(b)(2)	American Samoa Economic Development Credit—Special Rules for Application of Section—Separate Application	Generally, first two taxable years of a corporation to which Act Sec. 119(a) applies which begin after December 31, 2005, and before January 1, 2008
...	119(b)(3)	American Samoa Economic Development Credit—Special Rules for Application of Section—Foreign Tax Credit Allowed	Generally, first two taxable years of a corporation to which Act Sec. 119(a) applies which begin after December 31, 2005, and before January 1, 2008
...	119(c)	American Samoa Economic Development Credit—Definitions	Generally, first two taxable years of a corporation to which Act Sec. 119(a) applies which begin after December 31, 2005, and before January 1, 2008
...	123(a)	Special Rule for Elections Under Expired Provisions—Research Credit Elections	December 20, 2006
...	123(b)	Special Rule for Elections Under Expired Provisions—Other Elections	December 20, 2006
...	210(b)	Expenditures Permitted From the Leaking Underground Storage Tank Trust Fund—Conforming Amendments	December 20, 2006
..	402(b)(2)	Credit to Prior Year Minimum Tax Liability Made Refundable After Period of Years—Conforming Amendments	Tax years beginning after December 20, 2006
..	403(a)(1)	Withdrawal of Certain Federal Land and Interests in Certain Federal Land From Location, Entry, and Patent Under the Mining Laws and Disposition Under the Mineral and Geothermal Leasing Laws—Definitions—Bureau of Land Management	December 20, 2006

Code Sec.	Act Sec.	Act Provision Subject	Effective Date
. . .	403(a)(2)	Withdrawal of Certain Federal Land and Interests in Certain Federal Land From Location, Entry, and Patent Under the Mining Laws and Disposition Under the Mineral and Geothermal Leasing Laws—Definitions—Eligible Federal Land	December 20, 2006
. . .	403(a)(3)(A)	Withdrawal of Certain Federal Land and Interests in Certain Federal Land From Location, Entry, and Patent Under the Mining Laws and Disposition Under the Mineral and Geothermal Leasing Laws—Definitions—Forest Service Land	December 20, 2006
. . .	403(a)(3)(B)	Withdrawal of Certain Federal Land and Interests in Certain Federal Land From Location, Entry, and Patent Under the Mining Laws and Disposition Under the Mineral and Geothermal Leasing Laws—Definitions—Forest Service Land	December 20, 2006
. . .	403(a)(4)	Withdrawal of Certain Federal Land and Interests in Certain Federal Land From Location, Entry, and Patent Under the Mining Laws and Disposition Under the Mineral and Geothermal Leasing Laws—Definitions—Map	December 20, 2006
. . .	403(b)(1)(A)	Withdrawal of Certain Federal Land and Interests in Certain Federal Land From Location, Entry, and Patent Under the Mining Laws and Disposition Under the Mineral and Geothermal Leasing Laws—Withdrawal	December 20, 2006
. . .	403(b)(1)(B)	Withdrawal of Certain Federal Land and Interests in Certain Federal Land From Location, Entry, and Patent Under the Mining Laws and Disposition Under the Mineral and Geothermal Leasing Laws—Withdrawal	December 20, 2006
. . .	403(b)(2)	Withdrawal of Certain Federal Land and Interests in Certain Federal Land From Location, Entry, and Patent Under the Mining Laws and Disposition Under the Mineral and Geothermal Leasing Laws—Withdrawal—Availability of Map	December 20, 2006

Code Sec.	Act Sec.	Act Provision Subject	Effective Date
. . .	403(c)(1)	Withdrawal of Certain Federal Land and Interests in Certain Federal Land From Location, Entry, and Patent Under the Mining Laws and Disposition Under the Mineral and Geothermal Leasing Laws—Tax Incentive for Sale of Existing Mineral and Geothermal Rights to Tax-Exempt Entities—Exclusion	Sales occurring on or after December 20, 2006
. . .	403(c)(2)	Withdrawal of Certain Federal Land and Interests in Certain Federal Land From Location, Entry, and Patent Under the Mining Laws and Disposition Under the Mineral and Geothermal Leasing Laws—Tax Incentive for Sale of Existing Mineral and Geothermal Rights to Tax Exempt Entities—Qualifying Gain	Sales occurring on or after December 20, 2006
. . .	403(c)(3)(A)	Withdrawal of Certain Federal Land and Interests in Certain Federal Land From Location, Entry, and Patent Under the Mining Laws and Disposition Under the Mineral and Geothermal Leasing Laws—Tax Incentive for Sale of Existing Mineral and Geothermal Rights to Tax-Exempt Entities—Conservation Sale—Transferee is an Eligible Entity	Sales occurring on or after December 20, 2006
. . .	403(c)(3)(B)	Withdrawal of Certain Federal Land and Interests in Certain Federal Land From Location, Entry, and Patent Under the Mining Laws and Disposition Under the Mineral and Geothermal Leasing Laws—Tax Incentive for Sale of Existing Mineral and Geothermal Rights to Tax-Exempt Entities—Conservation Sale—Qualifying Letter of Intent Required	Sales occurring on or after December 20, 2006
. . .	403(c)(3)(C)	Withdrawal of Certain Federal Land and Interests in Certain Federal Land From Location, Entry, and Patent Under the Mining Laws and Disposition Under the Mineral and Geothermal Leasing Laws—Tax Incentive for Sale of Existing Mineral and Geothermal Rights to Tax-Exempt Entities—Conservation Sale—Nonapplication to Certain Sales	Sales occurring on or after December 20, 2006

Code Sec.	Act Sec.	Act Provision Subject	Effective Date
...	403(c)(4)(A)	Withdrawal of Certain Federal Land and Interests in Certain Federal Land From Location, Entry, and Patent Under the Mining Laws and Disposition Under the Mineral and Geothermal Leasing Laws—Tax Incentive for Sale of Existing Mineral and Geothermal Rights to Tax-Exempt Entities—Qualifying Mineral or Geothermal Interest	Sales occurring on or after December 20, 2006
...	403(c)(4)(B)	Withdrawal of Certain Federal Land and Interests in Certain Federal Land From Location, Entry, and Patent Under the Mining Laws and Disposition Under the Mineral and Geothermal Leasing Laws—Tax Incentive for Sale of Existing Mineral and Geothermal Rights to Tax-Exempt Entities—Qualifying Mineral or Geothermal Interest—Entire Interest	Sales occurring on or after December 20, 2006
...	403(c)(5)(A)(i)-(ii)	Withdrawal of Certain Federal Land and Interests in Certain Federal Land From Location, Entry, and Patent Under the Mining Laws and Disposition Under the Mineral and Geothermal Leasing Laws—Tax Incentive for Sale of Existing Mineral and Geothermal Rights to Tax-Exempt Entities—Other Definitions—Eligible Entity	Sales occurring on or after December 20, 2006
...	403(c)(5)(B)	Withdrawal of Certain Federal Land and Interests in Certain Federal Land From Location, Entry, and Patent Under the Mining Laws and Disposition Under the Mineral and Geothermal Leasing Laws—Tax Incentive for Sale of Existing Mineral and Geothermal Rights to Tax-Exempt Entities—Other Definitions—Qualifying Letter of Intent	Sales occurring on or after December 20, 2006
...	403(c)(6)(A)(i)-(ii)	Withdrawal of Certain Federal Land and Interests in Certain Federal Land From Location, Entry, and Patent Under the Mining Laws and Disposition Under the Mineral and Geothermal Leasing Laws—Tax Incentive for Sale of Existing Mineral and Geothermal Rights to Tax-Exempt Entities—Tax on Subsequent Transfers	Sales occurring on or after December 20, 2006

Code Sec.	Act Sec.	Act Provision Subject	Effective Date
...	403(c)(6)(B)(i)-(ii)	Withdrawal of Certain Federal Land and Interests in Certain Federal Land From Location, Entry, and Patent Under the Mining Laws and Disposition Under the Mineral and Geothermal Leasing Laws—Tax Incentive for Sale of Existing Mineral and Geothermal Rights to Tax-Exempt Entities—Tax on Subsequent Transfers—Amount of Tax	Sales occurring on or after December 20, 2006
...	403(c)(6)(C)	Withdrawal of Certain Federal Land and Interests in Certain Federal Land From Location, Entry, and Patent Under the Mining Laws and Disposition Under the Mineral and Geothermal Leasing Laws—Tax Incentive for Sale of Existing Mineral and Geothermal Rights to Tax-Exempt Entities—Tax on Subsequent Transfers—Liability	Sales occurring on or after December 20, 2006
...	403(c)(6)(D)(i)-(iii)	Withdrawal of Certain Federal Land and Interests in Certain Federal Land From Location, Entry, and Patent Under the Mining Laws and Disposition Under the Mineral and Geothermal Leasing Laws—Tax Incentive for Sale of Existing Mineral and Geothermal Rights to Tax-Exempt Entities—Tax on Subsequent Transfers—Relief from Liability	Sales occurring on or after December 20, 2006
...	403(c)(6)(E)	Withdrawal of Certain Federal Land and Interests in Certain Federal Land From Location, Entry, and Patent Under the Mining Laws and Disposition Under the Mineral and Geothermal Leasing Laws—Tax Incentive for Sale of Existing Mineral and Geothermal Rights to Tax-Exempt Entities—Tax on Subsequent Transfers—Administrative Provisions	Sales occurring on or after December 20, 2006
...	403(c)(7)	Withdrawal of Certain Federal Land and Interests in Certain Federal Land From Location, Entry, and Patent Under the Mining Laws and Disposition Under the Mineral and Geothermal Leasing Laws—Tax Incentive for Sale of Existing Mineral and Geothermal Rights to Tax-Exempt Entities—Reporting	Sales occurring on or after December 20, 2006
...	404(b)(4)	Partial Expensing for Advanced Mine Safety Equipment—Conforming Amendments	Costs paid or incurred after December 20, 2006
...	414(a)	Modification of Special Arbitrage Rule for Certain Funds Made Permanent	May 17, 2006
...	426(b)	Technical Corrections—Technical Corrections Regarding Authority to Exercise Reasonable Cause and Good Faith Exception	Documents provided on or after December 21, 2005

¶20,005

¶25,001 Code Section to Explanation Table

¶25,005 Code Sections Added, Amended or Repealed

The list below notes all the Code Sections or subsections of the Internal Revenue Code that were added, amended or repealed by the Tax Increase Prevention and Reconciliation Act of 2005 (P.L. 109-222) and the Tax Relief and Health Care Act of 2006 (P.L. 109-432). The first column indicates the Code Section added, amended or repealed, and the second column indicates the Act Section.

Tax Increase Prevention and Reconciliation Act of 2005

Code Sec.	Act Sec.	Code Sec.	Act Sec.
1(g)(2)(A)	510(a)	871(k)(2)(E)	505(c)(2)
1(g)(2)(A)-(C)	510(c)	897(h)(1)	505(a)(1)(A)-(C)
1(g)(4)(C)	510(b)	897(h)(4)(A)(i)(II)	504(a)
26(a)(2)	302(a)(1)-(2)	897(h)(4)(A)(ii)	505(a)(2)
54(l)(2)	508(d)(3)	897(h)(5)	506(a)
55(d)(1)(A)-(B)	301(a)(1)-(2)	911(b)(2)(D)(ii)	515(a)(1)-(2)
142(d)(2)(B)	209(b)(2)	911(c)(1)(A)	515(b)(2)(A)
143(l)(3)(B)	203(b)(1)(A)-(C)	911(c)(1)(B)(i)	515(b)(1)
143(l)(4)	203(a)(1)	911(c)(2)-(4)	515(b)(2)(B)
144(a)(4)(F)	208(b)	911(d)(4)	515(b)(2)(C)(i)
144(a)(4)(G)	208(a)	911(d)(7)	515(b)(2)(C)(ii)
148(f)(4)(D)(ii)(II)-(IV)	508(c)	911(f)-(g)	515(c)
149(f)(1)	508(d)(1)	953(e)(10)	103(a)(1)(A)-(B)
149(f)(2)(A)	508(a)	954(c)(6)	103(b)(1)
149(f)(4)-(7)	508(b)	954(h)(9)	103(a)(2)
149(f)(7)(B)	508(d)(2)	1221(b)(3)-(4)	204(a)
163(j)(8)-(9)	501(a)	1355(a)(4)	205(a)
163(j)(9)(B)-(D)	501(b)	1445(b)(8)	506(b)
167(g)(8)	207(a)	1445(e)(6)-(7)	505(b)
167(h)(5)	503(a)	3402(t)	511(a)
170(e)(1)(A)	204(b)	4965	516(a)(1)
179(b)-(d)	101	6011(g)-(h)	516(b)(2)
199(a)(2)	514(b)(2)	6033(a)(1)	516(b)(1)(B)
199(b)(2)	514(a)	6033(a)(2)-(3)	516(b)(1)(A)
199(d)(1)(A)(iii)	514(b)(1)	6049(b)(2)(B)-(D)	502(a)
355(b)(3)	202	6049(b)(2)(C)	502(b)
355(g)	507(a)	6159(f)	509(c)
408A(c)(3)(B)(i)	512(a)(2)	6652(c)(1)	516(c)(2)
408A(c)(3)(B)-(D)	512(a)(1)	6652(c)(3)-(5)	516(c)(1)
408A(d)(3)(A)(iii)	512(b)(1)	7122(c)-(e)	509(a)
408A(d)(3)(E)	512(b)(2)(B)	7122(d)(3)(A)-(C)	509(b)(1)
408A(d)(3)(E)(i)	512(b)(2)(A)	7122(f)	509(b)(2)
468B(g)	201(a)	7872(g)(6)	209(b)(1)
852(b)(3)(E)	505(c)(1)	7872(h)-(i)	209(a)

Tax Relief and Health Care Act of 2006

Code Sec.	Act Sec.	Code Sec.	Act Sec.
25D(a)(1)	206(b)(1), Div. A	170(e)(4)(B)(ii)	116(b)(1)(A), Div. A
25D(b)(1)(A)	206(b)(1), Div. A	170(e)(4)(B)(iii)	116(b)(1)(B), Div. A
25D(d)(2)	206(b)(2)(A)-(B), Div. A	170(e)(6)(B)(ii)	116(b)(2)(A), Div. A
25D(e)(4)(A)(i)	206(b)(1), Div. A	170(e)(6)(D)	116(b)(2)(B), Div. A
25D(g)	206(a), Div. A	170(e)(6)(G)	116(a)(1), Div. A
32(c)(2)(B)(vi)(II)	106(a), Div. A	179D(h)	204, Div. A
38(b)(29)-(31)	405(b), Div. A	179E	404(a), Div. A
41(c)(4)(A)	104(b)(1)(A)-(C), Div. A	198(d)(1)(A)-(C)	109(b), Div. A
41(c)(5)-(7)	104(c)(1), Div. A	198(h)	109(a), Div. A
41(h)(1)(B)	104(a)(1), Div. A	199(d)(8)-(9)	401(a), Div. A
45(d)	201, Div. A	220(i)(2)-(3)	117(a), Div. A
45A(f)	111(a), Div. A	220(j)(2)	117(b)(1)(A)-(B), Div. A
45C(b)(1)(D)	104(a)(2), Div. A	220(j)(4)(A)	117(b)(2), Div. A
45D(f)(1)(D)	102(a), Div. A	222(b)(2)(B)	101(b)(1)-(2), Div. A
45D(i)(4)-(6)	102(b), Div. A	222(e)	101(a), Div. A
45G(d)	423(a)(1)-(2), Div. A	223(b)(2)(A)-(B)	303(a)(1)-(2), Div. A
45K(g)(1)	211(b), Div. A	223(b)(4)	307(b), Div. A
45K(g)(2)(D)	211(a), Div. A	223(b)(8)	305(a), Div. A
45L(g)	205, Div. A	223(c)(1)(B)	302(b), Div. A
45N	405(a), Div. A	223(d)(1)(A)(ii)(I)	303(b), Div. A
48	207(1)-(2), Div. A	223(g)(1)	304, Div. A
48A(f)(1)	203(a), Div. A	263(a)(1)(J)-(L)	404(b)(1), Div. A
51(c)(4)(B)	105(a), Div. A	280C(e)	405(c), Div. A
51(d)(1)(G)-(I)	105(e)(1), Div. A	312(k)(3)(B)	404(b)(2), Div. A
51(d)(4)	105(b), Div. A	355(b)(3)	410(a), Div. A
51(d)(8)(A)(i)	105(c), Div. A	408(d)(9)	307(a), Div. A
51(d)(10)-(13)	105(e)(2), Div. A	468B(g)(3)	409(a), Div. A
51(d)(12)(A)(ii)(II)	105(d), Div. A	613A(c)(6)(H)	118(a), Div. A
51(e)	105(e)(3), Div. A	664(c)	424(a), Div. A
51A	105(e)(4)(A), Div. A	954(c)(6)(A)	426(a)(1)(A), Div. A
51A(f)	105(a), Div. A	954(c)(6)(A)	426(a)(1)(B), Div. A
53(e)	402(a), Div. A	1043(b)(1)(A)-(B)	418(a)(1)(A)-(B), Div. A
54(f)	202(a)(1)-(2), Div. A	1043(b)(2)(A)-(B)	418(a)(2)(A)-(B), Div. A
54(l)(3)(B)	107(b)(2), Div. A	1043(b)(5)(B)	418(a)(3), Div. A
54(m)	202(a)(3), Div. A	1043(b)(6)	418(b), Div. A
62(a)(2)(D)	108(a), Div. A	1221(b)(3)	412(a), Div. A
62(a)(21)	406(a)(3), Div. A	1245(a)(2)(C)	404(b)(3), Div. A
106(e)	302(a), Div. A	1245(a)(3)(C)	404(b)(3), Div. A
121(d)(9)	417(d), Div. A	1355(a)(4)	413(a), Div. A
121(d)(9)(A)	417(a), Div. A	1355(g)-(h)	415(a), Div. A
121(d)(9)(C)(iv)-(v)	417(b), Div. A	1397E(d)(1)(C)-(E)	107(b)(1)(A), Div. A
121(d)(9)(C)(vi)	417(c), Div. A	1397E(e)(1)	107(a), Div. A
143(d)(2)(B)-(D)	416(a), Div. A	1397E(f)-(l)	107(b)(1)(B), Div. A
143(l)(3)(B)(iv)	411(a), Div. A	1400(f)	110(a)(1), Div. A
163(h)(3)(E)	419(a), Div. A	1400A(b)	110(b)(1), Div. A
163(h)(4)(E)-(F)	419(b), Div. A	1400B(b)	110(c)(1), Div. A
164(b)(5)(I)	103(a), Div. A	1400B(e)(2)	110(c)(2)(A)(i)-(ii), Div. A
168(e)(3)(E)(iv)-(v)	113(a), Div. A	1400B(g)(2)	110(c)(2)(B), Div. A
168(j)(8)	112(a), Div. A	1400C(i)	110(d)(1), Div. A
168(l)	209(a), Div. A	1400F(d)	110(c)(2)(C), Div. A

Code Sec.	Act Sec.	Code Sec.	Act Sec.
1400N(d)(6)	120(a), Div. A	6330(c)(4)	407(b)(2)(A)-(D), Div. A
1400N(e)(2)	120(b), Div. A	6330(g)	407(b)(1), Div. A
1400N(l)(7)(B)(ii)	107(b)(2), Div. A	6427(i)(4)(A)	420(b)(3)(A)-(B), Div. A
4041(b)(2)(B)	208(c), Div. A	6427(l)(1)	420(b)(4), Div. A
4041(b)(2)(C)(ii)	208(b), Div. A	6427(l)(4)	420(a), Div. A
4041(b)(2)(D)	208(a), Div. A	6427(l)(5)-(6)	420(b)(1), Div. A
4082(d)(2)(B)	420(b)(2), Div. A	6702	407(a), Div. A
4132(a)(1)(O)	408(a), Div. A	6724(d)(1)(B)	403(c)(1), Div. A
4132(a)(1)(P)	408(b), Div. A	6724(d)(2)(B)	403(c)(2), Div. A
4980G(d)	306(a), Div. A	7122(f)	407(d), Div. A
5382(a)(1)(A)	3007, Div. D	7443A(b)(5)-(7)	406(a)(2)(A), Div. A
5388(c)(3)	422(a), Div. A	7443A(c)	406(a)(2)(B), Div. A
5754(c)(1)	401(f)(2)(B), Div. C	7608(c)(6)	121, Div. A
5761(c)	401(f)(2)(A), Div. C	7623	406(a)(1)(A)-(D), Div. A
5761(d)-(f)	401(f)(1), Div. C	7652(f)(1)	114(a), Div. A
6015(e)(1)	408(a), Div. C	7872(h)(4)	425(a), Div. A
6015(e)(1)(A)(i)(II)	408(b)(1), Div. C	9502(d)(2)-(3)	420(b)(5)(A)-(B), Div. A
6015(e)(1)(B)(i)	408(b)(2)(A)-(B), Div. C	9503(c)(7)	420(b)(6)(A)-(B), Div. A
6015(e)(1)(B)(ii)	408(b)(3), Div. C	9508(c)	210(a)(1)-(2), Div. A
6015(e)(4)	408(b)(4), Div. C	9701(c)(8)	211(d), Div. C
6015(e)(5)	408(b)(5), Div. C	9702(b)	213(a), Div. C
6015(g)(2)	408(b)(6), Div. C	9704(d)	212(a)(2)(A), Div. C
6015(h)(2)	408(b)(7), Div. C	9704(e)(1)	212(a)(2)(B)(i), Div. C
6039	403(c)(3), Div. A	9704(e)(3)(A)	212(a)(2)(B)(ii), Div. C
6039(a)	403(a), Div. A	9704(f)(2)(C)	212(a)(2)(C), Div. C
6039(a)	403(c)(4), Div. A	9704(j)	211(a), Div. C
6039(b)-(d)	403(b), Div. A	9705(b)	212(a)(1)(A)-(C), Div. C
6050H(h)	419(c), Div. A	9706(h)	212(a)(3), Div. C
6103(b)(5)	421(a), Div. A	9707(a)	213(b)(1), Div. C
6103(d)(5)(B)	122(a)(1), Div. A	9711(c)	211(b), Div. C
6103(d)(6)	421(b), Div. A	9712(a)(3)-(4)	212(b)(1), Div. C
6103(i)(3)(C)(iv)	122(b)(1), Div. A	9712(d)(1)	212(b)(2)(A), Div. C
6103(i)(7)(E)	122(b)(1), Div. A	9712(d)(2)-(3)	212(b)(2)(B)(i)-(ii), Div. C
6103(l)(13)(D)	122(c)(1), Div. A	9712(d)(4)	211(c), Div. C
6211(b)(4)(A)	402(b)(1), Div. A	9721	213(b)(2), Div. C
6320(b)(1)	407(c)(1), Div. A	9812(f)(3)	115(a), Div. A
6320(c)	407(c)(2), Div. A		
6330(b)(1)	407(b)(3), Div. A		

¶25,010 Table of Amendments to Other Acts

Tax Increase Prevention and Reconciliation Act of 2005

Amended Act Sec.	H.R. 4297 Sec.	Par. (¶)	Amended Act Sec.	H.R. 4297 Sec.	Par. (¶)
American Jobs Creation Act of 2004			**FSC Repeal and Extraterritorial Income Exclusion Act of 2000**		
101(f)	513(b)	7025	5(c)(1)	513(a)	7025
Jobs and Growth Tax Relief Reconciliation Act of 2003					
303	102	7010			

Tax Relief and Health Care Act of 2006

Amended Act Sec.	H.R. 6408 Sec.	Par. (¶)	Amended Act Sec.	H.R. 6408 Sec.	Par. (¶)
Employee Retirement Income Security Act of 1974			**Title 31 United States Code**		
712(f)	115(b)	7040	1324(b)(2)	402(b)	7065
Public Health Service Act			**Tax Increase Prevention and Reconciliation Act of 2005**		
2705(f)	115(c)	7040	206	414(a)	7075
Solid Waste Dispoal Act			**American Jobs Creation Act of 2004**		
9014(2)	210(b)	7060	903(d)(2)(B)(iii)	426(b)	7085

¶25,015 Table of Act Sections Not Amending Internal Revenue Code Sections

Tax Increase Prevention and Reconciliation Act of 2005

	Paragraph		Paragraph
Sec. 1. Short title, etc.	¶7005	Sec. 401. Time for payment of corporate estimated taxes.	¶7020
Sec. 206. Modification of special arbitrage rule for certain funds.	¶7015		

Tax Relief and Health Care Act of 2006

	Paragraph		Paragraph
Sec. 1. Short title, etc.	¶7030	Sec. 403 (Div. C). Withdrawal of certain federal land and interests in certain federal land from location, entry, and patent under the mining laws and disposition under the mineral and geothermal leasing laws	¶7090
Sec. 100. Reference	¶7035		
Sec. 117. Availability of medical savings accounts	¶7045		
Sec. 119. American Samoa economic development credit	¶7050		
Sec. 123. Special rule for elections under expired provisions	¶7055		
Sec. 406. Whistleblower reforms	¶7070		
Sec. 420. Modification of refunds for kerosene used in aviation	¶7080		

¶25,020 Act Sections Amending Code Sections

Tax Increase Prevention and Reconciliation Act of 2005

Act Sec.	Code Sec.	Act Sec.	Code Sec.
101	179(b)-(d)		148(f)(4)(D)(ii)(II)-
103(a)(1)(A)-(B)	953(e)(10)	508(c)	(IV)
103(a)(2)	954(h)(9)	508(d)(1)	149(f)(1)
103(b)(1)	954(c)(6)	508(d)(2)	149(f)(7)(B)
201(a)	468B(g)	508(d)(3)	54(l)(2)
202	355(b)(3)	509(a)	7122(c)-(e)
203(a)(1)	143(l)(4)	509(b)(1)	7122(d)(3)(A)-(C)
203(b)(1)(A)-(C)	143(l)(3)(B)	509(b)(2)	7122(f)
204(a)	1221(b)(3)-(4)	509(c)	6159(f)
204(b)	170(e)(1)(A)	510(a)	1(g)(2)(A)
205(a)	1355(a)(4)	510(b)	1(g)(4)(C)
207(a)	167(g)(8)	510(c)	1(g)(2)(A)-(C)
208(a)	144(a)(4)(G)	511(a)	3402(t)
208(b)	144(a)(4)(F)	512(a)(1)	408A(c)(3)(B)-(D)
209(a)	7872(h)-(i)	512(a)(2)	408A(c)(3)(B)(i)
209(b)(1)	7872(g)(6)	512(b)(1)	408A(d)(3)(A)(iii)
209(b)(2)	142(d)(2)(B)	512(b)(2)(A)	408A(d)(3)(E)(i)
301(a)(1)-(2)	55(d)(1)(A)-(B)	512(b)(2)(B)	408A(d)(3)(E)
302(a)(1)-(2)	26(a)(2)	514(a)	199(b)(2)
501(a)	163(j)(8)-(9)	514(b)(1)	199(d)(1)(A)(iii)
501(b)	163(j)(9)(B)-(D)	514(b)(2)	199(a)(2)
502(a)	6049(b)(2)(B)-(D)	515(a)(1)-(2)	911(b)(2)(D)(ii)
502(b)	6049(b)(2)(C)	515(b)(1)	911(c)(1)(B)(i)
503(a)	167(h)(5)	515(b)(2)(A)	911(c)(1)(A)
504(a)	897(h)(4)(A)(i)(II)	515(b)(2)(B)	911(c)(2)-(4)
505(a)(1)(A)-(C)	897(h)(1)	515(b)(2)(C)(i)	911(d)(4)
505(a)(2)	897(h)(4)(A)(ii)	515(b)(2)(C)(ii)	911(d)(7)
505(b)	1445(e)(6)-(7)	515(c)	911(f)-(g)
505(c)(1)	852(b)(3)(E)	516(a)(1)	4965
505(c)(2)	871(k)(2)(E)	516(b)(1)(A)	6033(a)(2)-(3)
506(a)	897(h)(5)	516(b)(1)(B)	6033(a)(1)
506(b)	1445(b)(8)	516(b)(2)	6011(g)-(h)
507(a)	355(g)	516(c)(1)	6652(c)(3)-(5)
508(a)	149(f)(2)(A)	516(c)(2)	6652(c)(1)
508(b)	149(f)(4)-(7)		

Tax Relief and Health Care Act of 2006

Act Sec.	Code Sec.	Act Sec.	Code Sec.
101(a), Div. A	222(e)	104(b)(1)(A)-(C), Div. A	41(c)(4)(A)
101(b)(1)-(2), Div. A	222(b)(2)(B)	104(c)(1), Div. A	41(c)(5)-(7)
102(a), Div. A	45D(f)(1)(D)	105(a), Div. A	51(c)(4)(B)
102(b), Div. A	45D(i)(4)-(6)	105(a), Div. A	51A(f)
103(a), Div. A	164(b)(5)(I)	105(b), Div. A	51(d)(4)
104(a)(1), Div. A	41(h)(1)(B)	105(c), Div. A	51(d)(8)(A)(i)
104(a)(2), Div. A	45C(b)(1)(D)	105(d), Div. A	51(d)(12)(A)(ii)(II)

Act Sec.	Code Sec.	Act Sec.	Code Sec.
105(e)(1), Div. A	51(d)(1)(G)-(I)	207(1)-(2), Div. A	48
105(e)(2), Div. A	51(d)(10)-(13)	208(a), Div. A	4041(b)(2)(D)
105(e)(3), Div. A	51(e)	208(b), Div. A	4041(b)(2)(C)(ii)
105(e)(4)(A), Div. A	51A	208(c), Div. A	4041(b)(2)(B)
106(a), Div. A	32(c)(2)(B)(vi)(II)	209(a), Div. A	168(l)
107(a), Div. A	1397E(e)(1)	210(a)(1)-(2), Div. A	9508(c)
107(b)(1)(A), Div. A	1397E(d)(1)(C)-(E)	211(a), Div. A	45K(g)(2)(D)
107(b)(1)(B), Div. A	1397E(f)-(l)	211(a), Div. C	9704(j)
107(b)(2), Div. A	54(l)(3)(B)	211(b), Div. A	45K(g)(1)
107(b)(2), Div. A	1400N(l)(7)(B)(ii)	211(b), Div. C	9711(c)
108(a), Div. A	62(a)(2)(D)	211(c), Div. C	9712(d)(4)
109(a), Div. A	198(h)	211(d), Div. C	9701(c)(8)
109(b), Div. A	198(d)(1)(A)-(C)	212(a)(1)(A)-(C), Div. C	9705(b)
110(a)(1), Div. A	1400(f)	212(a)(2)(A), Div. C	9704(d)
110(b)(1), Div. A	1400A(b)	212(a)(2)(B)(i), Div. C	9704(e)(1)
110(c)(1), Div. A	1400B(b)	212(a)(2)(B)(ii), Div. C	9704(e)(3)(A)
110(c)(2)(A)(i)-(ii), Div. A	1400B(e)(2)	212(a)(2)(C), Div. C	9704(f)(2)(C)
110(c)(2)(B), Div. A	1400B(g)(2)	212(a)(3), Div. C	9706(h)
110(c)(2)(C), Div. A	1400F(d)	212(b)(1), Div. C	9712(a)(3)-(4)
110(d)(1), Div. A	1400C(i)	212(b)(2)(A), Div. C	9712(d)(1)
111(a), Div. A	45A(f)	212(b)(2)(B)(i)-(ii), Div. C	9712(d)(2)-(3)
112(a), Div. A	168(j)(8)	213(a), Div. C	9702(b)
113(a), Div. A	168(e)(3)(E)(iv)-(v)	213(b)(1), Div. C	9707(a)
114(a), Div. A	7652(f)(1)	213(b)(2), Div. C	9721
115(a), Div. A	9812(f)(3)	302(a), Div. A	106(e)
116(a)(1), Div. A	170(e)(6)(G)	302(b), Div. A	223(c)(1)(B)
116(b)(1)(A), Div. A	170(e)(4)(B)(ii)	303(a)(1)-(2), Div. A	223(b)(2)(A)-(B)
116(b)(1)(B), Div. A	170(e)(4)(B)(iii)	303(b), Div. A	223(d)(1)(A)(ii)(I)
116(b)(2)(A), Div. A	170(e)(6)(B)(ii)	304, Div. A	223(g)(1)
116(b)(2)(B), Div. A	170(e)(6)(D)	305(a), Div. A	223(b)(8)
117(a), Div. A	220(i)(2)-(3)	306(a), Div. A	4980G(d)
117(b)(1)(A)-(B), Div. A	220(j)(2)	307(a), Div. A	408(d)(9)
117(b)(2), Div. A	220(j)(4)(A)	307(b), Div. A	223(b)(4)
118(a), Div. A	613A(c)(6)(H)	401(a), Div. A	199(d)(8)-(9)
120(a), Div. A	1400N(d)(6)	401(f)(1), Div. C	5761(d)-(f)
120(b), Div. A	1400N(e)(2)	401(f)(2)(A), Div. C	5761(c)
121, Div. A	7608(c)(6)	401(f)(2)(B), Div. C	5754(c)(1)
122(a)(1), Div. A	6103(d)(5)(B)	402(a), Div. A	53(e)
122(b)(1), Div. A	6103(i)(3)(C)(iv)	402(b)(1), Div. A	6211(b)(4)(A)
122(b)(1), Div. A	6103(i)(7)(E)	403(a), Div. A	6039(a)
122(c)(1), Div. A	6103(l)(13)(D)	403(b), Div. A	6039(b)-(d)
201, Div. A	45(d)	403(c)(1), Div. A	6724(d)(1)(B)
202(a)(1)-(2), Div. A	54(f)	403(c)(2), Div. A	6724(d)(2)(B)
202(a)(3), Div. A	54(m)	403(c)(3), Div. A	6039
203(a), Div. A	48A(f)(1)	403(c)(4), Div. A	6039(a)
204, Div. A	179D(h)	404(a), Div. A	179E
205, Div. A	45L(g)	404(b)(1), Div. A	263(a)(1)(J)-(L)
206(a), Div. A	25D(g)	404(b)(2), Div. A	312(k)(3)(B)
206(b)(1), Div. A	25D(a)(1)	404(b)(3), Div. A	1245(a)(2)(C)
206(b)(1), Div. A	25D(b)(1)(A)	404(b)(3), Div. A	1245(a)(3)(C)
206(b)(1), Div. A	25D(e)(4)(A)(i)	405(a), Div. A	45N
206(b)(2)(A)-(B), Div. A	25D(d)(2)	405(b), Div. A	38(b)(29)-(31)

¶25,020

Act Sec.	Code Sec.	Act Sec.	Code Sec.
405(c), Div. A	280C(e)	417(a), Div. A	121(d)(9)(A)
406(a)(1)(A)-(D), Div. A	7623	417(b), Div. A	121(d)(9)(C)(iv)-(v)
406(a)(2)(A), Div. A	7443A(b)(5)-(7)	417(c), Div. A	121(d)(9)(C)(vi)
406(a)(2)(B), Div. A	7443A(c)	417(d), Div. A	121(d)(9)
406(a)(3), Div. A	62(a)(21)	418(a)(1)(A)-(B), Div. A	1043(b)(1)(A)-(B)
407(a), Div. A	6702	418(a)(2)(A)-(B), Div. A	1043(b)(2)(A)-(B)
407(b)(1), Div. A	6330(g)	418(a)(3), Div. A	1043(b)(5)(B)
407(b)(2)(A)-(D), Div. A	6330(c)(4)	418(b), Div. A	1043(b)(6)
407(b)(3), Div. A	6330(b)(1)	419(a), Div. A	163(h)(3)(E)
407(c)(1), Div. A	6320(b)(1)	419(b), Div. A	163(h)(4)(E)-(F)
407(c)(2), Div. A	6320(c)	419(c), Div. A	6050H(h)
407(d), Div. A	7122(f)	420(a), Div. A	6427(l)(4)
408(a), Div. A	4132(a)(1)(O)	420(b)(1), Div. A	6427(l)(5)-(6)
408(a), Div. C	6015(e)(1)	420(b)(2), Div. A	4082(d)(2)(B)
408(b), Div. A	4132(a)(1)(P)	420(b)(3)(A)-(B), Div. A	6427(i)(4)(A)
408(b)(1), Div. C	6015(e)(1)(A)(i)(II)	420(b)(4), Div. A	6427(l)(1)
408(b)(2)(A)-(B), Div. C	6015(e)(1)(B)(i)	420(b)(5)(A)-(B), Div. A	9502(d)(2)-(3)
408(b)(3), Div. C	6015(e)(1)(B)(ii)	420(b)(6)(A)-(B), Div. A	9503(c)(7)
408(b)(4), Div. C	6015(e)(4)	421(a), Div. A	6103(b)(5)
408(b)(5), Div. C	6015(e)(5)	421(b), Div. A	6103(d)(6)
408(b)(6), Div. C	6015(g)(2)	422(a), Div. A	5388(c)(3)
408(b)(7), Div. C	6015(h)(2)	423(a)(1)-(2), Div. A	45G(d)
409(a), Div. A	468B(g)(3)	424(a), Div. A	664(c)
410(a), Div. A	355(b)(3)	425(a), Div. A	7872(h)(4)
411(a), Div. A	143(l)(3)(B)(iv)	426(a)(1)(A), Div. A	954(c)(6)(A)
412(a), Div. A	1221(b)(3)	426(a)(1)(B), Div. A	954(c)(6)(A)
413(a), Div. A	1355(a)(4)	3007, Div. D	5382(a)(1)(A)
415(a), Div. A	1355(g)-(h)		
416(a), Div. A	143(d)(2)(B)-(D)		

IRS Guidance

¶28,001 Introduction

Reproduced below are IRS News Release IR-2006-195 and IRS Publication 600, State and Local General Sales Taxes, which provide guidance to help tax filers in 2007 claim the extended deductions and other tax advantages in the Tax Relief and Health Care Act of 2006 (P.L. 109-432). Use CCH Tax Tracker News and other CCH Tax and Accounting products to keep up to date with all of the IRS's guidance on the new law.

¶28,005 IRS News Release IR-2006-195, December 22, 2006

WASHINGTON—The Internal Revenue Service announced new guidance today to help tax filers in 2007 claim the extended deductions and other tax advantages in the Tax Relief and Health Care Act of 2006 signed into law this week.

The start of the 2007 filing season will begin on time. However, the recent changes in the law mean the IRS will not be able to process a small percentage of individual tax returns until early February, primarily involving three tax deductions—the state and local sales tax, higher education tuition and fees, and educator expenses.

"The IRS is taking a number of steps to ensure taxpayers have the correct information on these deductions when they prepare and file their tax returns," IRS Commissioner Mark W. Everson said.

Among the ways taxpayers can get information:

- Taxpayers will be able to visit IRS.gov for updated information on the late legislation.

- The IRS will conduct a special mailing of Publication 600, which will include the state and local sales tax tables and instructions for claiming the sales tax deduction on Schedule A (Form 1040), to 6 million taxpayers. Publication 600, State and Local General Sales Taxes, will be sent to taxpayers who will receive the 2006 Form 1040 package in early January. Publication 600 was posted to IRS.gov today, with the special mailing for taxpayers arriving in mid-January.

- For people using IRS e-file or Free File, tax software will be updated to include the three key tax provisions. E-file gets refunds to taxpayers faster than paper returns.

The IRS urged taxpayers to use e-file instead of the paper forms to minimize confusion over the late changes and reduce the chance of making extender-related errors on their returns.

"As we always do, we encourage taxpayers who think they may claim these deductions to file electronically," Everson said. "They will get their refunds faster through e-file. Even more importantly, e-file will greatly reduce the chances for making an error compared to claiming the deductions on the paper 1040."

This new legislation affects a number of areas of tax law, but the most significant effect on individual taxpayers involves the deductions for state and local sales tax, higher education tuition and fees, and educator expenses. The sales tax deduction was claimed on approximately 11.2 million tax returns filed in 2006 for Tax Year 2005. The tuition and fees deduction was claimed on about 4.7 million returns, and the educator expense deduction was claimed on 3.5 million returns.

The IRS will not be able to process tax returns claiming these extender-related deductions until early February. Based on filings earlier this year, only about 930,000 tax returns claimed any of the three extenders provisions by Feb. 1. This year, the IRS expects to receive about 136 million tax returns.

Form 1040 Changes

The IRS also announced details today on how taxpayers can use existing lines on the current Form 1040 and other tax documents to claim the three major extenders provisions. The key forms (Forms 1040, 1040A, Schedule A&B, and instructions) went to print in early November and reflected the law in effect at that time. The instructions contain a cautionary note to taxpayers that the legislation was pending at the time of printing.

The majority of taxpayers file electronically, but taxpayers using a paper Form 1040 will have to follow special instructions if they are claiming any of the three deductions. Form 1040 will not be updated. Instead, taxpayers should follow these steps:

State and Local General Sales Tax Deduction:

- The deduction for state and local general sales taxes will be claimed on Schedule A (Form 1040), line 5, "State and local income taxes." Enter "ST" on the dotted line to the left of line 5 to indicate you are claiming the general sales tax deduction instead of the deduction for state and local income tax.

- The IRS also will issue Publication 600 for 2006, which includes the state and local sales tax tables, a worksheet and instructions for figuring the deduction.

- This option is available to all taxpayers regardless of where they live, though it's primarily designed to benefit residents of the eight states without state and local income taxes.

Higher Education Tuition and Fees Deduction:

- Taxpayers must file Form 1040 to take this deduction for up to $4,000 of tuition and fees paid to a post-secondary institution. It cannot be claimed on Form 1040A.

- The deduction for tuition and fees will be claimed on Form 1040, line 35, "Domestic production activities deduction." Enter "T" on the dotted line to the left of that line entry if claiming the tuition and fees deduction, or "B" if claiming both a deduction for domestic production activities and the deduction

for tuition and fees. For those entering "B," taxpayers must attach a breakdown showing the amounts claimed for each deduction.

Educator Expense Adjustment to Income:

- Educators must file Form 1040 in order to take the deduction for up to $250 of out-of-pocket classroom expenses. It cannot be claimed on Form 1040A.

- The deduction for educator expenses will be claimed on Form 1040, line 23, "Archer MSA Deduction." Enter "E" on the dotted line to the left of that line entry if claiming educator expenses, or "B" if claiming both an Archer MSA deduction and the deduction for educator expenses on Form 1040. If entering "B," taxpayers must attach a breakdown showing the amounts claimed for each deduction.

The new law also affects an even smaller number of business taxpayers who don't use the Form 1040 series. There could be minimal processing delays for some of these business filers in January and early February.

January is the slowest part of the filing season for the IRS, with less than 6 percent of all individual returns coming in during the agency's first two weeks of processing. Typically, early returns are from taxpayers with simpler refund returns who do not claim the extender provisions. Earlier this year, the IRS had less than 2.5 million returns filed by Jan. 20. An additional 4.2 million returns came in by Jan. 27.

¶28,010   IRS Publication 600, December 22, 2006

Department of the Treasury
Internal Revenue Service

Publication 600
Cat. No. 46600Y

State and Local General Sales Taxes

For use in preparing

2006 Returns

**Get forms and other information
faster and easier by:**

Internet • www.irs.gov

Introduction

The Tax Relief and Health Care Act of 2006 extended the election to deduct state and local general sales taxes for 2006. The act was enacted after Schedule A (Form 1040), Itemized Deductions, and its instructions were printed. Because we were not able to include the instructions for figuring the deduction in the Schedule A instructions, we are providing this publication to help you figure this deduction.

You can elect to deduct state and local general sales taxes instead of state and local income taxes as a deduction on Schedule A. **You cannot deduct both.** To figure your deduction, you can use either:

- Your actual expenses, **or**

- The optional sales tax tables **plus** the general sales taxes paid on certain specified items.

Actual Expenses

Generally, you can deduct the actual state and local general sales taxes (including compensating use taxes) you paid in 2006 if the tax rate was the same as the general sales tax rate. However, sales taxes on food, clothing, medical supplies, and motor vehicles are deductible as a general sales tax even if the tax rate was less than the general sales tax rate. If you paid sales tax on a motor vehicle at a rate higher than the general sales tax rate, you can deduct only the amount of tax that you would have paid at the general sales tax rate on that vehicle. Motor vehicles include cars, motorcycles, motor homes, recreational vehicles, sport utility vehicles, trucks, vans, and off-road vehicles. Also include any state and local general sales taxes paid for a leased motor vehicle. Do not include sales taxes paid on items used in your trade or business.

To deduct your actual expenses, enter the amount on Schedule A, line 5, and enter "**ST**" on the dotted line to the left of the line 5 entry space.

   You must keep your actual receipts showing general sales taxes paid to use this method.

Refund of general sales taxes. If you received a refund of state or local general sales taxes in 2006 for amounts paid in **2006**, reduce your **actual** 2006 state and local general sales taxes by this amount. If you received a refund of state or local general sales taxes in 2006 for prior year purchases, do not reduce your 2006 state and local general sales taxes by this amount. But if you deducted your **actual** state and local general sales taxes in the earlier year and the deduction reduced your tax, you may have to include the refund in income on Form 1040, line 21. See *Recoveries* in Pub. 525 for details.

Optional Sales Tax Tables

Instead of using your actual expenses, you can use the tables on pages 5 through 7 to figure your state and local general sales tax deduction. You may also be able to add the state and local general sales taxes paid on certain specified items.

To figure your state and local general sales tax deduction using the tables, complete the worksheet below.

 If your filing status is married filing separately, both you and your spouse elect to deduct sales taxes, and your spouse elects to use the optional sales tax tables, you also must use the tables to figure your state and local general sales tax deduction.

State and Local General Sales Tax Deduction Worksheet
(See the instructions that begin on page 3.)

Keep for Your Records

Before you begin:	See the instructions for line 1 on page 3 if:
	✓ You lived in more than one state during 2006, **or**
	✓ You had any **nontaxable** income in 2006.

1. Enter your **state** general sales taxes from the applicable table on page 5 or 6 (see page 3 of the instructions) . . . . **1. $** _____

Next. If, for all of 2006, you lived only in Connecticut, the District of Columbia, Hawaii, Indiana, Kentucky, Maine, Maryland, Massachusetts, Michigan, Mississippi, New Jersey, Rhode Island, Virginia, or West Virginia, skip lines 2 through 5, enter -0- on line 6, and go to line 7. Otherwise, go to line 2

2. Did you live in Alaska, Arizona, Arkansas (Texarkana only), California (Los Angeles County only), Colorado, Georgia, Illinois, Louisiana, New York State, or North Carolina in 2006?

☐ **No.** Enter -0-

☐ **Yes.** Enter your **local** general sales taxes from the applicable table on page 7 (see page 3 of the instructions) } . . . . **2. $** _____

3. Did your locality impose a **local** general sales tax in 2006? Residents of California, Nevada, and Texarkana, Arkansas, see page 3 of the instructions

☐ **No.** Skip lines 3 through 5, enter -0- on line 6, and go to line **7**

☐ **Yes.** Enter your **local** general sales tax rate, but omit the percentage sign. For example, if your local general sales tax rate was 2.5%, enter 2.5. If your local general sales tax rate changed or you lived in more than one locality in the same state during 2006, see page 3 of the instructions. (If you do not know your local general sales tax rate, contact your local government.) . . . . **3.** ___.___

4. Did you enter -0- on line 2 above?

☐ **No.** Skip lines 4 and 5 and go to line **6**

☐ **Yes.** Enter your **state** general sales tax rate (shown in the table heading for your state), but omit the percentage sign. For example, if your state general sales tax rate is 6%, enter 6.0 . . . . **4.** ___.___

5. Divide line 3 by line 4. Enter the result as a decimal (rounded to at least three places) . . . . **5.** ___.___

6. Did you enter -0- on line 2 above?

☐ **No.** Multiply line 2 by line 3

☐ **Yes.** Multiply line 1 by line 5. If you lived in more than one locality in the same state during 2006, see page 4 of the instructions } . . . . **6. $** _____

7. Enter your state and local general sales taxes paid on specified items, if any (see page 4 of the instructions) . . . . **7. $** _____

8. Deduction for general sales taxes. Add lines 1, 6, and 7. Enter the result here and the total from all your state and local general sales tax deduction worksheets, if you completed more than one, on Schedule A, line 5. **Be sure to enter "ST" on the dotted line to the left of the entry space** . . . . **8. $** _____

¶28,010

Instructions for the State and Local General Sales Tax Deduction Worksheet

Line 1. If you lived in the same state for all of 2006, enter the applicable amount, based on your 2006 income and exemptions, from the optional state sales tax table for your state on page 5 or 6. Read down the "At least–But less than" columns for your state and find the line that includes your 2006 income. If married filing separately, do not include your spouse's income. Your 2006 income is the amount shown on your Form 1040, line 38, **plus** any nontaxable items, such as the following.

- Tax-exempt interest.
- Veterans' benefits.
- Nontaxable combat pay.
- Workers' compensation.
- Nontaxable part of social security and railroad retirement benefits.
- Nontaxable part of IRA, pension, or annuity distributions. Do not include rollovers.
- Public assistance payments.

The exemptions column refers to the number of exemptions claimed on Form 1040, line 6d. Do not include any additional exemptions you listed on Form 8914 for individuals displaced by Hurricane Katrina.

What if you lived in more than one state? If you lived in more than one state during 2006, look up the table amount for each state using the above rules. If there is no table for your state, the table amount is considered to be zero. Multiply the table amount for each state you lived in by a fraction. The numerator of the fraction is the number of days you lived in the state during 2006 and the denominator is the total number of days in the year (365). Enter the total of the prorated table amounts for each state on line 1. However, if you also lived in a locality during 2006 that imposed a local general sales tax, do not enter the total on line 1. Instead, complete a separate worksheet for each state you lived in and enter the prorated amount for that state on line 1.

Example. You lived in State A from January 1 through August 31, 2006 (243 days), and in State B from September 1 through December 31, 2006 (122 days). The table amount for State A is $500. The table amount for State B is $400. You would figure your state general sales tax as follows.

State A:	$500 x 243/365 =	$333
State B:	$400 x 122/365 =	134
Total	=	$467

If none of the localities in which you lived during 2006 imposed a local general sales tax, enter $467 on line 1 of your worksheet. Otherwise, complete a separate worksheet for State A and State B. Enter $333 on line 1 of the State A worksheet and $134 on line 1 of the State B worksheet.

Line 2. If you checked the "No" box, enter -0- on line 2, and go to line 3. If you checked the "Yes" box and lived in

the same locality for all of 2006, enter the applicable amount, based on your 2006 income and exemptions, from the optional local sales tax table for your locality on page 7. Read down the "At least–But less than" columns for your locality and find the line that includes your 2006 income. See the line 1 instructions on this page to figure your 2006 income. The exemptions column refers to the number of exemptions claimed on Form 1040, line 6d. Do not include any additional exemptions you listed on Form 8914 for individuals displaced by Hurricane Katrina.

What if you lived in more than one locality? If you lived in more than one locality during 2006, look up the table amount for each locality using the above rules. If there is no table for your locality, the table amount is considered to be zero. Multiply the table amount for each locality you lived in by a fraction. The numerator of the fraction is the number of days you lived in the locality during 2006 and the denominator is the total number of days in the year (365). If you lived in more than one locality in the same state and the local general sales tax rate was the same for each locality, enter the total of the prorated table amounts for each locality in that state on line 2. Otherwise, complete a separate worksheet for lines 2 through 6 for each locality and enter each prorated table amount on line 2 of the applicable worksheet.

Example. You lived in Locality 1 from January 1 through August 31, 2006 (243 days), and in Locality 2 from September 1 through December 31, 2006 (122 days). The table amount for Locality 1 is $100. The table amount for Locality 2 is $150. You would figure the amount to enter on line 2 as follows. Note that this amount may not equal your local sales tax deduction, which is figured on line 6 of the worksheet.

Locality 1:	$100 x 243/365 =	$ 67
Locality 2:	$150 x 122/365 =	50
Total	=	$117

Line 3. If you lived in California, check the "No" box if your combined state and local general sales tax rate is 7.25%. Otherwise, check the "Yes" box and include on line 3 only the part of the combined rate that is more than 7.25%.

If you lived in Nevada, check the "No" box if your combined state and local general sales tax rate is 6.5%. Otherwise, check the "Yes" box and include on line 3 only the part of the combined rate that is more than 6.5%.

If you lived in Texarkana, Arkansas, check the "Yes" box and enter "4.0" on line 3. Your local general sales tax rate of 4.0% includes the additional 1.0% Arkansas state sales tax rate for Texarkana and the 1.5% sales tax rate for Miller County.

What if your local general sales tax rate changed during 2006? If you checked the "Yes" box and your local general sales tax rate changed during 2006, figure the rate to enter on line 3 as follows. Multiply each tax rate for the period it was in effect by a fraction. The numerator of the fraction is the number of days the rate was in effect during 2006 and the denominator is the total number of days in the year (365). Enter the total of the prorated tax rates on line 3.

Example. Locality 1 imposed a 1% local general sales tax from January 1 through September 30, 2006 (273 days). The rate increased to 1.75% for the period from October 1 through December 31, 2006 (92 days). You would enter "1.189" on line 3, figured as follows.

January 1 –		
September 30:	1.00 x 273/365 =	0.748
October 1 –		
December 31:	1.75 x 92/365 =	0.441
Total	=	1.189

What if you lived in more than one locality in the same state during 2006? Complete a separate worksheet for lines 2 through 6 for each locality in your state if you lived in more than one locality in the same state during 2006 and either of the following applies.

- Each locality did not have the same local general sales tax rate.
- You lived in Texarkana, AR, or Los Angeles County, CA.

To figure the amount to enter on line 3 of the worksheet for each locality in which you lived (except a locality for which you used the table on page 7 to figure your local general sales tax deduction), multiply the local general sales tax rate by a fraction. The numerator of the fraction is the number of days you lived in the locality during 2006 and the denominator is the total number of days in the year (365).

Example. You lived in Locality 1 from January 1 through August 31, 2006 (243 days), and in Locality 2 from September 1 through December 31, 2006 (122 days). The local general sales tax rate for Locality 1 is 1%. The rate for Locality 2 is 1.75%. You would enter "0.666" on line 3 for the Locality 1 worksheet and "0.585" for the Locality 2 worksheet, figured as follows.

Locality 1:	1.00 x 243/365 =	0.666
Locality 2:	1.75 x 122/365 =	0.585

Line 6. If you lived in more than one locality in the same state during 2006, you should have completed line 1 only on the first worksheet for that state and separate worksheets for lines 2 through 6 for any other locality within that state in which you lived during 2006. If you checked the

"Yes" box on line 6 of any of those worksheets, multiply line 5 of that worksheet by the amount that you entered on line 1 for that state on the first worksheet.

Line 7. Enter on line 7 any state and local general sales taxes paid on the following specified items. If you are completing more than one worksheet, include the total for line 7 on only one of the worksheets.

1. A motor vehicle (including a car, motorcycle, motor home, recreational vehicle, sport utility vehicle, truck, van, and off-road vehicle). Also include any state and local general sales taxes paid for a leased motor vehicle. If the state sales tax rate on these items is higher than the general sales tax rate, only include the amount of tax you would have paid at the general sales tax rate.
2. An aircraft or boat, if the tax rate was the same as the general sales tax rate.
3. A home (including a mobile home or prefabricated home) or substantial addition to or major renovation of a home, but only if the tax rate was the same as the general sales tax rate and any of the following applies.

   a. Your state or locality imposes a general sales tax directly on the sale of a home or on the cost of a substantial addition or major renovation.
   b. You purchased the materials to build a home or substantial addition or to perform a major renovation and paid the sales tax directly.
   c. Under your state law, your contractor is considered your agent in the construction of the home or substantial addition or the performance of a major renovation. The contract must state that the contractor is authorized to act in your name and must follow your directions on construction decisions. In this case, you will be considered to have purchased any items subject to a sales tax and to have paid the sales tax directly.

Do not include sales taxes paid on items used in your trade or business. If you received a refund of state or local general sales taxes in 2006, see *Refund of general sales taxes* on page 1.

¶28,010

2006 Optional State and Certain Local Sales Tax Tables

Income		Alabama 4.0000%						Arizona 5.6000%						Arkansas 6.0000%						California[1] 7.2500%						Colorado 2.9000%					
At least	But less than	Exemptions 1	2	3	4	5	Over 5	Exemptions 1	2	3	4	5	Over 5	Exemptions 1	2	3	4	5	Over 5	Exemptions 1	2	3	4	5	Over 5	Exemptions 1	2	3	4	5	Over 5
$0	$20,000	201	238	263	282	298	320	200	216	226	233	239	247	314	359	388	410	428	453	247	266	278	287	294	304	99	108	114	119	123	128
20,000	30,000	314	370	408	437	461	494	358	387	404	418	428	442	519	591	638	674	703	744	437	471	493	508	521	537	167	183	194	201	208	216
30,000	40,000	371	436	480	514	542	582	444	480	502	518	531	549	625	712	768	811	846	894	541	583	609	628	644	664	203	223	236	245	252	263
40,000	50,000	419	493	543	581	612	656	521	563	589	608	623	644	717	816	881	930	970	1025	632	681	712	735	753	777	235	258	272	283	292	303
50,000	60,000	463	544	598	640	675	723	592	639	669	691	708	731	801	911	982	1037	1081	1143	716	772	807	832	853	880	264	289	306	318	327	341
60,000	70,000	503	590	649	694	731	784	658	710	743	767	787	813	877	997	1076	1135	1184	1251	794	856	895	923	946	976	290	319	336	350	360	375
70,000	80,000	540	634	696	745	785	841	721	779	815	841	862	891	950	1080	1164	1228	1281	1353	869	937	979	1010	1035	1068	316	346	366	380	392	408
80,000	90,000	575	674	741	792	834	893	781	843	882	911	934	964	1017	1156	1246	1315	1371	1448	939	1013	1058	1092	1118	1155	339	372	393	409	421	438
90,000	100,000	608	713	782	836	881	943	838	905	947	977	1002	1035	1082	1229	1325	1397	1457	1539	1007	1085	1134	1170	1199	1237	362	397	420	436	449	467
100,000	120,000	652	763	837	895	942	1009	914	987	1033	1067	1093	1130	1167	1325	1428	1506	1570	1658	1097	1183	1236	1275	1306	1348	392	430	454	472	487	506
120,000	140,000	711	832	913	975	1027	1099	1021	1103	1153	1191	1221	1261	1284	1458	1571	1657	1726	1823	1222	1318	1377	1421	1456	1502	434	476	503	522	538	560
140,000	160,000	763	892	979	1045	1100	1177	1116	1205	1261	1302	1334	1379	1387	1574	1696	1788	1864	1968	1334	1438	1503	1550	1588	1639	471	517	545	567	584	607
160,000	180,000	815	953	1044	1115	1173	1255	1212	1309	1369	1414	1449	1497	1490	1691	1821	1920	2001	2112	1446	1559	1629	1681	1722	1778	508	557	588	611	630	655
180,000	200,000	862	1007	1103	1178	1239	1325	1299	1403	1468	1516	1554	1605	1584	1796	1935	2040	2125	2243	1549	1670	1745	1801	1845	1904	542	594	627	652	672	698
200,000 or more		1098	1278	1399	1491	1568	1675	1751	1892	1979	2043	2095	2164	2055	2328	2505	2640	2750	2902	2078	2240	2341	2415	2474	2554	714	783	826	858	884	919

Income		Connecticut 6.0000%						District of Columbia 5.7500%						Florida 6.0000%						Georgia 4.0000%						Hawaii 4.0000%					
$0	$20,000	197	208	215	220	223	229	163	172	179	183	186	191	209	228	241	250	257	267	145	159	168	174	179	186	224	255	275	290	302	319
20,000	30,000	354	374	386	395	402	412	296	314	325	333	339	348	373	407	429	445	458	476	245	268	282	293	302	314	369	419	451	476	496	523
30,000	40,000	440	465	480	491	500	512	369	391	405	415	423	434	462	505	532	552	568	589	297	325	343	356	367	381	445	504	543	572	596	629
40,000	50,000	517	546	564	577	587	601	434	461	477	489	498	511	541	592	623	646	665	691	343	376	396	411	423	440	510	578	622	656	683	721
50,000	60,000	587	621	641	656	667	683	495	525	543	557	567	582	614	671	707	734	755	784	385	421	444	461	475	493	569	645	694	731	761	803
60,000	70,000	653	690	713	729	742	759	551	584	605	620	632	648	682	746	785	815	838	870	423	463	488	507	522	542	623	706	760	800	833	879
70,000	80,000	716	757	781	799	814	833	605	642	665	681	694	712	748	817	860	892	918	953	460	503	531	551	567	589	675	764	822	866	901	951
80,000	90,000	776	820	846	866	881	902	656	696	721	739	753	772	809	884	931	965	993	1031	494	541	570	592	609	633	722	818	880	927	965	1017
90,000	100,000	833	880	909	929	946	968	705	748	775	794	809	830	868	948	998	1036	1065	1106	527	577	608	631	649	674	768	869	935	985	1025	1081
100,000	120,000	909	960	992	1015	1033	1057	771	818	847	868	885	907	946	1034	1089	1129	1162	1206	571	624	658	683	703	730	828	937	1008	1061	1105	1165
120,000	140,000	1016	1073	1108	1133	1153	1181	863	916	948	971	990	1015	1056	1154	1215	1260	1296	1346	631	690	727	755	777	807	911	1030	1108	1167	1214	1280
140,000	160,000	1110	1173	1211	1239	1261	1291	945	1002	1038	1063	1084	1111	1154	1260	1327	1376	1416	1470	684	748	788	818	842	875	984	1113	1196	1259	1311	1381
160,000	180,000	1206	1274	1315	1346	1370	1402	1028	1090	1129	1157	1179	1209	1252	1368	1440	1494	1537	1595	738	806	850	882	908	943	1057	1195	1284	1352	1407	1483
180,000	200,000	1294	1366	1411	1443	1469	1503	1104	1171	1212	1242	1266	1298	1342	1466	1544	1601	1647	1710	786	860	906	940	967	1005	1123	1269	1364	1436	1494	1574
200,000 or more		1744	1843	1903	1946	1981	2027	1496	1587	1643	1684	1717	1760	1806	1973	2077	2154	2216	2300	1033	1129	1190	1235	1270	1319	1455	1643	1765	1857	1932	2035

Income		Idaho[3] 5.2521%						Illinois 6.2500%						Indiana 6.0000%						Iowa 5.0000%						Kansas 5.3000%					
$0	$20,000	265	311	341	365	384	411	240	265	280	292	301	314	225	250	266	278	288	302	195	210	219	225	230	238	269	311	338	360	377	401
20,000	30,000	418	489	536	572	602	643	413	455	481	501	517	538	372	414	440	460	476	498	346	372	388	399	409	421	441	509	553	588	616	655
30,000	40,000	496	579	635	677	712	761	505	556	588	612	632	658	449	499	531	555	574	600	428	459	479	494	505	521	530	611	664	705	739	785
40,000	50,000	563	657	719	767	806	861	586	645	682	710	732	763	516	573	610	637	659	689	500	537	560	577	591	609	607	700	760	807	845	898
50,000	60,000	623	727	795	848	891	952	660	726	768	799	824	858	577	641	681	712	736	770	567	609	635	654	669	690	677	780	847	899	941	1000
60,000	70,000	678	790	864	921	968	1034	728	801	847	882	909	947	633	703	747	780	807	844	628	675	704	725	742	765	741	853	926	983	1029	1093
70,000	80,000	730	850	929	990	1041	1111	793	873	923	960	990	1031	686	762	810	846	875	914	688	739	770	794	812	837	802	922	1002	1062	1112	1181
80,000	90,000	778	905	990	1055	1108	1183	854	940	994	1034	1066	1110	736	817	868	907	938	980	743	798	833	858	878	905	858	987	1072	1136	1189	1263
90,000	100,000	824	958	1047	1115	1172	1250	912	1004	1061	1104	1139	1186	783	869	924	964	997	1042	797	856	892	919	941	970	912	1048	1138	1207	1263	1341
100,000	120,000	884	1027	1122	1196	1256	1340	990	1089	1151	1198	1235	1286	846	938	997	1041	1077	1125	868	932	972	1002	1025	1056	983	1129	1226	1300	1360	1444
120,000	140,000	967	1123	1226	1306	1371	1462	1098	1207	1276	1328	1369	1426	933	1034	1099	1147	1187	1240	967	1039	1083	1116	1142	1177	1081	1241	1347	1428	1494	1586
140,000	160,000	1039	1206	1317	1402	1472	1569	1193	1312	1387	1443	1488	1549	1009	1119	1189	1241	1283	1341	1055	1133	1182	1217	1246	1284	1167	1339	1453	1540	1611	1710
160,000	180,000	1111	1289	1407	1497	1572	1676	1289	1417	1498	1558	1607	1673	1086	1204	1279	1335	1380	1442	1144	1228	1281	1320	1351	1392	1253	1437	1559	1652	1728	1834
180,000	200,000	1177	1364	1488	1584	1662	1772	1376	1513	1599	1664	1715	1786	1156	1281	1360	1420	1468	1533	1225	1316	1372	1413	1446	1491	1330	1526	1655	1753	1834	1946
200,000 or more		1504	1740	1896	2016	2115	2252	1822	2002	2116	2201	2269	2361	1509	1671	1774	1851	1913	1998	1641	1762	1838	1893	1937	1997	1723	1973	2138	2263	2367	2510

Income		Kentucky 6.0000%						Louisiana 4.0000%						Maine 5.0000%						Maryland 5.0000%						Massachusetts 5.0000%					
$0	$20,000	214	238	253	264	273	285	155	165	171	175	178	183	144	153	159	164	167	172	179	194	204	210	216	223	158	168	175	180	183	188
20,000	30,000	359	398	423	441	456	476	275	292	303	311	317	325	258	275	286	294	300	308	313	339	355	367	376	389	275	294	305	313	320	329
30,000	40,000	435	482	512	534	552	577	340	361	375	384	392	402	320	342	355	365	373	383	385	416	436	451	462	478	339	361	375	385	393	404
40,000	50,000	501	555	590	615	636	664	397	423	438	450	459	471	375	401	416	428	437	449	448	485	508	525	538	556	395	421	437	449	458	471
50,000	60,000	562	622	660	689	712	744	450	479	497	510	520	534	426	455	473	486	497	511	506	548	573	592	608	628	446	475	493	507	517	531
60,000	70,000	617	684	726	757	782	817	500	531	551	565	577	592	474	506	526	541	552	568	560	606	634	655	672	694	493	526	546	560	572	588
70,000	80,000	670	742	788	822	849	886	547	582	603	619	631	648	520	555	577	593	605	622	612	661	692	715	733	758	539	574	596	612	625	642
80,000	90,000	720	797	846	882	911	951	591	629	652	669	682	700	563	601	625	642	656	674	660	714	747	772	791	818	581	619	643	660	674	693
90,000	100,000	767	849	901	940	971	1013	634	674	699	717	731	751	604	645	670	689	704	724	706	764	799	825	846	875	622	663	688	707	721	741
100,000	120,000	830	918	974	1016	1050	1096	690	734	761	781	797	818	659	704	732	752	768	790	768	830	869	897	920	951	676	721	748	768	784	806
120,000	140,000	916	1014	1075	1122	1159	1210	769	818	848	870	888	911	736	787	818	840	858	882	854	923	965	997	1022	1057	752	801	832	854	872	895
140,000	160,000	993	1098	1165	1215	1255	1310	839	893	926	950	969	995	805	860	894	919	938	965	930	1005	1051	1086	1113	1150	819	872	906	930	949	975
160,000	180,000	1070	1183	1255	1308	1352	1411	910	968	1004	1030	1051	1078	874	934	971	998	1019	1048	1006	1087	1138	1175	1204	1245	886	944	980	1006	1027	1055
180,000	200,000	1140	1260	1336	1393	1439	1502	975	1037	1075	1103	1125	1155	938	1002	1042	1070	1094	1124	1076	1162	1216	1256	1288	1331	948	1010	1048	1076	1098	1128
200,000 or more		1495	1652	1751	1825	1885	1966	1306	1390	1441	1479	1508	1548	1266	1352	1406	1445	1476	1518	1434	1548	1619	1672	1714	1771	1263	1345	1396	1433	1463	1503

Income		Michigan 6.0000%						Minnesota 6.5000%						Mississippi 7.0000%						Missouri 4.2250%						Nebraska 5.5000%					
$0	$20,000	216	233	244	252	258	267	213	225	233	239	243	249	367	422	458	486	508	540	164	184	196	205	213	223	213	227	235	242	246	253
20,000	30,000	378	409	428	442	453	468	380	402	416	426	434	445	600	689	746	791	827	877	275	307	328	343	356	373	378	403	418	429	438	449
30,000	40,000	466	504	527	545	558	577	471	499	516	528	538	551	721	826	895	948	991	1051	334	372	397	416	431	451	468	498	517	531	541	556
40,000	50,000	544	588	615	635	651	673	551	584	604	618	630	645	825	945	1024	1084	1133	1201	384	429	457	479	496	520	547	583	605	621	633	650
50,000	60,000	615	665	696	718	737	761	626	663	685	702	715	732	919	1052	1139	1206	1260	1336	431	480	512	536	556	582	620	660	685	703	718	737
60,000	70,000	681	736	770	796	816	843	695	736	761	779	794	813	1005	1150	1245	1318	1377	1459	473	528	563	589	610	639	688	733	760	780	796	817
70,000	80,000	744	804	842	869	891	921	761	806	833	853	869	891	1087	1243	1346	1424	1488	1576	514	573	611	639	662	693	753	802	832	854	871	895
80,000	90,000	804	869	909	939	963	995	823	872	902	923	940	964	1163	1330	1439	1522	1590	1685	552	615	656	686	711	744	814	867	899	923	942	967
90,000	100,000	860	930	973	1005	1031	1065	883	935	967	990	1009	1034	1235	1412	1528	1616	1688	1788	588	655	698	731	757	793	872	929	964	989	1010	1037
100,000	120,000	936	1012	1059	1094	1122	1159	963	1020	1054	1080	1100	1127	1330	1520	1645	1739	1817	1924	636	709	755	790	818	857	950	1012	1050	1078	1100	1130
120,000	140,000	1042	1126	1179	1217	1248	1290	1074	1138	1176	1205	1227	1257	1462	1670	1806	1910	1994	2112	702	782	833	872	903	945	1059	1128	1170	1201	1226	1259
140,000	160,000	1136	1227	1284	1327	1360	1406	1173	1242	1285	1316	1340	1373	1577	1801	1947	2059	2150	2276	761	847	903	944	978	1024	1156	1231	1277	1311	1337	1373
160,000	180,000	1230	1329	1391	1437	1473	1522	1273	1348	1394	1428	1454	1490	1692	1932	2088	2208	2305	2440	819	913	972	1017	1053	1102	1253	1335	1385	1421	1450	1489
180,000	200,000	1316	1423	1489	1538	1576	1629	1365	1445	1494	1530	1559	1597	1797	2050	2216	2342	2446	2589	873	972	1035	1083	1121	1173	1342	1429	1483	1522	1553	1595
200,000 or more		1758	1900	1989	2054	2106	2176	1835	1943	2009	2058	2096	2147	2322	2646	2858	3019	3151	3333	1144	1273	1355	1417	1466	1534	1799	1916	1987	2040	2082	2138

(Continued on next page)

2006 Optional State and Certain Local Sales Tax Tables *(Continued)*

Income: At least	Income: But less than	Nevada[2] 6.5000%						New Jersey[4] 6.4658%						New Mexico 5.0000%						New York[3] 4.0000%						North Carolina[3] 4.4788%					
		Exemptions 1	2	3	4	5	Over 5	Exemptions 1	2	3	4	5	Over 5	Exemptions 1	2	3	4	5	Over 5	Exemptions 1	2	3	4	5	Over 5	Exemptions 1	2	3	4	5	Over 5
$0	$20,000	293	251	262	270	277	286	217	232	242	248	254	261	205	219	227	234	238	245	136	146	152	157	160	165	171	187	197	205	211	219
20,000	30,000	409	440	460	474	486	501	383	409	425	437	447	459	365	389	404	415	424	436	241	259	270	278	285	294	296	323	340	353	363	377
30,000	40,000	504	542	566	584	598	617	473	505	525	539	551	566	452	482	501	514	525	540	299	321	334	345	353	363	362	396	417	433	445	462
40,000	50,000	587	633	661	681	698	720	552	589	612	629	643	661	529	564	586	602	615	632	350	375	391	403	413	425	421	460	484	503	517	537
50,000	60,000	664	715	747	771	789	814	624	666	693	712	727	747	600	640	664	683	697	716	396	426	444	457	468	482	474	518	546	566	583	605
60,000	70,000	735	792	827	853	874	902	692	738	767	788	805	828	665	710	737	757	773	795	440	472	492	507	519	535	524	572	603	625	643	668
70,000	80,000	804	866	904	933	955	986	756	807	838	861	880	904	728	777	807	829	847	870	482	517	539	555	568	585	571	624	657	682	702	728
80,000	90,000	868	935	976	1007	1081	1064	816	871	905	930	950	977	787	840	873	897	915	941	521	559	583	600	614	633	616	673	708	735	756	785
90,000	100,000	929	1001	1045	1078	1104	1140	874	933	969	996	1017	1046	844	901	936	961	981	1009	559	599	625	643	658	678	658	719	757	785	806	839
100,000	120,000	1011	1089	1138	1173	1202	1240	951	1015	1055	1084	1107	1138	920	982	1020	1047	1070	1099	609	653	681	701	717	739	715	781	822	853	877	910
120,000	140,000	1125	1212	1266	1305	1337	1380	1059	1138	1174	1206	1231	1266	1026	1094	1137	1168	1192	1225	679	728	759	781	799	824	793	866	912	946	973	1010
140,000	160,000	1226	1321	1379	1423	1457	1504	1154	1231	1279	1314	1342	1379	1119	1194	1241	1274	1301	1338	741	795	828	853	872	899	863	942	992	1029	1058	1098
160,000	180,000	1328	1431	1494	1541	1578	1629	1250	1334	1385	1423	1453	1494	1214	1295	1346	1382	1411	1451	804	862	898	925	946	975	932	1018	1072	1112	1144	1187
180,000	200,000	1421	1531	1599	1649	1689	1743	1337	1427	1482	1523	1555	1598	1301	1388	1441	1481	1512	1554	861	923	962	991	1013	1044	996	1088	1145	1188	1222	1268
200,000 or more		1896	2045	2136	2203	2256	2328	1785	1905	1978	2032	2075	2133	1745	1862	1934	1986	2028	2085	1156	1239	1291	1329	1359	1400	1322	1443	1519	1575	1620	1682

Income: At least	Income: But less than	North Dakota 5.0000%						Ohio[3] 5.5000%						Oklahoma 4.5000%						Pennsylvania 6.0000%						Rhode Island 7.0000%					
		1	2	3	4	5	Over 5	1	2	3	4	5	Over 5	1	2	3	4	5	Over 5	1	2	3	4	5	Over 5	1	2	3	4	5	Over 5
$0	$20,000	178	194	204	212	218	226	212	227	237	244	249	256	218	248	268	282	295	311	194	209	219	226	232	239	225	242	253	260	267	275
20,000	30,000	314	342	359	372	382	397	375	402	418	430	439	452	363	413	445	469	489	516	341	367	384	396	406	419	392	422	440	454	465	479
30,000	40,000	387	421	443	459	471	489	463	496	516	531	542	558	439	499	537	566	590	623	420	452	473	488	500	516	482	519	541	558	571	589
40,000	50,000	452	491	516	535	550	570	541	579	602	620	633	652	506	574	618	651	679	716	489	527	551	568	582	601	562	604	630	650	665	686
50,000	60,000	511	556	584	605	622	644	612	655	682	701	717	738	566	641	691	728	758	800	553	596	623	642	658	679	635	682	712	734	751	774
60,000	70,000	566	616	647	670	688	714	678	726	756	777	794	818	621	704	757	798	832	877	612	660	689	711	728	752	702	755	787	811	831	856
70,000	80,000	619	673	707	732	752	780	742	794	826	850	869	894	673	763	821	865	901	951	669	721	753	776	795	821	767	824	860	886	907	935
80,000	90,000	668	727	763	791	812	842	801	858	893	918	938	966	722	818	880	928	966	1019	722	778	812	836	858	886	827	889	928	956	978	1009
90,000	100,000	716	778	817	847	870	901	858	919	956	983	1005	1035	769	871	937	987	1028	1084	773	832	870	897	919	948	885	952	992	1023	1047	1079
100,000	120,000	779	847	889	921	946	961	934	1000	1041	1071	1094	1126	831	940	1012	1066	1110	1170	841	905	946	975	999	1031	963	1034	1079	1112	1138	1173
120,000	140,000	867	942	990	1025	1053	1091	1040	1113	1159	1192	1218	1254	916	1037	1115	1174	1222	1289	935	1007	1051	1084	1111	1146	1070	1150	1199	1235	1264	1303
140,000	160,000	945	1027	1079	1117	1148	1189	1134	1214	1263	1299	1328	1367	992	1121	1206	1270	1322	1393	1018	1096	1145	1181	1210	1248	1165	1252	1306	1345	1377	1419
160,000	180,000	1024	1113	1168	1210	1243	1288	1229	1315	1369	1408	1439	1481	1067	1206	1297	1365	1421	1498	1102	1187	1239	1278	1309	1351	1262	1355	1413	1456	1490	1536
180,000	200,000	1096	1191	1250	1294	1330	1378	1315	1408	1465	1507	1540	1585	1136	1283	1379	1452	1511	1593	1179	1269	1326	1367	1400	1445	1349	1449	1511	1557	1593	1642
200,000 or more		1464	1591	1670	1729	1776	1839	1758	1882	1958	2015	2059	2119	1482	1672	1796	1890	1966	2072	1572	1691	1766	1821	1865	1924	1797	1930	2012	2072	2121	2185

Income: At least	Income: But less than	South Carolina 5.0000%						South Dakota 4.0000%						Tennessee 7.0000%						Texas 6.2500%						Utah 4.7500%					
		1	2	3	4	5	Over 5	1	2	3	4	5	Over 5	1	2	3	4	5	Over 5	1	2	3	4	5	Over 5	1	2	3	4	5	Over 5
$0	$20,000	244	280	304	322	337	357	212	242	262	278	290	307	351	399	430	454	474	500	237	256	268	276	283	292	244	281	305	323	339	360
20,000	30,000	400	459	497	526	550	583	349	399	431	456	476	504	580	659	710	749	781	824	422	456	476	491	503	520	401	461	500	530	555	589
30,000	40,000	481	551	597	632	660	699	421	480	519	549	573	606	700	794	856	902	940	993	523	564	589	608	623	643	482	554	601	637	666	707
40,000	50,000	551	631	683	723	755	800	483	551	595	629	657	695	804	912	982	1035	1079	1138	612	660	690	712	729	753	553	635	688	729	763	809
50,000	60,000	615	703	761	805	841	891	539	614	664	701	732	774	898	1018	1096	1155	1204	1270	694	748	782	807	827	853	617	708	767	813	850	902
60,000	70,000	673	770	833	861	920	975	590	673	727	768	801	848	984	1115	1201	1265	1318	1391	770	830	867	895	917	947	676	775	840	889	930	986
70,000	80,000	728	833	901	953	995	1054	639	728	786	831	867	917	1066	1208	1300	1370	1427	1505	843	909	950	980	1004	1036	731	838	908	962	1005	1066
80,000	90,000	780	891	964	1019	1065	1127	684	780	842	889	928	981	1142	1294	1392	1467	1528	1612	911	982	1027	1059	1085	1121	783	897	972	1029	1076	1141
90,000	100,000	828	947	1024	1083	1131	1197	727	829	895	945	986	1042	1214	1376	1480	1560	1624	1713	977	1053	1101	1136	1164	1201	832	953	1033	1093	1143	1211
100,000	120,000	893	1020	1103	1166	1218	1289	785	893	964	1018	1063	1123	1310	1484	1597	1682	1751	1847	1064	1148	1199	1238	1268	1309	897	1027	1113	1178	1231	1305
120,000	140,000	983	1122	1213	1282	1338	1417	863	983	1061	1120	1168	1235	1443	1633	1757	1851	1927	2032	1187	1279	1337	1380	1413	1459	987	1130	1223	1294	1353	1434
140,000	160,000	1061	1211	1309	1383	1444	1528	933	1061	1145	1209	1261	1333	1560	1765	1898	1999	2081	2194	1295	1396	1459	1506	1543	1592	1066	1219	1320	1397	1460	1547
160,000	180,000	1140	1300	1405	1485	1550	1640	1002	1140	1229	1298	1354	1431	1676	1896	2039	2147	2235	2357	1406	1514	1583	1633	1673	1727	1145	1309	1417	1499	1566	1659
180,000	200,000	1211	1381	1492	1577	1646	1741	1065	1211	1306	1378	1437	1519	1782	2015	2167	2281	2375	2503	1505	1622	1695	1749	1792	1850	1216	1390	1504	1592	1663	1762
200,000 or more		1570	1789	1981	2039	2128	2250	1381	1569	1691	1784	1860	1964	2315	2615	2810	2958	3078	3243	2018	2176	2274	2346	2403	2481	1576	1799	1946	2057	2148	2275

Income: At least	Income: But less than	Vermont 6.0000%						Virginia[5] 5.0000%						Washington 6.5000%						West Virginia 6.0000%						Wisconsin 5.0000%					
		1	2	3	4	5	Over 5	1	2	3	4	5	Over 5	1	2	3	4	5	Over 5	1	2	3	4	5	Over 5	1	2	3	4	5	Over 5
$0	$20,000	135	139	141	143	144	146	199	227	245	258	269	285	251	270	282	290	297	306	316	360	389	410	428	452	193	206	214	220	225	231
20,000	30,000	252	259	263	266	269	272	324	369	397	419	437	462	443	477	498	513	525	541	522	593	639	674	703	743	344	367	382	392	401	412
30,000	40,000	317	326	332	335	339	343	389	442	476	502	524	553	548	589	614	633	648	668	629	714	769	811	846	893	426	455	473	486	496	510
40,000	50,000	376	387	393	398	401	406	445	506	545	574	598	632	640	688	718	740	757	781	721	819	882	930	969	1023	499	533	554	569	581	597
50,000	60,000	431	443	450	456	460	465	496	563	606	639	666	703	724	779	812	837	857	884	805	913	984	1037	1081	1141	566	604	628	645	659	677
60,000	70,000	482	496	504	510	515	521	543	616	663	699	728	768	803	863	900	928	950	979	882	1000	1077	1135	1183	1249	628	670	697	716	731	752
70,000	80,000	532	547	556	562	568	575	587	666	717	755	787	830	878	944	985	1015	1039	1071	955	1083	1166	1229	1280	1351	688	734	763	784	801	823
80,000	90,000	578	595	605	612	618	625	629	712	767	808	841	887	948	1020	1064	1096	1122	1157	1023	1159	1248	1315	1370	1446	744	794	825	848	866	890
90,000	100,000	624	641	652	660	666	674	668	757	814	858	893	942	1016	1092	1140	1175	1202	1240	1087	1232	1326	1398	1456	1536	797	851	885	909	929	955
100,000	120,000	684	704	716	724	731	740	720	815	877	924	962	1014	1106	1189	1241	1279	1309	1350	1173	1329	1430	1507	1569	1655	869	928	964	991	1012	1041
120,000	140,000	770	792	805	815	822	832	792	896	964	1015	1057	1114	1232	1324	1382	1424	1457	1503	1290	1461	1572	1657	1725	1820	969	1035	1075	1105	1129	1160
140,000	160,000	846	870	885	895	904	915	855	967	1040	1095	1140	1202	1343	1444	1506	1552	1589	1638	1394	1578	1698	1788	1862	1964	1058	1130	1174	1206	1232	1267
160,000	180,000	923	950	966	978	987	999	918	1038	1116	1175	1223	1289	1456	1565	1632	1682	1722	1775	1497	1695	1823	1920	1999	2109	1148	1225	1273	1308	1336	1374
180,000	200,000	995	1023	1040	1053	1063	1076	976	1103	1185	1248	1299	1369	1558	1675	1747	1801	1843	1900	1591	1801	1937	2040	2124	2239	1229	1313	1364	1402	1432	1472
200,000 or more		1366	1405	1429	1446	1460	1478	1265	1429	1534	1614	1679	1768	2084	2240	2337	2408	2464	2541	2064	2333	2508	2640	2748	2896	1650	1762	1831	1882	1922	1976

Income: At least	Income: But less than	Wyoming 4.0000%					
		1	2	3	4	5	Over 5
$0	$20,000	177	197	210	219	227	238
20,000	30,000	302	386	357	373	386	404
30,000	40,000	368	409	435	455	470	492
40,000	50,000	426	473	503	526	544	569
50,000	60,000	479	532	566	591	611	639
60,000	70,000	528	586	623	651	673	704
70,000	80,000	574	637	677	708	732	765
80,000	90,000	618	685	728	761	787	823
90,000	100,000	659	731	777	812	839	877
100,000	120,000	714	792	842	879	909	950
120,000	140,000	790	876	931	972	1006	1051
140,000	160,000	857	951	1010	1055	1091	1140
160,000	180,000	925	1026	1090	1138	1176	1229
180,000	200,000	986	1094	1162	1213	1254	1310
200,000 or more		1298	1439	1528	1595	1648	1722

Note. Alaska does not have a state sales tax. Alaska residents should follow the instructions on the next page to determine their local sales tax amount.

1 The California table includes the 1% uniform local sales tax rate in additon to the 6.25% state sales tax rate.

2 The Nevada table includes the 2.25% uniform local sales tax rate in addition to the 4.25% state sales tax rate.

3 The rate for Idaho increased and the rate for North Carolina decreased during 2006, so the rates given are averaged over the year. The rates for New York and Ohio decreased during 2005, so the rates given for 2006 are lower than the rates given in 2005, which were averaged over the year.

4 The rate for New Jersey increased during 2006, so the rate given is averaged over the year. Residents of Salem County should deduct only half of the amount in the state table.

5 The state and local general sales taxes are combined in the Virginia table.

Which Optional Local Sales Tax Table Should I Use?

IF you live in the state of...	AND you live in...	THEN use Local Table...
Alaska	Any locality	C
Arizona	Chandler, Gilbert, Glendale, Peoria, Scottsdale, Tempe, or Yuma	C
	Any other locality	B
Arkansas	Texarkana	B
California	Los Angeles County	B
Colorado	Centennial, Colorado Springs, City of Denver, Greeley, Jefferson County, or Longmont	B
	Arvada, Aurora, City of Boulder, Fort Collins, Lakewood, City of Pueblo, Thornton, or Westminster	C
	Boulder County, Denver County, Pueblo County, or any other locality	A
Georgia	DeKalb County, Rockdale County, Taliaferro County, or Webster	B
	Any other locality	C
Illinois	Any locality	B
Louisiana	Any locality	C
New York	New York City	A
	The cities of Fulton, Oneida, or Oswego, or one of the following counties: Albany, Allegany, Cattaraugus, Cayuga, Chemung, Clinton, Cortland, Erie, Essex, Franklin, Fulton, Genessee, Herkimer, Jefferson, Lewis, Livingston, Monroe, Montgomery, Nassau, Niagara, Oneida, Onondaga, Ontario, Orange, Orleans, Oswego, Otsego, Putnam, Rockland, St. Lawrence, Saratoga, Schenectady, Schoharie, Seneca, Steuben, Suffolk, Sullivan, Tompkins, Ulster, Warren, Washington, Westchester, Wyoming, or Yates	B
	Any other locality	D
North Carolina	Any locality	C

2006 Optional Local Sales Tax Tables for Certain Local Jurisdictions
(Based on a local sales tax rate of 1 percent)

Income At least	But less than	Local Table A						Local Table B					
		1	2	3	4	5	Over 5	1	2	3	4	5	Over 5
$0	$20,000	34	37	39	41	42	43	39	43	46	48	50	52
20,000	30,000	58	63	67	69	71	74	66	73	78	82	85	88
30,000	40,000	70	77	81	84	87	90	80	89	95	99	103	108
40,000	50,000	81	89	94	97	100	104	93	104	110	115	119	125
50,000	60,000	92	100	106	110	113	117	105	116	124	129	134	140
60,000	70,000	101	110	116	121	124	129	115	128	136	143	147	154
70,000	80,000	110	120	127	131	135	140	126	140	148	155	160	168
80,000	90,000	118	129	136	141	145	151	135	150	160	167	173	180
90,000	100,000	126	138	145	151	155	161	144	160	170	178	184	193
100,000	120,000	137	150	158	163	168	175	156	174	185	193	200	209
120,000	140,000	152	166	174	181	186	193	173	192	204	213	221	231
140,000	160,000	165	180	189	197	202	210	188	209	222	232	240	251
160,000	180,000	178	194	204	212	218	227	203	225	239	250	259	270
180,000	200,000	190	207	218	226	233	242	216	240	255	267	276	288
200,000 or more		250	273	288	299	307	319	286	317	337	351	363	380

Income At least	But less than	Local Table C						Local Table D					
		1	2	3	4	5	Over 5	1	2	3	4	5	Over 5
$0	$20,000	52	60	65	69	72	76	34	36	38	39	40	41
20,000	30,000	85	97	105	111	116	123	60	65	68	70	71	73
30,000	40,000	102	116	126	133	139	147	75	80	84	86	88	91
40,000	50,000	117	133	144	152	159	168	87	94	98	101	103	106
50,000	60,000	130	148	160	169	177	187	99	106	111	114	117	120
60,000	70,000	142	162	175	185	193	204	110	118	123	127	130	134
70,000	80,000	153	175	189	200	209	221	120	129	135	139	142	146
80,000	90,000	164	187	202	214	223	236	130	140	146	150	153	158
90,000	100,000	174	199	215	227	237	250	140	150	156	161	165	170
100,000	120,000	188	214	231	244	255	269	152	163	170	175	179	185
120,000	140,000	206	235	254	268	279	296	170	182	190	195	200	206
140,000	160,000	222	253	273	289	301	318	185	199	207	213	218	225
160,000	180,000	239	272	293	310	323	341	201	215	225	231	237	244
180,000	200,000	253	288	311	328	343	362	215	231	241	248	253	261
200,000 or more		327	372	401	423	441	466	289	310	323	332	340	350

¶28,010

Topical Index

References are to paragraph (¶) numbers

References are to paragraph (¶) numbers

References are to paragraph (¶) numbers